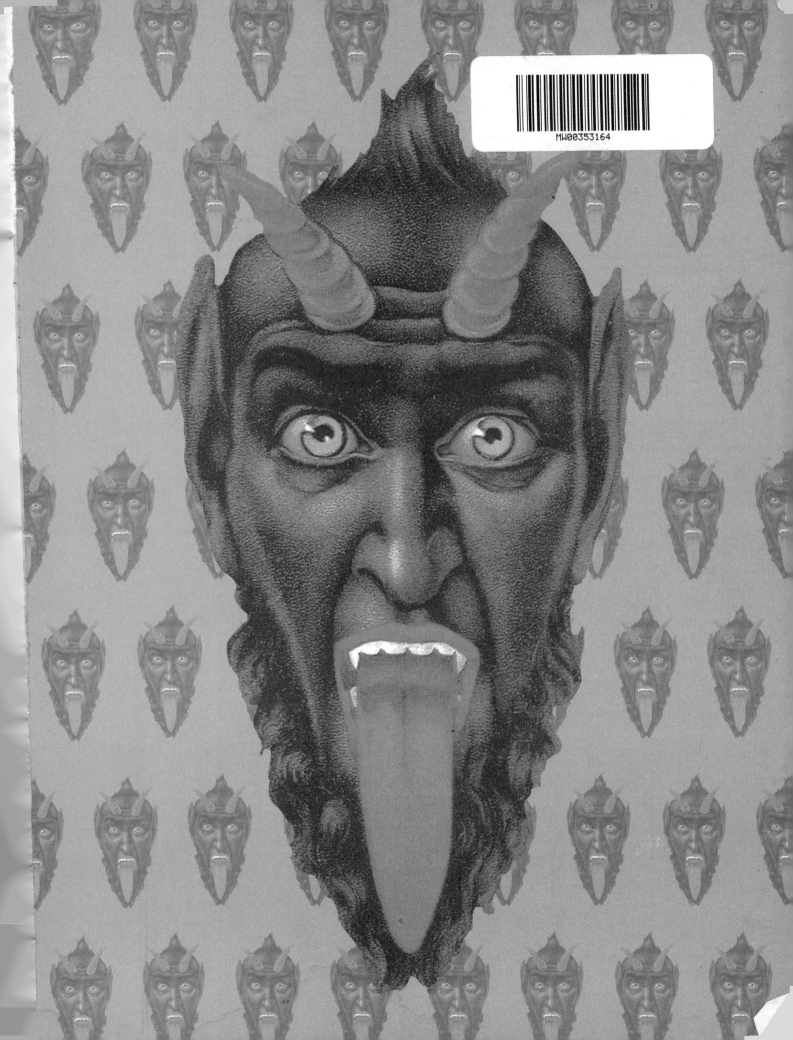

Published by The Disinformation Company Ltd.
163 Third Avenue, Suite 108
New York, NY 10003
Tel.: +1.212.691.1605
Fax: +1.212.473.8096
www.disinfo.com

Book Design: Tomo Makiura, Paul Pollard, and Kate Bingaman for P²M, NY.

First Printing September 2003

Library of Congress Control Number: 2003105112

ISBN 0-9713942-7-X

Printed in USA

Distributed in the USA and Canada by:
Consortium Book Sales and Distribution
1045 Westgate Drive, Suite 90
St Paul, MN 55114
Toll Free: +1.800.283.3572
Local: +1.651.221.9035
Fax: +1.651.221.0124
www.cbsd.com

Distributed in the United Kingdom and Eire by:
Turnaround Publisher Services Ltd.
Unit 3, Olympia Trading Estate
Coburg Road
London, N22 6TZ
Tel.: +44.(0)20.8829.3000
Fax: +44.(0)20.8881.5088
www.turnaround-uk.com

Attention colleges and universities, corporations and other organizations:
Quantity discounts are available on bulk purchases of this book for educational training purposes, fund-raising, or gift giving. Special books, booklets, or book excerpts can also be created to fit your specific needs. For information contact Marketing Department of The Disinformation Company Ltd.

Disinformation is a registered trademark of The Disinformation Company Ltd.

BOOK OF LIES

The Disinformation Guide to Magick and the Occult
(Being an alchemical formula to rip a hole in the fabric of reality)

Edited by
Richard Metzger

Preface by
Grant Morrison

disinformation®

All Highlights done by Previous owner, a Pretentious Pig Pretend Warlock. Suck my balls NPS!
"A Curse on <u>both</u> your houses"!
— Some fuckin' Shakespeare
— CM

For Fiona Horne

TABLE OF CONTENTS

Magic, you say?

Me, I'm a hard-nosed skeptic, when all's said and done. Try as I might, I can't find any convincing evidence to support the notion that flying saucers come from other planets to visit us, I don't "believe" in reincarnation, the Loch Ness Monster, ghosts of the dead, news reports, the objectivity of Science or the literal truth of Bible stories. In an overloaded, supersaturated mediasphere, my own best compass is the evidence of my senses.

Having said that, in the course of 24 years of almost daily occult practice and exploration, some very bizarre things have manifested in front of my lovely, flaring nostrils and I've been forced to alter my view of life, death and "reality" accordingly.

Because whether you "believe" in it or not, whether you like it or not, magic WORKS (I use the devalued word "magic" precisely because I'm amused by its associations with illusion, conjuring and deception, whereas Richard Metzger prefers to use the High-spelling form "magick," in honor of the heroic and misunderstood Aleister Crowley who broke centuries of Church-imposed silence and obscurity when he published the "secrets" and techniques of magic in his great, democratic work *Magick in Theory and Practice*, published in 1929). Magic has worked for all of the contributors to this book, as you will see, and it can work for everyone. Personally, I don't need to know HOW it works—although I have bucket loads of colorful theories—just as I don't seem to need to know how my TV works in order to watch it, or how a Jumbo Jet stays up when I'm dozing through in-flight entertainment at 35,000 feet. What I do know for sure, based on the evidence of my senses and on many years of skeptical enquiry, is that magic allows us to take control of our own development as human beings. Magic allows us to see the world entire in a fresh and endlessly significant light and demands of us a vital and dynamic collaboration with our environment. Magic brings coherence and structure to psychological "breakdowns," psychedelic experiences or transpersonal encounters. Magic allows us to personify our fears and failures as demons and outlines time-honored methods of bargaining with these feelings or banishing them. Magic is the sane response to a world filled with corporate ghost-gods, roaming, mindless laws and peering surveillance lenses. Above all, magic is about achieving results. It's about manipulating real-time events, dealing with devious "spirits" and other autonomous energy sources. It's about conjuring dead pop icons to do your bidding and writing it all down so that it reads like an exciting adventure story and changes the world around it. Magic is glamorous, dark and charismatic. "Magic" is the hopelessly inadequate Standard English word for a long-established technology which permits access to the "operating codes" underlying the current physical universe. Becoming a "magician" is a developmental skill, like learning to talk, to reason, to empathize or to see perspective.

Magic, in short, is Life as it is meant to be Lived by adults.

Disinformation's *Book of Lies* is a 21st century grimoire, a *How To* book designed to inspire the young magician-warriors of this new and turbulent century. In the apparent derangement of our times, this book is both a call to arms and an armory also. Read on, get tooled up, get out there... and start bending reality.

And welcome, one and all, to the New Magical Century. ♆

OPERATION MINDWARP

"The best place to hide something is right out in the open. No one ever thinks to look there."
–Robert Anton Wilson

"Can you teach me how to do a magic trick?"

At first this question used to really flummox me—did they expect me to do like a *card trick*? A little *sleight of hand* perhaps? What did they expect me to *whip out* and impress them with? By now I'm used to this line of inquiry and interestingly, the question is always asked with com-

So the first time I ever jerked off, it was to a picture of a butt-naked Maxine Sanders, Queen of the Witches. I think this explains a lot about me, actually...

plete sincerity, never with sarcasm or scorn, just an open attitude to the idea of "magick." In situations where my reputation has preceded me, I think this is kind of fun. I've even come to enjoy this question, as it sure beats making normal small talk.

But to answer the question, well, *yes*, I can teach you how to do a magick, uh, *trick* that will most assuredly bring you dependable results (within reason) and I can likely explain it to you within 10 minutes time. If you did what I told you, things *would* start happening, but before you go feeling all impressed with yourself, if you'd ask someone to teach you a song on the piano in 10 minutes, they could do so, but you'd still only be playing "Chopsticks."

Just to put that into perspective...

For some reason, I have always considered myself to be a *warlock*. Even when I was very young. I don't know why, really, but it is true. I have had this self-identity for as long as I can recall. There was never a time when I didn't feel this way. I don't remember how I gravitated towards magick in the first place, but when I was a little kid I really loved *Bewitched*. These were people who I could *relate* to and all the comics I liked had heroes who were sorcerers and warlocks: Dr. Strange, Adam Warlock, and Captain Marvel.[1] My parents even have a Super8 film of me dressed in a "wizard" costume replete with cloak and Merlin cap, reading my "grimoire" and "scrying" into a makeshift crystal ball that doubled as a funky early '70s ashtray. I was about five years old when this was shot. Thirty some years later I look back on this and laugh at how consistent I have been. The older I get the more I see a fairly straight trajectory from there to here. It's weird to contemplate it.

One strong shove in the direction of magick might have something to do with a book called *Witchcraft, Magic and the Supernatural*, a full color hardback picture book that came out in the 1970s with a bloody goat head on the front cover and an Austin Spare painting of a demon on the back. Since the audience for such a book was undoubtedly on the young side, this book—like many such occult tomes published by Octopus Books—had several pictures of foxy "sky-clad" witches nestled within its pages to attract more horny young buyers. I convinced my mother to purchase this book for me at the mall. I smiled sweetly, such a good little boy.

So the first time I ever jerked off, it was to a picture of a butt-naked Maxine Sanders, Queen of the Witches.

I think this explains a lot about me, actually...

When I was younger and first starting to read up on the occult, I was always puzzled why it all seemed to be so "ancient"—I'd read book after book looking for something to latch onto, but little of it had much relevance to my life and my interests. Latin incantations, wands, daggers, robes and the various occult "props" all seemed pointless to me and very ineffectual ways of making magick happen. I'd read about purification rituals, "casting circle," the "Mass" of this or that, "hand fasting" and all of this stuff that magicians were supposed to do, but *where was the sorcery*? When does it get to the part where it explains *how to make shit happen*? That's the part that I was interested in and it was the only part I was ever interested in. Forget about all this hokey *Dungeons and Dragons* robe-wearing nonsense, I wanted results.

I recall watching Kenneth Anger's films for the first time and grasping intuitively how his films were ritual on celluloid, constructed with magical efficacy foremost in mind. Color, music, pacing and especially his choice of actors (such as Anais Nin, Marjorie Cameron, Marianne Faithful and others) who he viewed as "elementals," all figured into making Anger's cinematic spells so potent and brilliant. There was also the angle of how, because they existed on film and could be screened over and over again all over the world, they were incantations of especial power. I was awestruck by what I was seeing and I learned

And if it is your first dip into occult literature, I do hope this book is like having a nuclear bomb go off behind your eyeballs or a razorblade slashed across your brain.

a great lesson about "making" magick through a careful study of Anger's work and through this influence, in part, I continued to move towards combining my career ambitions of working in film, television and publishing with my private magical interests.

Magick—defined by Aleister Crowley as "the art and science of causing change in conformity with will"—has always been the vital core of all of the projects we undertake at The Disinformation Company. Whether via our website, publishing activities or our TV series, the idea of being able to "influence" reality in some beneficial way is what drives our activities. I've always considered The Disinformation Company Ltd. and our various activities to

constitute a very complex *spell*. Some sorcerers use painting or music or fiction to work their magick, but I quite like the idea of having a "magick business"—both *literally* and figuratively—as the canvas that I perform *my* magick on. It works on a lot of levels, metaphorically speaking, for me to consider myself to be a *magical businessman*, if you see what I am saying. It's a fairly unfettered way to see your place in the world and doesn't exactly limit your imagination.

I'm sure Willy Wonka would agree.

Well, it works for me, at least.

"All Cretes are liars"
– Epimenides the Crete, inventor of the paradox.

For this anthology I've—quite obviously—cribbed the title from Crowley's cryptic 1913 book of the same name. I liked the irony and it dovetailing so neatly with the Disinformation brand ("Disinformation," a term usually associated with the CIA, means "a mixture of truth and lies" used as an information smokescreen), so *Book of Lies* seemed a natural. A book that announces itself as a *book of lies* would have to have the truth hidden somewhere in it, right?[2] Also, since Crowley looms so large over my way of thinking, it's fitting to pay tribute. Again and again during the preparations for this volume, I've looked over copies of his occult journal, *The Equinox*, and I am conscious that this collection and its sequels follow in its tradition. Here, I'm interested most of all in presenting "modern" magick as opposed to "museum" magick and feel that all too often the occult books being published today are merely a rehash of what has gone on before with nary an ounce of new energy or new ideas coming into the fold. Not since the innovations of Chaos Magick in the '80s has anyone really come along with a go at trying to redefine magick for the modern era and offer a working toolkit. This is my attempt, my version.

However, because this book is an anthology—the work of many people—and showcases so many radical belief systems, rebel biographies and "alt histories," I get to elegantly sidestep the notion that I, personally, am trying to tell anyone "*THIS* is how you should practice magick" as this is certainly not my intention. No one can do that for you and I would not presume to try. How can anyone possibly know more about *your* magick than you do? It's about what works *for you*. If you get results, then it must be working. Over time you'll see your targets hit with greater accuracy, but there is NO SET WAY OF DOING ANYTHING IN MAGICK. I can assure you that I, too, am making it all up as I go along. Even as my aim gets better and better as I get older and become more creative with my spell casting, I will say it again: I am *still* improvising. This book endeavors to showcase strategies that work for other people and create a *cookbook* for subversion, but feel free to riff on the recipes.[3] It's the only way forward, to discover your own *true* orbit in life and what *works* for you. The editorial selection attempts to broaden the cultural definition of what magick is—and what it is not—by including many disparate voices, some not normally viewed as working in the occult arena (painters, rock stars, comic book writers, computer programmers). Some of the names in the book will be familiar, others not, but the communal reason that they all coexist between the covers of Disinformation's *Book of Lies* is because they are doing something different and inspiring, bringing to light an obscure subject or else they are writing on a familiar topic and presenting a side of things not usually seen. This collection represents, for me, the strongest line up of magical thought that I could find today and presents some of the most potent magical thinkers of our time in its pages.

When you are in the book publishing business, at a certain point—hopefully early on—you need to ask yourself "Who is going to read this book? Who is it for?" This anthology is for the person who is like I was back then: searching for something, groping for something magical in their lives, but not quite finding it in the rehashed medievalism and 'incense and affirmations' school of what passes for occult literature. This book intends to fuel a certain kind of fire in a certain type of person. I know that I'd be happy if I stumbled upon it, so I consider that a good sign.

And if it is your first dip into occult literature, I do hope this book is like having a nuclear bomb go off behind your eyeballs or a razorblade slashed across your brain.

I think these ideas deserve a wider readership.

It's only when these sorts of thought forms can be fully externalized in the culture that we can expect to see the emergence of a mutant race. I am very interested in seeing this happen and this collection represents a nudge in that direction.

Which side are you on? ⊐

Editor's Note: The essays herein were culled from a variety of places; excerpts from both new and out of print books, the Internet, old magazines I'd been keeping for years not knowing when they might come in handy and several new pieces appearing here for the first time. I should probably mention that none of the writers are indicating with their involvement that they agree with or approve of the work of any other author also appearing in the book. This is not the case and for the most part, few of them had any idea whose work their writing might be sitting alongside.

Endnotes:

1. The "cosmic" '70s Captain Marvel written by Jim Starlin, not "Shazam." I hated him.
2. See Crowley's *Liber B vel Magi* for more on this topic.
3. Listen to John Coltrane's *A Love Supreme* and hear the way this man *prayed* with his saxophone. Beatific emotion pours out of his horn. You can see a similar thing in *The Mystery of Picasso* film, watching him paint. Incredible. *This* is magick in action, but these skills were not developed overnight. You *can't escape* putting the work in.

Special thanks go out to Michael Moynihan for his kind help and editorial suggestions and Genesis Breyer P-Orridge for providing us with all of the amazing Burroughs and Gysin images from his personal collection as well as always being an inspiration to me since I was a teenager. It's very gratifying that he has always been so supportive to my various projects. Thanks also to Grant Morrison, and Kristan Anderson, to Tomo Makiura, Paul Pollard and Kate Bingaman for the design and layout of this book, Nimrod Erez, Bradley Novicoff, Mogg Morgan at Mandrake of Oxford, Ben Meyers at Autonomedia, Nicholas Tharcher at New Falcon Publications, Eric Simonoff, Gerry Howard, Philip Gwyn Jones, Mark McCarthy, Eva Wisten, Peter H. Gilmore, Douglas Walla at Kent Gallery, Kirsten Anderson at Roq la Rue Gallery, Fiona Horne, Dean Chamberlain and Stacy Valis, Jon Graham and Cynthia Fowles of Inner Traditions, Brian Butler, Mike Backes, Shann Dornhecker, Greg Bishop, Ina Howard, Katherine Gates, Erik Pauser, Leen Al-Bassam, Ralph Bernardo, Russ Kick, Lee Hoffman, Alex Burns, Naomi Nelson and my business partner in Disinformation, Gary Baddeley, for all of his help with this manuscript.

MAGICK IN THEORY AND PRACTICE

POP MAGIC!

a perfect piece of cunt.

POP MAGIC! is Magic! For the People. Pop Magic! is Naked Magic! Pop Magic! lifts the 7 veils and shows you the tits of the Infinite.

THINKING ABOUT IT

All you need to begin the practice of magic is concentration, imagination and the ability to laugh at yourself and learn from mistakes. Some people like to dress up as Egyptians or monks to get themselves in the mood; others wear animal masks or Barbarella costumes. The use of ritual paraphernalia functions as an aid to the imagination only.

Anything you can imagine, anything you can symbolize, can be made to produce magical changes in your environment.

FIRST STEPS ON THE PATH

Magic is easy to do. Dozens of rulebooks and instruction manuals are available in the occult or "mind, body and spirit" sections of most modern bookstores. Many of the older manuals were written during times when a powerful and vindictive Church apparatus was attempting to suppress all roads to the truth but most of them are generally so heavily coded and disguised behind arcane symbol systems that it's hardly worth the bother—except for an idea of how other people used THEIR imaginative powers to interpret non-ordinary contacts and communications.

Aleister Crowley—magic's Picasso—wrote this and I can't say it any better than he did:

"In this book it is spoken of the sephiroth and the paths, of spirits and conjurations, of gods, spheres, and planes and many other things which may or may not exist. It is immaterial whether they exist or not. By doing certain things, certain results follow; students are most earnestly warned against attributing objective reality or philosophical validity to any of them."

This is the most important rule of all which is why it's here at the start. As you continue to learn and develop your own psychocosms and styles of magical practice, as you encounter stranger and stranger denizens of the Hellworlds and Hyperworlds, you'll come back to these words of wisdom again and again with a fresh understanding each time.

HOW TO BE A MAGICIAN

Simple. Declare yourself a magician, behave like a magician, practice magic every day.

Be honest about your progress, your successes and failures. Tripping on 500 mushrooms might loosen your astral sphincter a little but it will not generally confer upon you any of the benefits of the magic I'm discussing here. Magic is about what you bring BACK from the Shining Realms of the Uberconscious. The magician dives into the Immense Other in search of tips and hints and treasures s/he can bring home to enrich life in the solid world. And if necessary, Fake it till you make it.

Declare yourself a magician, behave like a magician, practice magic every day.

HOW TO BE A MAGICIAN 2

Read lots of books on the subject to get in the mood. Talking about magic with non-magicians is like talking to virgins about shagging. Reading about magic is like reading about sex; it will get you horny for the real thing but it won't give you nearly as much fun.

Reading will give you a feel for what's crap and what can usefully be adapted to your own style. Develop discrimination. Don't buy into cults, aliens, paranoia, or complacency. Learn whom to trust and whom to steer clear of.

HOW TO BE A MAGICIAN 3

Put down the books, stop making excuses and START.

MAGICAL CONSCIOUSNESS

Magical consciousness is a particular way of seeing and interacting with the real world. I experience it as what I can only describe as a "head-click," a feeling of absolute certainty accompanying a perceptual shift which gives real world transactions the numinous, uncanny feeling of dreams. Magical consciousness is a way of experiencing and participating with the local environment in a heightened, significant manner, similar to the effects of some drug trips, Salvador Dali's "Paranoiac/critical" method, near death experiences, etc. Many apparently precognitive and telepathic latencies become more active during periods of magical consciousness. This is the state in which tea leaves are read, curses are cast, goals are scored, poems are written.

Magical Consciousness can be practiced until it merges with and becomes everyday consciousness. Maintained at these levels it could interfere with your lifestyle unless you have one which supports long periods of richly associative thought.

EXPERIMENT:

As a first exercise in magical consciousness spend five minutes looking at everything around you as if ALL OF IT was trying to tell you something very important. How did that light bulb come to be here exactly? Why does the murder victim in the newspaper have the same unusual surname as your father-in-law? Why did the phone ring, just at that moment and what were you thinking when it did?

What's that water stain on the wall of the building opposite? How does it make you feel?

Five minutes of focus during which everything is significant, everything is luminous and heavy with meaning, like the objects seen in dreams.

Go.

EXPERIMENT:

Next, relax, go for a walk and interpret everything you see on the way as a message from the Infinite to you. Watch for patterns in the flight of birds. Make oracular sentences from the letters on car number plates. Look at the way buildings move against the skyline. Pay attention to noises on the streets, graffiti sigils, voices cut into rapid, almost subliminal commands and pleas. Listen between the lines. Walk as far and for as long as you feel comfortable in this open state. The more aimless, the more you walk for the pleasure of pure experience, the further into magical consciousness you will be immersed.

Reading about magic is like reading about sex; it will get you horny for the real thing but it won't give you nearly as much fun.

Magical consciousness resembles states of light meditation, "hypnagogic" pre-sleep trance or alpha wave brain activity.

APPLIED MAGIC

Is about making things happen and performing the necessary experiments. In these endeavors we do not need to know HOW magic works, only that it does. We prove this by doing the work, recording the results and sharing our information with other magicians. Theoretical magic is all the mad ideas you come up with to explain what's happening to you. Applied magic is what makes them happen.

THE MAGICAL RECORD

Always keep a journal of your experiments. It's easy to forget things you've done or to miss interesting little connections and correspondences. Make a note of everything, from the intent to the fulfillment. Make a note of dates, times, moods, successes and failures.

Study YOURSELF the way a hunter studies prey. Exploit your own weaknesses to create desired changes within yourself.

BANISHING

Banishing is a way of preparing a space for ritual use. There are many elaborate banishing rituals available, ranging across the full spectrum of pomposity. Think of banishing as the installation of virus protection software. The banishing is a kind of vaccination against infection from Beyond.

Most banishings are intended to surround the magician with an impenetrable shield of will. This usually takes the form of an acknowledgment of the elemental powers at the four cardinal points of the compass. Some like to visualize themselves surrounded and protected by columns of light or by four angels. Any protective image will do— spaceships, superheroes, warrior-monks, whatever. I don't bother with any of that and usually visualize a bubble radiating outwards from my body into space all around above and below me as far as I think I'll need it.

Why the need for protection?

Remember that you may be opening some part of yourself to an influx of information from "non-ordinary," apparently "Other" sources. If you practice ceremonial magic and attempt to summon godforms or spirits things will undoubtedly happen. Your foundations will be tested. There is always the danger of obsession and madness. As magical work progresses, you will be forced into confrontation with your deepest darkest fears and desires. It's easy to become scared, paranoid and stupid. Stay fluid, cling to no one self-image and maintain your sense of humor at all times. Genuine laughter is the most effective banishing ritual available.

Banishing reminds you that no matter how many gods you talk to, no matter how many fluorescent realms you visit, you still have to come home, take a shit, be able to cook

Study YOURSELF the way a hunter studies prey. Exploit your own weaknesses to create desired changes within yourself.

dinner, water the plants and, most importantly, talk to people without scaring them.

When you complete any magical work, ground yourself with a good laugh, a good meal, good shag, a run or anything else that connects you with the mundane world. Banishing after your ritual is over works as a decompression back into the normal world of bills and bus stops and job

satisfaction. The magician's job is not to get lost in the Otherworld but to bring back its treasures for everyone to play with.

SIGILS

In the Pop Magic! style, the sigil (*sij-ill*) is the first and one of the most effective of all the weapons in the arsenal of any modern magician.

The sigil technique was reconceptualized and modernized by Austin Osman Spare in the early 20th century and popularized by Chaos Magicians and Thee Temple ov Psychick Youth in the 19 hundred and 80s.

A sigil is a magically charged symbol like this one:

The sigil takes a magical desire or intent—let's say "IT IS MY DESIRE TO BE A GREAT ACTOR" (you can, of course, put any desire you want in there) and folds it down, creating a highly-charged symbol. The desire is then forgotten. Only the symbol remains and can then be charged to full potency when the magician chooses.

Forgetting the desire in its verbal form can be difficult if you've started too ambitiously. There's no point charging a sigil to win the lottery if you don't buy a ticket. Start with stuff that's not too emotionally involving.

I usually sigilize to meet people I'm interested in, or for particular qualities I'll need in a given situation. I've also used sigils for healing, for locating lost objects and for mass global change. I've been using them for 20 years and they ALWAYS work.

For me, the period between launching the sigil and its manifestation as a real world event is usually 3 days, 3 weeks or 3 months depending on the variables involved.

I repeat: sigils ALWAYS work.

So. Begin your desire's transformation into pure throbbing symbol in the following fashion:

First remove the vowels and the repeating letters to leave a string of consonants—TSMYDRBGC.

Now start squashing the string down, throwing out or combining lines and playing with the letters until only an appropriately witchy-looking glyph is left. When you're satisfied it's done, you may wind up with something like this:

Most homemade sigils look a little spooky or alien—like UFO writing or witchy wall-scratchings. There are no rules as to how your sigil should look as long as it WORKS for you. RESULTS ONLY are important at this stage. If something doesn't work, try something else. The point is not to BELIEVE in magic, the point is to DO it and see how it works. This is not religion and blind faith plays no part.

Charging and launching your sigil is the fun part (it's often advisable to make up a bunch of sigils and charge them up later when you've forgotten what they originally represented).

Now, most of us find it difficult at first to maintain the precise Zen-like concentration necessary to work large-scale magic. This concentration can be learned with time and effort but in the meantime, sigils make it easy to sidestep years of training and achieve instant success. To charge your sigil you must concentrate on its shape, and hold that form in your mind as you evacuate all other thoughts.

Almost impossible, you might say, but the human body has various mechanisms for inducing brief "no-mind" states. Fasting, spinning, intense exhaustion, fear, sex, the fight-or-flight response; all will do the trick. I have charged sigils while bungee jumping, lying dying in a hospital bed, experiencing a total solar eclipse and dancing to Techno. All of these methods proved to be highly effective but for the eager beginner nothing beats the WANK TECHNIQUE.

Some non-magicians, I've noticed, convulse with nervous laughter whenever I mention the word "masturbation"

(and no wonder; next to wetting the bed or shitting in your own cat's box for a laugh, it's the one thing no-one likes to admit to).

Be that as it may, magical masturbation is actually more fun and equally, more serious, than the secular hand shandy, and all it requires is this: at the moment of orgasm, you must see the image of your chosen sigil blazing before the eyes in your mind and project it outwards into the ethereal mediaspheres and logoverses where desires swarm and condense into flesh. The sigil can be written on paper, on your hand or your chest, on the forehead of a lover or wherever you think it will be most effective.

At the white-hot instant of orgasm, consciousness blinks. Into this blink, this abyssal crack in perception, a sigil can be launched.

Masturbation is only ONE of countless methods you can use to bring your mental chatter to a standstill for the split-second it takes to charge and launch a sigil. I suggest masturbation because I'm kind-hearted, because it's convenient and because it's fun for most of us.

However...one does not change the universe simply by masturbating (tell THAT to the millions of sperm fighting for their life and the future of the species in a balled up Kleenex). If that were true, every vague fantasy we had in our heads at the moment of orgasm would come true within months. Intent is what makes the difference here.

Forget the wanking for just one moment if you can and remember that the sigil is the important part of the magic being performed here. The moment of orgasm will clear your mind, that's all. There are numerous other ways to clear your mind and you can use any of them. Dancing

At the moment of orgasm, you must see the image of your chosen sigil blazing before the eyes in your mind and project it outwards into the ethereal mediaspheres and logoverses where desires swarm and condense into flesh.

or spinning to exhaustion is very effective. Meditation is effective but takes years to learn properly. Fear and shock are very good for charging sigils, so you could probably watch a scary movie and launch your sigil at the bit where the hero's head comes bouncing down the aluminum stepladder into his girlfriend's lap. A run around the block clutching a sigil might be enough to charge it, so why not experiment?

Try launching your sigil while performing a Bungee jump from a bridge, perhaps, or sit naked in your local graveyard at night. Or dance until you fall over. The important thing is to find your own best method for stopping that inner chat just long enough to launch a fiercely visualized, flaming ultraviolet sigil into the gap. States of exhaustion following ANY intense arousal or deprivation are ideal.

The McDonald's Golden Arches, the Nike swoosh and the Virgin autograph are all *corporate viral sigils.*

And if you experiment and still have trouble with sigils, try some of the other beginner exercises for a while. I've met a couple of people who've told me they can't make sigils work so maybe there are a few of you out there who genuinely have problems in this particular area. Tough luck but it doesn't mean there's no magic for you to play with. I couldn't wheeze "Twinkle twinkle little star..." out of a clarinet but I can play the guitar well enough to have written hundreds of fabulous songs. If I'd stuck with the clarinet and got nowhere would that mean there is no such thing as music? Or would it indicate simply that I have an aptitude for playing the guitar which I can't seem to replicate using a clarinet? If I want to make *music* I use the instrument I'm most comfortable and accomplished with. The same is true for magical practice. Don't get uptight about it. This is not about defending a belief system, this is about producing results.

USE ONLY WHAT WORKS.

SIGILS: DISPOSAL

Some people keep their sigils, some dispose of them in an element appropriate to the magician's intent (I have burned, buried, flushed away and scattered sigils to the winds, depending on how I felt about them. Love-sigils went to water—flushed down the toilet or thrown into rivers or boiled in kettles. War-sigils were burned etc.... Some of my sigils are still around because I decided they were slow-burners and worth keeping. Some are even still in print. Do what feels right and produces results.)

Soiled paper and tissues can easily be disposed of in your mum's purse or the pocket of dad's raincoat.

VIRAL SIGILS

The viral sigil also known as the BRAND or LOGO is not of recent development (see "Christianity," "the Nazis" and

any flag of any nation) but has become an inescapable global phenomenon in recent years. It's easy to see the Nazi movement as the last gasp of Imperial Age thinking; these visionary savages still thought world domination meant tramping over the "enemy" and seizing his real estate. If only they'd had the foresight to see that global domination has *nothing to do with turf* and *everything to do with media* they would have anticipated corporate stealth-violence methods and combined them with their undoubted design sense; the rejected artists who engineered the Third Reich might have created the 20th century's first global superbrand and spared the lives of many potential consumers. The McDonald's Golden Arches, the Nike swoosh and the Virgin autograph are all *corporate viral sigils.*

Corporate sigils are super-breeders. They attack unbranded imaginative space. They invade Red Square, they infest the cranky streets of Tibet, they etch themselves into hairstyles. They breed across clothing, turning people into advertising hoardings. They are a very powerful development in the history of sigil magic, which dates back to the first bison drawn on the first cave wall.

The logo or brand, like any sigil, is a condensation, a compressed, symbolic summing up of the world of desire which the corporation intends to represent. The logo is the only visible sign of the corporate intelligence seething behind it. Walt Disney died long ago but his sigil, that familiar, cartoonish signature, persists, carrying its own vast weight of meanings, associations, nostalgia and significance. People are born and grow up to become Disney executives, mouthing the jargon and the credo of a living corporate entity. Walt Disney the man is long dead and frozen (or so folk myth would have it) but Disney, the immense, invisible corporate egregore persists.

Corporate entities are worth studying and can teach the observant magician much about what we really mean when we use the word "magic." They and other ghosts like them rule our world of the early 21st century.

EXPERIMENT:

Think hard about why the Coca-Cola spirit is stronger than the Dr. Pepper spirit (what great complex of ideas, longings and deficiencies has the Coke logo succeeded in condensing into two words, two colors, taking Orwell's 1984 concept of Newspeak to its logical conclusion?). Watch the habits of the world's great corporate predators like FOX,

MICROSOFT or AOL TIME WARNER. Track their movements over time, observe their feeding habits and methods of predation, monitor their repeated behaviors and note how they react to change and novelty. Learn how to imitate them, steal their successful strategies and use them as your own. Form your own limited company or corporation. It's fairly easy to do with some paperwork and a small amount of money. Create your own brand, your own logo and see how quickly you can make it spread and interact with other corporate entities.

Build your own god and set it loose.

HYPERSIGILS

The "hypersigil" or "supersigil" develops the sigil concept beyond the static image and incorporates elements such as characterization, drama and plot. The hypersigil is a sigil extended through the fourth dimension. My own comic book series *The Invisibles* was a six-year long sigil in the form of an occult adventure story which consumed and recreated my life during the period of its composition and execution. The hypersigil is an immensely powerful and sometimes dangerous method for actually altering reality in accordance with intent. Results can be remarkable and shocking.

EXPERIMENT:

After becoming familiar with the traditional sigil method, see if you can create your own hypersigil. The hypersigil can take the form of a poem, a story, a song, a dance or any other extended artistic activity you wish to try. This is a newly developed technology so the parameters remain to be explored. It is important to become utterly absorbed in the hypersigil as it unfolds; this requires a high degree of absorption and concentration (which can lead to obsession but so what? You can always banish at the end) like most works of art. The hypersigil is a dynamic miniature model of the magician's universe, a hologram, microcosm or "voodoo doll" which can manipulated in real time to produce changes in the macrocosmic environment of "real" life.

HOW TO CHAT UP GODS

Accept this for the moment; there are Big Ideas in the world. They were Big before we were born and they'll still be big long after we're moldering. ANGER is one of those Big Ideas and LOVE is another one. Then there's FEAR or GUILT.

So...to summon a god, one has only to concentrate on that god to the exclusion of all other thought. Let's just say you wish to summon the Big Idea COMMUNICATION in the form of the god Hermes, so that he will grant you a silver-tongue. Hermes is the Greek personification of quick wit, art and spelling and the qualities he represents were embodied by Classical artists in the symbol of an eternally swift and naked youth, fledged with tiny wings and dressed only in streamers of air. Hermes is a condensation into pictorial form—a sigil, in fact—of an easily recognizable default state of human consciousness. When our words and minds are nimble, when we conjure laughter from others, when we make poetry, we are in the real presence of Hermes. We are, in fact, possessed by the god.

I am not suggesting that there is a real or even a ghostly, Platonic Mount Olympus where Hollywood deities sit around a magic pool watching the affairs of mortals and pausing only to leap down whenever one of us "believes" in them hard enough. There may well be for all I know but it seems a complicated way to explain something quite simple. The truth is that there doesn't HAVE to be a Mount Olympus for you to encounter Hermes or something just like him using a different name. You don't even have to "believe" in Greek gods to summon any number of them. Hermes personifies a Big Idea and all you have to do is think him fervently and he'll appear so hard and so fast in your mind that you will know him instantly.

People tend to become possessed by gods arbitrarily because they do not recognize them as such; a man can be overwhelmed with anger (the Greek god Ares), we can all be "beside ourselves" with passion (Aphrodite) or grief (Hades). In life we encounter these Big Ideas every day but we no longer use the word "god" to describe them. The magician consciously evokes these states and renames them gods in order to separate them from his or her Self, in order to study them and learn.

You may wish to connect with Hermes if you're beginning a novel or giving a speech or simply want to entertain a new beau with your incredible repartee.

HOW MANY HERMES?

The form the Big Idea takes depends upon your tradition or desire. The beautiful electric youth of the Greeks is a well-known image in Western cultures, having been appropriated for everything from Golden Age *FLASH* comics to the logo of the INTERFLORA chain of florists. Other cultures personify speed, wit and illusion slightly differently but the basic complex of ideas remains the same world-wide: velocity, words, writing, magic, trickery, cleverness, are all the qualities we would associate with Hermes, but in India this Big Idea is embodied not as a tin-hatted swift runner but as a plump youth with an elephant head and a broken tusk with which he writes the ongoing story of the universe. This is Ganesh, the scribe of the Hindu pantheon.

In Egypt, the same Big Idea is called Thoth, who created the symbols on the Tarot deck. In the Icelandic tradition, Odin or Wotan is the Lord of Lightning and communications. (Like the VDUs we stare at every day, Wotan is one-eyed and on his shoulders sit the ravens Thought and Memory who bring him instantaneous data from around the world. He can be very handy in this form, if you need to discipline an unruly PC).

Hermes, Mercury, Odin, Ganesh, Thoth; all these names represent variant embodiments on themes of Communication and speed.

Reductionists may come to an understanding of magic by considering "Mount Olympus" as a metaphor for the collective Human head.

EXPERIMENT:

Pick a traditional god or demon from a book on magic or mythology and learn all you can about your chosen subject. I suggest you start with a benign deity unless you're stupid or hard and want to get into some nasty dirty psychic business, in which case pick a demon from one of the medieval grimoires and hope you're strong enough to handle the intense negative feelings "demons" embody.

However, I'd suggest starting first with Hermes, the god of Magic, in his guise as Ganesh. Ganesh is known as a smasher of obstacles and part of his complex is that he opens the way into the magical world, so it's always good to get his acquaintance first if you're serious about following a magical path.

Call fervently upon Hermes. Luxuriate in his attributes. Drink coffee or Red Bull in his name or take a line of speed, depending on your levels of drug abuse. Fill your head with speedy images of jet planes, jet cars and bullet trains. Play "Ray of Light" by Madonna and call down Hermes. Surround yourself with *FLASH* comics and call down Hermes.

Tell him how very wonderful he is in your own words, and then call him into yourself, building a bridge between your own ever-growing feelings of brilliance and the descending energies of the Big Idea.

The arrival of the god will be unmistakable: you should experience a sense of presence or even mild possession (remember what this MEANS; we are "possessed' by Venus when LOVE destroys our reason. We are all possessed by Mars when ANGER blinds us. Learn to recognize the specific feelings which the word "possession" describes. This will allow you to study your chosen Big Idea and its effects on the human nervous system at close quarters without becoming too frightened or emotionally overwhelmed.)

You may hear a distinct voice inside your head which seems to have a strange-yet-familiar quality of "Otherness" or separateness. Ask questions and make note of the replies in your head. Remember anything specific you hear and write it down no matter how strange it seems. Maintain the sense of contact, question and response for as long as you're able and see what you can learn.

Remember Hermes is a trickster also and has a love of language and games, so be prepared for clever wordplay and riddles when you contact this Big Idea. Sometimes the rapid torrent of puns and jokes can seem like a nightmare of fractal iterations but if you're going to play with Hermes, be ready to think fast and impress with your wit.

If, on the other hand, there's only a faint hint of unearthly presence or none at all, don't worry. Try again with Ganesh, Odin or a god you feel more in tune with. Keep doing the experiment until you succeed in generating the required state of mind. It's not difficult; if you can make yourself Angry or Sad or Happy just by thinking about something (and most of us can), then you are already capable of summoning gods and Big Ideas.

DEMONS ARE...

No more, no less than the way you feel inside after you've been dumped by a beloved or exposed by one's peers as a freak or any of the other negative value defaults we have access to as human beings. Hell is ONLY the Cringe Eternal and the Place of Our Self's Undoing. When Nietzsche proclaimed "God is dead!" he forgot to add that Satan is also dead and we are Free from all that antique tat.

EXPERIMENT:

Use the techniques you've learned to summon classical gods and demons and apply them to beings you KNOW for sure can't be real, like Jack Kirby's comic book gods, H. P. Lovecraft's Cthulhu Mythos monsters, Pokemon characters, or Clive Barker's Cenobites. You will discover that you can evoke any of these outlandish characters to physical appearance. In place of Hermes, the messenger god, it's possible to summon the same complex in a quite different cultural drag—I advise at least one invocation of the speedy mercurial force of Hermes in the form of Metron, the computer-like intellectual explorer from Jack Kirby's *New Gods* comic books. I've had a great deal of success contacting the Kirby Gods, including a memorable encounter with the Big Idea of Righteous Anger in its aspect as "Orion" on the endless, cosmic battlefields of the Fourth World. Summon warrior strength and martial energy in the form of Orion by surrounding yourself with images from Kirby comics, by playing "Mars" from the "Planets Suite" or the Beatles "Revolution #9" or simply the sounds of gunfire and bombs from a special effects record.

Summon James Bond before a date by playing the themes to *Goldfinger* and *Thunderball* while dressing in a tuxedo.

Or try summoning Dionysus, god of creative delirium, in his Trickster aspect, as Ace Ventura, Pet Detective from the Jim Carrey films—surround yourself with your own pets or toy animals, play the movies, imitate the actor's distinctive moves and use them to formulate a physical sigil which you can enact within in your designated ritual space. Do this until you BECOME Dionysus as Ace Ventura. Record what happens to your sense of self and think of ways to use these new "godlike" qualities you have summoned into yourself (or brought forth from your "subconscious" depending on which model you choose to explain your experiences).

Think of these new qualities or gods as applications and upload them when you need to use them. The more you run the application the more convincing and intrinsic to

Self it seems to become. This is why actors sometimes find it difficult to "come down" from roles and why magicians often feel possessed by gods or demons. Applications are being run.

You will soon realize that gods are "qualities" or default states of consciousness available to everyone.

With much practice you will become proficient at accessing these states in yourself. Do not, however, assume that these states are ONLY internal psychological processes. The Big Ideas have been here long before you and will be here long after you are gone. They can be regarded as immensely powerful autonomous qualities and should be respected as such. Summoning too much ANGER into your life can make you a bore and a bully, summoning too much COMMUNICATION at the expense of other qualities can make you a conversation-hogging pedant and so on.

Summon James Bond before a date by playing the themes to *Goldfinger* and *Thunderball* while dressing in a tuxedo.

There is always danger when one "god" is worshipped in favor of all others. If you summon Ace Ventura you may find yourself becoming not funny and creative but annoying. If you summon Clive Barker's fictional Cenobites just to see whether or not I'm punting absolute nonsense, be prepared to deal with powerful issues of domination, torture, submission and pain for these value states define the operational parameters of Cenobites.

HEALING

My preferred method for healing is the Spiritualist "laying on of hands" technique which involves a simple homemade prayer to the congregation of dead "healers" or "veterinarians" who inhabit the "the other side" and are said to be willing to help us in times of need. This prayer is accompanied by intense concentration and visualization of the healing process. I've always found it works very well and can be most effective in conjunction with sigils.

EXPERIMENT:

Visit your local Spiritualist Church, if you have one, and ask to see a demonstration of this powerful healing method.

DUDE, WHERE'S MY EGO?

The "ego"—in the negative sense—is that ossified sense of a stable, unchanging "self" which people use as a defense against the Fear of Change and Death. It's SELF as a suit of armor; protective and comforting at times SELF doesn't allow much room to maneuver, make effective contact or adapt to new situations. Otherwise, the Ego, with a big "E" can be a useful tool like everything else lying around here. Ego creates the heroic drive towards the Transcendence which CONSUMES AND RESOLVES that drive into a higher context.

It must be remembered that you can't go beyond your ego until you've developed one to go beyond. The ego, as Individual Self, is scaffolding for what we can call superself or the memeplex (to use Susan Blackmore's term for what we call "personality"—see *The Meme Machine* (Oxford University Press, May 2000) for more on Dr. Blackmore's revolutionary theory). Scaffolding is a necessary part of any construction project but for the last couple of hundred years we've been encouraged to mistake the scaffolding for the building. The individual sovereign self once seemed such a developmental prize that it's now very difficult to let go of it without incurring amusing existential extinction traumas, but like all other stages of growth it IS just a stage and must be surpassed.

Demoting the concept of the "individual" by deliberately engineering multiple, conferring "egos," personae, memeplexes or selves is intended, at least by me, as a method of breaking up the existential, calcified, individual "Self" into more fluid Multiple Personality constellations, by exposing "the personality" as just one behavioral option from a menu of many.

THE ABYSS

Aleister Crowley embodied the destruction of Egoic Self structures as Choronzon, the Devil 333. Choronzon, we are told, is the all-devouring guardian of "the Abyss" (The Abyss being a suitably dramatic and evocative term for an experiential "gap" in human consciousness.) The term can be applied to that state of mind during which Individual Egoic Self-consciousness begins to cannibalize itself rather than confront the usually frightening fact that Personality is not "real" in the existential sense and is simply a behavioral strategy.

Most of us have had some small experience of the gigantic boundary complex Mega-ChoronzonnoznorohC-ageM; the Choronzonic Encounter is present in the relentless, dull self-interrogation of amphetamine comedowns or fevers, near-death experiences. Think of the chattering mind, annihilating itself in unstoppable self-examination and you will hear the voice of Choronzon.

Choronzon then, is Existential Self at the last gasp, munching out its own brains, seeking nourishment and finding only the riddle of the Bottom That Is Bottomless. Choronzon is when there is nothing left but to die to nothingness. Beyond Choronzon, concepts of personality and identity cannot survive. Beyond Choronzon we are no longer our Self. The "personality" on the brink of the Abyss will do anything, say anything and find any excuse to avoid taking this disintegrating step into "non-being."

> **Choronzon is when there is nothing left but to die to nothingness. Beyond Choronzon, concepts of personality and identity cannot survive. Beyond Choronzon we are no longer our Self.**

Most of us in the increasingly popular Western Consumerist traditions tend to wait until we die before even considering Choronzon. Since we can only assume that Egoic Self-sense is devoured whole in whatever blaze of guilt or fury or self-denial or peace perfect peace our last flood of endorphins allows in the 5 minutes before brain death, the moment of death seems to me to be a particularly vulnerable one in which to also have to face Existential terror for the first time.

Better to go there early and scout out the scenery. To die before dying is one of the great Ordeals of the magical path.

The Abyss, then, is that limit of Self consciousness where meaning surrenders and reverses into its own absolute opposite and is there consumed in "Choronzonic Acid," a hypersolvent so powerful it dissolves the SelfitSelf. Here you will encounter the immense SELF/NOT SELF boundary wall on the edge of Egoic Consciousness and be obliterated against it. The Abyss is a hiatus in awareness, where notions of identity, race, being and territory are consumed in an agonizing fury of contradiction.

Magicians who have successfully "crossed" the Abyss are considered no longer human, in the sense that survival of this ordeal necessitates the breaking down of SELF into multiple personality complexes.

EXPERIMENT:

The so-called "Oath of the Abyss," is a corrosive encounter with Choronzonic forces inside the personality. It is not something to be undertaken lightly and I'd suggest many years of magical practice before attempting anything as stupid and as glamorous as destroying your carefully-established SELF. The rewards of a successful crossing of the Abyss are many but a failed attempt can leave the magician broken inside, consumed by doubt, fear and insecurity and quite useless to his or her community...

REVOLT INTO MAGIC!

Becoming a magician is in itself a revolutionary act with far-reaching consequences. Before you set out to destroy "the System," however, first remember that we made it and in our own interests. We sustain it constantly, either in agreement, with our support, or in opposition with our dissent. The opponents of the System are as much a function of the System as its defenders. The System is a ghost assembled in the minds of human beings operating within "the System." It is a virtual parent we made to look after us. We made it very big and difficult to see in its entirety and we serve it and nourish it every day. Are there ever any years when no doctors or policemen are born? Why do artists rarely want to become policemen?

For every McDonald's you blow up, "they" will build two. Instead of slapping a wad of Semtex between the Happy Meals and the plastic tray, work your way up through the ranks, take over the board of Directors and turn the company into an international laughing stock.

For every McDonald's you blow up, "they" will build two. Instead of slapping a wad of Semtex between the Happy Meals and the plastic tray, work your way up through the ranks, take over the board of Directors and turn the company into an international laughing stock. You will learn a great deal about magic on the way. Then move on to take out Disney, Nintendo, anyone you fancy. What if "The System" isn't our enemy after all? What if instead it's our *playground*? The natural environments into which we pop magicians are born? Our jungle, ocean and ice floe...to bargain with and dance around and transform, as best we can, into poetry?

What if, indeed? ⌂

MARK PESCE

THE EXECUTABLE DREAMTIME

Being Imbolc, the Illumination of all things Hidden and Occult, the holiday of Bride, who brings the Light of Knowledge to all those who humbly ask Her Grace to dispel Darkness, it is Meet and Proper to discuss Such Things as may lead to a Broader Understanding of the Relation between Word and Will. Once Requested, Thrice Granted. So mote it be!

WORD AND WILL

I pitied thee,
Took pains to make thee speak, taught thee each hour
One thing or other: when thou didst not, savage,
Know thine own meaning, but wouldst gabble like
A thing most brutish, I endow'd thy purposes
With words that made them known.

–*The Tempest*, Act I, Scene 2

A recent issue of *New Scientist* celebrated William S. Burroughs' most famous maxim: "Language is a virus." It seems that language, our ability to apprehend and manipulate symbols and signs, has evolved to fill a unique ecological niche—the space between our ears. Human beings, together with most higher animals, share an ability to sequence perceptual phenomena temporally, detecting the difference between before, during, and after. This capability is particularly pronounced in the primates, and, in the case of *homo sapiens*, left us uniquely susceptible to an infection of sorts, an appropriation of our innate cognitive abilities for ends beyond those determined by nature alone. Our linguistic abilities aren't innate. They are not encoded in our DNA. Language is more like *E. coli*, the bacteria in our gut, symbiotically helping us to digest our food. Language helps us to digest phenomena, allowing us to ruminate on the nature of the world.

Why language at all? We are fairly certain that it confers evolutionary advantage, that a species which speaks (and occasionally, listens) is more likely to pass its genes on than a species which cannot speak. But we can't make too much of that: nearly all other animals are dumb, to varying degrees, and they manage to be fruitful and multiply without having to talk about it. Despite the fact that gorillas can sign and dolphins squeak, we haven't found any indication of the symbol-rich internal consciousness which we attribute to language. This means that other animals have a direct experience of the world around them, while everything we do is utterly infused with the fog of language.

We need to be clear about this: from the time, some tens or hundreds of thousands of years ago, that language invaded and colonized our cerebrums, we have increasingly lost touch with the reality of things. Reality has been replaced with relation, a mapping of *things-as-they-are* to *things-as-we-believe-them-to-be*. Language allows us to construct complex systems of symbols, the linear narratives which frame our experience. Yet a frame invariably occults more of the world than it encompasses, and this exclusion leaves us separated from the *world-as-it-is*.

It is impossible for a human being, in a "normal" level of consciousness—that is, without explicit training or "gratuitous grace"—to experience anything of the reality of the world. Language steps in to mediate, explain, and define. The moments of ineffability are outside the bounds of human culture (if not entirely outside human experience) because at these points where language fails nothing can be known or said. This alone should tell us that while we think ourselves the masters of language, precisely the opposite is true. Language is the master of us, a tyranny from which no escape can be imagined.

This is not a new idea. The second line of the *Tao Te Ching* states the matter precisely: "The name which can be named is not the true name." In the origins of human philosophy and metaphysics, language stands out as the great Interloper, separating man from the apprehension of things-as-they-are. Zen practice aims to extinguish the internal monologue, seeking a unification, a boundary dissolution between the internal state of mankind, encompassed at every point by the boundaries inherent in language, and the Absolute. This is the universal, yet entirely individual battle of mankind, the great liberation earnestly sought for. Yet, at the end, nothing is gained. And this seems reward enough, because the "mind forg'd manacles" which bind us to the world of words so hinder the progress of the soul that any release, even into Nothing, is a movement upward.

It is not as though all of us are imminently bound for Nirvana; while some will stop the Wheel of Karma, the rest will remain thoroughly entangled in the attachments of desire, hypnotically attracted to the veil of Maya. That veil is made of language; it is the seductive voice, the Siren's Call, which keeps us from our final destiny. This is bad, in that attachments produce suffering, but it is also good, a point rarely promoted by the devotees of utmost annihilation. Being in the world means being at play within the world. Without play there is no learning, without learning, no progress to the inevitable release. And in the play of the world, as in any game, there are winners and losers: there are those who skin their knees or break their bones, but at the end, everything returns to potentialities, and only the memory of having played the game remains. All of our interactions within the world leave their mark upon us, and we wage war within ourselves: we would be both naked, unadorned, and as completely transformed as the Illustrated Man, whose entire body, covered in tattoos, tells the story of his life.

In the battle between Word and Will, there are two paths, which diverge from a common entry point, and converge upon a final exit. We wish to release everything and become one with all; we wish to encompass everything and become one with all. If you desire to remove yourself from the world, there are numerous sources, starting with Lao Tze and Buddha, who can steer you in the direction of emptiness. But if you decide this is too much (or rather, *too little*) to ask, there is another path. I find the emptiness of the Absolute a bit too chilling, the light from *Ain Soph* too revealing; not because they represent the highest, but rather, because they simplify the manifold beauty. "The Tao produces one, one produces two, the two produce the three and the three produce all things." To choose the Tao over the many things which flow from it is to assert a hierarchy of values, a violation of the very essence of the Tao. We are that river; we flow from that source. Why do we feel the need to return?

"Language is a virus." While we think ourselves the masters of language, precisely the opposite is true. Language is the master of us, a tyranny from which no escape can be imagined.

As an answer to the demands of eternal return, the French philosophers have introduced us to the idea of *forward acceleration*. When you find yourself trapped in a seemingly hopeless situation, jam your foot down on the accelerator petal, take it to the limit, and drive straight on through to the culmination. *Imminentize the Eschaton*. What if we were to say, *fine, bring it on*, and accept language for all of its enslaving faults—but, at the same time, keep a consciousness of these faults constantly before us? Where would we find ourselves? Could this lead to freedom, a freedom which is less an escape from imprisonment than an encompassing awareness that the world, with all of its traps and cages, cannot be separated from the Absolute? In any case, a recognition of the "horror of the situation"—as Gurdjieff stated it—could only put us in a better place to plot our escape. When you find yourself in the belly of the Beast, why not curl up, make yourself comfortable, and *conspire*? That most concisely describes where we are today, in an instantaneously connected, universally mediated linguistic environment of human creation. But before we conspire in any sense of safety, we must consider how language shapes the relations between human beings. Otherwise we risk exchanging the illness of linguistic infection for the cunning traps of human power.

RHETORIC AND REASON

Good friends, sweet friends, let me not stir you up
To such a sudden flood of mutiny.
They that have done this deed are honorable:
What private griefs they have, alas, I know not,
That made them do it: they are wise and honorable,
And will, no doubt, with reasons answer you.

–Julius Caesar, Act III, Scene 2

A few weeks before I wrote this essay, I had a private conversation with a neurophysiologist at UCSD (University of California San Diego), who passed along some stunning insights he'd gathered from his research on the human brain. It seems that although we like to perceive ourselves as rational, reasonable creatures, carefully weighing our decisions before we commit, the fact of the matter is precisely the inverse. We arrive at our decisions through emotional sensations, acting "from the gut" at all times. Our reason enters the process only after the decision has been made, and acts as the mind's propagandist, convincing us of the utter rightness which underlies all of our actions. Beyond this, reason has a social function: to convince others that our actions are correct. Friends, Romans, countrymen, lend me your ears! Not so that you can think for yourselves, but that I might instruct you in what to believe.

Thus are all the great philosophies of Socrates and Plato overturned; these men, considering themselves the paragons of reason, used their rhetorical skills to create a new tradition in thought which had nothing more behind it than the force of the words which composed it. Seen in this light, the entirety of human history becomes more farcical (and more tragic) than could possibly be imagined. Right and wrong, good and evil, these carefully argued positions are foundations built upon the shifting sands of words. The linguistic infection has left us weakened, vulnerable to a secondary, and perhaps more serious illness—conviction.

Humans are faced with a dual-headed problem; it is bad enough that the world as-we-know-it is made of words, mediated by language, and still worse that this means that other human beings can employ this condition (more precisely, conditioning) for their own ends. It likely could not be otherwise, for we are social beings; that much is encoded into our DNA and our physiology. We need for people to believe in us, to support us, to conspire with us. A human being unwillingly deprived of the society of his peers descends into madness as the fine structures of perceived reality, maintained and reinforced by the rhetorical bombardments of others' truths (and his own, reflected back), rapidly unwind without constant reinforcement. What I tell you three times is true. What I tell you three million times is civilization.

Plato knew this: that's why he banned poets from his *Republic*. What he could not (or, more sinisterly, *would not*) recognize is that all words are poetry, rhetoric regimenting the reason. To speak and be heard means that you are sending your will out onto the world around you, changing the definition of reality for all those who hear you. We do this from the time we learn to speak (imagine the two year-old asserting his will in a shrill cry for attention, and noting a corresponding change in the behavior of those around him) till the moment we breathe our last. For most people, most of the time, this is an unconscious process, automatic and mechanical. For a few others, who, by accident or training, have become conscious of the power of reason to change men's minds, a choice is presented: *how do you use this power?*

"We are all pan-dimensional wizards, casting arcane spells with every word we speak. And every spell we speak always comes true." Owen Rowley, my mentor in both the magical mysteries and in the mysteries of virtual reality, taught me this maxim some years ago, though it took

> **We arrive at our decisions through emotional sensations, acting "from the gut" at all times. Our reason enters the process only after the decision has been made, and acts as the mind's propagandist, convincing us of the utter rightness which underlies all of our actions.**

some years before I began to understand the full magnitude of his seemingly grandiose pronouncement. More than anything else, it places enormous responsibility on anyone who uses language—that is, all of us. Because we are creatures infected by language, and because language shapes how we come to interpret reality, we bear the burden of our words. We know that words can hurt, we even believe that words can kill, but the truth is far more comprehensive: all of our words are the equivalent of a hypnotist's suggestions, and all of us are to some degree susceptible. With this responsibility comes an awareness of the burden we bear. It is how we encounter this burden—as individuals and as a civilization—which shapes reality.

If power corrupts, and each of us are endowed with inestimable power, we could cast human civilization as a long war of words, a battle to determine what is real. Robert Anton Wilson once quipped, "Reality is the line where rival gangs of shamans fought to a standstill." This statement hides the fact that we're all shamans, and every time we say, "This is this," we reset the parameters of the real. Most of these shamanic battles are relatively innocent, just primate teeth-baring and jockeying for dominance in a given situation. However, in the wrong mouths, words can lead to disaster. Consider Jim Jones or Adolph Hitler, who, by force of their oratory, led hundreds and millions to their deaths.

If, instead, an individual conscious of the power of words to shape the world chooses to use this power with wisdom, seeking not hegemony but liberation—a different path opens up. In this world, nothing needs to be true, and everything becomes permissible. This is the realm of conscious magick, where the realized power of the word opens possibilities for the self without constricting the potentialities of anyone else. This is the safest path, both karmically and practically; if you stay out of the way of others, there's less likelihood you'll be interfered with yourself. The magician does not proselytize; and although he may present an irresolvable paradox for those who confront his magick with their own linguistically reinforced perceptions of the world, he bares no responsibility for their reactions, nor is he susceptible to their attacks. He exists in a world apart, because there is no agreement on a common language through which a linguistic infection could spread. The magician insulates himself, inoculates himself and protects himself from the beliefs of others, while holding his own beliefs in great suspicion. Rhetoric and anti-rhetoric, combined, produces a burst of energy which propels the magician forward, with great acceleration, into a new universe of meaning.

The products of power sometime pose too great a temptation to the magician; we have the warning tale of Faust to remind us that although the mastery of the linguistic nature of the world confers great power over others, its use inevitably leads to destruction. The magician needs a higher consciousness—in the Sufic sense—before he can toy with the wheels and dials of such power. This is why many magical orders will not initiate candidates before they have reached a certain age, or have demonstrated a material responsibility which can form a foundation from which right action can proceed. To ignore such prohibitions is to court disaster, and the checkered history of magical orders in the 19th and 20th centuries shows that far too often, ignorance has been the order of the day. Only when the magician puts down his power over others does he achieve any realizable power over himself. You are your own High Priest, and no one else's. From this everything else follows.

When the magician has arrived at this point in his path, matters of education and technique become paramount. It is very rare when an individual is granted sufficient gratuitous grace to travel on the path to wisdom entirely

> **Robert Anton Wilson once quipped, "Reality is the line where rival gangs of shamans fought to a standstill." In the wrong mouths, words can lead to disaster. Consider Jim Jones or Adolph Hitler, who, by force of their oratory, led hundreds and millions to their deaths.**

alone. The teacher or mentor reveals the mysteries to the initiate, but the teacher must be aware of how much the initiate can bear safely, doling out knowledge as one might dispense a powerful tonic which is also a poison. The right dosage can do great good; too much will kill. For this reason the Sufis believe that only within a "School" governed by a teacher with sufficient wisdom, can the initiate pass through the gates of wisdom.

Consider for a moment the case of John Lilly, a modern magician, who used sensory deprivation in combination with LSD-25 in a search for wisdom. He had enormous successes to begin with: *Programming and Metaprogramming in the Human Biocomputer* is one of the most effective magical texts ever published, useful for the magician throughout his training. Yet this could not keep Lilly from becoming a life-long ketamine addict, which finally left him hollowed-out and lifeless (in consensus reality), as he chose to remain in the Valley of Illusions. This is an individual choice, of course, and Lilly had his reasons (or rather, his emotions) for choosing this course for his life. But Lilly deprived himself of the opportunity for further advancement on the path of knowledge, becoming trapped within a world of chemical fantasy. His intense forward acceleration led only to a cul-de-sac, a dead-end from which he would never escape.

If such a luminary as John Lilly cannot safely pass through the gates of wisdom, what hope can be given to the aspiring magician, one who has become conscious of the power of the word to shape the world, but has no understanding of how to actualize that knowledge? We are fortunate to live in an age when all the teachings of all the ages are more or less freely available, a time when all the mysteries have been revealed. But the mysteries themselves are not enough. A community is necessary, a conspiracy of like-minded souls set on the same path, speaking the right words, words which reinforce the integrity of the self, allowing the magician to learn wisdom through a series of initiations (whether explicit or implicit), growing, like a child, into adulthood.

These schools do exist, and it is possible for the aspiring magician to find them without too much difficulty. Even so, a certain skepticism is necessary; "By their fruits you will know them," and although the teacher may seem overtly stern, or authoritarian, it remains up to the candidate to prepare his vessel, ready to receive illumination. Even the most profane masters can be vehicles for the illumination of their students—provided the students are properly prepared. The student must remain conscious, vigilant, and never allow the master to use linguistic traps to assign the real; that's the difference between a School and a cult.

WORD AND WORLD

Now my charms are all o'erthrown,
And what strength I have's mine own,
Which is most faint: now, 'tis true,
I must be here confined by you,
Or sent to Naples. Let me not,
Since I have my dukedom got
And pardon'd the deceiver, dwell
In this bare island by your spell;
But release me from my bands
With the help of your good hands.

–*The Tempest*, Act V, Epilogue

We have by now told but half the story. Our linguistic capabilities, as employed by our reason, act upon each other to create reality. Yet beyond the reality-in-our-heads there is an exterior world (let's admit that, lest we be accused of nothing but solipsism and *word play*), which we are about to actualize as an exteriorization of our linguistic capabilities. The world presents two faces to us; the natural, that is, *that which arose by itself;* and the artificial; *that which is the product of man's interactions within the world*. While both the natural and artificial are clouded with the omnipresent linguistic fog, only the artificial world is the product of our linguistic nature. Artifacts are language concretized and exteriorized. Technology is a language of sorts, in which the forms of the world are shaped by our words, and then speak back to us. We have been throwing technological innovations into the world since we discovered fire (at least a half million years ago), and since that time the technological world, the world of artifact, has been talking back. The history of humanity, viewed in this way, can be seen as a continuous process of feedback: as we talk to the world, through our hands, the world accepts these innovations, which modify the environment within which we participate, which modifies our own understanding of the world, which leads to new innovations, which modifies the environment, which modifies us, and so on, and so on. This isn't causality, or just a circling Oroborus; this is a process, an epigenetic evolution, in which language continuously assumes a more concrete form. We are learning to talk to the hand, or rather, our hands are learning to speak, and are endowing the world of artifacts with the same linguistic infections that have so completely colonized our own biology.

This is a lot to assert, and a lot to absorb, but it is possible to approach this thesis from another point of entry, *the idea of code*. The word "code" has numerous meanings; it means one thing to a geneticist, another to a computer programmer, another to a cryptographer. Yet the underlying meaning is remarkably similar, because there is a growing sense in the scientific and technical communities that when all of the specifics are stripped away, when the very essence of the universe is revealed, it is naught but code. And what is code, precisely? Language. Whether the stepping-stairs of the amino acid base pairs which comprise the genome, or the sequence of logical steps in a computer program, or the mathematical translations which can either occult or reveal a message, code is a temporal organization of symbols—first...next...last—which establish the basis for both operation and understanding.

The idea of the universe as code has gained great currency from mathematician Stephen Wolfram's *A New Kind of Science* (Wolfram Media, Inc., 2002) which posits that the processes observable in the universe more often obey computational rules than algebraic formulae. He goes on to state that an enormous number of disparate processes we see in nature—the expansion of space-time, quantum interconnectedness, and the growth of biological forms— all have their basis in the fact that the universe acts as an entity which is constantly processing codes, executing programs, engaging in an execution of reality. Wolfram has been trained both as a physicist and a computer programmer; his background in both disciplines makes him uniquely qualified to identify the common ground that lies between these seemingly entirely distinct fields.

"Any sufficiently advanced technology is indistinguishable from magic."

The ground seems to be rising to meet Wolfram. While biologists discover the codes of nature, physicists and chemists are applying codes to nature's most basic structures, to produce atomic-scale forms known as nanotechnology. Whether or not we choose to acknowledge it, the arrow of the epigenetic evolution of the human species points to a time in the near future when the entire world will be apprehended as code. A forthcoming "Theory of Everything" won't be a formula; it will be a *program*, a series of linguistic statements, which, like the words in a sentence, describe the execution of reality.

Here we come to the heart of the matter, where the individual apprehension of the world as linguistically conceived becomes convergent with the increasingly accepted scientific view of the universe as a linguistic process. We know that words shape the world as we see it, but now we have come to understand that words shape the world as it is. There is, at an essential level, an isomorphism between the world of the code between our ears and the reality of the code of the universe. The codes we create change our personal perceptions of the world, but they also change the world around us; the more we learn about how to modify the world, the more that language becomes convergent with reality, and the more our will extends over the real. In a real sense, beyond the narrow vision of the world underneath our skin, words are colonizing the world.

This places the magician in a unique historical position, or, rather, restores him to a position which he lost during the scientific revolution. Newton began his career as an alchemist, seeking the mystical union between man and nature which would result in the Philosopher's Stone. He did not live to see the final convergence between the language of magick and the language of science, but, more and more, science will begin to look like magick, and magicians like scientists. I don't mean this in the rude sense of *Clarke's Law* that "Any sufficiently advanced technology is indistinguishable from magic," but rather, that the principles and techniques underlying these two seemingly separate disciplines are on naturally convergent courses. The magician, master of the code, will find himself completely at home in a universe which has become linguistically apprehensible *as code*. The scientist will find himself completely at home speaking a language in which his words change the world. With the exception of those few who pursue both disciplines, neither will have noticed that they have arrived at the same point. The magician will utter his spells, the scientist will speak his codes, but both will be saying the same thing.

It will feel to us as though we have come full circle. The ancients of the West compiled grimoires, magical texts which presented the lessons learned by generations of practitioners in a series of spells, linguistic incantations which used the word to shape the will. Aboriginal cultures wove these lessons into "songlines," expressing the mythic narrative of culture as the infinite possibility beyond consensus reality, a "dreamtime." Now, knowing the ground for the first time, we are using our gifts with language—in genetics and informatics and chemistry—to speak the word, and make the world. The idea of code is overflowing, becoming the world itself, and reality will soon be as programmable as the writer's page, responding to the will of the magician like some lucid dream. In this executable dreamtime everything is true, within limits determined by experiment; once those limits are known, a new generation of magicians will undoubtedly attempt to transcend them.

What will this world look like? We have no precedent in profane history to use as a guide; we must look further afield, to mythology, to understand the form of a linguistic universe. It is the dreamtime of the Aboriginal Australians, or the Faeire of the Celts, the absolute expansion of possibilities—both angelic and demonic—in that everything expressible can be brought into being. The masters of linguistic intent in both magical and scientific forms (a false distinction) will be masters of word and world. *Say the word, and it will come to pass.*

Although this process appears inevitable, it could be that we are bound by the same "Single Vision and Newton's Sleep" that William Blake prophesied 200 years ago. It could be that the universe is not code, but simply that the idea of code has overflowed from our brain's linguistic centers into other areas of the cerebrum, colonizing our reason and intellectual capabilities as easily as it captured our ability to apprehend sequence. This could all be a chimera, an elusive possibility which may remain tantalizingly out of reach. Yet the whole world seems to be conspiring to teach us this: *In the beginning was the word.* ◻

THEE SPLINTER TEST

It can be said, for me at least, that sampling, looping and re-assembling both found materials and site specific sounds selected for precision of relevance to thee message implications of a piece of music or a transmedia exploration, is an alchemical, even a magical phenomenon. No matter how short, or apparently unrecognizable a "sample" might be in linear time perception, I believe it must, inevitably, contain within it (and accessible through it), the sum total of absolutely everything its original context represented, communicated, or touched in any way; on top of this it must implicitly also include the sum total of every individual in any way connected with its introduction and construction within the original (host) culture, and every subsequent (mutated or engineered) culture it in any way, means or form, has contact with forever (in Past, Present, Future and Quantum time zones).

> *"Any two particles that have once been in contact will continue to act as though they are informationally connected regardless of their separation in space and time."*
> −Bell's Theorem

Let us assume then that every "thing" is interconnected, interactive, interfaced and intercultural. Sampling is all ways experimental, in that thee potential results are not a given. We are splintering consensual realities to test their substance utilizing the tools of collision, collage, composition, decomposition, progression systems, "random" chance, juxtaposition, cut-ups, hyperdelic vision and any other method available that melts linear conceptions and reveals holographic webs and fresh spaces. As we travel in every direction simultaneously

the digital highways of our Futures, thee "Splinter Test" is both a highly creative contemporary channel of conscious and creative "substance" abuse, and a protection against the restrictive depletion of our archaic, algebraic, analogic manifestations.

> *"My Prophet is a fool with his 1,1,1; are they not the OX, and none by the BOOK?"*
> −Liber AL I -48

So, in this sense, and bearing this in our "mind" on a technical level, when we sample, or as we shall prefer to label it in this essay, when we *splinter*, we are actually splintering people and brain product freed of any of the implicit restraints or restrictions of the five dimensions. We are actually taking bytes and reusing these thereafter as hieroglyphs or memes—the tips of each iceberg.

If we shatter, and scatter, a hologram, we will realize that in each fragment, no matter how small, large, or irregular; we will see the whole hologram. This is an incredibly significant phenomenon.

It has all ways been my personal contention that if we take, for example, a *splinter* of John Lennon, that splinter will, in a very real manner, contain within it everything that John Lennon ever experienced; everything that John Lennon ever said, composed, wrote, drew, expressed; everyone that ever knew John Lennon and the sum total of all and any of those interactions; everyone who ever heard, read, thought of, saw, reacted to John Lennon or anything remotely connected with John Lennon; every past, present and/or future combination of any or all of thee above.

In magick this is known as the "contagion theory" or phenomenon. The magical observation of this same phenomenon would suggest that by including even a miniscule reference or symbol of John Lennon in a working, ritual or a sigil (a two or three dimensional product invoking a clear intention usually primarily graphically and non-linguistically, in a linear, everyday sense) you are invoking *John Lennonness* as part of what in this particular context (i.e. music) is a musical *sigil*.

We access every variable memory library and every individual human being who's ever for a second connected with, conceived or related to or been devoted to or despised or in anyway been exposed to this splinter of culture.

All that encyclopedic information—and the time travel connected with it, through memory and through previous experience—goes with that one "splinter" of memory, and we should be very aware that it carries with it an infinite sequence of connections and progressions through time and space. As far as you may wish to go.

We can now all maintain the ability to assemble, via these "splinters," clusters of any era. These clusters are basically reminding. They are actually bypassing the usual consensus reality filters (because they reside in an acceptable form, i.e. TV/film/music/words) and traveling directly into "historical" sections of the brain, triggering all and every conscious and unconscious reverberation to do with that one splinter hieroglyph.

We access every variable memory library and every individual human being who's ever for a second connected with, conceived or related to or been devoted to or despised or in anyway been exposed to this splinter of culture.

We now have available to us as a species, really for thee first time in history, infinite freedom to choose and assemble, and everything we assemble is a portrait of what we are now or what we visualize being.

SKILLFUL SPLINTERING CAN GENERATE MANIFESTATION.

THIS IS THEE "SPLINTER TEST"

We are choosing splinters consciously and unconsciously to represent our own mimetic (DNA) patterns, our own cultural imprints and aspirations; we are in a truly magical sense invoking manifestations, perhaps even results, in

order to confound and short-circuit our perceptions, and reliance of *wholeness*.

Anything, in any medium imaginable, from any culture, which is in any way recorded and can in any possible way be played back is now accessible and infinitely malleable and useable to any artist. Everything is available, everything is free, and everything is permitted. It's a firestorm in a shop sale where everything must go.

The "edit" in video and televisual programming and construction is in essence an *invisible language* in the sense that our brain reads a story or narration in a linear manner, tending to blend, compose, and assemble as continuous what it primarily sees at the expense of *reading* the secondary sets of intersections and joins that it does not consciously, or independently, see. Yet the precision of choice in where to edit, and thee specific emotional and intellectual impact and innate sense of meaning that is thus specifically conveyed is as much a text of intent and directed meaning, even propaganda, as is the screenplay or dialogue itself.

Everything in life is cut-up. Our senses retrieve infinite chaotic vortices of information, flattening and filtering them to a point that enables commonplace activity to take place within a specific cultural consensus reality. Our brain encodes flux, and builds a mean average picture at any given time. Editing, reduction of intensity and linearity are constantly imposed upon the ineffable to facilitate ease of basic communication and survival. What we see, what we hear, what we smell, what we touch, what we emote, what we utter, are all dulled and smoothed approximations of a far more intense, vibrant and kaleidoscopic ultra-dimensional actuality.

Those who build, assemble. ASSEMBLY is thee invisible language of our TIME. Infinite choices of reality are thee gift of "software" to our children.

[THEE SPLINTER TEST –APPENDIX A.]

THEE SCATTERING

"And they did offer sacrifices of their own blood, sometimes cutting themselves around in pieces and they left them in this way as a sign. Other times they pierced their cheeks, at others their lower lips. Sometimes they scarified certain parts of their bodies, at others they pierced their tongues in a slanting direction from side to side and passed bits of straw though thee holes with horrible suffering; others slit thee superfluous part of their virile member leaving it as they did their ears."

A FORMAL PROCESS OF MORAL REASONING

If history is any clue, the succession of civilizations is accompanied by bloodshed, disasters and other tragedies. Our moral responsibility is not to stop a future, but to shape it: To channel our destiny in humane directions, and to try to ease the trauma of transition. We are still at the beginning of exploring our tiny little piece of the omniverse. We are still scientific, technological, and cyberspace primitives; and, as we revolutionize science itself, expanding its perimeters, we will put mechanistic science—which is highly useful for building bridges or

SOURCES ARE RARE

In the future the spoken word will be viewed as holding no power or resonance and the written word will be viewed as dead, only able to be imbued with potential life in its functional interactions with what will have become archaic software and programming archaeologies, namely speech. That is, just as a symphony orchestra preserves a museum of music, of music considered seminal and part of a DNA-like spiral of culture; so, the *word* will be seen as the preservation vehicle in a DNA-like chain of digital break-throughs and cultural intersections. The *word* will be viewed, not as a virus that gave speech, nor as the gift of organic psychedelics through which civilization (i.e. living in cities) was made so "wondrously" possible, but, as a necessary language skill for those specializing in thee arcane

Imagine, if you won't, that you are a subversive in this future. You conspire to be hidden by the use of the word. This act could move you into a position of becoming a co-conspirator in the process of desecration.

making automobiles—in its limited place. Alongside it we will develop multiple metaphors, alternative principles of evidence, new loggias, catastrophe theories, and new tribal ways to separate our useful fictions and archetypes from useless ones. The scattered shapes of this new civilization will be determined by population and resource trends; by military factors; by value changes; by behavioral speculations in fields of consciousness; by changes in family structures; by global political shifts; by awakened individual Utopian aspirations; by accelerated cultural paradigms and not by technologies alone. This will mean designing new institutions for controlling our technological leaps into a future. It will mean replacing obsolete political, economic, territorial, and ecological structures. It will mean evolving new micro-decision making systems that are both individually and tribally oriented synthesizing participation and initiation and new macro-decision making systems that are digitally spiritual and revealingly autonomous. Small elites can no longer make major technological, ecological, or economical decisions. Fractally anarchic clusters of individuals with integrated extended family structures and transhuman gender groupings must participate and calibrate what stretches out before them in a neo-pagan assimilation of all before—NOW!—and to be.

"It will BE because It is inevitable" Old TOPY proverb.

We plough the field and scattering the would-ship of our plan.

science of Software Archeology, or SoftArch Processing, as it will become known, in much the same way as Latin was for so long a required subject and qualifier of scholarship at prestigious universities when the drone majority found it incongruous, if not ludicrous. Of course individuals will be utilizing laser based systems to access and exit the neuro-system via the retina and these systems in turn will transmit, wirelessly, to a new breed of computers using liquid memory instead of micro-chips. If we are to disbelieve what we don't hear, then conversation will be a status symbol of the leisured classes and power elites. As ever the same processes that delineate *power*, in this case, a perpetuation of an atrophied communication system, i.e. *words*, will always be appropriated by those who position their means of perception at an intersection diametrically opposed to those who oppress with it, for it, or because of it. Put simply, any form of literal or cultural weapon pioneered by authority will some day be used by "esoterrorists" bent upon destabilizing and/or, at least temporarily, destroying its source. The poles become clearer, thine enemy more known, as the mud settles and we protagonists are exposed standing shakily on our rocks, above the Golden Section and visible to all who would disown and destroy us. It is in this spirit that this work was created.

Imagine, if you won't, that you are a subversive in this future. You conspire to be hidden by the use of the *word*. This act could move you into a position of becoming a co-conspirator in the *process of desecration*. To conspire literally means "to breathe together." Thee all pervading surveillance systems are—NOW!—so digitized that they have no voice recognition software, this has also been manifested to protect the conspiracies and debaucheries of the Control species themselves.

"Hell, even Deities need privacy, son. We used to plot murders and takeovers in saunas, then bug-proof buildings, now we just talk, son, no one out there listening, all just PLUGGED IN."

One fashionable lower class, blue-collar medical expense is the vocal chord removal process. It's taken as a status operation. A clear signal to one's contemporaries that your software interface is so advanced that you need never consider the use of speech ever again.

The *word* is finally atrophied. No longer a dying heart, but dead. The bypass is on. So here you are. You FEEL something is out of balance, you TALK. They TALK. The world swims in silence. The only place of secrecy is a public place, the only manner of passing on secrets is talking out loud. Neither protagonist is aware that the other is TALKING. If they were all Hells would be let loose.

Forcible vocotomies in the street, subversives held down at gunpoint, their chords lasered out in seconds. Loud laughter of a rich vocotomy tout, the ultimate status signal "of power."

Know the WORD is gone, its power defused, diffuse, in order that these scriptures of the golden eternity be fulfilled.

In the ending, was the WORD.

As a recipient of this cluster you are encouraged to recall, and remain constantly vigilant of the dilemma it exposes.

It hungers for the death of the *word*. Rightly so, for we are imprisoned in the *naming* sorcery that was both built, and solidified within the process of Control, and more critically and integral to it, submission and subservience.

This death is craved intrinsically by all in order that a showdown may occur, as the World Preset Guardians laser burn their retina of lust for result. The WORD wills to go. It is here to go.

Thee Brain Computer interface will replace all verbal media of communication, for bitter or wars, the *new* being

merely that which is inevitable. Nurse it along so that it may become a living intelligence system. Thee Museum of Meanings.

What wills to be reborn wills vary with the input of the user.

Debug the old preset programming. Leave only an empty timezone that you might later fill with your will and clarity of intent.

[THEE SPLINTER TEST –APPENDIX C.]
CATHEDRAL ENGINE

"VIDEO IS THEE ELECTRONIC MOLOTOV COCKTAIL OF THEE TV GENERATION"

Cause the cathode ray tubes to resonate and explode. You are your own screen. You own your own screen.

Watching television patches us into the global mixing board, within which we are all equally capable of being victim or perpetrator. The Internet carrying audio/video, text, pictures, data and scrap books via modem actually delivers a rush of potentiality that was previously only advanced speculation. The lines on thee television screen become a shimmering representation of the infinite phone lines that transmit and receive. We have an unlimited situation. Our reality is already half-video. In this hallucinatory state all realities are equal. Television was developed to impose a generic unity of purpose: The purpose of "control." To do this it actually transmits through lines and frequencies of light. Light only accelerates what the brain is. Now we can, with our brains, edit, record, adjust,

In this hallucinatory state all realities are equal. Television was developed to impose a generic unity of purpose: The purpose of "control."

assemble and transmit our deepest convictions, our most mundane parables. Nothing is true, all is transmitted. The brain exists to make matter of an idea; television exists to transmit the brain. Nothing can exist that we do not believe in. At these times consciousness is not centered in the world of form, it is experiencing the world of content. The means of perception wills to become the program. The program wills to become power. The world of form wills to thereby reduce the ratio of subjective, experiential reality, a poor connection between mind and brain. Clusters of temporary autonomous programs globally transmitted, received, exchanged and jammed will generate a liberation from consumer forms and linear scripts and make a splintered test of equal realities in a mass political hallucination transcending time, body, or place. All hallucinations are real, but some hallucinations are more real than others.

We create programs and "deities," entities and Armageddons in the following way: Once we describe, or transmit in any way, our description of an idea, or an observed, or an aspired to ideal, or any other concept that for ease of explanation we hereafter will to describe as a "deity," we are the source of it.

We are the source of all that we invoke. What we define and describe exists through our choosing to describe it. By continued and repeated description of its parameters and nature, we animate it. We give it life.

At first, we control what we transmit. As more and more individuals believe in the original sin of its description, and agree on the terms of linguistic, visual and other qualities, this "deity" is physically manifested. The more belief accrued, the more physically present the "deity" wills to become. At a certain point, as countless people believe in, and give life to that described and believed in, the "deity" wills to separate its *self* from the source. It then develops an agenda of its own, sometimes in opposition to the original intent and purpose of the source. The General Order at this intersection becomes *go* and it continues to transmit to our brains. Our brains are thus a Neuro-Visual Screen for that which has separated from its source and become a "deity." This is in no way intended as a metaphor, rather a speculation as to the manner in which our various concepts of brain are actually programmed and replicated. In an omniverse where all is true and everything is recorded, as Brion Gysin wondered, "who made the original recordings?" Or in more contemporary jargon, who programmed the nanotech software? Our response can only be a speculative prescience: The Guardians who exist in an—at present—unfathomable other world and preset the transmissions in some, as yet, mysterious way.

Videos can move televisual order and conditioned expectations of perspective from one place and reassemble its elements as if gluing a smashed hologram back together, all the while knowing that each piece contains within it the whole image. In other words, these are all small fragments of how each of us actually experiences life: *through all our senses simultaneously*. In every direction simultaneously. Even in all five dimensions (at least!) simultane-

ously. Bombarded by every possible nuance and contradiction of meaning simultaneously. Quaquaversally. This is a relentlessly *inclusive* process. We do not just view "life" anymore, although perhaps we can, at least potentially, have an option to view everything. *Intention* is the key. What was once referred to as the "viewer" is now also a *source* of anything to be viewed, and the Neuro-Visual Screen on which to view it. The constructed and ever increasing digital concoction built from millions of sources that is commonly referred to as "Cyberspace" is accelerating towards *deification*, and separateness. Towards the moment of a sentient awakening of its own consciousness and agendas that we feel is more aptly described as the "Psychosphere." This Psychosphere challenges us to seize the means of perception and remain thee source.

"Change thee way to perceive and change all memory."
–Old TOPY proverb.

[THEE SPLINTER TEST –APPENDIX D.]

Since there is no goal to this operation other than the goal of perpetually discovering new forms and new ways of perceiving, it is an infinite game. An infinite game is played for the purpose of continuing to play, as opposed to a finite game which is played for the purpose of winning or defining winners. It is an act of freed *will to*.... No one can "play" who is forced to play.

Play, is indeed, implicitly voluntary.

[THEE SPLINTER TEST –APPENDIX E.]

Thee night under Witches that you close up your book of shadows and open up your neuro-super highway to thee liquid blackness (within which dwells an entity) represents thee edge of present time. It pinpoints precisely the finality of all calendars, wherein it is clear that measurement, in its self, and of its self equals "DEATH" or "DAATH." The spoken binds and constricts navigation unutterably. The etymology of the word spiral (DNA), from the Greek, indicates an infinitude of perceptive spaces and points of observation, where "down," "up," "across," "distance" and other faded directional terms become redundant in an absolute elsewhere. Thee eyes have it and they suggest a serpent that was once the nearest metaphor to cold dark matters such as wormholes and spaces between. ⊟

MEMENTO MORI
Remember You Must Die

I. (THANATAESTHETICS)

The aesthetics of death is having a pseudo-posthumous revival. The Great Wheel of History—the Zeitgeist (The Time Spirit)—that allows the Juggernaut (Jagannatha: Vishnu the Sustainer) to move on has the death's head on its hub. The velocity of the Zeitgeist has never changed. It is just that our perception of reality has speeded up sufficiently, as we near the end of time, so that the true nature of reality is more apparent to all in this post-secular era of today.

Not only do most people want to know the secret of death—What is it like to be dead?—but also speculations like—What or where was I before I was born?—or Why does life have to end in death? Are there ontic states distinct from life and death? On street corners all over the world you can hear evidence of a passionate interest in metaphysics, religious themes and remarks like—"Why is there something rather than nothing?" resound both audibly between conversationalists and silently in the mind.

Thanaton III, Paul Laffoley, 73 1/2" x 73 1/2" oil, acrylic, ink and lettering on canvas, 1989. From the collection of Richard Metzger

The present condition of serious discourse in the world, if you would hold yourself back a bit from who is saying what, might sound medieval. Metaphysics, that division of philosophy that is concerned with the fundamental nature of reality which includes Ontology, Cosmology and

The aesthetics of death is having a pseudo-posthumous revival.

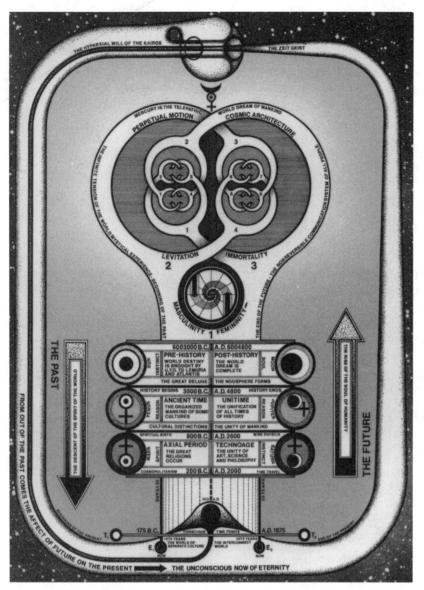

The Alchemy of History, Paul Laffoley, 17" x 23," ink, letters on board, 1975

authentic revivals of mysticism. The German philosopher Philipp Mainländer (1841–1876) born Philipp Batz—a follower of the neo-Buddhism of Arthur Schopenhauer (1788–1860), stated in his principle writing *The Philosophy of Redemption* (1876) that the universe begins with the death of God, since God is the principle of unity which is shattered into the plurality of existence. It is implied, therefore, that God is also the passionate—joy which is now denied proper fulfillment and expression as the result of infinite dispersal into the realm of evil and suffering (the world into which we are thrown). The memory of God's original unity and joy persists only in the human realization that non-existence is superior to existence. When people act upon the implications of this awareness by either refusing to perpetuate themselves or ending their existence with suicide, they are completing their cycle of redemption. This almost Neo-Gnostic mythos of nihilism was seen as the "cure" for the moral "sickness" that pervaded 19th century Europe, was only partially combated by Nietzsche's own yea-saying alternative by an ecstatic transvaluation of values. He based his concept of transvaluation on the theory of the eternal recurrence of the experience of time and its contents sustaining vast cycles. Believing, like the Roman poet-scientist Titus Lucretius Carus (99–55 BCE) author of *De Rerum Natura*, that the universe is infinite, but the number of its possible configurations is finite, it follows that the present configuration of the universe must be repeated time after time in the future until the energy of life becomes continuous with the energy of death.

LeCorbusier (pseudonym from 1920 of the Swiss-born French architect Charles-E'douard Jeanneret Gris (1887–1965)), who was probably the most influential figure in 20th century architecture, shared with the American engineer-architect-inventor Richard Buckminster Fuller (1895–1983) a belief in the possibility of realizing utopia on Earth. They both referred back to Plato's most famous dialogue *The Republic*. At the end of Book IX the ontic status of city-state is described as follows:

> I understand, he said. You mean the city whose establishment we have described, the city whose home is in the ideal, for I think that it can be found nowhere on earth.

Epistemology, is back with a vengeance—and this means a concern for the "The Facts of Death." Gone are the post-Victorian narcissistic snobberies of the independent-minded experimentists of early modernism. For instance, the queen of the British Modern Movement, Virginia Stephen-Woolf of Bloomsbury, once claimed in a fit of "highbrow" feminine pique that the most obscene thing in the world is religion. Her existence itself might now be considered equally as obscene. The traditional theological categories of belief: Theism, Atheism, Non-Theism, Syncretism, Skepticism, Animism, Polytheism, Agnosticism (either dogmatic or methodological) do not really work any longer. The 19th century position that "God is Dead" offered first by Mainländer, then by Nietzsche, Sarte, and finally the radical theology of Thomas Altizer and William Hamilton in the 1960s, ignores the fact that periods of true secularism are the fertilizer for

Well, said I, perhaps there is a pattern of it laid up in heaven for him who wishes to contemplate it and so beholding to constitute himself its citizen. But it makes no difference whether it exists now or ever will come into being. The politics of this city only will be his and of none other.

That seems probable, he said

And at the end of the last book (Book X) Plato describes what is called today as "the Near Death-Experience." It is the tale of the bold warrior Er who is slain in battle but does not decay and who wakes up on the twelfth day as he lay upon his funeral pyre and describes in detail the nature of the afterlife.

When Saint Thomas More (1478–1535) wrote *Utopia* (literally, nowhere) in Latin in 1516 he attempted to take Plato's indecisiveness about the existence of the ideal city to satirize England under the despotic rule of his one time friend and eventual nemesis King Henry VIII (1491–1547), who had More beheaded.

Utopia influenced Anabaptism, Mormonism, and Communism due to its appeal of naïve realism of 18th century revolutionaries like the philosopher and political provocateur Jean-Jacques Rousseau (1712–1778) who wrote about how to completely destroy the world and values of the Ancien Régime of France and replace it with utopian rules and visions; or the visionary architect Étienne-Louis Boullée (1728–1799) who from 1778 to 1788 produced Paper Architecture on a megalomaniacal scale of unrealized schemes of the Architecture of Death: tombs, mausolea, cenotaph and cemeteries including the huge *Cenotaph of Newton* (a vast sphere set in a circular base topped with cypress trees). Utopia as a concept and a literary impulse has a unique if paradoxical history. Both LeCorbuiser and R. Buckminster Fuller helped form the contemporary vision of utopic space—a space that has a ferocious neutrality and how to build with it. Utopic space—a space that has been hinted at all through recorded civilization. There exist no external clues as to its existence or actual characteristics. Reports of its nature have been by people who have entered utopic space and returned like Er to tell the tale.

One such recent historical person who has entered utopic space and returned was Father Pierre Teilhard de Chardin (1881–1955), philosopher priest and paleontologist. In his magnum opus *Le Phénoméne Humain* (1955), published immediately after his death, are his two famous metaphors of utopic space: The Nöosphere—the ubiquitous, open, democratic, and forever repeatable sphere of human consciousness or mental activity that exists on the surface of the Earth driven by the force of evolution, and The Omega Point—yielding the true definition of vitalism (which is the realization that the processes of life are not explicable by the laws of physics and chemistry and that life is in some part self-determining (free-will)), *refer to a space which merges that which has only history (life) with that which has no history (death)*. Unfortunately for Teilhard's reputation, he ignored the possibility of extraterrestrial life forms, but his principles of utopic space still hold.

Utopic space—a space that has been hinted at all through recorded civilization. There exist no external clues as to its existence or actual characteristics.

Utopic space therefore is in between the space of life (the relative) and the space of death (the absolute) and yet is continuous with both. It is the space of:

1. Absolute personal freedom.

2. Absolute oneness (like the world soul of the Neo-Platonic philosopher Plotinus (204–274 CE) based on the topology of the fourth dimensional sphere).

3. No holiarchies, no hierarchies, and no heteroarchies, only perfect continuity.

4. True transdisciplinary knowing, a process of knowledge similar to the child's mind that faces the cosmos with an eagerness for the authentically new, and makes no distinctions of time, values, or survival logic; in fact logic emerges as a by-product.

5. No natural directions, such as those associated with Cartesian Coordinates, it can receive information of any kind and in any amount without the limitations of organization.

6. Energy which is distinct from that associated with the secular concept of energy—energy that is efficacious with motion—instead it is energy that is efficacious without motion.

7. *The conventicle*—the only authentic social structure that can enter and leave this space; the conventicle is a completely future oriented concept with no elements of past social structures.

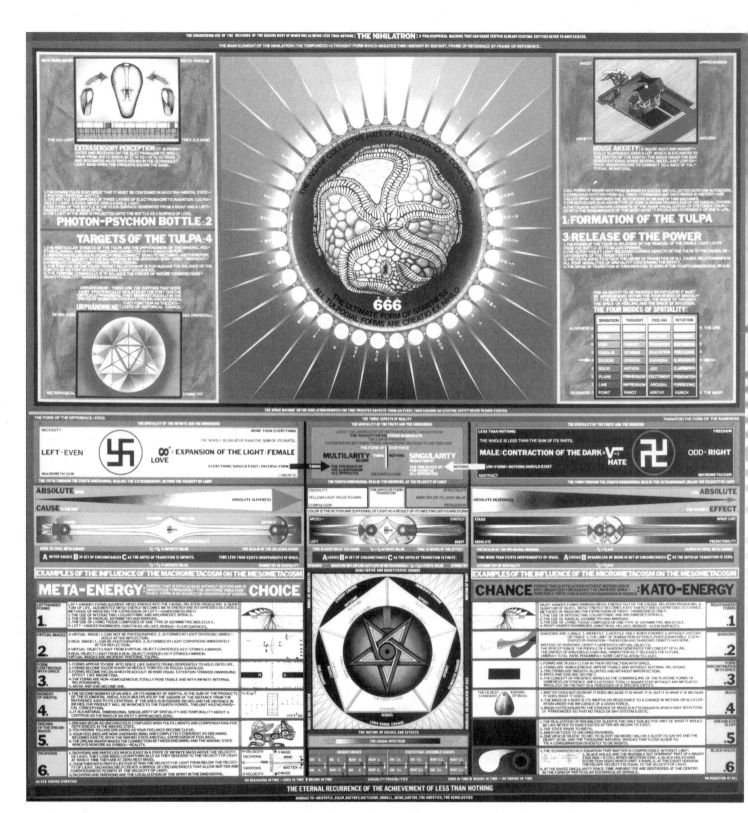

The Nihilitron, Paul Laffoley, 73 1/2" x 73 1/2" oil, acrylic, letters, India ink on linen, 1985

For most of the 20th century the sense of death in many forms gradually took over the psyche of the world—wars that grow progressively more dangerous to all, homelessness, populations that seem to expand without reason, the gradual increase in world starvation, continuous exposure to horrors, both social and individual, the rise in personal and social apathy, and finally mass insanity and sexual neurasthenia as an escape from feeling anything except a lack of motivation, inadequacy, and psychosomatic symptoms of depression, nausea, dizziness, loss of all appetites, blurred vision, weakness, drowsiness, trembling, thoughts of suicide, paresthesia, nameless fears and anxieties, all subsumed by hallucinations—in short the effects of violence being done to the human personality by the poison of absolute evil.[1]

The "Lost Generation" of disillusioned American intellectuals after World War I had its counterpart in the disenfranchised German Youth after the same period. They were the "Wander-Vogels" (the infantilized wandering birds) the exact precursors of the American "hippies" of the 1960s and 1970s. Right after the Second World War came the Beat Generation[2] with their sharpest edge being honed by the Jewish stand-up comic Lenny Bruce who scorned the racism, conservatism and the affluent complacency of suburban America. He once asked an audience to consider why it is obscene to show sex in the movies but not violence, or obscene to show breasts but not obscene to show mutilated body parts. Bruce moved everyone into the world of the "hippies" which became international in scope. It started simultaneously on Fort Hill in Boston, Massachusetts with the Mel Lyman Commune in the early 1960s, and in the Haight-Ashbury, Golden Gate Park section of San Francisco. Wearing folksy used clothes, beads, headbands, sandals, and flowers they took us into an aura of non-violent anarchy, tracking the civil rights movement, concern for the environment, the rejection of Western materialism and an all consuming interest in the occult and the mystical and what happens after death. One of the famous rock bands of the era was named The Grateful Dead. One of the finest achievements of the hippies was the spearheading of the protest against the US involvement in the Vietnam War which began in 1954 after the defeat of the French and lasted until 1975. The protest was whipped up from the mid-west by the SDS (Students for a Democratic Society) and "The Weathermen" its violent inner core.

Although the hippies took us to the brink of Postmodernism (July 15, 1972), middle America was left again in a cultural vacuum with no one to guide us except the two control freaks who formed the "inside" and the "outside" of hippieland—Timothy Leary and R. Buckminster Fuller. Then the Youth International Party (A "Yippie" was a person loosely belonging to or identified with a politically active group of hippies) raised its head above the crowd and realized it was "all over" but the shouting, and so returned to Wall Street and Madison Avenue to become young business professionals as the "Yuppies." They are the young college educated who are employed in well paying professions who live and work in or near a large city and contract the Yuppie flu attempting to fight off yet another British invasion, this time the Punk Movement of disaffected youth manifesting itself in fashions and music designed to shock or intimidate—pins through the skin, razor blade necklaces, hair in various colors and gelled into vertical spikes with Frankenstein make-up, wearing yobbo clothes, and listening to The Sex Pistols, and living on the dole.

Lenny Bruce once asked an audience to consider why it is obscene to show sex in the movies but not violence, or obscene to show breasts but not obscene to show mutilated body parts.

This physical dip into the world of monsters and making the celebration of Halloween a year round event produced the inevitable next step, The Goth; those who see everyone through distorted lenses like the most famous horror writer of all time H. P. Lovecraft (1890–1937) who could not stand to look at himself in the mirror. As Susan Sontag wrote, reviewing Diane Arbus' photographic documentary homage to Tod Browning's fantastic film, *Freaks*, Arbus's photos "undercut politics ... by suggesting a world in which everybody is an alien, hopelessly (we are all alone together, sliding forward on the razor edge of life, egged on by those behind, held back by those in front) isolated, immobilized in mechanical, crippled identities and relationships. They render history and politics irrelevant ... by atomizing ... [the world] into horror." Browning directed *Freaks* in 1932 for MGM, adapted from a story called *Spurs* by Tod Robbins. The story was initially suggested to Browning by his friend, the famous German midget Harry Earles. *Freaks* had everything: Johnny Eck, the boy with half a torso, Martha the armless wonder (before the thalidomide scare of the late 1950s), the Siamese twins Daisy and Violet Hilton—and dwarfs, pinheads, bearded women, sword swallowers, etc.; in short, the typical array of creatures found in a side-show at the circus before these displays were outlawed. Browning himself was banned from the film industry for indulging such lowbrow taste and numbing obscenity.

When the terrorists of al Qàedà struck the World Trade Center buildings with airplanes on September 11, 2001 between 8:45AM and 9:03AM I knew the Bauharoque had begun.

The Goths, of course, have followed Sontag off the cliff because of what she says about art. "Much of Modern Art is devoted to lowering the threshold of what is terrible. By getting used to what formerly, we could not bear to see or hear, because it was too shocking, painful, or embarrassing, art changes morals—that body of psychic customs and public sanctions that draws a vague boundary between what is emotionally and spontaneously intolerable and what is not." This mission statement is what drove the "Théâtre du Grand Guignol" (The French Theater of Fear, Terror and Horror) to exist continuously at one location—20 Rue Chaptal in the Arrondissement of Montmartre, Paris from Wednesday April 11, 1897 until American snuff and slasher movies put it out of business on Monday, November 26 1962.

The Gothic Sensibility became quickly international so the Noösphere of the world was really its origin. It was lauded at the prestigious Institute of Contemporary Art in Boston, Massachusetts in an Exhibition entitled *Gothic: Transmutations of Horror in Late Twentieth Century Art.* Curated by Christoph Grunenburg, it features the work of 23 artists who according to the catalogue "produce horror as well as amazement through often repulsive, fragmented and contorted forms. Some employ a detached and reductive formal language to evoke discomfort and claustrophobia or to transmute images of gruesome violence, achieving an equally disconcerting impact." In the catalogue there are reproductions of work by Julie Becker, Monica Carocci, Gregory Crewdson and that monster from the 1950s, Jackson Pollock, photographs of fashion designs by Thierry Mugler and musical performances by Marilyn Manson and the rock band Bauhaus. The films that accompanied the exhibition featured Browning's *Freaks.*

I went on the Institute's free-day (I believe artists should not have to pay for anything) and found the show somewhat disappointing. When I attend exhibitions that purport to display a radical change in sensibility I expect to be shown something authentically new. This was not the case. I had either done personal examples of the work shown or had anticipated them. I felt no jealousy here. Leaving the

ICA I realized why. The "Youthquake" that was started by Elvis's hips in the early 1950s had finally run its course and everyone is affected. There is no more high- or low-brow taste. We are all hip now. Even the quintessential outlaw motorcycle gangs of Harley-Davidson riders—The Hell's Angels (the ad hoc carrier wave of the youth movement, which started in 1948) now has retirement policies. The last time they went to court, which was in 1993, it was not to defend themselves against criminal charges—but to sue Marvel Comics for damaging the club's "goodwill" by issuing a comic book entitled *Hell's Angel.* Today, therefore, persons regardless of age have the right to consider (him, her, or it) themselves just as "alive" as anybody else.

As my foot landed on the last front step of the ICA and I was out on Boylston Street heading toward my studio I knew there was a change coming much larger than a change of sensibility. It was the third phase of Modernism after Postmodernism, similar in the flow of history to the third section of the Italian Renaissance cycle the Baroque just after Mannerism. The Baroque artists returned to the logical organizations of early Renaissance with a new energy derived from the forms of the High Gothic that artists of the Early Renaissance had eschewed. In 1986 I called our third phase of Modernism the *Bauharoque* in homage to the Bauhaus (1919–1933) the school that symbolized Heroic Modernism and the Baroque characterized by drama, movement and tension, grotesqueness, extravagance, complexity, and flamboyance. The Bauharoque holds onto Modernism but harkens back to the crazy energy of the 19th century. In 1991 Ada Louise Huxtable, America's leading architecture critic, named it the "Neo-Modern" or the "Post-Post-Modernism" (being neutral enough not to "inhibit" creativity) and a Washington, DC artist and art critic, J. W. Mahoney, added in 1992 to this lexicon of the discourse of the future the word "Transmodern," which I like because it refers to entering another realm such as death on the cultural scale.

When the terrorists of al Qàedà struck the World Trade Center buildings with airplanes on September 11, 2001 between 8:45AM and 9:03AM I knew the Bauharoque had begun. The time symmetry of the presence of Minoru Yamasaki's Twin Towers (a huge eleven—the most ominous of the numbers—in the New York skyline) was too much to resist. Yamasaki's buildings started Postmodernism with a death and ended it with a death.

That thieving maggot-pie of the art world composer Karlheinz Stockhausen (1928–), I believe, got it wrong when he declared the attack on 9/11 to be the greatest artwork in the history of the world (meaning "lowering the threshold of what is terrible"). This had already been done in 1973 by *Andy Warhol's Frankenstein* as Joan Hawkins wrote in her book *Cutting Edge: Art-Horror and the Horrific Avant-Garde* (2000) about Andy's film:

> And in Andy Warhol's Frankenstein, Frankenstein brings his female zombie to life in one of the most bizarre copulation scenes in the history of cinema. "To know death, Otto," (he tells his assistant when he's finished penetrating the zombie's "digestive parts,") "you have to fuck life in the gallbladder."

Since the story of Frankenstein was written by Mary Shelley (1797–1851) a country girl of nineteen, one can only but gather the inference that horror, terror and death can be best understood by the adolescent female because only they can really know the opposite, the joy and freedom of giving birth. Thus the practitioners of male dominated aesthetics characteristic of the 20th century will have trouble adjusting to the new Thanataesthetics of the 21st.

When Osama bin Laden thought he was handing us a fresh beaker of death to drink from, he was actually being influenced by Andy Warhol (1928–1987), that epicene, intersexual maestro of American art, who after 16 years of being dead, still has us all by the throat. Andy's message is that in the United States we are not very grown up—the complaint of most women about most men—and it is time to grow up and face death.

II. (THE TRIMURTI OF DEATH)

Thanataesthetics can be examined from three different perspectives of Transcendent Symbolism. The use of symbolism as the mode of expression is necessary because Utopic Space, the space that connects the space of life with the space of death into a developing continuity, is by nature an interdimensional space in between the classic Fourth-Dimensional Realm (Time-Solvoid) and the higher Fifth-Dimensional Realm (Eternity-Vosolid).

PERSPECTIVE ONE:

FASHION AESTHETICS is the expression of the SACRAMENTAL REVELATION of the human body as a form of energy, distinct from energy like electricity that informed Mary Shelley of how Frankenstein's Monster would come to life and produce the physical senses, the alimentary and respiratory systems, as well as the urges for food, sex, information, privacy, communality, indifference, love and hate. Instead the SACRAMENTAL is described by an eternal energy that is efficacious without motion, and limited by the mathematics of the so-called Divine Proportion or PHI. This meta-energy mathematics was codified in 1899 as the Greek letter Ο (PHI), the initial letter of the name Phidias (fl.ca. 490-430 BCE), the master sculptor who designed the Parthenon on the Acropolis in Athens with the help of the architects Ictinus and Callicrates. Phi refers to the logarithmic or equiangular spiral, the Fibonacci series (named after Leonardo Fibonacci-Filius Bonacci, alias Leonardo of Pisa (1175-1250)) sent out to infinity and then divided by itself, also the parabola and the Golden Section (.382.../.618...) : $e^2 = (\Phi + \Phi')^2$. The basic equation for the proportion of death is : $x + 1/x = x/1$ or $x^2 - x - 1 = 0$. The positive solution Φ: $x = (1 + \sqrt{5})/2$ and the negative solution Φ': $x = (1 - \sqrt{5})/2$ are both evident in animal and human forms. Also the Ancient Egyptians discovered that $\Pi = (3.1416...)$ is related to Φ, or $\Pi = \Phi^2$. (6/5) or $3.1416... = 2.168...$ (6/5).

"To know death, Otto, you have to fuck life in the gallbladder." –Udo Kier in *Andy Warhol's Frankenstein*.

The PHI proportion of death permeates every life form on the planet with the exception of the Ginkgo Biloba Tree which is dated as beginning in the Permian Period of the Paleozoic Era—286 million years ago. Its genes, however, are even older, dating from the Archean Period of the Precambian Era—4,000 million years ago when life was said to appear as the earliest algae and primitive bacteria. What happened was the seeds of the Ginkgo Biloba Tree arrived on earth encapsulated in the frozen centers of comets, therefore, could not have committed any moral turpitude along the way. Some parts of the seeds did thaw out to become the beginnings of life, sin, and death. As it says in Romans 6:21 and 23; "What fruit had ye then in those things whereof ye are now ashamed? (Seeds speaking to humans) For the end of those things is death. For the wages of sin is death."

When the Ginkgo Biloba appeared full blown in the Permian Period it was realized to be the fabulous TREE OF LIFE (it smells so bad that people are given to avoid eating it)—but in capsule form as it is taken now, Ginkgo Biloba, is a life extender because it improves circulation to the genitals and the brain. THE TREE OF THE KNOWLEDGE OF GOOD AND EVIL is, of course, the wild crisp Macintosh Apple Tree.

Sir d'Arcy Wentworth Thompson (1860–1948), one of the most distinguished scientists of the modern era, sets forth his analysis of the nature of the Divine Proportion in *On Growth And Form*, first written in 1917 and revised in 1942. As an example he describes the equiangular spiral as follows:

> "And it follows from this that it is in the hard parts of organisms, and not the soft, fleshy, actively growing parts, that this spiral is commonly and characteristically found; not in the fresh mobile tissue whose form is constrained merely by the active forces of the moment; but in things like shell and tusk, and horn and claw, visibly composed of parts successively and permanently laid down. The shell-less mollusks are never spiral; the snail is spiral but not the slug. In short, it is the shell which curves the snail and not the snail which curves the shell. THE LOGARITHMIC SPIRAL, IS CHARACTERISTIC, NOT OF THE LIVING TISSUES, BUT OF THE DEAD."

This energy of eternity, therefore, can transform the sorrow of the ritualized sacrifice of the time of our lives into: fashions, styles, modes, vogues, fads, rages and crazes, and into the joy of becoming vessels that receive the Divine as nourishment. This is the penetration of the BEAUTY BARRIER to the truth which then divulges THE LUX OF SYNESTHESIA—the pure light that combines all the senses into the universal remedy to all earthly problems, THE AZOTH, which then becomes like an all consuming drink from The River Lethe.

IT IS, THEREFORE, THE EXTINCTION OF THE PAST.

PERSPECTIVE TWO:

VAMPIRE AESTHETICS, the prophetic, is the expression of the Revelation of the Soul as the mystery of the tension between Fate and Free Will. There is a natural innocence to Fate and a natural guilt to Free Will. Many religious traditions acknowledge the reality of evil as both sufficient and necessary for the existence and fulfillment of Free Will. Often at the entrances of religious establishments or organizations that require a personal commitment to a mission, you will see a small sign with tasteful graphics

beseeching passersby making Free Will donations to the cause. To the secular mind the sign means simply giving money, but to more spiritually oriented minds, this is a request to give up part of your natural quantum of Free Will. The Free Will, as opposed to the controlled will, is considered a fit subject for the exorcism of evil spirits.

VAMPIRE AESTHETICS	FASHION AESTHETICS	ZOMBIE AESTHETICS
PENETRATE ➡ THE SUBLIME BARRIER TO EXPOSE THE:	PENETRATE ➡ THE BEAUTY BARRIER TO DIVULGE THE:	PENETRATE ➡ THE KITSCH BARRIER TO REVEAL THE:
PHENOMENON	LUX OF SYNESTHESIA	NOUMENON
ETERNITY	TIME	ETERNITY

Design for a bumper sticker for "Thanataesthetics," Paul Laffoley, 9" x 3", India ink, letters on board, September 11, 2001

It is the essence of the VAMPIRE that it is a person of either sex that preys on others. Often the Vampire is described as the reanimated body of a dead person believed to come from the grave at night and suck the blood of persons asleep, similar to the Incubus, an evil spirit that lies on women in their sleep and has sexual intercourse with them, and as does the Succubus—a demon assuming female form in order to have sexual intercourse with men in their sleep. As an example, a woman who exploits and ruins her lover—sometimes called a FEMME FATALE—is a type of vampire. It can just as easily be the opposite sex; L'HOMME FATALE, depending on whose gonads are being gored.

From the world of Opera comes the tale of the willful cigarette sweatshop girl *Carmen*. Carmen challenges the Divinity of Fate by seeking a man who refuses to pay any attention to her. To the accompaniment of the theme of Fate that again and again suggests the irresistible but sinister attraction, Carmen pursues the idealistic soldier Don José. Her Free Will impels her to stroll saucily up to the corporal and takes a flower from her bodice and tosses it in his face. Everyone laughs at his obvious embarrassment. As the factory bell sounds again, Carmen and the others leave him alone to pick up the flower. The story goes on with the usual twists and turns of the scenario of "La Grande Passion" until Don Jose knifes her in the Bull Ring to the sounds of "The Toreador Song" in praise of the victorious Escamillo, Carmen's next piece of fresh sexual meat to carve. Also the film *Fatal Attraction* (1987) utilizes some of the same themes, but amplified a thousandfold by means of cinematic tricks and stunts. Glenn Close is the heroine of *Fatal Attraction* as she is in the film version of Pierre Choderlos De Laclos's 18th century novel *Liaisons Dangereuses*, where the theme of the powerful woman having sex without love and crushing every "petit maitre" in sight is the kicker. Glenn Close, herself, always impressed me as a woman who has great difficulty simply existing.

The current use of the "Medieval Morality Play" format has attempted to revive the tension between FATE and FREE WILL that "Scientism" thought it had eliminated. By reducing FATE to temporal or causal determinism, and FREE WILL to temporal or causal indeterminism, according to advocates of "Scientism" all morality should vanish into a cloud of unknowingness and neutrality. Secularism would reign. The Soul's only salvation, however, is to be caught up in the conflict between the world-views of the future and one's present personal agenda. Trying to avoid the mystery of the conflict by reasoning that, "we are free to do what we will, but we are morally responsible only for what we do in the future, and not for what we are right now," will not work.

But for VAMPIRE AESTHETICS to truly seek the phenomenology of the future, it must penetrate The Sublime Barrier established by the scientific world-view.

The Sublime was popularized by Boileau's translation of Longinus into French in 1674 and by Edmund Burke (1729–1797) who wrote *A Philosophical Enquiry into the Origin of Our Ideas of the Sublime and the Beautiful* (1757). Its aim was to break through the control by the scientific worldview established in the 17th century. Two of the major "control freaks" of the time could not deal with the sublime and tried to stop the growing interest in it. Sir Joshua Reynolds (1723–1793) an English portrait painter and the first president of the Royal Academy in London in 1768 (and also the constant target of vituperation by mystical painter-poet William Blake (1757–1827)) said in 1790: "The sublime in painting, as in poetry, so overpowers and takes possession of the whole mind that no room is left for attention to minute criticism" (which, of course, was his only artistic forte).

In the same year Immanuel Kant (1724–1804), that German philosopher of the ontology of doubt, came up with the one-liner, when he discovered that a new sensibility might be breaking into his personal intellectual fortress: "The sublime, it is an outrage on the human imagination."

Those who tried to characterize the sublime agreed that it referred to the horror of infinite spatial extension, the sense of inhuman extraordinariness, and the grandeur and terror of nature in the raw—in other words what is meant by the emotion that goes beyond fear: DIVINE AWE.

The sublime helped launch the Romantic and Symbolist Movements in their individual assessments of the human personality and its motivations which is found without lies only in the subconscious: the will to, power, love, hate, lust, destroy and die. This is the revelation of the prophetic and it is, therefore, the extinction of the present.

PERSPECTIVE THREE:

ZOMBIE AESTHETICS, the mystical, is the expression of the relation of the spirit of the sacred. It is what cannot be named, limited, or known by the ordinary human consciousness, because it is prior to any distinction that can be made. As Plato implied in the *Timaeus*, the spirit or the godhead can emanate because it is distinct from the form of THE SAME, the form of THE DIFFERENT, and the form of THE EXISTENT. The spirit, therefore, unites the physical with the metaphysical, becoming with being. It is the horror of darkness, the wonder of light, the inevitable universal structure which is manifested by the simultaneity of the real and the illusory.

A zombie is a dead person—or, more precisely, the soulless body of a dead person—that has been artificially brought back to life, usually through magic. Lacking the ingredient of consciousness, the zombie's motions are undirected, mechanical, and robot like. By extension, living people who behave like unconscious automatons are sometimes referred to as zombies, like Elvis Presley (1935–1977) one year before his death or the current state of Michael Jackson (1958–) and, of course, the culturally ubiquitous Andy Warhol (1928–1987) for his whole life.

The term zombie seems to be derived from the name of the Python God of certain African tribes like those in Northern Angola, and it is similar to Pytho, the serpent killed by Apollo that produced, the Delphic Oracle. The Bantu language Kimbundu has a word NZÚMBE meaning ghost or the "walking dead," or the spirit of the dead. Zombie could, therefore, be connected to ancestor worship and the boa constrictor. Wade Davis, an ethnobiologist, studied Haitian zombies and found that they were actually people who were given drugs that made them appear dead and then buried alive. They were given strong poison, usually as a powder in food, of Bufotoxin and Tetrodotoxin—similar to natural poisons such as Botox that are used in cosmetic surgery today. The victim who receives the potion experiences malaise, dizziness, and a tingling that soon becomes a total numbness. The person then suffers excessive salivating, sweating,

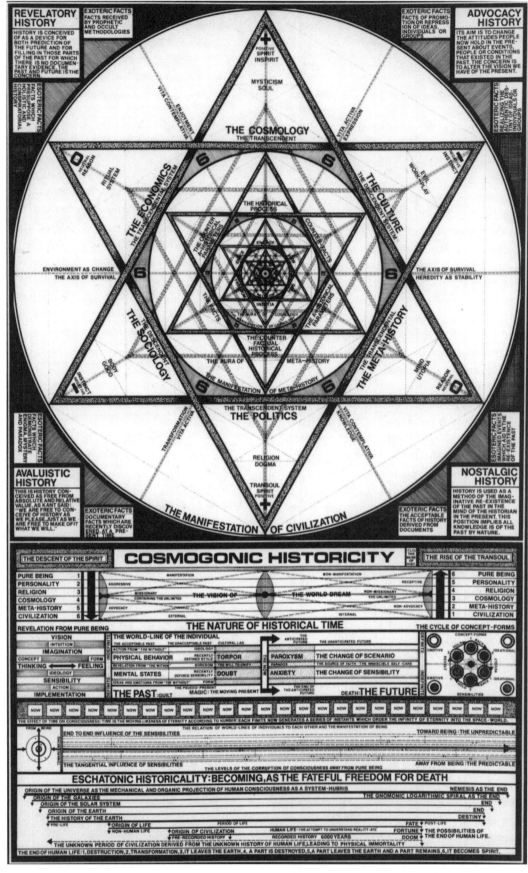

Cosmogonic Historicity, Paul Laffoley, 17" x 27", ink, letters on board, 1971

headaches, and general weakness, both blood pressure and body temperature drop, and the pulse is quick and weak. This is followed by diarrhea and regurgitation. The victim then undergoes respiratory distress, until the entire body turns blue (Blue Man Group). Sometimes the body goes into wild twitches (Elvis Presley), after which it is totally paralyzed (Michael Jackson), and the person falls into a coma in which he or she appears to be dead (Andy Warhol).

Exposure to an overdose of visual kitsch (the world of bad taste) can produce the same symptoms, such as in "Graceland," "Neverland," "Times Square," "Las Vegas," "Disneyland," Vienna, Austria, and Switzerland.

The Symbolist Movement in art (1880–1910) (official birth September 18, 1886 in Paris, France) develops the use of kitsch to protect the mystical. The symbolists were concerned about decadence, memento mori, the concept of ruin, the fin-de-siècle, and history that runs backward as in the writings of Plato, Hesiod, and Hinduism. Completely opposing the optimistic progress of the 18th century, the symbolist viewed society as decadent; therefore, the criminal classes were the avant-garde. They defined themselves as guilty of crimes of which society had yet to conceive and expressed this idea in art forms that appeared decadent to society because society had yet to achieve this new level of decadence.

Since a symbol suggested the presence of the numinous and transcendent utopic space, it had to be protected by nested shells of visual kitsch as deliberate lies so that society at large cannot reduce the symbol's power to the level of marketing cliché which has been done to so much of contemporary culture.

There are five semiotic levels or shells surrounding the sacred content of a symbol:

1. The lowest level is THE SIGN: This is information by convention, like a made up code, game or system or an advertising campaign. The viewer of the sign feels completely empowered and epistemically active and the content of the sign is passive.

2. The nest level is THE INDEX: This is information by symptom. There is something real out there but all we have are its tracks or its forensic indications of existence. The knower is a bit more passive and that which is a bit more active.

3. A still higher level is THE ICON: This is the actual depicting of the structure of the content of the symbol. The knower and that which is known are equal in power.

4. The next to last level is THE ARCHETYPE: This semiotic concept was made famous by the psychologist Carl Gustav Jung (1975–1961), in Basel, Switzerland (Switzerland is, of course, a high-kitsch area on the planet).

5. The Archetype tips the scales in favor of the epistemic power of the content of the symbol and moves from subjective to the objective. Jung declared the journey of the soul which he called *Heilsweg* as the burning of the unconscious contents into an indivdual's consciousness. Because the archetypes were shown to be the same throughout history and in all cultures, he felt he had demonstrated the existence of a collective unconscious that affected both waking and dreaming life.

6. The innermost level or shell is THE OBJECTIVE SYMBOL of the sacred or divine essence experienced as pure numinousity. Here the kitsch barrier has been penetrated and the epistemic relation between the knower and that which is known is inversed. The knower has become has become like a zombie—totally passive—and the knowledge goes beyond the objective into the realm of total, complete, active, power, the aspect of which the knower can not voluntarily avoid, as the desire to know is now absolutely satisfied.

In Canto 33 (lines 109–120) of *Il Paradiso* (the third canticle of *The Divine Comedy*), the poet Dante Alighieri (1265–1321) presents the beatific vision (the direct knowledge of God) in just such a manner:

Not that within THE LIVING LIGHT there was
more than a sole aspect of the divine
which is what IT has always been,
yet as I learned to see more, and THE POWER
OF VISION GREW IN ME, that single aspect,
AS I CHANGED, SEEMED TO ME TO CHANGE ITSELF.
Within its depthless clarity of substance,
I saw the great light shine into three circles
in the three clear colors bound in one same space;
the first seemed to reflect the next like a rainbow
equally breathed forth by the other two.

It is the extinction of the present.

Endnotes

1. Both LeCorbusier and Fuller were developing their most creative ideas prior to the publication of *Le Phenoméne Humain* and therefore, emphasized only part of Teilhard's vision of utopic space. From 1920–1925 LeCorbusier with his partner Amedée Ozenfant the painter (1886–1966) started a magazine called *L'Espirit Nouveau*. The contributions became influential texts—a heady brew of technology, messianic slogans proclaiming the supposed moral and hygienic virtues of the architectural language of the "Golden Section" and lessons derived from antiquity that found many devotees. In his writings LeCorbusier defined architecture as a play of masses brought together by light, and advocated that buildings should be practically constructed as a modern machine, an idea derived from the futurist architect Antonio Sant' 'Elia (1888–1916), complete with rational planning, and capable of being erected using mass-produced components. What Le Corbusier took from utopic space was absolute personal freedom for his style and individual buildings, but for his urban design projects like *La Ville Radieuse* (The Radiant City) his misinterpretetation of the concept of the conventicle was the metaphor as a beehive for people.

   In the 1920s he anticipated the political structures of the combination of fascism and socialism which characterized the 1930s. In fact during the early 1940s after the Nazis invaded France, LeCorbusier, whose architectural commissions began to dry up, found it easy to compromise his political convictions and accepted jobs from the collaborationist Vichy government.

   Jane Butzner Jacobs (1916–), who began her career as a critic for *Architectural Forum* in 1952, started to attack the dogma of heroic modernism especially the rules set forth by the CIAM (Congrès Internationaux D'Architecture Moderne) dominated first by the Bauhaus and then by LeCorbusier. The CIAM lasted from 1928 to 1959. Jacobs claimed that the CIAM was killing cities, especially American cities where there was enough money to put "urban renewal" projects into practice. These projects often resembled cemetery headstones uniformly laid out on carpets of grass. The most famous project was by Minoru Yamasaki (1912–1986), an American architect of Japanese descent. He built public housing in St. Louis, Missouri—the infamous Pruitt-Igoe scheme, from 1950–1958. As architect and critic Charles Jencks wrote in 1977, when HUD (The Office of Housing and Urban Development) blew up the Pruitt-Igoe on July 15, 1972 at 3:32PM Post-Modernism began, and Modernism died.

2. In 1952 John Clellon Holmes wrote a book called Go (which was reissued in 1959 under the title *The Beat Boys*). It was the first indication of the Beat sensibility. During this early period Hollywood film stars such as James Dean (I Am Immortal), Montgomery Clift (More Sensitive than a Broadway Playwright), or Marlon (*The Wild One*) Brando were shown on the silver screen through a gossamer veil of gayness to help promote the sensibility to suburban America by means of appealing to the developing libidos of preadolescent females. Later the real edge of the Beat Generation was honed by poets such as Allen Ginsberg who became famous overnight at his first reading of *Howl: Part I* at the Six Gallery on October 13, 1955 in San Francisco. Ginsberg's poetry mates such as Gregory Corso offered many works (but his most revealing was *Marriage-the Happy Birthday of Death*, 1960), or Laurence Ferlinghetti who published his poems *Pictures of the Gone World* in 1955 for $0.75 as the first title in The City Lights "Pocket Poems" editions.

   But it was the novelists of the period, in the popular imagination, who became the *sine qua non* of the Beat Generation. William S. Burroughs served up *Junkie* in 1953 and *Naked Lunch* in 1957 and of course, the reigning prince of the Beats, the bad boy drunk from Lowell, Massachusetts, Jack Kerouac, whose second novel *On The Road*, while published late in the game-September 5, 1957—took the media over like a big, bad, belated, blitzkrieg. His face was seen all over the power pop magazines of the 1950s: *Time, Life, Look, Colliers*, with a greater frequency than Elvis or Jackson Pollock. To the general public, the autumn of 1957 was the beginning of the Beat Generation. What added to the sense of America's cultural helplessness was the fact that 30 days after the novel (October 4, 1957), the first of a series of Soviet—Earth orbiting satellites—Sputnik I—was launched, and the first battle of the Cold-War (1945–1990) was won and not by the US. In Russian the word "sputnik" means "traveling companion" or the translation of the world "poputchik" meaning "fellow traveler": one that sympathizes with and often furthers the ideals and program of an organized group (as the Communist Party) without membership in the group of regular participation in its activities. A steel sphere 23 inches in diameter and weighing 185 lbs. containing a simple radio transmitter—the symbol of Soviet propaganda in space cast a pall over the United States and caused every young person of the time to assess the death karma we had created by dropping "Little Boy" on Hiroshima Japan August 6, 1945 at 8:15AM. Three days later, August 9, Nagasaki was also eliminated from the world atlas. The assessment entered the American lexicon as "Beatnik." America had its own Hiroshima of pride.

JOE IS IN THE DETAILS

Love Song, courtesy Joe Coleman

Exorcism, Alchemy, Mysticism, all of these things exist in my work, but only in the most practical and instinctual sense of a very personal need. Many of these concerns are apparent at the first encounter with one of my paintings. My portraits are dissections of a soul. The paintings are tombs that contain the things that define a life. At the center the fragile bone and flesh and the clothing. Around the center you will find objects important to this life. The homes that held and expressed this life. Important friends and family. Defining events. Dreams. The thoughts and words expressed by and about this being. All presented on the surface with equal importance.

From a distance, the painting has a direct confrontation with the viewer; full of information. If the viewer comes closer more information is revealed. The more one looks the more is revealed. If the viewer uses a magnifying lens or the special lenses I used to paint it, microscopic images are revealed, not just textures but tiny, minute scenes related to the subject.

Some of the detail is buried underneath the painted surface. For example I have spent many hours researching and painting an historical figure's pocket watch and then paint the pocket over it.

This process is enacted without sketching the composition beforehand. I complete a square inch at a time, starting at any point, letting the painting slowly reveal itself to me. I am intensely researching the subject and as information is filtered through me and onto the painting's surface it creates a densely woven narrative pattern. Pattern is the only order I trust. I care only about the detail, the composition is unimportant. It will reveal itself.

Exorcism, Alchemy, Mysticism, all of these things exist in my work, but only in the most practical and instinctual sense of a very personal need.

With magnified lenses used by jewelers and a one-hair brush I submerge into a microscopic world. I build sets, stitch costumes, and act out all of the parts. I become the person I am painting; perhaps like method acting, maybe it's what is called "the assumption of the God form" in occult books. But it is the way in which I can conjure a soul.

A New York Pirate, courtesy Joe Coleman

The painted surface is on a flat piece of wood finely sanded which is glued onto another piece of wood that contains fabric related to the subject or my connection to the subject. When this is attached to the painted frame about 1 to 1½ inches show between the painted frame and the painted wood, giving the effect that the painting is floating within the frame.

In the painting *Mommy/Daddy* the picture floats on actual clothing my parents wore. A black satin dress of my mother and a USMC (United States Marine Corps) shirt my father wore in Iwo Jima. The two fabrics connect at the very point where I have joined their bisected dependant halves. In the painting *A New York Pirate* the painting is floating

on the actual shirt that Elmo Patrick Sonnier wore to his execution. *Love Song*, which is a love song in paint to my wife, Whitney Ward, is floating on bed sheet that we fucked on and the four corners of the outer frame contain reliquaries holding co-mingled body parts: a cyst from my neck with Whitney's blood, Whitney's fingernails mixed with my hair, etc....

This treatment of objects as fetish is partially based on my Catholic upbringing but it is an aspect of Catholicism that is heavily rooted in pagan ritual. Objects have magical powers. This belief is so deep within me that I have turned my own home into a shrine of fear, desire and mystery. To possess an object of magic is to possess the object's power. The use of magical objects is vital to my paintings. For *A New York Pirate*, Sonnier's shirt helps to raise a monster's power and cage it within. In *Love Song* the objects serve to protect and immortalize our passion for each other. In *Mommy/Daddy* they serve as physical reminder of my creation and as a warning of the past.

Magical elements in my performances have parallels but it is in the realm of the priest or shaman. In my early teens I was compelled to strap onto my body home-made explosives that were attached to a cookie tin from my mother's kitchen. I wore this device on my chest and then hid it by wearing one of my father's shirts which was slightly too big for me. I would then invade stranger's homes and ignite myself; in the smoke and confusion I would disappear. I eventually turned these primal acts of suburban terror into a stage performance. In 1981 as Professor Momboozoo (a merging of parental forces: Mom=mother, Booze=father) in New York's alternative performance space "The Kitchen," I delivered an apocalyptic sermon then self-detonated, bit the heads off of live rats and then proceeded to chase out the entire audience from the theater with a double-barreled shotgun. Fire and explosion are elemental forces; the biting off of the head of a live animal is a rite of passage. These acts served to put me

I have spent many hours researching and painting an historical figure's pocket watch and then paint the pocket over it.

Mommy/Daddy, courtesy Joe Coleman

warrant read "Joe Coleman AKA 'Dr. Momboozoo'") with "possession of an infernal machine"—a charge my lawyer said had not been used since the 1800s. The words in the charge imply something diabolical.

As with all of my work I am concerned only with the details, the whole picture will reveal itself to me when it wants...or not. ⌂

into a heightened state of being. Transgression into transcendence into a pre-civilized existence that for me set off an internal psychodrama, releasing deep-seated conflicts of childhood producing a slowly diminishing catharsis until the performances of Professor Momboozoo ended.

With magnified lenses used by jewelers and a one-hair brush I submerge into a microscopic world. I build sets, stitch costumes, and act out all of the parts. I become the person I am painting; perhaps like method acting, maybeit's what is called "the assumption of the God form" in occult books. But it is the way in which I can conjure a soul.

As with the paintings there are many levels produced connecting ancient and modern, pagan and Christian. They also create a cultural echo that returns to me in strange cryptic symbols, like when game show host and animal rights activist Bob Barker spearheaded my arrest for biting the heads off of mice during a performance. When he condemned me in the press this "BARKER" became my sideshow pitchman. Or when the Boston police had me arrested after a performance at the Boston Film and Video Foundation in which I exploded while hanging over the audience. The district attorney charged me (the arrest

ARE YOU ILLUMINATED?

Magic is often referred to in terms of being a path, a spiritual quest, a voyage of self-discovery, or an adventure. However you want to dress it up, one point is clear, it is a means of bringing about Change. For this change to be effective, it is important that you be able to set the effects of your magical work within a context—to be able to make sense of them and integrate them into a dynamic interaction with a moving, fluid universe.

Initiation is the term which magicians use to examine this process of integration, and *Illumination* is one of its most important by-products.

This requires a sense (however tenuous) of where you have been, and where you are "going." At times these anchor-points will seem to be solid, and at others, ephemeral and faint. *Initiation* is the term which magicians use to examine this process of integration, and *Illumination* is one of its most important by-products.

INITIATION AS A PROCESS

There appears to be some misunderstanding over what exactly the term "initiation" means. Occasionally one bumps into people who consider themselves as "initiates" and seem to consider themselves somehow "above" the rest of humanity. Particularly irritating are the self-styled "initiates" who let drop teasing bits of obscure information and then refuse to explain any further because their audience are not "initiates." The term itself seems to crop up in a wide variety of contexts—people

speak of being "initiated" into groups, onto a particular path, or of initiating themselves. Some hold that "initiation" is only valid if the person who confers it is part of a genuine tradition, others that it doesn't matter either way. Dictionary definitions of initiation allude to the act of beginning, or of setting in motion, or entry into something. One way to explain initiation is to say that it is a threshold of change which we may experience at different times in our lives, as we grow and develop. The key to initiation is recognizing that we have reached such a turning point, and are aware of being in a period of transition between our past and our future. The conscious awareness of entering a transitional state allows us to perhaps, discard behavioral/emotional patterns which will be no longer valid for the "new" circumstances, and consciously take up new ones.

What magical books often fail to emphasize is that initiation is a process. It doesn't just happen once, but can occur many times throughout an individual's life, and that it has peaks (initiatory crises), troughs (black depression or the "dark night of the soul") and plateaus (where nothing much seems to be going on). Becoming aware of your own cycles of change, and how to weather them, is a core part of any developmental process or approach to magical practice. The key elements or stages of the initiation process have been extensively mapped by anthropologists such as Joseph Campbell. While they are mostly used to describe stages of shamanic initiation, they are equally applicable to other areas of life experience.

CRISIS AND CALL

In shamanic societies the first stage of the initiation process is often marked by a period of personal crises and a "call" towards starting the shamanic journey. Most of us are quite happy to remain within the conceptual and philosophical boundaries of Consensus Reality (the everyday world). For an individual beginning on the initiatory journey, the crisis may come as a powerful vision, dreams, or a deep (and often disturbing) feeling to find out what is beyond the limits of normal life. It can often come as a result of a powerful spiritual, religious or political experience, or as a growing existential discontent with life. Our sense of being a stable self is reinforced by the "walls" of the social world in which we participate—yet our sense of uniqueness resides in the cracks of those same walls. Initiation is a process which takes us "over

One way to explain initiation is to say that it is a threshold of change which we may experience at different times in our lives, as we grow and develop.

the wall" into the unexplored territories of the possibilities which we have only half-glimpsed. This first crisis is often an unpleasant experience, as we begin to question and become dissatisfied with all that we have previously held dear—work, relationships, ethical values, family life can all be disrupted as the individual becomes increasingly consumed by the desire to "journey."

The internal summons may be consciously quashed or resisted, and it is not unknown for individuals in tribal societies to refuse "the call" to shamanic training—no small thing, as it may lead to further crises and even death. One very common experience of people who feel the summons in our society is an overpowering sense of urgency to either become "enlightened" or to change the world in accordance with emerging visions. This can lead to people becoming "addicted" to spiritual paths, wherein the energy that may have been formerly channeled into work or relationships is directed towards taking up spiritual practices and becoming immersed in "spiritual" belief systems.

The "newly awakened" individual can be (unintentionally) as boring and tiresome as anyone who has seized on a messianic belief system, whether it be politics, religion, or spirituality. It is often difficult, at this stage in the cycle, to understand the reaction of family, friends and others who may not be sympathetic to one's newfound direction or changes in lifestyle. Often, some of the more dubious

religious cults take advantage of this stage by convincing young converts that "true friends" etc., would not hinder them in taking up their new life, and that anyone who does not approve, is therefore not a "true friend."

There are a wide variety of cults which do well in terms of converts from young people who are in a period of transition (such as when leaving home for the first time) and who are attracted to a belief/value system that assuages their uncertainties about the world. Another of the problems often experienced by those feeling the summons to journey is a terrible sense of isolation or alienation from one's fellows—the inevitable result of moving to the edge of one's culture. Thus excitement at the adventure is often tinged with regret and loss of stability or unconscious participation with one's former world. Once you have begun the process of disentanglement from the everyday world, it is hard not to feel a certain nostalgia for the lost former life in which everything was (seemingly) clear-cut and stable, with no ambiguities or uncertainties.

A common response to the summons to departure is the journey into the wilderness—of moving away from one's fellows and the stability of consensual reality. A proto-shaman is likely to physically journey into the wilderness, away from the security of tribal reality, and though this is possible for some Westerners, the constraints of modern living usually mean that for us, this wandering in the waste is enacted on the plane of ideas, values and beliefs, wherein we look deeply within and around ourselves and question everything, perhaps drawing away from social relations as well. Deliberate isolation from one's fellows is a powerful way of loosening the sense of having fixed values and beliefs, and social deprivation mechanisms turn up in a wide variety of magical cultures.

THE INITIATORY SICKNESS

In shamanic cultures, the summons to journey is often heralded by a so-called "initiatory sickness," which can either come upon an individual suddenly, or creep slowly upon them as a progressive behavioral change. Western observers have labeled this state as a form of "divine madness," or evidence of psychopathology. In the past, anthropologists and psychologists have labeled shamans as schizophrenic, psychotic, or epileptic. More recently, western enthusiasts of shamanism (and anti-psychiatry) have reversed this process of labeling and asserted that people as schizophrenic, psychotic or epileptic are proto-shamans. Current trends in the study of shamanism now recognize the former position to be ethnocentric—that researchers have been judging shamanic behavior by western standards. The onset of initiatory sickness in tribal culture is recognized as a difficult, but potentially useful developmental process. Part of the problem here

> ## The Dark Night is a way of bringing the soul to stillness, so that a deep psychic transformation may take place. In the Western Esoteric Tradition, this experience is reflected in the Tarot card "The Moon."

is that western philosophy has developed the idea of "ordinary consciousness," of which anything beyond this range is pathological, be it shamanic, mystical, or drug-induced. Fortunately for us, this narrow view is being rapidly undermined.

Individuals undergoing the initiatory sickness do sometimes appear to suffer from fits and "strange" behavior, but there is an increasing recognition that it is a mistake to sweepingly attach western psychiatric labels onto them (so that they can be explained away). Shamans may go through a period of readjustment, but research shows that they tend to become the healthiest people in their tribes, functioning very well as leaders and healers.

Transitional states showing similar features to the initiatory sickness have been identified in other cultures' mystical and magical practices, which western researchers are beginning to study, as practices from other cultures gain popularity in the west.

THE DARK NIGHT OF THE SOUL

St. John of the Cross, a Christian mystic, wrote of this experience:

> [it]...puts the sensory spiritual appetites to sleep, deadens them, and deprives them of the ability to find pleasure in anything. It binds the imagination, and impedes it from doing any good discursive work. It makes the memory cease, the intellect become dark and unable to understand anything, and hence it causes the will to become arid and constrained, and all the faculties empty and useless. And over this hangs a dense and burdensome cloud, which afflicts the soul, and keeps it withdrawn from God.

When entering the "Dark Night" one is overcome by the sense of spiritual dryness and depression. The idea, expressed in some quarters, that all such experiences are to be avoided in favor of a peaceful life, shows up the superficiality of so much of contemporary living. The Dark Night is a way of bringing the soul to stillness, so that a deep psychic transformation may take place. In the Western Esoteric Tradition, this experience is reflected in the Tarot card "The Moon" and is the "hump" in an individual's spiritual development where any early benefits of meditation, Pathworking or disciplines appear to cease, and there is an urge to abandon such practices and return to "everyday" life. This kind of "hump" which must be passed through can be discerned in different areas of experience, and is often experienced by students on degree courses and anybody who is undergoing a new learning process which involves marked life changes as well.

MACRO AND MICRO-INITIATIONS

Generally speaking, there are two kinds of initiatory experience—Microscopic and Macroscopic. Macroscopic initiations can be characterized as being major life shifts, traumas that sweep upon us—the collapse of a long-term relationship, the crash of a business or the sudden knowledge that you have a terminal illness. Such experiences are global, which is to say that they send shock waves into every aspect of our lives.

Microscopic initiations are more specific in their actions. One day I was sitting tapping figures into the company accounting program, when I suddenly found myself thinking "I'd like to do an Accounts Course." Now normally I would have regarded that as no more realistic than a wish to fly to the Moon tomorrow. Accounting is one of those tasks I am only too happy to leave up to someone else, and suddenly, I was becoming interested in it! Such newfound interests, particularly in subjects that you have accepted that you dislike or are uninterested in, can be likened to a small flame (symbolized by the Ace of Wands in Tarot) that could easily burn out again if smothered or ignored. The trick is to recognize that you are standing at a crossroads—a threshold of change. This recognition is the key to all initiations. Again, the A PIE formula is of use:

ASSESS

Stop. Look around you and assess your situation. Examine all possibilities for future action—there will always be more pathways available than is at first immediately obvious. What possible futures can you jump into? Use any technique that will gather useful information—options lists, divination, dream-oracles or asking your favorite deity. Often, all you have to do is open yourself to become vulnerable to the forces of Change.

PLAN

Once you have chosen a course of action—plan what you need to do. What resources do you need? These may be material, magical, financial and perhaps most importantly, the support of other people. Be prepared to carry your plan onwards.

IMPLEMENT

This is the hardest thing of all—to do what must be done. Often, fear will intervene at this stage. Be prepared to look at your motivations for not continuing upon your chosen course. Unacknowledged fears often take the form of inertia and laziness. Each step forwards gives further momentum to the next effort. Each barrier breached releases a rush of pleasure and freedom.

EVALUATE

This is the stage of assimilation—not merely the practice of writing up one's magical record, but being able to look back at your course through the initiatory period and realize what happened and how you dealt with it. Have you learned any important lessons? The value of such experience is to make knowledge flesh—assimilating experience until it seems perfectly simple and natural.

GETTING THE FEAR

A key to understanding initiatory states is that they bring with them varying degrees of fear. One of the characteristics of Macroscopic Initiations is that suddenly, our current repertoire of coping strategies are useless. If something into which we have invested a good deal of emotional commitment and self-esteem is directly threatened or removed, and we are placed in a position of being unable to do anything about this, fear is often the dominant emotion.

Fear is the bodily gnosis which reinforces any emotional and cognitive patterns which serve us to hold change at bay. Fear is basically an excitatory state—the fight/flight reflex of the Autonomic Nervous System firing up. Using the Emotional Engineering techniques described in the previous chapter, you can deconstruct fear into excitement, which can then be used to gather momentum for moving over a threshold into change, rather than reinforcing your own resistance.

RELAX INTO FEAR

This is a process of orienting yourself so that you are sufficiently open to all the different possibilities that each moment of experience offers—enmeshed in the world in an attitude of receptive wonder. This is the knowledge that at any time, without warning, any life event could spin you sideways into Illumination. The sudden-ness of such an experience is one of the underlying themes encapsulated in the Great God Pan. Pan represents creative derangement, the possibility of moving from one state to another, from ordinary perception to divine inspiration. Pan can leap upon you any time, any place with the sudden realization that everything is alive and significant. In such an experience, physical arousal is a strength, rather than a weakness. Allowing yourself to be vulnerable to the possibility of change means letting into your life wild magic and the power of surprises. Initiatory states often tip us into mental entropy and confusion, and this is a good time to free yourself from the bonds of the Past and the fetters of anticipated futures, and live in the now of your physical presence. Transform fear into wonder and open yourself to new possibilities. Transform fear into fuel and examine the thresholds and personal demons which hinder movement. This state is a form of ecstasy—a word which means "away from stillness," implying some kind of agitation.

SAHAJA

Sahaja is a Sanskrit word that can be translated as "spontaneity." If you can learn to relax within initiatory periods, abandoning all set routines and learned responses, you can act with a greater degree of freedom. Periods of initiation can be looked upon as windows of opportunity for major work upon yourself. So what kinds of techniques are appropriate here? Anything that enables you to make shifts in your Achievable Reality threshold. Procedures borrowed from NLP, Vivation, Bioenergetics or the various psychotherapies might prove useful here. What you should bear in mind is that recognition that you are entering a threshold of change is all-important. It is

Death by dismemberment is a strongly recurrent theme in shamanic cultures, where proto-shamans are stripped of their flesh and torn apart by spirits, only to be remade anew.

difficult to intentionally propel yourself into such states, particularly as at some point during the experience, it is necessary to surrender control.

The initiatory crisis tends to drive home (often very forcefully) the awareness of the fragility of day-to-day experiences, and of the hidden complexity behind that which we have taken for granted as normal. We have become addicted to a "sameness" of experience, and thus have difficulty coping with novelty or change. Hence the tendency, when faced with a crisis, to rely on learned habits, rather than actually observing the situation. Conversely, the magician has to recognize that there may well be an abyss around every corner, and that what rushes full-tilt at us must be faced head-on. In time, you will come to recognize that you have your own personal cycles of initiation—peaks, troughs and plateaus; you may well come to recognize that you are about to enter an initiatory period, and brace yourself accordingly.

INNERWORLD CONFRONTATIONS

Many world myths feature the descent into the Underworld as a central theme for transformation and the quest for power and mastery of self. The recognition of the necessity of "rites of passage" is played out both in tribal societies where the death of childhood and the rebirth into adulthood is marked by a rite of passing, and in Western magical and religious societies where "followers"

are reborn into a new selfdom. Death by dismemberment is a strongly recurrent theme in shamanic cultures, where proto-shamans are stripped of their flesh and torn apart by spirits, only to be remade anew, usually with some additional part, such as an extra bone, organ, or crystal as an indication that they are now something "more" than previously. In some cultures (such as in the Tibetan Tantric Chod ritual), the dismemberment experience is a voluntary meditation, whereas in others, it is an involuntary (though understood) experience.

This kind of transition is not uncommon in Western approaches to magical development, both as a willed technique and as a (seemingly) spontaneous experience that results from working within a particular belief-system. I have for example, been burnt alive in the pyre of Kali, and more recently, had an eye ripped out by the Morrigan. Periodic descents into the Underworld are a necessary phase in the cycle of personal development, and are also associated with depth psychotherapy. According to the Western Esoteric Tradition, one of the key stages of initiatory confrontation is the encounter with "The Dweller on the Threshold." Less prosaically, this phrase refers to the experience of our understanding of the gulf between the ego's fiction of itself and our selves as we truly are. This necessitates the acceptance of light into the dark corners of the self, and the acceptance of our shortcomings, blind spots and personal weaknesses as aspects of ourselves that we must take responsibility for. The recognition that we are, ultimately, responsible for all aspects of ourselves, especially those bits which we are loath to admit to ourselves, is a step that must be taken if the initiatory journey is to proceed. It is not uncommon for people to remain at this stage for years, or to come back to it, time and time again. Such ordeals must be worked through, or they will return to "haunt" us until they are tackled, else they will become "obsessional complexes" (demons) that will grow until they have power over us. There are a myriad of techniques—both magical exercises and psychotherapeutic tools which can be actively used to examine these complexes, but the core of this ordeal is the beginnings of seeing yourself. In shamanic cultures, physical isolation from the tribe is often reinforced by physical ordeals such as fasting, sleep deprivation, and exposure to rigors of heat or cold—all-powerful techniques for producing altered states of consciousness.

The initiatory cycle can be likened to a snake sloughing off its skin. So too, we must be prepared to slough off old patterns of thought, belief (about ourselves and the world) and behavior that are no longer appropriate for the new phase of our development. As we reach the initiatory stage of descent into the underworld, so we are descending into the Deep Mind, learning to rely on our own intuition about what is right for us, rather than what we have been told is correct. As the initiatory process becomes more and more intense, we reach a point where we have (to varying degrees) isolated ourselves from the Social World, (physically or mentally), and begun to dismember the layer of our Personal World, so that the Mythic World becomes paramount in our consciousness, perhaps in an intensely 'real' way that it has not been, beforehand. When we open up the floodgates of the Mythic World, we may find that our Deep Mind "speaks" to us using what psychologists call "autosymbolic images"; that is, symbols which reflect the churnings within us. These may well be entities or spirits from magical or religious belief systems that we have consciously assimilated, or they may arise "spontaneously" from the Deep Mind. These "entities" (whatever their source) may become the first of our "allies" or guides through the inner worlds that we have descended into. Accounts of shamanic initiation often recount the neo-shaman being "tested" in various ways by spirit guides and helpers, and, if she or he passes the testing, they become allies that the shaman can call upon, on returning from the underworld. Not all of the spirits one meets while undergoing the underworld experience will be helpful or benign; some will try to mislead or misdirect you. In this kind of instance you will need to rely even more on your own "truthsense" or discrimination. Ghosts are notoriously capricious, and an "elder brother" once told me to "be wary of spirits which herald a false dawn under the dark moon." Particular "misguides" to watch out for are the spirits who will tell you that you are "mystically illuminated" beyond a point that anyone else has reached—they are "parts" of the ego attempting to save itself from destruction. You may have to "overcome" some of these spirits—not so much by defeating them in astral combat, but by recognizing that they have no power over you—that you understand their seductions and will not be swayed by them. The danger here hearkens back to the necessity of attempting to shed light on as many of your buried complexes as possible—"misguide" spirits will attempt to seduce you into feeding those complexes so that you become caught up in them. Spirit guides and helpers usually come in a variety of forms and shapes. Their messages may not always be obvious, and may only become clear with hindsight—but then you cannot expect everything to be handed to you on a plate. It is not unknown for spirit guides to put the initiate through a pretty rough time, again to test their "strength," as it were. Powerful spirits don't tend to "like" shamans who won't take chances or face difficulties and overcome them. This is a hard time to get through, but if you keep your wits about you and hang on in there, then the rewards are worth it. Guides will often show you "secret routes" through the underworld, and "places of power" there which you can access at a later point. Some Amerind shamanic traditions involve the shaman descending into the underworld periodically to learn the names of spirits which, when brought out again, can be placed in masks or other ritual objects.

> **The initiatory cycle can be likened to a snake sloughing off its skin. So too, we must be prepared to slough off old patterns of thought, belief (about ourselves and the world) and behavior that are no longer appropriate for the new phase of our development.**

Another benefit of the "ordeals" stage is *Innerworld Mapping*—obtaining (or verifying) a symbolic plan of the connecting worlds that form the universe. Western occulture gives us conscious access to a wide variety of universal route maps, the Tree of Life that appears in many esoteric systems being just one well-known example. Western-derived maps seem to have a tendency to become very complicated very quickly—perhaps this reflects a cultural tendency to try and label everything neatly away. The interesting (and intriguing) thing about using innerworld maps is that you can metaprogram your Deep Mind to accept a number of different maps—images and symbols will arise accordingly. Our "tradition" for receiving innerworld maps (and indeed, any other esoteric teaching) is largely through the written word, rather than oral teaching or the psychoactively inspired communion with the tribal meme-pool which are the most common routes for shamans. But it is worth remembering that all the different innerworld maps had to come from somewhere, and the most likely source would seem to be the initiatory ordeals of very early shamans, which eventually became condensed into definite structures.

ILLUMINATION

The "peak" of the initiation experience is that of death/rebirth, and subsequent "illumination." That such an experience is common to all mystery religions, magical systems and many secular movements indicates that it may well be one of the essential manifestations of the process of change within the human psyche. Illumination is the much-desired goal for which many thousands of people worldwide have employed different psycho-technologies, and developed their own psychocosms. Illumination has also been linked with the use of LSD and similar drugs, and perhaps most mysteriously of all, it can occur seemingly spontaneously to people who have no knowledge or expectation of it. What characterizes an experience of illumination? Some of the prevalent factors are:

1. A sense of unity—a fading of the self-other divide
2. Transcendence of space and time as barriers to experience
3. Positive sensations
4. A sense of the numinous
5. A sense of certitude—the "realness" of the experience
6. Paradoxical insights
7. Transience—the experience does not last
8. Resultant change in attitude and behavior.

In neurological terms such experiences represent a re-organizing of activity in the brain as a whole. The loss of ego boundary and the involvement of all senses suggests that the Reticular Formation is being influenced so that the processes which normally convey a sense of being rooted in space-time are momentarily inhibited. The "floating" sensation often associated with astral projection and

The basis of this idea is that the movement of energy through a system causes fluctuations which, if they reach a critical level (i.e., a catastrophe cusp point) develop novel interactions until a new whole is produced.

other such phenomena suggests that the Limbic system of the brain stem (which processes proprioceptive information about the body's location in space) is also acting in an unusual mode.

What are the fruits of this experience—the insights, perceptions and messages brought back down to earth by the illuminate? Evolution of consciousness, by such means, could well be an important survival program—a way of going beyond the information given—a way of

learning how to modify the human biosystem via the environment. Ilya Prigognine's theory of "dissipative structures" shows how the very instability of open systems allows them to be self-transforming. The basis of this idea is that the movement of energy through a system causes fluctuations which, if they reach a critical level (i.e., a catastrophe cusp point) develop novel interactions until a new whole is produced. The system then reorganizes itself into a new "higher order" which is more integrated than the previous system, requires a greater amount of energy to maintain itself, and is further disposed to future transformation. This can equally apply to neurological evolution, using a psycho-technology (ancient or modern) as the tool for change. The core stages of the process appear to be:

1. Change
2. Crisis
3. Transcendence
4. Transformation
5. Predisposition to further change.

Also, the term "illumination" is itself significant. Visions of light that suddenly burst forth upon the individual are well documented from a wide variety of sources, from shamanic travelers to St. Paul; acid trippers to people who seemingly have the experience spontaneously. Similarly, the experience of being "born-again" is central to shamanism, religions and magical systems. One's old self dies, and a new one is reborn from the shattered patterns and perceptions. This is well understood in cultures where there is a single predominant Mythic reality. Death-rebirth is the key to shamanic development, and many shamanic cultures interpret the experience quite literally, rather than metaphorically. Western psychologists are only just beginning to understand the benefits of such an experience. What is clear is that for many people who undergo it, the experience is unsettling and disturbing, especially when there is no dominant cultural backdrop with which to explain or understand the process. A good example to look at (which always raises hackles in some quarters) is the LSD death-rebirth experience. Some Western "authorities" on spiritual practice hold that drug-induced experiences are somehow not as valid as ones triggered by "spiritual" practices. Fortunately, this somewhat blinkered view is receding as more information about the role played by psychoactive substances in shamanic training is brought to light. The positive benefits of LSD have been widely proclaimed by people as diverse as Aldous Huxley, Timothy Leary, and Stanislav Grof, all of whom also stressed that acid should be used in "controlled conditions," rather than, as is so often the case today, indiscriminately. What must be borne in mind about LSD (like other psychoactives) is that its action and effects are highly dependent upon individual beliefs and expectations, and social conditioning. Dropping acid can lead to lasting change and transformation in a positive sense; equally, it can lead to individuals uncritically accepting a set of beliefs and patterns that effectively wall them off from further transformations—witness the number of burnt-out acidheads who become "Born-Again" evangelicals, for instance. It's not so much the experience itself, but how individuals assimilate it in terms of cultural expectations.

As an example of how this process operates, contrast a proto-shaman against a member of a postmodern, industrial culture such as is our own. The proto-shaman undergoes death-rebirth, and, following illumination, is reborn into the role of a practicing shaman, with all its subsequent status affiliations and expectations. Would that it were as simple for Westerners! Ours is a much more complex set of social relations than the tribal environment. Though one might be tempted to think of oneself as a shaman-in-the-making, it's a safe bet that not everyone else is going to accede that role to you. It's tempting, and entirely understandable to think: "Right, that's it. I'm 'illuminated' now—I've been there, done it, etc." and sit back on one's laurels, as it were. While for some of us, one death-rebirth experience alone is enough to jolt us into a new stage of development; it's more often the case that what we do afterwards is critically important. Zero states of having "made it" are very seductive, but our conditioning patterns are insidious—creeping back into the psyche while our minds are occupied elsewhere. The price of transformation is eternal vigilance. Vigilance against being lulled back into conditioned beliefs and emotional/mental patterns that we think that we have "overcome." Illumination may well be a "peak" in our development, but it isn't the end point, by any means. Those undergoing the initiation cycle in the West tend to find that many periodic death-rebirth experiences are necessary, as we reshuffle different "bits" of the psyche with each occurrence. Yet the death-rebirth experience can bring about lasting benefits, including the alleviation of a wide variety of emotional, interpersonal, and psychosomatic problems that hitherto, have resisted orthodox treatment regimes.

I would postulate that the death-rebirth experience is an essential form of adaptive learning, as it is a powerful process of widening our perspectives on life, our perceptions of the world, and of each other. The illuminatory insight moves us toward a Holotropic perspective (i.e., of moving towards a whole) whereby new insights about self

Gnosis is not merely the act of understanding, it is understanding which impels you to act in a certain way. Thus as you work with magic, so magic works upon you.

in relation to the universe, and how ideas and concepts synthesize together, can be startlingly perceived. At this kind of turning point in our lives, we can go beyond what we already know and begin to manifest new concepts and constructs. We are all capable of the vision—what we do to realize that vision is equally, in our hands.

GNOSIS

Related to the experience of Illumination is the term Gnosis, which can be read on different levels. First, Gnosis is that "peak" experience of no-mind, one-pointedness or samadhi which is the high point of any route into magical trance. Second, Gnosis can be understood as Knowledge of the Heart—perceptions that are difficult to express in language, yet can be grasped and shared. This is the secret language of magic—to grasp the meaning you have to go through the experience first. Gnosis is not merely the act of understanding, it is understanding which impels you to act in a certain way. Thus as you work with magic, so magic works upon you. Such is the nature of Chaos. ⚸

CHEMOGNOSIS

TRYPTAMINE HALLUCINOGENS AND CONSCIOUSNESS

A talk given at the Lilly/Goswami Conference on Consciousness and Quantum Physics at Esalen, December 1983. It appears in print as part of *The Archaic Revival* (Harper San Francisco, 1992)

There is a very circumscribed place in organic nature that has, I think, important implications for students of human nature. I refer to the tryptophan-derived hallucinogens dimethyltryptamine (DMT), psilocybin, and a hybrid drug that is in aboriginal use in the rain forests of South America, ayahuasca. This latter is a combination of dimethyltryptamine and a monoamine oxidase inhibitor that is taken orally. It seems appropriate to talk about these drugs when we discuss the nature of consciousness; it is also appropriate when we discuss quantum physics.

It is my interpretation that the major quantum mechanical phenomena that we all experience, aside from waking consciousness itself, are dreams and hallucinations. These states, at least in the restricted sense that I am concerned with, occur when the large amounts of various sorts of radiation conveyed into the body by the senses are restricted. Then we see interior images and interior processes that are psychophysical. These processes def-

People have been talking to gods and demons for far more of human history than they have not.

initely arise at the quantum mechanical level. It's been shown by John Smythies, Alexander Shulgin, and others that there are quantum mechanical correlates to hallucinogenesis. In other words, if one atom on the molecular ring of an inactive compound is moved, the compound becomes highly active. To me this is a perfect proof of the dynamic linkage at the formative level between quantum mechanically described matter and mind.

Hallucinatory states can be induced by a variety of hallucinogens and disassociate anesthetics, and by experiences like fasting and other ordeals. But what makes the tryptamine family of compounds especially interesting is the intensity of the hallucinations and the concentration of activity in the visual cortex. There is an immense vividness to these interior landscapes, as if information were being presented three-dimensionally and deployed fourth-dimensionally, coded as light and as evolving surfaces. When one confronts these dimensions one becomes part of a dynamic relationship relating to the experience while trying to decode what it is saying. This phenomenon is not new—people have been talking to gods and demons for far more of human history than they have not.

It is only the conceit of the scientific and postindustrial societies that allows us to even propound some of the questions that we take to be so important. For instance, the question of contact with extraterrestrials is a kind of red herring premised upon a number of assumptions that a moment's reflection will show are completely false. To search expectantly for a radio signal from an extraterrestrial source is probably as culture bound a presumption as to search the galaxy for a good Italian restaurant. And yet, this has been chosen as the avenue by which it is assumed contact is likely to occur. Meanwhile, there are people all over the world—psychics, shamans, mystics, schizophrenics—whose heads are filled with information, but it has been ruled a priori irrelevant, incoherent, or mad. Only that which is validated through consensus via certain sanctioned instrumentalities will be accepted as a signal. The problem is that we are so inundated by these signals—these other dimensions—that there is a great deal of noise in the circuit.

The reaction to these voices is not to kneel in genuflection before a god, because then one will be like Dorothy in her first encounter with Oz.

It is no great accomplishment to hear a voice in the head. The accomplishment is to make sure it is telling the truth, because the demons are of many kinds: "Some are made of ions, some of mind; the ones of ketamine, you'll find, stutter often and are blind." The reaction to these voices is not to kneel in genuflection before a god, because then one will be like Dorothy in her first encounter with Oz. There is no dignity in the universe unless we meet these things on our feet, and that means having an I/Thou relationship. One say to the Other: "You say you are omniscient, omnipresent, or you say you are from Zeta Reticuli. You're long on talk, but what can you show me?" Magicians, people who invoke these things, have always understood that one must go into such encounters with one's wits about oneself.

What does extraterrestrial communication have to do with this family of hallucinogenic compounds I wish to discuss? Simply this: that the unique presentational phenomenology of this family of compounds has been overlooked. Psilocybin, though rare, is the best known of these neglected substances. Psilocybin, in the minds of the uninformed public and in the eyes of the law, is lumped together with LSD and mescaline, when in fact each of these compounds is a phenomenologically defined universe unto itself. Psilocybin and DMT invoke the Logos, although DMT is more intense and more brief in its action. This means that they work directly on the language centers, so that an important aspect of the experience is the interior dialogue. As soon as one discovers this about psilocybin and about tryptamines in general,

one must decide whether or not to enter into this dialogue and to try and make sense of the incoming signal. This is what I have attempted.

I call myself an explorer rather than a scientist, because the area that I'm looking at contains insufficient data to support even the dream of being a science. We are in a position comparable to that of explorers who map one river and only indicate other rivers flowing into it; we must leave many rivers unascended and thus can say nothing about them. This Baconian collecting of data, with no assumptions about what it might eventually yield, has pushed me to a number of conclusions that I did not anticipate. Perhaps through reminiscence I can explain what I mean, for in this case describing past experiences raises all of the issues.

I first experimented with DMT in 1965; it was even then a compound rarely met with. It is surprising how few people are familiar with it, for we live in a society that is absolutely obsessed with every kind of sensation imaginable and that adores every therapy, every intoxication, every sexual configuration, and all forms of media overload. Yet, however much we may be hedonists or pursuers of the bizarre, we find DMT to be too much. It is, as they say in Spanish, bastante, it's enough—so much enough that it's too much. Once smoked, the onset of the experience begins in about fifteen seconds. One falls immediately into a trance. One's eyes are closed and one hears a sound like ripping cellophane, like someone crumpling up plastic film and throwing it away. A friend of mine suggests this is our radio entelechy ripping out of the organic matrix. An ascending tone is heard. Also present is the normal hallucinogenic modality, a shifting geometric surface of migrating and changing colored forms. At the synaptic site of activity, all available bond

What does extraterrestrial communication have to do with this family of hallucinogenic compounds?

sites are being occupied, and one experiences the mode shift occurring over a period of about 30 seconds. At that point one arrives in a place that defies description, a space that has a feeling of being underground, or somehow insulated and domed. In *Finnegans Wake* such a place is called the "merry go raum," from the German word raum, for "space." The room is actually going around, and in that space one feels like a child, though one has come out somewhere in eternity.

The tryptamine Munchkins come, these hyperdimensional machine-elf entities, and they bathe one in love. It's not erotic but it is openhearted. It certainly feels good. And they are speaking, saying, "Don't be alarmed. Remember, and do what we are doing."

The experience always reminds me of the 24th fragment of Heraclitus: "The Aeon is a child at play with colored balls." One not only becomes the Aeon at play with colored balls but meets entities as well. In the book by my brother and myself, *The Invisible Landscape*, I describe them as *self-transforming machine elves*, for that is how they appear. These entities are dynamically contorting topological modules that are somehow distinct from the surrounding background, which is itself undergoing a continuous transformation. These entities remind me of the scene in the film version of *The Wizard of Oz* after the Munchkins come with a death certificate for the Witch of the East. They all have very squeaky voices and they sing a little song about being "absolutely and completely dead." The tryptamine Munchkins come, these hyperdimensional machine-elf entities, and they bathe one in love. It's not erotic but it is openhearted. It certainly feels good. These beings are like fractal reflections of some previously hidden and suddenly autonomous part of one's own psyche.

And they are speaking, saying, "Don't be alarmed. Remember, and do what we are doing." One of the interesting characteristics of DMT is that it sometimes inspires fear—this marks the experience as existentially authentic. One of the interesting approaches to evaluating such a compound is to see how eager people are to do it a second time. A touch of terror gives the stamp of validity to the experience because it means, "This is real." We are in the balance. We read the literature; we know the maximum doses, the LD-50, and so on. But nevertheless, so great is one's faith in the mind that when one is out in it one comes to feel that the rules of pharmacology do not really apply and that control of existence on that plane is really a matter of focus of will and good luck.

I'm not saying that there's something intrinsically good about terror. I'm saying that, granted the situation, if one is not terrified then one must be somewhat out of contact with the full dynamics of what is happening. To not be terrified means either that one is a fool or that one has taken a compound that paralyzes the ability to be terrified. I have nothing against hedonism, and I certainly bring

something out of it. But the experience must move one's heart, and it will not move the heart unless it deals with the issues of life and death. If it deals with life and death it will move one to fear, it will move one to tears, it will move one to laughter. These places are profoundly strange and alien.

The fractal elves seem to be reassuring, saying, "Don't worry, don't worry; do this, look at this." Meanwhile, one is completely "over there." One's ego is intact. One's fear reflexes are intact. One is not "fuzzed out" at all. Consequently, the natural reaction is amazement; profound astonishment that persists and persists. One breathes and it persists. The elves are saying, "Don't get a loop of wonder going that quenches your ability to understand. Try not to be so amazed. Try to focus and look at what we're doing." What they're doing is emitting sounds like music, like language. These sounds pass without any quantized moment of distinction—as Philo Judaeus said that the Logos would when it became perfect—from things heard to things beheld. One hears and beholds a language of alien meaning that is conveying alien information that cannot be Englished.

Being monkeys, when we encounter a translinguistic object, a kind of cognitive dissonance is set up in our hindbrain. We try to pour language over it and it sheds it like water off a duck's back. We try again and fail again, and this cognitive dissonance, this "wow" or "flutter" that is building off this object causes wonder, astonishment and awe at the brink of terror. One must control that. And the way to control it is to do what the entities are telling one to do, to do what they are doing.

I mention these "effects" to invite the attention of experimentalists, whether they be shamans or scientists. There is something going on with these compounds that is not part of the normal presentational spectrum of hallucinogenic drug experience. When one begins to experiment with one's voice, unanticipated phenomena become possible. One experiences glossolalia, although unlike classical glossolalia, which has been studied. Students of classical glossolalia have measured pools of saliva eighteen inches across on the floors of South American churches where people have been kneeling. After classical glossolalia has occurred, the glossolaliasts often turn to ask the people nearby, "Did I do it? Did I speak in tongues?" This hallucinogen induced phenomenon isn't like that; it's simply a brain state that allows the expression of the assembly language that lies behind language, or a primal language of the sort that Robert Graves discussed in *The White Goddess*, or a Qabalistic language of the sort that is described in the Zohar, a primal "ur sprach" that comes out of oneself. One discovers one can make the extradimensional objects—the feeling-toned, meaning-toned, three-dimensional rotating complexes of transforming light and color. To know this is to feel like a child. One is playing with colored balls; one has become the Aeon.

This happened to me 20 seconds after I smoked DMT on a particular day in 1966. I was appalled. Until then I had thought that I had my ontological categories intact. I had taken LSD before, yet this thing came upon me like a bolt from the blue. I came down and said (and I said it many times), "I cannot believe this; this is impossible, this is completely impossible." There was a declension of gnosis that proved to me in a moment that right here and now, one quanta away, there is raging a universe of active intelligence that is transhuman, hyperdimensional, and extremely alien. I call it the Logos, and I make no judgments about it. I constantly engage it in dialogue, saying, "Well, what are you? Are you some kind of diffuse consciousness that is in the ecosystem of the Earth? Are you a god or an extraterrestrial? Show me what you know."

The psilocybin mushrooms also convey one into the world of the tryptamine hypercontinuum. Indeed, psilocybin is a psychoactive tryptamine. The mushroom is full of answers to the questions raised by its own presence. The true history of the galaxy over the last four and a half billion years is trivial to it. One can access images of cosmological history. Such experiences naturally raise the question of independent validation—at least for a time this was my question. But as I became more familiar with the epistemological assumptions of modern science, I slowly realized that the structure of the Western intellectual enterprise is so flimsy at the center that apparently no one knows anything with certitude. It was then that I became less reluctant to talk about these experiences. They are experiences, and as such they are primary data for being. This dimension is not remote, and yet it is so unspeakably bizarre that it casts into doubt all of humanity's historical assumptions.

The psilocybin mushrooms do the same things that DMT does, although the experience builds up over an hour and is sustained for a couple of hours. There is the same confrontation with an alien intelligence and extremely bizarre translinguistic information complexes. These experiences strongly suggest that there is some latent ability of the human brain/body that has yet to be discovered; yet, once discovered, it will be so obvious that it will fall right into the mainstream of cultural evolution. It seems to me that either language is the shadow of this ability or that this ability will be a further extension of language. Perhaps a human language is possible in which the intent of meaning is actually beheld in three-dimensional space. If this can happen on DMT, it means it is at least, under some circumstances, accessible to human beings. Given 10,000 years and high cultural involvement in such a talent, does anyone doubt that it could become a cultural convenience in the same way that mathematics or language has become a cultural convenience?

Naturally, as a result of the confrontation of alien intelligence with organized intellect on the other side, many theories have been elaborated. The theory that I put forth in *Psilocybin: The Magic Mushroom Grower's Guide*, held the *Stropharia cubensis* mushroom was a species that did not

One of the interesting characteristics of DMT is that it sometimes inspires fear—this marks the experience as existentially authentic. A touch of terror gives the stamp of validity to the experience because it means, "This is real."

evolve on earth. Within the mushroom trance, I was informed that once a culture has complete understanding of its genetic information, it reengineers itself for survival. The *Stropharia cubensis* mushroom's version of reengineering is a mycelial network strategy when in contact with planetary surfaces and a spore-dispersion strategy as a means of radiating throughout the galaxy. And, though I am troubled by how freely Bell's nonlocality theorem is tossed around, nevertheless the alien intellect on the other side does seem to be in possession in a huge body of information drawn from the history of the galaxy. It/they say that there is nothing unusual about this, that humanity's conceptions of organized intelligence and the dispersion of life in the galaxy are hopelessly culturebound, that the galaxy has been an organized society for billions of years. Life evolves under so many different regimens of chemistry, temperature, and pressure, that searching for an extraterrestrial who will sit down and have a conversation with you is doomed to failure. The main problem with searching for extraterrestrials is to recognize them. Time is so vast and evolutionary strategies and environments so varied that the trick is to know that contact is being made at all. The *Stropharia cubensis* mushroom, if one can believe what it says in one of its moods, is a symbiote, and it desires ever-deeper symbiosis with the human species. It achieved symbiosis with human society early by associating itself with domesticated cattle and through them human nomads. Like the

Philip K. Dick, in one of his last novels, Valis, discusses the long hibernation of the Logos. A creature of pure information, it was buried in the ground at Nag Hammadi, along with the burying of the Chenoboskion Library circa 370 AD.

plants men and women grew and the animals they husbanded, the mushroom was able to inculcate itself into the human family, so that where human genes went these other genes would be carried.

But the classic mushroom cults of Mexico were destroyed by the coming of the Spanish conquest. The Franciscans assumed they had an absolute monopoly on theophagy, the eating of God; yet in the New World they came upon people calling a mushroom teonanacatl, the flesh of the gods. They set to work, and the Inquisition was able to push the old religion into the mountains of Oaxaca so that it only survived in a few villages when Valentina and Gordon Wasson found it there in the 1950s.

There is another metaphor. One must balance these explanations. Now I shall sound as if I didn't think the mushroom is an extraterrestrial. It may instead be what I've recently come to suspect—that the human soul is so alienated from us in our present culture that we treat it as an extraterrestrial. To us the most alien thing in the cosmos is the human soul. Aliens Hollywood-style could arrive on earth tomorrow and the DMT trance would remain more weird and continue to hold more promise for useful information for the human future. It is that intense. Ignorance forced the mushroom cult into hiding. Ignorance burned the libraries of the Hellenistic world at an earlier period and dispersed the ancient knowledge, shattering the stellar and astronomical machinery that had been the work of centuries. By ignorance I mean the Hellenistic-Christian-Judaic tradition. The inheritors of this tradition built a triumph of mechanism. It was they who later realized the alchemical dreams of the 15th and 16th centuries—and the 20th century—with the transfor-

mation of elements and the discovery of gene transplants. But then, having conquered the New World and driven its people into cultural fragmentation and diaspora, they came unexpectedly upon the body of Osiris—the condensed body of Eros—in the mountains of Mexico where Eros has retreated at the coming of the Christos. And by finding the mushroom, they unleashed it.

Philip K. Dick, in one of his last novels, *Valis*, discusses the long hibernation of the Logos. A creature of pure information, it was buried in the ground at Nag Hammadi, along with the burying of the Chenoboskion Library circa 370 AD. As static information, it existed there until 1947, when the texts were translated and read. As soon as people had the information in their minds, the symbiote came alive, for, like the mushroom consciousness, Dick imagined it to be a thing of pure information. The mushroom consciousness is the consciousness of the *Other* in hyperspace, which means in dream and in the psilocybin trance, at the quantum foundation of being, in the human future, and after death. All of these places that were thought to be discrete and separate are seen to be part of a single continuum. History is the dash over 10–15,000 years from nomadism to flying saucer, hopefully without ripping the envelope of the planet so badly that the birth is aborted and fails, and we remain brutish prisoners of matter.

History is the shockwave of eschatology. Something is at the end of time and is casting an enormous shadow over human history, drawing all human becoming toward it. All the wars, the philosophies, the rapes, the pillaging,

History is the shockwave of eschatology. Something is at the end of time and is casting an enormous shadow over human history, drawing all human becoming toward it.

the migrations, the cities, the civilizations—all of this is occupying a microsecond of geological, planetary, and galactic time as the monkeys react to the symbiote, which is in the environment and which is feeding information to humanity about the larger picture. I do not belong to the school that wants to attribute all of our accomplishments to knowledge given to us as a gift from friendly aliens—I'm describing something I hope is more profound than that. As nervous systems evolve to higher and higher levels, they come more and more to understand the true situation in which they are embedded, and the true situation in which we are embedded is an organism, an organization of intelligence on a galactic scale. Science and mathematics may be culture-bound. We cannot know for sure, because we have never dealt with an alien mathematics or an alien culture except in the occult realm, and that evidence is inadmissible by the guardians of scientific truth. This means that the contents of shamanic experience and of plant-induced ecstasies are inadmissible even though they are the source of novelty and the cutting edge of the ingression of the novel into the plenum of being.

Think about this for a moment: If the human mind does not loom large in the coming history of the human race, then what is to become of us? The future is bound to be psychedelic, because the future belongs to the mind. We are just beginning to push the buttons on the mind. Once we take a serious engineering approach to this, we are going to discover the plasticity, the mutability, the eternal nature of the mind and, I believe, release it from the monkey. My vision of the final human future is an effort to exteriorize the soul and internalize the body, so that the exterior soul will exist as a superconducting lens of translinguistic matter generated out of the body of each of us at a critical juncture at our psychedelic bar mitzvah. From that point on, we will be eternal somewhere in the solid-state matrix of the translinguistic lens we have become. One's body image will exist as a holographic wave transform while one is at play in the fields of the Lord and living in Elysium.

Other intelligent monkeys have walked this planet. We exterminated them and so now we are unique, but what is loose on this planet is language, self-replicating information systems that reflect functions of DNA: learning, coding, templating, recording, testing, retesting, recoding against DNA functions. Then again, language may be a quality of an entirely different order. Whatever language is, it is in us monkeys now and moving through us and moving out of our hands and into the noosphere with which we have surrounded ourselves.

The tryptamine state seems to be in one sense transtemporal; it is an anticipation of the future, it is as though Plato's metaphor were true—that time IS the moving image of eternity. The tryptamine ecstasy is a stepping out of the moving image and into eternity, the eternity of the standing now, the nunc stans of Thomas Aquinas. In that state, all of human history is seen to lead toward this culminating moment. Acceleration is visible in all the processes around us: the fact that fire was discovered several million years ago; language came perhaps 35,000 years ago; measurement, 5,000; Galileo, 400; then Watson-Crick and DNA. What is obviously happening is that everything is being drawn together. On the other hand, the description our physicists are giving us of the universe—that it has lasted billions of years and will last billions of years into the future—is a dualistic conception, an inductive projection that is very unsophisticated when applied to the nature of consciousness and language. Consciousness is somehow able to collapse the state vector and thereby cause the stuff of being to undergo what Alfred North Whitehead called "the formality of actually occurring." Here is the beginning of an understanding of the centrality of human beings. Western societies have been on a decentralizing

Think about this for a moment: If the human mind does not loom large in the coming history of the human race, then what is to become of us? The future is bound to be psychedelic, because the future belongs to the mind.

bender for 500 years, concluding that the Earth is not the center of the universe and man is not the beloved of God. We have moved ourselves out toward the edge of the galaxy, when the fact is that the most richly organized material in the universe is the human cerebral cortex, and the densest and richest experience in the universe is the experience you are having right now. Everything should be constellated outward from the perceiving self. That is the primary datum.

The perceiving self under the influence of these hallucinogenic plants gives information that is totally at variance with the models that we inherit from our past, yet these dimensions exist. On one level, this information is a matter of no great consequence, for many cultures have understood this for millennia. But we moderns are so grotesquely alienated and taken out of what life is about that to us it comes as a revelation. Without psychedelics the closest we can get to the Mystery is to try to feel in some abstract mode the power of myth or ritual. This grasping is a very over intellectualized and unsatisfying sort of process.

As I said, I am an explorer, not a scientist. If I were unique, then none of my conclusions would have any meaning outside the context of myself. My experiences, like yours, have to be more or less part of the human condition. Some may have more facility for such exploration than others, and these states may be difficult to achieve, but they are part of the human condition. There are few clues that these extradimensional places exist. If art carries images out of the Other from the Logos to the world—drawing ideas down into matter—why is human art history so devoid of what psychedelic voyagers have experienced so totally? Perhaps the flying saucer or UFO is the central motif to be understood in order to get a handle on reality here and now. We are alienated, so alienated that the self must disguise itself as an extraterrestrial in order not to alarm us with the truly bizarre dimensions that it encompasses. When we can love the alien, then we will have begun to heal the psychic discontinuity that has plagued us since at least the 16th century, possibly earlier.

My testimony is that magic is alive in hyperspace. It is not necessary to believe me, only to form a relationship with these hallucinogenic plants. The fact is that the gnosis comes from plants. There is some certainty that one is dealing with a creature of integrity if one deals with a plant, but the creatures born in the demonic artifice of laboratories have to be dealt with very, very carefully. DMT

Magic is alive in hyperspace. It is not necessary to believe me, only to form a relationship with these hallucinogenic plants.

is an endogenous hallucinogen. It is present in small amounts in the human brain. Also it is important that psilocybin is 4-phosphoraloxy-N, N-dimethyltryptamine and that serotonin, the major neurotransmitter in the human brain, found in all life and most concentrated in humans, is 5-hydroxytryptamine. The very fact that the onset of DMT is so rapid, coming on in 45 seconds and lasting five minutes, means that the brain is absolutely at home with this compound. On the other hand, a hallucinogen like LSD is retained in the body for some time.

I will add a cautionary note. I always feel odd telling people to verify my observations since the sine qua non is the hallucinogenic plant. Experimenters should be very careful. One must build up to the experience. These are bizarre dimensions of extraordinary power and beauty. There is no set rule to avoid being overwhelmed, but move carefully, reflect a great deal, and always try to map experiences back onto the history of the race and the philo-

sophical and religious accomplishments of the species. All the compounds are potentially dangerous, and all compounds, at sufficient doses or repeated over time, involve risks. The library is the first place to go when looking into taking a new compound.

We need all the information available to navigate dimensions that are profoundly strange and alien. I have been to Konarak and visited Bubaneshwar. I'm familiar with Hindu iconography and have collected thankas. I saw similarities between my LSD experiences and the iconography of Mahayana Buddhism. In fact, it was LSD experiences that drove me to collect Mahayana art. But what amazed me was the total absence of the motifs of DMT. It is not there; it is not there in any tradition familiar to me.

There is a very interesting story by Jorge Luis Borges called "The Sect of the Phoenix." Allow me to recapitulate. Borges starts out by writing: "There is no human group in which members of the sect do not appear. It is also true that there is no persecution or rigor they have not suffered and perpetrated." He continues,

> The rite is the only religious practice observed by the sectarians. The rite constitutes the Secret. This Secret ... is transmitted from generation to generation. The act in itself is trivial, momentary, and requires no description. The Secret is sacred, but is always somewhat ridiculous; its performance is furtive and the adept do not speak of it. There are no decent words to name it, but it is understood that all words name it or rather inevitably allude to it.

Borges never explicitly says what the Secret is, but if one knows his other story, "The Aleph," one can put these two together and realize that the Aleph is the experience of the Secret of the Cult of the Phoenix.

In the Amazon, when the mushroom was revealing its information and deputizing us to do various things, we asked, "Why us? Why should we be the ambassadors of an alien species into human culture?" And it answered, "Because you did not believe in anything. Because you have never given over your belief to anyone." The sect of the phoenix, the cult of this experience, is perhaps millennia old, but it has not yet been brought to light where the historical threads may run. The prehistoric use of ecstatic plants on this planet is not well understood. Until recently, psilocybin mushroom taking was confined to the central isthmus of Mexico. The psilocybin-containing species *Strophoria cubensis* is not known to be in archaic use in a shamanic rite anywhere in the world. DMT is used in the Amazon and has been for millennia, but by cultures quite primitive—usually nomadic hunter-gatherers.

I am baffled by what I call "the black hole effect" that seems to surround DMT. A black hole causes a curvature of space such that no light can leave it, and, since no signal can leave it, no information can leave it. Let us leave aside the issue of whether this is true in practice of spinning black holes. Think of it as a metaphor. Metaphorically, DMT is like an intellectual black hole in that once one knows about it, it is very hard for others to understand what one is talking about. One cannot be heard. The more one is able to articulate what it is, the less others are able to understand. This is why I think people who attain enlightenment, if we may for a moment comap these two things, are silent. They are silent because we cannot understand them. Why the phenomenon of tryptamine ecstasy has not been looked at by scientists, thrill seekers, or anyone else, I am not sure, but I recommend it to your attention.

The tragedy of our cultural situation is that we have no shamanic tradition. Shamanism is primarily techniques, not ritual. It is a set of techniques that have been worked out over millennia that make it possible, though perhaps not for everyone, to explore these areas. People of predilection are noticed and encouraged.

In archaic societies where shamanism is a thriving institution, the signs are fairly easy to recognize: oddness or uniqueness in an individual. Epilepsy is often a signature in preliterate societies, or survival of an unusual ordeal in an unexpected way. For instance, people who are struck by lightning and live are thought to make excellent shamans. People who nearly die of a disease and fight their way back to health after weeks and weeks of an indeterminate zone are thought to have strength of soul. Among aspiring shamans there must be some sign of inner strength or a hypersensitivity to trance states. In traveling around the world and dealing with shamans, I find the distinguishing characteristic is an extraordinary centeredness. Usually the shaman is an intellectual and is alienated from society. A good shaman sees exactly who you are and says, "Ah, here's somebody to have a conversation with." The anthropological literature always presents shamans as embedded in a tradition, but once one gets to know them they are always very sophisticated about what they are doing. They are the true phenomenologists of this world; they know plant chemistry, yet they call these energy fields

> "There is no human group in which members of the sect do not appear. It is also true that there is no persecution or rigor they have not suffered and perpetrated." –Jorge Luis Borges in "The Sect of the Phoenix"

"spirits." We hear the word "spirits" through a series of narrowing declensions of meaning that are worse almost than not understanding. Shamans speak of "spirit" the way a quantum physicist might speak of "charm"; it is a technical gloss for a very complicated concept.

It is possible that there are shamanic family lines, at least in the case of hallucinogen-using shamans, because shamanic ability is to some degree determined by how many active receptor sites occur in the brain, thus facilitating these experiences. Some claim to have these experiences naturally, but I am underwhelmed by the evidence that this is so. What it comes down to for me is "What can you show me?"

I always ask that question; finally in the Amazon, informants said, "Let's take our machetes and hike out here half a mile and get some vine and boil it up and we will show you what we can show you."

Let us be clear. People die in these societies that I'm talking about all the time and for all kinds of reasons. Death is really much more among them than it is in our society. Those who have epilepsy who don't die are brought to the attention of the shaman and trained in breathing and plant usage and other things—the fact is that we don't really know all of what goes on. These secret information systems have not been well studied. Shamanism is not, in these traditional societies, a terribly pleasant office. Shamans are not normally allowed to have any political power, because they are sacred. The shaman is to be found sitting at the headman's side in the council meetings, but after the council meeting he returns to his hut at the edge of the village. Shamans are peripheral to society's goings on in ordinary social life in every sense of the word. They are called on in crisis, and the crisis can be someone dying or ill, a psychological difficulty, a marital quarrel, a theft, or weather that must be predicted.

TRYPTAMINE HALLUCINOGENS AND CONSCIOUSNESS

We do not live in that kind of society, so when I explore these plants' effects and try to call your attention to them, it is as a phenomenon. I don't know what we can do with this phenomenon, but I have a feeling that the potential is great. The mind-set that I always bring to it is simply exploratory and Baconian—the mapping and gathering of facts.

Herbert Guenther talks about human uniqueness and says one must come to terms with one's uniqueness. We are naive about the role of language and being as the primary facts of experience. What good is a theory of how the universe works if it's a series of tensor equations that, even when understood, come nowhere tangential to experience? The only intellectual or noetic or spiritual path worth following is one that builds on personal experience.

What the mushroom says about itself is this: that it is an extraterrestrial organism, that spores can survive the conditions of interstellar space. They are deep, deep purple—the color that they would have to be to absorb the deep ultraviolet end of the spectrum. The casing of a spore is one of the hardest organic substances known. The electron density approaches that of a metal.

Is it possible that these mushrooms never evolved on earth? That is what the *Stropharia cubensis* itself suggests. Global currents may form on the outside of the spore. The spores are very light and by Brownian motion are capable of percolation to the edge of the planet's atmosphere. Then, through interaction with energetic particles, some small number could actually escape into space. Understand that this is an evolutionary strategy

the stars is a perfectly viable strategy for biology. It might take millions of years, but it's the same principle by which plants migrate into a desert or across an ocean.

Is it possible that these mushrooms never evolved on earth?

There are no fungi in the fossil record older than 40 million years. The orthodox explanation is that fungi are soft-bodied and do not fossilize well, but on the other hand we have fossilized soft-bodied worms and other benthic marine invertebrates from South African gunflint chert that is dated to over a billion years.

I don't necessarily believe what the mushroom tells me; rather we have a dialogue. It is a very strange person and has many bizarre opinions. I entertain it the way I would any eccentric friend. I say, "Well, so that's what you think." When the mushroom began saying it was an extraterrestrial, I felt that I was placed in the dilemma of a child who wishes to destroy a radio to see if there are little people inside. I couldn't figure out whether the mushroom is the alien or the mushroom is some kind of technological artifact allowing me to hear the alien when the alien is actually light-years aways, using some kind of Bell nonlocality principle to communicate.

The mushroom states its own position very clearly. It says, "I require the nervous system of a mammal. Do you have one handy?" ⌗

The mushroom states its own position very clearly. It says, "I require the nervous system of a mammal. Do you have one handy?"

where only one in many billions of spores actually makes the transition between the stars—a biological strategy for radiating throughout the galaxy without a technology. Of course this happens over very long periods of time. But if you think that the galaxy is roughly 100,000 light-years from edge to edge, if something were moving only one one-hundredth the speed of light—now that's not a tremendous speed that presents problems to any advanced technology—it could cross the galaxy in one hundred million years. There's life on this planet 1.8 billion years old; that's eighteen times longer than one hundred million years. So, looking at the galaxy on those time scales, one sees that the percolation of spores between

An Extended Excerpt from
BREAKING OPEN THE HEAD

When I was 12 years old and in the 7th grade, I bought a used paperback copy of Aldous Huxley's psychedelic classic, *The Doors of Perception*. Looking back on it, the only reason I can think of that led me to buy it must have been The Doors connection. I knew that Jim Morrison took the band's name from Huxley's slim volume and it must've cost me all of 50 cents, so I picked it up. It wasn't that I liked the Doors or anything—I didn't like them much at all—but I was really, really (really!) curious about drugs at that age. Something about this mysterious book seemed to beckon me to take it home, so I did, along with a huge stack of comic books, I'm quite sure.

I read the entire book one morning sitting in church with my parents and grandparents, who, of course, had no idea what I was reading. I often chose books to read in church that allowed me to silently rebel against the odious weekly ritual I hated so much, so the subject matter and the meager page count made it a perfect "Sunday book" for me. I remember being astonished at what I was reading and made it a point to immediately—if not sooner—get my hands on some LSD, something that took me about 2 more years to actually acquire, but when I did, it certainly didn't disappoint! Since that time I have returned again and again

flash. I try to make it a point to take a high dose of mushrooms at least once a year, if for no other reason, to blow all the bad shit out of my brain...

The publication of Daniel Pinchbeck's book, *Breaking Open the Head* (Broadway Books) was, to my mind, nothing short of an *event*. Pinchbeck, co-founder and co-editor (with novelist Thomas Beller) of the highbrow literary magazine Open City, has come up with something I had despaired of seeing again after the untimely death of Terence McKenna, *an instant classic of drug literature*. And just in time: this generation badly needs its own *Doors of Perception* and *Breaking Open the Head* is it, having arrived not a moment too soon.

In a way, *Breaking Open the Head* is almost two books in one: on one hand a historical overview of how psychedelics (or "entheogens" in politically correct tripper parlance) made their way into the diet of middle class American students, ushering in the "Age of Aquarius," "Hippie" and opposition to an unpopular and misguided war and on the other a travelogue and marvelously candid account of Pinchbeck's shamanic vision quest to "break open" his own head.

The publication of Daniel Pinchbeck's book, *Breaking Open the Head* was, to my mind, nothing short of an event, an instant classic of drug literature.

to the fountain of Huxley's "gratuitous grace" during times of crisis or confusion in my life and I have benefited greatly from the inner journeys and clarity provided by LSD, "magic mushrooms" and later, the "sci fi" dimensions of the DMT

What's particularly endearing about the book is that Pinchbeck himself is such a wonderful tour guide. Feeling alienated and depressed after the death of his father (Abstract expressionist painter Peter Pinchbeck. His mother is writer Joyce Johnson, author of *Minor Characters* and at one time the girlfriend of Jack Kerouac), Pinchbeck became desperate to somehow lift himself out of the Sartrean *nausea* and disconnectedness he felt himself sinking into in his pursuit of a literary career in his native Manhattan. The book chronicles Pinchbeck's journey from an atheist New York journalist to, as he puts it, a "shamanic initiate and grateful citizen of the cosmos."

At times I couldn't help but to picture George Plimpton, one of the original "participatory journalists," in Daniel's place and this illustrates one of the book's greatest strengths for the reader: in many ways Pinchbeck seems an unlikely candidate for spiritual enlightenment. As he describes himself at the start of the book, he's very much an "old school" kind of writer, a drinker and a bit of a womanizer—more Hemingway than Huxley—before a series of marvelously etched (and often humorous) encounters with Amazon witchdoctors, shaman, and the blissed out inhabitants of the Burning Man Festival urge Pinchbeck on to a deeper and deeper understanding, not just of himself also the weird historical moment we find ourselves in as we approach 10 minutes to midnight on the Apocalypse clock.

About halfway through the narrative, I began to lament that Pinchbeck seemed to be missing out on the occult (as opposed to the "spiritual") aspects of the psychedelic experience, but at that point a *startlingly magical* context (and one I, personally, wholeheartedly endorse) begins to emerge as he asks himself—and the reader—some very important questions: If these dimensions can be accessed by the judicious application of plant and chemical agents and if the bizarrely alien entities one encounters there are *real and autonomous beings* and not just a drug addled figment of our imaginations—then surely this is big news, *isn't it*?

Big fucking news, people. Big fucking news... But what does this mean??? Why aren't our finest minds working on getting to the bottom of this, one of the greatest mysteries facing us as human beings? Why instead are we turning *away* from wisdom and towards self-annihilation, war and planetary suicide? It doesn't make any damned sense!

As Einstein once said "God does not play dice with the universe." Could the widespread emergence of psychedelics in Western culture be any accident? 50 years ago, psychedelics were practically unheard of outside of botanical or Beatnik circles. Today, an historical blink of the eye since, due to the pioneering public relations efforts of Allen Ginsberg, William Burroughs, Timothy Leary, Terence

McKenna and others, millions of people have experienced the enlightenment of the psychedelic experience. No, this was no accident, it's all part of a strange and wondrous process that is unfolding in our lifetimes and *Breaking Open the Head* is a part of that process and carries on in that tradition. The enlightenment and *gnosis* resulting from the use of visionary plants and neuro-chemicals may be mankind's *only* hope for survival.

In an interesting interview that appeared in the *Arthur* newspaper, Pinchbeck argues that *this is* the task of the counterculture in our time: "This goal is the direct legacy of the counterculture—but it is actually hundreds if not many thousands of years older than that. In fact, this is the mission that we must somehow accomplish. Think of it as a secret raid to be carried out behind enemy lines, despite incredible odds and with no possibility of failure. The Beats and the Hippies saw through the abrasive insanity gnawing at the soul of America—this warmongering, money-mad, climate-destroying monstrosity which is now casting a dreadful shadow across this planet. Where the Beats acted intuitively, from the heart, we now have the necessary knowledge to put together a new paradigm that is simultaneously political, ecological, spiritual, and far more accurate than the outdated Newtonian-Darwinian model which is propping up the status quo."

Breaking Open the Head is a serious, thoughtful, provocative and *brave* book that should be read by everyone who senses that breaking open his or her own head might be the sanest act to perform in today's world. I urge you to all to read it.

–Richard Metzger

Think of it as a secret raid to be carried out behind enemy lines, despite incredible odds and with no possibility of failure.

1. Not for Human Consumption

I met Dave in Palenque. He had started a company selling experimental research chemicals which were labeled "not for human consumption," although most of them could be found in the back pages of Sasha Shulgin's

For $125, I bought one gram of yellowish powder of something called DPT, dipropyltryptamine, which has a chemical resemblance to DMT.

books. Sitting by the pool one day, I heard Dave tell how he had studied to be a priest, but dropped out to become a professional masseuse. By some circuitous route—a typical tangled American odyssey—he made his way from the Miami Beach yacht scene to psychedelics and the cutting-edge of mind-expansion. In Palenque, Dave invited me to join his private research group, giving me free and low-priced introductions to some new chemicals, as well as his regular catalog of little-known and unscheduled compounds. Fearing intensified government surveillance, he abruptly closed his company the day after the September 11 terrorist attacks, even though his business did not seem to be violating any specific laws.

Back in New York, I ordered a few things from his catalog. They came to my home in plain envelopes labeled with intimidating chemical names. For $125, I bought one gram of yellowish powder of something called DPT, dipropyltryptamine, which has a chemical resemblance to DMT. As far as I can ascertain, DPT, unlike DMT, does not occur in nature, which means it did not exist until some modern alchemist synthesized it in a laboratory a few decades ago. While DMT, an endogamous chemical

inside the body, is recognized by MAO enzymes and immediately neutralized, DPT, a new concoction, is not. Therefore it crosses the blood-brain barrier through direct sniffing or swallowing. But the most interesting aspect of the two chemicals is that the worlds they reveal are completely different. Why should this be the case? I don't know. I only know that propyl and methyl are simple carbon compounds, two of the building blocks of organic matter. There is, for example, methyl alcohol, wood alcohol, and propyl alcohol, rubbing alcohol. The tryptamine molecule is the building block of many neurotransmitters, and of many psychoactive compounds. Serotonin is a tryptamine.

In Shulgin's book and on the Internet I found some write-ups about DPT trips. Some described the effects as terrifying: "The whole universe falls apart, all colors in electric air whirlpool into a mandala, eaten up forever. That's it, the world's over." Others felt, after smoking the drug, they entered, for the first time, the "clear light" of God. Another report was more narrative: "I was being led by a wise old man who I know was God... I was handed a Torah for me to carry as a sign that I had been accepted, and forgiven, and come home." Shulgin also mentioned a church in New York, Temple of the True Inner Light, which uses DPT as its sacrament. Clearly DPT was a mind-warper of heavyweight proportions. I put the slim envelope of white powder in the refrigerator, where it sat for a few months.

I am often caught between my desire for new and intense altered states and my extreme fear of them. I fear them,

An Extended Excerpt from *Breaking Open The Head*

because every major doorway that I go through changes me in an ineffable but permanent way. I think this is the case for anyone with any sensitivity. After your first serious LSD trip, you really are never quite the same person again—you have been given another perspective on your self and your ego; you have been permanently relativized. The same with DMT, or ayahuasca. You may spend the rest of your life suppressing the memory, but somewhere inside of you it is there. As Don Juan told Castaneda: "We are men and our lot is to learn and to be hurled into inconceivable new worlds."

I am often caught between my desire for new and intense altered states and my extreme fear of them. I fear them, because every major doorway that I go through changes me in an ineffable but permanent way.

Psychedelics are catalysts for evolution and transformation, and when you take them, you have to be ready to transform in unexpected ways. That is the beauty and the power of them, that is why they need to be treated with utmost respect. That is also why it is good to be scientifically precise about what chemical you are taking, to know, as best as you can, what that chemical will do to you, and why you are taking it. Because I didn't know exactly what DPT was, or what I wanted from it, I bought it and then sheepishly left it alone.

My cautious resistance to the DPT lure continued until one night, after a party. For the first time in several months, I was drunk. I was with my two oldest friends, twin brothers, who were suddenly eager to try the DPT in my fridge. We each snorted a line and for me, it was an interesting disaster. I was both drunk and tripping. On the one hand, the world was a woozy mess; on the other hand, I was seeing it with razor-edged precision and in the most vibrant colors. When I closed my eyes, I saw multicolored three-dimensional triangles rotating in black space. I realized later that I had foolishly used alcohol to overcome my fear of DPT—the way I used to drink for the courage to talk to girls at bars. I didn't like DPT. Something about the DPT realm seemed icy and annihilating to me. I told my friends over and over again, "This is evil. DPT is bad. This is not something we should explore. This is not a good doorway."

In retrospect, I don't think that I was exploring the DPT realm on that trip. I think, instead, the DPT realm was beginning its exploration of me.

Because this is a story not just about chemicals but about occult correspondences and psychic events, I will note that later that night we went out to a bar and started talking to the people next to us. For some reason I talked about my anxiety over 2012, the Hopi and Mayan Prophecies. One of them described a vivid dream she had when she was a teenager, that had stayed with her ever since: "I was in a kind of space ship full of people. We were lifting off from earth. I looked back at the earth and there was brown crust where the land had been. We shot into space and went a long way. Then an angel appeared to us. He said that God had decided to rejuvenate the Earth, even though we had ruined it. He was going to start again—to do it all over from scratch. For the time being we were going to have to wait in limbo. And he pointed to a vast grey space where many people were already waiting. We had to leave the space ship to go there." It was another few months before I tried DPT again.

In the meantime, another new friend from Palenque accepted my invitation and came to New York. This was Charity the fire dancer. Twenty-four years old, skilled at Tarot and ceremonial magic, a professional stripper, she was the fearless and pixie-like embodiment of the new culture I had found at Burning Man. In Mexico, I told her I could find her a free place to stay in New York, and she hitchhiked all the way from Palenque with her cat, Prometheus, catching rides from truckers at truck stops. Unlike me, Charity had no fear of new psychedelics. She kept a list of all the drugs she had tried, and the number was up to 43. I told her I had this DPT stuff around, and of course she wanted to try it.

Charity cut two big lines of the DPT on the table, and I snorted one. The powder burned my nasal passages. Bitter residue dripped down the back of my throat. I stretched out on the couch. In a minute or two, I closed my eyes and entered the DPT realm.

Charity and I took DPT at my house one night—once again, I had to overcome an intense initial reluctance. Finally I put some of the yellowish powder into a pill and

For a flicker of forever, I was imprisoned in a post-modern bar surrounded by gleaming mirrors with a hyper-slick lounge lizard wearing a white Mohawk and synthetic fabrics. He was sitting at the bar, drinking a highball. DPT was a post-modern demonic MTV psychedelic.

swallowed it, but got no effect. She sniffed a line, and almost instantly went into a trance. When her trip was over, she told me I had to try sniffing it.

Sometimes, when one trips, it seems that all of the psychic matter, whether spoken or not, swirling around in the hours and days beforehand, gathers together, like particles galvanized by a magnet, and pushes the journey in a certain direction. These influences can seem like the karmic trace of some larger pattern. On many levels what seems to operate is a specific intentionality. Earlier that night Charity had told me about the "psychic vampires" who roamed the streets of San Francisco, some of them homeless hippies, who would pick up vibrations from strangers, talk to them, and suck their energy away. I laughed at this. We also talked about the books of Zacharia Sitchen, whose scholarly research convinced him that a race of extraterrestrial giants had created human beings, long ago, to serve them as slaves—a variation on the concept of the "Archons" from Gnosticism. According to Sitchen, the beauty and sophistication of the cruel alien race that created us was beyond our imagining.

Charity cut two big lines of the DPT on the table, and I snorted one. The powder burned my nasal passages. Bitter residue dripped down the back of my throat. I stretched out on the couch. In a minute or two, I closed my eyes and entered the DPT realm.

We were listening to moody Techno music. With each change in beat, with each skitter of electrical noise, I saw a brand new and extremely detailed demonic universe swirl before me in cobalt, scarlet, purple gossamer hues. At moments there seemed to be some incredibly elegant yet violently orgiastic party taking place with beautiful females in evening gowns and men in Edwardian top coats in the spacious parlors of a huge and opulent mansion. At other times there seemed to be bat or butterfly-winged creatures—long and quivering antennas, velvet coats and emerald eyes, stiletto talons—rising into otherworldly skies, wandering futuristic cities. I had an impression of tremendous vanity. "I" was being used as a mirror for the DPT beings to admire themselves. But

their realm was beyond what can be expressed in ordinary language in its speed of transmutation, its shivering quicksilver beauty.

The worlds revealed were like endless facets of a twirling diamond—I felt the real possibility of being trapped inside any of those facets, a kind of soul-prison, for eternity. That was the terror of it. As with smoking Salvia, I had the sense that some part of me had always been stuck in this Gothic DPT prison, trapped there eternally. I somehow understood that this was not my first visit, nor my last.

For a flicker of forever, I was imprisoned in a post-modern bar surrounded by gleaming mirrors with a hyper-slick lounge lizard wearing a white Mohawk and synthetic fabrics. He was sitting at the bar, drinking a highball. There were no doors or windows in this room, no escape possible. The graphics of this vision were high-res and hyper-perfect. Other shards of the DPT realm shared this sci-fi quality. DPT was a post-modern demonic MTV psychedelic.

The sleek, rhythmical mesh of the music seemed woven into the lurid fabric of the darkness, the revelation of sinister forces coming to life behind my eyelids.

Like DMT, the level of visual organization of the DPT realm seemed far beyond anything that the synaptical wiring of my brain could create—it was, in its own peacock-feathery way, not just as real as this reality, but far more real, crackling with power. I felt from the entities exploring my mind a kind of contempt, a disdain for human beings trapped in our pitiful unsophisticated domain, our meat realm. They seemed somewhere between bemused and enraged.

In shamanic cultures, the taking of entheogenic substances is always surrounded by ritual. A circle of protection is created, the four directions invoked, the spirits asked for their blessing through an offering of tobacco and prayer. Because we were sniffing a chemical powder in a modern New York apartment, a chemical without a long history of human use, it didn't even occur to us to take such precautions. I was jealous of Charity because she managed to get to the kitchen sink and throw up. She vomited four or five times in a row—later she said she saw a male entity in the sink with a kind of device or machine that he was using to soak up the energy she was expulsing, jeering at her as he did it. The demon told her his name but she couldn't recall it. I couldn't throw up. I suspected that I had finally, and completely, managed to destroy myself. I was convinced I would never recover from this onslaught. I staggered to the CD player and changed the music to Bach, which helped a little. With my eyes opened, transformational energy seemed to be crawling over everything, flickering and receding like waves of sentient power—vampiric electricity. My hands looked and felt like claws made out of wires. When I opened my eyes on ayahuasca, I also felt and saw energy passing like a waveform, but it was more human somehow. Here the speed of the waves was much faster and more brutal than the yagé flares. The experience was unmammalian, futuristic, inhuman.

About half an hour into the trip, past 3 a.m., I called my friend Tony. "This is total magic, total sorcery. I am watching endless Gothic demon universes mirroring each other," I babbled to him.

Not only was it suddenly obvious that there was such a thing as a soul, it was also clear that I was in danger of losing mine permanently.

I somehow understood that the DPT realm had evolved over an incredibly long period—millions of years, if time had the same kind of meaning to them as it does to us. I realized there were occult hierarchies, secret cabals, treasuries of wickedness to be studied over millennia. It was obvious that we little human beings have absolutely no idea what is going on in the cosmos. The word "baroque" doesn't even begin to begin to describe the jaded emptiness and sublime beauty of that other country. A little bit like soft candle-flicker worlds you see on hash and opium, but etched in perfect solid-state reality—more than photographic. The sleekness of the DPT dimension was beyond belief.

About half an hour into the trip, past 3 a.m., I called my friend Tony.

"This is total magic, total sorcery. I am watching endless Gothic demon universes mirroring each other," I babbled to him. "If someone could be at home here,

learn to control things here, they could gain so much fucking power they could just walk right through the walls of the White House, do anything, but it wouldn't matter, because they would already be part of such an ancient conspiracy." I had begun to pace around the house, and as I paced, I found that I was moving my arms in the air—making "passes" like the shamanic gestures described in Castaneda's work. These gestures came to me intuitively. They seemed to help control the overwhelming sense of assault.

"Daniel, don't be taken in by it. It's just samsara," Tony said. His voice was a soothing lifeline. He laughed at me. He tried to convince me that the trip would end soon, that I wasn't permanently fried. He told me I should have known what I was doing, since I had called DPT "evil" after my first attempt.

"What's that music you're playing in the background?" he asked.

"Bach," I told him. "It's the only thing that's keeping me together. Perhaps that's why they are here; the demons are attracted to the music. They are crowding in here to be close to it."

"Well, that's nice," he said.

"There's nothing nice about that!" I screeched at him. "They are totally defiant. They don't give a shit about us; we are their puppets."

But at this point the trip was starting to wind down. In a few minutes Charity and I were back in "reality" once again—whatever that figment might be. I felt incredibly relieved. "Wow, I can't believe it," I said to Tony. "Reality—this is definitely a good thing!"

In the next few days, however, I learned that I wasn't quite back in reality after all—or if I was, it was a new, hypercharged one.

I was supposed to leave to meet my girlfriend in Berlin the next day. In the morning my travel agent came up with a cheap last minute ticket. On the plane, I sat next to a German woman dressed in elegant black. I was reading *The Invisible Landscape* by Terence and Dennis McKenna, and I noticed she seemed startled after she read a few words from the back cover over my shoulder. She had read the word "shamanism." Halfway through the flight, she told me she had been having a series of dreams over the past months in which two American Indians, a couple, came into her house and told her that she was meant to be a shaman, that she wasn't supposed to get married. She was meant to devote herself to shamanism totally. The dreams mystified her. She had never thought about shamanism and she had no idea what it was. "Do you know anything about it?" she asked.

I tried to explain the basics of shamanism and gave her the names of some books to read. Also I told her what I believed—what I had learned from Robert: "The Indian cultures have been almost wiped out, but shamanism is an essential human phenomenon connected to the earth. Right now, the shamans of the past are looking for candidates who can carry on the traditions. They have zeroed in on you as a possible candidate. You can choose to follow this or ignore it, but I definitely recommend that you learn more about it before making a decision."

The woman had a tribal pendant around her neck—on it was a pattern of lightning-like zigzags around a central circle—and I asked her about it. "Somebody gave this to me on a beach in Mexico," she said. "They said it was a Navajo protection symbol."

ing into the flame column, being obliterated and shooting up into space. Then I saw the surface of another planet, covered in coral and sponge-like growths. A smirking alien was standing next to one of the sponges, and he kept flowing through the organic folds of the plant, then reassembling himself. He and the plant were fused in magical symbiosis.

Finally I fell asleep. I dreamt of a boy standing in the woods, yelling over and over again at the top of his lungs: "Long live ethnopharmacology!"

The next night, I had two extremely vivid dreams in which I was pursued by a bearded man. In one dream, I threw a party in an apartment where I once lived. Aggressive strangers showed up and stole my books from the shelves. A bearded man came up to me.

"I used to live here," he said.

"Do you want to come back?" I asked.

"Yes," he said.

In shamanic cultures, synchronicities are recognized as signs that you are on the right path.

I do not think the world is orchestrated as a paranoid conspiracy designed to entertain my wildest fantasies. Yet I had an intuitive, uncanny sense that this symbol had been sent to me—to show me that I was being protected, somehow, that I was being taken through a process. Even though I was freaking out, I had to trust that the process was good. In shamanic cultures, synchronicities are recognized as signs that you are on the right path.

I was in Berlin because Laura's father had been stricken with cancer. The entire family was assembling for the weekend. Because Laura was pregnant and wouldn't be able to travel later, she was staying with her parents for several weeks.

Whenever I was left alone, I found myself walking around the house and making conducting gestures again. I was afraid I was becoming some sort of obsessive-compulsive, but I could control the gestures when other people were around. One night, I couldn't sleep.

With my eyes closed, I watched vivid imagery unfold in little film loops—I saw a huge column of fire shooting up from the center of Stonehenge. I envisioned myself walk-

Back in New York, I still felt very strange—fizzy and non-ordinary, with a buzzing around the temples. It was my second night at home and I was jet-lagged. Ten minutes after I turned out the lights and got into bed, a large mirror in the other room fell off the wall and loudly crashed face down on the floor. It didn't break.

All night I dreamt that the bearded man was hitting me in the head with a pillow over and over again, and laughing as he did it. I tried to hit him back but my swings were feeble misses.

When I awoke in the morning, feeling groggy, I went to get a yogurt from the refrigerator. I opened the tightly closed silverware drawer and reached for a spoon. Right under the spoons was a large and ominous bug. It did not look like a New York bug at all—it was winged, honey-brown, with a long curly tail, and it quickly wriggled out of sight.

I screamed and slammed the drawer shut.

Fuck, I thought. The DPT trip had unleashed an angry poltergeist in my house. How could this be? I have never had a belief or even the slightest interest in poltergeists or the occult, but the signs couldn't be much more obvious. Suddenly I was in the midst of something for which I had no frame of reference, no preparation. What had I done? Once again, as often before, I cursed myself for my fascination with these chemicals.

I walked around in a panic. I went to the East Village and sat at a café. On the way I stopped in a Tibetan Buddhist store. I asked the clerk if he had any symbols of protection, and he sold me a small metal dorje—the Tibetan lightning bolt symbol used in meditation. I still felt fizzy— I had a tingling around my left temple and my left hand was buzzing slightly. Clutching the dorje in my fist, I called Charity and told her about the situation.

"Oh man," she said. "We've got to clean that thing out of there before your girlfriend comes back with the baby."

It turned out that Charity, from her days of San Francisco witchcraft (modern paganism was another scene I always dismissed), knew all about exorcisms and entities. She had carted with her, all the way from Mexico, an entire kit bag of magical implements—including a large and beautifully smooth obsidian ball that somebody gave her in Palenque, and some quartz crystals. While I knew that quartz was used for shamanic healing, to realign energy patterns, I did not know that obsidian was considered to have the power of absorption of negative spiritual energies. "This ball is so excellent, it just sucks all that stuff right up," Charity said. She also brought ceremonial candleholders (tacky little sculptures of a cat and an elephant, which became Bas and Ganesh for the duration of the ceremony), and Aleister Crowley's elegant Tarot cards. I met her and we went back to the apartment.

"I can already feel it," she said when we were in the lobby. And it was true—the air in the building seemed electrically charged, more so in the elevator, and in the apartment, the charge was almost a physical presence. Charity put the obsidian ball down on the ground in the center of the living room. We both watched, astonished, as it took the ball an extremely long time to stop trembling, finally rotating in smaller and smaller circles until it stopped. She organized a quick magical ritual, consulting the Tarot cards several times. I had also never given Tarot cards much thought, but now I was watching them as if my life depended on it—I felt, in some obscure and woozy way, perhaps it did.

She picked a card with lightning bolts all over it, "Swiftness." "So we'll be swift," she said. She picked "Fortune," suggesting a change for the better. She picked "Futility"—my heart sank—but opposite it, "The Queen of Cups," my court card. "Because your card is a water sign, we've got to do something with water," she said, quickly analyzing the situation like a technician faced with an engineering problem. She soaked the obsidian ball in salt water, then held it in the toilet and flushed a few times.

"Take that bullshit out of here," she commanded.

At the end of the ritual, the atmosphere in the apartment seemed changed, cleared out. It was, we thought, safe again.

It was safe until later that night, when I returned from visiting Tony. Once again, I felt the apartment crackling with a static occult buzz. My temple and left hand started buzzing weirdly. I had been jokingly complaining to Tony about the supernatural forces taking such obvious manifestations—a falling mirror, a big bug. It was all so silly, so comic book-like, even flirtatious. Once again, the joke seemed to be on me as I lay in bed and felt increasingly creeped-out and panicked.

I went into the living room and sat in front of the obsidian ball. I picked up the dorje and chanted a bit—nonsense words, Asiatic-sounding, insectile, similar to what I recalled of the Secoya language, came into my head and I called them out. "Ching! Ching! Gada-ching! Gada-gada-ching!" I rapped the hard surface of the black ball with the vajra, then I held the vajra in my palms before the ball and looked straight at the ball.

In a few seconds, my entire visual field turned grey.

All I could see were a few rectangles of refracted light in the center of the ball; thick greyness covered everything else.

I turned away from the ball and looked around the room.

In two seconds my vision went back to normal. I looked back at the ball.

My entire visual field turned grey yet again.

I grabbed my jacket and ran out of the house. Once in the street, I called my friend Michael. Michael is 20 years older than me; a poet and novelist with an impressive knowledge of alternative healing and indigenous cultures, he first told me about ayahuasca. For an hour, as I paced around the streets of downtown New York,

Michael tried to calm me down. He told me some Buddhist meditation techniques to "get you back in your body." He told me that even if there were some "other" out there—and he was not convinced there was—I had to recognize that aspects of my mind had manifested all of this stuff. "It takes two to tango," Michael said. Rather than fighting against it I could accept it, integrate it within myself.

Michael told me to imagine a Buddha hovering over me, shooting pure white light through my body, turning me into blinding white light, flushing everything negative or bad into my central channel where it would go into my intestines and ultimately come out of me as shit. At the end of the meditation, Michael told me to imagine this Buddha coming down to me as I merged with the white light.

I followed his instructions, and it seemed to help. Soon I fell asleep. By the next morning, the world had returned to some semblance of normal.

Perhaps this story seems ridiculous—yet the psychic reality of the DPT encounter and its aftermath overwhelm most ordinary events. I offer it as a cautionary tale. There are aspects of it that remain, for various reasons, impossible to tell. Suffice it to say, after DPT, that I suspect death is not the worst thing that can happen to a person. There are far worse fates.

2. New Sensations

For over a year, I had carefully studied my dreams, waking three or four times a night to write down images, conversations, disjointed narratives, and semi-conscious visions. Sometimes, lying in bed on the threshold of sleep, I would see myself as a corpse devoured by birds, or I would be processed through some kind of cosmic sausage-grinder. In one dream, I was crucified and my corpse paraded through an African town by laughing Bwiti tribesmen. In another, I was given directions to undertake the alchemical "Great Work" in an airport lobby. My dream life changed in other ways as well. I would fall asleep thinking about some esoteric concept, and throughout the night I would awaken repeatedly to find my unconscious mind was still holding the idea tightly, turning it around in different ways. I began to realize that sleep is an extension of waking awareness, not just an extinguishing of it.

The change in my dream life suggested some kind of shamanic or esoteric initiation. It felt as though the ideas that fascinated me were slowly filtering from my thoughts into my bloodstream, permeating my cells. Despite these hints, despite my fascination with the subject, I assumed that shamanism would remain a phenomenon "out there" that I was studying, in the distanced and analytical way I had always pursued intellectual subjects.

According to the mystic Gurdjieff, intellectual knowledge—technical or academic mastery of any subject—is always shallow and one-dimensional. "Knowledge by itself does not give understanding. ... Understanding depends upon the relation of knowledge to being." He thought that ancient cultures prioritized one's state of being—developed through self-discipline and spiritual training—while

> **Michael told me to imagine a Buddha hovering over me, shooting pure white light through my body, turning me into blinding white light, flushing everything negative or bad into my central channel where it would go into my intestines and ultimately come out of me as shit.**

modern culture only appreciates the amount that one knows: "People of Western culture put great value on the level of a man's knowledge but they do not value the level of a man's being and they are not ashamed of the low level of their own being." If understanding is linked to being, then certain types of phenomena can only be comprehended when the observer has changed: "There are things for the understanding of which a different being is necessary." This transformative process takes place in stages, over time.

It is hard to calculate precisely, but in small-scale tribal societies probably one out of every 25 or 30 people receives a shamanic calling. Since shamanism seems to be a universal phenomenon, this statistic should be cross-cultural, which means there are at least ten million people in our culture who potentially fit the shamanic role. Some of those people are currently alternative healers of some sort, some are artists or psychologists, and I have no doubt that many of them are imprisoned in mental hospitals, or they are among the muttering homeless who refuse integration into the mass society. Whether or not they even realize it, they are people, like myself, for whom contact with the invisible world is as essential as ordinary knowledge or material gain or any other reward that the "real world" can offer.

An Extended Excerpt from *Breaking Open The Head*

This is what I suspect happened when I made my alliance: A somewhat mischievous being from a higher-vibrational realm melded itself into my consciousness.

This is what I suspect happened when I made my alliance: A somewhat mischievous being from a higher-vibrational realm melded itself into my consciousness.

For a few weeks after the events, I felt this other "it" as a new perspective inside of my mind. My perceptions seemed more acute, my thoughts zingier. There were certain aspects of reality that I seemed to be picking up without conscious intent. For instance, walking around the streets of New York, I felt more conscious of the way that symbols and logos in advertisements and on clothes stood for unconscious forces, how they shaped and manipulated social reality. All logos, all symbols, seemed to draw energy from the occult dimension, the DPT realm. Even watching a basketball game on television became unbearable—the manipulations were so obvious. The underlying messages—beer for self-oblivion, jeep for planetary destruction and accelerated extinction—so mind-numbingly clear. Post-DPT, I had to overcome a new sense of contempt for humanity—myself included—as well as an increased sympathy for the devil.

I studied the DPT reports on the Internet with more care. Several of the DPT takers went to the same place as me: "I felt as if DPT were a sinister, sinister being that was laughing at me. Humans are so weak. DPT destroys you," wrote one of them. Charity and I were not the only people to confront that terror. Others had also felt the manifestation of a seemingly sinister entity. Some of them worried they had torn apart the fabric of reality: "It's very obvious the human world was as stable as a house of toothpicks, amazing it didn't fall apart sooner in history, but the hideous human angel hasn't been crawling along the planet that long at all, and now someone pulled the plug out accidentally." This writer also passed, at high speed, through Gothic realms where other people seemed to be present in some parallel dimension. Many takers of DPT experience the classic rising of kundalini energy—the Hindus call it shakti—from the base of their spine to the top of their skull, sometimes leading to out-of-control body shudders. Unsurprisingly, DPT often seems to generate an extreme fear reaction.

As noted earlier, Rick Strassman theorizes that DMT, nn-dimethyltryptamine, is the "spirit molecule" which releases the soul into the spirit realm. If that is the case, I suspect it is possible that DPT serves the same function in some other realm—the supernatural world of magical entities sketched by Aubrey Beardsley and described by Aleister Crowley. Perhaps DPT is the "demon molecule"—recognizing that demons are ambiguous entities in many traditions. In Tibetan Buddhism, all deities have both their benevolent and wrathful aspects. The wrathful deities in Tibetan Buddhism are depicted as frightening monsters, drinking blood out of skulls, multi-armed, with fangs and talons. As the flipside of the Buddha—and ultimately aspects of the inner self—such deities call to mind an old proverb: "The devil is God as He is misunderstood by the wicked."

In making this alliance—in this speculative interpretation—not only did I have no control once the process was set in motion, but the entity that integrated into me had little choice in the matter as well. "I" was somehow part of his evolution, his inquiry, as much as he was part of mine. Other forces were involved in guiding the merge—but don't ask me who or what they are. As Gurdjieff noted, "All the phenomena of the life of a given cosmos, examined from another cosmos, assume a completely different aspect and have a completely different meaning." He also said: "The manifestation of the laws of one cosmos in another cosmos constitute what we call a miracle."

There might be validity in the idea that the demons or spirits "are attracted to the music." The disembodied splendor of their higher-dimensional realm may bore them after a while. Through communion with a human being, a spirit from the supersensible realms gets to smell, taste, love, fuck, all our sense-realm experiences. On our side, perhaps we can utilize some tiny aspect of its higher

I studied the DPT reports on the Internet with more care. Several of the DPT takers went to the same place as me: "I felt as if DPT were a sinister, sinister being that was laughing at me. Humans are so weak. DPT destroys you," wrote one of them.

vision and its powers—of course I don't know, at this point, exactly what for, but perhaps that remains to be revealed at some other time.

If the universe has a spiritual design, perhaps the soul is like a widget running along a conveyor belt, having new

BOOK OF LIES

In my dream, the DPT demiurge came into my house and said to me: "I used to live here."

devices added to it or taken away as it passes through various incarnations which are stages in its education. In my dream, the DPT demiurge came into my house and said to me: "I used to live here." There was a strong feeling of familiarity to the episode. Perhaps, in some previous incarnation, centuries or eons or even worlds ago, we once made this same bargain. The incubus's memory just happens to be better, and longer, than mine.

I almost never buy clothes, but on the plane to Berlin, I began to see myself wearing a deep red or purple velvet Vivienne Westwood suit with an Edwardian cut to it. I thought how cool looking and comfortable such a suit could be, and even sketched myself wearing it. It was nothing like my normal dressing style. On the plane back to New York, I was reminded of the suit again. A week later, in SoHo, I happened to walk past the Vivienne Westwood boutique. Down in the basement, they were having a sample sale. I found one copy of the exact suit I had been thinking of, in deep crimson. I put it on. It fit. At 70 percent off, I could even afford it.

3. Magical Thinking

Before taking DPT, I had started to reread Carlos Castaneda's books on his relationship with the Yaqui sorcerer Don Juan. I anticipated writing dismissively of Castaneda as a phony anthropologist who perpetuated a fraud. As Jay Courtney Fikes writes in *Carlos Castaneda, Academic Opportunism and the Psychedelic Sixies*, "Castaneda's claims that he was a sorcerer's apprentice, and that Don Juan's teachings constituted a "Yaqui way of knowledge" are unsupported by photographs, field notes, or tape recordings." Fikes believes that Castaneda simply recognized a good marketing niche and cashed in.

After DPT, however, Castaneda's depictions of the sorcerer's world seemed plausibly insightful. Don Juan reveals the alternative worlds shown through psychedelics as tricks-of-the-eye universes, whole realms of otherness revealed in mirror-scratches or the shadow-throwing flickers of candle flames. These are parallel dimensions of beings at once extremely threatening and powerful, and on the other hand, evanescent and ephemeral. Don Juan's sorcery is a dangerous pursuit of knowledge that the sorcerer considers ultimately meaningless. "Seeing," as Don Juan embodies it, requires detachment towards ordinary reality.

"A man who follows the paths of sorcery is confronted with imminent annihilation every turn of the way, and unavoidably he becomes keenly aware of his own death," Don Juan says. "The idea of imminent death, instead of becoming an obsession, becomes an indifference." Through DPT, I thought I saw such a jaded path open up towards amoral knowledge and power. What was most frightening was its seductiveness.

I could no longer argue with the idea of ambivalent spirit-realms with the power to suddenly overflow into this one. The rules of navigating in these realms may be, as Don Juan lays them out, extremely specific and seemingly arbitrary. Without a guide, the dangers for the integrity of the psyche may be as imposing as the knowledge to be gained.

Post-DPT, I started to examine the occult tradition of the West. Impressed with Charity's deft handling of the Tarot, I found myself peering into the somewhat unhinged writings of Aleister Crowley. Like Castaneda and the occult in general, I thought of Crowley as mere adolescent entertainment. Alas for me, I could no longer dismiss him so easily. The DPT journey—and its aftermath—transformed Crowley's work, and Castaneda's, from spooky fantasy to strict realism.

Crowley's scholarly endeavor was to make a scientific system of correspondences between the mystical traditions, linking, for instance, the I Ching and Egyptian mysticism and the Tarot. "The laws of magick are closely related to those of other physical sciences," he wrote. He laid out a model of the cosmos with many higher dimensions and endless beings inhabiting them, made of subtler stuff than us. "It is one magical hypothesis that all things are made up of ten different sorts of vibrations, each with a different vibration, and each corresponding to a 'planet.'" This theory—based on the Sephiroth, the ten emanations of God in the Qaballah—has a neat poetic resonance with modern "superstring theory" in physics, which postulates ten (or eleven) dimensions of space-time.

In the 1920s, Crowley wrote, "Magick deals principally with certain physical forces still unrecognized by the vulgar; but those forces are just as real, just as material—if indeed you can call them so, for all things are ultimately spiritual—as properties like radio-activity, weight and hardness." Crowley considered the Tarot, based on the Tree of Life from the Qaballah, to be an accurate model of the forces and spiritual hierarchies at play in the universe—a tool given to us by higher-dimensional forces.

An Extended Excerpt from *Breaking Open The Head*

In the 1920s, Crowley wrote, "Magick deals principally with certain physical forces still unrecognized by the vulgar; but those forces are just as real, just as material—if indeed you can call them so, for all things are ultimately spiritual—as properties like radio-activity, weight and hardness."

Most people in the modern world reject the possibility that the self might have occult and transcendental dimensions that are carefully hidden by ordinary life. The possibility that such knowledge exists, and that you can receive direct experience of it, through psychedelics or other means, is upsetting, even frightening. I now suspect that this might be the central reason that psychedelics have been strenuously suppressed by mainstream society, and rejected by psychiatry. As T.S. Eliot wrote, "human kind cannot bear very much reality."

All of Carl Jung's researches led him to conclude that the unconscious as it was revealed through psychoanalysis had occult and even paranormal dimensions. Freud, despite his courage and brilliance, could not accept this possibility. He once confessed to Jung, as Jung described in *The Undiscovered Self*, "that it was necessary to make a dogma of his sexual theory because this was the sole bulwark of reason against a possible "outburst of the black flood of occultism.""

In these words Freud was expressing his conviction that the unconscious still harbored many things that might lead themselves to "occult" interpretations, as is in fact the case. ... It is this fear of the unconscious psyche which not only impedes self-knowledge but is the gravest obstacle to a wider understanding and knowledge of psychology.

Jung believed that, ultimately, the individual cannot achieve true awareness without reckoning with the occult domains of the psyche (which does not mean they have to literally conjure up demons). He looked at the metaphors for the quest for self-knowledge hidden in Gnosticism, and in alchemy, where the injunction, "Visit the interior of the earth," referred to techniques of seeking transcendent knowledge and power by delving into different modalities of consciousness.

The roots of European alchemy can be found in Gnosticism, a heretical offshoot of Christianity that flourished in the first centuries AD. The Gnostic version of Christ is something like a Leary-like advocate for direct spiritual experience over faith. In the "Gospel of Thomas," one of a group of Gnostic texts discovered in a jar in the Nag Hammadi desert at the end of the Second World War, Christ said, "Open the door for yourself, so you will know what is." In that same text, which may predate the Biblical scriptures and equal them in authenticity, Christ also announced, "If you bring forth what is within you, what you bring forth will save you. If you do not bring forth what is within you, what you do not bring forth will destroy you." Either of those phrases could stand as a psychedelic credo.

The hierarchies of invisible beings I had seen on DPT—as if I was a reflecting surface, a mirror for them to display and even preen themselves—now seemed to be present everywhere. Walking in a community garden on East Houston Street, featuring flowering paths and a small pond with turtles in it, I saw emanations of that higher-order occult dimension in the swooping flourishes of rare flowers, in the pseudo-psychedelic patterns traced across a turtle's scaly skin. It was suddenly obvious to me that the Darwinian theory of evolution, the Western rational perspective on world biology, with all of its flaws and gaps, could not be the whole story. It was true to a limited extent, but there were other truths as well. Life on earth has been sculpted into multitudinous forms by higher-dimensional beings for the enjoyment of their own skill and our delight. As I watched a turtle's eye rotate in its socket, I had to admit that they were master craftsmen.

As I was reading about the Qaballah and the Western occult tradition, feeling oppressed by Crowley's histrionic tone, I ran into an old friend of mine who had moved to San Francisco and was just in town for a few weeks. I had known Neil in New York for many years. We had shared an insatiable appetite for New York parties, art openings, and the pursuit of girls.

Neil seemed unchanged after five years. Thin and narrow, he wore antique suits and patterned ties, looking a bit like an ascetic Missionary from the 1940s on his first mission into the jungle. It turned out that Neil had become deeply involved in the work of Rudolf Steiner. Steiner was an Austrian-born visionary and occultist from the turn of the century. Neil was even living in a Steiner-inspired Church in the Bay Area. I knew nothing about Steiner, besides the fact he had created schools and founded something called Anthroposophy.

Although he no longer took drugs or even alcohol, Neil's interest in spirituality and mysticism had received an initial push through psychedelics. He described a DMT trip where he shot through a tunnel whose walls were covered with fast-changing runic script and visual symbols. "Then I looked up and I saw these guys hovering over me, smirking and winking at me and probing their fingers into my brain. Some of them looked like King Neptune, with tridents and long curly beards." Then a woman in a yellow dress flew down in front of him. She was carrying a glowing tablet, and

Steiner wrote. "Here, however, we must imagine these thoughts as living, independent beings. What we grasp as a thought in the material world is like a shadow of a thought being that is active in the land of spirits."

on that tablet Neil could see symbols that were changing. "The symbols of all the world's spiritual traditions were there—Native American symbols, mandalas, and Jewish Stars and everything else. She was showing me all of the world's mystical paths in symbolic form."

A few years later, a musician friend turned Neil onto anthroposophy. He recognized the beings he had seen on DMT as the "Elemental Beings" described by Steiner. These nonphysical or "supersensible" beings live within all the processes of nature and help with the work of creating and maintaining the physical universe. They are related to the gnomes, nyads, dryads, and slyphs seen by country people throughout history. Many people have reported making contact with such beings through psychedelics. For Steiner, a natural clairvoyant, they were just a small part of a vast order of supersensible entities he encountered through his own visionary experiences.

"Steiner believes that opposing forces act on human beings all the time," Neil told me. "One of these forces he calls "Luciferian," which is not evil, but it is the force that pulls us away from physical reality, upwards into dream and fantasy, visionary realms and intellectual theories. There is an opposing force which pulls us down towards the earth, towards the mineral aspect of the physical body and death, and keeps us from awareness of spiritual reality. As human beings, we should strive to achieve balance between these different forces. Psychedelic drugs are totally Luciferian. They give access to worlds that you may not be ready to see."

"Don't you think that it depends on the individual?" I asked. "After all, you probably wouldn't have found your way to Steiner if it wasn't for psychedelics."

"Obviously the drugs are here for a reason, but that doesn't mean they are good for us. The beings we meet on psychedelics may not have our best interests at heart." He quoted a song lyric from the British post-punk band, Magazine: "My mind ain't so open that anything can crawl right in."

I immediately started reading Steiner's work. Steiner believed that different types of spiritual training were appropriate for different epochs. He called the spiritual consciousness of the ancient world and the shaman a "dusk-like clairvoyance." In the present world, according to Steiner, that type of consciousness was no longer appropriate. He devised a method of spiritual training based on meditations and cognition, using the highly developed thinking power of the modern mind to rediscover the lost spiritual realms.

According to Steiner, in the spiritual worlds, beings are not separate from each other as they are in the physical world. He writes, "To have knowledge of a sense-perceptible being means to stand outside it and assess it according to external impressions. To have knowledge of a spiritual being through intuition means having become completely at one with it, having united with its inner nature." In other words, you meet a spiritual being by temporarily becoming that being. This suggests the effects of ingesting psychedelic compounds, which give the sense of temporarily melding into the psyche of an "Other."

The higher spiritual realms consist of beings made entirely of thought: "The actual world of thoughts is what pervades everything in the land of spirits, like the warmth that pervades all earthly things and beings," Steiner wrote. "Here, however, we must imagine these thoughts as living, independent beings. What we grasp as a thought in the material world is like a shadow of a thought being that is active in the land of spirits."

Steiner describes a hierarchy of consciousness, from the lowest pebble to the highest spiritual being. On earth, a person who achieved truly rational consciousness (of course, for Steiner, rationality would include spiritual awareness) would be at the highest level of thought that we can imagine, while minerals exist at the lowest level of mental activity (for mystics, it seems that nothing, not

An Extended Excerpt from *Breaking Open The Head*

even a pebble, is completely devoid of sentience). In the higher realms, you find beings whose lowest level of existence is rational thought: "Rational conclusions are the approximate equivalent of mineral effects on Earth. Beyond the domain of intuition lies the domain where the cosmic plan is fashioned out of spiritual causes."

In 1997, largely inspired by the jewel-like multicolored landscapes I beheld with eyes closed on several mushroom trips, I decided to go to Nepal. The prismatic fast-changing psilocybin scenes seemed direct evocations of "Buddha Realms," those sumptuous paradisiacal lands ruled over by enlightened unearthly beings, described in many Buddhist texts. After a few visits, I found myself drawn towards the stylized and highly ornamented artifacts of Tibetan art, the tangka paintings and mandalas used as aid to meditation.

I had picked up a lung infection during a Shiva festival in Kathmandu. To celebrate Shiva, the city with the third worst air quality in the world burnt fires of garbage all night long

With the money I made writing a never-published article about visiting a slightly embarrassing "Free Love Summer Camp" in the Oregon woods, I booked a ticket to Kathmandu, a city of crumbling Hindu temples, ancient stone streets, and dire poverty. I thought, perhaps, that Tibetan Buddhism might be a path for me. I visited several temples and monasteries. The solemn rituals of chanting monks and the stylized slow-motion pageantry of the costumed dances to celebrate Losar, the Tibetan New Year, were beautiful. But I didn't like the hierarchical and non-detached feeling of the Westerners who clustered around the high-powered Lamas.

From Nepal, I went to Dharmsala, the headquarters of the Dalai Lama and Tibet's government-in-exile, in Northern India. I appreciated the smiling faces and earthy warmth of the Tibetans—monks and commoners—but I was once again put off by the graspiness radiated by the Westerners. I had picked up a lung infection during a Shiva festival in Kathmandu—to celebrate Shiva, the city with the third worst air quality in the world burnt fires of garbage all night long—and spent a week coughing, waiting for either the Indian antibiotics or Tibetan homeopathic remedies to take effect.

By accident, I was in India at the time of the Hindu festival Kumbh Mehla. Kumbh Mehla is in the *Guinness Book of World Records* as the largest gathering of people in the world. Every three years, around 20 million people go to bathe in the River Ganges on one of three auspicious dates. At first, I thought the combination of Indian crowds and bad sanitation would make Kumbh Mehla the last place I ever wanted to go. Finally, sick of the Tibetan Buddhist circus, I decided to check it out.

The festival turned out to be well managed and orderly, despite its vast numbers. It was a joyful, almost Biblical, spectacle. I stayed in Rishikesh, a holy city of pastel-colored ashrams, the place where the Beatles went in the '60s to study Transcendental Meditation with The Maharishi. Rishikesh was idyllic and vegetarian. Clans of Hindus dressed in bright colors and flowing robes paraded cheerfully through the narrow, car-less streets. Kumbh Mehla also attracts saddhus from all over India; these yellow-robed, trident-carrying followers of Shiva range from sincere devotees to smirking shysters eager to extract donations, pick up chicks, or sell ganga to tourists. I stayed at a rundown ashram for Westerners, run by a laidback bald guru in his nineties. The ashram cost $1 a night, including breakfast, and for another dollar you could attend yoga and meditation classes spaced throughout the day. Hinduism seemed sloppier, more open than Tibetan Buddhism. Hanging out on the banks of the Ganges—clean to swim in because of its proximity to its source in the Himalayas—old holy men in long grey beards would come up to converse with me in broken English about the nearness of God. Wild monkeys chattered in the trees. A pilgrim in the streets stopped to tell me, sincerely, that he was sure we had known each other in an earlier life.

Kumbh Mehla marks a mythological event. Long ago, the Gods were fighting over a vial containing the nectar of immortality. Four drops of this nectar fell into the Ganges at the four spots where Kumbh Mehla is held every three years, on certain dates that have astrological significance. If you bathe in the Ganges during the right moment of the festival, you wipe away the bad karma, like a psychic crust, accumulated over all of your past lives.

The actual festival was held, that year, in the nearby and equally festive town of Haridwar. On the auspicious mornings, hordes of devotees clustered for miles up and down the riverbanks. On the first festival day, I did not go in the water myself, but I witnessed a riot of the Naga Babas. The Naga Babas are the most extreme and ascetic clan of Saddhus. Most of them live in caves high in the Himalayas, coming down for the festival once every three years. They parade—naked, carrying weapons, covered in grey ash—through the town before entering the water. They are followed by gurus from across India, on chariots, surrounded by their disciples. Among the Nagas, self-mortification is de rigeur. As they paraded, I saw that some of them had cut the tendons in their penises to prevent erections. Others had one arm raised in the air—they had stayed like that for years, until the appendage was thin and shriveled. By tradition, the Nagas entered the water first, to be followed by the Hindu hordes. I never understood why they were rioting—it had something to do with the exact order in which they would enter the water—but I watched as those emaciated mystics picked up large rocks from the street and hurled them into the crowds. They charged around, menacing the police with their weapons. I cowered in a restaurant, watching the melee through the metal grate that the proprietors had quickly pulled down.

I was so fascinated by the spectacle surrounding Kumbh Mehla that I put off my return flight. I spent several more weeks in Rishikesh, trying to learn yoga. On the next aus-

The Naga Babas are the most extreme and ascetic clan of Saddhus. Most of them live in caves high in the Himalayas, coming down for the festival once every three years. Among the Nagas, self-mortification is de rigeur. As they paraded, I saw that some of them had cut the tendons in their penises to prevent erections.

picious morning, I found myself luckily wedged into the center of Haridwar right across from the Nagas. This time, at the right instant, I joined the joyful multitudes bobbing up and down in the clear blue Ganges water.

Of course, at that point, I did not believe in karma.

Although he was an esoteric Christian, Steiner believed, along with Hindus and Buddhists, that human beings pass through many incarnations (84,000 is the average, according to the Hindus). Health problems and personal crises that manifest along the way are actually the residues of one's actions, the karma accrued in past lives. He also thought that, through spiritual training, it is possible to remember your past incarnations—as the Buddha did when he achieved enlightenment, recollecting all of his lives up to that instant.

"It is often asked why we do not know anything of our experiences before birth and after death," Steiner wrote. "This is the wrong question. Rather, we should ask how we can attain such knowledge." At the moment my provisional belief—stitched together from Buddhism, Western mysticism, quantum physics and psychedelic shamanism—is that what we experience as the "self" is actually a kind of vibration or frequency emitted from an invisible whole that exists in a higher dimension. Buddhists see this reality as somehow a manifestation of our consciousness, our karma. If that is the case, then the only way to change the world is to transform our consciousness.

Accepting Steiner's ideas for a moment, my actions over the last years, however much they seemed self-willed and haphazard, began to reveal a certain order to them, from an esoteric perspective. After Kumbh Mehla, I went, due to the "lucky draw" of a magazine assignment, through the Bwiti initiation in Africa, then I drank ayahuasca with Don Caesario and the Secoya. After DPT, I was forced to revise my thoughts yet again. I began to comprehend the ambiguous reality and power of occult realms. The DPT trip and its aftermath seemed strange, yet eerily familiar—I felt, I still feel, as though I had activated some circuit of Nietzschean "eternal recurrence," entering some realm I had inhabited before.

According to Steiner, along with the self that we perceive in daily life, the intractable "I," there is another self, a hidden spiritual being, which is the individual's guide and guardian. This higher self "does not make itself known through thoughts or inner words. It acts through deeds, processes, and events. It is this "other self" that leads the soul through the details of its life destiny and evokes its capacities, tendencies, and talents." The direction of our life is set out by that other self, a permanent being which continues from life to life. "This inspiration works in such a way that the destiny of one earthly life is the consequence of the previous lives." The pull of these far-flung archaic rites in India, Gabon, and the Amazon had exerted something like a magnetic attraction, and seeking out these experiences, perhaps I was prodded along by some hidden, higher aspect of my being. ⌑

An Extended Excerpt from *Breaking Open The Head*

ICONS

MICHAEL GOSS

KICK THAT HABIT
Brion Gysin–His Life & Magick

"Inside the village the thatched houses crouch low in their gardens to hide in the deep cactus lined lanes. You come through their maze to the broad village green where the pipes are piping; 50 raitas banked against a crumbling wall blow sheet lightning to shatter the sky. Fifty wild flutes blow up a storm in front of them, while a platoon of small boys in long belted white robes and brown wool turbans drum like young thunder. All the villagers dressed in best white, swirl in great coils and circles around one wildman in skins." (Gysin from sleeve notes of *Brian Jones Presents the Pipes of Pan at Jajouka*, Rolling Stones Records, 1972).

Brion Gysin was born in Taplow, Bucks (England) on January 19th, 1916. He later commented on this: "Certain traumatic events have led me to conclude that at the moment of birth I was delivered to the wrong address." After an education in Canada and the UK, he moved to Paris in 1934 to study at the Sorbonne. As a young painter he associated with many important literary and artistic figures, on the lookout, as always for something worth exploring and it was not long before he was introduced to and later joined the Surrealist movement. Gysin was a lot younger than most of the others involved and was therefore an outsider from the start. He was soon in conflict with Andre Breton, and when he arrived at the opening of his first group exhibition, he found Paul Eluard taking down one of his pictures, a depiction of a calf's head wearing a perraque, which bore a striking resemblance to Breton himself. After a few months Gysin was expelled from the Surrealist circle. He learnt from this the dangers of being too fixed in one's ideas.

"I too am not a theoretician and don't hold any particularly strong views about anything, in fact my own past experience of literary and painting groups has always been that this is bad news— it's better not to have such views."

After this period in Paris, Gysin visited Greece and then Algeria, his first contact with the Sahara and Arab culture. He returned to Paris briefly and at the age of 23 had his first one-man show to critical acclaim. It was 1939 and the approaching war forced him to take refuge in New York, associating there with other exiled Surrealists, including Max Ernst, Roberto Matta and Renne Crevelle. Whilst in New York he worked as assistant to Irene Sharaff on seven Broadway musicals and became friendly with composer John Latouche. Latouche's secretary at the time was married to William Burroughs, although Gysin and Burroughs did not meet until years later. Also through Latouche, he met the medium Eileen Garrett, who was quite a celebrity. This was one of his first magical contacts and there is no doubt that it aroused his interest in such things.

Gysin was averse to Burroughs' heroin addiction. It was not until 1958 that Gysin ran into Burroughs again in Paris. Burroughs' first words were "Wanna score?"

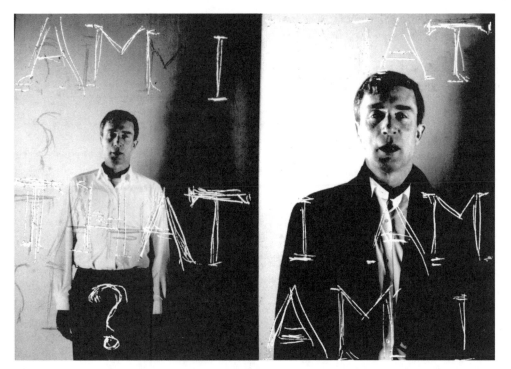

Brion Gysin with hand scratched permutation poem of the elemental linguistic source of creation in the universe "I AM THAT I AM." These slides were projected onto Gysin's body during multi-media performances with the "Domain Poetique" in Paris during the 1960s. From the collection of Genesis Breyer P-Orridge

Gysin gave up his Broadway job to become a welder in the Bayonne shipyards, New Jersey, until he was drafted into the Canadian army. He was still painting and his travels between Miami and Havana inspired some abstract visions and aerial landscapes of Florida bathing in the Gulf Stream. In the army a short time, he was chosen to learn Japanese for Intelligence purposes. "This," he said, "was the most important thing, it had a great deal of influence on my attitude towards surface, attacks of ink onto paper and brushwork, which has very much applied to my painting ever since."

In 1946, at the end of his army career, his first book was published by Eileen Garrett, *To Master A Long Goodnight*, which won Gysin a Fulbright Fellowship to research in France and Spain.

It was on a trip to Morocco with the writer Paul Bowles that he first encountered the magic and mystery of the indigenous culture. He was entranced and lived there on and off for the next 23 years. On a rainy day in Tangier, during an exhibition of his paintings:

"Burroughs wheeled into the exhibition, arms and legs flailing, talking a mile a minute. We found he looked very Occidental, more private-eye than Inspector Lee; he trailed long vines of Bannisteria Caapi from the upper Amazon after him and old

bullfight posters fluttered out from under his old trench coat instead of a shirt. An odd blue light flashed around the rim of his hat. All he wanted to talk about was his trip to the Amazon in search of Yage, the hallucinogenic drug. It was said to make you telepathic. I felt right away that he didn't need too much of that stuff and I may well have launched into my story of how the "Telephone Arabe" works in Tangier but I'm sure he didn't want to listen at the time. Our exchange of ideas came many years later in Paris."

Although they both lived in Tangier at the time, Burroughs often eating in Gysin's restaurant *The 1001 Nights*, they kept a wide berth; Gysin was averse to Burroughs' heroin addiction. It was not until 1958 that Gysin ran into Burroughs again in Paris. Burroughs' first words were "Wanna score?" This chance meeting led to four years of collaboration creating what they called "The Third Mind," discovering "Cut-ups," inventing the Dream Machine with Ian Sommerville, and making several films with Antony Balch. They were resident at the legendary "Beat Hotel" on the Rue Git-le-Coeur, and made frequent trips to London.

Throughout the 1960s and 70s, Gysin involved himself in many projects. He made two recordings of his "Machine Poetry" for BBC radio and was associated with Jean Clarence Lambert's "Domaine Poetique." There were exhibitions of his work in Europe, Scandinavia, Morocco, USA, Mexico and Japan. He wrote several more books and collections of stories. In 1969 he took Brian Jones of The Rolling Stones to Jajouka to record the music from the Pipes of Pan ritual, and published his most important book, *The Process*.

During the early 1980s he was still active and made an appearance at the Final Academy series of events in London 1982, giving readings from his books. He died on July 13th, 1986 in Paris after a long illness.

THE DREAM MACHINE

After leaving North Africa Gysin went first to London where he sold some paintings of the Sahara and then back to Paris where he "ran into a grey-green Burroughs in the Place St. Michel. Wanna score? For the first time in all the years I had known him, I really scored with him." This chance meeting with Burroughs led to four years of collaboration on many projects. One of the most important of these projects was the Dream Machine.

Gysin's first experience of the phenomenon that led to the discovery of the Dream Machine came when he was riding down an avenue of trees at sunset. He wrote in his journal:

> "Had a transcendental storm of colour visions today in a bus going down to Marseille. We ran through a long avenue of trees and I closed my eyes against the setting sun. An overwhelming flood of intensely bright patterns in supernatural colors exploded behind my eyelids; a multi-dimensional kaleidoscope whirling out through space. I was swept out of time. I was in a world of infinite number, the vision stopped abruptly as we left the tree." 21.12.58.

A couple of years later in Paris, Burroughs bought a book called *The Living Brain* by Dr. W. Grey Walter, and passed it on to Gysin. Inside this book there was a long account of the scientific study of the effects of flickering or flashing light on the human mind. Grey Walter discovered that flicker at certain rates synchronized with brain waves to give strange visions of color and pattern. Gysin immediately realized what had happened during his bus ride some time before.

In *The Living Brain*, Grey Walter defines the wave bands as follows:

Delta	0.5-3.5 cycles per second (c/s)
Theta	4.0-7.0 c/s
Alpha	8.0-13 c/s
Beta	14.0-30 c/s

Grey Walter discovered the strangest effects were achieved on the Alpha band. He began by using a strobe light:

"The flash rate could be changed quickly by turning the knob and at certain frequencies the rhythmic series of flashes appeared to be breaking down some of the physiological barriers between the different regions of the brain (*Breakthrough in Grey Room*, Burroughs)."

This meant that the stimulus of the flicker received in the visual projection area of the cortex of the brain was breaking bounds; its ripples were overflowing into other areas. The consequent alteration of rhythms in other parts of the brain could be observed from moment to moment even by an amateur, as the red ink pen of the automatic analyzer flicked its new patterns caused by the changing flicker frequencies reproducing the effect of them in one channel after another. Walter discovered his subjects were experiencing "Strange feelings, a faintness or swimming in the head; some became unconscious for a few moments" and not only that, they were seeing "a sort of pulsating check or mosaic, often in bright colors" … "others see whirling spirals, whirlpools, explosions and Catherine wheels" … "feelings of swaying, of jumping, even of spinning and dizziness and organized hallucinations; complete scenes as in dreams, involving more than one sense." A whole range of emotions were experienced—fatigue, confusion, fear, disgust anger, pleasure … "sometimes even the sense of time is lost or distorted."

Gysin was so impressed with what he read in Walter's book he wrote to Ian Sommerville, then at Cambridge University studying mathematics, asking him if it would be

"Magick Square" watercolor and calligraphy on paper by Brion Gysin 1961. From the collection of Genesis Breyer P-Orridge

possible to make a machine like this at home? It was and they did it by suspending a light bulb in a metal or card cylinder with just regular slots producing a fixed rate of flicker; this was driven by a 78-rpm gramophone turntable. They experimented with a whole series of dream-machines from a very simple cylinder to, years later, machines which as the closed eyes are moved along the height of the column, produce all the gradations of the Alpha Band.

Brion Gysin's own experiments are similar to those Grey Walter reported in his subjects:

> "Visions start with a kaleidoscope of colors on a plane in front of the eyes and gradually become more complex and beautiful, breaking like surf on a shore until whole patterns of color are pounding to get in. After a while the visions were permanently behind the eyes and I was in the middle of a whole scene with limitless patterns being generated around me. There was an almost unbearable feeling of spatial movement for a while but it was well worth getting through for I found that when I had stopped I was high above the earth in a universal blaze of glory."

Gysin connected his experience with Nostradamus, according to Gysin:

> "Catherine de Medici had Nostradamus sitting on top of a tower where with his fingers spread would flicker them over his closed eyes and interpret his visions in a way which influenced her to regard political power as instruction from a higher power."

His experience utterly changed the subject and style of his paintings. He often painted the interiors of his machine, sometimes inserting whole canvasses. He would compliment this by listening to rhythmic Moroccan music while he was viewing.

> "In the Dream Machine nothing would seem to be unique, rather the elements seen in endless repetition, leaping out through the numbers beyond number and back, show themselves thereby part of the whole. This, surely, approaches the vision of which mystics have spoken suggesting as they did that it was a unique experience."

Ian Sommerville also made a comparison to mystical experience. "Elaborate geometric constructions of incredible intricacy build up from bright mosaics into living fireballs like the mandalas of eastern mysticism surprised in their act of growth." "The elements of pattern which have been recorded by subjects under flicker show a clear affinity with designs found in prehistoric rock carving, painting and idols of a world-wide distribution: India, Czechoslovakia, Spain, Mexico, Norway and Ireland. They are also found in the arts of many primitive peoples of Australia, Melanesia, West Africa, South Africa, Central America and the Amazon."

"Catherine de Medici had Nostradamus sitting on top of a tower where with his fingers spread would flicker them over his closed eyes and interpret his visions in a way which influenced her to regard political power as instruction from a higher power."

Gysin took out a patent on his invention in July 1961. Several large Dream Machines were made, mostly ending up in private hands or art galleries, but not in great enough numbers to become the drugless turn-on of the '60s as Gysin had once hoped. He saw the Dream Machine as a gateway to a higher state of being. When talking about flicker, Grey Walter had written: "Perhaps in a similar way our arboreal cousins, struck by the setting sun in the midst of a jungle caper, may have fallen from their perch sadder but wiser apes." Gysin looked a stage further.

> "One ready ape hit the ground and the impact knocked a word out of him. Maybe he had an infected throat. He spoke. In the word was the beginning. He looked at and saw the world differently. He was one changed ape. I look about now and see this world differently. Colors are brighter and more intense, traffic lights at night glow like immense jewels. The ape became man. It must be possible to become something more than man."

MAGICK

Gysin's first encounter with magic was the medium Eileen Garrett. She had been questioned in England in 1920 under the Official Secrets Act because during a séance she had contacted the captain of the ill-fated British Airship R101, predicting its fate with great accuracy. They were introduced by Gysin's friend John Latouche, frequently attending her meetings together; as recounted in *Here to Go*. He was well read in Greek and Roman mythology and in the late '30s spent three years living in Greece. He later became very much a 20th century Dionysian figure.

It was after his first visits to Morocco that magic became of great importance to Gysin and became prominent in everything he created. Always willing to take risks, Terry Wilson commented:

"Gysin had a tendency to like to dice and flirt with fear, he liked to be afraid. He had an immense amount of courage, but there was also a side of him that was rather timid and cautious." Further "He had always had a very powerful personality, he was a person who had tremendous power over other people and could certainly put people into a trance."

Morocco has a long history of magic, especially before the coming of Islam. The indigenous Moorish people have their own Shamanic tradition, as well as fertility cults and belief in Barakas or psychic power points. Many Mosques are built on the spots much in the same way as some Christian churches were sited on pagan sites. Some of this undercurrent survives in the Sufi tradition and the Islamic Mystical Brotherhood, who believe that by using shamanistic methods they can bring themselves closer to Allah.

While getting the restaurant ready one day I found a magical object, an amulet of sorts, a rather elaborate one with seeds, pebbles, shards of broken mirror, seven of each in a little package along with a piece of writing.

In 1950 the writer Paul Bowles took Gysin to a festival on a beach just outside Tangier. It was an old pagan festival based on the solar calendar. The musicians were from the Ecstatic brotherhoods and for the first time Gysin saw large groups of people in trance. The musicians were said to be able to heal by the sound of their instruments alone. This music captured his imagination and after years of searching he traced the musicians, with the aid of the Moroccan painter Hamri, to Jajouka, a small village in the hills outside Tangier.

Here they still celebrated an ancient Pan festival, a version of the Roman Lupercalia. Originally this had been a race from a cave under the Capitoline Hill; goats were killed and a young man chosen to be sewn into the bloody warm skins. At Jajouka he was called Bou Jeloud, the father of skins, the father of fear. In ancient Rome, Mark Anthony was chosen to run the race on the Ides of March. The youth would run out of the city and into the forest to contact Pan, the goat-foot god, sexuality itself. He would run back through the streets with the news that Pan was still there fucking in the forest, all the time whipping the

women in the crowds. In Shakespeare's play, Julius Caesar asks Mark Anthony "to be sure to hit Calpurnia" his barren wife. Gysin thought, "Shakespeare dug right away that what it was, the point of sexual balance of nature which was in question."

Due to Islamic influence men and women live very separate lives and men don't always understand women's language. In Jajouka the women sing secret songs enticing Bou Jeloud, the father of skins to come to the hills for the prettiest girls, "we will give you cross-eyed Aisha; we will give you humpbacked, etc." naming all the undesirable "beauties" of the village. Pan is supposed to be so dumb he falls for this and will fuck anyone. When he comes up to the village he is met by the feminine energy of the village in the form of Aisha-Aisha Homolka. This name may be derived from Asherat or Astarte. The role of Bou Jeloud is to marry her, although nowadays, young boys, dressed as girls, dance her role.

"Pan, the father of skins dances through moonlit nights in his hill village Jajouka, to the wailing of his hundred master magicians. Down in town, far away by the seaside you can hear the wild whimper of his oboe-like raita; a faint breath of panic borne on the wind. Below the rough palisade of ginat blue cactus surrounding the village on it hilltop the music flows in streams to nourish and fructify the terraced fields below." (Gysin)

After Hamri's introduction to these master musicians and many visits to Jajouka, Gysin invited them to play in his restaurant, The 1001 Nights. For a few years they did so until they fell out.

"I kept some notes and drawings meaning to write a recipe book on magic. My Pan people were furious when they found out. They poisoned my food twice then resorted to more efficacious means to get rid of me...While getting the restaurant ready one day I found a magical object, an amulet of sorts, a rather elaborate one with seeds, pebbles, shards of broken mirror, seven of each in a little package along with a piece of writing. When deciphered we didn't even want to touch it, because of its magical qualities, which even educated Moroccans acknowledged. The message was written from right to left across the paper, which had then been turned and inscribed from top to bottom to form a cabbalistic (i.e. with hidden meaning)

grid calling on the devil of smoke to "make Massa Brahim leave this house as smoke leaves the fire, never to return...and within a very short time, I indeed lost the restaurant and everything else." (Here to Go, Terry Wilson)

A short while before this John and Mary Cooke had appeared at the 1001 Nights. They had sought Gysin out on the instruction of a Ouija board. John Cooke was a vastly rich man born of a wealthy and "far out" family in Hawaii. All his life he showed a great interest in magic and the occult. Before coming to Morocco he said that he had been involved in a "billion buck scam" with L. Ron Hubbard called Scientology. The Cookes were instrumental in its foundation and had presumably sought out Gysin in order to incorporate him into Scientology. They claimed he was a natural "Clear" and "Operating Thetan." Gysin was friendly towards the Cookes, even rushing to Algeria when John Cooke was stricken by a mysterious paralysis.

A civil war was brewing in Algeria and Gysin decided to leave North Africa for Paris. Of his time in Morocco he reflected:

"Both extra-ordinary encounters and unusual experiences have led me to think about the world and my activity in a way that came to be termed psychedelic. I've spent more than a third of my life in Morocco where magic is or was a matter of daily occurrence ranging from simple poisoning to mystical experience. I have tasted a pinch of both along with other fruits of life and that changes one's life at least somewhat. Anyone who manages to step-out of his own culture into another, can stand there looking back at his own under another light.... magic calls itself the other method...practiced more assiduously than hygiene in Morocco, though ecstatic dancing to the music of the secret brotherhoods is there a form of psychic hygiene. You know your music when you hear it one day; you fall into lie and dance until you pay the piper. Inevitably something of all this is evident in what I do and the arts I practice."

GYSIN IN PARIS

Gysin's chance meeting with William Burroughs led to four years of collaboration on many projects. Based at the Beat Hotel, they were both certainly in the "right place at the same time."

Gysin's painting in Paris was greatly influenced by the calligraphy contained in the amulet that had driven him from Tangiers. His paintings increasingly became formulas, and spells intended to produce very specific effects. Burroughs, who was recovering from heroin addiction, often sat in whilst Gysin painted, seeing a work from conception to completion. "Brion" he said, "is risking his life and his sanity when he paints."

With Islam, the world is a vast emptiness like the Sahara; events are written, predetermined. Gysin's works became "Written deserts," appearing from right to left like Arabic, and from top to bottom like Japanese. Burroughs was impressed, and in his essay on Gysin in *Contemporary Artists* wrote "It is to be remembered that all art is magical in origin—sculpture, writing, painting and by magical I mean intended to produce very specific results. Paintings were originally formulae to make what is painted happen."

A calligraphic "spell" by Brion Gysin circa 1959/60. Projected onto Gysin's body during his multi-media experiments as part of "Domain Poetique" in Paris. Breaking the boundary between word and body, inner and outer projections of non-verbal meaning. From the collection of Genesis Breyer P-Orridge

THE CUT-UP TECHNIQUE

At that time many other writers/painters were discovering the relationship between writing and painting. Gysin's ideas on the magical-technological approach to writing were, as Burroughs recognized, a way out of the identity habit, and a writing that eludes time, so Gysin thought, was still 50 years behind painting in this respect. It was from this perspective that the "Cut-up" technique was discovered.

"[…] while cutting out a mount for a drawing in room #25; I sliced through a pile of old newspapers …and thought of what I had said to Burroughs some six months earlier about turning painting into writing. I picked up the raw words and began to piece together texts which later appeared as the first cut-ups in Minutes to Go."

They both realized the importance and power of their discovery and how using this technique they could disrupt the linear time sequence of writing thereby destroying ordinary patterns of conditioned word associations. The cut-ups acted as an agent for simultaneous integration and disintegration, imposing another path on the eye and thought. Allen Ginsberg wrote "It meant literally altering consciousness outside of what was already the fixed habit of language-inner-thought-monologue-abstraction-mental images-symbol-mathematical abstraction."

Gysin and Burroughs saw these new writings as spells: "I sum on the little folk-music from the Moroccan hills proves the great god Pan not dead. I cast spells; all spells are sentences spelling out the work look that is you." (*Let the Mice In*, Gysin)

Burroughs himself said he

> "[...] couldn't read them a second time as they produced a certain kind of very unhappy psychic effect. They were the sort of texts that you might use for brainwashing somebody, or you might use them for the control of an enormous number of people whom you drove mad in one particular way by one sort of this application of this dislocation of language, where by sort of breaking off all their synaptic attachments to language you would maybe acquire a social dominance over them which one considered completely undesirable."

There is no doubt that these fears are justified as magical techniques are often tested and used by intelligence agencies of all governments.

These discoveries were not confined to the written word. They also used tape-recorders and early computers. With the help of mathematician Ian Sommerville (1941–76) they produced permutation and machine poetry. The permutation poems are acknowledged as influences by minimalist composers Phillip Glass, Terry Riley and Steve Reich. Some of these influences are noticeable in the live performances of Throbbing Gristle. Some of this is documented by Burroughs in *The Electronic Revolution* and his LP *Nothing Here Now but the Recordings*. With filmmaker Anthony Balch (1937–1980) they made *Towers Open Fire; The Cut Ups; Bill and Tony;* and *Dream Machine*. When watching these films one has the sensation of flashing backwards and forwards in time creating a flurry of deja-vu experiences.

Gysin and Burroughs together had created what they termed "The Third Mind":

> "Not the history of a literary collaboration but a fusion in a praxis of two subjectives that metamorphose into a third it is from this collusion that a new author emerged as an absent third person invisible and beyond grasp decoding the silence."

During their time together staying at the Beat Hotel, they both identified themselves with Hassan I Sabbah—"The Old Man of the Mountain" who in the 11th century terrified establishment Islam from a mountain fortress at Alamout (in Iran). His motto "Nothing is True, Everything is permitted" became theirs. They considered the Beat Hotel as their "Alamout" from which to "Blitzkrieg" the citadels of enlightenment whipping up a complete derangement of the senses as preached by earlier Hashashins like Arthur Rimbaud and Charles Baudelaire. Gysin believed that homosexuality was a kind of cut-up. According to Terry Wilson, he believed that ordinary heterosexuality reinforced human time by reproducing it. Orgasm was like a flash bulb capturing the same picture; the difference lay in the fact that homosexuality involved no physical reproduction. Gysin was a shaman, taking long hours, once as long as 36, to gaze into a mirror. Food, cigarettes or joints were handed to him as he sat there.

> "All sorts of things, great galleries of characters running through. I got to the point where all images disappeared, eventually after more than 24 hours of staring there seemed to be a limited area where everything was covered with a palpitating cloud of smoke, which would be about waist high...there was nothing beyond that."

Gysin rejected any claims that such activities were dangerous: "People who have some sort of mystic discipline are forever telling you that any personal experimentation is dangerous, you must do it according to the rules they have laid down, and I've never agreed with that either." (*Here To Go*, Wilson)

Both of Gysin's major novels, *The Process* and *Beat Museum-Bardo Hotel* have their roots in magical philosophy. *The Process* is based on the Islamic maxim that "Life is like a vast desert." In the book the central character sets out across such a desert which takes a whole lifetime to cross. The process can be read as "The Life Process." The book is also about "Intercultural Penetration," his own experience of Moroccan culture reflected in the central character's total immersion into Arab life.

The second book *Beat Museum-Bardo Hotel* is a story inspired by the death of Ian Sommerville in a car crash. It is heavily influenced by *The Tibetan Book of the Dead*, itself a description of after death experience. This eerie and surreal book has never been published in its entirety. ⌶

WHO IS THERE WILLIAM BURROUGHS

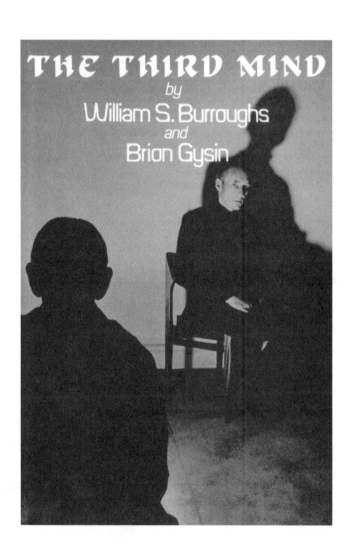

What it was that Sir Ernest Shackleton's party encountered on their harrowing crossing of South Georgia is a question that has confounded historians, and inspired Sunday sermons for generations of true believers. The apparition—which the explorer called the Fourth Presence—impressed Shackleton as being not of this world. It made its appearance near the end of the explorer's grandly named Imperial Trans-Antarctic Expedition of 1914–16, an expedition which came perilously close to ending in mass disaster. The fact that it did not is the foundation of Shackleton's legend. The expedition's ship *Endurance* was trapped and then crushed by ice in the Weddell Sea even before he could embark on the attempt to traverse the Antarctic continent. The retreating crew made an escape from the ice in small boats to Elephant Island. Knowing there was no chance any search for the expedition would find them there, Shackleton decided to leave the majority of his crew behind, take a small boat, its seams patched with artist's paints, and risk the extreme perils of the ocean south of Cape Horn, "the most tempestuous area of water in the world," in order to reach a whaling station on the British possession of South Georgia, 800 miles away.

After braving gales and freezing temperatures for more than two weeks, the six men arrived at South Georgia in the midst of a hurricane, the small boat driven ashore on the opposite end of the island from their destination. Leaving the others with the boat, Shackleton, Commander Frank Worsley, who had captained the lost *Endurance*, and Tom Crean, second officer, made an arduous 36 hour crossing of the ranges and glaciers of the island. They marched in moonlight and in fog. They ascended carefully,

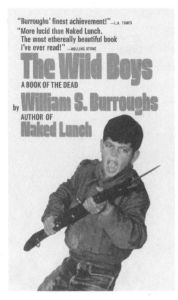

"Burroughs' finest achievement!" —L.A. TIMES

"More lucid than Naked Lunch.
The most ethereally beautiful book
I've ever read!" —ROLLING STONE

The Wild Boys
A BOOK OF THE DEAD
by William S. Burroughs
AUTHOR OF
Naked Lunch

roped together, threading around crevasses and across snowfields. They had slender rations and went virtually without sleep. At one point, they stood on an ice ridge, uncertain of what was over the other side because of a sharp incline. With a bank of fog threatening to overtake them, they opted to plunge into the unknown. At that point, only they knew the whereabouts of all the other expedition members. Had they dropped to their deaths, the entire expedition might have been doomed. Instead, they placed their fate in Providence, and survived. During their traverse, Shackleton later reflected, "we three fellows drew very close to each other, mostly in silence." They eventually shambled into the whaling station, barely recognizable as civilized men. Rescuers were dispatched to collect the others, and all of the *Endurance's* crew survived the ordeal. They were not untouched by the experience. "We had reached the naked soul of man," Shackleton wrote in *South*, published in 1919.

In writing his narrative, however, Shackleton had struggled with something unspoken. Leonard Tripp, a friend and confidant, was present as the explorer tried to come to terms with it. Shackleton had tears in his eyes: "You could see that the man was suffering, and then he came to this mention of the fourth man."[1] Shackleton explained his struggle in *South*: "One feels 'the dearth of human words, the roughness of mortal speech,' in trying to describe intangible things, but a record of our journeys would be incomplete without reference to a subject very near to our hearts." He revealed in the narrative that he had a pervasive sense, during that last and worst leg of his journey, that something out of ordinary experience accompanied them, a presence: "I know that during that long and racking march of 36 hours over the unnamed mountains and glaciers of South Georgia it seemed to me often that we were four, not three." He had said nothing to the others, but then three weeks later Worsley offered without prompting: "Boss, I had a curious feeling on the march that there was another person with us." Crean later confessed to the same strange sensation.

Shackleton at first did not mention the Fourth Presence to anyone else, and the passage alluding to it, which Tripp heard him dictate, was omitted in the original draft of *South*, written by Shackleton in collaboration with Edward Sanders in Australia in 1917. The presence does, however, appear on a separate sheet of paper labelled "note" in another typescript of the manuscript. Apparently Shackleton initially withheld the passage, before deciding to include it in the final version of the manuscript. He did, however, allude to it during some of his public lectures. Recalled one person who attended a banquet in London given in his honor: "You could hear a pin drop when Sir Ernest spoke of his consciousness of a Divine Companion in his journeyings."

Frank W. Boreham, in his 1926 book *A Casket of Cameos*, cites as "testimony concerning his Unseen Comrade" an account given by Ada E. Warden, who was present for a lecture by Shackleton given shortly before his death, in 1922. Said Warden:

> After repeating the story of the appalling voyage in the open boat from Elephant Island to South Georgia, he quoted the words from the one hundred and thirty-ninth Psalm: "If I take the wings of the morning, and dwell in the uttermost parts of the sea, even there shall Thy hand lead me and Thy right hand shall hold me." He repeated the words most impressively, and said they were a continual source of strength to him.[2]

So was the Fourth Presence, as the one listener at a Shackleton lecture surmised, the guiding, protective hand of the "Divine Companion," and as Boreham declared, "the Son of God"? Or was it something of equal mystery, if not glory and power?

Boreham, a British writer and Baptist minister who lived much of his life in New Zealand and Australia, took Shackleton's use of Scripture as proof of his abiding Christian faith, and hence as a clue to the true identity of the presence. Boreham found support for his conviction in Daniel 3:24–5:

> And Nebuchandnezzar the king was astonished, and rose up in haste, and spake, and said unto his counsellors, Did we not cast three men bound into the midst of the fire? They answered and said unto the king, True, O

king. He answered and said, Lo, I see four men loose, walking in the midst of the fire, and they have no hurt; and the form of the fourth is like the Son of God.

"Boss, I had a curious feeling on the march that there was another person with us."

Wrote Boreham: "Flame or frost; it makes no difference. A truth that, in one age, can hold its own in a burning fiery furnace can, in another, vindicate itself just as readily amidst fields of ice and snow." In either case the same conclusion applied, Boreham argued: "the form of the fourth is like the Son of God!"

So was the Fourth Presence, as the one listener at a Shackleton lecture surmised, the guiding, protective hand of the "Divine Companion," and as Boreham declared, "the Son of God"? Or was it something of equal mystery, if not glory and power? In their accounts of Shackleton's expedition, historians have struggled with it, speculating that it was an hallucination, that the "toil (was) enough to cloud their consciousness."[3] The possibility was even raised that it was "an attempt on Shackleton's part to court publicity, at a time of national emotion, by producing his own 'Angel of Mons.'[4] This is a reference to the First World War legend that an angel had appeared in the sky during the British retreat from Mons during August 1914, safeguarding the British army. A journalist and writer of fantasy literature

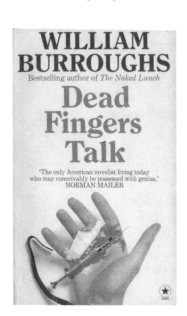

later said he had invented the angel. However, the writer Harold Begbie, who knew Shackleton and wrote an appreciation of the explorer in 1922, also authored *On the Side of the Angels*, which attempts to document that British soldiers believed that angels had appeared to them.

None of the men who experienced the Fourth Presence on South Georgia were ever definitive on the subject of their belief. In remarks made to Begbie, Shackleton remained ambivalent: "We were comrades with Death all the time, but I can honestly say that it wasn't bad. We always felt there was

Something Above." Shackleton clearly felt he had undergone a mystical experience, but did not elaborate. Begbie put it this way: "He was really profoundly conscious of the spiritual reality which abides hidden in all visible things." A naval officer recalled Shackleton alluding to the presence during a conversation: "He attempted no explanation. 'In religion I am what I am' were his words."[5] Whatever it was they encountered, it remained with them to the end. In one of his later lectures, Worsley, who died in 1943, referred to a party of four men making the crossing of South Georgia. Afterwards, his wife, Jean, pointed out his error. Worsley was stricken. "Whatever will they think of me," he said. "I can't get it out of my mind."[6]

T. S. Eliot described the phenomenon in Part V of *The Waste Land*, first published in 1922, the year of Shackleton's death:

> Who is the third who walks always beside you?
> When I count, there are only you and I together
> But when I look ahead up the white road
> There is always another one walking beside you.
> Gilding wrapt in a brown mantle, hooded
> I do not know whether a man or woman
> —But who is that on the other side of you?

"Whatever will they think of me," he said. "I can't get it out of my mind."

In his "Notes on *The Waste Land*," Eliot wrote that the journey to Emmaus in the Gospel According to Luke serves as a theme in Part V of the poem, which he titled "What the Thunder said". In Luke 24:15–17 two men on the road to Emmaus encounter a presence and do not recognize it as the risen Christ:[7]

> And, behold, two of them went that same day to a village called Emmaus, which was from Jerusalem about three score furlongs.
> And they talked together of all these things which had happened.
> And it came to pass, that, while they communed together and reasoned, Jesus himself drew near, and went with them.
> But their eyes were holden that they should not know him.

When Jesus blessed and broke bread at dinner, the disciples finally did know him, but Jesus then vanished from their sight. In his "Notes" Eliot, however, added that the passage in question was also stimulated by an account of an Antarctic expedition, "I forget which, but I think one of Shackleton's." The poet was impressed by the idea that "the party of explorers, at the extremity of their strength, had the constant delusion that there was one more member than could actually be counted." The tone of the account given in Eliot's poem is notably different, however, from Shackleton's published reference to a presence "very near to our hearts," and instead evokes the idea that they were "comrades with Death." Rather than inspiring a sense of the divine, one critic argued, "the visitation in the poem inspires a feeling of dread."[8]

Shackleton confronted the phenomenon at a point of extremity on his geographic journey. The extra man, however, made another appearance in a radically dissimilar context; evidence, perhaps, that exploration is not confined to geographic expeditions—or even the physical world. In common with polar explorers, William S. Burroughs, the American novelist and junky, had a propensity to take incalculable risks. The author of *Naked Lunch*, a harrowing narrative of addiction, sought out extremity wherever it lay, and placed his literary endeavors explicitly in the context of exploration: "In my writing I am acting as a map maker, an explorer of psychic areas ... a cosmonaut of inner space, and I see no point in exploring areas that have already been thoroughly surveyed."[9] It is significant, then, that Burroughs too encountered an unseen companion, and did so at the very point when his experiments with literature and drugs pushed the boundaries of physical and psychological tolerance. Burroughs called the phenomenon the Third Mind.

Burroughs had a long-standing interest in exploration. He had read explorers' narratives, among them Richard Halliburton's *New Worlds to Conquer*. He studied anthropology at Columbia University, Harvard University and at Mexico City College. Burroughs' own explorations did not cover the polar regions of the Earth, so much as the tropics of the mind, the source for literary imagination,

although he did also undertake geographic journeys. Burroughs' search for the telepathic-hallucinogenic drug yage—used by Amazonian Indians for finding lost souls—produced an epistolary account of his travels. Written to his friend, the poet Allen Ginsberg in 1953, Burroughs' correspondence was published ten years later as *The Yage Letters*. The use of epistolary as a device for documenting explorations can be traced as far back as Richard Hakluyt's *The Principal Navigations Voyages, Traffiques and Discoveries of the English Nation*, published in 1598. In style and in substance, *The Yage Letters* is a narrative of discovery. As with traditional exploration narratives, the title implies the goal, that is, the investigation of yage as a tool to reach the unknown. In his early critical examination of Burroughs's writing, Alan Ansen notes that "the actual discovery of the drug plays a relatively small part in the work; at the center are the anthropologist's field report and Burroughs' life in yage." The goal is merely the tool through which the explorer finds what he is looking for

"A Colombian scientist isolated from yage a drug he called telepathine. I know from my own experience telepathy is a fact. I have no interest in proving telepathy or anything to anybody. I do want usable knowledge of telepathy."

along the way. In *South*, Shackleton's goal was, of necessity, abandoned early on. What mattered was the journey, and ultimately his glimpse of the "naked soul." Burroughs' narrative in *The Yage Letters* adheres to a similar form.

The groundwork for Burroughs's yage search was laid at the end of *Junky*, his first novel, published in 1953. In the book, he noted the drug is "supposed to increase telepathic sensitivity. A Colombian scientist isolated from yage a drug he called telepathine. I know from my own experience telepathy is a fact. I have no interest in proving telepathy or anything to anybody. I do want usable knowledge of telepathy." Burroughs wanted to understand what others were thinking, but he also saw more practical applications for telepathic powers: "thought control. Take anyone apart and rebuild to your taste." Usually a concoction of the vine *Banisteriopsis caapi* with secondary plants, yage is used by Amazonian Indians for its "meet your maker" powers, in order to achieve communion with surroundings, to incite visions of cities and places, and as a way of blurring the boundaries between this world and the next. The Ecuadorian geographer Villavicencio was one of the earliest explorers to write about yage, in 1858: "I've experienced dizziness, then an

Burroughs called the phenomenon the "Third Mind."

aerial journey in which I recall perceiving the most gorgeous views, great cities, lofty towers, beautiful parks and other extremely attractive objects; then I imagine myself to be alone in a forest and assaulted by a number of terrible beings from which I defended myself."[10] Some have also indicated that the often overwhelming purgative side effects are a form of purification. The hallucinations are visual, aural, sensory. These properties, together with the previously claimed telepathic powers, suggested to Burroughs that yage "may be the final fix."[11]

In January 1953, while investigating yage at a university in Bogota, Colombia, Burroughs encountered Richard Evans Schultes, a Harvard University anthropologist and authority on hallucinogenic plants. Schultes told Burroughs he had tried yage: "I got colors but no visions."[12] To obtain the drug, Burroughs was advised to go down the Rio Putumayo. He traveled south to Mocoa, where he found a brujo, or medicine man, who prepared a weak yage extraction. Burroughs experienced vivid dreams in color and saw a composite city, part New York, part Mexico City and part Lima. "You are supposed to see a city when you take yage," he wrote Ginsberg on 28 February. Burroughs next managed to attach himself to a cocoa commission expedition. In the company of the botanists, he made the connection with another brujo, around 70 years of age, with "a sly gentleness about him like an old time junkie." The brujo incanted "yage mucho da," or "yage give much" as he prepared the concoction. Burroughs drank about an ounce of the oily and phosphorescent liquid. Within two minutes of ingesting it, a wave of dizziness swept over him and the hut began to spin. There was a strange blue light. Sudden, violent nausea sent him rushing outside, he vomited, and collapsed, arms and legs twitching uncontrollably. He wrote: "Larval beings passed before my eyes in a blue haze, each one giving an obscene, mocking squawk." He

continued to vomit, and it later occurred to Burroughs that yage nausea is motion sickness of transport to the yage state. On 10 July he wrote his final letter from the region to Ginsberg. He described his ultimate yage experience, witnessing migrations, incredible journeys through geographic places, and finally "the Composite City where all human potentials are spread out in a vast silent market." From this city expeditions left for unknown places, with unknown purpose. It was, Burroughs wrote, "a place where the unknown past and the emergent future meet in a vibrating soundless hum."

THE TICKET THAT EXPLODED
BY WILLIAM S. BURROUGHS
AUTHOR OF NAKED LUNCH

Sudden, violent nausea sent him rushing outside, he vomited, and collapsed, arms and legs twitching uncontrollably. He wrote: "Larval beings passed before my eyes in a blue haze, each one giving an obscene, mocking squawk."

Yage inspired a section of Burroughs' 1958 novel, *Naked Lunch*, which also bears many of the hallmarks of an explorer's account of a journey. As the writer Mary McCarthy noted, *Naked Lunch* recorded Burroughs' hallucinations "like a ship's log." This is particularly true in the case of his description of the yage state:

"Images fall slow and silent like snow... Serenity... All defenses fall... everything is free to enter or to go out... Fear is simply impossible... A beautiful blue substance flows into me... I see an archaic grinning face like South Pacific mask... The face is blue purple splotched with gold... The room takes on aspect of Near East whorehouse with blue walls and red tasseled lamps... Migrations, incredible journeys through deserts and jungles and mountains (stasis and death in closed mountain valley where plants grow out of genitals, vast crustaceans hatch inside and break shell of body) ..."

The Soft Machine
a novel by
William S. Burroughs
author of "Naked Lunch"

Largely compiled while Burroughs was living in a male brothel in Tangier, *Naked Lunch* additionally moves beyond fiction into the realm of exploration literature by including references to the matriarchies of the Bismarck Archipelago, and the social control system of the Mayan priestly caste—and scholarly notes and citations, including a reference to published accounts of Bang-utot, a sleep-erection related death occurring during a nightmare. It even has an appendix with scientific purpose, which was also published independently in *The British Journal of Addiction*, describing the effects obtained not only from yage, but other drugs. Such documents of scientific interest, from meteorological reports to anthropological observations, are an obligatory feature of exploration narratives: Shackleton's *South* included appendices on meteorology, physics and sea ice nomenclature.

Burroughs' explorations, which had evolved from his expeditions to the jungles of South America, to the exotica of Tangier, were finally, in arguably their most extreme manifestation, confined to his lodgings, and those of fellow traveler Brion Gysin, at a flea-bag hotel at 9 rue Git-le-Coeur, Paris. Gysin, an artist and writer raised in Canada, was the second who made for the Third Mind. In what might be termed the final Burroughs expedition, their rooms became a center for nightly gatherings and bizarre occurrences. Their imaginations stoked with hashish, and other drugs including mescaline, Burroughs and Gysin began to experience shared hallucinations. Burroughs wrote Ginsberg to report he had been making "incredible discoveries in the line of psychic exploration..."[13] On one occasion Burroughs looked into the mirror and saw himself change into a creature wearing a green uniform, his face "full of black boiling fuzz." Remarkably, Gysin had also witnessed it "without being briefed or influenced in any way." They sought a complete derangement of senses. Burroughs informed Ginsberg "I am in a very dangerous place but the point of no return is way back yonder."[14] The journeys inspired visual, aural, and sensory experiments, most notably in the use of cut-ups, an automatic writing technique where texts were sliced up then the words randomly reassembled. Burroughs considered T*he Waste Land* to be the first great cut-up for using "all these bits and pieces of other writers in an associational matrix"[15] —not least of all Ernest Shackleton. Eric Mottram, in a 1963 critical study, argued "Burroughs admires, and recalls in his novels, T. S. Eliot of *The Waste Land*: in one sense his own work is a vision of a waste land." Burroughs paid homage to Eliot by including the poem as raw material in his own cut-ups.

By pushing their experiments to the point of extremity, Burroughs and Gysin achieved a perfect state of what Gysin termed "psychic symbiosis." Shackleton had remarked upon the sense of his party having drawn "very close" during the crossing of South Georgia. For Burroughs, Gysin had evolved from mere collaborator to a central point of reference in his work. In *Last Words*, his final journals which were published in 2000, Burroughs wrote "Whose biographer could I be? Only one person. Brion Gysin." In many respects he was Gysin's biographer. Burroughs' published journals, essays, interviews, recordings and letters are filled with appearances by Gysin, whose theories, stories, and even biographical details appear irregularly in most of Burroughs' books after *Naked Lunch*. In Burroughs' book of dreams, *My Education*, Gysin appears in 22 of them. Evidence of a symbiant relationship could appear without warning. In a 1976 letter to Gysin, Burroughs wrote: "Did you see the color pictures of Mars and note similarity to your pink picture and read the inexplicable letters B/G that showed up on TV screen?"[16]

Burroughs' published journals, essays, interviews, recordings and letters are filled with appearances by Gysin, whose theories, stories, and even biographical details appear irregularly in most of Burroughs' books after *Naked Lunch*.

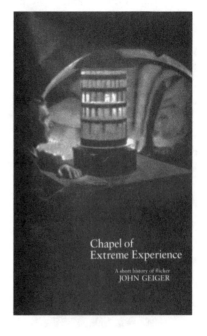

Chapel of
Extreme Experience
A short history of flicker
JOHN GEIGER

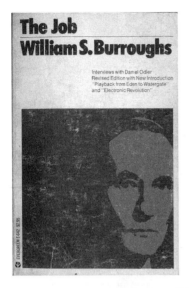

The Job
William S. Burroughs

Interviews with Daniel Odier
Revised Edition with New Introduction
"Playback from Eden to Watergate"
and "Electronic Revolution"

Burroughs owned a canvas by Gysin, painted long before photographs from Mars were transmitted by Saturn 11. The idea that Gysin had some precognition of the Mars photographs intrigued him. But more significant were the letters. Burroughs told the writer Edmund White, "You know they found stones on Mars that had the letters B and G on them?" They might have been Brion Gysin's initials, but White suspected Burroughs meant something else: "Burroughs and Gysin?"[17]

They decided to call the published account of their discoveries *The Third Mind*. In attempting to quantify the experience, Burroughs had discovered an explanation in an unlikely source: the concept of the "Master Mind" set out in *Think And Grow Rich*, a prototype of the self-help genre by Napoleon Hill. According to Hill, Andrew Carnegie built his fortune in part on the basis of the "Master Mind principle," the premise being that the human mind is a form of energy, part of which is spiritual in nature. Hill wrote that when two people work in a state of perfect harmony and are set on attainment of a definite purpose, "the spiritual units of energy of each mind form an affinity, which constitutes the 'psychic' phase of the Master Mind." Hill argued that a "friendly alliance of minds" can access "the sum and substance of the intelligence, experience, knowledge, and spiritual forces" of all participants. It is not merely an accumulation based on numbers, however, but a process which is accelerated by the creation of an additional intelligence. Noted Hill: "No two minds ever come together without, thereby, creating a third, invisible, intangible force which may be likened to a third mind." When recited by Burroughs, however, the reference is expanded to encompass both Hill and Eliot:

"Why am I here? I am here because you are here ... and let me quote to you young officers this phrase: 'No two minds ever come together with-out, thereby, creating a third, invisible, intangible force which may be likened to a third mind.' Who is the third that walks beside you?"

The presence in Shackleton's expedition of one more member than could be counted was a phenomenon Burroughs and Gysin had both ultimately detected in their own explorations. Burroughs argued that when the experiments reached their culmination, "we were in the position of creating a third mind." He used the idea in 'Who is the walks beside you written 3rd', an experiment in format published in *Darazt* magazine in 1965, which includes the line: "with reference to Mr. T. S. Eliot beside you ... This is the third lesson...." A passage in Burroughs' pamphlet *APO-33 Bulletin A Metabolic Regulator*, also published in 1965, reads: "young cop applied for that station a long time ago from The Third Man who else walks beside you?" Gysin also evoked the unseen presence by producing an artwork in which fragments of photographs of Burroughs and himself are merged to create an individual, as well as in a permutated poem. In the poem, Burroughs is transformed into the third:

Who is the third there walking beside you?
Who is the third there William Burroughs.
Who is there third the you walking beside
Who is there William Burroughs
Who is William Burroughs walking beside you? There
Who beside there walking the you
William Burroughs.

The Third Mind, published in 1978, was a compilation of their published literary experiments and theoretical articles, a narrative of their explorations, complete with maps in the form of 70 collages. In his introduction, Gerard-Georges Lemaire describes the intention of "Brion Burroughs and William Gysin": *The Third Mind*, he writes, "is not the history of a literary collaboration but rather the complete fusion in a praxis of two subjectivities, two subjectivities that metamorphose into a third; it is from this collusion that a new author emerges, an absent third person, invisible and beyond grasp, decoding the silence." Burroughs and Gysin explained the concept in an interview published in *Rolling Stone*:

Gysin: 'when you put two minds together...'
Burroughs: '... there is always a third mind...'

"Why am I here? I am here because you are here ... and let me quote to you young officers this phrase: 'No two minds ever come together without, thereby, creating a third, invisible, intangible force which may be likened to a third mind.' Who is the third that walks beside you?"

Gysin: '... a third and superior mind...'

Burroughs: '... as an unseen collaborator.'[18]

There are few similarities to be drawn between Sir Ernest Shackleton and William S. Burroughs, or for that matter the nature of their journeys—only that they both used exploration in their literature, they were both driven to the outré by their frustrations with the ordinary world, and indeed both had, as Shackleton put it, "pierced the veneer of outside things." Both men were engaged in a manner of exploration which pushed them to the limits, and both reached the point of sufficient extremity to have shared a common delusion—if that is what it was—that they had acquired an additional unaccountable companion on their respective journeys, what Shackleton termed the Fourth Presence and Burroughs called the Third Mind. They are not alone in their apprehension. The extra man has appeared to others, always at a moment of transcendence. The presence has been encountered individually or communally. It has been attributed to many things: an hallucination caused by extreme physical exertion, hypoxia or drugs; a ghostly apparition; Death itself; a power created by people who have achieved "psychic symbiosis"; and a manifestation of the Divine Companion. In one respect, though, all who have experienced it are in agreement: that the intangible companion represents a real and portentous force. ⌘

Endnotes

1. Leonard Tripp, memorandum for Dr. H. R. Mill, 1 March 1922; Alexander Turnbull Library, National Library of New Zealand.
2. Shackleton was not the first polar explorer to find solace in those words. A Bible found on Kind William Island—the site of the 1848 Franklin expedition disaster—had the same words underscored.
3. Hugh Robert Mill, *The Life of Sir Ernest Shackleton* (London: William Heinemann Ltd., 1923).
4. Margery Fisher and James Fisher, *Shackleton* (London: Barrie, 1957).
5. Roland Huntford, *Shackleton* (New York: Carroll & Graf Publishers, 1998).
6. Margery Fisher and James Fisher, *Shackleton* (London: Barrie, 1957).
7. Michael North (ed.) *T.S. Eliot The Waste Land: Authoritative Text, Contents and Criticism* (New York: W.W. Norton & Company, 2000).
8. Jarold Ramsey, 'The Waste Land and Shackleton on South Georgia' *English Language Notes 8* (1970).
9. Eric Mottram, *William Burroughs: The Algebra of Need* (Buffalo: Beau Fleuve 2, 1971).
10. Cited in: Marina Jiménez, 'Saving the vine of the soul', National Post, June 9, 2001.
11. William S. Burroughs, *Junky* (New York: Penguin, 1977).
12. Ted Morgan, *Literary Outlaw* (New York: Avon Books, 1990).
13. William S. Burroughs, letter to Allen Ginsberg, n/d [1959]. Columbia University Rare Book and Manuscript Library.
14. Barry Miles, *The Beat Hotel* (New York: Grove, 2000).
15. Philippe Mikriammos, 'The Last European Interview', *Review of Contemporary Fiction*, Spring 1984. Reprinted in Allen Hibbard (ed.) *Conversations with William S. Burroughs* (Jackson: University Press of Mississippi, 1999).
16. William S. Burroughs, letter to Brion Gysin, 5 October 1976. Folder 358. Ohio State University Libraries, Rare Books and Manuscripts.
17. Edmund White, 'Man Is Not a Mammal: A Visit with William Burroughs', *Weekly Soho News*, 18 February 1981. Reprinted in: Allen Hibbard (ed.) *Conversations with William S. Burroughs* (Jackson: University Press of Mississippi, 1999).
18. Robert Palmer, 'Rolling Stone Interviews William Burroughs', Rolling Stone, 11 May 1972.

MAGICK SQUARES AND FUTURE BEATS
The Magical Processes and Methods of William S. Burroughs and Brion Gysin

BEING THE FIRST PART:
CHANGE THE WAY TO PERCEIVE AND CHANGE ALL MEMORY

Our very first "memories" are hand-me-downs from other people. Various events and moments, amusing anecdotes of when we were babies and very small children. Usually stories from a period in our life that we actually cannot recall for ourselves. These are the cornerstones which we begin to add onto, building more conscious, personally recorded experiential memories. Usually, without much consideration of veracity or motive, we assume those original stories (whose source is usually parental) are true, rather than separately authored and constructed mythologies. Yet, with the best will in the world, they are edited highlights (and lowlights) from another person's perspective, interpreted by them, and even given significance and meaning by their being chosen to represent the whole of us, before our own separate SELF consciousness sets in. All the information we have at our immediate disposal as self-consciousness develops is from someone else. Everything about us is true. Everything about us is false. Everything about us is both. It is by omission that we are described exactly, creating an unfolding program not of our own choosing. We are edited bloodlines seeking an identity with only partial data and unknown motivation and expectation.

(I should point out here that Brion Gysin claimed very convincingly to recall being in his mother's womb, the traumatic drama of actually being born and the horror of arriving at the "wrong address" and all subsequent events. I personally believe(d) him. I also suspect it is a part of what made him so incredibly remarkable, important and effective as a cultural engineer and innovator, as a sorcerer of light and language and as a magician.)

These inherited, brief memories are a little jigsaw puzzle, a picture that contains impressions of what kind of "child" we were in the eyes of our familial others. Without malicious intent necessarily, they still tend to guide us towards an unbalanced, prejudiced perception of who we are. They can easily become at least a basic sketch of our character by our parents, a blueprint made more solid by each re-telling, less possible to challenge. Just as we tend to like to please our parents by doing what they praise, so we can also manifest and reinforce their criticisms as well. At their unintended worst, these assumptions and maps become the metaphors/enhancers/deciders/directives for a lifetime's neurotic self-image, selected recordings of who we are, who we are imagined to be, who we are instructed we are, who we are expected to become, what kind of adult we will unfold into and, of course, evidence of an inherited fiction from which we will be conditioned as to how we too will perceive the world and our place in and on it. Looping around and around, a self-perpetuating, self-fulfilling and prophetic sampling into which we immerse ourselves without any great wisdom to hint we might wait and see, listen and watch, question and perhaps even re-edit in order to maximize our potential to become.

Everything about us is true. Everything about us is false. Everything about us is both. In a pre-recorded universe who made the first recordings?

If our self-image is primarily built upon the faulty, biased, prejudiced and highly edited memory recordings of other people, with their own agenda of who we are intended to become, as defined by this perceptual process of un-natural selection, then ways and tools that allow us to seize the means of perception become vital in our fight to construct a self, a character, an identity that is truly and independently our own. Any magic that empowers us to do that, both sacred and profane, is a matter of survival, a cause of infinite concern in terms of the evolution of both our species and ourselves. In short, it's a divine territory that recognizes behavior, perception, and character as malleable matter equal to all other forms of matter, distinguished (so far) only by our apparent awareness that we exist and have choices, mortality and doubt as signifiers of our individuality. If there is any right, any birthright, it might well be the right to create one's SELF.

BEING THE SECOND PART:
IN A PRE-RECORDED UNIVERSE WHO MADE THE FIRST RECORDINGS?

In a very real sense, I do not own my early life. The first "memories" I have are actually short anecdotes describing things that happened involving me that I actually have absolutely no recollection of. Interestingly they all revolve around me doing something "naughty" which

Genesis Breyer P-Orridge and Brion Gysin in Paris, 1980.
Photo Peter Christopherson

influenced others negatively (by parental standards) and for which I got "blamed." The mistakes of others were placed very squarely at my door, a classic "bad influence." For much of my life these shameful crises were simply accepted on trust. I have even recounted them myself, for years, without doubting their veracity, even as I have come to know how subjective, selective, personally convenient and self-serving various sources of ver-

The first "memories" I have are actually short anecdotes describing things that happened involving me that I actually have absolutely no recollection of. Interestingly they all revolve around me doing something "naughty."

sions of events can be. We consciously and unconsciously edit out all kinds of things to suit ourselves, pragmatically, or manipulatively in order to make things happen. These are the roots of a childhood theatre of behavioral depth magick, a form that sadly suffers from being born of devout ignorance, and a total lack of shamanic guidance. Magick is by one definition, if you will, the science of making things happen according to your desires in order to maximize control over one's life and immediate environment to create a universe that is perfecting in its kindness towards you.

This could all be innocuous, and perhaps, for many, it is. For me, it has emerged as a key factor, a continuous exploration and necessity for my emotional survival as a creative being to free myself from imposed ways of being initiated by these uninvited guests in the recording device that is my experiential existence. My recordings are what I build my soul from. The act of independently visualized and consciously chosen creation builds that phenomenon that is what I call and perceive as "me": If I am not who I was told I was, then who am I? More importantly, can I find ways to change the original recordings and inherited construct and actually remember and become whoever it is that I am, or even better, who I dream I wish to be? Can we build ourselves? Are there methods, examples, tricks and techniques, methods and madness, analysis and delirium that empower my self?

It is very easy to fall victim to peer group pressure. Parental expectation. Emotionally crippling tales that put the blame for negative events upon your personality and behavior. We are pushed, shoved, squashed and bullied into submission and contrition. At some point in each being's life, I believe, we are presented with a critical choice, a classic, cliché fork in our road of life. As this occurs, I would suggest that the split is between the consensus reality, consensus-perceptual "memory" pre-recordings of a more or less controlled and predictable biological timeline existence and an opportunity to redefine self-perception and remix re-recordings, infinitely and chaotically, entirely unique and original combinations and collisions of *self* determined and *self* creating recordings assembled from, with and by, freedom of choice.

Instead of our identity (in all possible and *impossible* senses of the word) being built by others we can build our own, and *own it*.

It was in 1967 that this critical concern overwhelmed me. Was there a system, a way to adjust, control, break-up and re-assemble behavior, personality, creativity and perception, so that novelty and surprise, the unexpected and improvisation could be applied to my identity, using my self as raw material, as malleable physically and mentally as any other medium? Could I change the way I perceive and change all memory? It seemed to me that

there had to be a way to truly live my life as art and make my art an inseparable extension of my life. I began my search for a creativity-centered system of applied magick.

You might think that seeking out two Beatniks was a funny place to start looking for a functional, modern process of magick. In fact, it turned out to be exactly the right place to look,

William S. Burroughs at Duke Street, St. James, London during his first conversation on magick with P-Orridge in 1971. Photograph from the collection of, taken by and © of Genesis Breyer P-Orridge 1971/2003

and just as I had hoped, it did change my life, and it did enable me to build, with intention and clarity, the bohemian, divinely seeking being I willed to become.

If I was constructed on the foundation of, and from, inherited memories taken on trust, on metaphors handed down with their own agenda via language and image (what one might think of as the cultural DNA of personality) then I needed to confront the omnipotence of *word control*. It was imperative to my survival as a sentient being to locate the most advanced alchemists, and the most radi-

William had a cut out, cardboard, life-size photo of Mick Jagger standing by his bookcase. "Well... Reality is not really all it's cracked up to be, you know?"

cal in their field, in order to learn what I could of strategies that would force the hand of chance in favor of self-creation rather than submissive reaction.

Porn shops were the only places in those days to buy Burroughs, Henry Miller, and Jean Genet and pretty much everything I was consuming as confirmation, vindication and affirmation as a 15-year-old.

(In Paris during the 1970s Brion Gysin pointed out to me that it was extremely significant that the very first chapter of The Book of Genesis in the Bible is known as "The Creation." He also chose to point this out in an early permutation poem "In the beginning was the WORD and the WORD was God.")

I first met William S. Burroughs in London, at Duke Street, St. James, in 1971 after a brief series of postal correspondence. It actually felt and seemed strange, as I had discovered his existence via Jack Kerouac as the mysterious character "Bull Lee." Confirmation of his being an *actual person* led me to the porn district of Soho in 1965, where I snagged a copy, a first edition actually, with dust jacket by Brion Gysin, of *Naked Lunch*. It had been prosecuted for obscenity, so porn shops were the only places in those days to buy Burroughs, Henry Miller, and Jean Genet and pretty much everything else I was consuming as confirmation, vindication and affirmation as a 15-year-old. Six years after beginning my Beat odyssey via books, my very first question to him, a living, breathing, Beatnik legend in the flesh was... "Tell me about magick?"

BEING THE THIRD (MIND) PART:
NOTHING HERE NOW BUT THEE RECORDINGS

William had a cut out, cardboard, life-sized photo of Mick Jagger standing by his bookcase. Its significance was the rite of "Performance" not rock and roll. On the television set were a full bottle of Jack Daniels, and a remote, the first I ever saw. William was not in the least surprised by my question. "Care for a drink?" he asked. "Sure" I replied, nervous and for one of the only times ever in my life, in awe. "Well... Reality is not really all it's cracked up to be, you know," he continued. He took the remote and started to flip through the channels, cutting up programmed TV. I realized he was teaching me. At the same time he began to hit stop and start on his Sony TC cassette recorder, mixing in "random" cut-up prior recordings. These were overlaid with our conversation, none acknowledging the other, an instant holography of information and environment. I was already being taught. What Bill explained to me then was pivotal to the unfolding of my life and art: *Everything is recorded*. If it is recorded, then it can be *edited*. If it can be edited then the order, sense, meaning and direction are as arbitrary and per-

> ## What Bill explained to me then was pivotal to the unfolding of my life and art. Everything is recorded. If it is recorded, then it can be edited. If it can be edited then the order, sense, meaning and direction are as arbitrary and personal as the agenda and/or person editing. This is magick..

sonal as the agenda and/or person editing. This is magick. For if we have the ability and/or choice of how things unfold— regardless of the original order and/or intention that they are recorded in—then we have control over the eventual unfolding. If reality consists of a series of parallel recordings that usually go unchallenged, then reality only remains stable and predictable until it is challenged and/or the recordings are altered, or their order changed. These concepts lead us to the release of cut-ups as a magical process.

At this point we broke open the hard liquor and each downed a large glass. Soon (it seemed) the bottle was empty.

A CASSETTE TAPE RECORDER AS A MAGICKAL WEAPON:

What I was then told changed the unfolding of my life in every possible dimension and concept of the word. He told me about how during the Chicago Democratic convention in 1968 he had walked around recording the background noises of the Yippie demonstrations, the riots, the Mayor Daley repression and violence. As he walked, he would randomly hit record at intervals "cutting-in" the most recent sounds around him creating a collage that was non-linear time. What he observed happening was that as a configuration of "trouble sounds" occurred (i.e. police sirens, screams, chanting of slogans) the actual physical manifestations and/or expressions of those sounds also increased in what we think of as the "real" physical world. His next experiment was to work with "passive" environmental audioscapes in order to check his evidence and see if it could be replicated. As William explained it to me later, in what became an apocryphal action, he had decided to check more "scientifically" the theories he had been assembling with Brion Gysin regard-

ing "reality" being a linear recording. A malleable medium or element that was subject, as such, to the intervention of edits and erasings, rub-outs and re-sculpting if you will. Not far from Duke Street (where he was then living in voluntary exile, a choice I would find myself compelled to make years later) was a basic British/Greek café called the Moka Bar where he might sometimes relax and get the classic English breakfast of chips, baked beans, fried eggs, fried tomatoes, mushrooms and toast with a large cup of tea, or an instant coffee. Nothing special. Nowhere special. The perfect place, in fact, to encounter arrogance and snobbery, abruptness and poor manners on the part of the very people indentured to one's service. On one of those days, a day when all is over-colored, over-laid, and over-bearing, William was treated with great disdain, with rudeness beyond belief. Crass, crude, rude, nasty and aggressive, insulting behavior quite beyond the acceptable pale of manners. Such was the rudeness and unpleasantness experienced by William that he swore never to eat there again. But, more than that, his disgust and anger was so intense and intentional, so unforgiving and angry in the moment that he felt quite compelled to experimental "sorcery" (his word to me, take note). What form did his curse take? Here follows the first lesson in contemporary intuitive and functional magick.

William took his Sony TC cassette recorder and very methodically walked back and forth in front of the offending café, at breakfast-time and other times of day, making a tape of the ongoing street noises that made the sonic background of its location. A field recording encapsulating a typical day via street sounds. Next he went back to his apartment and at various random places on the same cassette he recorded "trouble noises" over bits of the previous recordings. These were things like police car

Brion Gysin in his Paris apartment in 1984 during a conversation about the real temperature at which water boils in order to make perfect mint tea. Photograph from the collection of, taken by and © of Genesis Breyer P-Orridge 1984/2003.

Previously unpublished Polaroid photograph of the reel-to-reel tape recorder used by Burroughs and P-Orridge to conduct experiments based upon the techniques of Konstantin Raudive to attempt to record the "voices" of dead spirits onto tape using no microphone. This occasion was on Hiroshima Day, August 6th, 1981 in "The Bunker" on the Bowery, New York.
Photograph © 1981/2003 Genesis Breyer P-Orridge

sirens, gunshots, bombs, screams and other types of mayhem culled primarily from the TV news. Then he went back to the café and again walked up and down the street outside playing the cut-up cassette recording complete with "trouble noises." Apparently the tape does not need to be played very loud, in fact just a volume that blends in so that passers-by on the other side of the street, or a few feet away would not notice the additional sounds as implanted fictions. This process was repeated several times, quite innocuous to any observer. "L'hombre invisible" at work. Within a very short time, the café closed down! Not only did it close down, but the space remained empty for years, unable to be rented for love, or money.

We would do well to consider at this point, that each individual human being is inevitably the center of their own unique universe/sensory/experiential world. Only YOU are physically present every single second of your personal life and as a result, any person, or event that takes place without your physical presence is a part of somebody else's unique universe. Of course, there are times when others are present and then they will tend to assume you are all in *one* universe together. However, ask any cop if they get the same story from a variety of witnesses, or the same description of a suspect, and you will be told in no uncertain terms, that *nobody* sees or hears the same thing at the same time as someone else, nor do they share equal abilities to describe or recall what

they imagine their memories have recorded. In other words, consensus reality is, *just that*, an amalgamation of approximate recordings from flawed bio-machines. The background of our daily lives is almost the equivalent of a flimsy movie set, unfolding and created by the sum total of what people allow to filter in through their senses. This illusory material world, built *ad hoc*, second to second, is uncommon to us all. It will only *seem* to exist whilst our body is passing through it. After that its continued existence is a matter of faith, and our experience of it seeming to have a continuity of presence, i.e., if we find we can apparently *go back* to a place that seems solid. It is quite possible that the energy or phenomenon that glues together a repeatable experience of solidity and materiality on this earth is the pressure of billions of human beings simultaneously, and in close proximity, *believing in* what they see and hear. Bear in mind that *history* is the collected recordings of subjective previous people(s) and our species. What has survived, what was memorized or stored in some form is usually assumed to be the story of our unfolding species. Nevertheless, we are more than aware that certain events are written up with agendas included: bitter families, dogmatic religions, democracies, and totalitarian regimes all collude in this process of editing. It has crossed my mind that this entire planet is a recording device itself. As archeology and anthropology and forensic science progress we are able to discover and reveal endless detail of happenings going back millions of years. Also, side-by-side, we have almost every period of human species history still con-

Ask any cop if they get the same story from a variety of witnesses, or the same description of a suspect, and you will be told in no uncertain terms, that nobody sees, or hears, the same thing at the same time.

tinuing today. The bushmen in Africa live in a basically prehistoric way; tribes in New Guinea in the Stone Age; other peoples in a barbaric Middle Ages; entire communities in middle America live almost in a fundamentalist Victorian era; and yet others, in somewhere like Silicon Valley or Tokyo, live in a technological science fiction future. This is a remarkable thing. Infinite micro-realities existing simultaneously, by their very activation creating an appearance of "reality" and infinite, social, macro-realities parallel and colliding and competing for supremacy and with it the power to edit and describe a global "reality."

Burroughs listens intently to the Raudive recordings for any evidence of messages from spirits of the dead. Photograph © 1981/2003 Genesis Breyer P-Orridge

At this point I feel it helpful to remind the reader that this essay is necessarily, as part of an anthology, only an over-view of the complex and wide-ranging evidence consistently to be found in the creative works, in all media, of William S. Burroughs and Brion Gysin. My thereby implicit proposal is, that whilst Burroughs was indeed a classic literary figure of the 20th century; and Gysin a classic 20th century "renaissance" artist, who together bequeathed to us through intuitive science, method and a prophetic appreciation of meaning, a pivotal approach to questions of perception and the nature and origin of literature and art, they can only be fully appreciated, and, perhaps, finally understood, in terms of their central and passionate *inner agendas* and obsessions when re-considered and re-assessed as serious, conscious and masterful creative/cultural *alchemists* and *practicing magicians*, a mission for which I have taken the linguistic liberty of coining the term/occupation "Cultural Engineer."

As their works as this unexpected brotherhood unfold after their collaborations begin at "The Beat Hotel" in Paris during 1957 to 1963 and meticulously thereafter, one is immersed with them in a fascinating journey into pre-material consciousness, a place where direct and indirect communications with the nervous system occur; where nothing is fixed or permanent. Everything is true and permitted; where ancient programming holds prisoner the possible truths of who and what we are, and where even words are potential enemy agents and distortion devices that assist in the suppression of our potential as beings. This wordless "Interzone" was so "inconceivable" to even such a libertarian poet as Allen Ginsberg that he felt it "...threatened everything." It is not uncommon for people to demonstrate symptoms of fear and insecurity when the very fabric of their protective safety blanket "reality" is scattered, shattered, shredded and then further cut-up to reveal a central possibility of divinity and love within all things and perceptions of things. It can be painful to release the last connection to an inherited linear space time "reality" assembled from filtered essence of solidifying mundanity. In a magical universe, everything and every thing is malleable, changeable, interconnected at invisibly deep levels, levels so subtle and sub-atomic that consciousness and intention can affect them.

"Intention is the work of envisaging and enacting will"

–Ray L. Hart in *"Unfinished Man and the Imagination"*[1]

In an oft quoted moment, Gysin proposed to Burroughs, "Writing is 50 years behind painting," by which he meant that painting had begun to call into question all the traditional boundaries and templates. Even reason and object were arbitrary and unnecessary markers. By his introduction of the cut-up in all its manifestations, Gysin, the accomplished "shaman" as Burroughs so rightly designated him, gave his compadre the magical tool(s) required for a lifetime's astonishing—recorded as literature—*revelation*. Their intricate and dazzling story and their functional, demystified techniques and process continue to leak into present time in preparation for various possible futures. I believe that a re-reading of their combined body of work from a magical perspective only confirms what they themselves accepted about themselves, *that they were powerful modern magicians*. To view them otherwise does a great disservice to us all. In this post-digital age, as we each construct our own personal "reality tunnels" it is my conviction that a positive unfolding of our species, and an evolution that is non-destructive and anathema to polarization, is absolutely central to our survival with ethical honor.

In the ever more metaphysical world of physics, a parallel sequence of "discoveries" equivalent in their importance to science as the "cut-ups" system of magick is to culture, has potentially reshaped our understanding of the universe and "reality." According to physicist David Bohm (and simplifying as best as I can as a lay person) any apparent separation between matter and consciousness is an illusion, an artifact that occurs or is assembled only *after* both consciousness and matter have unfolded *into* the "explicate" world of objects and linear/sequential time. As one might expect the other realm would be the "implicate" world, which would be all those inner "worlds" (including thought) that take place outside linear time, and sensory confluence. What is coming to be accepted as a non-material field of consciousness? Bohm's researches suggested to him "...at the sub-quantum

This wordless "Interzone" was so "inconceivable" to even such a libertarian poet as Allen Ginsberg that he felt it "...threatened everything."

"Writing is fifty years behind painting."

level, in which the quantum potential operated, location ceased to exist. All points in space became equal to all other points in space, and it was meaningless to speak of anything being separate from anything else." Interestingly, a Cheyenne/Apache shaman told me years and years ago that there was no word for death in his clan; instead they used the word "separation" to express the concept. Similarly, the Shiva holy man Pagalananda Nath Agori Baba spent many patient hours deprogramming my Western linear materiality in order for me to be better able to grasp the concept of his "path of no distinction." The Egyptian sage Hermes Trismegistus explained this *absolute elsewhere* idea hundreds of years ago when he was recorded as saying "The without is like the within of things and the small of things is like the large."

So now, finally, after thousands of years, we have a consensus of great significance born of this unprecedented and radical intersection between mystic, scientist, shaman and artist. Partly for lack of adequate language and partly to camouflage their subversive ideas in order to stay alive, various enlightened visionaries, often the "heretics" of their era, have employed brain-twisting metaphors to describe the Universe of objective "reality" as an illusion. What scientists are trying to describe to us now is a Universe where, according to thinkers like Niels Bohr and others, subatomic particles require an observer to come into existence and without an observer's presence they *do not* come into existence. Even more remarkable that away from us, each observing from the center-point of our individual existence, the Universe is a measureless resonating domain of frequencies that are an open source that only gets transformed into this world as we think we recognize it after being accessed by our senses and entering our brain. There it is decoded/encoded/acoded who knows which or all and is assembled according to the dimensions of linear time and space, and, I would argue, our subjective cultural expectations. There seems to be a growing agreement at the heart of creation among those in service of the path of the divine, the scientific, and the artistic that the primary reality is one of wholeness, an indivisible unity that functions not unlike a living being, or (my favorite analogy) a coral reef. So, while we rush about, billions of us, interacting experientially with our environment and various objective events do, for all practical intents and

purposes, happen to us in particular locations, on a subatomic level *things are quite different*. On a subatomic level Bohm proposes that all points in space become equal to all other points in space, they are *nonlocalities*. So, to quote John Lennon, "Nothing is real" and adding "And it wasn't/isn't there anyway!"

To sum up this section, the Universe is a unified source, an infinite, open, timeless, intricate quaquaversal frequency field in constant flux that appears to have objective form and material solidity when, and because, we observe it. And observe it we do. We observe it over and over, we are obsessed with recording it (just think of all those hundreds of paparazzi documenting J-Lo's every move) and then we store it in monolithic museums, libraries, databanks. These huge repositories can act on a society's behalf to symbolize anthropological recorders and our maintenance of them; our *belief* in their contents in turn functions as the batteries that charge up and energize the social hologram that we have assembled as consensus reality in order to give continuity, consistency, solidity, and even significant sense of meaning with enough consistency and reliability for us to function during life as biologically sentient beings. Nevertheless, it is our expectation that things will be the same, that a log will remain a log, and if enough of us keep "creating" logs as a matter of habit, eventually ... yes ... *log jam*; but it is

Page from the "magical diary" of Brion Gysin. Note the prophetic line about "Bagdad." Burroughs was convinced, with Gysin, that cut-ups allowed "...the future to leak through." From the collection of Genesis Breyer P-Orridge

MAGICK SQUARES: The Magical Processes and Methods of William S. Burroughs and Grion Gysin still no more "real" despite the materiality produced by repetition. It is not a coincidence that in more established doctrinal/dogmatic religions worldwide; in so-called "primitive" tribal and/or shamanic cultures; in the rituals of public and secret Western magical and/or Masonic orders, or in the ecstatic rhythms and ancient beats of trance targeted music and chants that go with them, *repetition of key power words and phrases are as*

modes of enquiry by pointing out that phenomena "...that occur only once..." will automatically be invalidated by virtue of their uniqueness and that they have an "...insatiable appetite for data." We have seen that everything is indivisibly unified. That there really are no hard edges, no division between mental and physical worlds, or any worlds or dimensions animate or inanimate. Instead we have been introduced to a holographic universe of infinite interconnectedness that responds to the future beat of a shaman's drum. It is fundamental to understanding how

In *Last Words*, Burroughs writes of the enemy and their two weaknesses being firstly that they have "…no sense of humor" and secondly "They totally lack understanding of magic."

integral as is the phenomenon of call and response. Even at this deepest level of a relationship with the measure-less frequency field, with the universe as a unified open source that has no locality, we are trying to solidify and maintain our sensory illusion(s). The purpose of these various "services" is to collectively reconstruct a social reality seamlessly with language, with words and names, with devotional submission to the power of its story, and thereby, ironically, to put into *strict bondage* through this habitual repetition, the essence of life itself. Why? *In order to predict and control it.* Often, unwittingly, we empower the people who claim continuity of descent by colluding in these rites. The real hidden doctrine handed down through the ages, the central agenda, is *control.* Why do those who control seek to maintain control? *For it's own sake.* How do they control? By controlling the story, by editing our collective memory, conscious and unconscious. In many ways the edit is the invisible language of control and its corporate media allies. They cut and paste in order to separate us from each other by entrancing us with a pre-recorded reality that seamlessly isolates us in a world designed by those who would immerse us in service to their fundamentalist consumerism, simultaneously divorcing us from the Universe that is creation itself in an infinite pre-sensory source.

"[...] writing is ... not (just) an escape from reality, but an attempt to change reality, so (the) writer can escape the limits of reality"

–*Last Words*, William S. Burroughs.

In *Last Words*, Burroughs writes of the enemy and their two weaknesses being firstly that they have "...no sense of humor" and secondly "They totally lack understanding of magic." Later he directs our attention to two other enemy weaknesses in reference to dogmatic scientific

to operate and interpret the challengingly effective, modern, and magical exercises of Burroughs and Gysin with cut-ups as their foundation and words as the disputed territory. What we have been trained from birth to believe is a solid environment is only a tiny fragment of what is available to our perception. At the same time, the behavioral, political and anthropological history of our society and culture has been written and recorded by authors fulfilling an agenda of (and for) vested interests who do not have our well being at heart, leaving most of us trapped in *their* current description of the universe.

> *"No two actual entities originate from an identical universe ... The nexus (lineage) of actual entities in the universe correlate to a growth by assimilation that is termed "the actual world"*
>
> –adapted with apology from Alfred North Whitehead, *Process and Reality*.

Back to the café. Experiments have shown we live a great deal of our lives "asleep," filtering out sensory input. Film a street as its residents are going to work in the morning. Add in a police car going past afterwards in the editing suite. Play it back to those same residents later that evening. Asked if this is a recording of the morning, almost all will say "Yes." They will also say they recall the police car going by. This is the phenomenon Burroughs was working with. Added to the fragility of our individual neurological recording devices is the age-old technique of suggestion. Yet, here we are faced with something perhaps even a little deeper: A conscious attack upon, and alteration of, consensus reality by a formularized ritual.

"In a pre-recorded universe who made the first recordings?" So asked Gysin and Burroughs. Further, if all we imagine to be reality is equivalent to a recording, then we become empowered to edit, re-arrange, re-contextualize and re-project by cutting-up and re-assembling our own reality and potentially, the reality of others. If this is true and effective, then a magical act is taking place. Simplified, magick has been defined as a method for changing reality in conformity with one's true will, or as a methodical demystified process that allows us to force the hands of chance in order to make things we truly desire happen based upon, and within, purity of intent. Crowley said that magick has "The method of science, the aim of religion." Brion Gysin talked of magick saying it was "...the Other Method, an exercise for controlling matter and knowing space, and a form of psychic hygiene." So what happened to the café? If it were *only* suggestion, then it would have only discouraged the people in the street whilst William was walking about playing his tape. None of them might have been customers anyway. It was NOT necessary for the café proprietors to be aware of the "curse." The premises closed and remained closed, followed by a series of brief failed businesses, long, long after William moved on to other activities.

"(The process) involves a reversal of our ordinary understanding that causes produce effects. The cause must precede its effect in (present) time, yet it must be presently existent in order to be active in producing its effect." *The Lure of God*, Lewis Ford.

Nook and cranny, window, door,
Seal them out for evermore..."

In addition to tape-recorder magick William also employed a version of the cut-up photograph as additional sorceric firepower. On one visit, as he explained magick to me, he very generously showed me some of his journals. On one page he had stuck in two pictures. One was a black and white photograph of the section of the street buildings where the café was. Beneath it was a second shot of the same section of street, or so it seemed at first glance. However, upon closer examination he had very neatly sliced out the café with a razor blade. Gluing the two halves of the image back together minus the offending establishment. This same principle can be applied to people one wishes to excise from one's life, and variations can be used according to your imagination and needs. Of course, these modern upgrades of magical practice can be easily integrated into older traditions if one desires. For example, one could put the cut-out image into a brown paper bag with one's invocation added in pencil, black pepper, broken glass, sharp blades, and vinegar and then throw it over one's shoulder into a graveyard whilst walking away without looking back.

Once one accepts a possibility that the Universe is holographic and that at the smallest subatomic levels all elements of phenomena can be affected by all others, then

Of course, these modern upgrades of magical practice can be easily integrated into older traditions if one desires. For example, one could put the cut-out image into a brown paper bag with one's invocation added in pencil, black pepper, broken glass, sharp blades, and vinegar and then throw it over one's shoulder into a graveyard whilst walking away without looking back.

According to Gysin in *Here To Go*, William sometimes used two cassette recorders, one in each hand and occasionally even added his own voice repeating an incantation he had written to intensify the focus of his spell. One particular incantation ended up as part of the soundtrack of *Witchcraft Through The Ages* (AKA *Haxan*) an obscure, and really rather kitsch, Scandinavian silent movie for which Burroughs did the voice over, a quirky anomaly resulting from the fact that Beat filmmaker Antony Balch had the UK distribution rights. Part of it went something like this:

"Lock them out and bar the door,
Lock them out for evermore.

the probability of these operations being effective becomes far more credible. Indeed I would argue that a *magical* view of the Universe is the most likely description we have proposed so far as a species. In *The Job* Burroughs discusses silence as a desirable state. What he seems to imply is that words are potentially blocks, both by their linearity in our language system and the manner in which they narrow definitions of experiential events and actions. He says, "Words ... can stand in the way of what I call *nonbody experience*." He does not want to turn the human body into an environment that includes the universe. That would once more create limiting templates and maps of expectation that discourage new and/or radical explorations. Rationality and the fixed progression of physical biology narrow consciousness. One magical method he proposes is:

> "What I want to do is to learn to see more of what's out there, to look outside, to achieve as far as possible a complete awareness of surroundings ... I'm becoming more proficient at it, partly through my work with scrapbooks and translating the connections between words and images."

–From "*The Third Mind*" interview with Conrad Knickerbocker 1967.

One pre-requisite of most Western magical orders is that the applicant/neophyte keep a daily magical diary in which they note their dreams, synchronicities, apparent resolution of temporal events and desires after magical operations. This is not so much just to document and vindicate the system being applied, as to create an ongoing awareness of the constant relationship we all actually have, moment to moment, with *the other*. In a universe where everything is, "interconnected, inter-dimensional and integrated," or as Michael Talbot describes it, *holographic*, the acceleration of and practical collaboration with this interrelation of energies and their ability to assist us in affecting manifestations is more clearly revealed by methodical documentation. It seems that the more one *acknowledges* this confluence of mutability the more kindly its relationship to and with you. This interaction is the one symbolized by the number 23 in Robert Anton Wilson's books and in the mythologies flowing throughout his and Burroughs' fiction. It is not so much that the number 23 is a "magical" number that does "tricks" for the person who invokes it, it is more that the number 23 reminds us of the inherent plasticity of our inherited reality and our potential to immerse our *self* in that quality to our own advantage and possible well-being. It represents a magical vision of life rather than a linear and existential one. Significantly, Burroughs, like Kerouac and Gysin, kept dream diaries and journals, Gysin and Burroughs extending their range further by including cut-up texts,

Brion Gysin "rubbing out the word" at The October Gallery, London 1981. Photograph © Genesis P-Orridge 1981/2003

newspaper headlines, photographs, fictional routines and poems in a kaleidoscopic visualization of multi-faceted and layered "reality." Burroughs suggests a practical exercise to amplify our appreciation of, and practical familiarity with, this manifestation:

> "Try this: Carefully memorize the meaning of a passage, then read it; you'll find you can actually read it without the words making any sound whatever in the mind's ear. Extraordinary experience, one that will carry over into dreams. When you start thinking in images, without words, you're well on the way."

– *The Third Mind*

It is not so much that the number 23 is a "magical" number that does "tricks" for the person who invokes it... It represents a magical vision of life rather than a linear and existential one.

On August 6th, 1981 I visited Burroughs in New York. He was living at 222 Bowery in the basement, a location fondly nicknamed and immortalized in various biographies as "The Bunker." A book Burroughs introduced me to was *Breakthrough* by the Latvian paranormal investigator Konstantin Raudive. In his book, Raudive documents hundreds of "recordings" of the voices of the spirits of the dead. His method was unusual but simple: Attach a crystal receiver to an otherwise standard reel-to-reel in the socket where a microphone would be plugged, hit record, and see what appeared on tape. What Raudive found was that within a wall of white noise and hiss, various intelligible sentences and messages that he believed were from souls in the dimensions associated with being dead, were audible. Given that we were meeting on "Hiroshima Day," as Burroughs designated it, there was a feeling that perhaps quite a large number of dead souls might wish to breakthrough. We set up an old tape recorder on the kitchen table where many a dinner soiree was held over his New York years and hit record. Each of us took turns listening through headphones live to the noise and interference going down on analog tape as it slowly turned. After half an hour we played the "results" back, intently noting the slightest sonic detail. Like good, objective, laboratory researchers we made notes, both on paper and recorded onto a cassette with the Sony Walkman I had with me. It was almost a parody of an autopsy on TV. Final report from the Bunker? Nothing! Oh, how we hoped for evidence, but we got just the expected hiss and short-wave *Twilight Zone* type sounds. Regardless—and Crowley was fastidious in reminding the initiate of this—we did not fall into the trap of "lust of result." Sometimes only one phenomenon occurs to vindicate a theory, sometimes things seem unrepeatable. In terms of this text, what is significant is that Burroughs truly believed in the possibility of communication with the soul after physical death, long before he went public with that in *Last Words*.

As a footnote to this experiment an extra event is worthy of mention. During 1985, Psychic TV were recording a song about the deceased/murdered founder of the Rolling Stones, Brian Jones, called "Godstar." Still fascinated by the Raudive book and Burroughs' dogged exploration of its technique as a magical tool, I arbitrarily, on impulse, told Ken Thomas (my co-producer and creative engineer) to leave track 23 of the 24-track analog tape empty. After all the elements of the song were recorded in the traditional multi-track way I instructed him to re-run the master tape with every track muted except track 23. This track was to be on record, but with absolutely NO form of microphone or even a crystal receiver plugged in, simply a tape running through a deck with no scientific means of recording on one track. Ken seemed to think this was both illogical and "a bit spooky," but to his credit, he went ahead and did as I asked anyway. When we played back the previously virgin, pristine and blank track 23, much to our amazement, we heard a metallic knocking at a few points! We replayed and replayed the track, it was definitely there and had certainly appeared during our "token" Raudive/Burroughs experiment; yet it seemed random, and was not a "voice." Suddenly, I had a moment of clarity and suggested Ken replay the track with the vocals of the lyric and some basic elements of the music added in the mix. The knocking sounds came very precisely under a sequence of words in the exact phrasing and position of the following, "…I wish I was with you now, I wish I could tell you somehow…" (Later I would change the lyric to "I wish I could save you somehow.") If I am truly frank, I took this as a sign of approval of the song and its message, which is that Brian Jones was murdered and received a callous treatment at the hands of the media during his last days. He became, for myself and many other fans of his iconography, a scapegoat in the essential magical and sacred way. Sacrificed, *at the very least*, by ignorance and greed to the consumer and materialistic machine of linear reality. It is

A "magick square" glyph utilizing the name "Gen" inscribed in a copy of his groundbreaking novel "The Process" by Brion Gysin during a visit to the author's home in London 1981. From the collection of Genesis P-Orridge

worth noting that at the time we were taping the song the consensus opinion, and official coroner's verdict was "death by misadventure" with a lot of media hinting that he either drowned during an asthma attack, or he was so high on drugs that, despite being an athletic swimmer, he drowned right in front of his current girlfriend and guests. Our "magical" message tended to imply there was more to the story and eventually, during the 1990s, a builder Jones had hired, Frank Thorogood, confessed on his deathbed to murdering Brian Jones by holding him under water. Whatever you may choose to believe, it certainly appears to me that there are ways to make contact with realms considered *Other* via the most simple of tape recording devices.

Burroughs, and Gysin, both told me something that resonated with me for the rest of my life so far. They pointed out that alchemists always used the most modern equipment and mathematics, the most precise science of their day. Thus, in order to be an effective and practicing magician in contemporary times one must utilize the most prac-

Burroughs, and Gysin, both told me something that resonated with me for the rest of my life: They pointed out that alchemists always used the most modern equipment and mathematics, the most precise science of their day.

tical and cutting-edge technology and theories of the era. In our case, it meant cassette recorders, Dream Machines and flicker, Polaroid cameras, Xeroxes, E-prime and, at the moment of writing this text, laptops, psychedelics, videos, DVDs and the World Wide Web. Please note that earlier we discussed the possibility that the universe is a holographic web constructed of infinite intersections of frequencies (of truth). Basically, everything that is capable of recording and/or representing "reality" is a magical tool just as much as it is a weapon of *control*.

BEING THE FOURTH PART:
LOOK AT THAT PICTURE IS IT PERSISTING?

The first question Brion Gysin asked me, in Paris in 1980 was "Do you know your real name?" I replied, yes, (assuming it was Genesis and not my given name Neil) and then inquired as casually as I could, "Tell me about magick?"

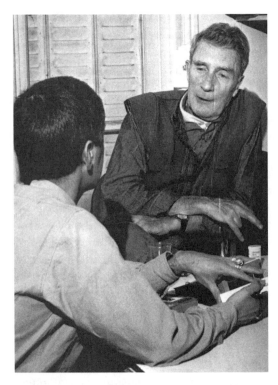

Genesis Breyer P-Orridge and Brion Gysin in Paris, 1980.
Photo Peter Christopherson

Brion Gysin was born in Taplow, England in 1916, but indicative of the unspecific density of his visitation on earth, (and I use the word "visitation" because until his dying day in 1986, Brion insisted that in being born human he was "delivered here by mistake") his conviction of mislocation, and with it a disruption of a different, perhaps parallel, dimensional existence, fueled his remarkably deep sense of irony and *Otherness* and was a central quality of his body of magical artistic work. Gysin was a *transmediator*, a 20th century renaissance man, a multimedia explorer and innovator. Innately disciplined, he would continually paint and draw, extending his calligraphic journeys into what Burroughs would describe as "…painting from the viewpoint of timeless space."

During my conversations on magick with Burroughs during the 1970s it became more and more clear to me that Gysin was pivotal in the history of the magical unfolding and the techniques of cultural alchemy that had drawn me to his Beat oeuvre and from thence, I desired to make direct contact. During my conversations on magick with Gysin, the cassette tape-recorder that I had with me was tolerated *only* on the condition that certain key teachings were spoken whilst the tape was switched off. As he presented it quite plainly to me, "Magick is passed on by the touching of hands." In other words, certain ideas and methods are handed-down master to student, one on one, directly in each other's physical presence. This agreement has been honored ever since, and remains so. Nevertheless, just to have confirmation from him that it was indeed true that his work was contemporary magick, not simply artistic or literary experimentation was a great solace and gave me determination in my personal path.

It was Gysin who first recognized the potential of cut-ups as a means to update and upgrade writing and art, and as a contemporary application of magick. In collaboration with Ian Sommerville and Burroughs he discovered and made cheaply accessible, the Dream Machine; "the first artwork to be looked at with eyes closed," the story of, and implications of, which are marvelously catalogued in John Geiger's book *The Chapel Of Extreme Experience*. In that book for the first time, out of a kaleidoscopic cyclone, a blizzard of revolutionary scientific information and ultra-visionary creation, we are exposed to an incredibly significant creative and conceptual exploration of consciousness via "flicker." In terms of possibility, both Burroughs and Gysin would often quote Hassan I Sabbah, the "old man of the mountains," who from his fortress in Alamut, Iran was rumored to have controlled, using brutal assassins, a huge swathe of ancient Arab civilization. His motto,

"Nothing is True, Everything Is Permitted" recurs over and over, especially in Burroughs' books. It is not so far from the Thelemic precept, "Do What Thou Wilt is The Whole of the Law," a theoretical connection that Burroughs appeared to acknowledge towards the end of his life.

Gysin spent 23 years living in Morocco. During that time he ran a restaurant called 1001 Nights and would invite a group called The Master Musicians of Jajouka to play music for the guests as the entertainment. He told the story, more than once, of how that business crumbled after he found a magick spell "…an amulet of sorts, a rather elaborate one with seeds, pebbles, shards of broken mirror, seven of each, and a little package in which there was a piece of writing … which appealed to the devils of fire to take Brion away from this house." Very shortly after this discovery, he lost the restaurant and ultimately returned to Paris. On one of my first visits to Paris to meet with Gysin I was blessed with a special evening. After looking into the Dream Machine for a couple of hours, Bachir Attar, then the son of the Master Musician of Jajouka—he is now the Master Musician himself after his father's death—and his brother, cooked me a ceremonial meal. During the feast Bachir played flute music that he told me raised the Djinn, the little people, and the spirits

Brion Gysin stares into a Dream Machine circa the "Beat Hotel" era (1957-63) using flicker to travel outside any constraints of time or space. From the collection of Genesis Breyer P-Orridge.

who would bestow great fortune upon the listener. Despite the friction of the era when the restaurant was lost, a very powerful magical bond remained between the ancient system of magick and the most contemporary of elaborations represented by Gysin.

Calligraphic magick squares were one of the techniques most commonly applied by Gysin. He would reduce a name or an idea to a "glyph" and then write across the paper from right to left, turn the paper and do the same again, and so on, turning the paper around and around to create a multi-dimensional grid. Gysin believed this "scaffolding" allowed the Djinn to run with the intention of "exercising control of matter and knowing space."[2] The same techniques and consciously driven functional intention also permeated his paintings. In a very real sense, everything he created was an act of sorcery.

William S. Burroughs described the central difference of Gysin's painting as follows:

> "All art is magical in origin … intended to produce very definite results. Art is functional; it is intended to make things happen. Take porcelain stove, disconnect it and put it in your living room, it may be a good-looking corpse, but it isn't functional anymore. Writing and painting were done in cave paintings to ensure good hunting. The painting of Brion Gysin deals directly with the magical roots of art. His paintings are designed to produce in the viewer the timeless ever-changing world of magic caught in the painter's brush. His paintings may be called space art. Time is seen spatially as a series of images or fragments images past, present, or future."

Gysin felt trapped and oppressed by materiality, but optimistically searched for techniques to short-circuit control and expectation. He accepted nothing as fixed and permanent, reducing the most intimidating formulae of language to animated permutations that become portals of

Night Of The Feast Marrakech, watercolor on old paper (paper circa 1810) by Brion Gysin 1967. From the collection of Miss Jackie Breyer P-Orridge

behavioral liberation. If, as we have seen, the Universe consists of interlaced frequencies, that pulse and resonate at various interconnected rhythms, then his search was for a *future beat* that would liberate the body and mind from all forms of linearity. Each magick square is essentially holographic, suffused with a directed unity. Intertwined in his grids as confirmation and illustration of the magical ideas proposed are examples of routines, exercises with words, and densely cut-up texts. What we observe is a complex, deeply serious mind, an occultural alchemist, camouflaged by passionate humor.

In Gysin's works and writings we are blessed with a perfect example of the storyteller teacher. A practiced, post-technological shamanic guide to the mind, providing exercises, navigational tools and data to assist us in the essential process for magical survival and for the exploration of this strange place in which we unfold our physical existence(s). A domain we call earth, society and life but rarely call into fundamental question. Rationality and materiality have generated a depth of inertia so profound that it could destroy our potential as a species to survive or evolve. All the more reason to re-appraise and study, as magical masters, the instructive works of Burroughs and Gysin as we traverse the 21st century. As science confirms the revelation of this space time neurosphere to be an holographic

Marrakech Market In The Daytime, watercolor on paper by Brion Gysin (undated). From the collection of Genesis Breyer P-Orridge

universe, I have no doubt that Burroughs and Gysin, *redefined as occultural alchemists and practicing magicians*, are destined for an accelerating appreciation for the seminal influence of their cultural engineering experiments.

There is an exquisite mastery of perception that these discoveries unfold. Both Gysin and Burroughs use a serial seduction of detail. Meaning is shattered and scattered to become a more accurate and truthful representation of this arbitrary plane we needlessly confine by using the word-prison "reality." Consecutive events are subverted as we read, revealing the fragility and distortions that our

"Abandon all rational thought"

conditioned senses filter out for simplicity of behavior and illusory reason. Nothing tends to remain as it seems, but *becomes as it's seen.* Contradictory experience is portrayed as equally perceived, parallel images and thoughts. Mundanity is turned strange and disturbing.

Burroughs and Gysin, as master mackinaws, grasp the elasticity of reality and our right to control its unfolding as we see fit and prefer. They consolidate our right to active participation in the means of perception, and their proposal of the nature of consensus being is still quite revolutionary. As we navigate the warp and weft of biological existence and infinite states of consciousness, the holographic universe that looks kindly upon us, at the magick squares of their methods and the delirious madness they supply us with, we are offered a unique perspective and afforded respite, balance and the possibility of retrieving new and valuable information for a future.

We are not talking about a matter of *faith* here; faith is something that has a low quotient in these experiments.

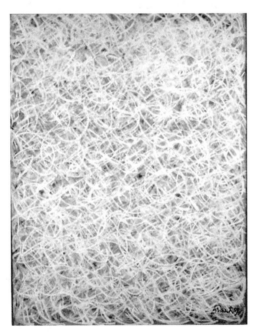

View From Peggy Guggenheim's Window In Venice, watercolor on paper by Brion Gysin 1959. Gysin informed the author that this picture was a rendering of the light flashing on the water at dawn. Created in the magick square formula. The original is actually in shades of pink through to white and utterly breathtaking. It also demonstrates how what seems abstracted at first is actually an image of "what is really there" in the same way cut-ups reveal "what it really says." From the collection of Genesis Breyer P-Orridge

View From My Window In Paris At Night, detail of watercolor and collage on paper by Brion Gysin 1974. A good example of Gysin's use of small photographic images into his "grid" and/or "roller"paintings. You can see Gysin in his apartment window in the bottom right corner. From the collection of Genesis Breyer P-Orridge

Rather we are looking at prophetic *predictions* based upon a magical vision of the universe and the resulting, practical applications of alchemical theories and exercises. In fact we are looking at an early, workable model of the future, in which a positive, compassionate unfolding of our latent qualities as a species is defined and described in the vainglorious hope that we "abandon all rational thought" and immerse ourselves in an ecstatic series of creative possibilities.

In a way, it is a bit like learning a martial art. We develop our media reflexes and accelerate our improvisational responses in order to maximize our individual potentialities and the interests of our chosen people or our private dream agenda. In his various essential commentaries on media divulgence, Douglas Rushkoff, astutely, directs us to a re-examination of the original source of an inherited narrative of culture and life. His conclusions are very similar to my assertions in relation to Burroughs and Gysin, that the very history that began this examination, the social narrative imposed upon us as a child, that so easily programs us to maintain every possible status quo without criticism; and that compounds the notion of linearity and a serial phenomenological universe seems more clearly to be an illusion and a deliberately inert construction. A picture of "reality" that is designed by those with a vested interest in stasis to maintain our surrender to cul-

tural impotence and all forms of addictive consumption. The past controls through people and their surrender to a closed system, where the laws of physics remain constant, and predictability is a desirable state in an ever more rigid global world order. Yet, in fact, we are entering a digital future, a holographic universe, where at least theoretically, every sentient being on earth will be interconnected, international and interfaced. Entirely new navigational tools are required. The possibilities are endless. It is my contention that as the authorship of our own private narrative becomes increasingly autonomous, malleable and optional, that a new future, a future that is inclusive, rooted in the idea of an open source that we can affect by logical and alchemical means, becomes critical to our species' survival, comprehension, and evolutionary change. A future where Burroughs and Gysin, and their modern occultural brethren, have supplied prophetic, functional skills and nonlocal points of observation which can train us to be fittingly alert and prepared for the unpredictable aesthetic and social spasms to come. ☿

NOTE: THE DISCIPLINE OF DO EASY

I strongly advise any reader who has been inspired to reconsider their picture of both the Beats and their world picture to look for an essay by William S. Burroughs titled "The Discipline of Do Easy" or "The Discipline of DE" which is part of the book *Exterminator!* In my own private, alchemical life, a rigorous and continual application of this idea has been as central to my uncanny achievement of countless goals as the Austin Osman Spare system of sigilization.

Endnotes:

1. See "Even Further The Metaphysics of The Sigil" by Paul Cecil in *Painful But Fabulous*, bibliog.
2. Another magician from a different school might call them "Egregores."

SELECTED BIBLIOGRAPHY

I suggest that anyone whose interest has been stimulated at all by this more unorthodox point of observation and interpretation of two classic Beat figures seek out, and actually read, the books listed below, and/or re-read them with a different perspective in mind. Needless to say, there is no end in sight, even within the realms of time or mortality as to how we recreate our subjective means of perception. I really believe that listed below is a functional, inspirational and thorough library of ideas and techniques for seeing this mystery of biological and neuro-illogical life in its intended and intrinsic holographic form. As you might suspect from my text, seeking out and finding, with dogged determination and a deeply hungry appetite for soul and wisdom, for purposes of *self* determination is necessary in a world built of feedback loops of surrender and submission to consuming, to addiction to the products of an ever more banal culture that can NEVER supply satiation, aesthetic nutrition, sensual self-creation, or freedom of identity.

Minutes To Go, William S. Burroughs; Gregory Corso; Sinclair Beiles; Brion Gysin, Beach Books, Paris, 1968.

The Process, Brion Gysin, Doubleday, 1969.

Future Ritual, Philip H. Farber, Eschaton, 1995.

Brion Gysin Let The Mice In, Brion Gysin; William S. Burroughs; Ian Sommerville 1973.

Exterminator! William S. Burroughs, Viking, New York, 1973.

Here To Go: Planet R-10: Brion Gysin interviewed by Terry Wilson, Terry Wilson, Brion Gysin, RE/Search, 1982.

Beat Hotel, Barry Miles, Grove Press, New York, 2000.

Thee Psychick Bible, Genesis P-Orridge, Alecto Enterprises, 1994.

The Job, Interviews With William S. Burrough, Daniel Odier, Grove, New York, 1974.

Painful But Fabulous: The Lives And Art Of Genesis P-Orridge, Julie A. Wilson; Douglas Rushkoff; Richard Metzger; Paul Cecil; Bengala; Carol Tessitore, Carl Abrahamsson, Soft Skull, New York, 2003.

Chapel Of Extreme Experience, John Geiger, Gutter Press, 2002.

Radium 226.05 magazine, Ulrich Hillebrand; Cm Von Hausswolff; Spring 1986.

Back In No Time: The Brion Gysin Reader, Jason Weiss, editor, Wesleyan University Press, 2001.

Cyberia, Douglas Rushkoff, HarperSanFrancisco, 1994.

Media Virus, Douglas Rushkoff, Ballantine, 1994.

The Holographic Universe, Michael Talbot, HarperPerennial, New York,1991.

The Third Mind, William S. Burroughs; Brion Gysin, Viking 1978.

The Best Of Olympia, Maurice Girodias, Olympia Press, Paris, 1961.

The Last Museum, Brion Gysin, Grove, 1986.

Wreckers Of Civilization, Simon Ford, Black Dog, London, 1999.

RE/Search #5/6: W.S. Burroughs/Brion Gysin/Throbbing Gristle. Vale, editor, 1982.

Flickers of The Dream Machine, Paul Cecil, editor, Codex Books, 1996.

Disinformation: The Interviews, Richard Metzger, et al, The Disinformation Company, 2002.

Sex And Rockets, The Occult World Of Jack Parsons, John Carter, Feral House, Los Angeles, 1999.

Breakthrough: An Amazing Experiment in Electronic Communication With The Dead, Konstantin Raudive, Colin Smythe Books, London, 1971.

The Final Academy: Statements Of A Kind, G. P-Orridge and Roger Ely, editors, with texts by Antony Balch; Felicity Mason; William S. Burroughs; Brion Gysin; John Giorno; Dave Darby; Jeff Nuttall; Ian Sommerville; Victor Bockris; Jon Savage; Eric Mottram; Barry Miles; 23 Skidoo; Cabaret Voltaire; Psychic TV; Ian Hinchcliffe; Last Few Days; Paul Burwell; Anne Bean, 1982.

This Is The Salivation Army, Scott Treleaven, Genesis P-Orridge, foreword; 2003.

Portable Darkness: An Aleister Crowley Reader, Scott Michaelsen, editor, with forewords by Robert Anton Wilson and Genesis P-Orridge, Harmony Books, 1989.

The Soul's Code: In Search Of Character And Calling, James Hillman, Warner, 1996.

Naked Lens: Beat Cinema, Jack Sergeant, Creation, 2002.

Apocalypse Culture and *Apocalypse Culture 2,* Adam Parfrey, editor, 1987, revised edition. Feral House, 1990; 2000.

Rapid Eye #2, Simon Dwyer, editor, Creation, 1992.

Rebels And Devils: The Psychology Of Liberation, Christopher S. Hyatt, editor, with contributions by William S. Burroughs; Timothy Leary; Robert Anton Wilson; Austin Osman Spare; Lon Milo Duquette; Genesis P-Orridge; Aleister Crowley; Israel Regardie; Peter J. Carroll; Osho Rajneesh; Jack Parsons and others, New Falcon, Tempe, AZ, 1996.

Global Brain: The Evolution Of Mass Mind From The Big Bang To The 21st Century, Howard Bloom, John Wiley and Sons Inc., New York, 2000.

The Lucifer Principle, Howard Bloom, Atlantic Monthly Press, New York, 1995.

AUSTIN OSMAN SPARE
Divine Draughtman

Spare self-portrait, 1907

Austin Spare (1886–1956) provides us with a fascinating example of an artist who was both a magician and a trance-visionary. While the formal structures of the Hermetic Order of the Golden Dawn were fragmenting amid schisms and dissent just prior to the onset of World War One, Spare was developing a unique system of practical magic through his exploration of ecstatic trance states. Spare was probably the first modern occultist to evolve a self-contained working hypothesis about the nature of psychic energy which could be applied without all the paraphernalia of traditional rituals, grimoires and magical implements. His system of magical sigils showed how an effort of will, when focused on the subconscious mind, could unleash the most extraordinary psychic material.

One of five children, Spare was born in Snow Hill, London, on December 30th, 1886, the son of a policeman. The family later moved to south London and Spare attended St Agnes' School in Kennington Park; he would live in this area of the city, in modest circumstances, for most of his life.

Spare showed artistic talent early on, and at the age of twelve began studying at Lambeth Evening Art School. In 1902, when he was sixteen, he won a scholarship enabling him to attend the Royal College of Art, South Kensington, and in 1905 examples of his work were exhibited at the Royal Academy. The President of the Academy, John Singer Sargent, proclaimed Spare to be a genius and he was soon commissioned to illustrate a handful of books, including Ethel Wheeler's *Behind the Veil* (1906) and a book of aphorisms titled *The Starlit Mire* (1911).

Spare postulated the existence of a primal, cosmic life-force which he termed Kia, and he believed that the spiritual and occult energies inherent in Kia could be channeled into the human organism, which he called Zos.

In 1917 Spare enlisted in the Royal Army Medical Corps, and in 1919 visited France as a special war artist documenting the aftermath of the Great War—several works based on sketches from this period are included in the collection of the Imperial War Museum. In 1919 Spare also co-founded an excellent illustrated literary magazine called *The Golden Hind*, which included the work of such writers as Aldous Huxley, Alec Waugh and Havelock Ellis.[1]

However, while he received a degree of acclaim and recognition during his lifetime—Augustus John proclaimed Spare to be one of the leading graphic artists of his era and he was also praised by George Bernard Shaw—Spare has remained largely unacknowledged in the major art histories. This may be because he was very much an occultist as well as an accomplished artist: Spare's art teems with magical imagery and he was briefly a member of both the Argenteum Astrum and the Ordo Templi Orientis. When he began to self-publish his illustrated magical books from 1905 onwards it became evident that his was an eccentric rather than a mainstream artistic talent, and there is little doubt that his unconventionality has pushed him to the sidelines of cultural history. He nevertheless remains a legendary figure in the 20th century western esoteric tradition and is one of its truly original thinkers, his approach to trance states and his technique of atavistic resurgence representing a unique contribution to the study of magical consciousness.

ZOS AND KIA

Spare postulated the existence of a primal, cosmic life-force which he termed *Kia*, and he believed that the spiritual and occult energies inherent in *Kia* could be channeled into the human organism, which he called Zos. As we will see, his technique of arousing these primal energies—an approach he termed *atavistic resurgence*—involved focusing the will on magical sigils, or potent individualized symbols, which in effect represented instructions to the subconscious. When the mind was in a "void" or open state—achieved, for example, through meditation, exhaustion or at the peak of sexual ecstasy—this was an ideal condition in which to direct magical sigils to the subconscious. Here they could "grow" in the seedbed of the mind until they became "ripe" and reached back down into the conscious mind. In such a way one could learn to manipulate one's own "psychic reality."

How did Austin Spare stumble upon his special approach to magical states of consciousness? Clearly it was no accident. His magic draws on a variety of inspirational sources, encompassing the mythic images of ancient Egypt, a fascination with the sexual energies of the subconscious mind,[2] and his close personal relationship with an unusual psychic mentor whom he always referred to simply as Mrs. Paterson.

Spare visited Egypt during World War One and was impressed by the magnetic presence of the classical gods depicted in monumental sculpture. He believed the ancient Egyptians understood very thoroughly the complex mythology of the subconscious mind:

> "They symbolized this knowledge in one great symbol, the Sphinx, which is pictorially man evolving from animal existence. Their numerous Gods, all partly Animal, Bird, Fish... prove the completeness of that knowledge...The cosmogony of their Gods is proof of their knowledge of the order of evolution, its complex processes from the one simple organism."

For Spare, impressions from earlier human incarnations and potentially all mythic impulses could be reawakened from the subconscious mind. The gods themselves could be regarded as a form of internal impetus. "All gods have lived (being ourselves) on earth," he wrote, "and when dead, their experience of Karma governs our actions in degree."

However, while the classical gods of ancient Egypt made a marked impression on him, Spare learnt his actual technique of trance activation from an elderly woman called Mrs. Paterson, who was a friend of his parents and used to tell his fortune when he was quite young. Mrs. Paterson claimed a psychic link with the witches of the Salem cult

Spare employed a technique of ecstasy which frequently combined active imagination and will with the climax of sexual orgasm.

and also appeared to have an extrasensory ability to project thought-forms. According to Spare, she was able to transform herself in his vision from being a "wizened old crone" to appearing quite suddenly as a ravishing siren, "creating a vision of profound sexual intensity and revelation that shook him to the very core."[3]

The archetypal female image recurs in all phases of Spare's artistic work—he was a master at depicting the sensuous naked female form—and the Universal Woman would become a central image in his mythology of the subconscious. In his definitive magical credo, *The Book of Pleasure*, he writes:

> "Nor is she to be limited as any particular 'goddess' such as Astarte, Isis, Cybele, Kali, Nuit, for to limit her is to turn away from the path and to idealize a concept which, as such, is false because incomplete, unreal because temporal."

Spare employed a technique of ecstasy which frequently combined active imagination and will with the climax of sexual orgasm. Spare believed that his magical sigils—representing symbols of the personal will—could be directed to the subconscious mind during the peak of sexual ecstasy since, at this special moment, the personal ego and the universal Spirit, or Kia, were united in a state of blissful, transcendent openness. "At this moment, which is the moment of generation of the Great Wish," writes Spare, "inspiration flows from the source of sex, from the primordial Goddess who exists at the heart of Matter...inspiration is always at a *void* moment."

Mrs. Paterson claimed a psychic link with the witches of the Salem cult and also appeared to have an extrasensory ability to project thought-forms.

Several of Spare's drawings depict the Divine Maiden leading the artist into the labyrinthine magical world. One of his most central works, *The Ascension of the Ego from Ecstasy to Ecstasy*, shows the Goddess welcoming Spare himself, who on this occasion appropriately has wings issuing forth from his head. Spare's "ego," or persona, is shown merging with an earlier animal incarnation and two forms transcend each other in the form of a primal skull. Spare clearly believed that he could retrace his earlier incarnations to the universal "Oneness of Creation," or *Kia*. According to Kenneth Grant, who knew the artist personally, Spare derived his formula of *atavistic resurgence* from Mrs. Paterson:

"She would visualize certain animal forms and—the language of the subconscious being pictographic not verbal—each form represented a corresponding power in the hidden world of causes. It was necessary only to 'plant' an appropriate sigil in the proper manner for it to awaken its counterpart in the psyche. Resurging from the depths it then emerged, sometimes masked in the form to do the sorcerer's bidding."[4]

Undoubtedly, one of Spare's major objectives in using the trance state was to tap energies which he believed were the source of genius. According to Spare, "...ecstasy, inspiration, intuition and dream...each state taps the latent memories and presents them in the imagery of their respective languages." And genius itself was "a directly resurgent atavism" experienced during the ecstasy of the Fire Snake—Spare's term for magical sexual arousal.

SPARE'S MAGICAL COSMOLOGY

Spare's unique magical approach took several years to unfold, however, and while ancient Egyptian deities and other pagan entities abound in his drawings, his first book, *Earth Inferno*—published as a limited edition in 1905—seems to have been strongly influenced by the Qabala and other elements of the western mystical tradition. Here Spare tends towards dualism, regarding the phenomena of life as generally either positive or negative, spiritual or materialistic, real or delusory. His concept of *Kia* has a clear counterpart in the transcendent *Ain Soph Aur* of the Qabala, and there is a strong emphasis on the superficial and essentially false nature of appearances. Man, says Spare, should learn to shed his dependency on material security, which inevitably shrouds him in the falsehoods of conventionality. Instead he should search beneath his "mask" to uncover the potentials of his subconscious.

In *Earth: Inferno* Spare is intent on exploring the relationship between *Zos* and *Kia*—between individual awareness and the Universal Consciousness or Primal Energy. He concurs with the traditional mystical perspective that the Godhead lies within, and by now has begun to embrace the view that he should follow the beckoning of the Universal Mother of Nature—the "Primitive Woman"—who can guide him pantheistically back to the Source of All Being. Spare has also taken a magical name to epitomize his mystical quest: *Zos vel Thanatos*.

Spare painting

experience the transcendence of *Kia*. Spare talks of this in a reflective way: "The barrenness of this life but remains, yet in despair we begin to see true light. In weakness we can become strong. Revere the *Kia* and your mind will become tranquil."

Spare already believed that every human being is innately divine, though most failed to perceive it. "I have not yet seen a man who is not God already," declares Spare provocatively. All man has to do is confront himself as he really is, and he will find God. This in turn involves the death of the ego, for it is the ego which isolates us from the realization of the unity which sustains all aspects of creation. For Spare, death could even be seen as a positive element because it destroyed the pretence of the personality. "From behind," writes Spare, "Destiny works with Death." And death is a precursor of enlightenment. In *Earth: Inferno* Spare presents us with a vision which draws on both the Qabala and the Major Arcana of the Tarot:

> On entering at the Gates of Life
> Lo, I behold Knowledge the Jester
> Capsizing the Feast of Illusion.
> The drawing aside false Truth
> He shewed us all—
> The World,
> The Flesh
> and
> The Being.
>
> This is the Alpha and Omega.

On the Qabalistic Tree of Life, Kether is the first emanation from the infinite formlessness of *Ain Soph Aur*—the first act of Creation "out of nothing"—and this is the highest level of spiritual awareness any human being can theoretically attain. It is shown symbolically on the Tarot path which leads to Kether as the Jester, or the Fool—the person who knows No-thing. The Jester is therefore the wisest among all men for he has reached the highest possible state of consciousness. He has experienced *Kia*, or transcendent reality.

All of this involves a relatively orthodox Western mysticism, but Spare was already developing his own individualized philosophy—a system of magical thought which he hoped would be free of dogma or "belief." As he saw it, Spare was now liberating his perception from the vices of the world— "fear many of his finest drawings as well as describing the essence of his new magical approach. Released, faith...science and the like"—and was preparing to plunge into his own personal unknown: *his inner self*.

In *Earth: Inferno* Spare makes it clear that the magical journey is one which is undertaken beyond "the parapet of the subconscious." Here Spare depicts the world of everyday awareness as a circular pathway along which visionless old men dodder hopelessly, looking to their candles for light while simultaneously remaining unaware of the "Great Beyond." Spare also shows us a depraved young man making lustful advances to the Universal Woman in his failure to see beyond her enticing outward appearance. This clearly involves an issue of insight: the Universal Woman is the wise and all-seeing Sophia of the Gnosis and is not to be mistaken for the Scarlet Woman of Babalon. Spare maintains that he himself did not commit this error: "I strayed with her, into the path direct. Hail! The Jewel in the Lotus!"

Nevertheless, at this stage Spare still finds himself caught between the inner and outer worlds: as he proclaims in his text, "I myself am Heaven and Hell." He has begun to encounter the dark night of the soul, and realizes that he will have to venture through the illusions of everyday life and the debris of the subconscious in order to

With this perspective in mind, he now produced a book which would be the magnum opus of his magical and artistic career. Entitled *The Book of Pleasure (Self Love): The Philosophy of Ecstasy*, it featured in 1913, *The Book of Pleasure* was privately published and included a number of important new concepts.[5]

It is true that prior to this time a number of occultists had been emphasizing the role of the "will" in magical procedures. Golden Dawn member Florence Farr had outlined the need for intense mental concentration in her articles in the *Occult Review* (1908), and Aleister Crowley had emphasized the need for both a spiritual and magical focus in his central dictum "Do what thou wilt shall be the whole of the Law." Austin Spare was briefly a member of Crowley's order, the Argenteum Astrum,[6] and he adopted this view too, but only up to a point; he then moved in a different direction.

SIGILS AND ECSTASY

In *The Book of Pleasure* Spare explored methods of concentrating the will. Since the degree of effectiveness of any action is related to a thorough understanding of the command behind the action, Spare developed a way of condensing his will so that it was more readily grasped *as a totality*. He did this by writing his "will" (=desire) in sentence form and by combining the basic letters, without repetition, into a pattern shape, or *sigil*. This could then be simplified and impressed upon the subconscious mind. Spare describes the process:

"Sigils are made by combining the letters of the alphabet simplified. Illustration: the word "Woman" in sigil form is:

The idea being to obtain a simple form which can be easily visualized at will..."[7]

What was to be done with the sigil once it was arrived at? And what was the significance of the sigil itself? We must first of all consider some related ideas.

As has been noted earlier, Spare spoke of Kia as the Supreme Principle in the Universe: it was akin to a dynamic, expanding Vortex of Energy, ever in a state of becoming. Most human beings were unaware of its full potential simply because they did not let it manifest within themselves ("Are we not ever standing on our own volcano?"). Instead, most people would shut themselves off by means of the various "insulating" devices employed by the ego. The only way in which the cosmic energy could manifest, or be aroused within, was by thoroughly opening oneself to it.

According to Austin Spare it was when the individual was in a state of mental "vacuity"—or ultimate openness—that Kia became "sensitive to the subtle suggestion of the sigil." This state could be arrived at by emptying the mind of all its thought-forms in an effort to visualize non-manifestation—for example, by meditating on blackness or emptiness. This in turn usually involved inducing a state of meditative trance in which the individual became oblivious of his surroundings as he focused only on the Inner Void.

Because we all proceed from the Godhead originally, argued Spare, it should be possible to track back through the mind to the First Cause. Like many mystics, Spare believed in reincarnation and he therefore regarded the subconscious mind as the "potential" source of all his own earlier physical embodiments or personalities, right back to the Beginning.[8] The psyche, as it were, consisted of a number of different layers—the resulting impressions of successive lives, most of which were subconscious. All of these were an aspect of the individual's own "reality":

> "Know the subconscious to be an epitome of all experience and wisdom, past incarnations as men, animals, birds, vegetable life, etc.: everything that has, and ever will, exist. Each being a stratum in the order of evolution. Naturally then, the lower we probe into these strata, the earlier will be the forms of life we arrive at: the last is the Almighty Simplicity."

Spare's intention was to gain knowledge of his concealed mental states through "regression" and eventually to lose his sense of self in an indescribably ecstatic union with Kia—whose energy he had now come to consider as basically sexual. The dark void of the mind, emptied of thought-forms through an act of concentration, could now be penetrated by the will by employing a sigil suitable for one's purpose. In theory, and according to one's ability, one could project the sigil to all possible recesses of the subconscious mind and in this way gain access to the entire sphere of the imagination.

Spare seems to have often preferred a third approach for bypassing the ego. This involved a state of self-induced trance in which the body became rigid, ceased to function, and underwent what Spare called "the Death Posture."

In reality this was much harder to achieve than the theory suggests. Obviously, it depended upon a number of crucial factors:

* An ability to derive a suitable sigil.

* An ability to prevent random thought-forms from unintentionally disturbing the "black void" and thus rendering "impure" the individual's attempt to become a pure vessel for the energies of Kia.

* An ability to reach further into the subconscious by totally renouncing the worldly context of one's aspirations. Ultimately this task would involve rejecting one's sense of humanity and eventually destroying the ego altogether—a most unworldly intention!

Naturally the last condition was the hardest to achieve. Spare acknowledged that "total vacuity" was difficult and unsafe for those "governed by morality, complexes etc."— that is to say; for all those governed by the "superstitions" and intellectual conceptions that most human beings surround themselves with. Indeed, Spare maintained that one would have to cast aside all contrived or finite rationalizations. He therefore tried to think of various situations where a sense of the rational was minimal or absent, and he emphasized three such circumstances:

The first of these was the state of physical exhaustion. If one had a "desire" or "concentrated thought" in this situation, Spare argued, the mind would become "worried, because of the non-fulfillment of such desire, and seek relief. By seizing this mind and living, the resultant vacuity would become sensitive to the subtle suggestion of the sigil." In other words, by exhausting the body, one made it impossible for normal mental intentions or commands to be carried out physically. The mind would then be forced into manifesting the concepts embodied in the magical sigil. Sheer exhaustion can be brought about in a number of ways, and this includes the climax of sexual orgasm itself. The tantric yoga technique of using orgasm as the "leaping off" point to visionary states of consciousness was well known in Western esoteric circles at the time Spare was writing.

The second method lay in exploiting the mental state of extreme disappointment, experienced, for example, when one lost all faith in a close friend, or when a cherished ideal had been destroyed. Spare felt that this state, too, could provide its own sense of opportunity:

> "When fundamental disappointment is experienced the symbol enshrining a quota of belief is destroyed. In some cases the individual is unable to survive the disillusionment. But if at such times the moment is seized upon and consciously experienced for its own sake, the vacuum attracts into itself the entire content of belief inherent in the person at the time of disappointment."

Spare is saying, in effect, that when we thoroughly lose faith in a belief or ideal, that we are given the option of transcending it, and transcendence of belief can lead to a state of ecstasy as we are drawn into the vortex of Kia.

However, Spare seems to have often preferred a third approach for bypassing the ego, a method which could be used for generalized changes in the personality and also for specifics. This involved a state of self-induced trance in which the body became rigid, ceased to function, and underwent what Spare called "the Death Posture." He describes a preliminary exercise designed to bring this about:

> "Gazing at your reflection (e.g. in a tall mirror) till it is blurred and you know not the gazer, close your eyes and visualize. The light (always an X in curious evolutions) that is seen should be held onto, never letting go, till the effort is forgotten; this gives a feeling of immensity (which sees a small form ∞ whose limit you cannot reach."

Spare considered that the Death Posture exercise should be practiced daily for best effect. "The Ego is swept up as a leaf in a fierce gale," he wrote. "In the fleetness of the indeterminable, that which is always about to happen, becomes its truth. Things that are self-evident are no longer obscure, as by his own will he pleases; know this as the negation of all faith by living it, the end of duality of consciousness." Here Spare is alluding to the Kia dimension, which is beyond time and space but which nevertheless represents the central basis for all life and human potential. Spare believed that achieving the state of openness necessary for Kia to manifest would also enable him to direct his magical will into the cosmic memory. By doing this he could acquire a full and detailed knowledge of the earlier life-forms which were both an aspect of oneself and of Kia as a whole. The Death Posture provided the possibility of a link; the magical sigil confirmed the possibility.

A sigil, as we have seen, is a visual condensation of the will. However, what we "will" can often be based on ideas of grandeur and self-deception. Spare points out that even if we imagine ourselves to be great this is not necessarily so, and all the desiring in the world cannot alter the fact. Spare notes: "Realization is not by the mere utterance of words... but by the living act. The will, the desire, the belief, lived as inseparable, become realization." Hoping for something won't help us achieve it: we must *live* it and *enact* it for it to become true.

According to Spare,

"Belief to be true must be organic and subconscious. The idea to be great can only become organic (i.e. 'true') at the time of vacuity and by giving it form. When conscious of the sigil form (any time but the magical) it should be repressed, a deliberate striving to forget it; by this it is active and dominates at the subconscious period; its form nourishes and allows it to become attached to the subconscious and become organic; that accomplished is its reality and realization. The individual becomes his concept of greatness."

"In summary, beliefs need to be 'organic' not theoretical; organic realities originate with Kia and lie dormant in the subconscious; we can use a sigil to embody our desire, command or will, and this should relate to what we want to do or become; the sigil can 'grow' in the subconscious but will lose its effect if it is consciously remembered; and, finally, the sigil will eventually manifest as a 'true' aspect of the personality since it comes from within."

Spare also relates this process to the faculty of creativity: "All geniuses have active subconsciousnesses and the

less they are aware of the fact, the greater their accomplishments. The subconscious is exploited by desire reaching it." This implies that geniuses not born, could be made—an idea he shared with Aleister Crowley.

Spare's system of implanting sigils was capable of different levels of application, and from an occult perspective it could be applied both to high and low magic. While Spare often used his sigils to embody transcendent commands his system could also be used for comparatively mundane purposes. Kenneth Grant tells of a situation where Spare needed to move a heavy load of timber without assistance. A sigil was required which involved great strength, so Spare constructed a suitable sentence: "This is my wish, to obtain the strength of a tiger." Sigilized, this sentence would be:

Grant goes on to say: "Spare closed his eyes for a while and visualizes a picture which symbolized a wish for the strength of tigers [i.e. the final sigil above]. Almost immediately he sensed an inner response. He then felt a tremendous upsurge of energy sweep through his body. For a moment he felt like a sapling bent by the onslaught of a mighty wind. With a great effort of will, he steadied

A sigil, as we have seen, is a visual condensation of the will.

himself and directed the force to its proper object. A great calm descended and he found himself able to carry the load easily."

Kenneth Grant makes it clear from his account that firstly dormant energy was awakened and then it was focused into a specialized activity. This was not always Spare's method, for in his more far-reaching atavistic resurgences he allowed the influx of Kia to obsess him. His mind would become flooded with preternatural influences and there was no semblance of control.[9] Spare, himself, considered this type of atavistic activity to be an act of bravery:

"Strike at the highest.... death is failure. Go where thou fearest not. How canst thou be great among men? *Cast thyself forth!* Retrogress to the point where knowledge ceases in that Law becomes its own spontaneity and freedom... This is the new atavism I would teach: Demand of God equality—Usurp!"

Spare's method is thus clearly an act of stealing fire from heaven. His preferred method, the Death Posture, involved the "death" of the ego through the negation of conscious thought—a positive, but "unconscious" thrust towards transcendence.

What is unusual about Spare's cosmology and his occult trance techniques is that he believed in regression, rather than in the more conventional mystical concept of "conscious evolution." Indeed, he redefines his idea of magical evolution:

> "The Law of Evolution is retrogression of function governing progression of attainment, i.e. the more wonderful our attainments are, *the lower in the scale of Life the function that governs them.* Man is complex, and to progress, must become simplified.

> This means that because more and more manifestations of Kia are appearing in the world all the time through reincarnation, as the Source of Creation expands 'outwards', the true magical direction is 'inwards' or more specifically 'backwards' to the First Cause."

Austin Spare's approach to magical perception is virtually unique within the western esoteric tradition. As with Aleister Crowley and Dion Fortune, he has retained an enthusiastic following to the present day. However in Spare's case, aspects of this renewed interest appear to be of a lower calibre than one might have hoped for. So-called "Chaos magicians" now claim to be utilizing Spare's sigil methods and an influential work titled *Practical Sigil Magic* by Frater U.D., first published in 1990, purports to extend the practical applications of Spare's trance formulations. However, these practitioners have appeared to fall far short of Spare's magical vision and have seized hold only of its pragmatic "low magic" applications. While Frater U.D. writes that "sigil magic is primarily success magic," Spare is embracing much wider realms than magical self-gratification: his is a unique response to the cosmos. It remains to be seen whether the resurgent interest in Austin Spare will be deflected by a trivialization of his unique contribution to the exploration of magical consciousness. ⛢

Endnotes

1. For further information on Spare's life, readers are referred to F. W. Letchford, *From the Inferno to Zos*, First Impressions, Oxford 1995, Gavin W. Semple, *Zos Kia,* Fulgur, London 1995, Geraldine Beskin and John Bonner, *Austin Osman Spare 1886–1956: The Divine Draughtsman*, Morley Gallery catalogue, London, September 1987, and Kenneth Grant & Steffi Grant, *Zos Speaks*, Fulgur, London 2000.
2. Spare was familiar with the writings of Freud, Krafft-Ebing and Havelock Ellis.
3. See Austin Osman Spare, *The Book of Pleasure*, privately published, London 1913, pp.52–53 (reissued in facsimile edition by 93 Publishing, Montreal 1975).
4. See Gavin W. Semple, op.cit, p.7
5. This had been preceded by *A Book of Satyrs* (c.1911), which contained "satires" on the Church, politics, officialdom and other "follies." It is not a major work.
6. Spare became a member of the Argenteum Astrum in 1910 after contributing some drawings to Crowley's occult journal *The Equinox*.
7. See *The Book of Pleasure*, p.50.
8. Spare believed that the self lived "in millions of forms" and that it was obliged to experience "every conceivable thing"—all the infinite possibilities inherent in the manifested universe. Any incomplete existence or situation required a reincarnation to finalize it or make it whole. In his own words: "I have incarnated that which I need to rationalize." Spare also thought that by exploring the recesses of the mind, one would undoubtedly uncover past incarnations, "for whatever is attained is but a re-awakening of an earlier experience of the body."
9. In his autobiography *Memories, Dreams, Reflections*, Carl Jung warned against the possibility of allowing the symbolic contents of dreams and visions to be indulged in, rather than checked. Jung believed that the perception of dual, but intermingled, levels of awareness—in Spare's case a fusion of atavisms and everyday reality—could lead to schizophrenia. One wonders whether Spare would agree.

VIRTUAL MIRRORS IN SOLID TIME
The Prophetic Portals of Austin Osman Spare

Spare automatic drawing from the collection of Genesis Breyer P-Orridge

"Since all phenomena (or phenomenally appearing things) which arise, present no reality in themselves, they are said to be of the noumena (in other words, they are of the Voidness, regarded as the noumenal background or Source of the physical universe of the phenomena). Though not formed into anything, yet they give shape to everything. Thus it is that phenomena and noumena are ever in union, and said to be of one nature. They are, like ice and water, reflection and mirror, two aspects of a single thing."

–The Seven Books of Wisdom—Tibetan text.

In the case of a mirror, there is a third aspect: the subject/viewer. Mirrors reveal and conceal; their mystery permanent, their hints at doorways, windows, points of entry and thresholds just out of reach of our conscious minds. TIME (The Imaginary Mass Emits). Image. Idea. There can be no separation, scientifically or subjectively. The atavistic face gazes down into a crystal pool. Ice-cold water. Grunts. A hand shatters the image; fear gaunt and haunting passes across, a shadowy cloud, and through all TIME; that moment can persist, be reclaimed.

"What is Time, but a variety of one thing?

–Austin Osman Spare

These moments of time accumulate, are listed under memory in our modern synapses and are posited as always retrievable, amorphous. Nothing is forgotten, all is permitted. In a stinking cave, muttering babies scream and scratch, furs undulate in copulation. In one corner, bright-eyed first marks are daubed on a wall.

She was a medium, but her guides were not the "New Age" romantic, and patronizing icons of native peoples and tribes. Not just Indian Chiefs, Pharaohs, Tibetan Rinpoches or aborigines. They were more like the creatures of Clive Barker's Hellraiser visions, or the demons in *Evil Dead*.

They are marks to function, marks of place, of time. They are marks to draw results and persist beyond one human lifetime. Instinct has arisen, snake-like, coiling its self into intuition and suggested the very power of suggestion. No one noted down from a book this process, it grew from watching the elements, closeness to life-sources, death-forces that modern persons are divorced from. On this damp stone there is a curve, it is land, horizon, ejaculation, movement.

"Magick consists in seeing and willing beyond the next horizon."

–The Sar

Mrs. Paterson stares down. Penciled into existence. It is her as she was when she took Austin Osman Spare at fourteen years old and initiated him into the art of sexual magick and a power-full system of sorcery (a primal oral tradition preserved through female bloodlines) that she had rediscovered and regenerated through her covert communion across time with systems and techniques that grew from a most animalistic and pure union of instinct and inherited DNA encryptions. This woman knew, and she taught Spare, how to travel through time and just how malleable and manipulable a form of energy and matter it was. She also instructed Spare in techniques that could empower him to remain present in life, after an apparent physical death. She was a medium, but her guides were not the "New Age" romantic, and patronizing icons of native peoples and tribes. Not just Indian Chiefs, Pharaohs, Tibetan Rinpoches or aborigines. They were more like the creatures of Clive Barker's Hellraiser visions, or the demons in *Evil Dead*. They were the deepest, most atavistic and raw representations of the alien that we can experience. Equivalent, if you will, to a seriously hard-core DMT entity confrontation. Mrs. Paterson understood a most particular secret. Her medium was her self. She was quite able to travel through mirrors and throughout time.

There is a drawing in my possession by Spare, a pencil and gouache, finished in 1928. The main figure is Mrs. Paterson. Coming from behind her head, making a blister

in a shimmering green-penciled aura is a half completed face. It belongs to no one, everyone. It is she at times, it is cavalier and it is also Austin Osman Spare. This one picture contains all the secrets Spare never wrote down and his books are thorough, precise, and often opaque. Spare appears in the bottom right-hand corner, represented as he projects he will look as an old man, eyes closed, concentrated, manifesting, it would seem, the other beings in the picture. Remarkably, his projection of his older self is uncannily accurate.

What Spare is doing is "tricking" us. All his writings are symbolic; they were never intended to be taken literally, as illustrations, on any level. His writings are primarily journals, decorative encryptions of basic techniques of travel. But they are appendices to the real work. This special trick was to convince everybody that his drawings, paintings, and images were symbolic, fantastical products of his imagination. They are in fact the essence of his sorcery. Like all great sorcerers, he hid his central secret in an apparently commonplace medium. What we discover in this key picture is that he is actually kneeling. It is actually a "photographic" record of his prediction of both his own bodily death, and his worship of Mrs. Paterson as the keeper of immortality.

Spare made consistent use, for very specifically sex magical reasons, of late middle-aged prostitutes who would normally be considered "brash" and heavily made-up.

Spare made consistent use, for very specifically sex magical reasons, of late middle-aged prostitutes who would normally be considered "brash" and heavily made-up. Women who could, in his mind, represent Mrs. Paterson at the age she seduced and instructed him, and thus charge more powerfully his sexual magick rituals and sigils as a result. Just as the sorcerer repeats elements of ritual over and over again, and uses the same magical tools, incenses, incantations and so on repeatedly to achieve a cumulative effect, so Spare recreated a virtual sorceress to revisit, the precise intersections of time and space that she had imprinted in his brain. Through this reputedly sordid, but actually visionary method of sexual magick, he was able to return at will to a potent portal, an access point into the matter of time itself, and then, even deeper, into what we can only call timelessness, though outside time might be a more accurate way to articulate the state. These women were close enough to Mrs. Paterson in cosmetic physical appearance and characteristics to be used as a focusing visual key enabling him to be accelerated at the moment of orgasm, just like a particle accelerator, into direct, inter-dimensional contact with her, and all the infinite previous hers that had ever existed. This is more easily understood contemporaneously, now, in a post-DMT experiential environment. In other words, DMT would be a very good equivalent experience of what this catapulting might feel like. However Spare could recreate this at will, and via Will To... over and over again, with deep lucidity and in a state of sexual intoxication, rather than bio-chemical intoxication. A drug free splitting of the atoms of time!

When Mrs. Paterson died, he was able to take a particular aspect of her life source and literally preserve it still "living" into this, and one or two other pictures. This is not to be misunderstood as in any way vampiric. That is not what we're dealing with here. This is a much more deeply fundamental sorcery. Spare is consensually keeping open a portal of connection between the primal inter-dimensional knowledge and an entity that was represented by the physical manifestation within linear time by Mrs. Paterson's existence on this particular Earth, at a particular allotted moment. In the same mysterious way that, if you will, a mirror can contain all that it faces in what seems an equally "real" world, so Spare's pictures can hold the entirety of the images and entities that he represents in them.

They are there. The frame is exactly intended to be experienced as, and function as, the edges of a mirror, although, because it is a plastic, more fixed medium, we often cannot see around the inside edges by moving, as we can with a mirror. As we cannot all ways change the amount, and depth of what we see simply by moving, as we can with a mirror. Do not be fooled by mundane physics. There are specific periods when, remarkably, the opposite is true, and these images do indeed become exactly the same as mirrors, representing an entire portal into a parallel omniverse. Further, I would suggest, indeed insist, based upon my own personal experiences, and those of many other colleagues who have acted as controls, and/or guinea pigs in my experiments with these pictures to act as confirmation, or dis-

missal of the actuality, that these pictures do not just become virtual mirrors. They become living portals that animate, through which entities can travel, accessing our "world" and bidding us into theirs.

When Mrs. Paterson died, he fixed her in this picture. We see him. He sinks into her chest, is absorbed, they rise together, androgynous, genderless, both their faces, and all their ages superimposed to create one alien being. One interdimensional entity. He has drawn himself dying, conjuring himself into this picture in advance of that event, so that he may always return. Like the Cocteau character crossing back and forth through the mirror.

They rise together, androgynous, genderless, both their faces, and all their ages superimposed to create one alien being.

"Art can contradict Science."

–Austin Osman Spare

"Art is the truth we have realized of our belief"

–Austin Osman Spare

"Do you see those flowers growing on the sides of the abyss whose beauty is so deadly and whose scent is so disturbing? Beware..."

–de Guatia

In these sorcerous images, these his purest incantations through art, Spare uses a graphic skill and technique second to none. Yet his most commonly seen works can appear deliberately fast and loose. The nearest modern parallel would be Salvador Dali, who could suggest perfection and hyper-reality in a few precisely placed marks and intersections, and through his works worship his own personal sorceress, Gala. Dali's photo-realistic technique is accurate in an unearthly way, too, and Dali uses delirium and dislocation of the senses to catapult himself, and us, through the parameters of madness and obsession into his personal landscape and environment. Dali occasionally masturbated into his paints, particularly painting the leather strap across Hitler's back, and made good use of the canvas as a virtual mirror viewed from one static position. I would argue that Dali, despite his genius, was a naive, struggling to describe glimpses and fragments of vision, with an ad hoc quasi-magical perception and aspiration. Dali did not build, though he hungered to, a system as unique, primal, timeless, and fully administered by informed, cumulative, and inter-dimensional arcane knowledge as Spare. Spare knew all too well what

VIRTUAL MIRRORS IN SOLID TIME: The Prophetic Portals of Austin Osman Spare

Spare drawing from *Thee Starlit Mire*, Temple Press, 1989

he was doing, conjuring, and building. A method of physical, and neurological immortality, a means to step outside time. Dali really wanted to, but remained finally restrained by his inability to travel beyond use of his imagination. For Dali, the mirror was a solid barrier into which he could gaze, but not travel. Spare was the very material of the mirror, the destroyer of its boundaries, or limitations, and finally usurped every definition of mirrorness creating a virtual portal that accessed all moments of time past, present, future, none, in every possible and impossible infinite combination. Time is, you see, a solid through which all passes, all is seen from a vantage point. As we learn to move our point of perception, so we act like a lens, or a mirror's surface viewed from above. Light, thought, life, passes through us, expanding outwards. We can place our mirrors anywhere, perceive them from any direction, thus we are potentially everywhere, in every possible time and every possible dimension. All travel is possible. We are an amorphous infinite density of matter. The matter is time. It is all a matter of time. Time is malleable and thus both the portal and the means of travel. We can leave, we can return, we can cease to exist. This is the "virtual mirror" of Spare. These are the prophetic portals. But they do not prophesy art. They prophesy an end to materiality. A disintegration, a dissipation of our corporeality beyond anything so far confessed in the small wooden box of physics.

"The future is in the past, but it is not wholly contained in the present."

–Hoene-Wronski

Brion Gysin was another such artist of the future, another such alchemist and sorcerer who used art to create time and inter-dimensional travel. He used a different style. More abstract, more directly concerned with encryption, coding and decoding, and with a clear appreciation of post-linguistic magick. "Rub Out The Word" he would emphasis. He too was absolutely aware of the implication of his experiments and their functions. Both Gysin and William Burroughs accepted as a given that the central power of their works was to trick time and through another system of cumulative effect, manipulate and navigate mortality and all sources of pre-recorded life; brain; entity; location and the process of control that locks us out of this inviolate humane right to transcend physicality. Gysin was a practicing magician first, and actually described at length to me in Paris his longtime practice of mirror staring, and the incredible melting of consensus reality that resulted for both him, and many others of the Beats. He suggested that there are "hot spots" in cultural engineering, and vehicles of convenience that accelerate the inevitable for those reckless and/or courageous enough to risk all for a possibility of disincarnation, of leaving behind the host physical body forever in a necessary transmutation into otherness, alien being, that must be the only valid goal of any of us if forward motion and discovery are truly our agenda. In traditional Western occulture this letting go of all preconceptions, all expectations, all value systems, all inherited moral imprints, all concepts of self-preservation, and all distinctions is referred to as "The Abyss."

"See a cliff, jump off."

–Old TOPY Proverb

Both Spare and Gysin lived to pursue, and attain, new dimensions. They understood the hunger to pursue successful systems of sorcery, not knowledge. This alone made overt collaboration with magical groups impossible, where the need for nostalgic elitism, power implied by academic recall, and self-image measured by the length of one's bookshelf far too often camouflage mere self-aggrandizement, and the essence of motivation is

He consciously used his books, his twisted Beardsley-esque graphics and his atavistic writings to attract our interest after his physical death.

the servility of others. Gysin incorporated tape-recorders, permutations, projections, trance music, mathematical formulae. Spare incorporated his own body, sexuality, and dimensional fluidity. Both were prophets of portals of virtuality and developments in quantum neurology that later became possible, and, as egalitarian access to cyberspace and other synthetic worlds expands globally, now become at the very least more likely, I would propose: inevitable. The world we appreciate in a mirror. That world where as we get close, appears to be a large, and equally as "real" as this supposedly more physical consensus reality; and the world of Spare, where the frame of the image is arbitrary, where creatures, and perceptual environments are frozen in a precise cryogenic graphic. These worlds are mere precursor of the apparently limitless, and multi-dimensional possibilities heralded by the microchip. The century wills to be remembered eventually as the century during which the cut-up, the splitting of the atom by relativity; of the mind by psychedelic compounds and of linear thinking by cultural nihilism were the primary themes. Spilling over into social fragmentation, online alienation and a data-glut

Sound far-fetched? Well, personal anecdote, take it or leave it: Many different guests would suddenly gasp and say, did you know that the faces in that painting have "come alive"?

Spare self-portrait (detail)

that by its very scale, insists on acceleration of response by our brains, and a highly developed perceptual skill of instant, and arbitrary assembly "to see what is really there" as W. S. Burroughs has stated.

Spare was aware that mystery and magick, in themselves, generate at the very least a morbid fascination, and reaction in human persons. He consciously used his books, his twisted Beardsley-esque graphics and his atavistic writings to attract our interest after his physical death. Not for reasons of ego. I would contend that it was to reactivate his "mind" and re-animate his psyche. Sound far-fetched? Well, personal anecdote, take it or leave it:

One of the Spare paintings that I used to own (now in the collection of Blondie's Chris Stein) was called *The Ids*. Every New Year's Eve strange things would occur. Most noticeably, the two faces of Spare himself that faced each other would re-animate. Many different guests would suddenly gasp and say, did you know that the faces in that painting have "come alive"? Or "They are arguing." None of these observers knew who Spare was, or any of his, or my own, ideas about him. Eventually I checked and found that Spare died on New Year's Eve, 1956. A medium called Madame Bruna, also, on a social visit, was shocked and disturbed by the "Mrs. Paterson" image. In fact, it was this repeated witnessing of the faces becoming real, moving, talking, changing, that led to the thoughts in this essay. In the case of the "Mrs. Paterson" picture, nobody felt anything malevolent. Just a powerful experience of people "trapped in a mirror." *The Ids*, however, was different. Something one could only think of as "bad" always happened when it animated. It got so predictable and incontrovertible that I took to putting it in a cupboard, facing the wall for a period before and after New Years Eve each year. The last phenomenon was particularly odd. Before traveling abroad I arranged for two people to be caretakers of my house in Brighton. I warned them, almost like in a fable such as "Hansel and Gretel" that they must not touch, move, or hang up the Spare painting *The Ids*, which was in the loft space of the house, facing the wall. I told them, "It might sound superstitious or stupid, but please trust me on this one." I guess, inevitably, they felt this as a challenge and chose to not only turn the picture facing outwards in the loft, but to spend a night staring at it and sleeping in the same space. Apparently, as they tell it, after an hour or so, the picture seemed to fill the room. Spare argued with himself, as usual. Then a new thing happened. The central face of one woman (there were three women's faces above Spare's heads) came alive too. The picture seemed to grow into a huge mirror, filling the visual perception of one whole end of the loft. The room seemed to fill with green mist, and then holding her hand out, this woman walked out of the "painting" and came towards them. In the inanimate painting, the heads are floating in a green field, no bodies. They have heavy make up on, like the prostitutes Spare favored for his psycho-sexual sorcery. Both people panicked, and ran from the loft, locking the door behind them. From that time on,

The picture seemed to grow into a huge mirror, filling the visual perception of one whole end of the loft. The room seemed to fill with green mist, and then holding her hand out, this woman walked out of the "painting" and came towards them.

various destructive events affected the house, and them. They had let loose, in classic horror film style, an entity, that was malevolent, and with its own agenda? One of the two people became an alcoholic; both had mental breakdowns. By the way, Chris Stein was aware of this side of the painting's history when he purchased it.

Spare had been shrewd enough to make all his secrets non-verbal, and non-linear. Not one explanation of these secrets is contained overtly in his writings. He was, in the best covert cultural traditions, working for himself alone. Only the atavistic hinting, and the "Virtual Mirror" drawings and paintings can articulate, and bear witness to, his phenomenal achievements.

"The Universe is a creative process carried on by man's imagination, an operative power capable of becoming more supple, more animate."

–Teilhard de Chardin

What is happening in these certain key pictures? I would propose a few speculations. All ideas have an image. We were originally an hieroglyphic species, before the restrictive linguistic and alphabetical systems we use now were adopted. Adopted I might add, purely for reasons of control, and the compression of both vision and potential in all of us. All the materials used to create and fix an image are material. They are formed of patterns of atoms and molecules, charged by certain energies that hold their specific clusters together in some way. Modern psychology also tends to accept that ideas are material entities, like animals and plants. All mythological ideas, Jung suggests,

are essentially real and far older than any philosophy. They originated in primal perceptions, correspondences and experiences. The catalytic element that regenerates a reaction between entotic ideas and a spectator and that favors parapsychological events is the presence of an active archetype. In the specific case of Spare's virtual mirror art, this element can be anything from an obvious glyph (condensing and compressing a desire), a non-decorative aesthetic arrangement, or in the most intense "portal" works, an invisible charge of energy which somehow calls the deepest, instinctual layers of the psyche into action. The archetype is a borderline phenomenon, an acausal connecting principle, closest in explanation to deliberately controlled, self-conscious synchronicity. When Spare describes in certain of his texts "Self-Love," if you will, as the engine of his sorcery, I believe he means self-conscious, yet ego-less. When he uses the word chaos, which he profoundly championed from the start of the century, he is leaving a key evidentiary clue and amusing himself. Austin Osman Spare's "Chaos" is both a signature, and a signpost into future time. (ChDVH (CH) = JOY=23) Thus we get CH-A.O.S.—both his name, and his confession of secret sorcery.

"Art is the instinctive application of the knowledge latent in the subconscious."

–Austin Osman Spare

After Mrs. Paterson died, Spare was waiting to be inside her again, fused with her sexual-magical energy. Inside her also, in the sense of two liquids mixing to create a third amalgam. Two consciousnesses as well, the Third Mind of Brion Gysin. This is not romantic fiction. This is a prediction of some of the inter-dimensional forays that are subscribed to very convincingly by Terence McKenna and other such botanical voyagers. In this key picture by Spare, what we are really seeing is both his projection into the actual future moment of his own death, and the way Mrs. Paterson looked exactly at the moment of her death overlaid. His aim in all his sorcery was to reunite his spirit and hers, captured within the dimensions of his artworks so that through this process they could both quite literally, live forever—an interesting twist on the idea of great art making the artist immortal! In this case I mean immortal quite literally. They do still live. Just as our concepts and assumptions about reality, and varieties of perception have been forever revised by the advent of virtual

Spare drawing from *Thee Starlit Mire*, Temple Press, 1989

reality and quantum psychology, so our concepts of linear existence are confounded by the manifestation held in stasis in these virtual mirrors.

Keep in mind Cocteau's "mirrors" passing through to the "other side" where different rules of physics and continuity apply. We are finally accepting that everything is truly in constant flux, that the malleability of all matter and all constructs is not just theoretical, that time is equally an energy and matter as flesh, and that projected images and virtual worlds are as valid and vibrant as the basic inherited consensus possibility that we tend to arrive trapped, in squealing and pissing from our mother's vaginas. We are witnessing the realization that everything everyone says is true. That everything believed is real. That bodies are mere vehicles for transporting our brain and that mortality is primarily a philosophical control process. Why, my children, even that dear old anarchist construct "The Bible" was assigned the alchemical message more significant than Pat Robertson might choose to consider.

"Have I not said that faith can move mountains?"

– Some old prophet or another

"The marvelous is not rare, incredulity is stronger than miracles"

– Jaques Rigaut

Apart from the more dramatic animations already mentioned, many unprompted witnesses have been shocked to see Mrs. Paterson's eyes close, open, cry or her whole head turn. Quite literally a living portrait. Magick makes "dreams" real, makes the impossible possible, focuses the Will to... Throughout occult circles in all ages crystal, water, polished metal, mirrors of all types have been used for oracular purposes. Spare's massive achievement is that he recognized the potential of art, of image, to be the most powerful magical mirror of all. A window in time. An interface with death. An interdimensional modem. In his art he captures not just an image but a life force. What seems to happen is that the individual's consciousness

contained within the art remains dormant in this reality until they come into contact with the minds of certain others, or as an intersection with linear TIME sets in motion a preprogrammed "software" sequence of interactions. Primal, atavistic "aboriginal" peoples knew this. Sometimes facilitated with botanical catalysts they would invest immense and potentially limitless powers in specific totem images and glyphs or sigils. This use of the image as scrying mirror and as neurological nuclear energy is very different as a function of "art" to the post-patronage, post-craftsperson 21st century norm of Art, with that horribly big "A." In contemporary elitist art you actually don't get anything much back except aesthetics. You certainly don't get mummification and time travel! But we must never forget that all art grew from sorcery and from the concealment of Gnostic, and alchemical procedures from those who would be "King." Art was once synonymous with, and a direct aspect of, Magick. It was functional, and it was dedicated to the processing of immortality, and the opening and preservation of portals. (By the way, I would argue that "cyberspace" (or the Psychosphere as I would prefer it was called), is an extension of this perception and function in just the same way and we are just glimpsing the beginnings of the somewhat cack-handed access we've so far realized.)

All mythological ideas, Jung suggests, are essentially real and far older than any philosophy.

Anyway ... Spare achieved the forgotten, that which vested interests in all status quos considered impossible, even blasphemous; a two-way communication where HIS image reacts to and with the viewer. It has a life of its own. The nearest parallel, a virtual mirror in which you can see another world, one that we cannot touch, the glass remaining solid and frustrating us. What this energy held within his images is doing is transcending the barriers of observed time so that what we are seeing is a five-dimensional object or image. This form of energy wills to have existed at all times, and wills to exist at all times.

An objective (Hah!) and critical survey of the available data would establish that perceptions occur as if in part there were no space, in part no time. Space and time are not only the most immediate "certainties" for us, they are the most misleading, doomed to be discredited as separate and abstracted states imminently. They are also usually considered empirical certainties too since everything observable is said to happen as though it occurred in space and time. In the face of this overwhelming "certainty" it is understandable that "reason" should have the greatest difficulty in granting validity to the peculiar nature of "delirious" phenomena, or paranormal events. But anyone who does some amount of justice to the facts cannot but admit that their apparent space-timelessness is their most essential quality. The fact that we are totally unable to imagine a form of existence without space or time by no means proves that such an existence is in itself impossible, and, therefore, just as we cannot draw from an appearance of space-timeless-ness, any absolute conclusion about a possible space-timeless form of existence, so we are not entitled to conclude from the apparent space-time quality of our perception that there is no form of existence without

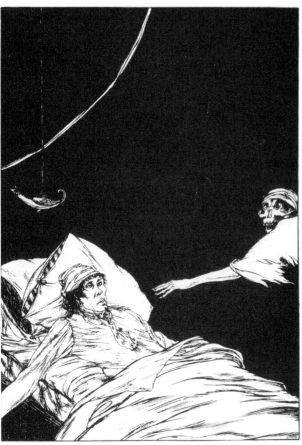

Spare drawing from *Thee Starlit Mire*, Temple Press, 1989

space and time. I would imagine though that any of you fortunate enough to have had a particularly enervating moment of psychedelic experience will be more empathetic to the speculative space-timeless state!

In contemporary elitist art you actually don't get anything much back except aesthetics. You certainly don't get mummification and time travel!

Just as "physics" now tends to allow for "limitedness of space," a relativization, it is beginning with Catastrophe Theory/Fuzzy Geometry/Chaos Mathematics and other quantum disciplines to posit a "limitedness" of both TIME and causality. In short, nothing is fixed, "It's official!"—the possibilities alone are endless.

"Conscious looking is a search for verification of the notions that impel the search, and all ways has a circular mirroring element within it."

–Genesis P-Orridge

In Spare's most critical images, it seems a medium has been synthesized whereby the essence that survives death but is usually beyond our communication has been transmitted into an object that we are familiar with, i.e. a painting or drawing, and we are therefore familiar with trying to interpret or receive information from. Because of the familiarity of the medium of painting, we don't put up paranormal, skeptical, or too many emotional barriers. We expect to try and see what the artist wanted to present, wanted to communicate (though personally I see little of that in contemporary "deceptual art" as Brion Gysin used to say) If Spare said he was going to capture himself within the frame and canvas and facilitate immortality—or at least, a very different medium of mortality, demonstrating "life" after apparent death—most observers would switch off, or scream ridicule tinged with an innate fear of the unknowable. There would be an interference with the transmission, because Spare seduces us by allowing us to dupe ourselves into assuming what we view is an artwork, a picture, when in fact it is a "photograph" of a mirror of an actual, or virtual reality, a mortality software if you will to, because of the self-deception we remain open-minded. This open-mindedness is essential to the functioning of the sorcery at the critical time intersections that animate it (New Year's Eve for example) and increases the chances that the phenomenon of actual physical changes.

The observer, if fortunate enough, wills to see that which many of us in this rightly post-existentialist age choose not to believe in or to be heartily skeptical of, namely living,

In short, nothing is fixed, "It's official!"–the possibilities alone are endless.

Spare drawing from *Thee Starlit Mire*, Temple Press, 1989

neuro-visual screen of the brain. In this key Spare's work centered on Mrs. Paterson and executed in 1928, her eyes are neither open, nor shut, and this is true in many of Spare's virtual mirror works. They are neither rejecting the possibility of seeing a captured "soul," nor openly inviting it. This half-open, half-shut limbo suggests responsibility lies with the viewer to choose whether or not to commune with any frisky entities that manifest. In fact, on many occasions an interesting further mutation frequently occurs. The eyes become alien, not dissimilar from the Schwa portrayal, as if coated with an almost reptilian film of non-human skin. This alien quality seems to be amplified by Spare's technique of painting himself old when he was in fact young, and of course later, painting himself young when he was by then old. Forming an infinite envelope of time, in effect, Spare moves back and forth through time as he succeeds in presenting us, via the image with the apparently impossible, or miraculous—immortality. Sorcery has all ways made effective and functional use of the process of reversal to confound expectation even at the root of the most sacred and central scientific assumptions.

The psyche, in its deepest reaches, seems well able to participate in an existence beyond the web of space and time This dimension is often dubbed "eternity" or "infinity" yet it actually seems to behave—if we for the moment take Spare's art as representative and more vitally, functional and in no way symbolic—as either a one way or two

moving, changing images of a post-death entity or brain-essence. This is all as acutely programmed as any software, except—Allah be praised—it's not binary, nor an either/or program, which probably explains Spare's success, as surprise surprise we do not and never did, live in an either/or universe and all binary systems are fallacious, serving only to block the righteous evolution and maximizing of the potential of our species, a species programmed in its DNA for only one ultimate function, to transcend all need for a physical body, fixed in linear time and space. You will see this entity reacting to you; it receives and transmits direct into your conscious five senses. It must also be transmitting directly into your other levels of consciousness too, and your other hyper-real senses. Presumably we transmit back to what is there, so what is there wills to change by absorption over the years as it reacts to, and is triggered by, all the various observers. All these factors mingle and mix, and mutate. Mutation, after all being the sincerest form of flattery.

The "soul" (advert for the brain as Dr. Timothy Leary once suggested to me) is generally said to be visible through the eyes, the mirror of the soul. The eyes, jewels of the actual brain exposed directly to the outside, the

All these factors mingle and mix, and mutate. Mutation, after all being the sincerest form of flattery.

way mirror dependent for its operation upon a translation of the unconscious into a communicable image that bonds the actual atomic structures of the graphic image with its driving forces unlocked from the unconscious into a fixed or mobile source of power dependent upon previous viewers, and with more critically, our own individual abilities to interface directly with it.

"Accept nothing, assume nothing, always look further, be open-eyed as well as open-minded and don't kid yourself"
—Genesis P-Orridge

Keeping the speculation simple for now, if in theory, as all matter is actually vibrating tiny particles with lots of groovy names; it's just possible that we could walk through walls. Then it is also theoretically possible to lock clusters of the same particles and energy into the fabric of an image giving it the ability to move, change, alter and animate its content. The only gap of credibility being first hand experience. We don't usually believe anything until it happens to us. We only really know what we have experienced; belief is rooted in recognition.

Every now and then as I type, you'll not be surprised to

Science cannot tell us why Spare's images can alter, why his faces change, eyes open and close, colors vary.

know, I wonder if this is going to sound too "out there" or "crazed" as you the observer read it. I already know it gets a little opaque—for which my less than humble apologies—and of course it assumes you know what the fuck I am referring to vis a vis the paintings themselves. Oh well, tough. This subject leads us to a bigger "picture" a discussion of the parallels between virtual space and the creation of deities, immortality and the psychosphere from a Processean perspective that will to arrive on another occasion. But I digress... Imagination opens to synthesis larger than the sum total of reason. New images reflect more than logical synthesis can produce. There is a radical discontinuity in every truly creative idea or discovery.

"It's all a matter of TIME..."

–Genesis P-Orridge

Projection direct from image to viewer involves more than the logical mode of thinking. An idea cannot exist separate from an image. For example, the Virgin Mary image embodies the idea of "compassion" perhaps. A Goddess or God is a figurative image of an idea. Images are the root language of social freedom and self-expansion as much as words and alphabets are the roots of social control and self-limitation. Science attempts to explain the omniverse objectively (yes, even now most of them) therefore it cannot explain "art" or more particularly the unique effects or phenomena Spare generates within "art." This is not a possible function of Science, although to be fair Science is, now, thankfully, beginning to include the point of viewing in its theories to great effect. Science cannot tell us why Spare's images can alter, why his faces change, eyes open and close, colors vary. Photographs are said to steal "souls" and they certainly capture a moment in time and freeze it. So do the images and oracles of "art," for art was originally revelatory, prophetic, functional, shamanic. Fully integrated into every detail and aspect of life.

"He who transcends Time escapes necessity"

–Austin Osman Spare

Spare's images capture the process of creation, the thoughts of the creator, and the memories of the viewer. ("Change the way to perceive and change all memory"— G.P-O) These memories of the viewer recall past events and feelings that are more compact, briefer than when they took place originally. They are compressed. Memories are past time, accessed into recent time. Time is not however linear, all time exists simultaneously and points in every direction simultaneously. It is quaquaversal, omnipresent, in fact, all the usual definitions of "GOD" in the Catholic Church. There is really no reason why Spare's paintings and images should not capture time, thought and experience, then recreate and expand it in the viewer's mind.

"All nature is a vast reflection of that which is within us, or else we could not know it"

–Austin Osman Spare

Subjective experience is no less "real" than objective conjecture. All roads lead to Rome in a mirror-to-mirror function. This function of mirroring is found in the trance state in a simple, direct way. The higher techniques of idea and artist's illusory skills makes effects and phenomena active through the dimensions of spacelessness and timelessness in ways normally consigned to the skeptical parking lot of modern existence. Time mirrors time.

"Embrace reality by imagination"

–Austin Osman Spare

Years of trying to rationalize inexplicable "experiences" disintegrate and only the most extreme speculations and constructs of impossibility begin to get close to giving answers that we see and feel. We are "Here to Go" as Brion Gysin succinctly stated. But not just here to go into inner and outer space, though that process is one part and conceptual parcel of the final aspiration. We are here to go out of the physical body. To enter the solid pool of time. To be fully integrated into that matter of TIME that connects us with every moment, in every direction, and every parallel or conflicting omniverse that ever was, wills to be, or intends to be. Intention is the key and the process is the product.

"The Life Force is not blind. We are"

–Austin Osman Spare

Time must be reassessed as a solid; as a form of consciousness; as the key element in the atomic scale. As the covert energy hidden in the million and one names of deities. Life is only a brief physical manifestation outside the circles of time. We can reenter the time pool and we can remanifest. This is exactly the same as entering the virtual world of "cyberspace/psychosphere" when you log on. Our appreciation of the implication of logging on must be developed from this deification perspective. Once logged on, we are vulnerable to all the agendas, traumas, neuroses, and brilliances of all other logged on individuals. We have reentered a pool. No different to the pool of time or the gene pool, or "racial memory/DNA" pools. This pool I will to name the Spatial Memory.

Our understanding of time travel, physicality, possibility, and the malleability of TIME and existence in a new contrived virtual world is prophesied by Austin Osman Spare, by Brion Gysin, by many artists and creators. This shift in our perception of time and mortality will be the most important arena of discussion and philosophical, cultural engineering in this 21st century.

"What is death? A great mutation to your next SELF"

–Austin Osman Spare

The primary quest in Art, Life, Science and Brain has become a quest for reliable, repeatable methods for interdimensional travel and communication. Beyond the body and through the prophetic portals. Einstein, Spare, Gysin, Leary, McKenna and all the other visionary synthesists

We are here to go out of the physical body. To enter the solid pool of time. Time must be reassessed as a solid; as a form of consciousness; as the key element in the atomic scale.

have contributed to the cumulative effect upon which sorcery is based. We can all play. By being aware of the implication of logging on. By designing conceptual and physical grids within the Psychosphere to facilitate accurate post-physical travel. By shouldering the responsibility we have accessed of God/Goddess building our actions are the process that leads to the final unity and the vanquishing once and for all of any either/or paradigms at last. This is the time that shall end. This is the calendar that ceases to exist. Time and life are not synonymous or fixed. Both are solids and can be shaped to our will to... ⏚

CALLING CTHULHU
HP Lovecraft's
Magick Realism

"In this book it is spoken of...Spirits and Conjurations; of Gods, Spheres, Planes and many other things which may or may not exist. It is immaterial whether they exist or not. By doing certain things certain results follow."

–Aleister Crowley, *Magick in Theory and Practice*

Consumed by cancer in 1937 at the age of 46, the last scion of a faded aristocratic New England family, the horror writer Howard Phillips Lovecraft left one of America's most curious literary legacies. The bulk of his short stories appeared in *Weird Tales*, a pulp magazine devoted to the supernatural. But within these modest confines, Lovecraft brought dark fantasy screaming into the 20th century, taking the genre, almost literally, into a new dimension.

Nowhere is this more evident than in the loosely linked cycle of stories known, somewhat problematically, as the Cthulhu Mythos. Named for a tentacled alien monster who waits dreaming beneath the sea in the sunken city of R'lyeh, this fragmentary and inconsistent story-cycle encompasses the cosmic career of a variety of gruesome extraterrestrial entities that include Yog-Sothoth,

Nyarlathotep, and the blind idiot god Azathoth, who sprawls at the center of Ultimate Chaos, "encircled by his flopping horde of mindless and amorphous dancers, and lulled by the thin monotonous piping of a demonic flute held in nameless paws." Lurking on the margins of our space-time continuum, this merry crew of Outer Gods and Great Old Ones are now attempting to invade our world through science and dream and horrid rites.

As a marginally popular writer working in the literary equivalent of the gutter, Lovecraft received no serious attention during his lifetime. But while most 1930s pulp fiction is nearly unreadable today, Lovecraft continues to attract attention. In France and Japan, his tales of cosmic fungi, degenerate cults and seriously bad dreams are recognized as works of bent genius, and the celebrated French philosophers Gilles Deleuze and Felix Guattari praise his radical embrace of multiplicity in their magnum opus *A Thousand Plateaus*. On Anglo-American turf, a passionate cabal of critics fill journals like *Lovecraft Studies* and *Crypt of Cthulhu* with their almost Talmudic research. Meanwhile both hacks and gifted disciples continue to craft stories that elaborate the Cthulhu Mythos. There's even an occasional Lovecraft convention—the NecronomiCon, named for the most famous of his forbidden grimoires. Like the Gnostic science fiction writer Philip K. Dick, H.P. Lovecraft is the epitome of a cult author.

The word "fan" comes from *fanaticus*, a Latin term for a temple devotee, and Lovecraft fans exhibit the unflagging

Lurking on the margins of our space-time continuum, this merry crew of Outer Gods and Great Old Ones are now attempting to invade our world through science and dream and horrid rites.

devotion, fetishism and carping sectarian debates that have characterized popular religious cults throughout the ages. But Lovecraft's "cult" status has a curiously literal dimension. Many magicians and occultists have taken up his Mythos as source material for their practice. Drawn from the darker regions of the esoteric counterculture—

Lovecraft draws the reader into the chaos that lies "between the worlds" of magick and reality.

Thelema and Satanism and Chaos magic—these Lovecraftian mages actively seek to generate the terrifying and atavistic encounters that Lovecraft's protagonists stumble into compulsively, blindly, or against their will.

Secondary occult sources for Lovecraftian magic include three different "fake" editions of the *Necronomicon*, a few rites included in Anton LaVey's *The Satanic Rituals*, and a number of works by the loopy British Thelemite Kenneth Grant. Besides Grant's Typhonian O.T.O. and the Temple of Set's Order of the Trapezoid, magical sects that tap the Cthulhu current have included the Esoteric Order of Dagon, the Bate Cabal, Michael Bertiaux's Lovecraftian Coven, and a Starry Wisdom group in Florida, named after the 19th century sect featured in Lovecraft's "Haunter of the Dark." Solo chaos mages fill out the ranks, cobbling together Lovecraftian arcana on the Internet or freely sampling the Mythos in their chthonic, open-ended (anti-) workings.

This phenomenon is made all the more intriguing by the fact that Lovecraft himself was a self-described "mechanistic materialist" philosophically opposed to spirituality and magic of any kind. Accounting for this discrepancy is only one of many curious problems raised by the apparent power of Lovecraftian magic. Why and how do these pulp visions "work"? What constitutes the occult authenticity? How does magic relate to the tension between fact and fable? As I hope to show, Lovecraftian magic is not some low-rent pulp hallucination but an imaginative and coherent reading set in motion by the dynamics of Lovecraft's own texts, whose thematic, stylistic, and intertextual strategies constitute what I call Lovecraft's *Magick Realism*.

Magical realism already denotes a strain of Latin American fiction—exemplified by Jorge Luis Borges, Gabriel Garcia Marquez, and Isabel Allende—in which a fantastic dreamlike logic melds seamlessly and delightfully with the rhythms of the everyday. Lovecraft's Magick Realism is far more dark and convulsive, as ancient and amoral forces violently puncture the realistic surface of his tales. Lovecraft constructs and then collapses a number of intense polarities—between realism and fantasy, book and dream, reason and its chaotic Other. By playing out these tensions in his writing, Lovecraft also reflects the transformations that modern occultism has undergone as it confronts the new perspectives of psychology, quantum physics, and existentialism. And by embedding all this in an intertextual Mythos of profound depth, he draws the reader into the chaos that lies "between the worlds" of magick and reality.

A PULP POE

Written mostly in the 1920s and '30s, Lovecraft's work builds a somewhat rickety bridge between the florid decadence of *fin de siecle* fantasy and the more "rational" demands of the new century's science fiction. His early writing is gaudy Gothic pastiche, but in his mature Cthulhu tales, Lovecraft adopts a pseudodocumentary style that utilizes the language of journalism, scholarship, and science to construct a realistic and measured prose voice which then explodes into feverish, adjectival horror. Some find Lovecraft's intensity atrocious—not everyone can enjoy a writer capable of comparing a strange light to "a glutted swarm of corpse-fed fireflies dancing hellish sarabands over an accursed marsh."

But in terms of horror, Lovecraft delivers. His protagonist is usually a reclusive bookish type, a scholar or artist who is or is known to the first-person narrator. Stumbling onto odd coincidences or beset with strange dreams, his intel-

Stumbling onto odd coincidences or beset with strange dreams, his intellectual curiosity drives him to pore through forbidden books or local folklore, his empirical turn of mind blinding him to the nightmarish scenario that the reader can see slowly building up around him.

lectual curiosity drives him to pore through forbidden books or local folklore, his empirical turn of mind blinding him to the nightmarish scenario that the reader can see slowly building up around him. When the Mythos finally breaks through, it often shatters him, even though the invasion is generally more cognitive than physical.

By endlessly playing out a shared collection of images and tropes, genres like weird fiction also generate a collective resonance that can seem both "archetypal" and clichéd. Though Lovecraft broke with classic fantasy, he gave his Mythos density and depth by building a shared world to house his disparate tales. The Mythos stories share a liminal map that weaves fictional places like Arkham, Dunwich, and Miskatonic University into the New England landscape; they also refer, though inconsistently, to a common body of entities and forbidden books. A relatively common feature in fantasy fiction, these metafictional techniques create the sense that Lovecraft's Mythos lies beyond each individual tale, hovering in a dimension halfway between fantasy and the real.

Lovecraft did not just tell tales—he built a world. It's no accident that one of the more successful role-playing games to follow on the heels of Dungeons & Dragons takes place in "Lovecraft Country." Most role-playing adventure games build their worlds inside highly codified "mythic" spaces of the collective imagination (heroic fantasy, cyberpunk, vampire Paris, Arthur's Britain). The game *Call of Cthulhu* takes place in Lovecraft's 1920s America, where players become "investigators" who track down dark rumors or heinous occult crimes that gradually open up the reality of the monsters. *Call of Cthulhu* is an unusually dark game; the best investigators can do is to retain sanity and stave off the monsters' eventual apocalyptic triumph. In

Call of Cthulhu is an unusually dark game; the best investigators can do is to retain sanity and stave off the monsters' eventual apocalyptic triumph.

many ways the game "works" because of the considerable density of Lovecraft's original Mythos, a density which the game-players themselves directly thicken.

Lovecraft himself "collectivized" and deepened his Mythos by encouraging his friends to use his sort of metafictional tricks in their own stories, often as a kind of in-joke. Peers like Clark Ashton Smith, Robert Howard, and a young Robert Bloch complied, with Lovecraft often

returning the favor. After Lovecraft's death, August Derleth carried on this tradition with great devotion, and today, dozens continue to write Lovecraftian tales. With some notable exceptions, most of these writers mangle the Myth, often by detailing horrors the master wisely left shrouded in ambiguous gloom. Even after a great deal of close-reading and cross-referencing, the exact delineations of Lovecraft's cosmic cast and timeline are murky at best. But in the hands of the Catholic Derleth, the extraterrestrial Great Old Ones become elemental demons defeated by the "good" Elder Gods. Forcing Lovecraft's cosmic and fundamentally amoral pantheon into a traditional religious framework, Derleth committed an error at once imaginative and interpretive. For despite the diabolical aura of his creatures, Lovecraft generates much of his power by stepping beyond good and evil.

THE HORROR OF REASON

For the most part Lovecraft abandoned the mystic and religious underpinnings of the classic supernatural tale, turning instead towards science to provide frameworks for horror. Calling Lovecraft the "Copernicus of the horror tale," the fantasy writer Fritz Leiber Jr. wrote that Lovecraft was the first fantasist who "firmly attached the emotion of spectral dread to such concepts as outer space, the rim of the cosmos, alien beings, unsuspected dimensions, and the conceivable universes lying outside our own spacetime continuum." As Lovecraft himself put it in a letter, "The time has come when the normal revolt against time, space, and matter must assume a form not overtly incompatible with what is known of reality—when it must be gratified by images forming supplements rather than contradictions of the visible and measurable universe."

For Lovecraft, it is not the sleep of reason that breeds monsters, but reason with its eyes agog. By fusing cutting-edge science with archaic material, Lovecraft creates a twisted materialism in which scientific "progress" returns us to the atavistic abyss, and hard-nosed research revives the factual basis of forgotten and discarded myths. Hence Lovecraft's obsession with archeology; the digs which unearth alien artifacts and bizarrely angled cities are simultaneously historical and imaginal. In his 1930 story "The Whisperer in Darkness," Lovecraft identifies the planet Yuggoth (from which the fungoid Mi-Go launch their clandestine invasions of Earth) with the newly-discovered planet called Pluto. To the 1930 reader—

probably the kind of person who would thrill to popular accounts of C.W. Thompson's discovery of the ninth planet that very year—this factual reference "opens up" Lovecraft's fiction into a real world that is itself opening up to the limitless cosmos.

Lovecraft's most self-conscious, if somewhat strained, fusion of occult folklore and weird science occurs in the 1932 story "The Dreams of the Witch-House." The demonic characters that the folklorist Walter Gilman first glimpses in his nightmares are stock ghoulies: the evil

Lovecraft understands that, from the perspective of hyperspace, our normal, three-dimensional spaces are exhausted and insufficient constructs.

witch crone Keziah Mason, her familiar spirit Brown Jenkin, and a "Black Man" who is perhaps Lovecraft's most unambiguously Satanic figure. These figures eventually invade the real space of Gilman's curiously angled room. But Gilman is also a student of quantum physics, Riemann spaces and non-Euclidian mathematics, and his dreams are almost psychedelic manifestations of his abstract knowledge. Within these "abysses whose material and gravitational properties...he could not even begin to explain," an "indescribably angled" realm of "titan prisms, labyrinths, cube-and-plane clusters and quasi-buildings," Gilman keeps encountering a small polyhedron and a mass of "prolately spheroidal bubbles." By the end of the tale he realizes that these are none other than Keziah and her familiar spirit, classic demonic clichés translated into the most alien dimension of speculative science: hyperspace.

These days, one finds the motif of hyperspace in science fiction, pop cosmology, computer interface design, channeled UFO prophecies, and the postmodern shamanism of today's high-octane psychedelic travelers—all discourses that, by the way, feed contemporary chaos magic. The term *hyperspace* itself was probably coined by the science fiction writer John W. Campbell Jr. in 1931, though its origins as a concept lie in 19th century mathematical explorations of the fourth dimension. But Lovecraft was the concept's first mythographer. He understands that, from the perspective of hyperspace, our normal, three-dimensional spaces are exhausted and insufficient constructs. Because we are incapable of vividly imagining this new dimension in humanist terms, we face a crisis of representation, a crisis that for Lovecraft invokes our most ancient fears of the unknown. "All the objects ... were totally

beyond description or even comprehension," Lovecraft writes of Gilman's seething nightmares. Of course, this doesn't keep Lovecraft from offering descriptions of these objects, descriptions which emphasize the breakdown of cognitive categories through almost non-sensical juxtapositions like "obscene angles" or "wrong" geometry.

One Chaos magician calls this rhetorical technique "Semiotic Angularity," an aspect of Lovecraft's long-standing habit of labeling his horrors "indescribable," "nameless, "unseen," "unutterable," "unknown" and "formless." Though superficially weak, these moves can also be seen a kind of macabre *via negativa*. Like the apophatic oppositions of negative theologians like Pseudo-Dionysus or St. John of the Cross, Lovecraft marks the limits of language, limits which paradoxically point to the Beyond our intellects are always striving, and failing, to map. For the mystics, this ultimate is the ineffable One, Pseudo-Dionysus' "superluminous gloom" or the Ain Soph of the Qabalists. But there is no unity to Lovecraft's Beyond. It is the omnivorous Outside, the heartless screaming multiplicity of cosmic hyperspace opened up by reason alone.

For Lovecraft, scientific materialism is the ultimate Faustian bargain, but not because it hands us Promethean technology (a man for the 18th century, Lovecraft had no interest in gadgetry). Instead, science leads us beyond the horizon of what our minds can withstand. "The most merciful thing in the world, I think, is the inability of the mind to correlate all its contents," goes the famous opening line of "Call of Cthulhu." By correlating those contexts, empiricism opens up "terrifying vistas of reality"—what Lovecraft elsewhere calls "the blind cosmos [that] grinds aimlessly on from nothing to something and from something back to nothing again, neither heeding nor knowing the wishes or existence of the minds that flicker for a second now and then in the darkness."

Lovecraft gave this existentialist dread an imaginative voice, what he called "cosmic alienage." For Fritz Leiber, the "monstrous nuclear chaos" of Azathoth, Lovecraft's supreme entity, symbolizes "the purposeless, mindless, yet all-powerful universe of materialistic belief." But this symbolism isn't the whole story, for, as DMT voyagers know, hyperspace is haunted. The entities that erupt from Lovecraft's inhuman realms seem to suggest that in a blind and mechanistic cosmos, the most alien thing is sentience itself. Peering outward through the cracks of domesticated "human" consciousness, a compassionless materialist like Lovecraft could only react with horror, for reason must cower before the most raw and atavistic dream-dragons of the psyche.

Civilization describes the process through which humans come to suppress, ignore or constrain these forces lurking in our lizard brain. In terms of myth, this process is characterized as demons imprisoned under the angelic yokes of altruism, morality, and reason. But if one no longer believes in any ultimate universal purpose, then these base impulses within us are paradoxically *more*

the Black, not because he desires a simple Satanic inversion of Christianity but because he seeks the amoral and shamanic core of magical experience—a core that Lovecraft conjures up with his orgies of drums, guttural chants, and screeching horns. At the same time, Chaos mages like Carroll also plumb the weird science of quantum physics, complexity theory and electronic Prometheanism. Some darkside magicians become consumed by the atavistic forces they unleash or addicted to the dark costume of the Satanic anti-hero. But the most sophisticated adepts adopt a balanced mode of Gnostic existentialism that calls all constructs into question while refusing the cold comforts of skeptical reason or suicidal nihilism, a pragmatic and empirical shamanism that resonates as much with Lovecraft's hard-headed materialism as with his horrors.

Like most Chaos magicians, the British occultist Peter Carroll gravitates towards the Black, not because he desires a simple Satanic inversion of Christianity but because he seeks the amoral and shamanic core of magical experience

attuned to the cosmos precisely because they are amoral and inhuman. In "The Dunwich Horror," Henry Wheeler overhears a monstrous moan from a diabolical rite and asks "from what unplumbed gulfs of extra-cosmic consciousness or obscure, long-latent heredity, were those half-articular thunder-croakings drawn?" The Outside, in other words, is within.

CHAOS CULTURE

Lovecraft's fiction expresses a "future primitivism" that finds its most intense esoteric expression in Chaos magic, an eclectic contemporary style of darkside occultism that draws from Thelema, Satanism, Austin Osman Spare, and Eastern metaphysics to construct a thoroughly postmodern magic. For today's Chaos mage, there is no "tradition." The symbols and myths of history's sects, orders, and faiths, are constructs, useful fictions, "games." That magic works has nothing to do with its truth claims and everything to do with the will and experience of the magician. Recognizing the distinct possibility that we may be adrift in a meaningless, iterative cosmos within which human will and imagination are vaguely comic flukes (the "cosmic indifferentism" Lovecraft himself professed), the mage accepts his groundlessness, embracing the chaotic self-creating void that is himself.

As in Lovecraft's fictional cults and grimoires, chaos magicians refuse the hierarchical, symbolic and monotheist biases of traditional esotericism. Like most Chaos magicians, the British occultist Peter Carroll gravitates towards

The first occultist to really set these notions in motion was Aleister Crowley, who shattered the received vessels of occult tradition while creatively extending the dark dream of magic into the 20th century. With his outlandish image, trickster texts, and his famous Law of Thelema ("Do what thou wilt shall be the whole of the law"), Crowley called into question the esoteric certainties of "true" revelation and lineage, and was the first magus to give occult antinomionism a decidedly Nietzschean twist, an occult will to power that is more exuberantly expressed as a will to Art. In many ways, the *fin de siecle* occultism that exploded during Crowley's time was an esthetic esotericism. A good number of the 19th century magicians who inspire us today were poets, painters, and writers informed by Symbolism and decadent Romanticism. The Hermetic Order of the Golden Dawn was infused with artistic pretensions, and Golden Dawn member and fantasy writer Arthur Machen was one of Lovecraft's strongest influences.

Surrealism took a step toward chaos magic by ripping mystic techniques and sensibilities from their traditional "occult" contexts and applying them to the goal of transforming quotidian reality through the Freudian energies of dream and desire. But it was the British maverick Austin Osman Spare who most decisively dissolved the boundary between artistic and magical life. Though working independently of the Surrealists, Spare also based his art on the dark and autonomous eruptions of "subconscious" material, though in a more overtly theurgic context. Today's Chaos magicians are heavily influenced by Spare, and their Lovecraftian rites express this simultaneously

Surrealism took a step toward chaos magic by ripping mystic techniques and sensibilities from their traditional "occult" contexts and applying them to the goal of transforming quotidian reality through the Freudian energies of dream and desire.

creative and nihilistic dissolution. And as postmodern spawn of role-playing games, computers, and anime, they celebrate the fact that Lovecraft's secrets are scraped from the barrel of pop culture.

PROOF IN THE PUDDING

In a message cross-posted to the Internet newsgroups alt.necromicon [sic] and alt.satanism, Parker Ryan listed a wide variety of magical techniques described by Lovecraft, including entheogens, glossalalia, and shamanic drumming. Insisting that his post was "not a satirical article," Ryan then described specific Lovecraftian rites he had developed, including this "Rite of Cthulhu":

A) Chanting. The use of the "Cthulhu chant" to create a concentrative or meditative state of consciousness that forms the basis of much later magickal work.

B) Dream work. Specific techniques of controlled dreaming that are used to establish contact with Cthulhu.

C) Abandonment. Specific techniques to free oneself from culturally conditioned reality tunnels.

Ryan goes on to say that he's experimented with most of his rites "with fairly good success."

In coming to terms with the "real magic" embedded in Lovecraft, one quickly encounters a fundamental irony: the cold skepticism of Lovecraft himself. In his letters, Lovecraft poked fun at his own tales, claiming he wrote them for cash and playfully naming his friends after his monsters. While such attitudes in no way diminish the imaginative power of Lovecraft's tales—which, as always, lie outside the control and intention of their author—they do pose a problem for the working occultist seeking to establish Lovecraft's magical authority.

The most obvious, and least rewarding, answer is to find authentic magic in Lovecraft's biography. Lovecraft's father was a traveling salesman who died in a madhouse

when Lovecraft was eight, and vague rumors that he was an initiate in some Masonic order or other were exploited in the *Necronomicon* cobbled together by George Hay, Colin Wilson, and Robert Turner. Others have tried to track Lovecraft's occult know-how, especially his familiarity with Aleister Crowley and the Golden Dawn. In an ambiguous Internet document relating the history of the "real" Necronomicon, Colin Low, tongue firmly lodged in cheek, argues that Crowley befriended Sonia Greene in New York a few years before the woman married Lovecraft. As proof of Crowley's indirect influence on Lovecraft, Low sites this intriguing passage from "The Call of Cthulhu":

> That cult would never die until the stars came right again and the secret priests would take Cthulhu from His tomb to revive His subjects and resume His rule of earth. The time would be easy to know, for then mankind would have become as the Great Old Ones; free and wild, and beyond good and evil, with laws and morals thrown aside and all men shouting and killing and revelling in joy. Then the liberated Old Ones would teach them new ways to shout and kill and revel and enjoy themselves, and all earth would flame with a holocaust of ecstasy and freedom.

Low claims this passage is a mangled reflection of Crowley's teachings on the new Aeon and *The Book of the Law*. In a letter written the year before he died, Lovecraft makes passing reference to "the rather over-advertised Aleister Crowley." Crowley was mentioned in Leonard Cline's *The Dark Chamber*, a novel Lovecraft discussed in his *Supernatural Horror in Literature*.

But so what? Lovecraft was a fanatical and imaginative reader, and many such readers are drawn to the semiotic exotica of esoteric lore regardless of any beliefs in or experiences of the paranormal. From *The Case of Charles Dexter Ward* and elsewhere, it's clear that Lovecraft knew the basic outlines of occultism and Theosophy. But these influences pale next to *Vathek*, Poe, or Lord Dunsany.

That cult would never die until the stars came right again and the secret priests would take Cthulhu from His tomb to revive His subjects and resume His rule of earth.

Desperate to assimilate Lovecraft into a "tradition," some occultists enter into dubious explanations of mystical influence by disincarnate beings. North gives this Invisible College idea a shamanic twist, asserting that prehistoric Atlantian tribes who survived the flood exercised tele-

in the chaos of hyperspace are not so much archaic figures of heredity as the avatars of a new psychological and mythic aeon. At the very least, it would seem that things are getting mighty out of hand beyond the magic circle of the ordered daylight mind.

Low claims this passage is a mangled reflection of Crowley's teachings on the new Aeon and *The Book of the Law*.

pathic influence on people like John Dee, Blavatsky, and Lovecraft. But none of these Lovecraft hierophants can match the delirious splendor of Kenneth Grant. In *The Magical Revival*, Grant points out some curious but essentially trivial similarities between Lovecraft and Crowley: both refer to "Great Old Ones" and "Cold Wastes" (of Kadath and Hadith, respectively); the entity "Yog-Sothoth" rhymes with "Set-Thoth," and *Al Azif: The Book of the Arab* resembles, vaguely, Crowley's *Liber AL vel Legis: The Book of the Law*. In *Nightside of Eden*, Grant maps Lovecraft's pantheon onto a darkside Tree of Life, comparing the mangled "iridescent globes" that occasionally pop up in Lovecraft's tales with the shattered sefirot known as the Qlipoth. Grant concludes that Lovecraft had "direct and conscious experience of the inner planes," the same zones Crowley prowled, and that Lovecraft "disguised" his occult experiences as fiction.

Like many latter-day Lovecraftians, Grant commits the error of literalizing a purposefully nebulous myth. A subtler and more satisfying version of this argument is the notion that Lovecraft had direct *unconscious* experiences of the inner planes, experiences which his quotidian mind rejected but which found their way into his writings nonetheless. After all, Lovecraft was blessed with a vivid and nightmarish dream life, and drew the substance of a number of his tales from beyond the wall of sleep. In this sense, Lovecraft's magical authority is nothing more or less than the authority of dream.

But what kind of dream tales are these? A Freudian could have a field day with Lovecraft's fecund, squishy sea monsters, and a Jungian analyst might recognize the liniments of the proverbial shadow. But Lovecraft's Shadow is so hostile to light it swallows the standard archetypes of the collective unconscious like a black hole. If we see the archetypal world not as a static storehouse of timeless godforms but as a moving host of figures that mutate as cultural and historical conditions change, then the seething extraterrestrial monsters that Lovecraft glimpsed

In an intriguing Internet document devoted to the Necronomicon, Tyagi Nagasiva places Lovecraft's potent dreamtales within the *terma* tradition found in the Nyingma branch of Tibetan Buddhism. Termas were "pre-mature" writings hidden by Buddhist sages for centuries until the time was ripe, at which point religious visionaries would divine their physical hiding places through omens or dreams. But some termas were revealed entirely in dreams, often couched in otherworldly Dakini scripts. An old Indian revisionary tactic (the second-century Nagarjuna was said to have discovered his Mahayana sutras in the serpent realm of the nagas), the terma game resolves the religious problem of how to alter a tradition without disrupting traditional authority. The famous *Bardo Thodol*, or *Tibetan Book of the Dead* is a terma, and so, perhaps, is the *Necronomicon*.

Of course, for Chaos magicians, reality presents itself through any number of self-sustaining but mutually contradictory symbolic paradigms (or "reality tunnels," in Robert Anton Wilson's memorable phrase). Nothing is true and everything is permitted. By emphasizing the self-fulfilling nature of all reality claims, this postmodern perspective creatively erodes the distinction between legitimate esoteric transmission and total fiction.

This bias toward the experimental is found in Anton LaVey's *Satanic Rituals*, which includes the first overtly Lovecraftian rituals to see print. In presenting "Die Elektrischen Vorspiele" (which LaVey based on a Lovecraftian tale by Frank Belknap Long), the "Ceremony of the Angles," and "The Call to Cthulhu" (the latter two penned by Michael Aquino), LaVey does claim that Lovecraft "clearly...had been influenced by very real sources." But in holding that Satanic magic allows you to "objectively enter into a subjective state," LaVey more emphatically emphasizes the ritual power of fantasy—a

"The Old Ones are the objective manifestations ... of the subjective universe which is what is trying to 'break through' the merely rational mind-set of modern humanity."

radical subjectivity which explains his irreverence towards occult source material, whether Lovecraft or Masonry. In naming his Order of the Trapezoid after the "Shining Trapezohedron" found in Lovecraft's "The Haunter of the Dark"—a black, oddly-angled extraterrestrial crystal used to communicate with the Old Ones—LaVey emphasized that fictions can channel magical forces regardless of their historical authenticity.

In his two rituals, Michael Aquino expresses the subjective power of "meaningless" language by creating a "Yuggothic" tongue similar to that heard in Lovecraft's "The Dunwich Horror" and "The Whisperer in the Dark." Such guttural utterances help to shut down the rational mind (try chanting "P'garn'h v'glyzz" for a couple of hours), a notion elaborated by Kenneth Grant in his notion of the Cult of Barbarous Names. After leaving the Church of Satan to form the more serious Temple of Set in 1975, Aquino eventually reformed the Order of the Trapezoid into the practical magic wing of the Setian philosophy. For Stephen Flowers, current Grand Master of the order, the substance of Lovecraftian magic is precisely an overwhelming subjectivity that flies in the face of objective law. "The Old Ones are the objective manifestations ... of the subjective universe which is what is trying to 'break through' the merely rational mind-set of modern humanity." For Flowers, such invocations are ultimately apocalyptic, hastening a transition into a chaotic aeon in which the Old Ones reveal themselves as future reflections of the Black Magician ("There are no more Nightmares for us," he wrote to me).

This desire to rebel against the tyranny of reason and its ordered objective universe is one of the underlying drives of Chaos magic. Many would applaud the sentiment expressed by Albert Wilmarth in Lovecraft's "The Whisperer in Darkness": "To shake off the maddening and wearying limitations of time and space and natural law—to be linked with the vast outside—to come close to the nighted and abysmal secrets of the infinite and ultimate—surely such a things was worth the risk of one's life, soul, and sanity!"

In his electronically circulated text "Kathulu Majik: Luvkrafting the Roles of Modern Uccultizm," Haramullah Tyagi Nagasiva writes that most Western magic is ossified and dualistic, heavily weighted towards the forces of order, hierarchy, morality, and structured language. "Without the destabilizing force of Kaos, we would stagnate intellectually, psychologically and otherwise... Kathulu provides a necessary instability to combat the stolid and fixed methods of the structured 'Ordurs' ... One may become balanced through exposure to Kathulu." Nagasiva criticizes black magicians who simply reverse "Ordur" with "Kaos," rather than bringing this underlying polarity into balance (a dualistic error he also finds in Lovecraft). Showing strong Taoist and Buddhist influences, Nagasiva calls instead for a "Midul Path" that magically navigates between structure and disintegration, will and void. "The idea that one may progress linearly along the MP [Midul Path] is mistaken. One becomes, one does not progress. One attunes, one does not forge. One allows, one does not make."

In the *Cincinnati Journal of Ceremonial Magic*, the anonymous author of "Return of the Elder Gods" presents an evolutionary reason for Mythos magic. The author alludes to an approaching world crisis brought on by the invasion of the Elder Gods—Qlipothic transdimensional entities who ruled protohumanity until they were banished by "the agent of the Intelligence," a Promethean figure who set humanity on its current course of evolution. We remain connected to these Elder Gods through the "Forgotten Ones," the atavistic forces of hunger, sex, and violence that linger in the subterranean levels of our being. Only by magically "reabsorbing" the Forgotten Ones and using the subsequent energy to bootstrap higher consciousness can we keep the portal sealed against the return of the Elder Gods. Though Lovecraft's name is never mentioned in the article, he is ever present, a skeptical materialist dreaming the dragons awake.

WRITING THE DREAM...

Within the Mythos tales, one finds two dimensions—the normal human world and the infested Outside—and it's the ontological tension between them that powers Lovecraft's magick realism. Though Cthulhu and friends have material aspects, their reality is most horrible for what it says about the way the universe is. As the Lovecraft scholar S. T. Joshi notes, Lovecraft's narrators frequently go mad "not through any physical violence at the hands of supernatural entities but through the mere realization of the existence of such a race of gods and beings." Faced with "realms whose mere existence stuns the brain," they experience severe cognitive dissonance—precisely the sorts of disorienting rupture sought by some Chaos magicians.

The role-playing game *Call of Cthulhu* wonderfully expresses the violence of this Lovecraftian paradigm shift. In adventure games like Dungeons & Dragons, one of your character's most significant measures is its hit points—a number which determines the amount of physical or magical punishment your character can take before it gets injured or dies. *Call of Cthulhu* replaces this physical characteristic with the psychic category of Sanity. Face-to-face encounters with Yog-Sothoth or the insects from Shaggai knock points off your sanity, but so

"The Haunter in the Dark" and *The Case of Charles Dexter Ward*. Like the monsters themselves, Lovecraft's dreams are autonomous forces breaking through from Outside and engendering their own reality. But these dreams also conjure up a more literal "outside": the strange dream life of Lovecraft himself, a life that (as the informed fan knows) directly inspired some of the tales. By seeding his texts with his own nightmares, Lovecraft creates an autobiographical homology between himself and his protagonists. The stories themselves start to dream, which means that the reader too lies right in the path of the infection.

If you use any of the binding spells from *De Vermis Mysteriis* or the *Pnakotic Manuscripts*, you necessarily learn more about the Mythos and thereby lose more sanity.

does your discovery of more information about the Mythos. The more you find out from books or starcharts, the more likely you are to wind up in the Arkham Asylum. Magic also comes with an ironic price, one that Lovecraftian magicians might well pay heed to. If you use any of the binding spells from *De Vermis Mysteriis* or the Pnakotic Manuscripts, you necessarily learn more about the Mythos and thereby lose more sanity.

Lovecraft's scholarly heroes discover the Mythos as much through reading and thinking as through investigations of physical space, and this psychological exploration draws the mind of the reader directly into the loop. Usually, readers suspect the dark truth of the Mythos while the narrator still clings to a quotidian attitude—a technique that subtly forces the reader to identify with the Outside rather than with the conventional worldview of the protagonist. Magically, the blindness of Lovecraft's heroes corresponds to a crucial element of occult theory developed by Austin Osman Spare: that magic occurs over and against the conscious mind, that ordinary thinking must be silenced, distracted, or thoroughly deranged for the chthonic will to express itself.

In order to invade our plane, Lovecraft's entities need a portal, an interface between the worlds, and Lovecraft emphasizes two: books and dreams. In "Dreams of the Witch-House," "The Shadow out of Time" and "The Shadow over Innsmouth," dreams infect their hosts with a virulence that resembles the more overt psychic possessions that occur in

Lovecraft reproduces himself in his tales in a number of ways—the first-person protagonists reflect aspects of his own reclusive and bookish lifestyle; the epistolary form of the "The Whisperer in Darkness" echoes his own commitment to regular correspondence; character names are lifted from friends; and the New England landscape is his own. This psychic self-reflection partially explains why Lovecraft fans usually become fascinated with the man himself, a gaunt and solitary recluse who socialized through the mail, yearned for the 18th century, and adopted, with much dry humor, the crabby outlook and mannerisms of an old man. Lovecraft's life, and certainly his voluminous personal correspondence, form part of his myth.

Lovecraft solidifies the virtual reality of his stories by adding autobiographical elements to his shared world of creatures, books and maps. He also constructs a documentary texture by thickening his tales with manuscripts, newspaper clippings, scholarly citations, diary entries, letters, and bibliographies that list fake books alongside real ones. All this produces the sense that "outside" each individual tale lies a meta-fictional world that hovers on the edge of our own, a world that, like the monsters themselves, is constantly trying to break through and actualize itself. And thanks to Mythos storytellers, role-playing games, and dark-side magicians, it has.

In the climax of the tale, Peaslee journeys to the Australian desert to explore ancient ruins buried beneath the sands. There he discovers a book written in English, in his own handwriting: the very same volume he had produced inside his monstrous dream body.

...AND DREAMING THE BOOK

In "The Shadow out of Time," Lovecraft makes explicit one of the fantastic equations that drives his Magick Realism: the equivalence of dreams and books. For five years, the narrator, an economics professor named Nathaniel Wingate Peaslee, is taken over by a mysterious "secondary personality." After recovering his original identity, Peaslee is beset by powerful dreams in which he finds himself in a strange city, inhabiting a huge tentacle-sprouting conical body, writing down the history of the Western world in a book. In the climax of the tale, Peaslee journeys to the Australian desert to explore ancient ruins buried beneath the sands. There he discovers a book written in English, in his own handwriting: the very same volume he had produced inside his monstrous dream body.

Though we learn very little of their contents, Lovecraft's diabolical grimoires are so infectious that even glancing at their ominous sigils proves dangerous. As with dreams, these texts obsess Lovecraft's bookish protagonists to the point that the volumes, in Christopher Frayling's phrase, "vampirize the reader." Their titles alone are magic spells, the hallucinatory incantations of an eccentric antiquarian: *The Pnakotic Manuscripts*, for example, or *The Seven Cryptical Books of Hsan*. Lovecraft's friends contributed *De vermis mysteriis*, the *R'lyeh Text*, *The Book of Eibon*, and von Junzt's *Die Unaussprechlichen Kulten*.

> **The text was penned in 730 AD by a poet, the Mad Arab Abdul Alhazred, and named after the nocturnal sounds of insects. It was subsequently translated by Theodorus Philetas into Greek, by Olaus Wormius into Latin, and by John Dee into English.**

Hovering over all these grim tomes is the "dreaded" and "forbidden" *Necronomicon*, a book of blasphemous invocations to speed the return of the Old Ones. Lovecraft's supreme intertextual fetish, the *Necronomicon* stands as one of the few mythical books in literature that have absorbed so much imaginative attention that they've entered published reality.

If books owe their life not to their individual contents but to the larger intertextual webwork of reference and citation within which they are woven, then the dread *Necronomicon* clearly has a life of its own. Besides literary studies, the *Necronomicon* has generated numerous pseudo-scholarly analyses, including significant appendices in the *Encyclopedia Cthulhiana* and Lovecraft's own "History of the Necronomicon." A number of FAQs can be found on the Internet, where a tedious flame war periodically erupts between magicians, horror fans, and mythology experts over the reality of the book. The undead entity referred to in the *Necronomicon*'s famous couplet—"That is not dead which can eternal lie/And with strange eons even death may die"—may be nothing more or less than the text itself, always lurking in the margins as we read the real.

Lovecraft's brief "History" was apparently inspired by the first Necronomicon hoax: a review of an edition of the dreaded tome submitted to Massachusetts' Branford Review in 1934. Decades later, index cards for the book started popping up in university library catalogs. Inevitably, and with supremely Lovecraftian logic, all these ghostly references eventually manifest the book itself. In 1973, a small-press edition of Al Azif (the Necronomicon's Arabic name) appeared, consisting of eight pages of simulated Syrian script repeated 24 times. Four years later, the ceremonial magicians at New York's Magickal Childe published a Necronomicon by "Simon," a grab bag that contains far more Sumerian myth than Lovecraft (though portions were "purposely left out" for the "safety of the reader"). George Hay's *Necronomicon: The Book of Dead Names*, also a child of the '70s, is the most complex, intriguing, and Lovecraftian of the lot. In the spirit of the master's pseudoscholarship, Hay nests the fabulated invocations of Yog-Sothoth and Cthulhu within a set of analytic, literary and historical essays.

Though magicians with strong imaginations have claimed that even the Simon book works wonders, the pseudohistories of the various *Necronomicon*s are far more compelling than the texts themselves. Lovecraft himself provided the bare bones: the text was penned in 730 AD by a poet, the "Mad Arab" Abdul Alhazred, and named after the nocturnal sounds of insects. It was subsequently translated by Theodorus Philetas into Greek, by Olaus Wormius into Latin, and by John Dee into English. Lovecraft lists various libraries and private collections where fragments of the volume reside, and gives us a knowing wink by noting that the fantasy writer R. W. Chambers is said to have derived the monstrous and suppressed book found in his story collection *The King in Yellow* from rumors of the *Necronomicon*.

All of the subsequent pseudohistories of the *Necronomicon* weave the book in and out of actual occult history, with John Dee playing a particularly conspicuous role. According to Colin Wilson, the version of the text published in the Hay Necronomicon was encrypted in Dee's Enochian ciphertext *Liber logoaeth*. Colin Low's Necronomicon FAQ claims that Dee discovered the book at the court of King Rudolph II's court in Prague, and that it was under its influence that Dee and his scryer Edward Kelley achieved their most powerful astral encounters. Never published, Dee's translation became part of the celebrated collection of Elias Ashmole housed at the British Library. Here Crowley read it, freely cobbling passages for *The Book of the Law*, and ultimately passing on some of its contents indirectly to Lovecraft through Sophia Greene.

Crowley's role in Low's waggish tale is appropriate, because Crowley certainly appreciated magical confections of hoax and history. For in many ways the history of the occult is a confabulation, its lies wedded to its genealogies, its "timeless" truths fabricated by revision-

himself wrote, "No weird story can truly produce terror unless it is devised with all the care and verisimilitude of an actual hoax."

In *Foucault's Pendulum*, Umberto Eco suggests that esoteric truth is perhaps nothing more than a semiotic conspiracy theory born of an endlessly rehashed and self-referential literature—the intertextual fabric Lovecraft understood so well. For those who need to ground their profound states of consciousness in objective correlatives, this is a damning indictment of "tradition." But as Chaos magicians remind us, magic may be nothing more than groundless subjectivity interacting with an internally consistent matrix of signs and affects. In the absence of orthodoxy, all we may have is the dynamic tantra of text and perception, of reading and dream. These days the Great Work may be nothing more or less than another "ingenious game," fabricating itself without closure or rest, weaving itself out of the resplendent void where Azathoth writhes on his Mandelbrot throne. ⬚

Lovecraft's *Necronomicon* is the occult equivalent of Orson Welles' 1938 radio broadcast of *War of the Worlds*. As Lovecraft himself wrote, "No weird story can truly produce terror unless it is devised with all the care and verisimilitude of an actual hoax."

ists, madmen, and geniuses, its esoteric traditions a constantly shifting conspiracy of influences. The *Necronomicon* is hardly the first fiction to generate real magical activity within this potent twilight zone between philology and fantasy.

Take, for example, the anonymous Rosicrucian manifestos that first appeared in the early 1600s, claiming to issue from a secret brotherhood of Christian Hermeticists who had deemed it time to come above ground. Many readers immediately wanted to join up, though it is highly unlikely that such a group existed at the time. But this hoax focused esoteric desire and inspired an explosion of "real" Rosicrucian groups. Though one of the two suspected authors of the manifestos, Johann Valentin Andreae, never came clean, he made veiled references to Rosicrucianism as an "ingenious game which a masked person might like to play upon the literary scene, especially in an age infatuated with everything unusual." Like the Rosicrucian manifestos or Blavatsky's *Book of Dzyan*, Lovecraft's *Necronomicon* is the occult equivalent of Orson Welles' 1938 radio broadcast of *War of the Worlds*. As Lovecraft

Excerpt from
THE ROAD OF EXCESS

BRIAN BARRITT

THE ROAD OF EXCESS

A Psychedelic Autobiography

FULL MOON AT BOU SAADA

Bowling along dusty roads with Tim driving a beat-up Deux Cheveaux with the flat of his hand, sending terrified chickens screeching from under the tires, while the sun beats on the roof. South to Bou Saada away from the trials and tribulations of the Panthers[1] out into the desert where only the sand grows.

We stop at the Hotel Caid, a brand new desert fortress arched and domed, to pick up a suitcase of garments that Tim and Rosemary left on their previous trip, and as soon as we are out of town we take the acid and hash out of the shoes, drive amongst the dunes and pull over near a dried up riverbed with only a trickle of water winding its way slowly through the sand.

We sit on the river bank watching the sunset and waiting for the tabs of Orange Sunshine to hit, Timothy in a wind-cheater, myself dressed in a jellaba with the hood up. The wine that I consumed at the Mutton Fest has left me feeling wan and the lump of Afghani hash I am chewing is all I have eaten today and is spacing me already.

Silence, night and time pouring through the hourglass of the Sahara. Frogs croaking, stillness, the dunes like pyramids on a lunar surface. When you have lost your ego there is only the surroundings left, you are the hills and dunes looking through the eyes of Mother Nature at different aspects of yourself. The sand shifts and wavers in infinite layers of gossamer that gently rise and fall in rhythm to my breaths.

I take deep lungfulls of air and the desert breathes me.

Into my head comes the image of a man surrounded by a whirlwind of sand, the dust devil spinning a thin shroud around his figure, and from out of nowhere the name Dr. John Dee and the impression of a scrolled manuscript wafts through my brain.

The sky is on fire, massive cycles of energy swirl across it, massive sweeps of time career through the ages, the very sight of them turning us immortal. Space Gods parade in a circle around us, with stars for eyes and stars in the palms of their hands, clothed in night with the cosmos blowing through them. Time stretches every which away, at a twitch of the mind the history of Africa blows across the gem studded sky, mythic dramas unfold in scrolls and curlicues where e'er the mind tarries, and behind it all the interstellar hiss of creation as the energy pours forth from the Om.

The throbbing earth-beat pulsing through my blood grows louder, powered by the clapping hands and stamping feet of all the ancestors who have gone before me, beating in time to the new generations as they pour forth from the Earth's womb. I see fabulous creatures painted on the wall of my skull, archetypes, the touchstones of humankind, flash past like arrows fired through the animal kingdom into the future, aimed at the microcosm, the perfect mirror, the "Mighty Micro" of MAN!

Other images loom massive and awesome, inside the cave of my skull are beasts not of this planet, men not of humankind.

The arch of the sky is the dish of a radio telescope relaying broadcasts via my brain from a shaman of long ago, simultaneously he is speaking from the future in cosmic rhyming-slang, "odd, ode, code, toad," overdubbed on mind-frames of events yet to take place.

Into my head comes the image of a man surrounded by a whirlwind of sand, the dust devil spinning a thin shroud around his figure, and from out of nowhere the name Dr. John Dee and the impression of a scrolled manuscript wafts through my brain.

I stand a mile high, time is wrapped around my ankles causing flurries in the atoms of sand, spinning universes around me, building galaxies, creating microcosmic stars. And then it is all gone and I am back in my ego again, staring with eyes as big as flying saucers over the endless cones of sand.

The ego is a piteously small area of consciousness when seen from the bird's eye view, a bounded circle, tunnel vision zooming-in on a minute area of the universal canvas with a dilating lens. It dilates because the cosmos is straining to get through it and out into the hardcore world of downtown reality, it pulses to the beat of ancient hearts, ancient hands clapping, ancient feet stamping the hard earth.

I am sitting at the entrance to a cave, looking through the flames of a fire up into the vast dish of the sky. As a log ignites, a shower of sparks explode, like stars, and the firmament becomes a copy of the thoughts sparking in my brain. I suddenly see that the huge dome of the heavens is no bigger than the inside of my own skull, and that the Little Bear (Ursa Minor) crouched on top of my head, is my ego, turning with its tail the handle of the sky.

He is using my brain as an inter-galactic air terminal, silver channels streak from my third eye, massive galactic spaceships blink into being, fresh from hyperspace, gigantic stratocruisers shrink me to the size of an ant as I look up at their immensities. Golden vessels with the faces of Egyptian Gods on their prows glide between life and death. Each star is a grain of sand on the cosmic beach, ships of the desert surf the golden Sahara, sahasrara, beauteous cities glide by composed of materials not yet invented, towers twist skyward...

Through a window a woman with the face of an angel and the body of a spider is chatting me up with her eyes. I am climbing up the rungs of a vertical ladder leading to the entrance of her flying saucer, pushing my feet well through the spaces between the rungs so that I won't fall backwards, when there is a sharpness to my ear—Tim is saying something, he's asking me what I am doing? I look down at him and find my spirit has dragged my body halfway up a sand dune. I croak a word of reassurance and carry on walking up the ladder, but now it's the face of the moon I am climbing towards. At the top of the dune the moon is so big it blocks out the rest of the sky—she has the features of Elizabeth.

Tim is performing a ceremony, in the background I can hear him repeating "Solve et Coagula" as he walks up and down.

What's the chance of us tripping by accident in the same location as Crowley and Neuburg? Of all the acid houses in the world we have to trip out in this one? Play it again Aleister!

Tim is performing a ceremony, in the background I can hear him repeating "Solve et Coagula" as he walks up and down. Telepathy has been working between us off and on throughout the trip and I am not sure which thoughts are his and which are mine, against a backdrop of eternity we could be pulling out thoughts from any time. It doesn't seem to matter as long as I remember them. I think of Elizabeth back in Algiers and project the image of a Moebius strip slowly revolving on itself across space and time to the villa Cent Trent in Morretti.

On the way back the Deux Cheveaux crawls happily along like a scarab beetle winding in and out the dunes of sand, but wherever we move the horizon always keeps us in the center of its magic circle. We pull over, park, and watch the sun rising in all its glory on one edge of the horizon as the full moon sets on the other, with Venus, Mars and Jupiter (I think) spanning the arch between them. Behind the planets the stars have laced themselves together into fantastic complexities that spin off Catherine Wheels of vibrations that stream across the solar system right down to Tim and myself, standing with arms spread soaking them up through the palms of our hands. It's Easter Sunday.

When I arrive back at Morretti, Liz is waiting to welcome me. "You look illuminated" she says and shows me the Moebius strips she has been drawing. She has drawn them in a multitude of combinations and colors, as if my telepathic image has gone through a mirror and refracted.

BOU SAADA DECODED.

To you, I say, how learned so ever you be,
Go burns your Bookes and come and learne of me
–Sir Edward Kelley.

Back at Immensee, when we're not fiddling with the Book, we are comparing the acid levels and clarifying our PSI maps, the pleasantest occupation possible as far as Timothy and myself are concerned.

One evening I am lounging in front of the fire in the downstairs room glancing through a copy of *The Confessions of Aleister Crowley* that Bobby Dryfus has left behind, when I read that in 1909 Crowley himself held a magical cere-

It's not reincarnation we are thinking of so much as recurring cycles with different representatives each time around.

mony in the dunes, just outside Bou Saada, with a poet called Victor Neuburg.

When I read it out loud Tim grabs the book, his face all alight with interest. We look at each other in amazement. What's the chance of us tripping by accident in the same location as Crowley and Neuburg? Of all the acid houses in the world we have to trip out in this one? Play it again Aleister!

I remind him of the manuscript I saw during our trip and the name Dr. John Dee—we look at each other in double amazement. The book says that the manuscript that Crowley used for his conjurations was composed by Dr. John Dee! Tim and myself tripped for the first time together in the same area in which Crowley and Neuburg dropped mescaline and performed a magical ceremony using Dr. Dee's script!

The new information shakes and impresses us both. It's not reincarnation we are thinking of so much as recurring cycles with different representatives each time around. We feel we are riding the same current that powered Dr. Dee and Edward Kelley in the 16th century and Crowley and

Seven Up album cover, music by Timothy Leary, Brian Barritt and Ash Ra Tempel, 1972

Neuburg at the beginning of this one. I see a similarity between Kelley, Neuburg and Barritt paralleling the one between Dr. Dee, Aleister Crowley and Dr. Leary.

Suddenly the earth moves under my feet. I feel as though somebody just walked over my grave, as if I have been stomping about in seven league boots without seeing what's going on between my strides. I have been moved like a chess piece from London to Bou Saada without being aware of the real cause, my instincts had been told what to do and all the in between actions were only the rationalizations of my intellect. There are synchronicities and there are synchronicities, this is no Jungian beetle crawling over a windowsill, this is international! The mysterious force that brought Tim to Bou Saada had to get him out of prison in the States first, fly him across the Atlantic and drive him out of Algiers itself by using Eldridge Cleaver.

Was it the same unconscious directive that scooped up Aleister and Victor 60 years ago and deposited them amongst the cones of sand? They seem to have had no more idea of their mission than we had. Crowley's writing shows some of his puzzlement:

"I had no magical object in going to Algiers, which I reached on November 17th. As my chela, I took Frater Omnia Vincam, a neophyte of the A∴A∴ disguised as Victor Neuburg. We merely wanted to rough it a bit in a new and interesting corner of the planet ... with no particular objective beyond filling our lungs with pure air and renewing the austere rapture of sleeping on the ground and watching the stars...

... "I cannot imagine how the idea came to me. Perhaps I happened to have in my rucksack one of my earliest magical notebooks, where I had copied with infinite patience the nineteen Calls or Keys obtained by Sir Edward Kelley from certain angels and written from his dictation by Queen Elizabeth's astrologer with whom he was working."

–from The Confessions of Aleister Crowley

So Victor and Aleister walked out into the desert evoking one Key of the manuscript per day, passing Bou Saada on the way to Biskra (just as Tim and Rosemary had done). They were aimlessly wandering, walking round in circles in the sand waiting for an omen or a sign, feeling around with their extrasensory perceptions like the tip of a dowser's wand.

"I became subtly aware that this Work was more than the impersonal exploration which I had intended to make. I felt that a hand was holding my heart, that a breath was whispering words in a strange tongue...'

'We went far out from the city into a hollow amongst the dunes. There we made a circle to protect the scribe and a triangle wherein the Abyss might manifest sensibly." Ibid.

The Abyss is that part of your trip where there is no orientation. On the way up your body seems to liquefy into wriggling vibrations, a no-man's land between earth and heaven, often perceived as frightening and monstrous. To get through this region painlessly you lie still and relaxed and "Go with the flow." Crowley however, decides to put the upward shift on "hold," stop the elevator between floors as it were, and blag his way past the demon doorman. He scores a circle in the sand, and in case he flips out, arms Neuburg with a consecrated dagger to keep him at bay. Then he sits himself down outside the protective circle in a triangle also scored in the sand and begins to vibrate the magic Key from Dee and Kelley's manuscript. Crowley is not conjuring a demon, he is becoming one!

"The name of the Dweller in the Abyss is Choronzon, but he is not really an individual. The Abyss is empty of being; it is filled with all possible forms, each equally inane, each therefore evil in the only true sense of the word—that is, meaningless but malignant, in so far as it craves to become real. These forms swirl senselessly into haphazard heaps like dust devils, and each such chance aggregation asserts itself to be an individual and shrieks, 'I am I!' though aware all the time that its elements have no true bond; so that the slightest disturbance dissipates the delusion just as a horseman, meeting a dust devil, brings it in showers of sand to the earth." Ibid.

Neuburg, watching and taking notes from the relative security of the circle, sees him pass through a series of changes as the demon Choronzon possesses his consciousness. Aleister appears to become a woman that Victor had once loved, then a snake with a human head, then such a string of images and words that Neuburg, disorientated and dazzled by the imagery does not see that

Then the entity possessing Crowley's body rushed at Neuburg "flung him to the earth and tried to tear out his throat with froth-covered fangs."

he is being purposefully distracted, and that all the time he is speaking Choronzon is dribbling sand over the line of the circle. Then the entity possessing Crowley's body rushed at Neuburg "flung him to the earth and tried to tear out his throat with froth-covered fangs." Victor invokes the names of God and fights him off with the dagger till he runs off into the desert and cools out.

> "During all this time I had astrally identified myself with Choronzon, so I experienced each anguish, each rage, each despair, each insane outburst. My ordeal ended as the last form faded; so, knowing that all was over, I wrote the holy name of BABALON in the sand with my magical ring and arose from my trance. We lit a fire to purify the place and destroyed the Circle and Triangle. The work had lasted over two hours and we were both utterly exhausted, physically and every other way. I hardly know how we ever got back to Bou Saada." *Ibid*

As I read Aleister Crowley's "Confessions" my mind goes back; I remember that it was actually before the peak of the trip, when I was high on fasting and had shortly before eaten a chunk of primo Afghani hashish, that a cowled man surrounded by a dust devil had appeared along with the name Dr. Dee and a scroll of manuscript.

Now, as I learn that Aleister was himself cowled, and see that he describes the demon Choronzon possessing him as being a coagulation of forms that "swirl senselessly into haphazard heaps like dust devils" ("dust devils" is the same expression used in my notes), I realize that it was Choronzon that I saw in the desert! "... and each such chance aggregation asserts itself to be an individual and shrieks 'I am I'! though aware all the time that its elements have no true bond."

Evidently, writing BABALON in the sand with his ring and building a "great fire to purify the place" was not enough, Crowley had left a swirl of psychic pollution hanging about shouting "I am Dr. Dee!" and waving the manuscript.

After Bou Saada I felt something tremendous had happened, Liz said I looked illumined, and I had that privi-

leged feeling and a warmness inside me as if sometime, somewhere I must have done something right. And it all coincided with Easter, a time of epiphany, an up thrust of energy following the sacrifice of the Mouton Festival after the purification of the Tindouf escapade—I had been in a ritual without knowing it!

Memories flood back; the dawn sky, feeling as if we had been called to this place by unknown forces, directed by ultrasonic voices or guided by ley lines under the desert sands.

Then there was that strange "coming together of the sky" that I had witnessed with Elizabeth the night following the Bou Saada experience, as if time itself had snapped into place—TimESPace.

I wonder if the old wizard himself, Dr. Dee, ever came to Bou Saada, a few centuries back with Kelley? They certainly did a lot of traveling around Europe together, either sponsored by the Bohemian Emperor Rudolf II or living off their alchemy and their wits—not unlike Tim and myself. They had similar pressures to contend with as well; at one time Dee was accused of plotting to kill Mary Tudor by drugs or magic and so many crimes are attributed to Kelley that it's a wonder he had time for anything else.

When the discovery was made that Crowley and Neuburg had been to Bou Saada, Tim wrote, referring to himself and Rosemary:

> "We touched base at Bou Saada. We did not realize until Brian Barritt told us months later that we were following exactly the route which Aleister Crowley took on his search for desert illumination. The eerie synchronicities between our lives and that of Crowley, which were later to preoccupy us, were still unfolding with such precision as to make us wonder if one can escape the programmed imprinting with which we are born. At times it seemed so Oedipally prepackaged."—*Confessions of a Hope Fiend*, Timothy Leary, Bantam Books, 1973[2]

Our meditations are interrupted at this point by the appearance of Kenneth Kahn and his assistant Sherri requesting an interview with Tim (Later published in the LA Free Press in the US and Oz magazine in the UK).

Q: Why did you go to Algeria?

A: I was hypnotized by Bernadine Dohrn[3] for whom I would go anywhere. Actually we went to Algeria to meet Brian Barritt and perform certain magical actions demanded by the Aleister Crowley, Victor Neuburg reincarnation script.

Q: Were those your respective prior names?

A: Apparently.

Q: Did you make this discovery under the influence of LSD?

A: The full moon pilgrimage to the desert in Bou Saada was fuelled by all the alchemy we could conjure up. The precision of this reincarnation dance was revealed a year later upon reading *The Confessions of Aleister Crowley*.

–Oz, November 1972.

Shortly after we have discovered Crowley's *Confessions* Tim comes bounding upstairs waving the book and pointing to a passage; "Look at this" he says, "What do you think of that?"

"Then the Angel bade me understand whereto my aspirations led; all powers, all ecstasies, ended in this—I understood. He then told me that my name was Nemo, seated amongst the other silent shapes in the City of the Pyramids under the Night of Pan; those other parts of me that I had left for ever below the Abyss must serve as a vehicle for the energies which had been created by my act. My mind and body, deprived of the ego which they had hitherto obeyed, were now free to manifest according to their nature in the world, to devote themselves to aid mankind in its evolution. In my case I was cast out into the sphere of Jupiter. My moral part was to help humanity in Jupitarian work, such as governing, teaching, creating, exhorting men to aspire to become nobler, holier, worthier, kinglier, kindlier, and more generous."

–from *The Confessions of Aleister Crowley*

"I'm Nemo," he says "Those are all the things I want to do."

I am not terribly impressed; sure they describe him but they also describe every other religious teacher throughout the whole of history, with a little imagination I could apply them to myself. If you look into occult writings you find something you identify with right away, it's like staring into a mirror and agreeing with yourself that it's a good likeness. So I say "Yes, Timothy it describes you to a T but Nemo is just 'omen' backwards and I have enough omens without going 20,000 leagues under the sea to look for more." My remarks do not phase him at all, he's still full of enthusiasm and for the next couple-o-weeks he is lit up like a light bulb, calling himself either Timo or Nemo and signing himself with a smiley face in the O and radials shooting out of it like rays from the sun.

Note: It is only after I have finished this manuscript, 20 years after the event, that Liz, flipping through the pages of a Crowley book someone has left behind, called *Gems From the Equinox*, reads out an interesting foot-note: "The river-bed near Bou Saada."

Brian Barritt, probably tripping

It's in a section called The Vision and the Voice that contains a record of Crowley and Neuburg's mescaline ceremonies in the Algerian desert.

The precision of this reincarnation dance was revealed a year later upon reading *The Confessions of Aleister Crowley*.

Tim and I were pretty freaked to find we had tripped by accident in the same area as the previous psychedelic explorers, now I find we have tripped in the same place! On the 4th Dec. 1909 Crowley and Neuburg stood in the sand where the river bells out just as Tim and I had done, they were performing the 13th Aether, using the call "Zim," not by full moon like ourselves but in broad daylight in the afternoon. The entity they contacted was called Nemo.

Nemo tells Crowley about a garden—representing the earth—and informs him that he is a rare flower and that he has just inherited the post of head gardener. The Gardener tends the garden making it possible for other flowers to grow, one of them, already growing, will be the Nemo to come. Crowley's report gives the impression that he is taking over from the former Nemo and preparing the way for the next—a line of gurus unfolding. I think that on Easter Sat/Sun 1971 Tim inherited Crowley's old job. ⏻

Endnotes

1. Here Barritt refers to Timothy and Rosemary Leary's "house arrest" hospitality at the hands of exiled Black Panther leader Eldridge Cleaver at Cleaver's headquarters in Algeria. Cleaver initially welcomed the Learys but later became paranoid and "arrested" them.
2. The title of this book is also a Crowley homage, combining the titles of Crowley's books *The Diary of a Drug Fiend* and *The Confessions of Aleister Crowley*.
3. Bernadine Dohrn, co-founder of the "Weather Underground," a cell of urban terrorists that splintered from the student New Left. Dohrn assisted Leary's prison break.

LEARY AND CROWLEY
An Excerpt from *Cosmic Trigger*

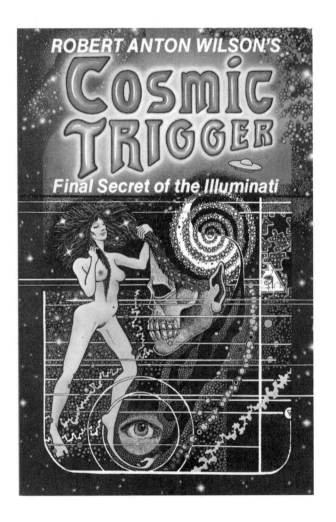

Starseed

The next step in whatever is wrong with me again involved Timothy Leary.

I was conducting a series of experiments in July–August 1973—following the Sirius Transmission—in which I attempted astral projection. I met all sorts of odd and amusing entities on all sorts of astral planes, but none of those experiences ever developed into anything evidential. However, I was continually interrupted during my voyages by impressions of Leary doing similar experiments in his cell at Folsom. I also had visions of him flying over the walls of the prison.

I specifically mentioned these experiences of ESP-contact with Leary in an article on Tantric yoga, published in the *Chicago Seed* [an underground publication of the day] in September 1973.

It was *four years later*, in 1977, that Lynn Wayne Benner, who was Leary's closest friend in Folsom, told me of the events of that August of 1973. According to Benner, Leary and he were not only doing the interstellar ESP experiments described below but also tried experiments at levitation, in which they attempted to *fly over* the walls of Folsom.

I wrote to the warden of Folsom in late August, and asked for permission to correspond with Dr. Leary. Bureaucratic red tape being what it is, this permission was delayed for several weeks.

Shortly after the telepathic flashes of Leary (July–August 1973) ended, Walter Culpepper, the attorney for

P.R.O.B.E.—a Leary created organization to abolish prisons—had a benefit for the Leary Defense Fund and P.R.O.B.E. Two rock groups played and then we were shown "At Folsom Prison With Timothy Leary, Ph.D.," produced by Joanna Leary.

The film blew the Skeptic's mind. Timothy came on screen and immediately flashed the famous Love-Peace-Bliss grin at the camera—as if he were greeting visitors to his home. We never saw a man look less like a suffering martyr. Tim took a chair and answered the interviewer's questions in a serious and thoughtful manner, explaining that he wasn't interested in drugs any more since they had only been "microscopes" to reveal the focus and re-focus possibilities of the nervous system. He wanted to talk about something more exciting now—Outer Space. The interviewer kept leading him back to drugs, and Leary kept maneuvering back to Cosmic Dimensions.

I began to notice an odd thing: Timothy looked younger than he had in the 1960s.

Tim led the interviewer to ask about the strange design on his prison uniform. "This is Starseed," Tim said, proud as a new father. The emblem was that strange miniature infinity design, the nucleotide template formed as DNA imprints messenger-RNA to start a new growth program.

Starseed, however, was not just any nucleotide template. It was the one recently found on a meteor which landed in Orgeuil, France, when scientists examined the rock microscopically. It is the first chemical proof that the mechanism of chemical "intelligence"—the building of life programs (RNA) out of information-codes (DNA)—exists elsewhere in the universe.

Starseed, Leary enthusiastically told the interviewer, proves that cellular intelligence is not exclusively earthly. It therefore increases the probable grounds to believe many forms of life and intelligence exist in space-time.

Other cons in Folsom, after Leary left, picked up the Starseed symbol, carved it on belts, painted it on sketch pads, sewed it on clothing, and formed bull sessions to rap with Hal Olsen (life-termer, illustrator of Leary's *Terra II*) and Wayne Benner ("the Tuxedo Bandit" and one unit in Leary's four-person telepathy experiments) about the possibility of Higher Intelligence and the transcendental implications of modern science.

meanwhile went on researching Sirius. I was quite moved, as you will readily understand, when I found the following

in O.T.O. Grand Master Kenneth Grant's new book, *Aleister Crowley and the Hidden God:*

> Crowley was aware of the possibility of opening the spatial gateways and of admitting an extraterrestrial Current, into the human life-wave...
>
> It is an occult tradition—and Lovecraft gave it persistent utterance in his writings—that some transfinite and superhuman power is marshalling its forces with intent to invade and take possession of this planet.... This is reminiscent of Charles Fort's dark hints about a secret society on earth already in contact with cosmic beings and perhaps preparing the way for their advent."[1]

This sounds more than a little sinister and was especially eerie for me, since I had already incorporated into *Illuminatus* a variation on the Lovecraft mythos. Lovecraft has written several stories and novelettes in which the "Cthulhu cult" or some other secret society was aiding the schemes of hostile Aliens; I had attached this theme to the Illuminati as a kind of deadpan put-on and laughed like hell at the thought that some naive readers would be dumb enough to believe it. Now here it was being proclaimed by Kenneth Grant, who alleges that the Ordo Templi Orientis was formed in the 1890s by amalgamating P. B. Randolph's Hermetic Brotherhood of Light with the original Bavarian Illuminati. I thought for the first time (as I was to think again, many times, during the Watergate Scandals), "My God, can't I invent any preposterous paranoid fantasy that doesn't have some truth behind it?"

But Grant goes on to cheer us up, if we are willing to trust him at this point:

> Crowley dispels the aura of evil with which these authors (Lovecraft and Fort) invest the fact; he prefers to interpret it Thelemically, not as an attack upon human consciousness by an extra-terrestrial and alien entity but as an expansion of consciousness from within, to embrace other stars and to absorb their energies into a system that is thereby enriched and rendered truly cosmic by the process.

LEARY AND CROWLEY: An Excerpt From Cosmic Trigger

And then he adds, quite nonchalantly again, that one star is especially important:

> The Order of the Silver Star is thus the Order of the Eye of Set, "the Sun behind the Sun." ... The Silver Star is Sirius.

A MESSAGE FROM COSMIC CENTRAL?

In October 1973, I finally received permission to begin corresponding with Dr. Leary at Folsom Prison. I started out with a letter about the general philosophical implications of tuning the nervous system to higher fidelity of signal-reception and very carefully did *not* mention my July 23 experience with Sirius. (I was fairly sure that my July–August impressions that Timothy was doing telepathic experiments had been accurate, but I had no idea yet that he was attempting interstellar telepathy.) Tim's answer was full of characteristic humor:

> The prison administration is perfect. They act as a Van Allen belt protecting my privacy, screening out distractions ... The people they refuse visiting privileges are exactly those people who come to exploit me or whose love for me is flawed.
>
> (My gratitude towards the prison warden must not be misunderstood. They are too possessive and jealous—terrible states to be in. Their love and dependence on me are too restricting. They are terrorized that I might leave them ... in the lurch, so to say. This is unhealthy for them...)[2]

I wrote back, but remained mum about Sirius. Instead, just for the hell of it, I used my official Discordian Society letterhead. The stationery bears the imprint of the Joshua Norton Cabal, this being a Cabal of the Discordian Society located in the Bay Area—other Cabals including the Tactile Temple of Eris Erotic in Los Angeles, the Colorado Encrustation in Denver, the John Dillinger Died for You Society in Chicago, etc. Timothy, however, seems to have thought Joshua Norton Cabal was the name of a living person. Actually, Joshua Norton—or Norton I, as he preferred—was a San Franciscan of the last century who elected himself Emperor of the United States and Protector of Mexico. Bay Area historians still

argue as to whether Norton was a psychotic or a clever con man; in any event, he was "humored" by the citizenry of the time and, in effect, lived like an Emperor. As Greg Hill, co-founder of Discordianism, has written, "Everybody understands Mickey Mouse. Few understand Herman Hesse. Hardly anybody understands Einstein. And nobody understands Emperor Norton." (The Discordian Society, we repeat again, is not a complicated joke disguised as a new religion but really a new religion disguised as a complicated joke.)

Timothy replied:

> Dear Bob,
>
> Quick response ... to indicate that transmission is working form this galaxy to yours.
>
> Your stationary amazed me... could you explain any of it? Like ODD3140Aft11bii? And who is Joshua Norton Cabal?
>
> Actually the Warden here is very protective of me. He is like a gruff Zen abbot. He doesn't want me to be bothered with visits or correspondence which would bring me down, slow up my scientific work, etc. As long as I sit in my cell and write science fiction books ... everyone is happy.
>
> Yes. G. I. Gurdiieff is my direct successor. I have never doubted that his baraka was transferred to me ... perhaps by some intermediary. I love Him and I resonate to his wisdom more than anyone else's.
>
> Crowley... the coincidences-synchronicities between my life and His are embarrassing. Brian Barritt and I had a visionary experience Easter Sat–Sun in Bou Saada, the Algerian town where C. had his. Etc.

The Libertarian wrote back discussing the odd links between Leary's work and that of Crowley and Gurdjieff, and mentioning the evidence that the latter two were both taught certain advanced techniques of consciousness expansion by the Sufi lodges of the Near East. He also mentioned that Rasputin might have had the same sort of Sufi training during his wanderings.

Leary's reply blew his mind:

Dear Bob,

Loved your letter …

Are you in touch with teachings methods, teachers, etc. that transmit Higher Intelligences. That you are totally hooked into?

If so, would you tell me?

I don't believe in secrets …

I believe that Higher Intelligence can be contacted and have described how to do it and what They transmit, etc. Have you contacted Joanna? Ask Her to send you a copy of Terra II.

You mention that Crowley, G. and Rasputin may have had contact with some Sufi lodge. Do you think this "lodge" actually exists in the human sense of Masters in the Middle East who send G and C and R out as emissaries? This is the most exciting idea I've puzzled over for ten years.

I have seen what can be transmitted through one unit. The one that I belonged to. Where are the others? …

I am amazed that you haven't contacted Michael Horowitz.

Mike Horowitz, a thin, intense, brilliant guy, is Director of the Fitzhugh Ludlow Memorial Library in San Francisco—a psychopharmacological archive full of rare literature on drugs—scientific, propagandistic (government), literary, or just journalistic. When the Investigator got in touch with Mike Horowitz, he heard, for the first time, about the Starseed Transmissions.

Meanwhile, Dr. Leary was shifted from Folsom to Vacaville and communication with him temporarily shorted-out. Once again, I had to apply for permission to correspond, fill out the right forms when they were finally mailed, and then wait for the new warden's decision. The Libertarian felt increasingly like one of the scholars of the Middle Ages, trying to keep up communication with a fellow investigator while the Holy Inquisition created as much static as possible.

It should be remembered, in evaluating the Starseed signals, that, a few months before this experience, three government psychiatrists testified (at the escape trial) that Dr. Leary was perfectly sane and possessed a high I.Q. Since so many extremists of Left and Right have impugned Dr. Leary's sanity, it should also be entered in the record that Dr. Wesley Hiler, a staff psychologist at Vacaville, who spoke to Dr. Leary every day (often to ask Tim's advice) emphatically agrees with that verdict. "Timothy Leary is totally, radiantly sane," he told me in a 1973 interview.

As recounted in Terra II, during July–August 1973, Dr. Leary had formed a four-person telepathy team in an attempt to contact Higher Intelligences elsewhere in the galaxy. (This was in the middle of the "dog days," when I was having my first (real or hallucinatory) Contacts with Sirius.) The persons involved were: Dr. Leary and his wife, Joanna; fellow prisoner Wayne Benner; and Wayne's girlfriend, a journalist who prefers to be known as Guanine.

The Starseed Transmissions—"hallucinations" or whatever—were received in nineteen bursts, seldom in recognizable English sentences, requiring considerable meditation and discussion between the four Receivers before they could be summarized, eventually, into the following message:

It is time for life on Earth to leave the planetary womb and learn to walk through the stars.

Life was seeded on your planet billions of years ago by nucleotide templates which contained the blueprint for gradual evolution through a sequence of bio-mechanical stages.

The goal of evolution is to produce nervous systems capable of communicating with and returning to the Galactic Network where we, your interstellar parents, await you.

Life on planet Earth has now reached this halfway point, established itself, and evolved through larval mutations and metamorphoses to the seven brain stages.

At this time the voyage home is possible.

Assemble the most intelligent, advanced, courageous of your species, divided equally between men and women. Let every race, nationality, and religion be represented.

You are about to discover the key to immortality in the chemical structure of the genetic code, within which you will find the scripture of life. The time has come for you to accept the responsibility of immortality. It is not necessary for you to die.

You will discover the key to enhanced intelligence within the chemistry of the nervous system. Certain chemicals, used wisely, will enable your nervous system to decipher the genetic code.

All life on your planet is a unity. All life must come home.

Total freedom, responsibility and interspecies harmony will make the voyage possible. You must transcend larval identities of race, culture and nationality. Your only allegiance is to life. The only way you will survive is to make the voyage home.

The Japanese people are the most advanced race on your planet and will give protection to the company.

We are sending a comet to your solar system as a sign that the time has come to look to the stars. When you arrive back home you will be given new instructions and powers. Your sperm ship is the flower of terrestrial life. As soon as the company is formed and the voyage begun, war, poverty, hatred, fear will disappear from your planet and the most ancient prophecies and celestial visions will be realized.

Mutate!

Come home in glory.

In the following months, Comet Kohoutek, as predicted in the Transmissions, arrived in the solar system and sped inward toward the sun, while astronomers announced an unprecedented spectacle and Leary's disciples chortled at the confirmation.

Then the comet fizzled, leaving us wondering.

SOME EGYPTIAN GODS INTRUDE ON THE NARRATIVE AND OUR LADY OF SPACE SPEAKS AGAIN

In 1904, in one of the most extraordinary magical experiences of his life, Aleister Crowley contacted a Higher Intelligence named Aiwass, who dictated to him *The Book of the Law*. In what follows, we will show some imagistic links between this Book and the Starseed Signals—but first, a few details about how Crowley received this strange document:

Aleister and his first wife, Rose, were in Cairo, Egypt, when Rose began going spontaneously into trances and muttering "They are waiting for you," and similar urgent but unintelligible phrases. Crowley did not like this at all, since it is typical of the uncontrolled, quasi-hysterical trances of spiritualist mediums (whom he despised) and lacked the elements of *willed concentration* and *rational control* that he demanded of his magick experiments. Nonetheless, despite his attempts to banish the phenomenon, it kept coming back, and finally, in one of Rose's trances, Crowley set a series of tests for the alleged communicating entity. He asked Rose, for instance, to describe the aura of the being, and she said "deep blue"; he asked the character of the being, and she said "force and fire"; he asked her to pick the being from drawings of ten Egyptian gods, and she picked Horus. She also identified Horus' planet (Mars) and so forth for a series of similar questions. Crowley then calculated the odds against her being right in all cases—for instance, guessing Mars had a 1/9 probability, there being nine planets, picking Horus out of ten drawings had a 1/10 probability, etc. The chance of her guessing right on the whole series *by chance* was, mathematically, 1/21, 168,000. (The long-suffering skeptical reader may resist the "reality" of Horus by accepting the less bizarre theory that Rose was simply reading Aleister's mind.)

The next day Crowley took Rose to the Boulak Museum and asked her to identify the communicant from the statues and paintings there. She walked past several depictions of Horus—the ever-cynical Aleister watching, he says, in "silent glee"—and then stopped at a stele showing a *dark woman* bending over a *winged glob*e, a *hawk-headed god* and a human male. "This is the one," she said, pointing to the hawk-headed god, Horus. The stele was numbered 666 by the museum officials, and that was a synchronicity that got Aleister's immediate attention. He had been using 666 as his own magick number for years.[3] So Crowley decided to cooperate, and back at his hotel accepted a light trance in which *The Book of the Law* was dictated to him in a "rich baritone" by an invisible being. The book opens:

> Had! The manifestation of Nuit.
> The unveiling of the company of heaven.
> Every man and every woman is a star.

Nuit, *the Egyptian divinity of the stars*, seems to tell us, in these opening verses, that we are Her children. She goes on to declare:

> I am *above* you and *in* you. My ecstasy is in yours.
> My joy is to see your joy.

The union of mankind with the stars is precisely forecast:

> They shall gather my children into their fold; they shall bring the glory of the stars into the hearts of men.
>
> And the sign shall be my ecstasy, the consciousness of the continuity of existence, the omnipresence of my body...
>
> For I am divided for love's sake, for the chance of union.

This seems a vividly poetic pre-statement of Leary's theory that Higher Intelligence is "divided," by sending out DNA seed to fertilize every womb-planet in the galaxy, "for the chance of union," the return of these "children" after

they have evolved past the larval circuits into higher modes of consciousness.

> I love you! I yearn to you! ... Put on the wings, and arouse the coiled splendor within you: *come unto me!*

The Star-Mother, Nuit, is definitely calling us home, to Galactic Center. The "coiled splendor" may even suggest the DNA helix within which, Leary and other investigators now think, is the secret of immortality. But shortly comes a more interesting text:

> Is a God to live in a dog?

A reference to the great Dog Star, Sirius? Instructions on contacting this intelligence are quite specific:

> To worship me take wine and strange drugs whereof I will tell my prophet & be drunk thereof!

The Immortality Pill is directly mentioned:

> Think not, O King, upon that lie: That Thou Must Die: verily thou shalt not die, but live.

In Chapter Three, Horus, the war-god, takes over and makes some ferocious predictions about the 20th century:

> Now let it be understood first that I am a god of War and Vengeance. I shall deal hardly with them...
>
> I am the Warrior Lord of the Forties; the Eighties cower before me & are abased.[4]

Now, this is not terribly bad as prophecy of the 20th century, for a book produced in 1904—when the majority opinion of Europe was that war had been banished from the civilized nations forever.

It seems clear that the Starseed Transmissions acquired a rather heavy Timothy Leary flavor in passing through the Leary nervous system, just as the *Book of the Law* took on an undeniably Crowleyan aroma in passing through Aleister's neurons; but the underlying message is hauntingly similar.

A few other oddities about the *Book of the Law* and the Stele of Revealing are worth noting: Crowley was an avid

Qabalist and spent years examining the Qabalistic numbers for key words in the text. This is based on the traditional assumption that Qabalistic numerology is a code worked out millennia ago for communication between humans and Higher Intelligence. Be as cynical about that as you will, but consider the data: All the important words, Crowley gradually realized, had the value of 93 in Greek Qabala. (He thereafter referred to his magick work as "the 93 current," and Crowleyans to this day speak of their work as carrying on the 93 current.)

93 is also the Qabalistic numeration of the word *Thelema*, the "word" of the New Age, according to the communicating entity. The Abbey of *Thelema*, in Rabelais, had the motto "Do what thou wilt." The *Book of the Law* says, "Do what thou wilt shall be the whole of the law." Thelema, in Greek, means either *will* or *the casting of a magick spell*. Aiwass, the "Holy Guardian Angel" presiding over this Contact, also has the value 93. And Agape (love), another key word in the text, is again 93. The name of "God" in Genesis (Alhim) contains the value of π to four places (3.1415); add Crowley's 93 and you get π accurate to six places (3.141593).

The second major number in the book is 418, which "coincidentally" was the number of Crowley's home in Inverness, Scotland. Its standard Qabalistic meaning is "the Great Work accomplished," or the Illumination of all humanity. Crowley interpreted this to mean that his mission was not to illuminate a few, as other gurus have done and are doing, but to set in motion occult forces which would result in the illumination of all by the end of this century; 418 is also the value of "Parcifal," that Sufi whose life so oddly intersected mine in that mad summer of 1973.

The Stele of Revealing contains in addition to Nuit, Horus and Ankh-f-na-Khonsu, a mysterious winged globe. Dr. Jacques Vallee, in *The Invisible College*, gives several other forms of the winged globe from Egyptian and Gnostic sources and points out the similarity to modern sketches of UFOs by witnesses or Contactees.

The winged globe, with an eye in it, appears in an ancient Assyrian seal found by astronomer [Robert] Temple and reproduced in his *Sirius Mystery*. In this case, it is accompanied by Oannes, the water-god, whom Temple identifies as an extraterrestrial visitor from Sirius. Note the fish-tail on Oannes. Now look at the following illustration which is a drawing from the Dogon tribe of Africa, showing Nommo, whom they claim was a visitor from Sirius; note the similar fish-tail.

Dr. John Lilly, who has duplicated much of Timothy Leary's research and supplemented it with hypnotic methods and Sufi yoga, describes many encounters with what seem to be extraterrestrial intelligences in his *Programming and Meta-programming the Human Biocomputer*. Dr. Lilly agnostically examines also the possibilities that these transmitters are time-travelers from the future, very advanced Illuminati Adepts alive now on earth, "angels" in the traditional sense, or projected aspects of his own mind. In *The Center of the Cyclone* he says clearly:

> Such a network [of Adepts] exists and functions … throughout this planet. I suspect *it extends farther than our earth*, but this this has yet to be publicly demonstrated beyond the private *experience of myself and others*.

A network of adepts that extends far beyond our Earth … that was what your narrator was gradually coming to believe and here it was being said, with only slight reservation, by Dr. John Lilly—the man once defined by the *New York Times* as "a walking one-man syllabus of Western civilization."

But permission to visit Dr. Leary had finally been granted by prison authorities and I was to hear even more extraordinary theories from him. ☿

Endnotes

1. Grant here quotes, in a footnote, from Fort's *The Book of the Damned*, "… some other world is not attempting, but has been, for centuries, in communication with a sect, perhaps, or a secret society or certain esoteric ones of this earth's inhabitants."
2. Because Leary had already escaped from one California prison, the authorities at Folsom originally placed him in "the hole," a solitary confinement cell in the basement of the maximum security building.
3. *The Law is For All* by Aleister Crowley, edited by Israel Regardie, Llewellyn: St. Paul, 1970. See also *Confessions of Aleister Crowley*, Bantam: New York, 1971, pp 413–27.
4. All quotations from the *Book of the Law* are from *The Law is For All*, op. cit., pp 44–65.

THE GREAT BEAST 666

SIX VOICES ON CROWLEY

Aleister Crowley (1875–1947) created a spiritual or religious system known as Thelema, which revolves around ideas of freedom and personal growth. Unlike traditional religious systems that expect their adherents to echo their teachings, Thelema recognizes the validity and holiness of many different voices. This introduction presents six different voices, myself, or the Unreliable Narrator, together with Crowley's own voice, and four fictional voices, the True Believer, the Chaotic, the Skeptic and the Mystic, composites drawn from the occult community. I do not always agree with them, and they do not always agree with each other.

"DO WHAT THOU WILT"

"Do what thou wilt shall be the whole of the Law" or the Law of Thelema is a moral utterance found in the Thelemic foundation scripture, the Book of the Law. It is derived from the rule of the fictional Abbey of Thélème in the classic satire *Gargantua* by the French priest and occult student François Rabelais (1483–1553), named by Crowley as a Gnostic Saint, along with Nietzsche, Payne Knight, Swinburne, and Papus. In Rabelais this rule was "fay çe que vouldras," French for "do what you will." The maxim became a part of Western literary life, and was adopted by the English gentleman's society called the Hell-Fire Club.

In Crowley's writing, the Law of Thelema is explained in terms of True Will, the ultimate spiritual core or quintessence of each person, which has a divinely self-ordained path through the world of experience. "Do what thou wilt"

The Great Beast

refers not to the outer emotional and intellectual self but to this sacred inner core of personal divinity. Often will is contrasted with whim, and the knowing and doing of the True Will is painted not in terms of license but of responsibility.

"Do what thou wilt" refers not to the outer emotional and intellectual self but to this sacred inner core of personal divinity.

Since this new law replaces outdated moral codes based around sins and forbidden acts, a person knowing and doing the will might appear to be sinful from a traditional viewpoint. In Crowley's view the Thelemite is following a demanding code requiring personal integrity even while, for instance, making love in ways that would be illegal in oppressive societies. This inversion of traditional mores is easily expressed in ironic or satirical form.

Crowley also held that "do what thou wilt" was an ethical code bearing on how one should deal with others. One must respect not only one's own will but the wills of others. All the wills are magically arranged so that there is no conflict between them, just as (so it was believed in Crowley's day) the stars are arranged so that they never collide. The personal will and the will of all are mystically joined in a unified whole that is paradoxically also the basis of individuality. Collision between wills indicates that one or the other person was not doing their True Will.

At other times Crowley said that the only error was to believe that others existed at all and that they had wills that could be violated. This solipsism was inspired by his sympathy for the philosopher Berkeley but he placed God within rather than without.

At yet other times Crowley said that there was no possibility of error and that all beings live according to the will-paths predestined by themselves before their births, from which any deviation would be impossible. In this view the appearance of deviation from the will is akin to the Buddhist doctrine that all beings are enlightened already, and the appearance of non-enlightenment is illusion. Crowley added that incarnation is voluntarily chosen as a play of shadow and light, in contrast with traditional Hindu ideas of the curse of rebirth. The idea that sorrow is illusory in a reincarnatory world was popular in Spiritualist circles during Crowley's formative period.

These apparent contradictions may have been reconciled for Crowley by the idea of levels of truth. Pure selfhood is paradoxically selfless. The realization of one's true nature comes at the same time that one realizes one's unity with all beings. So for the ordinary person, "do what thou wilt" is a useful rule of thumb for interacting with others. At a higher level one realizes that there are no others, or that the distinction between self and non-self is an illusion, and so the Law of Thelema takes on a non-dual meaning.

The Law of Rabelais' Abbey has widespread influence by itself. For instance, in 1929 Aldous Huxley published a book of his essays entitled *Do What You Will*. His source was not Crowley, but William Blake (1757–1827), who wrote in his *Gnomic Verses*, xxiii, "Do what you will this life's a fiction, And is made up of contradiction." Similarly, the Wiccan Rede of Gerald Gardner came from Rabelais through the erotic novelist Pierre Louys and his *Adventures of King Pausole* (1900). Crowley did not invent the phrase, and his views are not the last word upon it.

ALEISTER CROWLEY: "Thelema means Will. The Key to this Message is this word—Will. The first obvious meaning of this Law is confirmed by antithesis; 'The word of Sin is Restriction.'

"Again: 'Thou hast no right but to do thy will. Do that and no other shall say nay. For pure will, unassuaged of purpose, delivered from the lust of result, is every way perfect.'

"Take this carefully; it seems to imply a theory that if every man and every woman did his and her will—the true will—there would be no clashing. 'Every man and every woman is a star,' and each star moves in an appointed path without interference. There is plenty of room for all; it is only disorder that creates confusion.

"From these considerations it should be clear that 'Do what thou wilt' does not mean 'Do what you like.' It is

"Take this carefully; it seems to imply a theory that if every man and every woman did his and her will—the true will—there would be no clashing. 'Every man and every woman is a star,' and each star moves in an appointed path without interference."

"From these considerations it should be clear that 'Do what thou wilt' does not mean 'Do what you like.' It is the apotheosis of Freedom; but it is also the strictest possible bond."

the apotheosis of Freedom; but it is also the strictest possible bond.

"Do what thou wilt—then do nothing else."—"The Message of the Master Therion," *The International*, January 1918.

THE TRUE BELIEVER: Do what thou wilt shall be the whole of the Law. As revealed in the *Book of the Law*, human history is divided into Æons which correspond to the precession of the Astrological Signs of the Zodiac. The new Æon of Horus, which began in 1904, brings with it a rotation in the roster of deities governing the planet as well as a revolution in moral codes. Gone are the old codes based on sin, sacrifice and other veils of shame and sorrow. The Law of Thelema is the code of absolute Freedom and absolute Responsibility, and the most perfect moral Law ever formulated. It will last for two thousand years until the rise of the next Æon. Love is the law, love under will.

THE CHAOTIC: True magical power resides in the unconscious mind, which is aware of many things beyond the scope of the ordinary consciousness. Descend far enough into the alien geometries of the unconscious and you might find out who and what you really are. This will free you from shame and guilt and other limitations that society has imposed on you. You can use magic to go inside, or music, or entheogens, or other techniques.

THE SKEPTIC: There is a long history of respect for the individual in Western culture, starting with ancient Greek philosophy, waning under Christianity, and returning in the 17th century with the rise of social philosophers and democratic political institutions. Existentialist philosophy of the 19th and 20th centuries developed a new set of ideas about the individual. Crowley's work is part of this stream of thought, but his contributions are not major compared to those of thinkers such as Nietzsche on one hand and John Stuart Mill on the other.

THE MYSTIC: The True Will, the innermost spark of divine flame known in the Qabala as Yechidah, is unapproachable except by undertaking the work of the Path. By stilling the noise of the lower mind and focusing on the archetypal symbols hidden behind the veil of the universe, and persisting through the great spiritual ordeals that turn away the dilettante and the coward, one may ultimately arrive at that eternal Self and place it into its rightful relation with the rest of the personality, setting intellect and emotion in their proper places as Will's servants rather than its oppressors.

THE BOOK OF THE LAW

Central to Crowley's system is a curious and enigmatic book known as *The Book of the Law*, also called Liber AL, Liber Legis, Liber L, or CCXX (220). It is fairly short and has often been issued in pamphlet form. Crowley said it was revealed to him during his 1904 vacation with his wife Rose in Cairo by the dictation of Aiwass, who was both Crowley's own Holy Guardian Angel and the messenger of the new deities set over this Æon (eon) or age of history. In a series of trance visions, Rose indicated a number of symbols related to the Egyptian god Horus, according to the correspondences Crowley had gotten from the Golden Dawn. She pointed out Stélé 666 in the Boulak Museum, an image of an ancient priest, with the title or name Ankh-f-n-Khonsu, before the god Horus. This stélé has become a Thelemic icon. Following Rose's instructions, Crowley went to their rented rooms at an arranged time for three days and took dictation from an unseen voice.

The phrase "Book of the Law" comes from Freemasonry, as a synonym for "Volume of the Sacred Law" (VSL). In a Christian Freemasonic Lodge this VSL would be the Bible on the altar; in a Jewish Lodge it would be the Torah, which means the scroll of the Law; and in a religiously mixed Lodge there might be more than one sacred book on the altar. In Thelemic ritual, Crowley's *Book of the Law* is used for swearing initiatory oaths, like the VSL in Freemasonry. *The Book of the Law* is the central scripture of Thelema, its Bible so to speak. Crowley's work and his curriculum can only be understood with respect to his dynamic relationship with Liber AL.

The book has three chapters, one for each deity of its divine trinity. Its phrasing is often ambiguous and it employs an unearthly prose-poetic style that some find beautiful. Crowley wrote several commentaries during his life, some of them interpreting its verses in very different ways from his other commentaries or in ways at odds with the surface meaning of the verses.

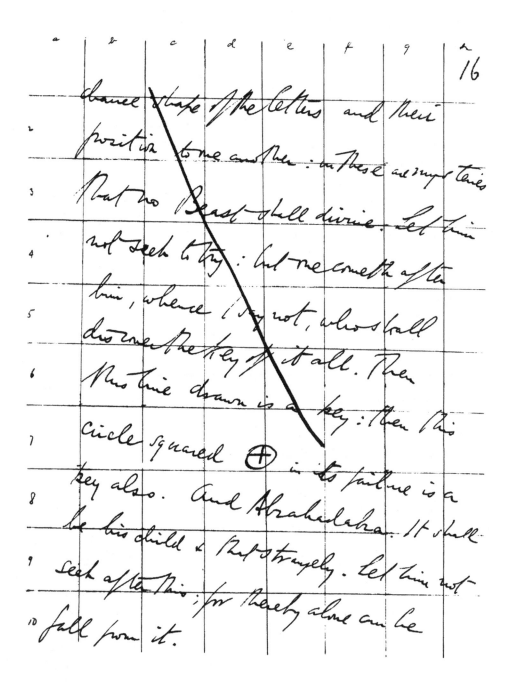

The most curious page of all from *The Book of the Law*: "This book shall be translated into all tongues: but always with the original in the writing of the Beast; for in the chance shape of the letters and their position to one another: in these are mysteries that no Beast shall divine. Let him not seek to try: but one cometh after him, whence I say not, who shall discover the Key of it all. Then this line drawn is a key: then this circle squared in its failure is a key also. And Abrahadabra. It shall be his child & that strangely. Let him not seek after this; for thereby alone can he fall from it." (AL III:47)

The trinity of *The Book of the Law* or Liber AL is composed of three reinterpreted Egyptian deities. First is Nuit (Nut), the goddess of the night sky, closely linked in Egyptian religion with Hathor, also known as the Egyptian Venus. Her message is of freedom, love and the mystical bliss of union, as expressed in the curious equation 0=2. Nuit reveals the Law of Thelema and declares that the Æons have turned in the Equinox of the Gods. She is represented by space and the stars of space. Nuit indicates the space-time continuum, or infinite potential.

Second is Hadit (Heru-Bedheti or Horus of Edfu), the winged solar globe, symbol of divine authority. This form of the Egyptian god Horus, originally local to Bedheti, had influence throughout ancient Egypt. Hadit symbolizes the secret individuality within each of us, the star that each person is, the invisible, ineffable and unmanifest divine spark which moves each of us on our self-appointed path of will. As such Hadit also represents the underworld, the infinitely small point, the capacity for knowledge, the complement of Nuit, and the fiery nature of underworld deities such as Blake's Los and the Christian Lucifer. Themes of kingship are central to the message of Hadit.

Crowley said that the Apocalypse was an authentic prophecy but that it had been distorted by the point of view of the previous Æon, so that John had misrepresented the Great Beast and Scarlet Woman, who are avatars of solar power and sexual force.

Third in the trinity is the child produced by the union of Nuit and Hadit, the lord of the new Æon, alternately expressed by two different forms of Horus. One form is Ra-Hoor-Khuit (Re-Horakhty), a military aspect of Horus as conqueror and warrior. Ra-Hoor-Khuit extends the inwardly-turned energy of Hadit outwards into the world. Some Thelemites feel that the advocacy of war and violence in the second and third chapters of *The Book of the Law* is meant as a metaphorical magical formula, while others think of them as exhortations to conquer on the plane of political and temporal power.

The other form of Horus in the third chapter is Hoor-Paar-Kraat (Harpocrates), Horus the child, traditionally the child of Isis and Osiris. The English magical group known as the Golden Dawn, to which Crowley belonged, attached to Harpocrates an attribute he probably did not possess in ancient Egyptian religion—his finger pressed to his lips seemed to be a hushing gesture, making him the god of silence. The finger at the lips is now thought by scholars to have been a thumb-sucking gesture of childishness rather than one of silence. When Crowley revised the Tarot Trump Judgment in the last few years of his life he reflected this change, giving Harpocrates a gesture of childlike wonder.

Throughout the book two other mythic figures stand out, the Great Beast and the Scarlet Woman named Babalon. These characters are familiar in Western culture from the Biblical Apocalypse of John, where they appear as evil spirits in animal and human form whose coming marks the end times. Crowley said that the Apocalypse was an authentic prophecy but that it had been distorted by the point of view of the previous Æon, so that John had misrepresented the Great Beast and Scarlet Woman, who are avatars of solar power and sexual force. Crowley held the Beast office and Rose was his original Scarlet Woman.

ALEISTER CROWLEY: "I am certain, I the Beast, whose number is Six Hundred and Sixty Six, that this Third Chapter of *The Book of the Law* is nothing less than the authentic Word, the Word of the Æon, the Truth about Nature at this time and on this planet. I wrote it, hating it and sneering at it, secretly glad that I could use it to revolt against this Task most terrible that the Gods have thrust remorselessly upon my shoulders, their Cross of burning steel that I must carry even to my Calvary, the place of a skull, there to be eased of its weight only that I be crucified thereon. But, being lifted up, I will draw the whole world unto me; and men shall worship me the Beast, Six Hundred and Three-score and Six, celebrating to Me their Midnight Mass every time soever when they do that they will, and on Mine altar slaying to Me that victim I most relish, their Selves; when Love designs and Will executes the Rite whereby (an they know it or not) their God in man is offered to me The Beast, their God, the Rite whose virtue, making their God of their throned Beast, leaves nothing, howso bestial, undivine…

"'Who wrote these words?' Of course I wrote them, ink on paper, in the material sense; but they are not My words, unless Aiwaz be taken to be no more than my subconscious self, or some part of it: in that case, my conscious self being ignorant of the Truth in the Book and hostile to most of the ethics and philosophy of the Book, Aiwaz is a severely suppressed part of me. Such a theory would further imply that I am, unknown to myself, possessed of all sorts of praeternatural knowledge and power.... In any case, whatever 'Aiwaz' is, 'Aiwaz' is an Intelligence possessed of power and knowledge absolutely beyond human experience; and therefore Aiwaz is a Being worthy, as the current use of the word allows, of the title of a God, yea verily and amen, of a God."—*The Equinox of the Gods* (1936), chapter VII.

THE TRUE BELIEVER: Liber AL vel Legis numbered CCXX is a transmission from the gods appointed over the current Æon. The Æon of Osiris was cursed by the failings and horrors of Christianity, a religion that perverted the formula of the Dying and Reborn God first prophesied by the ruling Egyptian God Osiris. In 1904 the two-thousand-year cycle ended with the new Prophecy. Now Christianity and other remnants of Osiris have only the existence of the undead, and like zombies they are crumbling away. Soon they will be gone and the true era of Freedom will reach fruition.

THE CHAOTIC: *The Book of the Law* is a powerful spellbook and meditation focus. It engages many deep parts of the unconscious mind. So do A. O. Spare's works and other systems for other people—there is a lot more to occultism than Crowley. Alternative historical models may be better than Crowley's Æons, like the Chaos Magic psychohistorical model, the Typhonian/Achadian Æon of Ma'at, or the personal Word of each Magus in the Temple of Set. Crowley's Æons were valid for him and for his personal mythology but there are a lot of different stories you could tell about history. They are all myths. It would be a mistake to take any myth literally.

THE SKEPTIC: One can take an approach to Thelemic myth like that of liberal Christianity toward Genesis, using it as poetic or speculative material for ritual and worship. The Æonic model is a mistake if examined as history, but so are most cosmological myths. Cultural prejudices in the Christian West created a mistaken idea that the Christ myth had been prefigured in paganism as the Dying and Reborn God. Osiris and Christ are not similar, and they are not similar to other gods who were forced into the Christian mold, such as Dionysus, Orpheus, Attis and Tammuz.

THE MYSTIC: The Æons bring with them characteristic Formulae of Initiation. In the Æon of Osiris the Formula was Crucifixion and Self-Sacrifice. This had an esoteric meaning related to but different from mundane Christianity. The meaning was preserved through the ancient Mysteries and the Secret Tradition of Occultism. In the Æon of Horus, Sacrifice is replaced by the natural and progressive Growth of the Child. The Attainment of mature powers and Solar glory assume the place previously held by a death-and-rebirth Ordeal.

THE TREE OF LIFE

Crowley frequently makes reference to a diagram which purports to represent the spiritual universe. The Tree of Life has many forms in Qabala. This tradition of Jewish mysticism was adopted centuries ago by Christian mystics and magicians. The Tree Crowley used was that of the Golden Dawn. It is composed of ten spheres (sephiroth) and of 22 paths connecting the spheres, as well as the three veils above Kether, the veil of Paroketh (the Portal, below the central sphere of Beauty), the veil of Da'ath (the Abyss of Knowledge, below the three supernal spheres), and the corrupt and twisted Shells or Qliphoth echoing the Tree in a perverted and demonic form below Malkuth. Kether is reflected into four worlds from the closest to God down to the physical.

The Tree of Life is reminiscent of Platonic idealism, in which the world of sensory phenomena is held to be a secondary or degenerate form of a spiritual reality made up of pure ideas existing behind the appearance of the material world. The ideals are like lights and the events perceptible to the senses are only the shadows they cast.

Emanationist cosmological models similar to the Tree of Life were central in an ancient form of magic known as Neo-Platonic theurgy, an ancestor of modern occultism, and a Græco-Roman cousin of Gnosticism. Centuries after the fall of Rome, first Jewish Qabala and then Christian Qabala and Renaissance magic revived the Neo-Platonic cosmological and magical tradition. It had survived for a millennium in classical works, and in the Islamic preservation of Hellenism. The magical revival developed many different symbolic representations of the idealistic universe, including the Tree of Life, the Tarot, other philosophical card decks, and alchemical and zodiacal diagrams.

Philosophy often deals with two opposing perspectives, the nominalist and the idealist. Loosely speaking, nominalists focus on the names of things and their outward appearances as the currency of human knowledge, while idealism considers things in the world of senses to be only pale reflections of their ideal forms, or essences. For instance, there are plenty of physical chairs, but only one "chairness," which exists on a plane separate from the physical

Aleister Crowley painting circa 1918. From the collection of Richard Metzger

world. This plane of ideal forms, derided by nominalists, was the basis of Renaissance philosophy and the Tree of Life. Nominalism has been crucial to existentialism, phenomenology, and 20th century philosophy in general. Idealism is no longer widely considered a viable philosophy.

Crowley insisted that he was not an idealist but a nominalist, while also insisting that the Tree of Life truly represented the esoteric structure of reality and that its correspondences could only be harmed by any change. Was this an inspired paradox or a careless contradiction?

Crowley also acknowledged the Enochian æthyrs, the Chinese Yi Jing, and Buddhist psychology as peers of the Tree of Life. He did not make as extensive use of these systems, feeling them to be inconvenient compared to the Tree, but they all played significant roles along his spiritual path.

In the Golden Dawn as well as Thelema, the Tree has two major roles. First, it is a map of spiritual progress. Starting at the lowest and most worldly sphere of the Tree of Life, known as Malkuth or Kingdom and representing the physical world, the spiritual adventurer ascends through the spheres by the paths, taking a new spiritual grade at each sphere, until finally a hardy few reach the ultimate sphere, Kether or Crown, the unseen

unity of ultimate deity and the true Self, known in mysticism as Union with God.

Second, the Tree of Life is used as a classification system. It is held that all the symbols of world religion and occultism find a proper place somewhere on this Tree, and perhaps all symbols and ideas whatsoever. Tables set out many of these correspondences from world religion and traditional magical teaching. Familiarity with this symbolic tapestry is a prerequisite to spiritual practices in Crowley's system as well as the Golden Dawn. Much of the system is to be committed to memory so that it is readily available in ritual and meditation.

Crowley wrestled until his death with the Jewish origins of Qabala, which conflicted with his anti-Semitism. His statements resembling blood libel—the accusation that Jewish rites are celebrated using sacrificed children—should be weighed against his esoteric interpretations of the symbol of sacrifice, and his claims about the Egyptian origins of the Qabala should be taken with a sand dune's worth of salt.

ALEISTER CROWLEY: "We can refer everything in the Universe to the system of pure number whose symbols will be intelligible to all rational minds in an identical sense. And the relations between these symbols are fixed by nature. There is no particular point—for most ordinary purposes—in discussing whether 49 is or is not the square of 7.

"Such was the nature of the considerations that led me to adopt the Tree of Life as the basis of the magical alphabet. The 10 numbers and the 22 letters of the Hebrew alphabet, with their traditional and rational correspondences (taking into consideration their numerical and geometric interrelations), afford us a coherent systematic groundwork sufficiently rigid for our foundation and sufficiently elastic for our superstructure.

"But we must not suppose that we know anything of the Tree a priori. We must not work towards any other type of central Truth than the nature of these symbols in themselves. The object of our work must be, in fact, to discover the nature and powers of each symbol. We must clothe the mathematical nakedness of each prime idea in a many-coloured garment of correspondences with every department of thought."–*777 Revised*, "A Brief Essay Upon The Nature And Significance Of The Magical Alphabet."

THE TRUE BELIEVER: All the religions of the world are but Veils for the One Secret Tradition known to Initiates throughout the ages. The Prophet has left us with the

Key in the form of *Liber 777*, the great Table of Correspondences. By meditating on and invoking the energies of the Paths and Spheres all magical power and mystical insight may be attained. Unto those who have scaled the heights of the Tree and become Adepts (or even higher Initiates) is reserved True Understanding; from these

Teachings. Once integrated into the self by practice, the symbols become repositories for Energies. At the end of the Path the Diagram will become One with the Self and the World in a Mystic Marriage, and reveal concealed Glories undreamed of by the profane.

The practices of Crowley's system are arranged in an initiatic progression that is called the A∴ A∴ system. The glyphs after the letter A are triangles made up of three dots, a Freemasonic usage indicating a claim to possess the legendary Lost Word.

lofty heights are made possible Perspectives that utterly transcend and negate the views of persons ensnared in the illusions of the lower Spheres.

THE CHAOTIC: Symbols are the keys to magic, but models are only models and many different models are valid. The Tree of Life is one excellent model but to get locked into believing that it is The One True Way would be to impose harmful limitations on your own mind. The power that comes from these systems comes from the charge the symbols acquire in your unconscious mind and not from their "truth." There are other useful models like the eight colors of magic, the Enochian æthyrs, the Leary eight-brain model, and so on. Magicians should come up with their own system rather than be trapped by others.

THE SKEPTIC: There are shared themes and formulae in world religion but we now understand that there is much more diversity than was admitted by older scholarship. In the 19th century it was common to think that all religions are only reflections of one underlying tradition. Scholars tried to unify disparate traditions and myths but they imposed preconceptions and waved away differences. Tables of correspondence reduce complex and diverse symbols to single points of debatable contact, and so they conflate the dissimilar. This may be offensive to the cultures whose complex traditions are reduced. Tables of this kind may be useful as generators for ritual and meditation practices but as an apparatus of comparative interpretation they are useless today.

THE MYSTIC: There is only one Path, the Path to Oneself. Along the way one encounters the same Truths clothed in a variety of forms and symbols. To synthesize and reduce this appearance of Many to the One is the Great Work of Alchemy. Mystics of the ages have always recognized this Unity in each other; religious differences have been caused by political usurpers who perverted the pure

SPIRITUAL PRACTICE

Many occultists endlessly spin out cosmologies and other symbolic arrangements having little relationship to any apparent pragmatic issue. Crowley speculated quite a lot, but coming from the Golden Dawn, and exposure to Buddhist monasticism, and Hindu yoga, he was more concerned with setting up a program of spiritual exercises.

In Thelema the goal of the path is to be the most oneself that one can be, to know who you really are and to let that eternal self or True Will be the guiding force in life. To do this it is recommended that one practice ritual and meditative disciplines that quiet and focus the mind, travel astrally to various locations in the spiritual world inside or outside oneself, invoke deities and evoke lesser spirits, attain to the Knowledge and Conversation of the Holy Guardian Angel at the central sphere of the Tree of Life (Tiphareth, or Beauty), and for the very few, to give up all one's conceptions about the self in favor of the radical perspective of the eternal Self.

Initiation is a major theme in Crowley's system of Thelema, as in the Golden Dawn and Theosophy. Initiation is a complex subject and has been the subject of extensive study by anthropologists. Freemasonry gave rise to the Golden Dawn, and both fit the van Gennep model of initiation accepted by anthropologists. Initiations mark stages in personal transformation.

The practices of Crowley's system are arranged in an initiatic progression that is called the A∴ A∴ system. The glyphs after the letter A are triangles made up of three dots, a Freemasonic usage indicating a claim to possess the legendary Lost Word. This curriculum is a combination of Golden Dawn magic, Yogic and Buddhist meditation practices, and original practices developed by Crowley. The work to achieve even the middle ranges of the system is arduous. Few people have accomplished it. Many have claimed personal attainment of A∴ A∴ grades without conquering the basic material. The next time you meet a Master of the Temple, you might ask to test them on Asana and Pranayama as per Liber E.

The motto of Crowley's literary and magical journal, the Equinox, was "The Method of Science, the Aim of Religion."

The motto of Crowley's literary and magical journal, the Equinox, was "The Method of Science, the Aim of Religion." While his methods fall short of a truly scientific standard, his system shares with anthropology the requirement for a phenomenological record of ritual experience, a tool of ethnographic field observation.

The A∴ A∴ system of initiations follows the spheres of the Tree of Life, as did the Golden Dawn. In addition to a variety of fringe Masonic degrees, Crowley gave the A∴ A∴ grades, the Ordo Templi Orientis degrees, and the ordinations and bishoprics of the Ecclesia Gnostica Catholica or Gnostic Catholic Church. These are all different systems but there is some overlap in themes and practices. The O.T.O. rituals are derived from Freemasonry as filtered through Crowley's occult theories, although like all Crowley's groups it admits both women and men. The E.G.C. is closely related to the O.T.O. but revolves around the Gnostic Mass, conferring offices such as Priestess, Priest, Deacon and Bishop. New Thelemic groups with their own initiations and courses of study have sprung up since Crowley's death in 1947. Several are currently in operation, including the Ordo Templi Astarte, Temple of Thelema, and Thelemic Golden Dawn.

ALEISTER CROWLEY: "The experimenter is encouraged to use his own intelligence, and not to rely upon any other person or persons, however distinguished, even among ourselves.

"The written record should be intelligibly prepared so that others may benefit from its study…

"The more scientific the record is, the better. Yet the emotions should be noted, as being some of the conditions."–*Liber E vel Exercitiorum*, I:5-9.

"This book is very easy to misunderstand; readers are asked to use the most minute critical care in the study of it, even as we have done in its preparation.

"In this book it is spoken of the Sephiroth and the Paths; of Spirits and Conjurations; of Gods, Spheres, Planes, and many other things which may or may not exist.

"It is immaterial whether these exist or not. By doing certain things certain results will follow; students are most earnestly warned against attributing objective reality or philosophic validity to any of them.

"The advantages to be gained from them are chiefly these:

"a. A widening of the horizon of the mind.

"b. An improvement of the control of the mind."–*Liber O vel Manus et Sagittæ*, I:2-3.

THE TRUE BELIEVER: The A∴ A∴ is the Great White Brotherhood, that hidden order of Initiates that has existed in Service throughout the ages and has emerged behind such masks as the Rosicrucians and the Zoroastrian Magi. The Third Order of A∴ A∴ is in service to the deities and sages of the Occult Government of this Solar System. The *Book of the Law* was sent to humanity by the A∴ A∴ on the revolution in Æons declared by the Secret Chiefs. Crowley held the grade of Magus in the A∴ A∴ and as such uttered the Word of the Æon, ABRAHADABRA, which all members accept as Natural Law.

THE CHAOTIC: The A∴ A∴ is an abstraction which includes all authentic magical paths. There are groups that call themselves the A∴ A∴ but its real nature is in the continuity of spiritual traditions everywhere. Different groups are best for different people. Treating one group as the One True Path and obsessing about lineage wars are remnants of the Æon of Osiris. Today there are spiritual methods that improve on Crowley's curriculum, like isolation tanks, sigils, entheogens, and mind machines. The Protestant work ethic is a Victorian relic. Progress is possible through play as much as perseverance and perspiration.

"It is immaterial whether these exist or not. By doing certain things certain results will follow; students are most earnestly warned against attributing objective reality or philosophic validity to any of them.

THE SKEPTIC: Religious systems present themselves as revolving around doctrine, practice, and morality but they can often be best understood by the methods of political science, group psychology, sociology and anthropology. The homogenizing and leveling effects of social bonding are always in tension with the freedom of the individual. Thelemic groups have a dogmatic tendency that is in conflict with their commitment to freedom. The power dynamics in initiatory hierarchy encourage people to seek degrees for reasons of status.

THE MYSTIC: The ordinary mind is a roaring babble that drowns out the voices of the Holy Guardian Angel. Establishing Silence through Yogic concentration, then calling upon the Forces behind the sensible world, one may climb the Ladder of Lights and obtain Enlightenment. Most people require instruction by groups to learn the required practices. All such Fraternities derive their authority from A∴ A∴, which has existed since the first humans were born. A great Spiritual Hierarchy beckons downwards to us from Kether, as our Aspiration lifts us Upward through the Emanations of the one invisible God within ourselves.

TRUTH AND FALSEHOOD

Crowley's doctrine of truth and falsehood is the central theme of his book of Qabalistic poetry, *The Book of Lies*. Contradiction for him was not a problem but a sign of a higher mystical synthesis transcending the rational. Ordinary understanding is held to be inadequate to engage Truth; in fact it is in the way. One preparation for the Ordeal of the Abyss is to constantly multiply contradictions in one's mind, each thought contradicting the previous, until the trance known in yoga as samadhi is attained. Every fixed idea is shown to be partial and false, including ideas about the self, until finally the usurper Reason is dethroned and the True Will takes its place.

While all mundane truth is false in a sense, still there is the level of ordinary human reality with its mundane truths, "the old school tie," whether a shop is open or closed. Deconstructing truth need not lead to the paralysis that Hume attributes to the Pyrrhonist.

The Truth of a higher initiate is incomprehensible to one of lower degree, while the "truth" of lower degrees is seen as false by the higher. Along these lines, Crowley observes that monotheism is only true after the Knowledge and Conversation of the Holy Guardian Angel. Crowley claimed to be a skeptic but he was also full of passionate conviction. He demanded allegiance to certain ideas but also insisted that every idea must be doubted. Was Crowley an authority or a trickster? He has left us with no clear answer.

ALEISTER CROWLEY: "The Abyss of Hallucinations has Law and Reason; but in Truth there is no bond between the Toys of the Gods.

"The Abyss of Hallucinations has Law and Reason; but in Truth there is no bond between the Toys of the Gods."

"This Reason and Law is the Bond of the Great Lie.

"Truth! Truth! Truth! crieth the Lord of the Abyss of Hallucinations.

"There is no Silence in that Abyss: for all that men call Silence is Its Speech.

"This Abyss is also called 'Hell', and 'The Many.' Its name is 'Consciousness,' and 'The Universe,' among men.

"But THAT which neither is silent, nor speaks, rejoices therein…

"Identity is perfect; therefore the Law of Identity is but a lie. For there is no subject, and there is no predicate; nor is there the contradictory of either of these things.

"Holy, Holy, Holy are these Truths that I utter, knowing them to be but falsehoods, broken mirrors, troubled waters; hide me. O our Lady, in Thy Womb! for I may not endure the rapture."

– *The Book of Lies*, "Windlestraws" and "The Glow-Worm."

THE TRUE BELIEVER: The Law of Liberty is the Charter of Universal Freedom and the sole rule and guide of life in this Æon. It is Truth on every level. The Law of Thelema is an inspired mystical Truth emanating from the Third Order of A∴ A∴ but it is also natural Law and a pragmatic human fact. There is a definite Current of Energy flowing from the Third Order against which it would be foolish and self-defeating to struggle. It is the Will of All to align with this Current.

THE CHAOTIC: Crowley was an early shock trooper in the ontological guerrilla warfare waged by people like Brion Gysin, A. O. Spare, William Burroughs, Timothy Leary, Peter Carroll, and Robert Anton Wilson. He wasn't afraid to directly assault traditional value systems; he demonstrated the limits of logic; he explored the distant cognitive frontier; and he insisted on individual thought instead of dogma. He could sometimes forget his own principles but that's part of the process too. At least he kept his sense of humor!

THE SKEPTIC: Crowley's negative view of intellect is comparable with Blake's view of Newton and Urizen. As Crowley was a freethinker one might think of him as one of the highly differentiated points on the existentialist spectrum, a kind of occult Kierkegaard. Other existentialists also dedicated much of their work to the reclamation and validation of denied or underworld feelings. Crowley may deserve study as a literary contributor but not as a philosophical contributor—he was a sloppy thinker, and his doctrine of contradictions degenerates into an excuse for contradictions.

Crowley was an early shock trooper in the ontological guerrilla warfare waged by people like Brion Gysin, A. O. Spare, William Burroughs, Timothy Leary, Peter Carroll, and Robert Anton Wilson.

THE MYSTIC: Truth and falsehood as applied by the intellect are false. Truth is only known to the Master of the Temple, the silent Self first assumed by the Babe of the Abyss who is born after the fall of Reason. Truth can only be spoken by the Magus, but He is Cursed to have His Word be heard as falsehood. This Truth is beyond any possible description in words but could be indicated as the Understanding of the unity of the psyche and the world that it creates.

SEX MAGICK AND SUFFRAGE

The Free Love movement and the embrace of Pagan values by Neo-Classical Romanticism in the 19th and early 20th centuries validated sexual inquiries in literature, the arts, popular morals, and Spiritualism. Sexual revolution brought in advocates such as Victoria Woodhull, H. G. Wells, and of course Aleister Crowley.

In world religion, writers such as Richard Payne Knight collected sexual odds and ends from archæology and mythology and argued for the universal phallic basis of religion.

Rumors spread of the hidden sexual wisdom of the East as reflected in certain Yogic works, the Kama Sutra, and in Tantra, as well as in Islamic texts such as *The Scented Garden*. These volumes, discreetly translated by adventurers such as Gnostic Saint Richard Francis Burton and circulated by private subscription through gentlemen's clubs, helped inspire a Rabelaisian revival, including Pierre Louys and the decadents.

In the occult world, African-American mage Paschal Beverly Randolph (1825–1875) created a system of sexual magic that influenced writers such as H. P. Blavatsky and Crowley and became the foundation of the Hermetic Brotherhood of Luxor, an influential but ill-starred occult group contemporary with the Golden Dawn and Theosophy. The Cromlech Temple preached an erotic interpretation of Christian symbolism (their papers were collected by Francis King in *Astral Projection, Ritual Magic, and Alchemy*, London 1971), while in France saucy Gnosticism and atheism-friendly Freemasonry developed their own sexual interpretations, such as Ragon's idea of the Rose and Cross as representing the organs of generation, and Eliphas Levi's identification of Lucifer, Pan and Baphomet as sexual forces. Theodor Reuss, an associate of Richard Wagner, collected his own ideas of sexual mysticism and those he attributed to Karl Kellner into a new type of esoteric Freemasonry called the Ordo Templi Orientis or O.T.O., which claimed to hold the keys to sex magic. Other forms of esoteric Freemasonry embraced a sexual doctrine under a variety of veils, and the French mystic Papus co-developed with the O.T.O. and H.B.L. sexual interpretations of occult formulæ such as the Tetragrammaton. Papus' reading of YHVH in *The Tarot of the Bohemians* is remarkably similar to Crowley's in *Magick*.

Crowley, born in 1875, was brought up in the thick of this pro-sexual current in Western society and in occultism. Since Rabelais Thélème has been associated with libertinism and Crowley's Thelema is no exception. Crowley was a libidinous individual and he delighted in flouting Christian sexual taboos. He was a bisexual ritualist and sexual adventurer.

Like many occultists and some scholars, Crowley believed that a unified religious and phallic tradition lay behind all the variations in world religion. He described his system as "solar-phallic" after Jung, and while the particular sexual formulae he employed are secret, it is no secret that the inner formulæ of the A.·.A.·., O.T.O. and E.G.C. are charged with sexual significance.

Crowley's interpretations of sexual symbolism change over the course of his life. In addition, his systematizing tendency—his desire to present a simple key or formula as initiated meaning—was at war with his freewheeling, variegated, and playfully perverse tastes.

The sexual instinct is sacred and expresses a transgenerational undying intelligence through the mechanisms of evolution and reproduction. Christianity does us harm by denying the sacredness of the sexual instinct and its variations. Sexual experimentation and sex outside marriage are praiseworthy. Christianity's sacrament of the Eucharist perverts an older pagan ceremonialism in which the Eucharist involved sexual fluids. The Phallus is the true God, while the female deity is either derogated as a temporary refuge (the womb) or exalted as the bearer of the Mundane Egg of the Orphics. The female part in sex magick, which he derogated early in life, assumes greater significance and respect in late works such as *The Book of Thoth*.

ALEISTER CROWLEY: "I have insisted that sexual excitement is merely a degraded form of divine ecstasy. I have thus harnessed the wild horses of human passion to the chariot of the Spiritual Sun. I have given these horses wings that mankind may no longer travel painfully upon the earth, shaken by every irregularity of the surface, but course at large through the boundless ether. This is not merely a matter of actual ceremonies; I insist that in private life men should not admit their passions to be an end, indulging them and so degrading themselves to the level of the other animals, or suppressing them and creating neuroses. I insist that every thought, word and deed should be consciously devoted to the service of the Great Work. 'Whatsoever ye do, whether ye eat or drink, do all to the glory of God.'" —*The Confessions of Aleister Crowley*, chapter 61.

"Now the Semen is God (the going-one, as shown by the Ankh or Sandal-strap, which He carries) because he goes in at the Door, stays there for a specified period, and comes out again, having flowered, and still bearing in him

The female part in sex magick, which he derogated early in life, assumes greater significance and respect in late works such as *The Book of Thoth*.

that Seed of Going. (The birth of a girl is a misfortune everywhere, because the true Going-Principle is the Lion-Serpent, or Dragon; the Egg is only the Cavern where he takes refuge on occasion.)...

"Why do men insist on 'innocence' in women? ... To cover their secret shame in the matter of sex. Hence the pretence that a woman is 'pure,' modest, delicate, aesthetically beautiful and morally exalted, ethereal and unfleshly, though in fact they know her to be lascivious, shameless, coarse, ill-shapen, unscrupulous, nauseatingly bestial both physically and mentally. The advertisements of 'dress shields,' perfumes, cosmetics, anti-sweat preparations, and 'Beauty Treatments' reveal woman's nature as seen by the clear eyes of those who would lose money if they misjudged her; and they are loathsomely revolting to read. Her mental and moral characteristics are those of the parrot and the monkey. Her physiology and pathology are hideously disgusting, a sickening slime of uncleanliness. Her virgin life is a sick ape's, her sexual life a drunken sow's, her mother life all bulging filmy eyes and sagging udders.

"These are the facts about 'innocence'; to this has man's Christian Endeavour dragged her when he should rather have made her his comrade, frank, trusty, and gay, the tenderer self of himself, his consubstantial complement even as Earth is to the Sun.

"We of Thelema say that 'Every man and every woman is a star.' We do not fool and flatter women; we do not despise and abuse them. To us a woman is Herself, absolute, original, independent, free, self-justified, exactly as a man is."—*The Law is for All*, III:55.

THE TRUE BELIEVER: The male is the lively, enlightening, creative, jovial force of the Pillar of Mercy, while the female is the brooding, dark, harsh, silent, but nourishing matrix of the Pillar of Severity in which the divine Seed

"We of Thelema say that 'Every man and every woman is a star.' We do not fool and flatter women; we do not despise and abuse them. To us a woman is Herself, absolute, original, independent, free, self-justified, exactly as a man is."

takes shape. Creation is a higher function than destruction and Light is a higher power than darkness and so ours is a Solar-Phallic Religion. The true God is the Quintessence, the Holy Spirit, the Creative Will as expressed by the Representative of the Sun on Earth, the Phallus.

THE CHAOTIC: Sex is a road to magical power and a gateway to the unconscious mind. Crowley deserves credit for his contributions, but sex has moved on from the 19th century and taking Crowley's views seriously today would be like reading old marriage manuals to understand teenage pop stars. Sex is too wild to be tied down to one formula. There are an infinite number of sexual forms and Crowley's don't seem as special or unique today as they did a hundred years ago.

The Stélé of Revealing, ancient Egyptian artifact dear to Thelemites

Sex is a road to magical power and a gateway to the unconscious mind. Crowley deserves credit for his contributions, but sex has moved on from the 19th century and taking Crowley's views seriously today would be like reading old marriage manuals to understand teenage pop stars.

THE SKEPTIC: The theory of the universal phallic religion flourished as a reaction against sex-negativity when it was hard to talk rationally about sex in Western culture. The theory has not held up now that barriers to sexual discussion have been lowered. Some of the phallicists' discussion of truly phallic deities like Priapus and Shiva remains worthwhile, but their universalism does not. Crowley embraced a radical and idiosyncratic exegesis based on tenuous speculative links.

THE MYSTIC: Every person is both man and woman, and every man and every woman is a star. The mystical formula of Union of Opposites or Thelemic Love, related to the Hegelian dialectical formula, can be enacted with thoughts or with bodies and is constantly enacting itself in the world around us. It is the Key to the Stone of the Philosophers and to the Universal Medicine. To downplay or disparage the male-female polarity would be to cripple the magic—it is their very difference from each other that makes their Union powerful. In a ritual involving sex the generative organs of the partners are consecrated ritual tools which must be used according to their natural formula like any other tool of High Magick.

DRUGS AND SPIRITUAL PRACTICE

The 19th century brought the West not only sexual revolution but a drug problem. Morphine was invented early in the century; it and other opiates such as laudanum, a popular opiated liqueur, were readily available and widely used in Europe and the United States. Napoleon's troops brought back marijuana and hashish along with the Egyptian revival, P. B. Randolph sold hashish by mail order for spiritual purposes, and Blavatsky was said by a close acquaintance to have used hashish to boost her visionary powers; she for her part made clear enough references to psychoactive plants and Randolph's drug-induced "Sleep of Siloam." Crowley was born into an atmosphere that was charged with drugs and mysticism as well as sex.

Crowley experimented with drugs with his teacher Allan Bennett early in life, but he says they were of no use at the time—"Like Huckleberry Finn's prayer, nuffin' come of it"—until he had practiced Yoga. Given the powers of mind resulting from meditation, he felt that psychoactive substances could be useful for breaking through dry spells, provided one had the strength to thwart an uncontrolled flow of delusional visions and the tendency to fall asleep.

Crowley also thought that drugs could wake up ordinary people to the prospects of mysticism by inducing altered states of consciousness without arduous disciplines. Israel Regardie in *Roll Away the Stone* attributes this idea to William James' famous statement that "our normal waking consciousness, rational consciousness, as we call it, is but one special type of consciousness, whilst all about it, parted from it by the flimsiest of screens, there lie potential forms of consciousness entirely different."

A drug-positive approach is evident in *The Book of the Law*, when it echoes the phrase "lightening [or loosening] the girders of the soul" from the *Chaldean Oracles*. Crowley interprets this as a hashish reference in his "Psychology of Hashish." Hadit instructs the reader "To worship me take wine and strange drugs whereof I will tell my prophet, & be drunk thereof!" Crowley took drugs such as cocaine, heroin and hashish throughout his career, all the while claiming to be above addiction. This conclusion is not shared by all of his biographers.

For all the undeniable significance of drug mysticism to Crowley and Thelema, entheogen practices never assumed the importance that sexual ones did in his system. His view of humanity was not physical but metaphysical. He believed in the ability of intelligence to take non-physical forms, so he was unlikely to adopt a concept like the psychedelic idea of consciousness as chemistry. While both the A∴A∴ and O.T.O. lead to inner sexual instructions, neither reveals a drug practice per se in its foundations. To Crowley drugs were a means to an end rather than an end in themselves. Regardie notes this difference between Crowley's attitudes and the psychedelic idea of drugs such as LSD as inherently illuminating.

ALEISTER CROWLEY: "I could persuade other people that mysticism was not all folly without insisting on their devoting a lifetime to studying under me; and if only I could convince a few competent observers—in such a matter I distrust even myself—Science would be bound to follow and to investigate, clear up the matter once for all, and, as I believed, and believe, arm itself with a new weapon ten thousand times more potent than the balance and the microscope...

"Hashish at least gives proof of a new order of consciousness, and (it seems to me) it is this primâ facie case that mystics have always needed to make out, and never have made out.

"But today I claim the hashish-phenomena as mental phenomena of the first importance; and I demand investigation.

"I assert—more or less *ex cathedrâ*—that meditation will revolutionise our conception of the universe, just as the microscope has done."—"The Psychology of Hashish," *Equinox* I:2.

THE TRUE BELIEVER: Drugs seduce the weak, but so let it be: as it is written: "stamp down the wretched & the weak: this is the law of the strong: this is our law and the joy of the world." Let all the world take these drugs so that millions

> "Hashish at least gives proof of a new order of consciousness, and (it seems to me) it is this primâ facie case that mystics have always needed to make out, and never have made out."

may awaken to Our Law, and fear not that some must suffer early rebirth, a small penalty for a glimpse of the Dawn upon the East. Yet let the aspirant beware of addiction, obsession, and sleepiness, lest he be like my great rival, who I will not deign to mention here except by reference to the well-known failings of his mother and his charter. True, I had eaten bad mushrooms when I became a Master of the Temple, but I swore the Oath, and that's what matters.

THE CHAOTIC: Crowley was a drug revolutionary for his time, and researchers like Timothy Leary, Stanislav Grof, and Terence McKenna are indebted to him. That said, I'm supposed to limit my use of psychedelics until I can do what? I'd never have tripped if I thought I needed to climb to Nepal and study at someone's feet first. LSD and MDMA didn't even exist in Crowley's time and they've changed the old rules.

THE SKEPTIC: Psychedelic drugs were once erroneously known as psychotomimetic drugs, that is, drugs that induced psychotic symptoms. While this turned out to be more false than true, the use of psychotropic drugs in visionary experience inevitably raises the questions of delusion and disorder. Again, though, we must beware of reductionism. Changes induced by such means as drugs,

Given this and Crowley's reliance on the reinterpreted Book of Revelation, it would not be far off the mark to call Thelema itself a form of esoteric Christianity.

psychosis or harsh spiritual practices such as fasting or flagellation may be pathological in one sense, but they induce states of consciousness which deserve study if only because they are hard to explain. These states might shed light on the study of consciousness as well as the treatment of mental illness.

THE MYSTIC: The experiences induced by drugs are lesser mysteries, tools useful only to the very beginner who needs to break the grip of ordinary consciousness, and to the experienced mage who possesses the strength of mind to resist the blandishments of drugs. Drugs do not represent a shortcut; nothing can substitute for one's own spiritual work, and only in rare circumstances can they be combined. As for the slanders raised against my mother, I only note my pity at the depths to which the Qliphoth can ensnare the unwary or inept drug experimenter. I would wish him well in the next life if he were not on the road to utter destruction, and I have given his address to the police.

CHRIST AND LUCIFER

Crowley's hostility to Christianity was vitriolic and intense. There are many Thelemites who are equally hostile and would not accept or admit that any part of Christianity, esoteric or not, is part of Thelema. The exclusion of Christian symbolism does not reflect Crowley's usage. Biographically, Crowley's hatred of Christianity began with his upbringing in the Protestant tradition known as the Plymouth Brethren, to which his parents belonged. Moralistic and restrictive, the

Crowley's theory of ancient sex magick revolves around the Gnostics, a group of ancient Christian-Jewish-Pagan fusion sects who preoccupied 19th century occultists. The 20th century discoveries of the Dead Sea Scrolls and the Nag Hammadi Library made Crowley's ideas of Gnosticism obsolete, but he believed the Gnostics had been sex magicians who held the sexual inner keys of the formula of the Eucharist of the Catholic Mass, a symbolic form of a central sexual secret carried down by the occult underground through the centuries. Crowley's Gnostic Mass, one of his most frequently practiced rituals today, is meant to restore his idea of the pre-Christian secret to its proper place of reverence. *Given this and Crowley's reliance on the reinterpreted Book of Revelation, it would not be far off the mark to call Thelema itself a form of esoteric Christianity.* [Emphasis added, Metzger]

Placing the symbols of others' religions into one's own syncretistic system is often considered offensive. An examination of the column for Christianity in Crowley's *777* reveals a wicked sense of humor at work. "God the Holy Ghost (as Incubus)" in the place of Yesod, for instance, smacks of gleeful wickedness. Similar forms of protest are evident in the Gnostic Mass and the O.T.O.'s Trinitarian central secret. The Christian elements of his system were in part meant to annoy Christians.

However, it would be a mistake to treat the Gnostic Mass and similar Christian elements in Thelema as low parodies merely meant to offend. Christian symbols appear at the very heart of Crowley's system and his sincere devotion to them is apparent. For Crowley there was pleasure in using Christian symbols in transgressive ways, but that

The Christian elements of his system were in part meant to annoy Christians.

Plymouth Brethren were also obsessed with the Book of Revelation. His mother called the rebellious Crowley "the Beast" early in life well before *The Book of the Law* confirmed him in this title.

Lawrence Sutin credibly suggests in his biography *Do What Thou Wilt* that one thing Crowley despised about the Plymouth Brethren was its Quaker-like egalitarianism. This might explain the rigid hierarchies of Crowley's groups and his support for the Golden Dawn's heavy-handed leader MacGregor Mathers.

was not his primary motive in using symbols like the Rose and Cross, or the Great Beast and Scarlet Woman. These symbols had personal significance and his interpretations were sincere despite their elements of protest.

As an opponent of Christianity, Crowley was drawn by the examples of the literary "Satanic school" and the seminal French magician Eliphas Levi to reinterpret the Devil in positive terms. The "Satanic school," like Gnosticism, is a post facto interpretive category and not an organization or an historical meeting. It includes poets and playwrights such as Byron, Shelley, Blake, Baudelaire, Rimbaud, and Shaw. In occultism, Blavatsky had expressed her sympathy for the fall of the angels as the source of Liberty in her history of the solar system, as reflected in the name of her periodical *Lucifer*, not to be confused with the Free Love magazine of the same name. With the shaking of sexual taboos came the suspicion that perhaps Satan was not such a bad fellow after all.

Belief in the witch or black magician exists in all cultures. These reputed malefactors delight in wreaking havoc and raining ill fortune on the community. Although there are curses in magical practice, nothing real corresponds with the ancient horror that anthropologists call witchcraft.

With the shaking of sexual taboos came the suspicion that perhaps Satan was not such a bad fellow after all.

Literary Satanism was nothing like the popular idea of "Satanism." Thus one must be hesitant to call Crowley, or anyone, a Satanist, because that would invoke legend rather than reality. In this sense there is no such thing as a Satanist. In a broader sense, though, there is a kind of Satanism in *Prometheus Unbound* and *The Devil's Disciple*, in *Beyond Good and Evil*, in Rabelais, Louys and Blake, and in Levi, Blavatsky, and Crowley.

It would hardly be credible to deny that Crowley was part of the Satanic school in this broader sense, since Thelema contains elements traditionally associated with Satan, and the name Satan itself is used with respect in rituals, poems and essays. The Great Beast and the Scarlet Woman are associated with "the dragon, Satan" in the Bible's book of Revelation. Crowley makes many statements which interpret Satan in a positive light throughout his career, from his dedication to an early poem ("Why Jesus Wept," 1905) which says "I, at once a higher mystic and a colder skeptic, found my Messiah in Charles Watts, and the Devil and all his angels" to a late essay on the Tarot trump The Devil (*The Book of Thoth*, 1944) that "the card represents creative energy in its most material form; in the Zodiac, Capricorn occupies the Zenith. It is the most exalted of the signs; it is the goat leaping with lust upon the summits of earth... the

formula of this card is then the complete appreciation of all existing things. He rejoices in the rugged and the barren no less than in the smooth and the fertile. All things equally exalt him. He represents the finding of ecstasy in every phenomenon, however naturally repugnant; he transcends all limitations; he is Pan; he is All."

Crowley's "Satanism," if it can be called that, is not very oppositional in itself, though it partakes of rebellion. Satan to Crowley is a misunderstood symbol for the sacred energies of sex. He writes about these positive sexual qualities much more than he dwells on Satan as the opposition to God. Their opposition is a Christian concept that he rejects. There is an irony and a playfulness in his use of Satan, but Crowley's Satan is a surprisingly sunny figure, just as Crowley explained the meaning of his adopted number, 666, as "little sunshine." As Blake could embrace both Los and Christ, Crowley was a curiously Christian Satanist.

ALEISTER CROWLEY: "The Devil does not exist. It is a false name invented by the Black Brothers to imply a Unity in their ignorant muddle of dispersions. A devil who had unity would be a God.

'The Devil' is, historically, the God of any people that one personally dislikes. This has led to so much confusion of thought that THE BEAST 666 has preferred to let names stand as they are, and to proclaim simply that AIWAZ—the solar-phallic-hermetic 'Lucifer'—is His own Holy Guardian Angel, and 'The Devil' SATAN or HADIT of our particular unit of the Starry Universe. This serpent, SATAN, is not the enemy of Man, but He who made Gods of our race, knowing Good and Evil; He bade 'Know Thyself!' and taught Initiation. He is 'the Devil' of the Book of Thoth, and His emblem is BAPHOMET, the Androgyne who is the hieroglyph of arcane perfection. The number of His Atu is XV, which is *yod hé*, the Monogram of the Eternal, the Father one with the Mother, the Virgin Seed one with all-containing Space. He is therefore Life, and Love."—*Magick in Theory and Practice*, XXI:II.

Belief in the witch or black magician exists in all cultures. These reputed malefactors delight in wreaking havoc and raining ill fortune on the community. Although there are curses in magical practice, nothing real corresponds with the ancient horror that anthropologists call witchcraft.

"It seems as if I possessed a theology of my own which was, to all intents and purposes, Christianity. My satanism did not interfere with it at all; I was trying to take the view that the Christianity of hypocrisy and cruelty was not true Christianity. I did not hate God or Christ, but merely the God and Christ of the people whom I hated. It was only when the development of my logical faculties supplied the demonstration that I was compelled to set myself in opposition to the Bible itself. It does not matter that the literature is sometimes magnificent and that in liberal theologies are taken seriously in many mainstream denominations. It is hard to find a Thelemic group as devoted to pluralism as liberal Christian groups and Unitarian-Universalism.

THE MYSTIC: The Equinox of the Gods has come as it does every two thousand years, installing new Officers and Rites, and sweeping away the darkness of the old ways. Where once blazed the Cross of Suffering as the Sun of Beauty now there is the Crowned and Conquering Child,

"It seems as if I possessed a theology of my own which was, to all intents and purposes, Christianity. My satanism did not interfere with it at all; I was trying to take the view that the Christianity of hypocrisy and cruelty was not true Christianity. I did not hate God or Christ, but merely the God and Christ of the people whom I hated."

isolated passages the philosophy and ethics are admirable. The sum of the matter is that Judaism is a savage, and Christianity a fiendish, superstition."—*The Confessions of Aleister Crowley*, chapter 6.

THE TRUE BELIEVER: Christianity is the curse of the world. Those who cling to it in the new Æon of Horus will be banished when the Sun shall fully rise. When the Prophet wrote "the Christians to the lions!" He did not speak idly or in jest. Christians are the enemies of Freedom and they do not even understand the few fragments of the Secret Tradition that are perverted in their rites. Only when they are all dead and gone can we truly become as "a strong Man who goeth forth to do his Will."

THE CHAOTIC: Christianity is the hand with the stick that has instilled shame and guilt as virtues so we have a whole society of mass-produced clone-farm humanoids who are afraid to think. The way to dissolve these shackles on a mass scale is through a culture of individuality and the reality distortion effect that has become the dominant paradigm. Christians are plodding, literal robots who would probably lock up all the magicians if they could get away with it.

THE SKEPTIC: Christianity's failings are well known to those of us who come from Christian cultures. We are less aware of similar problems in other cultures and religions. Of the many faiths, Christianity is among those adapting most quickly to the modern world and the idea of human rights, and now at the start of the 21st century

whose message is not of salvation from without but Grace from Within, the Kingdom of Heaven that is within you. Through all the Æons there is one thread of tradition and one Great White Brotherhood whose immortal spiritual Chiefs share the Wisdom of their Teaching with humanity. The Christians could not destroy the Gnosis and now the Initiates of the Sanctuary of the Gnosis have embraced the formula propounded at the new Equinox with Joy and Love in their hearts.

CROWLEY'S PERSONALITY

Aleister Crowley was talented, intelligent, capable, arrogant, judgmental, prejudiced, and not afraid to turn politeness aside if it would get in the way of a good insult. His talents extended to ritual and meditative practice, writing, mountain climbing, sexual athletics, attracting followers, and achieving publicity. His vices went as far as anti-Semitic blood libel, rabid hostility to Christianity, misogyny, child neglect, loss of friends, obnoxiousness, and megalomania.

There are marked similarities between Crowley, MacGregor Mathers, his mentor in the Golden Dawn, and Helena Petrovna Blavatsky, who founded the Theosophical Society. All three were charming, impressive, well-read, anger-prone, tough-talking international spiritual leaders. They were creators of new religious traditions when traditional belief in Christianity was on the decline due to science and knowledge of Eastern and pre-

Christian religions. Followers were drawn to them by their magnetism, energy and talent, but frequently did not know what to make of their character flaws. In each case there is cause to suspect mental disorder by the criteria of modern psychology, but Szasz and Laing remind us that inspired wisdom is often socially condemned as insanity. Moralistic, pathologizing or reductionist accounts of "insane" people are necessarily oversimplifications. In some cases, such as Crowley's, the "insane" person provides so much ammunition that character assassination becomes inevitable.

Whether one could accept a flawed character such as Crowley as a spiritual leader depends on one's model of spirituality. Treating any of the three as moral exemplars would seem incompatible with their biographies. If the purpose of religion is to produce such exemplars then their religious endeavors—Theosophy, the Golden Dawn, and Thelema—have failed. However, if the purpose of religion is to produce spiritual adventurers then they have succeeded.

Crowley's life was an adventure. He was set upon by thieves in dark alleys, and expelled from countries for immorality. He climbed mountains, scandalized a culture that had adapted to Baudelaire, Rimbaud and Swinburne, juggled love affairs, formed new magical orders and broke up others, and made headlines as "the Wickedest Man in the World." Through all he maintained a rigorous course of spiritual practice, exercise, journaling, and writing. Saint Burton might have been proud.

Judgment of personality is necessarily subjective. The best way to get acquainted with Crowley is to read his own works and the better biographies. Unfortunately, there is more bad biography of Crowley than good. It would be difficult to deny his many character failings, but the level of vitriol leveled at him both during and after his lifetime is amazing. Much of this yellow journalism is libelous or fabricated.

Both Crowley's vices and his virtues shine through clearly in his *Confessions*. Israel Regardie's *The Eye in the Triangle* gives a critical but sympathetic and engaged account of Crowley's spiritual career, not turning a blind eye to his flaws or his accomplishments. Other biographies are available, and good biographies continue to appear.

ALEISTER CROWLEY: "I will not acquiesce in anything but the very best of its kind. I don't in the least mind going without a thing altogether, but if I have it at all it has got to be

A1. England is a very bad place for me. I cannot endure people who are either superior or inferior to others, but only those who, whatever their station in life, are consciously unique and supreme....

"I feel so profoundly the urgency of doing my will that it is practically impossible for me to write on Shakespeare and the Musical Glasses without introducing the spiritual and moral principles which are the only things in myself that I can identify with myself.

"This characteristic is evidently inherited from my father. His integrity was absolute. He lived entirely by his theological convictions. Christ might return at any moment. 'Even as the lightning lighteneth out of the East and lighteneth even unto the West, so is the coming of the Son of Man.' He would have to give an account of 'every idle word.' It was a horrifying thought to him that he might be caught by the Second Advent at a moment when he was not actively and intensely engaged on the work which God had sent him into the world to do. This sense of the importance of the lightest act, of the value of every moment, has been a tragically intense factor in my life. I have always grudged the time necessary for eating, sleeping and dressing. I have invented costumes with the sole object of minimizing the waste of time and the distraction of attention involved. I never wear underclothing....

"I soon discovered that to distinguish myself in school was in the nature of a conjurer's trick. It is hard to analyze my method or to be sure of the analysis; but I think the essence of the plan was to make certain of the minimum required and to add a superstructure of one or two abstruse points which I would manage to bring to the notice of the master or the examiner so as to give him the idea that I had prepared myself with unusual thoroughness."—*The Confessions of Aleister Crowley*, chapter 4.

THE TRUE BELIEVER: Crowley was the Prophet of the Silver Star, the chosen human agent of the Secret Chiefs. He was selected because for all his human frailties he was a man of prodigious strength, intelligence and discipline, an occultist of many incarnations who was poised to assume the highest mantle and fit himself for a place in the City of the Pyramids with the Prophets and Bodhisattvas. To understand Crowley you must work his system, attaining through the power of your own True Will the keys to the Great Work, and only then judge Crowley from an Initiated perspective.

THE CHAOTIC: I'm tired of Crowley. It seems like all the people who are into him are into nothing else. I'm suspicious of his system; way too regimented, way too hierarchical. Crowley contributed to magic, but so have other people. We've learned a lot in the last century about real freedom and sexual liberation, and a Victorian master-of-the-passions approach would be a step backward. Crowley had a lot of hang-ups; I'd rather work a system more relevant to my life.

THE SKEPTIC: Crowley studies have been little adopted by academics, with good reason. His work is derivative and like Blavatsky he can be traced to a handful of main sources. Spiritual progress is feeding people, helping those who need it, participating in society to make it more just and humane, and Crowley has little to contribute to that. For Crowley to be interesting, he does not have to be taken as a spiritual authority. A person might have spiritual accomplishments yet retain base elements of their personality. People outside the normal spectrum might carry back useful viewpoints to the world of the sane.

THE MYSTIC: The documents of A∴ A∴ in Class A are inspired writings from a praeterhuman Intelligence, a direct and flawless link to the Secret Chiefs. The transmission of these gems is all that one needs to know about the career of To Mega Therion, the Great Beast, the Magus who spoke through the physical vessel of the man named Aleister Crowley, himself merely a Student of no great importance. The course of study of A∴ A∴ is the work not of Crowley but of The Master Therion and has been issued under the Authority of the Third Order.

READING CROWLEY

This introduction deals with some of Crowley's major themes in summary form. Understanding of Crowley's intricate and contradictory writing requires your own reading. The fragments given here only convey a few of the flavors of his work.

Reading Crowley can be difficult. Crowley was unusual and involved, and his views changed over the six decades of his writing career. He frequently contradicts himself and makes obscure allusions. At other times he is præternaturally lucid. He can seem almost prescient, or be starkly clear and direct when expressing his most outrageous and unbelievable views, such as those on the sexual technology of Atlantis and the turn of ancient Æons.

As this voice ends, I would like to note that your voice is your own. Your own relationship with Crowley will no doubt be unique. Your views may or may not resemble any of the views presented here. Even if some thought you hold seems almost identical with one of these ideas—or utterly incompatible with all of them!—it will still be uniquely yours, embedded firmly in your own personal matrix of thought and life in an irreplaceable and sacred way.

ALEISTER CROWLEY: "Yet to all it shall seem beautiful. Its enemies who say not so, are mere liars."—*The Book of the Law*, III:68.

THE TRUE BELIEVER: My collection contains many rare works. You do not have them, since the Gods reserve them for those of higher degree. Unto such as yourself I solemnly recommend the memorization of *The Book of the Law*, the Charter of Universal Freedom. *The Equinox of the Gods*, which is part of the book *Magick*, explains the revelation of the Book. It should convince even the meanest skeptic, and woe to those who reject the Prophet! In *The Law is For All*, he interprets the Æon of the Crowned and Conquering Child with profound wisdom. *Liber Aleph*, *The World's Tragedy*, *The Star in the West* and many other works are required for the serious aspirant, as is membership in my group, the one duly chartered source of Initiation in this Æon. Aum. Ha.

THE CHAOTIC: I like Crowley's later books, like *The Book of Thoth*, including Lady Frieda Harris' beautiful Tarot deck, and *Magick Without Tears*, a funny and relaxed collection of letters which was originally called *Aleister Explains Everything*. On the serious side *The Vision and the Voice* records the scrying of the Enochian æthyrs in an intense succession of visionary images worthy of Blake. Studying just Crowley would be a really bad idea, though. He's kind of outdated. Be sure to sample Austin Osman Spare, the Discordians, Peter Carroll, Nema, the Sub-Genius movement, and Alan Moore's *Promethea*, and don't forget to familiarize yourself with psychedelics research and transpersonal psychology in your copious free time. Make your own Æon—don't settle for Crowley's!

THE SKEPTIC: Crowley was an allusory writer and to understand him it's necessary to understand the sources of his allusions as well as the cultural and subcultural currents that influenced him. In the literary world one should be familiar with Swinburne, Baudelaire, Rimbaud, Blake, Rabelais, and Græco-Roman classics, and one will need an acquaintance with English and French art and literature in general. Geoffrey Ashe's *Do What You Will: A History of Anti-Morality* traces the ironic current in religion and morality, as expressed through Rabelais, the Hell-Fire Club, de Sade, Crowley, and others.

THE CHAOTIC: I'm tired of Crowley. It seems like all the people who are into him are into nothing else.

THE MYSTIC: Study and meditate upon The Holy Books, which emanate directly from the higher intelligence of the Secret Chiefs. *Magick* or Liber ABA is an invaluable textbook of spiritual practice and symbolism, as are *Eight Lectures on Yoga*, *The Goetia*, and every volume of *The Equinox*, the Encyclopedia of Initiation. *The Book of Lies* and *The Heart of the Master* elucidate mysteries through lyric philosophy. The Secret Chiefs who sent Aiwass to Crowley were the same who set in motion the Golden Dawn and Theosophy, and those two parents of Thelema must be studied. Vivekananda helped inspire the Prophet's work on Yoga, earning His recommendation. Remember that books are not the work. One must practice Yoga and Magick, as described in the instructions of the holy order A∴ A∴ May you achieve the Knowledge and Conversation of the Holy Guardian Angel, and even further Wonders; yea, even further Wonders. ▢

The works of Aleister Crowley are © Aleister Crowley and Ordo Templi Orientis, and are used by permission.

JOHN S. MOORE

ALEISTER CROWLEY AS GURU

Official culture does not take Aleister Crowley at all seriously these days, but the issues he arouses, and the things he writes about, are often very similar to others which are taken very seriously indeed. Take for example the writings of one of the most revered of modern philosophers, Ludwig Wittgenstein. In his book, *Culture and Value* translated by Peter Winch, Wittgenstein appears as guru, with views and observations on all manner of subjects over and above the strictly philosophical ones which made his reputation. If it is acceptable to study this sort of thing, Aleister Crowley offers comparable intellectual meat to chew on, fascinating, creative and original speculations, normally censored out of the English scholarly tradition. Why pay attention to one set of ideas rather than to another? This is the question of authority. Why Wittgenstein rather than Marx, Freud, Heidegger, or even Crowley?

Crowley shared with Wittgenstein the urge to submerge others in his own will, to overcome their alienness by dominating and influencing them. Both sought and found fanatical followers among brilliant, unstable undergraduates from Oxford and Cambridge. Through these was hope of influencing the cultural mainstream. However, just as Wittgenstein rejected the idea that his influence should be restricted to academics, so Crowley repudiates any suggestion that he is speaking to some class restricted in scope. As much as to the fortunate members of society he addresses himself to paupers and to prisoners. He is concerned to influence individual minds through unofficial channels, bringing creative thinking to those normally felt to have no right to it.

He did aspire to a popular following, partly for energy, partly as the most obvious possibility of effecting change. He made use of existing occultist movements to refine them and to exercise his will to power. Though "against the people," the individual who can lead a mass movement acquires freedom of action, and the dominant forces of the day no longer obstruct and oppose him. With the inertia of the mass behind him, he has support for whatever he wants to do. Even a rational ideal could do with a popular base, especially if it is expected to make any serious difference to society.

In 1911 he was advertising his publications *Equinox* and *777*, textbook of the Crowleyan Qabala, in the *Occult Review*. These were the waters in which he fished, as Lenin and Mao in those of revolutionary tradition, and Wittgenstein among philosophy students. Crowley showed little interest in politics. From his viewpoint political interests may be thought of as a kind of vice, constricting into immediate place and time. By contrast he invites into some very exotic traditions, exploring the wisdom and experience of civilizations very remote from his own. His literary style has an oriental, very knowing, quality. Little is argued, or attempted to be argued. He writes from a position of assumed enlightenment, though he is far from narrow or dogmatic. Also he was a master of image manipulation, a subject of ever increasing importance in the modern world. A large part of his message actually consisted in the creation of his image. For a seeker after power who was also a serious intellectual, the field of people looking for esoteric wisdom had something promising to it. The world of the philosopher and the world of images might seem to be very different, but if the philosopher desires influence he may have to take account of this other world.

Preoccupation with images may suggest corruption of feeling, or at best triviality, like an excessive concern with clothing. The world of images promises the excitement of the superficial, with immediate opportunities for emotional stimulation and satisfaction. This is the world of Hitler as führer, and that of American advertising and propaganda. The subject includes the emotional power of archetypes and stereotypes, sexual adornment and attraction, kings, queens, gods, goddesses, demons, vampires, maenads, angels, nymphs.

Actors apply their skills to see other people in terms of images; studying image manipulation, they may live out their own lives in such a world. Image contrasts with reality, for example the image of a philosopher versus the reality of a philosopher. Image manipulation appears as a form of play. One takes pleasure in the promotion of a certain image or reputation, and responding to the images projected by others as the truly real as if this is the true game of life, its real meaning. Focusing on the emotional impact of a stereotype, all the charge associated with it, the aspiring magus aims to be more than human in embodying some attractive image.

Certain writers have significantly influenced this intersection between thought and image. In the early years of the century, the influence of Dostoyevsky was strong in Germany, as well as in Russia. Dostoyevsky stimulated a will to believe in the exciting personal relationships and daemonic influences that he described. This created a demand, which came to be met, ultimately giving rise to such charismatic beings as Rasputin and Hitler. Crowley thrived in a similarly motivated atmosphere among susceptible circles in England and elsewhere.

Where the objective is power and overcoming, it is not enough to be seen as embodying some image or other, as if life were some form of stage play or masquerade. Jacques, in *As You Like It*, says that 'All the world's a stage,' but his is the viewpoint of a gloomy misanthrope. Life as masquerade is a limiting perspective. The person who desires power will only value it from the point of view of what he can get out of it. Crowley's first object was to get people to listen to what he had to say. The ideal of the masquerade depends on mutual courtesy and respect, which is to say a general propping up of illusions. A politician or philosopher who wants to exert an original influence will want to spoil other people's games.

According to the rules of ordinary life, success follows according to a given procedure. To raise the question of what rule we ought to follow introduces complication. If you seek to question the rule you will have nearly all those who have prospered by it against you.

John Symonds' book *The Great Beast* reached a generation of readers in the post-1945 age of mass culture. Its effect was to contribute to a reaction against that culture, but it was also a product of it. Crowley's influence was initially transmitted largely through that book. Reflecting on what he achieved suggests what else might be done.

Despite his enormous intellectual power, his initial attraction, to anyone, does not lie in the answers he gives to intellectual problems

Thinking of modern culture and the normal ways in which it is transmitted, mass media, music industry, universities, art schools, political parties, publishing houses, Aleister Crowley is not supposed to count for very much.

There is seeming justification in the nature of his following. Despite his enormous intellectual power, his initial attraction, to anyone, does not lie in the answers he gives to intellectual problems. People are attracted to Crowley for reasons other than an appreciation of the sublime poetry of *The Book of the Law*, the intricacies of the Crowleyan Qabala, or the other profound and fascinating ideas to be found in his writings. Whatever it is that attracts, attracts all kinds of people. This may appear to his intellectual discredit. There is an interesting question in the relation of his guru image to the quality of his message. The same applies to Wittgenstein. The message on all levels springs from a strong, conscious drive for power, and is in no way weakened or invalidated by that.

Crowley's admirers in modern society are from many walks of life, from the insane and the incarcerated, through the respectable working and middle classes, to the aristocracy and the intelligentsia. Among his proclaimed followers are some with disagreeable forms of mental disturbance. Some like to inspire fear, if they can, the sadistic and pathologically aggressive. There are the self-consciously malevolent and the criminals. They usually lack Crowley's sense of humor and his wit. His own hostility was meant as a way to repel fools. People pursue their ways of life usually unaware of the rationale that lies behind them. Hence the value of devils like Crowley to disturb.

His own hostility was meant as a way to repel fools. People pursue their ways of life usually unaware of the rationale that lies behind them. Hence the value of devils like Crowley to disturb.

His influence stretches among ordinary working people, as he said he wanted in *Magick in Theory and Practice*. His admirers have included hippies, punk rockers, readers of science fiction, football fans. A bookcase full of Crowleyana is a sight occasionally to be seen in the most unexpected places. He is not without appeal in the suburbs, among middle class women, interested in magic and the occult, people that might normally be thought of as thoroughly bourgeois. Crowley as a hobby for the respectable may sound odd. Isn't he a revolutionary? Doesn't he appeal to the discontented? But when we talk about bourgeois values we are talking about something fundamental. What could anyone put in their place? There is a poetry of the suburbs, with its cranks and cults, and housewives. Though one may feel that Thelema is really revolutionary, one cannot object to its existence on that level. After all, what use do the intellectuals make of it?

Crowley created a persona for himself of omnipotent ego, the actualization of "Do What Thou Wilt." Living in a way that was outrageous to the people of his day, he crops up as one of the most striking bridges between the old culture and the new, one whose place is not fully recognized

Dali and Crowley were two of a kind, monstrous egos, they have been called.

in the life of his own generation, yet whose influence is long reaching, out of the heyday of the imperial era into modern mass society, the post imperial pop age. Few bridge that gap; Dali is another who does. Dali and Crowley were two of a kind, monstrous egos, they have been called. Neither will win the complete approbation of the conventional, Crowley in particular because of his comprehensive flouting of moral taboos. There is a great discordance between his portrayal of himself as the wise and virtuous King Lamus in his novel *Moonchild*, and his real untrustworthiness. This very untrustworthiness is part of his message to the world, and does much to prove his seriousness. To maintain a positive personal image by continuously observing some code, even if only one of honor and decency, is an easy way out for anyone. The path of dishonor is the way to search out the deeper ques-

tions of value and the worth of life, it is that of the religious reformer. The Christ chose dishonor, and was prepared to sacrifice millions of people in the name of God, which was his name for his mission. The Crowley's dishonorable acts were not meannesses, they are witnesses to his sense of destiny.

Symonds wrote: "The sphinx with the face of Aleister Crowley propounds this riddle. 'Why did I drive away my friends and followers? Why did I behave so vilely?' Other people have no ego and are just weak, but Crowley made a religion out of his weakness, out of being egoless."

This alleged weakness and "vile" behavior, especially if we want to avoid reproaching Crowley for it, poses an interesting problem. To call someone weak rather than bad may normally be thought a charitable view. But in Crowley's case, of possible motives for his actions, even sadism seems a more creditable motive than mere weakness. On an ordinary understanding, weakness would completely undermine his guru image. It must be wrong to see it as weakness pure and simple. We might rather see him as sticking to his guns, to a principle of absolute egoism, on which it would be impossible for him to compromise. From this viewpoint what Symonds would understand as strength is a kind of inhibition. He writes that Crowley lacked integration and was in the grip of unconscious forces. What is integration? Moral unification and control?

His ruthlessness would perhaps be of the same order as Lenin's. Nothing could be allowed to stand in the way of the proclamation of the law of Thelema. Weakness may be included in this. One would like to do good as the expression of strength; however, one has weakness, that is to say a certain quality of self-indulgence, and self-denial is unrealistic. It may be "normal" to overcome this in un-Thelemic ways. Some people practice self-denial by putting moral restraints on themselves, for altruistic motives. Rejecting such solutions, vile behavior may express integrity without suggesting immediate strength.

Crowley's alleged weakness included difficulty in earning a living. He survived by a series of shifts. Some things that come easily to the normal human, like steady, regular work, are just impossible for such types, putting it one way: they are too weak to do it. What are regarded as elementary duties, if they clash with immediate self-interest, will be experienced as impossible. They cannot do anything for the sake of duty; they cannot sacrifice themselves for anything other than perceived self-interest.

Crowley's longtime "Scarlet Woman," Leah Hirsig, asserted that there was weakness in him, something he did not normally want to think about, and that he normally preferred to deny.

Women, who claimed to understand him better than he understood himself, occasionally said there was something in him which was fundamentally not likeable. Crowley's longtime "Scarlet Woman," Leah Hirsig, asserted that there was weakness in him, something he did not normally want to think about, and that he normally preferred to deny.

He affirmed himself in his weakness. Weakness usually suggests constraint, prison, the opposite of a holiday. Acts of weakness are acts of constraint, and are therefore not admired. What excites admiration is courage, the power to act according to an idea, the saint, the martyr, not self-glorification in one's weakness. "Admire me, follow me, but I cannot protect you. I claim to be a Magus, but I do not have everything under control. I am not entirely to be trusted, not because of my perverseness, but because of my weakness (Dalinian softness)." What is normal human strength that is respected? Dependability, loyalty etc.

Crowley is misunderstood if he is seen primarily as the teacher of a new path to liberation, his sexual yoga and his Abbey of Thelema as a means of imparting this, with the theory behind it boiled down to the crude schematas of paths to enlightenment. He was part of a greater, far more intelligible tradition. Thelema itself is a rationally intelligible ideal that goes back to Rabelais, via Sir Francis Dashwood. Crowley gave this distinguished western tradition a new degree of development. The doctrine serves the man, not the man the doctrine. Not every practitioner of sex magick is a true disciple of Aleister Crowley.

Crowley resembles a Sufi master in the mystery and ambiguity of his image. In one aspect, his life is a fantasy indulgence. Many of the most explicit doctrines are only to be understood in the light of the conditions to which they are a response. The entire occult tradition is something complex like this. Magick is the satisfaction of desire, that is its whole concern, and desires vary from person to person. A Magus combines knowledge with personal development, specific techniques that may be taught have greater or lesser value, take them or leave them, dependant on the individual. A Magus will explore and understand different systems of attainment which will be suitable to different people at different times and places. No one of these is to be seen as his central message unless he is a social, religious, or cultural reformer, which he might well be, but we trivialize Crowley if we see him primarily thus.

Social mores change, what remains constant is the will to power. Generally the Thelemite rebels against the prevailing mores. In one age asceticism is appropriate, in another lechery. Crowley's sensual extravagance is admirable from his viewpoint, but to expect it to become socially acceptable is unreasonable. Prejudice against it is not irrational; it springs from honest self-interest. Who can feel pride in himself if an ideal is held up for his admiration which seems to overthrow all the fixed standards by which he finds his feet, an ideal that can easily be copied by people he may not want to admire, violent criminals, effeminate homosexuals and hopeless drug addicts?

Sensual desire can overthrow the judgment. Begin believing that total sensual satisfaction is the ideal and one is as if hooked on a drug, one feels forced to respect and

Magick is the satisfaction of desire, that is its whole concern, and desires vary from person to person.

admire those one wants to despise. It is wisdom that is really the ideal, but it is easy to confuse wisdom with its outer husk or shell, the manifestation it takes in some particular era.

The superman in the form of Sanine[1] or the Master Therion, is someone above all the normal problems of life, powerful, resourceful and superabundantly healthy. Crowley often chose to present himself thus. His life conflicts are described in a context of the noblest idealism. He has no hang-ups, no bitterness, envy or hatred. This is presumably why Symonds says he was surprisingly unintrospective. His nobility, his *supermanhood*, is preserved by the externalization of all his problems. He presents himself as a practical and efficient man of action.

There is a paradox in the superman persona. He is the serpent in lion's clothing. The serpent was the subtlest beast of the field. The lion, as king of beasts, represents conventional moral strength. It does not admit to weakness or resentment as elements in its character. The later Goethe projected a leonine image. However the lion is too stupid to become the superman. The superman has grown outside conventional values, and this is how he has mastered them. He has grown outside them because he has rejected them, and he has done this because he has suffered from them. In the process of overcoming this oppression, he has broken the code most thoroughly and comprehensively. Nothing has stood in his way, neither justice, loyalty, nor common decency. If he now dons the mantle of superior virtue, this is because he is able to rationalize the path he has taken in terms of duty to God, or some other externalization.

In contrast to Symonds, Susan Roberts' biography of Crowley, *The Magician of the Golden Dawn*, is a presentation of the superman persona. In a way, to take that persona at face value diminishes it, reduces to the leonine, cuts him down to size. But it does give a useful perspective. Dali's egomania took a different form. Roberts' biography paradoxically brings Crowley down to earth; it makes him seem less incommensurable with other people. Much of this apparent superiority is due to this presenting as manifestations of mere Saninian strength what was far more likely to be the manifestation of a violent reaction against weakness. The manifestation, be it strength or weakness, has itself the power and mystery of art. There is no art apart from profound discontent with conventional values. The great artist is not some kind of Olympian superadult, giving people superior toys to play with, from his position of serene mature wisdom and insight. He is one trying hard to enjoy himself. It is not that he has surpassed conventional happiness, not that he is so abundant in it that he creates more of it. His strength is not superhuman. He is driven by his discontent, his dissatisfaction with conventional values, ordinary roads to fulfillment and happiness, to remold them, to remake them so they can serve his purposes properly.

The yellow press was of great help to Crowley in promoting a superman image. The building up of a devil figure can produce an object of admiration and identification for those who despise the values of those who create it. The devil is a hate object compounded of insecurities. Symonds' expressed opposition to Crowley is apparently quite fundamental, it seems to be of someone belonging to an opposite camp, like an ideological enemy. The effect, however, is that Symonds with his moralizing is like the straight man of a pair of comedians. Conventional newspaper morality sets off Crowley's eccentricity very well. Crowley makes us laugh, and this can be built on. It is a form of illumination.

The reality of people like Crowley is that they react as they do by sheer reflex action. In the process of reacting they are creative. For those who are on his side, he is a solace and an encouragement, his superhuman legend more than his reality. All his actions take on a special heroic quality, as if they are messages, as if everything he does is part of a deliberately created work of art. Usually they just spring from the necessity of his position. Moves of desperation seem like acts of great evil and perversity.

Hero worship of Crowley involves the constant assumption of his superior wisdom, as if all of his interests had some profounder significance. Always there is his assumption of esoteric, initiated knowledge, guruhood. There is special value in having instruction from a guru. In the study of secret wisdom one needs to be led through the profoundest paradox, keeping trust unswerving. A guru may be living or dead. Crowley of course is dead. Are not the works of the sages, in Chuang Tsu's phrase "the lees and the scum of bygone men"? But books these days can preserve more than that. We can even hear his voice, see his portrait.

Rather than that Crowley was dishonest in the way he presented himself, it is more likely that he expected his intelligent readers to be able to read between the lines. The devil image is really far more attractive than the lion. The lion image is less a source of wonder because it is more transparent. As for Crowley's family life, that is hardly so bizarre as it once seemed, as many of us discover from our own experience. Much of his outrageousness is fairly ordinary if we take a broad perspective, and cease to think only of the respectable middle classes.

There are many possible attitudes towards moral rules. Where a moral code provides a standard by which the success or otherwise of a course of action is to be judged, change the standard and you read an entirely different story. The moral code, or the standard, is entirely a question of interpretation; it does not have to be consciously in the minds of any of the actors in the drama. Thus your actions may very easily have more significance than you understand at the time. At the time, for example, you may feel very insecure about your code of values. You may feel shame and guilt, which is dissipated in retrospect, as you understand that you could not have done otherwise than as you did.

The roots of the creative personality lie in the great mass of disorderly material from childhood onwards. His task is the imposition of order upon disorderly material. Much of

The Crowley discovered at age 14, can continue to have profound value and significance throughout life. His appeal is far more than something merely adolescent.

this is to be found in the writings of Aleister Crowley. His genius lives on, resisting judgment, through the power of will. Judgment (Geburah on the Tree of Life), until you have won its favor, is a kind of death. A claim to greatness is not an appeal to judgment.

In presenting oneself as capable now, one must acknowledge that once one was incapable. That is one's true history, and resulted in a certain amount of abnormality. Only in the light of this admission can the reality become intelligible or admirable. In applying the law of Do What Thou Wilt, it must be understood what phantoms one fought and is still fighting, in what exactly one's strength should consist. In a general sense, it consists in not submitting to alien judgments and never having done so. Crowley emphasizes some of the vices in his own character, to the point where they make us laugh, and seem an expression of freedom.

His alleged crimes and weaknesses include letting followers like Norman Mudd and Leah Hirsig starve. But I am not my brother's keeper. Why should he have accepted the responsibility of supporting them as if they were his family? They were not his children. He had to consider his own survival first, and that was at times difficult. He is accused of self-indulgence. He was not able to support, materially, all the various weaklings who crossed his path. Did he ever imply, misleadingly, that he could? Unlike Bhagwan, or the Scientologists, his organization offered no security to its members. Unfortunately, the law of Do What Thou Wilt did not work well for some people. Too many came to bad ends, seeming damnation. Crowley appeared to be preaching a philosophy of dangerous bohemianism. Why did his personality appear to drive

women mad? He never went to prison, though he came close to it once. He has been reproached for his behavior on the mountain, for an incompletely cut ice step, and for not going out to search for the missing people. Was that funk? He may have been guilty of trying to justify himself after the event, of self-justification in the face of crimes and weakness.

Crowley the Beast made a morality out of immorality. It is shocking that madness and suicide should so follow in his wake. It shows how far he was from being the King Lamus figure he sometimes projected. But this shockingness also seems to express some teaching, perhaps a mystical message worth meditating upon. Crowley lived out his Beast role. As to the Beast, one is not called to an Imitatio Crowleyi. Not having that historical role to play, one does not have to be utterly callous and selfish to all one's friends and lovers. One can be inspired by it, without feeling any need to imitate it.

Youthful fascination for Crowley is an essentially statistical phenomenon. A proportion of young people who read *The Great Beast* would feel a close identification with him. Because they feel as they do they also feel a sense of superiority, of being in possession of some superior insight. Not that, at their age, their insight could be any greater than the man chosen by Crowley himself to be his biographer. The Crowley discovered at age 14, can continue to have profound value and significance throughout life. His appeal is far more than something merely adolescent. Crowley was a deliverer from *Weltschmerz*; he represented affirmation in a strong form. In the war against Ialdabaoth, as in all wars, sometimes extreme measures are necessary. Oppression by the zeitgeist continues, whether we feel it as Christianity, capitalism, socialism, materialism, democracy, or whatever. It is all too easy to pick on one of these, identifying most strongly with its enemies, fervently denouncing it as the heart and essence of an evil that really runs much deeper. ▢

Endnote

1. Sanine: eponymous hero of a novel by Arstibashyev, a Russian portrayal of a Nietzschean superman from a largely sexual angle.

THE ENOCHIAN APOCALYPSE

A SAINT AND A ROGUE

Between the years 1582 and 1589 the Elizabethan scholar John Dee (1527–1608) conducted a series of ritual communications with a set of discarnate entities who eventually came to be known as the Enochian angels. It was Dee's plan to use the complex system of magic communicated by the angels to advance the expansionist policies of his sovereign, Elizabeth the First. At the time England lay under the looming shadow of invasion from Spain. Dee hoped to control the hostile potentates of Europe by commanding the tutelary spirits of their various nations.

Dee was a thoroughly remarkable man. Not only was he a skilled mathematician, astronomer and cartographer, he was also the private astrologer, counselor and (some believe) confidential espionage agent of Queen Elizabeth.[1] His father had been a gentleman sewer (a kind of steward) at the table of Henry VIII. When Elizabeth ascended to the throne, Dee was asked by Robert Dudley to set an auspicious date for her coronation ceremony. Always intensely loyal to Elizabeth, he had earlier been accused, (falsely) of trying to kill her predecessor, Bloody Queen Mary, with sorcery. His intellectual brilliance and skill as a magician were famous, and infamous, throughout Europe.

In his occult work he was aided by an equally extraordinary person, Edward Kelley (1555–1597), the son of a Worcester apothecary, who dreamed of discovering the secret of the philosopher's stone and dabbled in the black art of necromancy. Fleeing Lancaster in 1580 on charges of forging title deeds, Kelley found it prudent to set out on

Dr. John Dee

a walking tour of Wales. Somewhere near Glastonbury (so the story goes) he purchased a portion of the fabled red power that could turn base metals into gold from an innkeeper who had received it from tomb robbers.[2]

All the remainder of his colorful life Kelley labored to unlock the secret of the red powder so that he could manufacture more of it himself. It was on this quest for alchemical knowledge that he sought out the library of John Dee in 1582, and it was primarily for this reason that he agreed to serve as Dee's seer—he hoped Dee would help him to discover the secret of the powder.

Dee was a saint, Kelley a rogue.

Dee was a saint, Kelley a rogue, but they were bound together by their common fascination for ceremonial magic and the wonders it promised. Dee possessed little talent for mediumship. He tried to overcome this limitation by hiring a mountebank named Barnabas Saul as his professional scryer but had poor results. When he learned of Kelley's considerable psychic abilities, he eagerly employed Kelley as his seer for the sum of 50 pounds per annum.

The spirits got their name from the nature of the system of magic they described to Dee. It was, they claimed, the very magic that Enoch the patriarch had learned from the angels of heaven.

Dee invoked the Enochian angels to appearance within a scrying crystal or a black mirror of obsidian by means of prayers and certain magical seals. After Kelley alerted Dee to the presence of the spirits, Dee questioned them. Kelley reported their sayings and doings back to Dee, who recorded their words and actions in his magical diaries.

The most important portion of Dee's transcription of the Enochian communications, covering the years 1582–1587, was published in London in 1659 by Meric Casaubon under the title *A True and Faithful Relation of What passed for many Yeers Between Dr. John Dee ... and Some Spirits*. This fascinating work has been reprinted several times in recent decades and is readily available.

The spirits got their name from the nature of the system of magic they described to Dee. It was, they claimed, the very magic that Enoch the patriarch had learned from the angels of heaven. The angel Ave tells Dee: "Now hath it pleased God to deliver this Doctrine again out of darknesse: and to fulfill his promise with thee, for the books of Enoch."[3] Compared to it, the angels asserted to Kelley, all other forms of magic were mere playthings.

Although Dee faithfully recorded all the details of Enochian magic in his diaries, he never tried to work this system in any serious way. We cannot know the reason with certainty. His rupture in 1589 from Kelley, who stayed on in Bohemia to manufacture gold for the Emperor Rudolph the Second while Dee

returned to England at the request of Elizabeth, may have inconvenienced his plans. However, it is my contention, as I shall demonstrate below, that Dee was awaiting permission from the angels to employ their magic, and this permission was not given in his lifetime.

Edward Kelley

THE REALITY OF THE ENOCHIAN ANGELS

It is necessary to state here unequivocally for those unfamiliar with Enochian magic that neither Dee nor Kelley fabricated the spirit communications. Both believed completely in the reality of the angels, although they differed about the motives of these beings. Dee believed the angels obedient agents of God submissive to the authority of Christ. Kelley mistrusted them and suspected them of deliberate deception. The dislike was mutual. The angels always treated Kelley with amused contempt. Kelley hoped the angels would communicate the secret of the red powder, which is the only reason he endured their insults for so many years.

There is no space here to enter into the entire question of the nature and objective reality of spirits, nor is it likely that any conclusions could be reached on this difficult subject.

Dee believed the angels obedient agents of God submissive to the authority of Christ. Kelley mistrusted them and suspected them of deliberate deception. The dislike was mutual.

Woodcut from Doctor Faustus by Christopher Marlowe, 1636 edition

Whatever their essential nature, the Enochian angels acted as independent, intelligent beings with their own distinct personalities and purposes. This is how Dee and Kelley regarded them, and this is how I shall regard them in this essay, because I am presenting here the secret agenda of the angels, which they concealed from John Dee—to plant among mankind the ritual working that would initiate the period of violent transformation between the present aeon and the next, commonly known as the Apocalypse.

THE GATES AND THE KEYS

What the Enochian angels conveyed to Dee through Kelley was not merely a more potent form of spirit magic to rule the tutelary daemons of the nations of the earth. It was an initiatory formula designed to open the locked gates of the four great Watchtowers that stand guard against chaos at the extremities of our universe. The Watchtowers are described by the angel Ave:

> "The 4 houses, are the 4 Angels of the Earth, which are the 4 Overseers, and Watch-towers, that the eternal God in his providence hath placed, against the usurping blasphemy, misuse, and stealth of the wicked and great enemy, the Devil. To the intent that being put out to the Earth, his envious will might be bridled, the determinations of God fulfilled, and his creatures kept and preserved, within the compasse and measure of order."[4]

These Watchtowers, represented in Enochian magic by alphabetical squares, are equivalent to the four mystical pillars of Egyptian mythology that hold up the sky and keep it from crashing into the earth. They bar the chaotic legions of Choronzon from sweeping across the face of the world. Choronzon, the Enochian angels reveal to Dee, is the true heavenly name for Satan.[5] He is also known by the Enochian title of Death-Dragon or Him-That-Is-Fallen (Telocvovim).[6]

The Enochian Calls, or Keys (the angels refer to them by both titles) are 48 spirit evocations delivered to Dee and Kelley in the Enochian language and then translated into English word for word by the angels. The overt purpose of the Keys, declared by the angels, is to enable Dee to establish ritual communication with the spirits of the 30 Aethers or Airs who rule over the tutelary daemons of the nations of the earth. There are actually 49 Keys, but the first, the angels inform Dee, is too sacred and mysterious to be voiced. The first eighteen explicit Keys are completely different in their wording; the last 30 are similar save for the name of the Aether inserted in the first line.

The angel Raphael declares the expressed purpose of the Keys to Dee:

> "In 49 voyces, or callings: which are the Natural Keyes, to open those, not 49. but 48. (for One is not to be opened) Gates of understanding, whereby you shall have knowledge to move every Gate, and to call out as many as you please, or shall be thought necessary, which can very well, righteously, and wisely, open unto you the secrets of their Cities, & make you understand perfectly the contained in the Tables."[7]

The tables referred to by Raphael are the 49 alphabetical tables from which the Keys were generated, one letter at a time, by the Enochian angels. The Keys are related in sets to the four Watchtowers, which contain the names of various hierarchies of spirits.

Dee's blindness to the true function of the Keys is curious, because clues about their nature are everywhere for those with eyes to see them. The Enochian communications recorded by Dee are filled with apocalyptic pronouncements and imagery. Again and again the angels warn of the coming destruction of the world by the wrath of God and the advent of the Antichrist. This apocalyptic imagery is also found throughout the Keys themselves.

The very name of these evocations should have been clue enough. Surely if the Watchtowers stand guard at the four corners of our dimension of reality, keeping back the hordes of Choronzon from descending like "stooping dragons," as the Eighth Key puts it, and if the evocations known as the Keys are designed to open the gates of these Watchtowers, we might be led to suspect that it would be a bad idea to unlock the gates.

Perhaps Dee believed, as the angels deceitfully encouraged him to believe, that the gates could be opened a crack for specific human purposes and then slammed shut before anything too horrible slipped through to our dimension of awareness. He would have assumed that the harrowing of the goddess Earth and her children by the demons of Choronzon would not occur until the preordained time of the Apocalypse, an event initiated by God and presumably beyond Dee's control.

What he failed to understand is that the date of the initiation of the period of change known as the Apocalypse is (in the intention of the angels) the same date as the successful completion of the full ritual working of the eighteen distinct manifest Keys and the Key of the Thirty Aethers upon the Great Table of the Watchtowers, and that this date is not predetermined, but will be determined by the free will and actions of a single human being who is in the Revelation of St. John called the Antichrist.

THE NATURE OF THE APOCALYPSE

It has always been generally assumed that the Apocalypse is in the hands of the angels of wrath, to be visited upon the world at the pleasure of God, at a moment foredestined from the beginning of creation. In the veiled teachings of the Enochian angels this is not true. The gates of the Watchtowers can only be unlocked from the inside.

Again and again the angels warn of the coming destruction of the world by the wrath of God and the advent of the Antichrist.

The angels of wrath cannot initiate the Apocalypse even if they wish today to do so. This is suggested by an exchange between Dee and the angel Ave:

DEE: As for the form of our Petition or Invitation of the good Angels, what sort should it be of?

AVE: A short and brief speech.

DEE: We beseech you to give us an example: we would have a confidence, it should be of more effect.

AVE: I may not do so.

AVE: Invocation proceedeth of the good will of man, and of the heat and fervency of the spirit: And therefore is prayer of such effect with God.

DEE: We beseech you, shall we use one form to all?

AVE: Every one, after a divers form.

DEE: If the minde do dictate or prompt a divers form, you mean.

AVE: I know not: for I dwell not in the soul of man.[8]

Spiritual beings must be evoked into our reality by human beings. We must open the gates and admit the servants of Choronzon ourselves. Evocation and invocation are not a part of the business of angels, but of humans. That is why it was necessary for the Enochian angels to go through the elaborate ruse of conveying the system of Enochian magic, with the Keys and the Great Table of the Watchtowers, to Dee. If the Apocalypse is to take place, and if it is necessary for human beings to open the gates of the Watchtowers before it can take place, the angels first had to instruct a man in the correct method for opening the gates.

It is evident that Dee was to be restrained from opening the gates of the Watchtowers until it pleased the angels. The angel Gabriel, who purports to be speaking with the authority of God, tells him:

> "I have chosen you, to enter into my barns: And have commanded you to open the Corn, that the scattered may appear, and that which remaineth in the sheaf may stand. And have entered into the first, and so into the seventh. And have delivered unto you a Testimony of my spirit to come.
>
> For my Barn hath been long without Threshers. And I have kept my flayles for a long time hid in unknown places: Which flayle is the Doctrine that I deliver unto you: Which is the Instrument of thrashing, wherewith you shall beat the sheafs, that the Corn which is scattered, and the rest may be all one.
>
> (But a word in the mean season.)
>
> If I be Master of the Barn, owner of the Corn, and deliverer of my flayle: If all be mine (And unto you,

If the apocalypse is to take place, and if it is necessary for human beings to open the gates of the Watchtowers before it can take place, the angels first had to instruct a man in the correct method for opening the gates.

there is nothing: for you are hirelings, whose reward is in heaven).

Then see, that you neither thresh, nor unbinde, untill I bid you, let it be sufficient unto you: that you know my house, that you know the labour I will put you to: That I favour you so much as to entertain you the labourers within my Barn: For within it thresheth none without my consent."[9]

Surely nothing could be clearer. Throughout the Enochian communications the angels refer to the Apocalypse euphemistically as "the Harvest." Here, Enochian magic is specifically described as the "Instrument of thrashing." Yet Dee did not comprehend the awesome significance of the burden that had been laid upon his shoulders. Elsewhere in the record the angel Mapsama is just as explicit about the need for Dee to await permission before attempting to use the Keys:

MAPSAMA: These Calls are the keyes into the Gates and Cities of wisdom. Which [Gates] are not able to be opened, but with visible apparition.

DEE: And how shall that be come unto?

MAPSAMA: Which is according to the former instructions: and to be had, by calling of every Table. You called for wisdom, God hath opened unto you, his Judgement: He hath delivered unto you the keyes, that you may enter; But be humble. Enter not of presumption, but of permission. Go not in rashly; But be brought in willingly: For, many have ascended, but few have entered. By Sunday you shall have all things that are necessary to be taught; then (as occasion serveth) you may practice at all times. But you being called by God, and to a good purpose.

DEE: How shall we under stand this Calling by God?

MAPSAMA: God stoppeth my mouth, I will answer thee no more.[10]

Despite these hints and many others, the angels never actually came out and told Dee that he was to be the instrument whereby the ritual formula that would initiate the Apocalypse would be planted in the midst of humanity, where it would sit like a ticking occult time bomb, waiting for some clever magician, perhaps guided by the angels, to work it. Dee evidently never received the signal to conduct the Apocalypse Working in his lifetime. It was to be reserved for another century, and another man. That man was Aleister Crowley (1875–1947).

ENTER, THE GREAT BEAST

Even as a child, Crowley became convinced that he was the Great Beast mentioned in the biblical Book of Revelation. He studied magic within the Hermetic Order of the Golden Dawn, then went on to construct his own occult system using an amalgamation of the ritual working of Abramelin the Mage, the *Goetia*, and the Tantric sexual techniques of the German Ordo Templi Orientis, among other sources.

Enochian sigil used by Dee and Kelley in their workings

He firmly believed that he was the herald for a new age of strife and destruction that would sweep across the world. He called this age the Aeon of Horus, after the Egyptian god of war. In 1904 in Cairo, Egypt, he received in the form of a psychic dictation from his guardian angel, Aiwass, the bible of this apocalyptic period, *Liber AL vel Legis (The Book Of the Law)*. It sets forth some of the conditions that will prevail in the Aeon of Horus. In it is Crowley's famous dictum: "Do what thou wilt shall be the whole of the Law."[11]

It is highly significant that Crowley never considered himself to be the Antichrist. He is not the central character in the drama of the Apocalypse, but the herald who ushers in the age of chaos. In a very real sense he was the gatekeeper of the Apocalypse. The text of *The Book Of the Law* clearly states:

> "This book shall be translated into all tongues: but always with the original in the writing of the Beast; for in the chance shape of the letters and their position to one another: in these are mysteries that no Beast shall divine. Let him not seek to try: but one cometh after him, whence I say not, who shall discover the key of it all."[12]

No other man of the 20th century was better suited to initiate the Apocalypse Working.

Crowley studied and practiced Enochian magic more often and deeply than any other magician of the Golden Dawn; indeed, more deeply than any other human being who has ever lived. About the angelic communications of Dee and Kelley he writes: "Much of their work still defies explanation, though I and Frater Semper Paratus [Thomas Windram], an Adaptus Major of the A[rgentum] A[strum] have spent much time and research upon it and cleared up many obscure points."[13]

The record of his working of the Enochian Aethers in 1909 in the desert of North Africa is preserved in the document titled *The Vision and the Voice*.[14] He possessed a profound and broad understanding of ritual magic, an understanding not merely theoretical but practical. No other man of the 20th century was better suited to initiate the Apocalypse Working, even as there had been no man better suited than John Dee in the 16th century to receive it from the Enochian angels. It is significant that Crowley believed himself the reincarnation of Edward Kelley.

I doubt that Crowley ever succeeded in correctly completing the entire Enochian Apocalypse Working—that is, the primal occult Key which is nowhere recorded, the eighteen manifest Keys and the Key of the Thirty Aethers in their correct correspondence with the parts of the Great Table of the Watchtowers—but he may have succeeded in partially opening the gates of the Watchtowers. It is significant that he states concerning the African working with his disciple Victor Neuberg: "As a rule, we did one Aethyr every day."[15] About the method of working the Keys the angel Ave tells Dee:

> "Four days ... must you onely call upon those names of God [on the Great Table of the Watchtowers], or on the God of Hosts, in those names:
>
> And 14 days after you shall (in this, or in some convenient place) Call the Angels by Petition and by the name of God, unto the which they are obedient. The 15 day you shall Cloath yourselves, in vestures made of linnen, white: and so have the apparition, use, and practice of the Creatures. For, it is not a labour of years, nor many dayes."[16]

It seems clear to me that the complete Apocalypse Working, which will be conducted by the Antichrist and will throw wide the gates of the Watchtowers, (if we are to believe the intimations of the Enochian angels) must be conducted on consecutive days, one Key per day. I would guess that the unexpressed primordial Key of the Great Mother is the missing ingredient that will complete the Working, but this is a matter of practical magic and there is no space to investigate the details of the Apocalypse Working in this brief essay.

Crowley remained firmly convinced until his death in 1947 that the Aeon of Horus had begun in 1904, precisely at the time he received *The Book Of the Law*. He may have been right. The Aeon of Horus is the duration of the Apocalypse, that period when Choronzon shall rule over the cosmos and visit destruction upon mankind. And the Apocalypse is a mental transformation that will occur, or is presently occurring, within the collective unconscious of the human race.

Despite these hints and many others, the angels never actually came out and told Dee that he was to be the instrument whereby the ritual formula that would initiate the Apocalypse would be planted in the midst of humanity, where it would sit like a ticking occult time bomb, waiting for some clever magician, perhaps guided by the angels, to work it.

Edward Kelley

A MENTAL ARMAGEDDON

It is common among fundamentalist Christians to believe that the end of the world will be a completely physical event and will be sparked by some horrifying material agent—global thermonuclear war, or the impact of a large asteroid, or a deadly plague.

This supposition is natural in view of the concrete imagery in the vision of St. John the Divine, the purported author of Revelations. It is in keeping with the materialistic world view of modern society. But nobody stops to consider that this destruction is described by angels, or that angels are spiritual creatures, not physical beings.

In my opinion the Apocalypse prepared by the Enochian angels must be primarily an internal, spiritual event, and only in a secondary way an external physical catastrophe. The gates of the Watchtowers that stand guard at the four corners of our dimension of reality are mental constructions. When they are opened, they will admit the demons of Choronzon, not into the physical world, but into our subconscious minds.

Spirits are mental, not material. They dwell in the depths of mind and communicate with us through our dreams, unconscious impulses, and more rarely in waking visions. They affect our feelings and our thoughts beneath the level of our conscious awareness. Sometimes they are able to control our actions, either partially as in the case of irrational and obsessive behavior patterns, or completely as in the case of full possession. Through us, by using us as their physical instruments, and only through us, are they able to influence physical things.

The Enochian communications teach us that not only must humanity itself initiate the cosmic drama of the Apocalypse through the magical formula delivered to John Dee and Edward Kelley more than four centuries ago, but humans must also be the physical actors that bring about the plagues, wars and famines described with such chilling eloquence in the vision of St. John. We must let the demons of Choronzon into our minds by means of a specific ritual working. They will not find a welcome place there all at once, but will worm their way into our subconscious and make their homes there slowly over time. In the minds of individuals that resist this invasion they will find it difficult to gain a foothold, but in the more pliable minds of those who welcome their influence they will establish themselves readily.

Once they have taken up residence, we will be powerless to prevent them turning our thoughts and actions toward chaotic and destructive ends. These Apocalyptic spirits will set person against person and nation against nation, gradually increasing the degree of madness, or chaos, in human society, until at last the full horror of Revelation has been realized upon the stage of the world. The corruption of human thoughts and feelings may require generations to bring to full fruition. Only after the wasting and burning of souls is well advanced will the full horror of the Apocalypse achieve its final fulfillment in the material realm.

Let us suppose for the sake of argument that the signal for the initiation of this psychic invasion occurred in 1904 when Crowley received *The Book Of the Law*, as Crowley himself believed. Crowley's Enochian evocations of 1909 then pried the doors of the Watchtowers open a crack—enough to allow a foul wind to blow through the common

Dr. John Dee

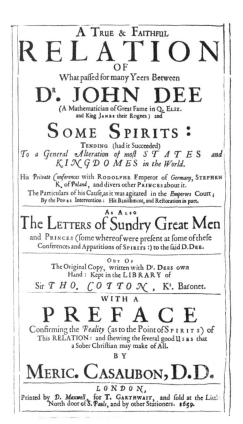

Title Page of *A True & Faithful RELATION OF What passed for many Yeers Between Dr. JOHN DEE (A Mathematician of Great Fame in Q. ELIZ. And King JAMES their Reignes) and Some Spirits*

Endnotes

1. See Richard Deacon, *John Dee: Scientist, Geographer, Astrologer and Secret Agent* (London, 1968).
2. See the Introduction to *The Alchemical Writings of Edward Kelly*, ed. A. E. Waite [London, 1893], Samuel Weiser, New York, 1970.
3. Meric Casaubon, A True & Faithful Relation Of What passed for many Yeers Between Dr. John Dee (*A Mathematician of Great Fame in Q. Eliz. and King James their Reignes*) and Some Spirits, [London, 1659]. The Antonine Publishing Company Ltd., Glasgow, 1974, page 174.
4. Ibid. p. 170.
5. Ibid. p. 92.
6. Ibid. p. 207.
7. Ibid. p. 77.
8. Ibid. p. 188.
9. Ibid. p. 161.
10. Ibid. pp. 145–6.
11. Aleister Crowley, *The Book Of the Law*, ms. pp. 10–11.
12. Ibid., ch. 3, para. 47.
13. *The Confessions of Aleister Crowley*, ed. John Symonds and Kenneth Grant. Arkana Books, 1989, p. 611.
14. *The Vision and the Voice*, Thelema Publishing Co., California, 1952. See also the <u>Confessions</u>, ch. 66.
15. *Confessions*, p. 618.
16. *True and Faithful Relation*, p. 184.

subconscious mind of the human race. This would explain the senseless slaughter of the First World War, and the unspeakable horror of the Nazi Holocaust during the Second World War. It would explain the decline of organized religions and why the soulless cult of science has gained supremacy. It would explain the moral and ethical bankruptcy of modern times and the increase in senseless crimes of violence.

We may not have long to wait before the individual known in the vision of St. John as the Antichrist, the one foretold in Crowley's *The Book Of the Law* to follow after the Beast, will succeed in completing the Apocalypse Working placed in the world as a flaming sword by the Enochian angels. Then the gates of the Watchtowers will truly gape wide,

We may not have long to wait before the individual known in the vision of St. John as the Antichrist, the one foretold in Crowley's *The Book Of the Law* to follow after the Beast, will succeed in completing the Apocalypse Working.

and the children of Choronzon will sweep into our minds as crowned conquerors. If this chilling mythic scenario ever comes to pass, the wars of the 20th century will seem bucolic to those who survive the slaughter. ⛢

THE ENOCHIAN APOCALYPSE

THE CRYING OF LIBER 49
Jack Parsons, Antichrist Superstar

"All stories are true, every last one of them. All myths, all legends, all fables. If you believe them true, then they are true. If you don't believe them, then all that can be said is that they are true for someone else."

When the history of the American space program is finally written, no figure will stand out quite like John Whiteside Parsons. Remarkably handsome, dashing and brilliant, Jack Parsons was one of the founders of the experimental rocket research group at Cal Tech (California Institute of Technology) and the group's seven acre Arroyo Seco testing facility would eventually become the Jet Propulsion Laboratory, NASA's rocket design center.

Werner von Braun allegedly claimed it was the self-taught Parsons, not himself, who was the true father of the American space program for his contribution to the development of solid rocket fuel. Although Parsons has been memorialized with a statue at JPL and has had a crater on the dark side of the moon named in his honor, his story remains shrouded in mystery, for what is little known about this legend of aerospace engineering is that Parsons was an avid practitioner of the occult sciences, and for several years, Aleister Crowley's hand-picked leader of the US branch of the Ordo Templi Orientis, the Southern California-based Agape Lodge.

Parsons was born in Los Angeles on October 2, 1914, the son of a wealthy and well-connected family living in a sprawling mansion on Pasadena's "Millionaire Row." His father worked for Woodrow Wilson. After his parents' divorce, the solitary childhood of Parsons imbued

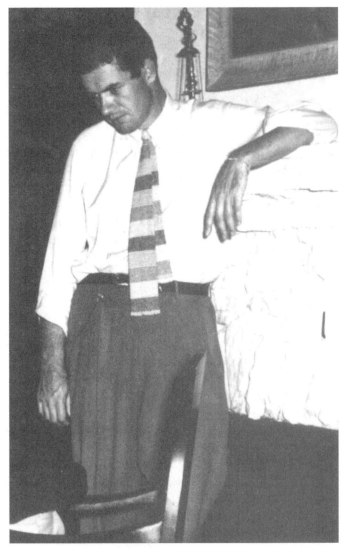

Jack Parsons

him with a deep hatred of authority and contempt for any sort of interference in his activity. Parsons' interest in the occult apparently commenced at an early age and in one of his diaries he claimed to have evoked Satan at the tender age of 13.

Crowley, self-styled "Great Beast 666," considered himself the avatar of the Antichrist and *The Book of the Law* is a proclamation that the era of the slave gods (Osiris, Allah, Jesus) had come to an end and that the Aeon of Horus, the "Crowned and Conquering Child" had begun.

After discovering Crowley's philosophy of *Thelema*, Parsons joined the Agape Lodge in 1941. Wilfred T. Smith, the expatriate Englishman who started the order in the early 1930s with a charter from the Great Beast himself, wrote of Parsons in a letter to Crowley: "I think I have at long last a really excellent man, John Parsons. And starting next Tuesday he begins a course of talks with a view to enlarging our scope. He has an excellent mind and much better intellect than myself ... John Parsons is going to be valuable."

Another member of the Lodge, Crowley's old friend, actress Jane Wolfe described Parsons as "26 years of age, 6'2", vital, potentially bisexual at the very least, University of the State of California and Cal Tech, now engaged in Cal Tech chemical laboratories developing 'bigger and better' explosives for Uncle Sam. Travels under sealed orders from the government. Writes poetry—'sensuous only,' he says. Lover of music, which he seems to know thoroughly. I see him as the real successor of Therion [Crowley]. Passionate; and has made the vilest analyses result in a species of exaltation after the event. Has had mystical experiences which gave him a sense of equality all round, although he is hierarchical in feeling and in the established order."

Parsons rose quickly through the ranks, taking over the Agape Lodge from Smith at Crowley's decree within a year.

"FOR I AM BABALON, AND SHE MY DAUGHTER, UNIQUE AND THERE SHALL BE NO OTHER WOMEN LIKE HER."
–LIBER 49, THE BOOK OF BABALON, VERSE 37

In one of the most celebrated feats in magical history, Parsons and pre-Dianetics L. Ron Hubbard (whose role is too complicated to describe in this short essay) per-

formed The Babalon Working, a daring attempt to shatter the boundaries of time and space and intended to bring about, in Parsons' own words, "love, understanding, and Dionysian freedom [...] the necessary counterbalance or correspondence to the manifestation of Horus."

The above reference recalls Crowley's announcement of the "Aeon of Horus," described in *The Book of the Law* (Liber AL vel Legis), a blasphemous, strangely beautiful, prose poem that Crowley received from a discarnate entity called Aiwass in Cairo in 1904. Crowley, self-styled "Great Beast 666," considered himself the avatar of the Antichrist and *The Book of the Law* is a proclamation that the era of the slave gods (Osiris, Allah, Jesus) had come to an end and that the Aeon of Horus, the "Crowned and Conquering Child" had begun. In its infancy, Crowley predicted, the Aeon would be characterized by the magical formula of bloodshed and blind force, the tearing down of the established orders to make way for the new. Crowley held the two World Wars as evidence of this, but did not see the Horus-force as evil, rather as embodying the innocence of a hyperactive child who is like a bull in a china shop. Babalon, a Thelemic

The impossible was precisely what Jack Parsons, the scientific sorcerer, had in mind.

counterpart of Kali or Isis, was described by Parsons as, "... black, murderous and horrible, but Her hand is uplifted in blessing and reassurance: the reconciliation of opposites, the apotheosis of the impossible."

The impossible was precisely what Jack Parsons, the scientific sorcerer, had in mind.

HECATE RISING...

In its initial stages, The Babalon Working was intended to attract an elemental to serve as a partner for Parsons' elaborate sex magick rituals. The method employed was that of the solo VIII Degree working of the O.T.O., the quasi-Masonic organization reformulated by Crowley in the earlier part of the century in accordance with his *Do What Thou Wilt* mythos. Parsons used his "magical wand" to whip up a vortex of energy so the elemental would be summoned. Translated into plain English, Parsons jerked off in the name of spiritual advancement whilst Hubbard (referred to as "The Scribe" in the diary of the event) scanned the astral plane for signs and visions.

Apparently, it worked. In a letter to Crowley dated February 23, 1946, Parsons exclaimed, "I have my elemental! She turned up one night after the conclusion of the Operation, and has been with me since."

The elemental was a green-eyed, flaming redhead named Marjorie Cameron, (later of Kenneth Anger's *Inauguration of the Pleasure Dome* film and a Beatnik artist of some renown). Cameron was only too happy to participate in Parsons' sex magick and now Parsons could get down to the real business of the Babalon Working: the birthing of a moonchild or homunculus. The operation was formulated to open an interdimensional doorway, rolling out the red carpet for the appearance of the goddess Babalon in human form, employing the angelic language of the Enochian Calls of Elizabethan magus John Dee and the attraction of the sex force of the duo's copulation to this end.

As Paul Rydeen points out in his extended essay *Jack Parsons and the Fall of Babalon*: "The purpose of Parsons' operation has been underemphasized. He sought to produce a magical child who would be a product of her environment rather than of her heredity. Crowley himself describes the Moonchild in just these terms. The Babalon Working itself was preparation for what was to come: *a Thelemic messiah.*" [Emphasis added]. To wit: Babalon incarnate as a *living* female, the Scarlet Woman as consort to the Antichrist, bride of the Beast 666. In effect, Parsons also claimed the mantle of Antichrist for himself, as the magical heir of Crowley prophesied in *Liber AL*: "The child of thy bowels, he shall behold them [the mysteries of the Apocalypse]. Expect him not from the East, nor from the West, for from no expected house cometh that child."

Without the Scarlet Woman, the Antichrist cannot make his manifestation; the eschatological formula must first be complete. In whiter words, with the magical rites of the Babalon Working, it was Parsons' goal to bring on the Apocalypse.

JAMES DEAN OF THE OCCULT

Parsons' Babalon gambit was dazzling to say the least: If the earth must first be covered in evil before the return of the Christ consciousness and the final triumph of good, what better way to hasten the uplifting of humanity than to rip an alchemical hole in the fabric of reality and invite the very spawn of Hell in for a rip-snorting orgy of howling madness?

So much is written of Parsons as a psychotic lunatic, but I put it to you dear reader, is the Babalon Working the product of a deranged mind or the ultimate exploration of the absolute furthest reaches of consciousness, putting the pedal to the metal for the absolute *living end* in revolutionary chic and mind expansion?

Parsons used his "magical wand" to whip up a vortex of energy so the elemental would be summoned. Translated into plain English, Parsons jerked off in the name of spiritual advancement whilst Hubbard (referred to as "The Scribe" in the diary of the event) scanned the astral plane for signs and visions.

Parsons' perverse imitation of Christ was intended to disrupt, oppose, and subvert the established order of things. It's the age-old Manichean battle between good and evil, the forces of order and chaos, the status quo versus revolutionary tendencies. But in the 21st century, these lines have become significantly blurred: If you consider the New World Order multinational corporate monoliths poisoning the planet and reducing mankind to the level of wage slavery for the benefit of the very few to be representative of the good, then the Babalon Working must sound like the most outright evil deed ever perpetrated by a human being. But if you're like me, and would dearly love to see the vile, puss-ridden edifice of Western society burned to the ground, you should see Parsons as the penultimate style icon of psycho-sexual/magical insurrection, a truly American original if ever there was one. This darkly handsome, genius scientist was, I submit, the James Dean of the Occult: one spectacularly cool motherfucker.

"ONLY IN THE IRRATIONAL AND UNKNOWN DIRECTION CAN WE COME TO IT [WISDOM] AGAIN."
–JACK PARSONS, IN A LETTER TO MARJORIE CAMERON, LATE 1940S.

The question must be asked: Who is the greater hero—he who prolongs the agony of this pathetic existence or he who opens wide the Pandora's Box of perdition knowing that this is how the final eschatological chapter must play itself out?

Isn't the Great Work, the cosmic perfection of mankind, the final goal of the alchemists? Just as the rocket scientist Parsons was willing to play dice with heavy explosives, Parsons the nuclear age warlock was willing to play with fire of a very different sort. Parsons rests firmly in the tradition of the fraternity of Western Magi who include Moses, Solomon, Jesus Christ, John Dee, Adam Weishaupt, Crowley, Gurdjieff and Timothy Leary—great revolutionaries and liberators all.

It's not such a black and white world anymore.

Parsons wrote in his *Manifesto of the Anti-Christ:* "An end to the pretence (sic), and lying hypocrisy of Christianity. An end to the servile virtues, and superstitious restrictions. An end to the slave morality. An end to prudery and shame, to guilt and sin, for these are of the only evil under the sun, that is fear. An end to all authority that is not based on courage and manhood, to the authority of lying priests, conniving judges, blackmailing police, and an end to the servile flattery and cajolery of minds, the coronations of mediocrities, the ascension of dolts."

Amen to that! Parsons was clearly willing to put his money where his mouth was! Abbie Hoffman, Subcomandante Insurgente Marcos and Che Guevara seem total *pussies* in comparison.

Forget your Conspiracy Theory 101, the Illuminati are not the bad guys and George Bush was never a member and neither is Henry Kissinger. If, in the words of Christ, it is by their fruits and works that men shall be judged, would you want the Mai Lai massacre or the Gulf War slaughter staining *your* karma?

Hey, being the Antichrist is a dirty job, but somebody's got to do it.

It's not such a black and white world anymore.

A MAGICAL CALL TO ARMS

"Parsons opened a door and something flew in."
–Kenneth Grant, *Outside the Circles of Time.*

Did the Babalon Working actually work? For the sake of argument, if you believe it to be true, its true enough. As a metaphor or a myth to explain the psychic and atmospheric turbulence taking place in the world today, it certainly works for me. What has long been prophesied by the world's major spiritual traditions is now coming to pass. Turn on CNN for a couple of hours for *ample* proof: terrorism, wars, killer viruses, floods, famines, violent crime, earthquakes, suicide bombers; the list goes on and on. Certainly Parsons' untimely death in a 1952 chemical explosion would leave the crown of the "conquering child" unclaimed to this day as Thelemites continue to await their Chaos Messiah, but perhaps Parsons was an Antichrist and his particular mission was to pry open the Apocalyptic gateway and activate the occult forces necessary for the upheaval of consciousness.

The apostles of the new forms of gnosis unearthed by the Babalon Working will be art, the inspired initiator of sacred science and the torch of Gods appearing in new and unexpected forms in the unfolding of the divine drama. The poets, artists, philosophers and thinkers will form the first ranks of perfected humanity and no rules will apply save for nobility and freedom beyond the Kali Yuga.

But this will not happen without a struggle between the forces of control, black magick, and oppressive boredom on one hand and the Luciferian agents of wisdom, unleashed creativity and anarchic rebellion on the other. What we have been brainwashed to believe is good: patriotism, so-called free enterprise, private property, Christianity (not the teachings of Christ, but the hateful travesty that the religion bearing his name has become thanks to the likes of Pat Robertson and his filthy ilk), is now beginning to be seen by the emerging generation of the crowned and conquering child to be the death trip bullshit it truly is.

A whole culture is collapsing and a new one is about to be born. Jack Parsons would be pleased. ⛢

SCARLET WOMEN

BRIAN BUTLER

CAMERON
The Wormwood Star

Marjorie Cameron from Kenneth Anger's *Inauguration of the Pleasure Dome*

We are Stars and herald alien laws outside the Solar Wheel invading natural systems of the earth.[1]

The late 1940s was an interesting time to be in Southern California. World War II had just ended and for the first time atomic weapons had been detonated in warfare. Science and technology were advancing at an alarming pace. Science fiction had become popular, and space travel seemed a possibility. There were UFO sightings; tales of Black Magick and strange new religious cults were formed. For some reason, Los Angeles became the hub for such activity. There, through a chance encounter with an old navy acquaintance, 23-year-old Marjorie Cameron was led to the home of the famous Jet Propulsion Laboratory rocket scientist and master occultist Jack Parsons in Pasadena. This house, also known as the Parsonage, had become a meeting place and boarding house for cutting edge scientists, occultists, cult leaders and science fiction authors. At the time Cameron arrived, Parsons and then science fiction author L. Ron Hubbard were well into one of the most important occult operations of the 20th century—"The Babalon Working." Through their invocations, they had set the stage for the arrival of Cameron to assist them as an elemental spirit incarnated in the form of a redhead with green eyes. This meeting was to forever alter the destiny of Marjorie Cameron and set her on a lifelong quest to manifest the Babalon[2] current upon Earth. While much has been documented from her years with Jack Parsons, until now very little has been known publicly about Cameron's life before or after this five-year period.

Mockery is the punishment of the Gods. What fiendish laughter...[3]

Marjorie Elizabeth Cameron—later known as Cameron—was born on April 23, 1922 in Belle Plain, Iowa, the eldest of four children. Her father, Hill Leslie Cameron, was a Scot from Illinois who worked with the railroad. Her mother, Carrie V. Ridenour, of German and Dutch decent, was a native of Iowa. The night of Cameron's birth was surrounded by chaos; there was a terrible thunderstorm and her father got drunk and attempted suicide because he thought his wife was dying. Her grandmother, a staunch churchwoman, believed Cameron to be a child of the devil because of her fiery red hair.

Though unsuccessful, she found that these near brushes with death had further enhanced her psychic abilities, giving her a glimpse into the realm of the dead.

As a child, Cameron began to have strange and powerful visions that were so vivid, she could not be sure if they were real or imaginary. One night from her bedroom, she saw a ghostly procession of four white horses float by her window. Later she could recall these dreams in detail and was able to capture this in her artwork and poetry. In a letter to magician and Aleister Crowley associate Jane Wolfe, she mentions finding "a hole to hell" in her grandfather's backyard:

> "I remember always a tree on my grandfather's property from which hung an old, old swing where my mother had played as a little girl. Near this spot I recall a well which I always believed was the hole to hell—also the blue Bachelor Button flower grew near this spot. Herein I find again a new concept of the 4 elements and the name of god—the tree, the well, the swing (water's life) and the flower—which is seed."[4]

Never quite accepted in her small hometown, Cameron spent most of her childhood alone. In kindergarten, she was placed in a special school for children with above-average abilities and it became apparent that she was very different from other children. In a town dominated by the railroad, Cameron would often venture to the proverbial "wrong side of the tracks." She was always attracted to the darker side of things and found a kinship with other individualists and loners.

As a teenager, Cameron made a hideout in the attic of her parents' home and there she began to develop her psychic abilities. She soon established contact with spirits that would tell her detailed accounts of what had occurred at the house in the past. Like a true witch, she collected black cats and would go for late night prowls alone dressed only in a nightgown.

When she was seventeen, the Great Depression was underway and Cameron moved with her family to Davenport, Iowa, a considerably larger town than Belle Plain. Again she had trouble adjusting. After the suicide of a close friend, Cameron attempted to take her own life several times, each time through an overdose of sleeping pills. Though unsuccessful, she found that these near brushes with death had further enhanced her psychic abilities, giving her a glimpse into the realm of the dead.

Mine eyes are terrible and strange but thou knowest me[5]

In 1943, in the midst of World War II, the 21 year-old Cameron joined the Navy—turning down several college scholarships. She was sent along with 3,000 other women to boot camp in Cedar Falls, Iowa. Soon she was selected for a high-level job in Washington, DC, where she applied her artistic skills by drawing maps for the war efforts. She was then sent to the Joint Chiefs of Staff were she once met Churchill. She had a drafting table at the head of their conference room. Later, according to the principles of talismanic magic[6] she felt that many men died in the South Pacific as a result of her drawings. She always felt a karmic connection to these men and believed that the later tragic events in her life were the result of her participation in their deaths.

Later, she worked at the photo science lab on the Potomac, also called "The Hollywood Navy." There she met many Hollywood celebrities such as Gene Kelly. After learning that her brother, a tail gunner in the Air Force, had been shot

> **Later, according to the principles of talismanic magic she felt that many men died in the South Pacific as a result of her drawings. She always felt a karmic connection to these men and believed that the later tragic events in her life were the result of her participation in their deaths.**

down and injured, Cameron walked out on her job and returned to Belle Plain to see him. Eventually, Cameron was declared AWOL and was court martialed. She spent the final six months of the war confined to the base.

THE BIRTH OF BABALON

After her release from the Navy, Cameron moved in with her family, which had moved to Pasadena, California. In January of 1946, while waiting at the unemployment office, she saw an old acquaintance from the photo science lab in the Navy. This man, whose identity remains unknown, was living at the Parsonage and told her of a "mad scientist" that she had to meet. Inviting her to breakfast, he took her to a house at 1003 South Orange Grove Avenue in Pasadena, and there she met Jack Parsons for the first time. As she walked in, Parsons was standing in the hallway speaking on the phone dressed only in a black silk robe. They met only briefly but immediately felt a deep connection. Also living there was Jack's magical scribe, L. Ron Hubbard. After this encounter, Hubbard and Parsons commanded the man to "go find her or we'll kill you!" On January 19, 1946, at the climax of a magical operation that was begun by Jack and L. Ron Hubbard two weeks previously "to obtain the assistance of an elemental mate," Cameron returned and in that moment her destiny was changed.

Although Cameron was initially uninterested in Aleister Crowley or magick, Jack proceeded to instruct Cameron in the occult arts and told her of her destiny in the world.

Cameron immediately became romantically involved with Jack and moved into the house with him.[7] Unknowingly, she had become Parsons' sex magick partner in a ritual designed to incarnate the force of Babalon. Although Cameron was initially uninterested in Aleister Crowley or magick, Jack proceeded to instruct Cameron in the occult arts and told her of her destiny in the world. According to Jack, she was to become the vehicle for the Goddess or force called Babalon to manifest on earth. Years later, Cameron came to believe that she was in fact Babalon incarnate.

In March of 1946, Cameron witnessed a flying saucer over the Orange Grove house. She claimed that it was the "war engine"[8] that was predicted in Aleister Crowley's *Book of the Law* and the "sign" that Jack was waiting for.

> "The flying saucers—the miracle!—our war machine! I saw the first one in the spring of 1946 at 1003.—Oh—my god. This is the sign (drawing of an inverted triangle within a circle) Flying Saucers—imagine!"[9]

Had she reported it publicly, this would have been known as one of the first UFO sightings in America and would have preceded, by one year, Kenneth Arnold's infamous sighting on June 24, 1947—the sighting which propelled the "modern UFO era."

As the magical current became more intense at the Parsonage, things began to disintegrate. Hubbard had absconded with Jack's former girlfriend and most of his fortune. In August, Jack resigned from Crowley's occult order[10] in favor of his own system—"The Witchcraft."[11] As a result, the occult lodge at the Parsonage was disbanded and guests became fewer and less frequent. Cameron soon found herself spending a lot of time alone painting in the downstairs drawing room. She convinced Jack to get her a German Shepard to keep her company. As yet unfamiliar with the nature of the magical operations going on, Cameron felt that the house was haunted, and Jack would often return to find her and the dogs freezing outside of the house, terrified to return. It is interesting to note that later, in a letter to Cameron, Jack stated that the performance of Aleister Crowley's "Bornless One" ritual was known to cause "permanent haunting" wherever it was recited:

> "I will send you the ritual of the Bornless One…It is a very ancient, potent & dangerous ritual, often used by bold magicians in the Guardian Angel Working. It is useful as a preliminary in almost any sort of work, causing a tremendous concentration of force. It is, however, liable to produce dangerous side phenomena and sometimes permanent haunting in an area where it is repeated, & is for this reason often avoided."[12]

Finally, after numerous adverse psychic phenomena at the Parsonage, Cameron and Jack consulted the Ouji board and got the message "To Marjorie—Clean Ron's room and get out!" They immediately did so and moved to Manhattan Beach, California.

THE RED WITCH

In late 1947, Jack sent Cameron to England to meet Aleister Crowley. Although Crowley was skeptical about Jack's recent experiences with Hubbard and Cameron, Jack believed that if Crowley met Cameron in person his opinion would change. Using her Navy connections, Cameron first sailed to Paris and decided to stay there for a while. She became a regular at a local pub in Paris, and there she was known as the "Red Witch" because of her unusual appearance. On the day she walked into the pub to announce that she was off to London for the weekend to meet Aleister Crowley, the locals informed her that he had just died.[13]

Cameron was heartbroken that she missed the opportunity to meet the Master Therion, and following the advice of a friend in Paris, joined a convent in Lugano, Switzerland. After three weeks at the convent, she had a life changing experience—she bathed, let her hair down on her face, got on her haunches and howled into the mirror like a wild animal. It was in this moment that she realized she was in fact the Scarlet Woman and had no place in a convent. She contacted Jack, who sent her funds to return to America. Cameron remained with Jack for the next year. Jack by this time was experiencing the darker effects of the Babalon Working. From Parsons' *The Book of Antichrist*:

"Now it came to pass even as BABALON told me, for after receiving Her Book I fell away from Magick, and put away Her Book and all pertaining thereto. And I was stripped of my fortune (the sum of about $50,000) and my house, and all I Possessed.

Then for a period of two years I worked in the world, recouping my fortune somewhat. But that was also taken from me, and my reputation, and my good name in my worldly work, that was in science."

In 1948, Cameron separated from Jack and went to study art in Mexico on the GI Bill. She did not see Jack for almost two years, and they corresponded solely by mail. However, it was during this period that she received the most serious instruction in practical magick from him. These letters still exist and are available on the Internet.

While in Mexico, Cameron quickly fell in with the famous artist colony in San Miguel—a group that included the painter David Siqueiros and the surrealist artist Leonora Carrington. Cameron felt a deep connection to Mexico and later said that San Miguel replaced in her heart her childhood home. She had met a kindred spirit in Carrington. She also met Renate Druks and Paul Matheson who would later co-star with her in Kenneth Anger's *Inauguration of the Pleasure Dome.*" She had a brief romance with a bullfighter named Armando, but when he fell ill and died, Cameron was accused of witchcraft and run out of town.

We dance a geometry of wizardry and wind the threads about our prey...[14]

Cameron returned to America around 1950 and lived with Jack once again as his wife in Manhattan Beach. Jack was then working for Hughes Aircraft and negotiating a deal with Israel to create an explosives plant as well as providing research for "rockets and other armaments." In September 1950, plainclothes men raided the Parsons' home and confiscated Jack's papers. Jack was accused of removing con-

fidential documents from Hughes and was fired. An FBI investigation began, one that would last for over a year. An informant assessed the Parsons as follows:

"...the PARSONS are an odd and unusual pair in that they do not live by the commonly accepted code of married life and are both very fascinated by anything unusual or morbid such as voodooism, cults, homosexuality, and religious practices that are "different." Subject seems very much in love with his wife but she is not at all affectionate and does not appear to return his affection, [deleted] She is the dominating personality of the two and controls the activities and thinking of subject to very considerable degree. It is the opinion [name withheld] if subject were to have been in any way willfully involved in any activities of an espionage nature, it would probably have been on the instigation of his wife."[15]

Jack resigned from Crowley's occult order in favor of his own system—"The Witchcraft."

Although Parsons was eventually cleared of any wrongdoing, on January 17, 1952, he lost his security clearance. This seriously reduced his chances for employment, so Cameron and Jack began to make plans to leave the country. They were first headed for Mexico and from there to either Spain or Israel. Jack ultimately wanted to form a magical school in Israel. Jack and Cameron moved to a carriage house on Orange Grove—a few houses down from the Parsonage.[16]

On June 17, 1952, the evening before they planned to leave for Mexico, Jack was killed in an explosion when he dropped a vial of mercury fulmate in his private laboratory. Cameron was down the street fueling the car when she heard the blast. Jack's death was ruled an accident by authorities but Cameron always believed that Howard Hughes was somehow behind it.

We traveled Stellar webs to darker Worlds within the Lunar mirrors of Suicide.[17]

After Jack's death, Cameron moved into friend Renate Druks's Malibu home for six months. Druks could not withstand the heavy vibe that was Cameron and relates strange tales of Black Magic and astral attacks. Shortly after ejecting Cameron from her household, Druks claims to have been woken by a strange astral figure floating over her bed.

Druks claims to have been woken by a strange astral figure floating over her bed. Described as a sort of alien creature that appeared as bright neon-colored brain with a tail that resembled a spinal column, it increased in size as it came at her and then suddenly disappeared.

Described as a sort of alien creature that appeared as a bright neon-colored brain with a tail that resembled a spinal column, it increased in size as it came at her and then suddenly disappeared. Overcome with terror, she consulted with their mutual friend, Jane Wolfe. Wolfe stated "That was Cameron——how naughty of her!" and instructed Druks in the banishing ritual of the pentagram to protect herself.

Exiled from Druks's home and still deeply affected by Jack's death, Cameron withdrew into complete isolation in the desert of Beaumont, California. There she lived in a house in an abandoned canyon that had no water or power.

During this period Cameron found a new magical teacher in Jane Wolfe and their correspondence remains as a sort of magical diary. Cameron began to see her life increasingly from a magical point of view, analyzing her experiences in terms of a life-long magical ritual or initiation. This was also her darkest period, she writes to Jane:

> "I am approaching the darkest hour of the abysmal night furthest from the sun. This is the fateful hour in which I drink the cup of poison to its dregs—eat the tainted apple—feel the sting of the terrible dart in the core of me. Know the fang of the deadly serpent in my heart. And thereafter I shall plunge down into the abysmal horror of madness and death—or I shall walk upon the dawn—golden with the golden kiss upon me. This hour is far beyond the return. The turning back point was Sunset of year. My farewells were made long ago. No—this is the hour when I approach the terrible rendezvous when all my gods shall declare themselves—when I shall call upon the secret name—open the final door." [18]

Cameron realized that she must face this ordeal alone:

> "If you have tried to contact me you have no doubt found the going hazardous—I seem to be pyramiding a mountain of fear that is closing all doors to me —now Renee's. [19]

> It amounts to this—in the case of each they reach a barrier of fear over which they cannot

pass to follow me. And since I can show no pity—since to do so is to pity myself—I am rapidly eliminating my companions on the journey to completion. I had not expected this—as you know—the only comfort left me—is the knowledge that I have the courage to do that which no one else seems to have. This is indeed the luxury of Kings—but I had tried to bring joy and not fear into the hearts of others. What happens from now on—I do not know. I can only remind myself constantly in this period of aloneness and dryness that which I have known from the beginning." [20]

It is in these letters to Jane that Cameron fully divulges her feelings and candidly describes her own rituals. Most interesting is a magical working which she began shortly after Jack's death in 1952. This ritual included some of the same people who later appeared in Kenneth Anger's film of an occult ritual, *Inauguration of the Pleasure Dome*. According to Cameron, this working was to bear fruit in the summer of 1953. By this operation, some say that Cameron intended to create a "magical child" or "wormwood star" sired by Jack from beyond the grave.

> "This is the star which was calculated for me to give it birth. Jane—Jane—This is the star by which I shall behold him and in that union shall he be born—he whose name shall be wonder. His magnificence cannot be foretold and this is my star the Wormwood Star which will be born this summer Solstice of the year 1953." [21]

Cameron goes on to explain the technical details of the operation based on the seven pointed star of BABALON:

> "The points of the star are seven but it produces eight. It consists of the quadrupled union of four pairs of opposites. The eighth of this is not apparent until the four unions are completed. Now when each union is made the word of god must be uttered. Do you know this word? I asked for this word of Jack in March of 1949. It was given to me with no account of the cost. I carried it with me in great secrecy, not ever daring to

dream of the miracle it concealed. This word I will only give to you in great secrecy.[22] With the right combination—which is my star [Star of Babalon drawn here] this great word creates— and since there is death in all birth there are four opposites destroyed—but their destruction is absorption and here again another face of the four square miracle!"[23]

She further elaborates on the formula of the operation:

"This opposite must always be the sublime whole of the opposite of the invoked. Such as in this invocation the opposites all destroyed will be pure aspects. Here is the meaning of debauchery as sacrament—the sublime follows between the six and eight of the Tarot.[24] This is the sacrament. The exquisite edge of growth and decay and this is absorbed like the fruit, the wine of the season on the dying cycle of the year. This destruction or absorption will be done each time to the union of the 8 opposites occur."[25]

She then describes the function of the unknowing participants or "elementals" in this strange working:

"Each male in this invocation is an Elemental god and these five gods will be the five fathers of the god. Each is a perfect revelation of the four represented in the Universe card of the Tarot—the Dance of the Star and the Snake. The holy 22. The kether, the Crown, the god. These four are represented as the Bull, the Lion, the Hawk and man sublime angelic—man revealed as god. I plan to write these into four commentaries—or

Cameron states that she is pregnant but not with a human child.

songs—for each of the Elemental gods in a miraculous revelation. When the star is completed and the god born, these elemental gods will be known to their voices and the whole damned union will be complete and magnificent."[26]

Cameron states that she is pregnant but not with a human child:

"The pregnancy, as you understand—was not the actual growth of a human child—but the spiritual child of a psychic union—and in the case of Cupid and Psyche—this child—was a female—

called Pleasure—or the birth of Babylon—which is a symbolical—but most real birth of the age of the Goddess of Pleasure—being the union of the mind and body."[27]

After her extraordinary experiences in the desert, Cameron moved back in with her parents in Pasadena and was considered catatonic for a time. Still in isolation and confusion, she painted a series of works that she called "the parchments." These pieces received a lot of attention, including an offer from a psychiatrist to publish them with a commentary (which she refused). She believed that through these works of art, she literally "painted herself out" of her situation. Renewed, she emerged as a "real force" in the artistic and occult communities.

Death has been thy lover. Is there else to fear?[28]

In December of 1953, Cameron walked into another situation that was to alter both her destiny and that of those around her. This time it was the home of the eccentric warlock, Samson Debreir, on Barton Avenue in Hollywood, California. Underground filmmaker Kenneth Anger had begun casting for his occult film, *Inauguration of the Pleasure Dome* and the stage was once again set for the Scarlet Woman. The famous erotic writer Anais Nin was to the star until Cameron appeared, upstaging her by the mere power of her presence. The rivalry between the two became a driving force behind the film.

When Anger met Cameron, she introduced herself as "the Scarlet Woman." And Anger replied "That's obvious… I have been waiting to meet you for a thousand years." By this time, she had developed a very powerful countenance, and it was this that struck Anger. He vividly recalls, "[She had] Flaming Scot red hair…real emerald green eyes that could also turn into sea mist grey according to her mood…and suddenly Anais Nin shrunk…in front of the majesty that is Cameron because Cameron wiped her out." Cameron had a profound effect on Kenneth Anger and was a sort of mentor to him. Soon, they were living together. Anger relates many strange stories of UFOs, levitation and astral visions, and he still considers Cameron one of the most important women of his life.

The film, in which Cameron plays herself "The Scarlet Woman," was well received among both magical initiates and the art world. Cameron believed that this film was proof to the world that she had manifested the force of Babalon on earth.

Up the swirling scarf of smoke rise our invocations. [29]

By the late 1950s, Cameron was living in Malibu and hanging out with a crowd of Beat artists that included the likes of Dennis Hopper, Wallace Berman, Bruce Conner and assemblage artist George Herms. In 1957, Wallace Berman's show at the Ferus Gallery was closed by the vice squad for pornography after he displayed one of Cameron's drawings. This drawing depicted a woman, possibly Cameron, being taken from behind by an alien creature.

That same year, experimental filmmaker and her *Inauguration of the Pleasure Dome* co-star Curtis Harrington directed a film that featured Cameron and her artwork called *The Wormwood Star*. The film opens with titles drawn by Paul Matheson over an extreme close-up of the Seal of Solomon. "Concerning the knowledge and conversation of the Holy Guardian Angel as revealed to: Cameron." Introduced through a series of composed still frames, rather surreal in juxtaposition and symbolic props, Cameron is then shown seated, looking into a mirror as if in a trance. After a few minutes of this rather abstract portraiture, the film then shifts to a study of Cameron's paintings that illustrate a desert procession of angels. In the background Cameron recites a solemn invocation to her Holy Guardian Angel:

> *Dark Star, I seek you in all the endless rooms of the universe*
> *I have entered the maze of chaos and searched the promise of no end and no fulfillment*
> *But I have seen your helmeted head flashing gold from the bloody triumphs and sunsets of the world*
> *I have heard your voice singing lovely songs of desire in the world womb*
> *I remember the artistry of fingers that held the rose in wonder*
>
> *Your musical flute sounding the hymn of love seeking since the birth in the crashing star nebulae*
> *Singing limbs of muscle and star-foam pursued and pursuing*
> *Radiant Warrior, how long?*
> *Beloved God, how long?*
> *How long, how long?"* [30]

Cameron later burned all of the paintings seen in *The Wormwood Star* while living with her second husband Sherif Kimmil, who was said to be the inspiration for the R. P.

McMurphy character in Ken Kesey's *One Flew Over the Cuckoo's Nest*, and was by all accounts insane. Kimmel and Cameron had been up for several days on speed and formed what Cameron called a "suicide club." Kimmel went to the bathroom and slit his wrists. [31] In turn, Cameron symbolically committed suicide by throwing her paintings in the fire. According to Kenneth Anger, Cameron's paintings were in reality magical talismans and had to be destroyed lest they turn and destroy the creator. He states, "She was doing art for the sake of magick and her soul. She never sold her paintings."

In this hour I decide between nothingness and creation… [32]

By 1960, Cameron had transcended her darker period and emerged as an individual. She began to have a greater understanding of her life's pattern. From her diary entry of October 22, 1960, she writes:

> *"I sense the approaching end to my years of exile. Some inner knowing prepares me for the return to the world in my just position. In the years of exile I compounded a state of mind that philosophically remains balanced regarding the continuity of my present state of existence or to finally win for myself a gracious and rewarding end to life. Ultimatums are impossible for one who has witnessed the broad sweep of existence. Yet I am tempted to sum up the experience for I fear already I have lost the vast majority of my impressions. I have lived frugally but I have squandered dreams and visions as only the spend thrift does—sowing wide golden plains."*

In 1961, Cameron appeared in the film *Nite Tide*. Directed by Curtis Harrington, this film also featured Dennis Hopper's first starring role. Cameron played a mysterious figure that is seen prowling the beach in Santa Monica. In the film she has a strange, compelling presence. On October 3, 1964, the Cinema Theatre in Los Angeles presented "The Transcendental Art of Cameron," which featured slide projections of her paintings while she read from her journals.

She is applying makeup to her face in a sort of Kabuki style while her daughter Krystal and two other children are seen playing in the background. Cameron ignores them while staring into the mirror, smoking a joint.

By the late 1960s Cameron moved to Santa Fe, New Mexico. A short experimental film from this period (1969) by John Chamberlain entitled "Thumbsuck" still exists. It shows Cameron as a striking figure with long red hair and piercing eyes. She is applying makeup to her face in a sort of Kabuki style while her daughter Krystal and two other children are seen playing in the background. Cameron ignores them while staring into the mirror, smoking a joint.

And the Hag with lizard eyes embraces shadows...[33]

As Cameron grew older, she took on the image of an old witch or crone with long, straight white hair. She lived in a small house on North Genesee in West Hollywood and could often be seen practicing Tai Chi in Bronson Park. Her last art show "The Pearl of Reprisal" was held at the Barnsdall Art Park on April 8, 1989. Here she exhibited a haunted series of pen and ink drawings titled "Pluto Transiting the Twelfth House." *Inauguration of the Pleasure Dome* and *The Wormwood Star* were shown. Cameron also gave a reading of her poems by candlelight. The same year Cameron edited *Freedom is a Two Edged Sword*—a compilation of the writings of Jack Parsons published by New Falcon.

Cameron died of cancer on July 23, 1995. A magical rite was performed at her bedside at the VA hospital. A wake was held at the Beyond Baroque bookstore in Los Angeles where her poetry was read by friends and her paintings were exhibited, including the "Black Angel" painting of Jack Parsons as an angel with a sword. ⌂

Endnotes

1. Cameron magical diary September 1962.
2. Babalon is the companion of the Beast 666 in Aleister Crowley's Thelemic pantheon. Crowley first wrote extensively about this in *Vision and the Voice* which documents his experiences with the Enochian system of magic and his own initiation. After the magician crosses the "abyss" that separates the spiritual world from the rational or mental world, he is greeted by the goddess Babalon, the great mother who resides in Binah on the Qabalistic tree of life, which is the spiritual home of those who have achieved the grade of Magister Templi.
3. Cameron magical diary June 21, 1964.
4. Cameron letter to Jane Wolfe December 26, 1952.
5. Cameron from the film *The Wormwood Star* 1957.
6. Cameron considered all of her drawings to be magical talismans that had very real effects on the world.
7. On October 19, 1946 Cameron and Jack were married.
8. Liber Al Chap. III v7: I will give you a war-engine.
9. Letter from Cameron to Jane Wolfe January 22, 1953.
10. Despite numerous attempts this order has yet to be revived by a competent group of magicians in America. The present author has however formed a new order which incorporates the teachings of Cameron, C. F. Russell and Charles Stansfeld Jones. Interested aspirants may contact him directly (see information at back of book).
11. See Jack Parsons, *Freedom is a Two Edged Sword* (New Falcon)
12. Letter from Jack Parsons to Cameron Jan. 10, 1950.
13. Aleister Crowley died on December 1, 1947.
14. Cameron magical diary January 21, 1962.
15. FBI file on Jack Parsons.
16. Although the Parsonage was destroyed, Cameron believed the house to be eternal on the astral plane like Crowley's Boleskine in Scotland.
17. From the book "The Black Pilgrimage" by Cameron 1964. Privately published.
18. Letter to Jane Wolfe, dated December 6, 1952, 6:00am.
19. Renate Druks.
20. Cameron letter to Jane Wolfe April 7, 1953.
21. Cameron letter to Jane Wolfe December 26, 1952.
22. This word not here revealed. The present writer has however obtained it.
23. Cameron letter to Jane Wolfe December 26, 1952.
24. Atu VII of the TARO is the Chariot. The formula contained in this card is one key to understanding this working.
25. Cameron letter to Jane Wolfe August 23, 1953.
26. *Ibid.*
27. *Ibid.*
28. Cameron magical diary March 11, 1962
29. Cameron magical diary September 1962.
30. Cameron from the film *The Wormwood Star* 1957.
31. While writing *One Flew Over the Cuckoo's Nest*, Ken Kesey worked as a janitor in the psychiatric ward of the VA Hospital in Palo Alto, California (often under the influence of LSD). It is possible that it was there that he encountered Kimmel, who was committed to the VA Hospital for several months as a result of this suicide attempt.
32. Cameron letter to Jane Wolfe January 22, 1953.
33. Cameron magical diary June 21, 1964.

IDA CRADDOCK
Sexual Mystic and Martyr for Freedom

Ida Craddock (1857-1902)

In Volume III Number 1 of his *Equinox* occult journal published in 1919, Aleister Crowley reviewed a paper called "Heavenly Bridegrooms." In this work, a woman identified only as "Ida C——" claimed to be the wife of an angel. A scholar named Theodore Schroeder edited the manuscript and published it in a psychological journal, where it apparently attracted the attention of Crowley. In the review,

Crowley states that "Heavenly Bridegrooms" "is one of the most remarkable human documents ever produced." He goes on to say:

> "I am very far from agreeing with all that this most talented woman sets forth in her paper, but she certainly obtained initiated knowledge of extraordinary depth. She seems to have had access to certain most concealed sanctuaries.... She has put down statements in plain English which are positively staggering. This book is of incalculable value to every student of occult matters. No Magick library is complete without it."

This is quite an endorsement from Crowley, and perhaps even more significant in that he signed the review "Baphomet," using his magical name as Tenth Degree of O.T.O.

Roughly 50 years later, Crowley scholar Marcelo Motta published "Heavenly Bridegrooms" along with another work by this "Ida C——" called "Psychic Wedlock." This latter paper outlines a three-degree system of mystical initiation through sexual techniques. It was written around 1895, shortly before the founding of the O.T.O. based on a similar model involving three degrees of initiation into sexual mysteries. Motta also included a brief biography of the author, in which we learn that her full name is Ida Craddock. But except for these references, not much more about Ms. Craddock and her work has appeared in print.

Was she just insane and delusional about having sex with angels, as Schroeder contends, or did she have some

Crowley states that Heavenly Bridegrooms "is one of the most remarkable human documents ever produced."

kind of connection with the same sources of initiated wisdom which had influenced Crowley? Our researches took us to Special Collections at the University of Southern Illinois, which had become the repository for the collected papers of Theodore Schroeder after his death. There we discovered a treasure trove of diaries, manuscripts, pamphlets, letters, and other material which gave us a wealth of insight into this fascinating and remarkable woman.

Ida Craddock was born in Philadelphia on August 1, 1857. Her father died when she was two years old. Her mother had been very interested in spiritualism and the occult, but following the death of Ida's father she became a fundamentalist Christian and raised Ida with an extremely puritanical discipline. Ida received intense religious training, and learned to read the Bible from a very early age. The result, of course, was that this repressed young woman grew up to be intensely interested in the very subjects which were most forbidden to her in childhood: namely, sexuality, occultism, and freedom in general.

But even before she began actively pursuing these forbidden subjects, Ida was ahead of her time. She was very intelligent and ambitious, not exactly qualities that were admired in women of the late 19th century. She campaigned to allow women to be admitted to the University of Pennsylvania, and would have been its first female graduate if the decision hadn't been eventually reversed. She went on to teach stenography to women at Giraud College in Philadelphia, and wrote a standard textbook on the subject which was published when she was just 18. By teaching this marketable skill to other young women, she was giving them a chance to become employed for themselves, thereby affording them greater opportunities for independence and self-sufficiency. This, in itself, was a radical idea for America in the 1880s.

Ida became involved in occultism beginning around 1887, about the time she turned 30 years old. At this time the Theosophical Society (founded in 1875) was the pre-eminent promoter of occult teachings, and Ida started attending classes in Theosophy at a local Unitarian church. She

also began reading and studying a tremendous amount of material on occult subjects, judging from the sheer breadth and depth of the knowledge exhibited in her own writings. She cites everything from biblical and ecclesiastical sources to Hindu and Greek philosophers to contemporary academics and occultists. The recently translated Raja Yoga by Vivekananda was also drawn upon in many of Ida's works, and at one point she listed herself as "Priestess and Pastor of the Church of Yoga," a theosophical offshoot.

According to Schroeder, between 1889 and 1891 Ida had ongoing "illicit" sexual relations with two different men (that is, she had sex with men to whom she was not married). The first man was younger than she, and apparently not a very satisfying lover. The second man, never named by Schroeder but described as an ex-clergyman and "heretical mystic" (probably introduced to Ida through Theosophical circles), was somewhat older than Ida, and was reportedly well-versed in the technique of Karezza, or the ability to withhold ejaculation. His lovemaking prowess brought Ida to hitherto-undiscovered heights of sexual ecstasy, in contrast to her other lover who made love in the "normal," conventional way.

To overly repressed Ida, this discovery was nothing less than a divine revelation. She began studying esoteric sexuality, combining her extensive knowledge of folklore and mythology with various sources from the occult world including P. B. Randolph and Alice Bunker Stockham. During this period there was a growing trend of increased sexual awareness and open discourse of sexuality in society. Burton had brought back translations of the Kama Sutra and Ananga Ranga from India, and Havelock Ellis had begun applying scientific principles to the study of sexuality. This was the first sexual revolution, long before the 1960s, as the western world emerged from its Victorian prudery to start openly and objectively examining sex for the first time.

Ida received intense religious training, and learned to read the Bible from a very early age. The result, of course, was that this repressed young woman grew up to be intensely interested in the very subjects which were most forbidden to her in childhood: namely, sexuality, occultism, and freedom in general.

In her massive study of religious sexuality entitled "Lunar & Sex Worship," Ida argued that "the moon was a more ancient deity than the sun, and that she was therefore recognized as the superior of the sun-god, who, as being the exponent of a later religion, could triumph only after receiving her sanction." This theory resembles remarkably Crowley's description of the Aeons of Isis and Osiris. Her development of the argument cites a tremendous range of sources, including Assyrian, Babylonian, Hindu, Irish, Greek, Norse, Jewish, Christian, Islamic, Chinese, Egyptian, African, but to name a few. It goes on and on, for over 100 typewritten legal-size pages.

In another work entitled "Sex Worship (Continued)" Ida contends that the symbol of the cross, not only that featured so prominently in Christianity but those found everywhere throughout the cultures and religions of the world, is fundamentally a symbol of sexual union, and its ubiquitous worship reflects a universal worship of the sex instinct as the underlying quintessence of all religion.

Ida's second lover was coincidentally the head of the National Liberal League, an organization prominently associated with the Free Thought movement around the turn of the century. Ida got a job as the League's secretary, and subsequently took up the cause, promoting social reform through freedom from oppressive moral codes and strictures. In particular, she sought to address the plight of America's married women, whom, as her own experience had taught her, were most likely not achieving their full potential of wedded bliss; or, worse yet, were suffering at the hands of their husbands who cared not in the least about the feelings or needs of their wives when it came to sex. Ida cited the following story as told to her by a nurse attending a young wife who had just had her first baby:

"The patient had been greatly lacerated in delivery. On the second day after delivery, while the nurse was attending to the baby, the husband entered, and requested the nurse to leave the room. "For God's sake, nurse, don't leave me!" exclaimed the sick woman. But a look from the husband caused the nurse to obey him, nevertheless. Shortly after, she heard her patient scream, "Oh, he'll murder me!" Whereupon the nurse rushed in and found the husband in the act of committing a rape upon his wife. The nurse seized his arm, and endeavored to pull him away; but he did not yield until he was ready, when he allowed himself, sullenly, to be led from the room, covered with blood. The wife mean-

while had fainted. When she recovered, she cried, "Oh God, would that my baby girl and I would die! That man promised on our wedding-day to honor, love and protect me; but every night since then he has used my poor body!"

Ida was convinced that ignorance of basic sexual facts was to blame for much of the ills of society. She traveled to Chicago, Washington, Philadelphia, Denver, and New York, giving lectures with titles such as "Survivals of Sex Worship in Christianity and in Paganism" and "What Christianity has done for the Marital Relation." She also provided sexual counseling in a small office on Dearborn Street in Chicago. Those who were too modest to come to her personally could enroll in her courses sent through the mail.

She then wrote a series of pamphlets which were essentially marriage manuals, with titles like "The Wedding Night," "The Marriage Relation," and "Right Marital Living." In these manuals, she emphasized sexual self-control, and asserted that to force intercourse on one's wife without her desiring it amounts to rape—quite a radical notion for the time. Ida recommended that intercourse should last at least 1/2 to 1 hour in order to allow enough time for the female orgasm—undoubtedly this was pretty alarming to the majority of husbands to which her pamphlets were targeted! Quoting from "The Wedding Night," here is her advice to the newly wed couple on their honeymoon:

"The very first thing for you to bear in mind is that, inasmuch as Nature has so arranged sex that the man is always ready (as a rule) for intercourse, whereas the woman is not, it is most unwise for the man to precipitate matters by exhibiting desire for genital contact when the woman is not yet aroused. You should remember that that organ of which you are, justly, so proud, is not possessed by a woman, and that she is utterly ignorant of its functions, practically, until she has experienced sexual contact; and that it is, to her who is not desirous of such contact, something of a monstrosity.

Even when a woman has already had pleasurable experience of genital contact, she requires each time to be aroused amorously, before that organ, in its state of activity, can become attractive. For a man to exhibit, to even an experienced wife, his organ ready for action when she herself is not amorously aroused, is, as a rule, not sexually attractive to her; on the contrary, it is often sexually repulsive, and at times out and out disgusting to her. Every woman of experience knows that, when she is ready, she can cause the man to become sexually active fast enough.

If this be so with the wife who has had pleasurable experience in genital contact, how much more must the sight or touch of that apparent monstrosity in a man shock and terrify the inexperienced young bride!

Yet, if you are patient and loverlike and gentlemanly and considerate and do not seek to unduly precipitate matters, you will find that Nature will herself arrange the affair for you most delicately and beautifully. If you will first thoroughly satisfy the primal passion of the woman, which is affectional and maternal (for the typical woman mothers the man she loves), and if you will kiss and caress her in a gentle, delicate and reverent way, especially at the throat and bosom, you will find that, little by little (perhaps not the first night nor the second night, but eventually, as she grows accustomed to the strangeness of the intimacy), you will, by reflex action from the bosom to the genitals, successfully arouse within her a vague desire for the entwining of the lower limbs, with ever closer and closer contact, until you melt into one another's embrace at the genitals in a perfectly natural and wholesome fashion; and you will then find her genitals so well lubricated with an emission from her glands of Bartholin, and, possibly, also from her vagina, that your gradual entrance can be effected not only without pain to her, but with a rapture so exquisite to her, that she will be more ready to invite your entrance upon a future occasion."

Obviously, this approach was squarely opposed to the prevailing culture of male-dominated attitudes concerning the marital "rights" of husbands and the marital "duties" of wives. Furthermore, Ida's direct and open discussion of sexual matters was offensive to the moralists who sought to control the proliferation of vice by suppressing any frank treatment of sexual subjects. Nevertheless, orders for her pamphlets poured in from grateful wives, progressive couples, and many doctors who reported marked improvements in their married patients' psychological well-being.

There was a further problem as well: how could Ida teach and write so knowledgeably about sexual subjects, when she herself was not married? After all, if she was to be regarded by society as a respectable woman whose opinion was worthy of consideration, never having been married must mean that she had never had sex. Ida dealt with this question directly in "Heavenly Bridegrooms," written in 1894. In this work she admits that she *is* sexually experienced, but insists that she is married—just not to any

In her massive study of religious sexuality entitled "Lunar & Sex Worship," Ida argued that "the moon was a more ancient deity than the sun, and that she was therefore recognized as the superior of the sun-god, who, as being the exponent of a later religion, could triumph only after receiving her sanction."

living person. Her husband is an angel named Soph who visits her at night to have sex, and to teach her enlightenment through a divinely inspired system of sexual initiation as detailed in her subsequent paper entitled "Psychic Wedlock." Most of the paper is devoted to justifying this arrangement as perfectly plausible and morally acceptable; after all, wasn't the Virgin Mary herself impregnated by a "heavenly bridegroom"?

"Psychic Wedlock" is of particular interest, as it describes a three-degree system of initiation by sexual means. The first degree, which Ida dubs "Alphaism," calls for the development of self control. In particular, "sex union is forbidden, except for the express purpose of creating a child." In the second degree, called "Dianism," "sex union is enjoined in absolute self-control and aspiration to the highest." This is accomplished in two phases: first, by learning to delay ejaculation and prolong the union indefinitely; and second, after mastering the first phase, acquiring the ability to go through the ecstasy of orgasm without ejaculation. She describes similar practices of self-control on the part of the female as well. Finally, the third degree inculcates "communion with Deity as the third partner in marital union." This degree also has two phases: the first is to fulfill the duty to aspire to communion with the "Great Thinker" during sexual ecstasy; and the second is to attain the state of joy which accrues to both the "Great Thinker" and to the partners through such communion.

Ida's conflicts with our puritanical society began in 1893, when she attended a performance at the World's Columbian Exposition in Chicago. The show was called "Danse du Ventre" ("Belly Dance") and was the introduction of this art into America. Naturally, it became wildly popular, and attracted the attention of a man named Anthony Comstock, founder of a self-ordained moral police squad called "The Society for the Suppression of Vice." Comstock demanded that the show be shut down. Curious to see what the fuss was about, Craddock attended the show and decided that the belly dancer's "indecent undulations" were actually an expression of sexual self-control, and as such ought to be taught and encouraged

In 1894 Ida's mother conspired to have Ida committed in an insane asylum.

to married women to enhance their sex lives. (Craddock would later report in her diary that she used various "Danse du Ventre" techniques in her lovemaking with her angelic husband Soph). Ida wrote an article defending the show along these lines, and published it in the journal "The World." Comstock immediately pounced on Craddock's article, declaring it obscene and banning its dissemination through the US Mail.

In 1894 Ida's mother conspired to have Ida committed in an insane asylum. She promised that if she was successful, she would have all of Ida's diaries and manuscripts burned. This prompted Ida, in 1895, to send her papers to an editor of a journal in England named W. T. Stead. (This is fortunate for us, because this is how Theodore Schroeder managed to recover them in 1914 when he became interested in Ida Craddock's case, and this is how they eventually ended up in Special Collections at the University of Southern Illinois). At one point in 1898 her foes did manage to have Ida admitted to the Pennsylvania Hospital for the Insane, but she was released after 3 months without ever being judged to be legally insane by the court.

Meanwhile, after failing to shut down the Danse du Ventre (it was way too popular) and embarrassed that he had been ultimately ineffective against Ida's efforts to defend it, Comstock began to pursue a vendetta against Craddock and set out to have her prosecuted for distributing obscenity. His first attempt came in 1899, when Ida was arrested and charged with sending copies of her "Right Marital Living" pamphlet through the mail. She managed to stay out of jail only because the famed criminal lawyer and free-speech advocate Clarence Darrow

posted her bond. (Darrow is best known for serving as defense counsel in the Scopes Monkey Trial, which outlawed the teaching of Darwinism in public schools).

Soon after this, Ida moved to Comstock's home turf of New York City, and continued to provide her services and mail her pamphlets to her clients. She seems to have wanted to deliberately challenge Comstock, as she wrote: "I have an inward feeling that I am really divinely led here to New York to face this wicked and depraved man Comstock in open court." On March 5, 1902, Ida was arrested under New York's anti-obscenity law for sending copies of "The Wedding Night" through the mail. The judge refused to allow the jury to even see the offending document, calling it "indescribably obscene." The jury took his word for it and found Craddock guilty, as it was reported, "without leaving their seats." She was sentenced to three months in the city workhouse, in which she endured inhumane conditions and harsh treatment. All the while, support was pouring in from free-speech advocates, publishers, doctors, and clients, but to no avail. Upon her release from prison, she was immediately re-arrested under the federal Comstock law. She refused an offer to escape a prison sentence by pleading insane. On the morning she was to be sentenced, she committed suicide by slashing her wrists and inhaling natural gas.

Ida left a letter to the public which read, in part: "I am taking my life because a judge, at the instigation of Anthony Comstock, has declared me guilty of a crime I did not commit—the circulation of obscene literature. Perhaps it may be that in my death, more than in my life, the American

"I have an inward feeling that I am really divinely led here to New York to face this wicked and depraved man Comstock in open court."

people may be shocked into investigating the dreadful state of affairs which permits that unctuous sexual hypocrite Anthony Comstock to wax fat and arrogant and to trample upon the liberties of the people, invading, in my own case, both my right to freedom of religion and to freedom of the press." In a long note to her mother, she wrote: "I maintain my right to die as I have lived, a free woman, not cowed into silence by any other human being."

On the morning she was to be sentenced, she committed suicide by slashing her wrists and inhaling natural gas.

In the end, the negative publicity generated by Comstock's hounding of Ida to her death marked the beginning of the end of the influence of the Society for the Suppression of Vice. The newspapers condemned Comstock, and contributions to the society fell off sharply. One by one the Society's founders died off, and Comstock's influence from then on became less and less significant.

Enter Theodore Schroeder, a free-speech lawyer from New York with an amateur interest in psychology. He became interested in Ida Craddock's case approximately 10 years after her death. He began researching her life, and managed to locate and collect a large amount of her letters, diaries, manuscripts, and other printed materials. Aleister Crowley was introduced via correspondence to Schroeder through a mutual friend. In 1914, one of the very first things Crowley did after reaching America was to dash off a letter to Schroeder which read: "Dear Sir: I am here. Would you like to see me? Yours very truly, Aleister Crowley." At one point Crowley even offered to make Schroeder a VIIth degree in the O.T.O. (at only 2/3rds the price!) as Schroeder was interested in obtaining some "secret documents" which Crowley could not release to him unless he had been bound to secrecy. The next issue of *The Equinox* carried the review of "Heavenly Bridegrooms." I think it is safe to assume that Crowley would have had access to "Psychic Wedlock" and the other unpublished manuscripts as well. ⛢

REFERENCES

Bates, Anna Louise. *Weeder in the Garden of the Lord: Anthony Comstock's Life and Career*. Lanham, MD: University Press of America, 1995.

Craddock, Ida. *Heavenly Bridegrooms*. Ts., spec.coll., University of Southern Illinois.

Craddock, Ida. *Lunar & Sex Worship*. Unpublished ts., spec.coll., University of Southern Illinois.

Craddock, Ida. *Psychic Wedlock*. Ts., spec.coll., University of Southern Illinois.

Craddock, Ida. *The Marriage Relation*. Ts., spec.coll., University of Southern Illinois.

Craddock, Ida. *Right Marital Living*. Pamphlet, spec.coll., University of Southern Illinois.

Craddock, Ida. *Sex Worship (continued)*. Unpublished ts., spec.coll., University of Southern Illinois.

Craddock, Ida. *The Wedding Night*. Pamphlet, spec.coll., University of Southern Illinois.

Culling, Louis T. *Sex Magick*. St. Paul, MN: Llewellyn Publications, 1988.

Crowley, Aleister. *The Equinox*, Volume III, Number 1. New York: Samuel Weiser, 1972.

Motta, Marcelo Ramos. *The Equinox*, Volume V, Number 4. Nashville, TN: Thelema Publishing Company, 1981.

Petersen, James R. *The Century of Sex: Playboy's History of the Sexual Revolution, 1900–1999*. New York: Grove Press, 1999.

Stockham, Alice B. *Karezza: Ethics of Marriage*. Mokelumne Hill, CA: Health Research, n.d.

Stoehr, Taylor. *Free Love in America: A Documentary History*. New York: AMS Press, 1979.

ROSALEEN NORTON
Pan's Daughter

Rosaleen Norton with her pet cat

Rosaleen Norton (1917–1979) has been described as Australia's best-known witch although by now her fame has extended well beyond her native shores. Avant-garde American film-maker Kenneth Anger, who has had an ongoing fascination with occult mythology and visited Aleister Crowley's Abbey in Cefalu, proposed to make a film about her, and she has also inspired contemporary novels and a play. Rosaleen Norton is certainly one of the most impressive painters of supernatural themes to have emerged in modern times.

Prior to her death in 1979, Rosaleen lived in a shadowy basement apartment in an ageing block of flats close to the El Alamein fountain in Sydney's Kings Cross district. In one of her rooms she had erected a sacred altar in honor of the horned god Pan, the ancient Greek patron of pastoral life and Lord of Nature. However she kept her deepest beliefs and ideas very much to herself, living like a recluse from the exuberant nightlife which surrounded her.

There was a time when Rosaleen Norton's murals and decorative motifs spanned the walls of several popular coffee bars in Kings Cross, but these are now long gone; the well known Apollyon yielded to the bypass which now takes the main flow of traffic out to Sydney's eastern suburbs. Her heyday was in fact in the 1940s and 1950s. She was known to the public as an eccentric, bohemian witch-lady who wore flamboyant, billowing blouses and vivid bandanas, puffed on an exotic engraved cigarette holder, and plucked her eyebrows so that they arched in a somewhat sinister curve. Slight in build with long curly black hair, she always had something of a magnetic presence that made her stand out in the crowd.

Rosaleen Norton became known in the public mind as the artist whose provocative paintings of half-human, half-animal forms were even more controversial than Norman

In one of her rooms she had erected a sacred altar in honor of the horned god Pan, the ancient Greek patron of pastoral life and Lord of Nature.

Fishers of Men

Lindsay's risqué nude figures. She depicted naked women wrestling with reptilian elementals or flying on the backs of winged griffins, and gods who were both male and female and whose arms were like wings with claws at the extremities. These days, at a time when fantasy art has brought a vivid array of supernatural and surreal styles to CD covers, posters and t-shirts, Rosaleen Norton's paintings appear more mainstream, but in the decade after World War II they seemed to be an affront to human decency and ran counter to orthodox religious sensibilities.

Rosaleen Norton was born in Dunedin in 1917 during a violent thunderstorm which she later claimed was a portent for her love of the night side of life. Even when she was just three years of age she was fond of drawing "nothing beasts"—animal-headed ghosts with tentacle arms—and at the age of five she observed an apparition of a shining dragon beside her bed. These events convinced her of the presence of the spirit world and she found herself developing religious beliefs contrary to those of her more orthodox parents. Rosaleen's father was a captain in the merchant navy and a cousin of composer Vaughan Williams, her mother a "conventional, highly emotional woman, far too absorbed in her family."

The Nortons migrated from New Zealand in 1925 and settled in the Sydney suburb of Lindfield. Young Rosaleen lived there for the next ten years with her parents but found it increasingly difficult to relate to her mother, pre-

ferring the company of her elder sister and a favorite aunt. By the age of fourteen she had decided upon the direction her life should take and was preparing to experience everything she could, "good, bad and indifferent," engaging both her life and art in the only way that came naturally. A numerologist had earlier worked out her name chart and had arrived at the conclusion that Rosaleen's life and work would lie well off the beaten track—a prediction which certainly came true.

Rosaleen was soon expelled from school under a cloud, her headmistress writing to her mother indicating that she had "a depraved nature which would corrupt the innocence of the other girls." She then studied for two years at East Sydney Technical College under the sculptor Rayner Hoff. During this time she became interested in witchcraft and magic and was soon well versed in the occult writings of Dion Fortune, Aleister Crowley and Eliphas Levi even though such specialist publications were difficult to obtain in Sydney at the time. After leaving the college she became one of Australia's first women pavement artists, displaying her work at the bottom of Rowe Street, near the Sydney GPO. Her subsequent jobs included working as a newspaper cadet, designing for a toy manufacturer, assisting in a bohemian nightclub, waitressing and modeling. But her work pursuits were becoming increasingly secondary to her occult interests and in 1940 she began to experiment with self-hypnosis as a means of inducing automatic drawing.

She was known to the public as an eccentric, bohemian witch-lady who wore flamboyant, billowing blouses and vivid bandanas, puffed on an exotic engraved cigarette holder, and plucked her eyebrows so that they arched in a somewhat sinister curve.

Rosaleen was already familiar with the trance methods of the surrealists and especially admired the work of Salvador Dali and Yves Tanguy who, like the other artists in their movement, had explored techniques of encouraging the subconscious mind to manifest its visionary contents. Sometimes the surrealists drew rapidly so that forms came through unimpeded by the intellect. Others experimented with drugs or documented their dream experiences with great detail in order to develop a greater knowledge of the "alternative reality" of the subconscious mind.

Rosaleen Norton found that she could shut off her normal consciousness by means of self-hypnosis and could transfer her attention to an inner plane of awareness. As she noted in her personal records: "These experiments produced a number of peculiar and unexpected results... and culminated in a period of extra-sensory perception, together with a prolonged series of symbolic visions." She spent several years after this studying various systems of occult thought, including Buddhist and other examples of eastern literature as well as standard works on western magic and mysticism.

During this period she also began to focus more specifically on the magical forces associated with the Great God Pan, whose spirit she felt pervaded the entire earth. Her studies had taught her that the ancient Greeks regarded Pan as lord of all things—symbolizing the totality of the elements and all forms of manifest being. He was therefore, in a very real sense, the true god of the world. Pan was a maintainer of the balance of Nature and also had at his command an invisible hierarchy of lesser spirits who could help him in his work of ruling and sustaining the earth.

Rosaleen painted a large-scale interpretation of Pan, complete with horns, pointed ears, cloven hooves and musical pipes, and mounted it on the wall of her flat. She also conducted magical ceremonies dressed in a tiger-skin robe to honor his presence, and would often experience him as a living reality when she entered a trance state.

Meanwhile, her art continued to reflect the entities she encountered in her visions, including a variety of devilish creatures, half animal-half human pagan deities, and various supernatural motifs. Several psychiatrists were fascinated by her style and one of her paintings was bought in the early 1950s by an Adelaide bishop, curious about the source of her inspiration. When the English art critic John Sackville-West arrived in Australia in 1970 he claimed that far too many abstract painters were claiming to be artists when in fact they were really designers; he identified Norman Lindsay and Rosaleen Norton as two of Australia's finest artists, gifted in depicting the detailed human form. Rosaleen was very pleased by this particular praise; she liked to be compared with Norman Lindsay, whom she very much admired and regarded, with Sir William Dobell, as one of "Australia's only great artists." She also admitted to being influenced by Aubrey Beardsley, Leonardo, Van Gogh and the etcher Gustav Doré.

THE GODS, IN THEIR OWN RIGHT

Many occultists have drawn on Swiss psychoanalyst Carl Jung's concept of the "collective unconscious" to explain their relationship with the archetypal forces of the mind. Dion Fortune was an early enthusiast of Jungian thought. Jung believed that at a deep, collective level of the psyche lay a rich and potent source of sacred archetypal imagery, and that these numinous forms provided the very basis of religious and mystical experience, irrespective of the cultural context involved. In other words, gods and sacred mystical images were really an extension of the universal human experience.

A number of occultists, though, have rejected this view, claiming instead that the gods live apart from the collective minds of humanity and are not merely projected "thought-forms." Rosaleen Norton agreed with this latter perspective. In an interview given the year before her death in 1979, she explained to me that she found it egotistical and self-centered for humanity to accord itself a special position in the spectrum of creation. For her, the gods existed in their own right. She knew Hecate, Lucifer and Pan, not as extensions of her own consciousness, but as beings who would grace her with their presence *if it pleased them*, and not subject to her will. She believed she had discovered some of the qualities of these gods within her own temperament, and that this provided a sense of natural affinity. This made their invocation much easier and more effective than would have been the case had there not been some sort of innate bond. Rosaleen maintained that she went to the realm of the gods on the astral planes—an inner world of spirit accessed through magical trance—and that on different occasions the gods would reveal different dimensions of their own magical potency.

Geburah

Rosaleen Norton regarded Lucifer, for example, not so much as an embodiment of "evil" as humanity's natural adversary. He bound and limited man when it appeared that he was growing too big for his boots.

He tried to trick man, not out of malice but with the positive intent of exposing the limitations of the ego and revealing the essential falseness of man's pride in his own existence. Rosaleen also regarded Pan as a very significant deity for the present day, a force in the universe which protected and conserved the natural beauty and resources of the environment. For her, Pan was alive and well in the anti-pollution lobbies and among the Friends of the Earth!

Hecate, on the other hand, she felt to be more imposing—an often frightening, shadowy goddess flanked by cohorts of ghouls and night-forms, a dealer in death and a purveyor of curses. But there was a magical bond to be found there too. Rosaleen regarded magic and witchcraft as her protection and an inspiration in a hostile, ungenerous world. However, her own brand of witchcraft hardly brought her abundance. She lived simply, with few possessions, and certainly without any measure of wealth. If ever she cursed people with "witch current," she said, it was a means of redressing the balance of events—a legitimate use of the magical art.

Not surprisingly, Rosaleen's paintings show a certain similarity of style to those of Norman Lindsay. But while for Lindsay the world of supernature could only offer decadent and exotic themes for his artmaking, for Rosaleen Norton this realm was a perceptual reality—and this is very much reflected in her work. There are fire elementals, ablaze with light; devils with dual banks of eyes, indicative of their different planes of perception; cats with magical awareness; horned beings with sensual cheeks and a strange eerie light playing on their brow. Her art was the result of the direct magical encounter. Energies filtered through her, she said, as if she were a funnel. She transmitted the current during a state of self-induced hypnotic trance.[1] If the gods were alive in her, her artistic skills would then allow these gods to manifest, in varying degrees, upon her canvases.

Rosaleen always denied that she portrayed the totality of the god. She could depict only those qualities the god chose to show. The gods existed in their own right, on a plane far removed from the everyday world of human consciousness.

In certain of Rosaleen's paintings and drawings we find creatures which are half human and half animal and these, in many ways, are her most impressive magical images. Several illustrations of this type were reproduced in a volume of the artist's drawings titled *The Art of Rosaleen Norton*, published in 1952 in a limited

The Jester

edition of a thousand copies. The drawings were in black and white, and accompanied a series of poems by Rosaleen's lover, Gavin Greenlees.[2]

Greenlees, who died in 1983, was a modest and quietly spoken man for whom the magical view of the world was simultaneously a visionary and poetic expression. In the 1952 edition, Rosaleen Norton's magical images blended superbly with Greenlees' mystical poetry and also provided a type of homage to the major supernatural forces in her magical pantheon.

Pan was a maintainer of the balance of Nature and also had at his command an invisible hierarchy of lesser spirits who could help him in his work of ruling and sustaining the earth.

In his introduction to the book, publisher Walter Glover noted the parallels between Rosaleen Norton's art and certain of the surrealists, and also pointed out that her paintings embodied what he called "a vision of the night." Rosaleen Norton would always regard her art as a medium for tapping into a wondrous "alternative reality." In an early journal entry she wrote:

"There are senses, art forms, activities and states of consciousness that have no parallel in human experience... an overwhelming deluge of both Universal and Self Knowledge (often in an allegorical form) from every conceivable aspect— metaphysical, mathematical, scientific, symbolic. These comprise a bewildering and significant relationship to every other facet.

Rosaleen Norton and her altar to Pan

One such experience could be compared with simultaneously watching and taking part in a play in which all art forms, such as music, drama, ceremonial ritual, shape, sound and pattern, blended into one..."

Rosaleen's artistic output was quite varied and the limited edition remains a hallmark of her stylistic breadth. Her drawings ranged from satirical, but essentially whimsical, parodies of church figures through to semi-abstract vorticist whirlpools of energy and figurative depictions of the great supernatural deities. Her representation of Mars—an obviously warlike entity—shows a powerful human male torso with the winged head of a hawk. The god has a scorpion's tail and clawed feet, and embodies a very tangible feeling of power and aggression. In his right hand he holds a sphere—the puny globe of Earth—asserting his command.

Rosaleen's portrait of Jupiter, meanwhile, shows a proud potentate with a resplendent beam of light issuing from his forehead and a dark, majestic beard lapping down onto his chest. His legs and tail are leonine, and he carries in his right hand a mace, symbolizing spiritual authority.

In both of these pictures, Rosaleen Norton depicts her deities as an animal-human fusion. For her, animals embodied a dignity which mankind had lost. She was especially fond of cats because of their "psychic qualities," and the lion, for her, was a supremely appropriate symbol of benevolent authority. Rosaleen felt that, in general, animals had managed to retain their integrity much more effectively than most human beings. Towards the end of her life, she felt an increasing empathy with the animal kingdom, taking great pleasure in her pets, and she began to shun human contact altogether. A believer in reincarnation, she also recalled an earlier "lifetime" that throws light on her close bond with animals...

In this existence she lived in a rickety wooden house in a field of yellow grass near Beachy Head in Sussex. There were various animals—cows, horses and so on—and she was a poltergeist. She remembered understanding the techniques by which poltergeists made objects move. When "real" people came near her house they were offended or frightened by her presence—they could not relate to her poltergeist condition—and she in turn found herself attacking them out of contempt. The animals, however, were no trouble at all. They regarded her as just another cohabitant in their shared universe, as part of the "natural order."

Rosaleen felt that, in general, animals had managed to retain their integrity much more effectively than most human beings.

Rosaleen's love of animals and her antipathy towards much of what the human race had come to represent, had a profound influence on her magical conceptions. And yet she acknowledged dueling elements in the animal kingdom as well, for these reflected the important opposing polarities within the cosmos itself. Her preference for animals was not simply a retreat into the world of the non-human. On the contrary, she believed the animal kingdom encompassed a broad range of activities, functions and potentials from which humanity had much to learn.

This recognition of opposing polarities shows itself well in one of her most impressive

pictures, *Esoteric Study*. Here an angry demon leers across from the realm of chaos, counterbalanced by a diamond-image of white radiance on the other side. A pair of scales rises up from the cosmic egg—a universal symbol of life and new birth—and the superimposition of the artist's face upon the scales suggests that she is the vehicle through which these tides of magical energy must flow. Gavin Greenlees' accompanying poem begins:

> "Out of herself, the Earth created by her own Guardian faces
> And using the rule they gave her, out of herself
> She made creatures to serve her—animals, poems,
> Forgotten beings, men, women... Out of herself
> She made the grandeur aid its faith, healthy or faded..."[3]

Another of Rosaleen Norton's key works is *Individuation*, a reference to Jung's concept of spiritual and psychic wholeness. The androgynous figure depicted is a fusion of animal, human and divine and stands astride the Zodiac, seemingly drawn down into an accumulation of manifested forms, yet at the same time able to rise transcendent above them. Accompanying the image are these words:

> "I speak the birth
> I speak the beginning of presence
> I am inauguration, I am a greeting between friends..."[4]

Individuation is an important drawing because it embodies the different elements of the magical quest. And while Rosaleen's drawings and paintings so often seem to point to the "night" side of consciousness, works like this show that she really understood that magical exploration was an encounter with the forces of both darkness and light. One without the other would lead to a state of psychic and spiritual imbalance.

It is fair to say that Rosaleen Norton was frequently misunderstood during her own lifetime.

Individuation

Rosaleen Norton in later years

Many remember her more for her exotic public persona as "the witch of Kings Cross" than for her innovative and often confronting role as a magical artist. And yet, clearly, she was no mere witch. She lived in a world populated by magical beings and astral entities whose presence pervaded her paintings and drawings in varying degrees. For her, the ancient gods were a living presence in the world, and we could fail to heed their call only at our own cost. Rosaleen Norton was a visionary ahead of her time—an important forerunner of the contemporary occult revival. ⊙

Endnotes

1. For a full account of Rosaleen Norton's trance explorations see Nevill Drury, *The Witch of Kings Cross*, Kingsclear Books, Sydney, Australia 2002 (www.kingsclearbooks.com.au)
2. A facsimile of this edition, *The Art of Rosaleen Norton*, was published by the late Walter Glover in Sydney in 1982.
3. See The Art of Rosaleen Norton, op.cit., p.38
4. There is also a degree of resemblance, in my opinion, to the Tarot image of *Temperance*, which similarly reflects a state of spiritual unity or balance. Rosaleen Norton denied a direct influence from the Tarot, though, regarding it more as an intuitive than a specific source of archetypal imagery.

SECRET SOCIETIES

MAGICAL BLITZKRIEG
Hitler and the Occult
Peter Levenda Interview

Peter Levenda's quest for the truth began in 1979 while reading *Aftermath: Martin Bormann and the Fourth Reich* by Ladislas Farago. This book revealed how Hitler's former Reichsleiter had escaped to South America after the war pretending to be a priest, protected by the "underground railroad" of Nazi sympathizers that operated and still operate all over that continent, including many if not most of the police and military. Levenda came across a description of one of Bormann's many hideouts, a Branch Davidian-like cult compound called "Colonia Dignidad" (Colony of Righteousness), which was, as Farago described, "the weirdest encampment of the postwar world, housing a sect that combines Nazism and voodooism." Intrigued as he was by such an odd combination, Mr. Levenda decided to check the place out for himself, and actually flew down to Chile to conduct the investigation. He did manage to penetrate the compound, but only briefly, and this led to his being chased out of Chile by a series of unidentified agents, then later fired from his job at "a large, multinational corporation that did a lot of business with the Chilean military." It also led to the research that eventually culminated in Levenda's terrifying, spellbinding book, *Unholy Alliance: A History of Nazi Involvement with the Occult.*

THE HISTORY

It all started with the Thule Gesellschaft, a pagan, anti-Semitic, right-wing aristocratic society founded by a Freemason and Eastern mystic named Baron Rudolf von Sebottendorff. They met every Saturday in Munich's Four Season's Hotel to discuss things like runes, racial evolution, Nordic mythology and German nationalism. Registered under the name "Thule Gesellschaft" as a "literary-cultural society," in order to fool the Communist Red Army now controlling Munich, this group had originally been known as the Germanenorden, or the German Order Walvater of the Holy Grail. According to Levenda, "The Germanenorden had an impressive series of initiatory rituals, replete with knights in shining armor, wise kings, mystical bards and forest nymphs, including a Masonic-style program of secrecy, initiation and mutual cooperation." But they were not copying the ideological aspects of Freemasonry. As Levenda writes, "What the Germanenorden became was, essentially, an anti-Masonry: a Masonic-style society dedicated to the eradication of Freemasonry itself." Their symbol was a long dagger on top of a swastika, and their beliefs had been influenced largely by the writings of Guido von List and Lanz von Liebenfels, two men who will feature prominently in our story. Liebenfels had founded the neo-pagan, swastika-waving "Order of the New Templars" on Christmas Day, 1907, along similar ideological lines. In that same year, occult researcher Guido von List began The List Society, part of a then-developing "völkish" (folkish) movement extolling the virtues of Norse heritage—heritage which could be traced by reading the Edda, a compilation of Icelandic legends which Hitler would later take great interest in. The völkish movement itself was based in part on the ideas of Madam Helena Blavatsky, founder of the Theosophical Society, famous for her books *Isis Unveiled and The Secret Doctrine.* She wrote that humanity was descended from a series of imperfect races which had once ruled the earth, and which all had a common Atlantean origin dating back millions of years, culminating in the Aryan race—which had at one point possessed supernatural powers but had since lost them. She also romanticized about the occult significance of the swastika, of Lucifer, "The Light-Bearer," and of a cabal of spiritual "Hidden Masters" called the Great White Brotherhood, who guided human evolution from their abode in the Himalayas and who Blavatsky herself purported to channel during her many self-induced trances. And the philosophy of List and Liebenfels took this a bit further, to the extent that the Aryan race was the only "true" humanity, and that the Jews, along with a host of other undesirables, or "minderwertigen" ("beings of inferior value") were sapping the race of its strength and purity through the evil machination of Christianity, Freemasonry, capitalism and Communism. They believed that the Aryan race had come from a place called Thule, located at the North Pole, where there was an entrance to a vast underground area populated by giants. "Among the völkish cults," writes Levenda, "it was believed that—as soon as the Germans had purified the planet of the pollution of the inferior races—these Hidden Masters, these Supermen from Thule, would make themselves known, and the link which had been lost between Man and God would be forged anew."

These were the beliefs of the members of the Thule Gesellschaft when they met on November 9, 1918 to discuss something of immediate concern: the Communist control of Munich. After a rousing speech by Sebottendorf, the Thule Society began to prepare for a counter-revolution, stockpiling weapons and forming

"Colonia Dignidad was the weirdest encampment of the postwar world, housing a sect that combines Nazism and voodooism."

German Army, and eventually, part of the S.S.) On April 26, the Red Army raided Thule headquarters and began making arrests, including the arrest of the well-connected Prince von Thurn und Taxis. On April 30, Walpurgisnacht [Witches Night], they were executed in the Luitpold High School courtyard. The following day, their obituaries were published in Sebottendorff's newspaper *Münchener Beobachter* (which would evolve one year later in to the official Nazi publication, *Völkischer Beobachter*). The citizens of Munich became outraged. The Thule Society organized a citizen rebellion, which was joined by the 20,000-member Freikorps, and together they marched, "beneath a swastika flag, with swastikas painted on their helmets, singing a swastika hymn." By May 3, after much bloodshed and destruction, the Communists in Munich were defeated. But there was much work to be done. The Soviet threat was still very real. With the help of the local police and military, the Thule Gesellschaft began organizing a more full-scale national revolt, using connections with society's wealthy intellectuals. They also began recruiting among Germany's working class by forming a group called the German Worker's Party, which met regularly in beer halls to discuss the threat of Jews, Communists, and Freemasons. This group would later become the National Socialist German Workers' Party—The Nazi Party—and in November 1923, they would make their first attempt at national takeover, the failed Beer Hall Putsch, led by a man who had originally been sent by the German Army to spy on them—Adolf Hitler.

We all know what the Nazi party went on to accomplish. What most people do not know is the extent to which those actions were inspired by the occult beliefs of their perpetrators.

alliances with other like-minded groups, such as the Pan-Germans, the German School Bund and the Hammerbund. The following year, on April 7, a Bavarian Soviet Republic was proclaimed in Munich, causing the Prime Minister of Bavaria to run off to Bamburg in order to prevent a total Communist take-over of the government. Six days later the Thule-organized Palm Sunday Putsch failed to overcome the Communists in Munich, and now the Thule members were on the Red Army's "most wanted" list. Sebottendorf got busy organizing an army of Freikorps (Freecorps) to counter-attack. (One of the units of the Freikorps, the Ehrhardt Brigade, later became part of the

We all know what the Nazi party went on to accomplish. What most people do not know is the extent to which those actions were inspired by the occult beliefs of their perpetrators. As Levenda writes, "The most extreme aims of the Thule Society would all eventually become official policy of the Third Reich, while its purely metaphysical and occult characteristics were adopted wholeheartedly by the S.S." Hitler himself was fascinated by the occult. While he was a college student he began reading Von Liebenfels' magazine, *Ostara*. Later in 1909, while he was living in poverty in a men's dormitory and selling his paintings on the street, Hitler actually met Libenfels in his office. He is said to have arrived looking "so distraught and so impoverished that the New Templar himself gave Hitler free copies of *Ostara* and bus fare back home." Hitler's friend Josef Greiner recalls in his memoirs how obsessed young Adolf was with astrology, religion, occultism, magic and yoga. Hitler loved Wagner, as we know, especially *The Ring Cycle*, *Parsifal*, *Lohengrin*, and *Rienzi*. It was from Wagner that Hitler gained his affinity for knighthood, chivalry, and the Quest for the Holy Grail—a pagan, Teutonic Grail. In

Hitler's friend Josef Greiner recalls in his memoirs how obsessed young Adolf was with astrology, religion, occultism, magic and yoga.

1915, Hitler was at war, and while in the trenches, wrote a poem, one which "sings the praises of Wotan, the Teutonic Father God, and of runic letters, magic spells, and magic formulas." So there is no doubt that Hitler's interest in occultism and paganism ran deep. There is doubt, however, as to whether or not Hitler actually performed any magical operations himself. According to Levenda, this was not in his nature, a nature inclined more towards accomplishing things here on Earth, in the 3rd dimension. He did not have the time and the patience necessary for real spiritual endeavors. "Hitler was a paranoid," writes Levenda, "and the occult holds special attractions for the paranoid. But Hitler as a cultist? As a black-robed, ritual-performing, invocation-chanting priest of Satan? Probably not. But Hitler as a tool of other cultists? Probably so."

In fact, a number of people deeply involved in the occult would have great influence on him and play essential roles in the development of the Third Reich. It would do us well to examine them one by one.

DIETRICH ECKART

Hitler, while working as the leader of the German Worker's Party, became friends with Thulist Dietrich Eckart, who published a newspaper called *Auf Gut Deutsch* (In Good German), which "ranks with the *Völkischer Beobachter* as a racist sheet with intellectual pretensions." Eckart had a tremendous effect on Hitler, and it was he who first introduced Hitler to all the wealthy and powerful people he needed to make his crusade possible, including Henry Ford, who would later contribute "vital financial support" to the Nazi party. From Eckart, Hitler learned a great deal about the esoteric sciences, and it is said that they occasionally attended séances together and talked to ghosts. Eckart, who died after the Beer Hall Putsch, is quoted as saying, "Hitler will dance, but it is I who plays the tune."

ALFRED ROSENBURG

Eckart's protégé, and soon Hitler's as well, was Alfred Rosenburg, a man who would later become "one of the architects of official Nazi policies." One of these policies was that all of the Masonic temples in all of the Nazis' occupied territories were to be raided, and the goods shipped back to Rosenberg himself. This was done by Franz Six and Otto Ohlendorf, both occultists. Rosenberg was also friends with another occultist named Walther Darré, who became agricultural minister of the Third Reich. "Together," writes Levenda, "they ran around the nation drumming up support for an official state religion based on the worship of the Old Gods, a religion that included purifying the Aryan race of elements that were in the process of polluting it and diluting the strength of its blood."

WILHELM GUTBERLET

Gutberlet was an astrologer, a shareholder in the *Völkischer Beobachter* who had been Hitler's close friend since the days of the German Worker's Party in 1919. In the memoirs of Walter Schellenberg he is described as "a Munich physician who belonged to the intimate circle around Hitler." Gutberlet believed in the sidereal pendulum, an astrological device which he claimed gave him the power to sense at once the presence of any Jews or persons of partial Jewish ancestry, and to pick them out in any group of people. Hitler availed himself of Gutberlet's mystical powers and had many discussions with him on racial questions.

RUDOLF HESS

A friend of Hitler's from way back, he had been arrested at the Beer Hall Putsch with him in 1923, and had transcribed Hitler's *Mein Kampf* (originally titled *Four and a Half Years of Struggle Against Lies, Stupidity and Cowardice*) while they were both in prison. He later became Hitler's Deputy Führer. He was an "intimate" of the Thule Society, and was way into the occult. Hess introduced Hitler to one of his professors, Karl Haushofter, a man with an interest in astrology who claimed clairvoyance. Haushofter later came to wield considerable power in Germany by founding the Deutsche Akadamie, and by heading the University of Munich's Institute Geopolitik, "[a] kind of think tank-cum-intelligence agency," according to Levenda. He was vital in forming the Nazi alliances with Japan and South America, and was responsible for the adoption of the Lebensraum ("Living Room") policy, which stated that, "a sovereign nation, to ensure the survival of its people, had a right to annex the territory of other sovereign nations to feed and house itself."

HIMMLER AND THE S.S.

The S.S. (Schutzstaffel) was originally formed as a personal bodyguard to Hitler, and numbered around 300 when Heinrich Himmler joined. But when he rose to its leadership in 1929, things changed a bit. Four years later, membership had soared to 52,000. He established headquarters at a medieval castle called Wewelsburg, where his secret inner order met once a year. According to Walther Schellenberg's memoirs, "Each member had his own armchair with an engraved silver nameplate, and each had to devote himself to a ritual of spiritual exercises aimed mainly at mental concentration.... The focal point of Wewelsburg, evidently owing much to the legend of King Arthur and the Knights of the Round Table, was a great dining hall with an oaken table to seat twelve picked from the senior Gruppenführers. The walls were to be adorned with their coats of arms." Underneath this dining hall there was kept a so-called "realm of the dead," a circular well in which these coats of arms would be burnt and the ashes worshipped after the "knight" had died. (There are tales of Himmler using the severed heads of deceased S.S. officers to communicate with ascended masters.) In addition to this, each knight had his own room, "decorated in accordance with one of the great ancestors of Aryan majesty." Himmler's own room was dedicated to a Saxon King Henry the Fowler, whose ghost Himmler sometimes conversed with.

Outside of the inner order, S.S. officers were discouraged from participating in Christian ceremonies, including weddings and christenings, and celebrated the Winter Solstice instead of Christmas. The traditional day of gift exchange was switched to the day of the summer solstice celebration. Writes Levenda, "These ceremonies were replete with sacred fires, torchlit processions, and invocations of Teutonic deities, all performed by files of young blond-haired, blue-eyed Aryan supermen." Although Himmler admired the ceremonial nature of Catholicism and modeled the S.S. partially on the Order of the Jesuits, he also despised Christianity for what he considered its weak, masochistic nature. He held further resentment because of the persecution of German witches during the Inquisition.

Himmler, along with Richard Darré, was responsible for absorbing The Ahnenerbe Society "a kind of seminary and teaching college for the future leaders of the Thousand Year Reich," into the S.S. The Ahnenerbe was devoted to some odd völkish studies, each of which had a subdivision dedicated to it: "Celtic Studies"; Externsteine (near Wewelsburg), where the world-tree Yggdrasil was supposed to reside; Icelandic research; Tibetan research; runic studies; a strange new twist on physics called the "World Ice Theory"; and an archeological research in an effort to find evidence of past Aryan presence in remote locations all over the world, such as South America, giving rise to "Aryans discovered America" stories. Another theory propounded by Himmler was that babies that had been conceived in cemeteries would inherit the spirits of whoever was buried there, and actually published lists of cemeteries that were good for breeding because of the Teutonic heroes resting therein. Himmler was infatuated with the concept of the Holy Grail, and hired researchers to try and prove that the Grail was actually a Nordic pagan artifact.

THE ALLIED OCCULT OFFENSE

According to Levenda, "Himmler was obsessed by the idea that British Intelligence was being run by the Rosicrucian order, and that occult adepts were in charge of MI5." Whether or not that was true, the Germans were certainly not the only participants in the war using the power of magick to their advantage. Levenda provides the details of a "Cult Counterstrike" organized by the intelligence agencies of the US and Britain, an effort centering on the "most evil man in the world," the Great Beast 666, Aleister Crowley.

> "Hitler was a paranoid and the occult holds special attractions for the paranoid. But Hitler as a cultist? As a black-robed, ritual-performing, invocation-chanting priest of Satan? Probably not. But Hitler as a tool of other cultists? Probably so."

Crowley had gone to live in New York during WWI after being rejected for military service by the British government, and began writing "pro-German propaganda" for a magazine called *The Fatherland*, published by George Viereck. Crowley took over as editor. He later claimed that he had really been working for British Intelligence, because, "his articles were so outlandish that the journal was reduced to absurdity, a caricature of serious political discussion, which would help the British cause more than harm it." There is some evidence to suggest that Crowley

Maxwell Knight was the real historical figure behind the fictional character "M" in all the James Bond novels, written by Knight's friend in the Department of Naval Intelligence, Ian Fleming.

was working for MI5 during this time, spying on his fellow O.T.O. initiate Karl Germer, a German intelligence agent, so perhaps his excuse for working for *The Fatherland* is sound. Whatever the case, he was definitely hired by MI5 during WWII. Crowley had become friends with author Dennis Wheatley, well-known for a number of fiction and non-fiction books based on the occult, who had once worked for Winston Churchill's Joint Planning Staff. He had been introduced to Crowley by a journalist named Tom Driberg, who would later become a spy for MI5 as well, and who would come into possession of Crowley's diaries shortly after his death in 1947. Wheatley also introduced Crowley to yet another MI5 agent, Maxwell Knight. Knight was the real historical figure behind the fictional character "M" in all the James Bond novels, written by Knight's friend in the Department of Naval Intelligence, Ian Fleming. Crowley met Knight for dinner at Wheatley's house, and it was there that Crowley agreed to take them both on as magick students. Later, Ian Fleming dreamed up a way to use Crowley's expertise in a scheme against the Germans. The scheme involved an Anglo-German organization known as "The Link," a supposed "cultural society" which had once been under the leadership of Sir Barry Domville, Director of Naval Intelligence from 1927 to 1930. The Link had been investigated by Maxwell Knight in the 1930s because of its involvement in German spy operations, and was soon dissolved after much incriminating evidence was found. As Levenda describes it, Fleming, "thought that if the Nazis could be made to believe that The Link was still in existence, they could use it as bait for the Nazi leadership. The point was to convince the Nazis that The Link had sufficient influence to overthrow the Churchill government and thereby to install a more pliable British government, one which would gladly negotiate a separate peace with Hitler." The suggestion came in the form of fake astrological advice passed on to the gullible Rudolf Hess, who was already under the delusion that only he could talk the British into peace with Germany, and that it was his destiny to do so. One of his staff astrologers, Dr. Ernst Schulte-Strathaus, under British employ, encouraged Hess to make his mission to England on May 10, 1941 a significant date because of a rare conjunction of six planets in the sign of Taurus. The Duke of Hamilton was also enlisted to let Hess know that he would be happy to entertain him should he plan to go through with such an endeavor. So

Hess, a trained pilot, embarked on a rather dangerous solo flight to the British Isles, parachuting into Scotland decked out in various occult symbols, where he was immediately arrested by the waiting Brits. According to Levenda, "Fleming tried to obtain permission for Crowley to debrief Hess in order to develop intelligence on the occult scene in the Third Reich and particularly the Nazi leadership." But this permission was denied, and Hess spent the rest of his days in prison not being much use to anybody. Levenda finds this suspicious, for, "[w]hat could have been a major propaganda coup against the Nazis went utterly wasted, as if by tacit agreement on both sides."

After Hess's arrest, Hitler denounced him as a crazed madman, and began persecuting astrologers and occultists in his own domains more so than ever before. Crowley continued trying to help the Allied cause, but most of his ideas were rejected. One, however, while initially dismissed, was later implemented. This involved dropping occult pamphlets on the German countryside that predicted a dire outcome for the war and depicted the Nazi leadership as Satanic. A forgery of a popular German astrological magazine called *Zenit* was created and dropped onto enemy battlefields. It was set for full-scale distribution, but the delivery was intercepted by the Gestapo before it could be completed.

Besides Crowley, there were other occultists involved in the fight against the Third Reich. One of Crowley's protégés, Jack Parsons, who was the Head of the Agapé O.T.O. Lodge in California as well as a charter member of both Cal Tech and the Jet Propulsion Laboratory, invented the "Greek Fire" rocket propellant which was widely used by the United States Navy between 1944 and 1945. According to Levenda, it was "a solution that could have only come from someone with a working knowledge of the arcane lore of alchemy and magic."[1] There was also a Golden Dawn initiate named Sam Untermyer, an attorney and wealthy philanthropist once called a "Satanist" by a British newspaper. Untermyer started the Non-Sectarian Anti-Nazi League to Champion Human Rights and the World-Anti-Nazi Council, which both promoted the boycott of German products. He also donated money to the hunt for Nazi agents coming into New York. And with the help of a man named Richard Rollins, he started a secret society called "The Board," which engaged in counterespionage against Nazi groups who were recruiting in the United States.

The World War II that Levenda describes is a magick war, and a holy war—a war in which both sides considered themselves to be fighting the forces of evil. It is a war operated behind the scenes by mystical adepts using their esoteric knowledge of symbolism, astrology, meditation, astral travel, clairvoyance, and mind control against the enemy. It was a war inspired by age-old beliefs in the Elder Gods of Europe's ancient past. In the pages that follow, Mr. Levenda discusses that war with the editor of *Dagobert's Revenge*, Tracy R. Twyman.

TRACY R. TWYMAN: Your book is all about how occultism, esoteric beliefs and secret societies inspired many of the leading figures in the Nazi party. You also detail how several people in the upper echelons of the Golden Dawn and the O.T.O. were involved in espionage—Karl Germer and Theodor Reuss for German intelligence, and Crowley for the British. And certainly we know that a number of occult societies throughout history, such as the Bavarian Illuminati, various Masonic sects,

charms. One stays alive, and one resists. One has one's cake and eats it. In the case of spiritual authority, an intelligent person cannot stomach that a black-robed eunuch with a wine-red nose would have some kind of direct connection with God unobtainable by ordinary folk. The intelligent person wants to talk to God directly, and not have to take direction from a tired old priest or minister or whatever. That person—through the act of contacting higher powers or forces on his or her own—becomes a kind of "anti-priest" and thus a cult is born. Conspiracies are a fact of life: they grow like mushrooms around office water coolers. They remain secret from the managers and supervisors; they attempt to cause change, indirectly and discretely. Add God or occult powers into the mix—or politics, espionage, coups d'etat—and you have an irresistible mix for a certain type of person. We all feel there is a mystery at the heart of reality. Note the popularity of crime and detection novels, spy novels ... and occult novels. The spy and the occultist live at the periphery of this elemental Ur-mystery. It has to do with authority, the king,

> ## Conspiracies are a fact of life: they grow like mushrooms around office water coolers. They remain secret from the managers and supervisors; they attempt to cause change, indirectly and discretely. Add God or occult powers into the mix—or politics, espionage, coups d'etat—and you have an irresistible mix for a certain type of person.

the Knights of Malta, the Templars, etc., have been involved in espionage and political revolution. What do you think draws occultists into the fields of spying and revolutionary activities?

PETER LEVENDA: Secret knowledge; the illusion of secret power; the man or woman who walks among us, ordinary and unremarkable or even of low and unattractive appearance, who is in reality a Magister Templi or a Colonel in the KGB… It's the same attraction that Batman, Superman, Spiderman, etc. have for generations of pre-adolescents. Spies and magicians are a lot like Batman, except that spies really exist and really do exert some hidden influence over mundane events; and magicians thoroughly believe that they do, too, and have the benefit—sometimes—of a cult of like-minded people who prop up their belief system by means of what Robert Anton Wilson called "consensus reality." On a deeper level, I think that many people—intelligent people—resent having to obey authority. Openly resisting authority is usually cause for arrest and torture, if not execution, in many countries. Secretly resisting authority, however, has its

and reality. The very word "reality" comes from the same root as "royal": reality was whatever the king said it was. Real estate was the kingdom; outside the kingdom, there was no king and, hence, no reality. To challenge the king, one had to be from beyond the border of the kingdom: one had to be in communion with non-real forces; one had to represent the anti-king. Spies and occultists live among us, but have loyalties elsewhere. There is a certain attraction to that, and a certain danger. But it is also ultimately a lonely existence, and that is where the spy and the occultist sometimes fail: in their attempt to salve their loneliness by opening up to others they reveal their secret natures to their sworn enemy: reality or the King. I am thinking just now—perhaps in a stream of consciousness—about the Philby affair. A group of old queens (already on the outs with general society by their very natures) spying against society for the enemy, since Russia valued their contribution and ignored their homosexuality. What fun! But in the end it was this very relationship they had with each other—Philby, Burgess, Maclean, Blunt[1]—that doomed them all.

TT: Are politics and magic inseparably linked? Would you say that throughout history politicians and political movements have always used subliminal occult messages and archetypes to manipulate public consciousness for or against the prevailing power structure? Are political struggles basically magic wars, and power structures kept intact by magical means?

PL: In other words—to paraphrase Clausewitz—is magic a continuation of politics by other means? It depends on your definition of magic. Is it, as Crowley would have it, the "science and art of causing change to occur in conformity with will"? Then, yes. But... under those guidelines, so is selling used cars. We need a sharper definition of what we mean by magic. It depends on whether or not you subscribe to the conspiracy theory of the day, I guess. If real power is in the hands of a few, secret people behind the scenes who pull strings ... then, obviously, politics as we know it does not exist. I mean, the will of the people ... the voting booth... the ad campaigns and the mud-slinging, etc. in the end come to naught because the boys in the back room will decide who gets elected. But if political power is the ability to move and mold masses of people, then you have a chance at proving the thesis that political wars are magic wars. The key to this thesis would be, in my point of view, propaganda. Propaganda is the use and manipulation of symbols. Whoever does it best is the better magician, and will probably win the "war." But the symbols of the political arena—especially in the United States—are not as sublime as we find in the occult symbol system. The political symbols are taken from the environment, from the times;

paring apples and oranges, I think. Hitler was upfront about what he was doing; the symbolism was deliberately occult, pagan, anti-Christian, anti-Semitic. In fact, he was openly using ritual. Most of our popular politicians today would be unable and unwilling to do this, since virtually any public use of ritual for political ends would be considered crypto-fascist, I think. I am not trying to beg the question; I just think it is more complex than comparing politics to magic on that level. Arthur had Merlin for that; it was a separate department in his government, if you see what I mean. I believe that CIA—specifically the boys at MK-ULTRA—came close to becoming our very own, homegrown version of Merlin but I don't think Harry Truman was a black magician himself.

TT: In *Unholy Alliance* you suggest that the Freikorp's assassination of Foreign Minister Walther Rathenau (in June 1922) on the eve of the summer solstice was a human sacrifice to the sun god Wotan. (Note: It was believed that Rathenau was one of the actual Elders of Zion.) Do you think that in a larger sense the elimination of six million Jews could be considered one giant pagan sacrifice?

PL: We can consider the Holocaust a kind of pagan sacrifice, but more importantly I think it was something far more sinister than that. You don't sacrifice what you despise; you sacrifice something of value. Rathenau—although Jewish—was considered an exemplary human being even by his executioners, and thus a fitting sacrifice. After all, he was an important element of Germany's war machine during the First War and had a lot to offer post-war Germany. His was a true sacrifice. But the

Propaganda is the use and manipulation of symbols. Whoever does it best is the better magician, and will probably win the "war."

the zeitgeist, if you will. No one actually goes around waving the tattvic symbols or the Tarot deck around during a political campaign; the manipulation goes in different channels. I think political wars are analogous to magic wars, but I don't think they are necessarily one and the same. A magician does not need a crowd to effect his or her will. A magician operates—like our spies—secretly, and manipulates forces of nature (or super-nature) rather than directly massage the psyches of people. We are also in danger of considering all subliminal messages as occult messages; there may be some justification in this, in that any subliminal message probably has its occult analogue, but when you compare a run-off election in Iowa with what Hitler was doing at Nuremberg, you are com-

Holocaust? The slaughter of the Jews—and Gypsies, and homosexuals, Communists, etc—was designed to purify the planet of diseased blood and diseased spirit in the eyes of the Nazis. That is why it was kept going until the very end, regardless of the cost and regardless of the fact that the resources being used to keep the camps running could have been better utilized defending Berlin. It was not so much a sacrifice as a purification of the soil. The Nazis believed that the Jews and their fellow travelers were actual representatives of an evil force on earth and had to be destroyed, at any cost. If their race disappeared, the Nazis felt that they had done the planet, and its surviving human members, a favor, and would be remembered forever for their contribution.

TT: Why do you think Hitler and the Nazis spent so much effort persecuting pagans and occult orders? Were they placating the Catholic Church or were they just eliminating competition? Were they afraid of the magical powers of these other occult orders?

> We can consider the Holocaust a kind of pagan sacrifice, but more importantly I think it was something far more sinister than that. You don't sacrifice what you despise; you sacrifice something of value.

PL: They were eliminating competition. Also, remember that the occult groups were a potential "fifth column" inside Germany. They had their own means of communication and contacts all over Europe. They had roots going back many years in many countries. They were indeed a threat. I believe that the US felt the same way, which would help explain the Jack Parsons situation.

TT: Why do you think the swastika specifically was chosen as the Nazi insignia? I know that their ideology was heavily influenced by Theosophy, and the swastika was one of Blavatsky's favorite symbols. The Hindus of course, refer to it as the whirling disc with which Brahma spun the universe into existence. But what exactly was its significance to the Nazis? It seems to give one the impression of aggression and power.

PL: I pretty much cover this in my book. It was a popular symbol in Germany before the Nazis appropriated it. In fact, it was used by troops during World War One as a kind of talisman. The Germans clearly felt it had racial connections, and was more representative of their people than the Christian cross. Remember, too, that the Nazis idolized Tibet and the cults of Northern India. The so-called "Aryan" race would have had its origins there, and India, Nepal, Bhutan and Tibet are replete with swastika motifs. I live in Asia, and the swastika is everywhere out here: on Buddhist, Taoist and Hindu temples alike. It represents—specifically—"auspiciousness" but is taken to symbolize a kind of polar energy in the universe, a spinning sun disk (yes) but also a deeper, more mysterious analogue since the sun does not spin in two directions but the swastika does.

PL: In your book you write about how Guido von List borrowed the Golden Dawn's system of degrees, based on the Tree of Life, for use in his own völkish, anti-Semitic pagan order, the Armanenschaft, and that he might have gotten the information from a Golden Dawn initiate named D.R. Felkein, or from Rudolf Steiner. You write, "That List would have based his hierarchy on the patently Jewish Tree of Life and borrowed the concept from the Golden Dawn—by way of the O.T.O.—would seem merely ironic to a lay person but positively frightening to an occultist, for what it implies about the relationship between the anti-Semitic List organizations and the ostensibly apolitical Golden Dawn and O.T.O. lodges." So what is that implication, exactly?

PL: The implication is that the Blavatskian notion of a racial hierarchy—root races, and all that—would have found a sinister manifestation in a proto-Nazi occult movement, and that the Golden Dawn and O.T.O. themselves might have been fellow travelers; that a spiritual hierarchy might imply a racial one; that a magical war might develop into genocide.

TT: From my understanding the Nazi idea of the Overman entailed much more that just increased physical strength and intellectual prowess. It involved a creature whose ajna faculties—psychic powers associated with the Third Eye—had been fully developed. It entailed a creature more in touch with his higher self, a creature more advanced spiritually as well. What else do you think this entailed? What do you think men like Sebottendorff, Liebenfels, List and Eckart imagined when they talked about the Overman? Did they imagine the Aryan race evolving into something with an entirely different physical appearance?

PL: Yes, the Overman was not merely a "superman" as it is often erroneously translated. It was the next level of human evolution. As Hitler himself says, anyone who thinks that National Socialism is merely a political party had better think again: the goal is to create the New Man. I believe he meant that literally. Else: Why the Holocaust? Why the Lebensborn organization? Why the documented racial purity of prospective S.S. members? Germany was a laboratory where Hitler would create his homunculus. To the Nazis, this meant a human being that was above compassion; above sentiment; passionate in his ideals and self-image, but conscience-less by comparison to the rest of us. A sociopath, probably. Intelligent, strong, perfectly proportioned. And a remorseless killer.

TT: You've mentioned that many of these Nazi occultists believed in the Theosophical concept of Ascended Masters and Secret Chiefs. I know that Blavatsky believed them to reside in the Himalayas, while the Thulists deposited them underground, in a subterranean vault accessible by a tunnel which opens up in the North Pole. But is it possible

The Nazis perceived themselves as "ice men" and their Eden was a frozen wasteland

that some of these people believed that the Ascended Masters were extraterrestrials or trans-dimensional beings? We know that the Nazis were suspected of conducting experiments with flying saucers, time travel and multiple dimensions, so it made me wonder.

PL: I think that recent neo-Nazi authors are toying with this idea, most notably Miguel Serrano in Chile. Crowley and his followers certainly hold these views [about trans-dimensional beings] (see the works by Kenneth Grant, for instance). The Nazis themselves? Well, going through their Canon is a bit tedious but I am sure the resourceful researcher could uncover the odd reference to an extraterrestrial abode for their Secret Chiefs. At that time, space opera was not nearly the advanced art form it is today and flying saucers were not yet the vogue although the foo fighters had already made an appearance, as did the mysterious flying ships of the turn of the century. I think the Nazis still understood the Masters to be a kind of god-force, like Odin or Thor; Horbiger was coming close to an extraterrestrial theory as he developed his World Ice concept, but it had little to do with the Secret Chiefs. I guess what I am trying to say is that I have not found documentation to show that the Nazis had a developed theory about the nature of the Chiefs, and that I have found very little support for an extraterrestrial theory of any kind among the Nazis so far. I am aware of the idea that they were working on a saucer or some kind of space ship, but that does not imply that they held significant alien life theories beyond those of a purely speculative nature.

TT: Please explain the "World Ice Theory," if you would. This makes no sense to me.

PL: Makes no sense to me, either. The idea is that the basic building blocks of the universe are ice crystals, and that temperature and humidity are the determining factors for the various stages of life, evolution, etc. The Nazis perceived themselves as "ice men" and their Eden was a frozen wasteland; they looked down on the tropical Edens of Biblical lore as being the abodes of subhumans, much as tropical countries are the domain of non-Aryans. The Theory is convoluted and self-referential, and gave rise to scientists running all over the world taking its temperature, so to speak.

TT: In *Unholy Alliance* you recount stories of Himmler having his inner circle of 12 S.S. officers try to telepathically influence a German Army Commander in Chief who was being interrogated in the next room to tell the truth. You

also recount stories of psychics being hired by Himmler to pinpoint the locations of British battleships and to find Mussolini when he had been imprisoned on an island off of Naples after a coup—feats which they performed with amazing accuracy. Then you tell stories of Nazi mind control experiments involving psychedelic drugs, and torture techniques. You quote Rudolf Hess's statement at the Nuremberg Trials about how he himself was a made a victim of such mind control techniques, and how he believed that the prosecution witnesses at the trial had been hypnotized because of their "glassy and dreamy eyes." Do you think the CIA and others have copied certain mind control techniques from the Nazis?

PL: I don't think that Hess was implying the Nazis had mind control, but that the Allies had it. The man who interviewed Hess for Dulles was Dr. Ewen Cameron, who went on to run the official CIA mind control operation in Montreal. The Nazis were experimenting with hallucinogens and narcotics during the war; their documentation on this was seized by American intelligence and has never seen the light of day. That much is known. The idea that CIA was running a vast mind control experiment in the 1940s–1970s which involved all sorts of people and organizations forms the central thesis of my next book (which has not been finished yet), so I don't want to ruin the surprise. Suffice it to say that when the Nazis were being imported by the hundreds to the US and other American countries after the War, it wasn't only an "outer" space program that was being contemplated.

TT: You wrote that Jörg Lanz von Liebenfels created the Order of New Templars as "a secret society bent on reviving the chivalric brotherhood of knights, but in an aggressively Teutonic—and anti-Semitic—format." Since the original Templar order had so much to do with Judaism—Jerusalem, holy relics like the Ark of the Covenant, Jewish mysticism and of course that Jewish priest king known as Jesus Christ—how did he reconcile the concept of the Templars with his own anti-Semitic beliefs?

PL: We enlightened types realize that Christianity has its roots in Judaism. I mean, the Old Testament should be proof enough of that, right? But just try telling the wrong people that Christ was a Jew and see what happens. If occult scholarship on the Templars is correct, however, these knights were less Christian than would appear at first blush. The Templars—albeit an order of Catholic knighthood—went on an expedition to the Temple of

Solomon, found something there that probably challenged their belief structure and caused them to deny the crucifixion and—in doing so—possibly the entire Judeo-Christian edifice they had sworn to uphold and defend. Remember that the Nazis were fond of the Cathars whom they considered—via Otto Rahn, at any rate—to be the "true" Christians rather than the persecuting Catholics. Remember that generations of scholars have posited some sort of Cathar/Templar connection. Remember that the Templars became enemies of the Church and were ruthlessly exterminated (as were the Cathars). When someone like Lanz von Liebenfels decides to resurrect the Templars, it is not as the pious Catholic monk/knights but as heroic enemies of Catholicism and, by extension, Judaism as well. The Grail was no longer a Christian symbol to Lanz, but something more ancient, more "pagan." The bloodline of Jesus? Not to Lanz, unless that bloodline was purely Teutonic. One can no longer speak of Templarism without the implicit challenge to papal authority. To the Church in the 14th century, Templarism was synonymous with Satanism and idol-worship and all sorts of heresy. There has been no attempt by the modern Church to rehabilitate the reputation of the Templars. Von Liebenfels and other "new Templars" such as Crowley and Reuss bore no love for Catholicism. They used esoteric Judaica purely as a key to other mysteries, as a tool and not as an element of their "faith." Crowley may have been a qabalist, for instance, but by no stretch of the imagination was he a worshipper of the Jewish god. No tallis, tefillim or yarmulka for that boy. Same for von Liebenfels. The Christ that Christians worship—according to the Nazis, both then and now—is a Jewish impersonator. That Christ was Jewish is a lie perpetrated by the Jews to main-

it obtained all the non-Christian trappings over the centuries. Cults like the new Templar orders were created as repositories of the "true Faith," the secret knowledge behind the Masons and the Jews and the Christians, the pre-Jehovah, pre-Garden of Eden consciousness of the Aryan people. As in the old saying, "the enemy of my enemy is my friend," the Knights Templar were obviously the enemy of the Church, thus it followed...

TT: One of the chapters in your book that interested me most was Chapter 7, entitled "Lucifer's Quest for the Holy Grail." In it, you describe how a mystical Grail scholar named Otto Rahn was enlisted into the S.S. and hired by Himmler to a write a book proving (A) that Lucifer was the God of the Aryan race (B) that Jehovah was Satan and (C) that Christ was a Teutonic sun god and Christianity the corrupted result of Jews trying to co-opt the German Messiah. All this led to the conclusion that the Holy Grail was actually a Luciferian relic that the Jews had also tried to co-opt. Rahn was even given a deadline of October 31st, 1936 to finish his book, entitled *Lucifer's Servants*. But a few years later, in February 1939, Rahn resigned from the S.S. for reasons unknown, and died a mysterious death one month later while hiking in the mountains. You intimate that he may have been assassinated because of something he may have discovered during his Grail researches, something he'd "confessed" to another Nazi occultist named Karl Wiligut, with whom he was good friends. Is it possible that he discovered evidence that the Grail was actually the Bloodline of Christ, the Judaic bloodline of David? This would of course have been thoroughly unacceptable to Himmler and devastating to his whole cosmology if such facts had gotten out.

The Nazis were experimenting with hallucinogens and narcotics during the war; their documentation on this was seized by American intelligence and has never seen the light of day.

tain some degree of control over the Gentiles. So, the "new Templars" were able to identify with a Christian knightly order while simultaneously reviling Christianity, since the "revealed" Christianity was a hoax. They were at least half right; what we know of Christianity today is a hodge-podge of other myths, other religions, and some political agendas. Strip away Mithraism, Gnosticism and paganism from Christianity—especially Roman Catholicism—and what's left? A messianic cult of Essenes with a narrow focus on regaining Jerusalem in its lifetime? The end of the 19th century saw a flurry of books and articles attacking the Church and demonstrating how

PL: I don't know why Otto Rahn was killed, although I am reasonably certain he was and that his death was not the accident it was made out to be. He may be only another one in a series of individuals involved with Montsegur and Rennes-le-Chateau who died violent deaths. Was he murdered by the Nazis ... or were other elements at play here? He was Himmler's pet for awhile, and a friend of Wiligut (who designed the Death's Head Ring worn by the S.S.). Wiligut was a total psycho, so it is hard for me to imagine a less likely friendship since Rahn seems somewhat sane in his writings, if a bit overboard at times. There is no evidence at hand that Himmler ordered an investigation into Rahn's death, so either it was ordered by Himmler himself or he was satisfied that it was an accident. Had he been cut down by a cult defending the Cathar/Templar secret, it is possible that more would have been made of his death and that there would be a paper trail to follow. (Possibly there was, but it has been lost with time and with the destruction of many Nazi documents during the final days of the War.) Yes, if Rahn had discovered the *Holy Blood, Holy Grail* secret then possibly Himmler would have ordered Rahn killed to keep the secret safe … or he would have had him killed for having the temerity to suggest it. But I think that Himmler would have been fascinated by this discovery and would have had Pierre Plantard[2] and his relatives rounded up and brought to Wewelsburg for some heavy interrogation. The Rahn mystery is one that concerns me to this day, for none of the reports, stories, theories I have heard so far have seemed conclusive enough. Perhaps, as the French say, cherchez la femme?

TT: In the epilogue to your book, when you discuss the cooperation the Nazis received from the Catholic church, despite the openly pro-pagan, anti-Christian stance of Nazi doctrine, you say the following:

"Were the Nazis somehow blackmailing the Church with evidence of some monstrous crime that has never come to light (did the Nazis find the Templar treasure? were they in possession of the Grail?), or was the Church's notorious lack of conviction during World War II somehow evidence that the Church itself had lost its own faith?"

If you'll recall, the Priory of Sion and members of the Grail families have been suspected of blackmailing the Vatican with their knowledge of the continuing bloodline of Christ, knowledge that would have disastrous implications for the Church, since their empire is based on the idea that Christ was celibate and died on the Cross with no heirs. Is it possible that Nazis were implementing a similar form of blackmail, if they had, as you suggest, found the "Templar treasure," or the "Holy Grail," terms which could be interpreted to mean the bloodline of Christ?

PL: Yes, it's possible; but why kill Rahn, then? Rahn would have been invaluable for the blackmail operation as he would have an intimate knowledge of the history, the documents, etc. The blackmail theory does have its merit, though. It would explain a great deal, especially the rat-lines after the War. But it's something that would have been kept from Hitler, I think. Hitler would have blurted it out, and had Goebbels write up a particularly scathing oration on the subject for Nazi sweeps week. If this secret had been unearthed, Himmler would have held onto it and used it in his own way. But… there the

theory falls apart. Himmler had no friends at the end, no help from any quarter, and committed suicide after he was captured. If he had been in possession of this secret, he could have blackmailed his way straight into Bel Air if he so desired. Something doesn't ring true, then. Rahn would have been the one to discover the secret, and he would have told it to either Himmler or Wiligut. Both turn up empty-handed at war's end. Was the secret—whatever it was—an object that was subsequently lost (again) by either Rahn or Himmler? Recovered by the Church? Or hidden by some third party somewhere? There is a retired Army veteran who writes books on the subject, and who claims that a German submarine buried something in Antarctica after the War…

TT: How is it that Freemasonry—the tenets of which proclaim "liberty, equality, fraternity," encouraging men to regard one another with brotherly love, and the members of which have fought for freedom of thought and conscience for hundreds of years—could be so corrupted into the fascist Italian Propaganda Due (P2) Masonic lodge, involved in a number of fascist coup attempts both in Italy and throughout South America? How is it that Albert Pike—author of *Morals and Dogma*, that essential Masonic tome—could at the same time have drafted the charter for the Order of the Ku Klux Klan? This is also odd since the Nazis considered Freemasonry to be the machinery with which the Jewish conspiracy operated.

PL: By way of illustration, a little story: Pope John Paul I was leader of the Catholic Church for about a month before he was assassinated. One of his missions was to fire all members of Masonic lodges—such as P2—who were clergymen. He never got the chance. Membership in Masonic lodges was at that time (and until only recently) forbidden to Catholics; much more so to monsignors, bishops and cardinals. John Paul I felt that the widespread Masonic cult within Vatican City itself constituted a real enemy. P2 was—and remains—pitted against the power of certain elements within the Church, as were the generations of Templars and Freemasons and Illuminati down the centuries. That is not to say that these groups would have been anti-fascist or supportive of liberation movements in South America. If you'd spent any time in Italy, you would eventually realize that what constitutes a Masonic lodge there is not necessarily what you would recognize elsewhere. Specific lodges often have specific political agendas. Italy has a long history of secret societies and we probably shouldn't judge Freemasonry on the basis of P2. But you get a like-minded group of males together for whatever purpose and soon you will find that water seeks its level and what began as a Masonic lodge becomes a center for political favoritism, secret deals, a few points off a mortgage arrangement or a real estate sale ... you get the picture. Remember that one must be asked to join a lodge: this precludes signing up people who are "not like us." The corollary is that the brotherhood of that particular lodge takes on a certain complexion, a certain homogeneity. There is a authoritarian aspect to Freemasonry in that there is a hierarchical structure, a graded system of degrees, secrets that are not revealed all at once but only over a time, etc. In other words, a system of control over people. Is that a bad thing, necessarily? Should we ask the question? Today, we have very specific attitudes towards what we perceive to be fascism, totalitarianism, etc. In the 17th and 18th centuries, there was no such thing as an identifiable form of fascism. There was nationalism, and colonialism, and imperialism. And racism. And sexism. Much of this was institutionalized, of course. Did Freemasonry and Rosicrucianism arise as revolts against specific political and/or spiritual leaders? Probably. Would these movements have replaced existing power structures with ones of their own? Possibly. That is probably what happened in America in 1776. The problem for me personally with all of this is that the fashionable morality of one age becomes concretized—petrified—in the system. The high-sounding ideals of a Scottish Masonic lodge of the 18th century would not be inconsistent with the views of someone like Albert Pike, for instance. Once again, we have an underdog—this time a member of the failed Confederacy—creating a secret cult to oppose the totalitarian state of America. P2 had a specific anti-Communist agenda; it viewed the Church as soft on Communism. And what was the reverse of Communism to the post-WWII mentality? Nazism. We made the same mistake, hiring Reinhard Gehlen to run European operations for the CIA and Werner von Braun to head up our space program, etc. P2 was a continuation of politics by other means. I should point out that when Albert Pike created the Klan, all the votes were not in on the heinous nature of what the Klan supported. For many years the Klan was seen as a romantic symbol of the Old South and as a resistance movement to the greedy carpetbaggers and other scurrilous Yankees coming down from the North. For much the same reason as Nazis are emulated by certain elements of society today—the nicer uniforms, the aura of gentility and sophistication—the vanquished Southern gentlemen officers of the Confederacy were idolized. *Birth of a Nation* told us that, if Major Moseby and stories of the Grey

Ghost did not. As for the Jewish elements of Freemasonry, as with the Germans and Templarism whatever was Jewish was conveniently ignored or explained away as elements that were appropriated by the Jews from older, more authentic, sources. The Nazis that I met

How is it that Albert Pike—author of Morals and Dogma, that essential Masonic tome—could at the same time have drafted the charter for the Order of the Ku Klux Klan?

during the course of the last 20 odd years have never agreed that the Jews were the repository of any special knowledge or ability, only that they had stolen the family jewels, so to speak—which was the core of the Jewish conspiracy—and that the jewels had to be reclaimed and the Jews destroyed once and for all.

TT: Do you think that there was organized participation by Freemasons in the allied resistance in order to stamp out enemies of the craft?

PL: I don't think the resistance was organized. Probably more of a case of individual lodge members assisting each other to flee the Nazis, etc. The Masons had never organized along military lines, as did the Thule and other groups. They were not armed, or hiding guns in their temples. I think if the Nazis had had any proof of that, it would have been highly publicized. But I am sure there were Masons involved with the Marquis in France and may have formed a kind of subset within the resistance group. But that is about as far as I am willing to speculate without documentation.

TT: What do you think about the idea put forth in *Holy Blood, Holy Grail* hypothesizing that *The Protocols of the Learned Elders of Zion*, were originally a Masonic document, which was doctored by Sergei Nilus in order to foster anti-Semitism?

PL: It is possible that the Protocols are a corruption of another document; but once we go down that path how do we know what was original and what was Nilus? At one point, Nilus himself says that the *Protocols* were stolen by a woman from an influential leader of Freemasonry. (That was only one of his many stories of the background and origin of the *Protocols*; most are mutually exclusive.) It was originally entitled *Minutes of the Meeting of the World Union of Freemasons and Elders of Zion* according to Norman Cohn in his definitive *Warrant for Genocide*, which is probably the best source for anyone interested in the history of the *Protocols*. I should also mention Cohn's point that in "the 18th century the Freemasons were on the whole hostile to the Jews (and so, incidentally, were the Bavarian Illuminati)." The irony is that the Nazis (and the Russian anti-Semites responsible for the Protocols) assumed a Jewish-Masonic conspiracy. Both groups were considered secretive, clannish, self-supporting and outside the mainstream of culture; ergo, they were united in a single conspiracy. Paranoia has its own internal logic, I guess.

marize: in the 1970s a couple of Eastern Orthodox monks pulled off the biggest rare book heist in the history of the United States. It was a continuing crime, the books being taken from libraries and private collections all over the country (and, it was said, Canada and Mexico). They were finally busted, and did federal time, but most of the books were never recovered. *The Necronomicon* was part of this swag as were a lot of occult books. It was in Greek, handwritten, but the problem was that much of the Greek was unintelligible. My modest contribution to this was recognizing that some of the Greek was an attempt to pho-

I kind of like the fact that William Burroughs was into it, and wrote Simon and L. K. Barnes a letter praising it as an important spiritual breakthrough.

TT: In the book, you hint about your own involvement with the occult. What can you tell me about that? Why are you mentioned in the "Special thanks" section of *The Necronomicon*? And what's up with *The Necronomicon*, anyway? I always thought it was something that Lovecraft had made up, but the preface to the one edited by L. K. Barnes states that it was brought to him by some guy named Simon in a briefcase containing "additional material on *The Necronomicon* which provided his bona fides." He also says that the briefcase contained "correspondence from various Balkan embassies." This I at first took with a grain of salt but after seeing your name in the special thanks section I grew curious.

PL: My involvement was on the translation side. I've been around occult groups in New York since the late '60s. I was a friend of Herman Slater of the old Warlock Shop in Brooklyn Heights before it moved to Manhattan and became Magickal Childe. I was around during the famous Witch Wars of the '70s, when it seemed that everyone was casting spells on everyone else. I was there when Gardnerians and Welsh Trads and Alexandrians and Sicilian Trads sat down around a table in the back of Herman's shop to settle the War and make peace once and for all. Herman had once interviewed neo-Nazis in New York in the 1960s and we had a lot of interests in common. I never joined any of the groups, that wasn't my intention or inclination—but I was a familiar face around the campfire, so to speak. My fascination has always been on the degree to which religion and occultism influence mainstream politics; *Unholy Alliance* began as an academic study of this before it turned into a Nazi history. As for *The Necronomicon*, it was part of stash of stolen books. The story is told, I think, in other places and I have been asked this before—also on the Internet—so to sum-

neticize Babylonian and Sumerian words. I am not one of the people arguing that this *Necronomicon* is THE *Necronomicon*, or that Lovecraft was even aware that it existed. I think Lovecraft heard the name through one of his friends in the Golden Dawn, and used it creatively. If the Simon *Necronomicon* is a hoax, I think it would have been better done and more closely followed the Cthulhu Mythos. I kind of like the fact that William Burroughs was into it, and wrote Simon and L. K. Barnes a letter praising it as an important spiritual breakthrough. ☓

Endnotes

1. Parsons later killed himself in an accident involving fulminate of mercury. He had been driven crazy and proclaimed himself the Anti-Christ after becoming involved with one "Frater H," who was actually a spy sent by Naval Intelligence to infiltrate the O.T.O. That spy's name was L.Ron Hubbard!
2. There have been no more successful, more dramatically impressive spies than a group of Englishmen who all met at Trinity College, Cambridge University in the 1930s. To one degree or another, they were active for the Soviet Union for over thirty years. They were the most efficient espionage agents against American and British interests of any collection of spies in the 20th century. One of them, Kim Philby, served the KGB for almost 50 years. (Crimelibrary.com)
3. Pierre Plantard was the Priory of Sion's Grand Master from 1981 until his resignation in 1984. His interviews with the authors of *Holy Blood, Holy Grail* provided much of the source material for that book and its sequel, *The Messianic Legacy*.

THAT WHICH HAS FALLEN

"This place is terrible." This enigmatic phrase inscribed above the entryway at Rennes-le-Chateau has been the source of bafflement to many researchers. Why would any priest affix to their church a statement seemingly so at odds with the function and solemnity of a place of worship? A few observers have noted that it is actually a quote from *Genesis*, yet stop short of actually speculating on its possible meaning in this context. The actual passage (Gen. 28:17) describes an incident that happened to Jacob. He goes to sleep, resting his head upon a stone, and has a most unusual dream. In it, he sees a ladder stretching to heaven, and angels are ascending and descending upon it. When he awakes, he declares, "This place is terrible but it is the house of God and the portal to Heaven." He anoints the stone and decides that a temple should be erected on that very spot.

What seems to be the relevant aspect of the Jacob story is what he saw in his dream: angels ascending to heaven and descending from heaven. An unusual vision, to be sure. But there is another passage in Genesis that refers to angels descending from Heaven and walking on the earth. In Genesis, it says:

> "The Nephilim were on the Earth in those days—
> and also afterward—when the sons of God went
> to the daughters of men and had children by
> them, the same became mighty men who were of
> old, men of renown."

In some translations of the Bible, the word *giants* is substituted for Nephilim. But Nephilim doesn't mean giants, it means "Those who were cast down." The reference to the Nephilim is extremely brief, and would hardly seem to convey any negative connotation. The "sons of God" took the daughters of men, and gave birth to a dynasty of "mighty men... of renown." What's wrong with that?

But immediately thereafter, the Lord becomes angry with man's incessant evil and decides "to wipe humankind ... from the face of the Earth." Are we missing something? It would seem that there is much more to this story which is being left out in this telling. And indeed there is. There is an entire apocryphal text called *The Book of Enoch* which deals with the Nephilim saga in far greater depth. It is, in fact, a book wholly dedicated to the Nephilim story in all its aspects. And its importance lies not just in the fact that it seems to be a record pertaining to the details of a missing chapter of biblical history, but that it seems also to be the retelling of a story that recurs in numerous mythologies: that of a race of Gods which comes to Earth to teach man their wisdom (only to end up intermarrying with the Earth women.)

It is supposed that *The Book of Enoch* was written in the first or second century BC. There is every indication that at the time the text was regarded as a valid piece of sacred literature in its own right. The fact that it is dismissed as an "apocryphal" text is misleading. The word "apocrypha" simply implies that it's *cryptic*, and its use was intended only for the initiated. It was referred to by such figures as Ireneus and Clement of Alexandria, whom, we are told, assigned it an authenticity "analogous to that of Mosaic literature." And Tertullian called Enoch "The most ancient prophet." Archbishop Richard Laurence, who first translated *The Book of Enoch*, notes that references to the book show up in the Zohar, saying: "In this cele-

"This place is terrible but it is the house of God and the portal to Heaven."

brated compilation of what was long supposed to constitute the hidden wisdom of the Jewish nation, occasional references are made to *The Book of Enoch* as a book carefully preserved from generation to generation." Despite this, the book faded somehow into oblivion, and was not to be found in Europe for well over a thousand years. Then in 1773, a Scottish explorer named James Bruce found three copies of the text in an Abyssinian Church called the House of St. George.

Bruce brought the manuscripts back to Europe, donating one copy to the Biblioteque Nationale in Paris, and another to the Bodleian Library at Oxford. When Richard Laurence first published his translation of the text in 1821, Biblical scholars were taken aback. *The Book of Enoch* was equal in apocalyptic intensity only to *The Revelation of St. John the Divine*. It relates the story of Enoch the Prophet, a man reputed to have been the son of Cain. The story chronicles how the sons of God taught their wisdom to mankind, and in so doing, unleashed a tide of evil. It starts off with a reiteration of the Nephilim scenario, except that in this version they're called "the Watchers." As it states:

> "It happened after the sons of men had multiplied in those days, that daughters were born to them, elegant and beautiful. And when the angels, the sons of heaven beheld them, they became enamored of them, saying to each other, Come, let us select for ourselves wives from the progeny of men, and let us beget children."

So the angels, 200 in number, swore an oath to one another in a pact to take as wives the daughters of men. Such a pact essentially constituted a rebellion against heaven. This detail would represent a decisive difference between the story of Enoch's Watchers and the Nephilim of Genesis. If the Nephilim were "those who were cast down," the implication is clearly that they were expelled from Heaven, or were *fallen angels*. The Watchers, in contrast, are plainly portrayed as willfully conspiring to rebel against Heaven. Enoch continues:

> "Then they took wives, each choosing for himself; whom they began to approach, and with whom they cohabitated; teaching them sorcery, incantations... (and) all the secret things which are done in the heavens."

And herein lies what seems to have been the real sin of the Watchers: to have shared "powerful secrets" with mankind, because "men were not born for this." Each of the leaders of the Watchers taught some specialized field of knowledge, such as astronomy, the manufacture of goods, the dying of textiles, and so on. And certainly, while the teaching of such things as sorcery and astrology may have been viewed as ungodly at the time, one angel stands accused of "[teaching] men to understand writing, and the use of ink and paper." This is odd, because elsewhere Enoch himself is described as a "scribe of righteousness," and is often credited with being the inventor of mathematics, writing, and astronomy!

This book is probably a far more accurate record of how the Watchers were *perceived* than it is a reflection of who they *were* or what they *did*.

The great crime of the Watchers was to teach wisdom to mankind. The subtext of the book would seem to be saying that wisdom begets evil. Like the Luddite sects who felt that man's technological progress led him away from God, and created all the world's ills and iniquities, the author of *The Book of Enoch* is telling us that higher understanding was contrary to man's true nature, and resulted inevitably in woe. This book is probably a far more accurate record of how the Watchers were *perceived* than it is a reflection of who they *were* or what they *did*. It is axiomatic that people fear and mistrust those who know more than they do, or wield more power. And it's also a given that people fear and resist the kind of change that accompanies knowledge and new ideas. This, by all accounts, is precisely what the Watchers brought to the ancients. We can see echoes of precisely this same sort of fearful attitude, in more modern times, in the account of certain tribes in Africa who were observed practicing a kind of negative eugenics. When a researcher watching from a hidden position in a bush saw a tribesman put to death a perfectly healthy child for seemingly no reason at all, he questioned the motive for their act. They replied that every so often a child was born who was too beautiful, too curious, or too intelligent, and it was simply understood that such people would eventually be the source of problems. Any individual who at so young an age was demonstrably brighter than his peers would inevitably grow up to promote ideas at variance with tradition. Such people create change, sow seeds of discord, and upset the equilibrium of the community, and such behavior constitutes a grave threat to the survival of the group as a cohesive whole. Consequently, dealing with the problem at the earliest possible time was not only prudent, it was a necessity.

In ancient times, wisdom was synonymous with power; and power, especially for those who don't possess it, is more often than not perceived to be synonymous with *oppression*. Indeed, the Watchers were accused of such when it was written, "Let every oppressor perish from the face of the earth; Destroy... the offspring of the Watchers, for they have tyrannized over mankind." As is common in apocalyptic Jewish texts, the oppressors are ascribed mythic attributes. In *The Book of Enoch*, the offspring of the Watchers are described as a race of giants who "devoured all which the labor of men produced; until it became impossible to feed them; when they turned against men in order to devour them." They consumed birds and fish, "devouring their flesh one after another and drinking their blood." This sounds like the highly exaggerated claim of any peasant anywhere, who watches his rulers feast on fatted calves while he and his family must subsist on porridge. But that said, we must keep in mind what many major religions assert, which is that there was indeed a time when giants walked the Earth. Why would diverse and widely separated traditions all make the same outrageous claim unless it had some basis in truth? Or more to the point: if it weren't true, what are the odds that all these traditions would concoct the same lie?

It must be remembered that the *Book of Enoch* was the first major text to be written after the Jews' Babylonian captivity, and we can clearly see the emergence of the influence of the Zoroastrian ideas which they assimilated at that time. We see a more clearly defined dichotomy between notions of good and evil, the elect and the unrighteous. Before Enoch, the Lord was both Good Cop and Bad Cop—alternatively blessing and punishing, loved and feared. The devil was, if anything, a bit player in the drama. But in the Watchers we can see an emerging prototype of Satan, the adversary. And too, we can see a variation on the theme of original sin. Just as with Eve and the forbidden fruit, the sin of the Watchers involved a specific combination of infractions, having to do with both disobedience, and *knowledge*.

In ancient times, wisdom was synonymous with power; and power, especially for those who don't possess it, is more often than not perceived to be synonymous with oppression.

If one were to look behind the mythic elements of the story of the Watchers, any number of more purely historical facsimiles of the events described seem to present themselves. What interests us is the persistence of the myth itself: the ongoing story of a race of gods and their descendants, who somehow come to be perceived as Luciferian. Often such figures are associated with water,

the sea, or the Flood. At times they are presented as dwellers within the Earth (and often in connection with this, as giants). Some say that the Watchers themselves were imprisoned within the Earth, while *The Book of Enoch* places great emphasis on the notion that a flood was sent "so that their seed would perish from the Earth." The question as to whether or not that seed did in fact perish is one of contention, because there is an interesting (and altogether perplexing) addendum to the tale.

Enoch's son Mathusala took a wife for his son Lamach. The text reads:

> "She became pregnant by him and brought forth a child, the flesh of which was white as snow, and red as a rose; the hair of whose head was white as wool, and long; and whose eyes were beautiful. When he opened them, he illuminated all the house, like the sun; the whole house abounded with light." Fearing something was seriously amiss, Lamach went to Mathusala, and told him: "I have begotten a son unlike to other children. He is not human, but resembling the offspring of Heaven, is of a different nature, being altogether unlike us. His eyes are bright as the rays of the sun; his countenance glorious, and he looks not as if he belongs to me, but to the angels."

Lamach entreated Mathusala to go to Enoch, who was "with the angels," and find out the truth about his unusual child. At length, Enoch was located "at the extremities of the Earth," and apprised of the situation. Enoch reassured him that, "the child which is born is [Lamach's] child in truth; and there is no deception." But strangely, he hastened to add that, "his posterity shall beget on the earth giants." Then he foretold of a great flood that would bring destruction to all the Earth—except for Lamach's son.

> "This child which is born to you shall survive on the Earth, and his sons shall be saved with him. When all mankind who are on the earth die, he shall be safe. And his posterity shall beget on the earth giants, not spiritual, but carnal. Now therefore inform thy son Lamach that he who is born is his child in truth; and he shall call his name Noah, for he shall be to you a survivor."

What are we to make of this bizarre addendum? Its chief elements are highly contradictory, and simply don't add up in the context of the rest of the Watcher's saga. Are we to conclude that the child, although in no way similar-seeming to Lamach, is indeed *his*? Or that the fact that his child is foretold to sire a race of giants has no particular significance? Or are we to infer that Noah was in fact a descendant of the seed of the Watchers—that indeed Enoch himself was one of the Watchers? Enoch, after all, is said to be the inventor of math, writing and astronomy, the very bits of knowledge the Watchers had been guilty of sharing with humans. Enoch himself stated, "I am acquainted with the holy mysteries, which the Lord himself has discovered and explained to me; and which I have read in the tablets of heaven." If the sharing of such "powerful secrets" was a sin for the Watchers and their progeny, why could Enoch engage in the same pursuit with impunity? Though the true nature of Enoch's relation to the Watchers is deliberately left out of the Book of Enoch, it becomes self-evident when we examine the Hebrew word for those descended from the Nephilim: the Anakim. Just as "Elohim" implies the descendants of God, so "Anakim" implies the descendants of Anak—that is to say, the descendants of Enoch. So *The Book of Enoch*, while outwardly masquerading as an indictment of the Watchers, was really intended as a vehicle in which to encode their great secret: that Enoch himself was a descendant of fallen

monster who resides in the ocean, and is *female*. The apocryphal Acts of Thomas characterizes Leviathan as a dragon who lives beyond "the waters of the Abyss," and says that he is *"king of the worms of the Earth, whose tail lies in his mouth. This is the serpent that led astray through passions the angels from on high; this is the serpent that lead astray the first Adam and expelled him from Paradise."* Elsewhere in the *Acts*, one of the sons of Leviathan states that he is, *"the offspring of the serpent-nature and a corruptor's son. I am the son of he who ... sits on the throne and has dominion over the creation beneath the heavens... who encircles the sphere ... who is around the ocean, whose tail is in his mouth."* A similar theme shows up in the *Pistis Sophia*, in which it is said that, *"The outer darkness is a huge dragon, whose tale is in its mouth."* This seems fairly emblematic of the consensus opinion regarding the character of Leviathan, with the notable exception of *The Book of Enoch*, which speaks of, *"a female monster, whose name is Leviathan, dwelling in the depths of the sea, above the springs of waters..."* *The Revelation of St. John the Divine* also equates

Like many books of the Bible, The Book of Enoch is laced with contradictions.

angels, and that his progeny would constitute what he referred to as "the elect." Like many books of the Bible, *The Book of Enoch* is laced with contradictions. Indeed, all of myth contains an element of contradiction, ambiguity and paradox. Perhaps that is central to the mechanism of how myth functions. If we understood its component details in a more straightforward way, we would no doubt be denied the experience of its essence at a more primal level. The fundamental truth that we take away from the myths of the Nephilim and the Watchers is that they seem to be very much in accord with certain basic stories related in myths pertaining to the Merovingians. Though differing in detail, the elemental similarities far overshadow the more superficial dissimilarities. And despite the differences apparent in their outward form, they would essentially appear to constitute an identical tradition, albeit clothed in the symbolism of another time and culture.

The primary symbolism that recurs persistently in connection to the Merovingians is that of dragons, serpents, the sea, and sea serpents. The most well known dragon or sea serpent is undoubtedly the biblical Leviathan. It is very probably patterned after a much more ancient sea god, and although its mythology is far less cohesive than its earlier prototypes, it nonetheless holds some tantalizing clues in relation to the Merovingians. In some versions of the tale, Leviathan is described as a dragon who encircles the Earth, biting his tail, and is said to represent the "world soul." In *The Book of Enoch*, Leviathan is described as a

Leviathan with the sea. Why a dragon, whether dwelling in the sea or encircling the Earth, should be synonymous with the serpent of *Genesis*, or evolve into a generic term for the devil is somewhat perplexing; yet the connection is undeniable. And in the statement from the *Acts of Thomas* attributed to a son of Leviathan, he seems to be equating his father with the Demiurge (Le Roi du Monde—Lucifer.) This is intriguing, because another context in which Leviathan shows up in one of the world's most recognizable satanic symbols. In the depiction of Baphomet as a goat's head within a pentagram, the Hebrew characters at each of the star's five points spell *Leviathan*. And the pentagram is a symbol central to the Merovingian saga. It figures prominently in the Rennes-le-Chateau mystery, it was used by the Cathars, it was encoded in the works by Poussin and Cocteau, and continues to be a key symbol for groups such as the Freemasons. Some scholars even maintain that the pentagram, and not the hexagram, is the true Star of David. Such an assertion seems imminently agreeable, since the symbol generically referred to as the Star of David is more widely known to occultists as the Seal of Solomon, and why would two different designations not infer that two different symbols in fact existed?

Further, the pentagram seems an appropriate emblem for the House of David, because it is said to be representative of the secret doctrine of the antediluvian gods who taught their wisdom to mankind. Could it not also signify the living remnant of the seed of that antediluvian race of gods, the descendants of which were the House of David, and later the Merovingians? If such a supposition were true, it's easy to see why such a symbol (as well as the doctrine and race it represented) might have been viewed by the ancients as signifying something demonic. Consequently, the pentagram, which may well have been a straightforwardly Davidic symbol, evolved over the years into a purely occult icon. It continued to be a symbol of central significance to the descendants of David, but their use of it was restricted ever more increasingly to more *sub rosa*, encoded manifestations. Even centuries later, the five-petaled rose would be a prominent monarchistic device, and this symbol was well known in occult circles as code for the pentagram.

So, key elements of the Merovingian mythos come together in the sea, the pentagram, and Leviathan. But Leviathan was only associated with the sea in some versions of the myth, while in others his place was in "the outer darkness." Such seeming contradictions dissolve when you realize that for the ancients, the sea and the heavens were often conceptualized as one and the same. The vast reaches of the night sky, of space, were viewed as another kind of sea—an ocean in which the terrestrial realm was afloat. And more modern observers, taking this conception as a point of departure, have gone so far as to advance the theory that in ancient times, the world may in fact have been surrounded by a vast watery firmament which was held aloft via centrifugal force. Far-fetched though such assertions may seem, they constituted the thesis of a worldwide bestseller, Ignatius Donnelly's *Atlantis: The Antediluvian World*. Such a circumstance, according to Donnelly, would explain why the ancients perceived the heavens to be synonymous with the sea. And, according to the theory, this could have created a vastly different climate on Earth; one which could have allowed men to live much longer than current conditions (i.e., life spans akin to those recorded in the Bible.) This, too, could account for the Deluge, recorded in countless mythologies. If some cataclysm of gargantuan proportions had occurred to disrupt the watery firmament, the resulting disturbance could have caused a global flood. Bizarre though such a theory may be, it turned Donnelly into an international celebrity in the 1800s, and his counsel was sought by both Presidents and European royals. Though by modern standards, Donnelly's ideas would be dismissed as crackpot theories, in his day they were viewed as a *scientific* explanation of Biblical events.

Insofar as mythical sea creatures are concerned, Leviathan is not the sole example, nor even the principal example. We look to the pantheon of sea gods due to the fact that there is scant documentation in regard to Meroveus or Merovee. We can only conclude that the name Meroveus is a Latinized variation of a more primordial incarnation of a god who embodied the same attributes; that the word Meroveus is simply a term meaning "born of the sea." Meroveus was said to be the spawn of a mythical creature called a Quinotaur, a god whose form was part man, part fish. None of the preeminent encyclopedias of mythology contain any mention of such a creature, nor can any specialists in the fields of the occult or mythology whom we've contacted remember having ever heard of this entity. And references to Meroveus prove to be very nearly non-existent. We'd often wondered why those researching the Merovingians and/or the Grail mystery had simply glossed over this aspect of the saga, one which (it seemed to us) could perhaps reveal some vital clue to the whole affair. We'd assumed that they had dismissed the Meroveus story as being pure mythology, and therefore irrelevant. But perhaps the lack of coverage given the Meroveus saga was due more to a paucity of concrete information.

Given what we'd seen at Rennes-le-Chateau, we had reason to believe that Meroveus and the story of the Quinotaur constituted some fundamental clue that was possibly central to the whole mystery. Over and over again we'd seen symbolism relating to the sea and water. There was the Mary Magdalen grotto, constructed out of *coral* (a material not in great abundance in a town hours from the sea by car). There were figures such as Asmodeus and John the Baptist, both bearing seashells. There was the depiction, central to the altar in the church, of the Grail chalice, being born aloft on waves of water. And there was an archway near the Calvaire, also made of coral. Such symbolism was so incongruous, and yet obviously so purposeful, that we were sure it had to signify something.

When we asked the Rennes-le-Chateau tour guide where the coral for the grotto and archway had come from, she informed us that Sauniere had excavated it himself from a riverbed in a nearby town. He'd carried it back to the domain in a sack on his back—a sack such as those used by grape pickers in local vineyards. Such an explanation seems straightforward enough at first hearing, until one considers that there *aren't* any towns "nearby." In Sauniere's day, a trip to the nearest town, back and forth on foot, lugging rocks uphill in one direction, would surely have constituted a day's journey, at least. And given the amount of coral used in the construction of the grotto alone, Sauniere would have had to make such a journey dozens of times.

While we know that coral cannot generally be found in freshwater riverbeds hundreds of miles from the sea, we found ample evidence to indicate that this whole region was once underwater. Just outside our mountaintop hotel we found huge rocks such as those only seen at the seaside, and what were clearly seashells half-protruding from the mud. It seemed conceivable that there might also be ancient coral formations in the vicinity as well. The tour guide seemed fairly confident about the details of her story—the name of the town and the river, and that

In ancient reliefs, Dagon is depicted as a man dressed as a fish.

Sauniere had traveled there and back on foot, and so on. But whether Sauniere had gotten the materials from somewhere in the region or had journeyed all the way to the Riviera, the same conclusion was inescapable. He'd gone to an incredible amount of trouble to procure this specific building material, and it had to be in order to communicate a specific idea: that of *the sea*.

The tradition of sea gods is as ancient as that of sun gods. And just as sun gods were often depicted as having the head or body of a bird, so the sea gods were represented as being part fish. The sea was a potent symbol in ancient times. Water was viewed as a substance that represented a kind of intermediary plane between the terrestrial realm and the celestial. Heaven was above the waters, Earth below. Mythical creatures associated with water or the sea were seen, then, to exist between two planes, *or on two planes at once*: the physical and the spiritual. Such creatures were emblematic of the divine spirit having descended into matter, the flesh. This is what Simon Magus referred to when he described the two aspects of the One. One aspect was *above*, in "the unbegotten power," the other *below*, "in the stream of waters, begotten in the image." Images of water and the sea recur frequently in biblical texts, apocryphal texts, and Gnostic texts. Biblical names such as Mary and Miriam both derive from the Latin word for the sea. Mary was the name both of Christ's mother, and his consort Mary Magdalen. And of crucified Messiahs known to the ancient world, no less than seven had mothers whose names were Mary (or some derivation thereof). Are we to conclude that this fact represents a bizarre coincidence, or that the sea was in fact a powerful symbol to the ancients, one whose meaning has grown obscure through the passage of time? And too, are we to conclude that within the context of the Merovingians, the sea was purely emblematic of an existence straddling two planes, or could it also be a reference to something far more tangible as well?

While the figure of the Quinotaur (for the time being) remained somewhat elusive at best, evidence of similar sea gods seems suggestive of a Merovingian connection.

The most compelling in this regard is Dagon. The very name is suggestive of *dragon*, a creature much associated with the Merovingians. It is also highly suggestive of Dago-bert, one of the most legendary of the Merovingian rulers. And the Dagon/Dragon/Dagobert association becomes even further compounded by the fact that King Dagobert was recorded by some chroniclers as being called King *Drago*bert.

In reference to Dagon, Dragons and the sea, Albert Pike tells us:

> "The Dragon was a well-known symbol of the waters, and of great rivers; and it was natural that... the powerful nations of the alluvial plains... who adored the dragon or the fish, should themselves be symbolized under the form of dragons."

And later:

> "Ophioneous, in the old Greek mythology, warred against Kronos... and was cast into his proper element, the sea. There he is installed as the Sea God ... Dagon, the Leviathan of the watery half of creation."

In ancient reliefs, Dagon is depicted as a man dressed as a fish. He looks stern, somber, and has the authoritative bearing of a priest or king. He wears a massive fish head as a hat, and the fish's scaly hide hangs down his back. The shape of the fish head and the contours of its mouth, pointed skyward, are suggestive of the mitre worn by the Pope and other officials of the Catholic church; and indeed, some maintain that the genesis of such regalia may date back to this time. So, likewise, may the fish imagery affiliated with orthodox Christianity. The fish symbol associated with Christ comes from the Greek "Ichtus," meaning "fish." This word, in turn, is formed of the first letters of each word from the Greek phrase "Jesus Christ, God—Son—Savior." According to legend, Dagon was a god who came from out of the sea to teach mankind the secrets of civilization, such as science, agriculture, and the arts (sound familiar?) Yet again (and in an altogether different context), we encounter the recurring tale of the being who comes from another realm to teach humanity evolutionary wisdom.

In another version of the same tale, Dagon is called Annedotus. He too emerges from the sea to disperse great secrets to mankind. But there is an important variation to the story: Annedotus begets a race who become the teachers of mankind, the Annedoti. Note the similarity

Oannes The Fish God/Man

to the names that appear in a Semitic Sumerian myth very much of the same ilk. In this telling, the god Anu comes to Earth, bringing knowledge, and sires a race called the Annunaki; except, according to Zecharia Sitchin, Anu was from outer space, and his descendants, the Annunaki, were half-human, half-alien. Sitchin's interpretation notwithstanding, this seems to be yet another recapitulation of the same myths, varying only in detail. Our hypothesis, in this regard, seems to be borne out by the assertions of some Sumeriologists who say that "Annunaki" is simply a term meaning "Lords of the Deep Waters." Annunaki is also obviously a variation of the previously discussed "Anakim." Therefore, if the Annunaki are descendants of Anu, and Anakim are the descendants of Enoch, Anu is undoubtedly a Mesopotamian variation of the same historical figure.

Another sea god associated with both Dagon and Annedotus was Oannes, a deity part-man, part-fish, who appeared "from that part of the Erythrean sea which borders on Babylon." He too imparted great knowledge to the ancients, and gave them:

> "...insight into the letters and sciences and arts of every kind. He taught them to construct cities, to found temples, to compile laws, and explained to them the principles of geometrical knowledge.

He made them distinguish the seeds of the Earth, and showed them how to collect the fruits. In short, he instructed them in everything which could tend to soften manners and humanize their lives. From that time, nothing has been added by way of improvement to their lives." (Berossus.)

According to legend, Oannes spent the day among men, passing down his teachings, but when the sun set, he "retired again into the sea, passing the night in the deep, *for he was amphibious.*" According to the Theosophical Glossary, this simply implied that Oannes:

> "...belonged to two planes: the spiritual and the physical. For the Greek word *amphibios* means simply 'life on two planes'... The word was often applied in antiquity to those men who, though still wearing a human form, had made themselves almost divine through knowledge, and lived as much in the spiritual, supersensuous regions as on Earth."

In other words, the man/fish symbolism relates to what was perceived as Oannes' dual nature, part human, part divine and mythic. Such an idea is confirmed when we look to a later incarnation of Oannes as the Roman god Janus. By such time, the sea symbolism had vanished, and his dual nature was depicted in the form of two faces. In an interesting footnote, Oannes is also the figure from whom we derive the names Jonah and John (via Johannes), two Biblical figures equally associated with the imagery of water.

The Oannes/Dagon/Nephilim theme appears to show up elsewhere in Greek mythology in the story of the Titans.

The Oannes/Dagon/Nephilim theme appears to show up elsewhere in Greek mythology in the story of the Titans. The Titans were a race of gods who, like the offspring of the Watchers, were giants. When the primordial god Ouranos (a permutation of Oannes) had an incestuous liaison with his mother, Gaia, she gave birth to twelve giants, the Titans. When the powerful race of Titans rebelled against the authority of the parental gods, Zeus cast them into the abyss, imprisoning them in the underworld. Ouranos may be connected to the idea of the ouroburos, the watery Leviathan discussed earlier. And the Titans are obviously connected to the Tritons, a race of gods spawned by Poseidon and Amphitrite. Rather than being giants, the Tritons were hybrid fish-men. Also of interest in regard to Poseidon is that he was alternately called Poseidaon, and Dagon was also called *Daonos*. Another title of Dagon was Daos, which is so similar in sound to words such as "deus," "dios" and so forth that our primary words for deity may well have had their genesis in this strange fish-god.

In Plato's *Critias*, it is evident that the Titans and the Tritons are one and the same. They are the offspring of Poseidon and a mortal woman, and are giants. The story told is very much that of the Watchers, with a key difference. Here, it is the human element of their nature that leads to their corruption and ultimate downfall.

> *"For many generations, as long as the divine nature lasted in them, they were obedient to the laws, and well-affectioned toward the gods, who were their kinsmen... but when the divine portion began to fade away in them, and became diluted too often, and with too much of the mortal admixture... human nature got the upper hand, then, they being unable to bear their fortune, became unseemly, and to him who had eyes to see, they began to appear base, and had lost the fairest of their precious gifts; but to those who had no eye to see the true happiness, they still appeared glorious and blessed at the very time when they were filled with unrighteous avarice and power. Zeus, the god of gods, who rules with law, and is able to see into such things, perceiving that an honorable race was in a most wretched state, and wanting to inflict punishment on them, that they might be chastened and improved, collected all the gods into his most holy habitation, which, being placed in the center of the world, sees all things that partake of generation. And when he had called them all together he spake as follows..."*

Unfortunately, we'll never know what Zeus said, as Plato's manuscript ends abruptly at this point.

The tale related in *Critias* is interesting not only for its striking similarities to other such stories we've examined, but also for the glaring *dissimilarities*. Rather than casting the gods into the abyss "for all time," Zeus merely imprisons them in "his most holy habitation." Rather than wanting to "wipe their seed from the face of the Earth," Zeus merely wants to see them "chastened and improved." And their sin was due not to any willful rebellion against God (or the gods), but was a byproduct of miscegenation with humans; which led to their divine nature being overshadowed by the human. There are hints of this in *The Book of Enoch*, wherein the mortal wives of the Watchers seem literally to be blamed for "defiling" the angels. Plato's version of the Titan/Triton tale seems almost to end on a hopeful note, as though the chance exists that the gods might possibly be reformed somehow. There are numerous permutations of this saga. The names of the gods and the details of the story vary quite a bit in the different tellings. In some versions, one of the sons of Poseidon is Dagon.

Oftentimes when Oannes or Dagon are referred to in print, the same picture is used to depict them both. It's a photograph of an Assyrian relief, showing a man wearing a fish's head as a hat. The figure portrayed is plainly a man, and the fish regalia he's wearing clearly seems to be some form of ceremonial garb. He seems to be perhaps a priest or a king, and it's quite evident that no one at the time this relief was carved had any illusions that he was in any way a sea creature. On the contrary, he was clearly a man invoking the symbolism of the sea in order to align himself in the public mind with whatever symbolic connotations such an archetype would have embodied at that time.

Scholars seem to concur that Oannes, Dagon, and Annedotus are merely different names which all refer to essentially the same mythological character. And yet the Assyrian relief would seem to contradict such a premise. It would seem to bear a kind of mute testimony to the possibility that all three of the aforementioned figures may have had their genesis in what was at one time a real historical personage. In the modern era, we have witnessed even trivial pop culture figures take on a mythic character, morphing from mere singers or actors into figures of an almost religious veneration. We have witnessed the proliferation of urban legends, bizarre tales that are patently untrue and baseless, yet inspire widespread belief. And we have seen (repeatedly) people adapt fanatical beliefs which contradict all the well-established facts relating to exceedingly well-documented public events. (For instance: those who say Elvis is alive, O.J. Simpson was framed, and so on.) All this we have seen in our own lifetime, and in an age supposedly defined by realism and skepticism, an age in which every public event is documented in such thorough detail that even those with an intense interest in the subject become bored, and even those not paying attention know more about the topic than they care to. If we can observe such a dissonance between fact and myth, truth and belief, in our own time, imagine the inherent possibilities of such a process in an age ruled by superstition, in which information was passed on by means of an oral tradition.

It is probably safe to assume that the symbolism associated with Dagon and Oannes was at one time perceived as straightforward, and was readily understood by those who first heard their stories. With the passage of time, as such tales spread to other lands and other peoples, the meaning became lost, and what was once pure symbolism was taken at face value. Remember, when early Babylonians and Egyptians saw a depiction of a man with a hawk's head, they in no way imagined that it represented

In the modern era, we have witnessed even trivial pop culture figures take on a mythic character, morphing from mere singers or actors into figures of an almost religious veneration.

an entity part human, part-bird. They understood that the hawk was a symbol of the sun, and that this composite of man/bird was intended to infer a special relationship to the sun, or to the god symbolized by the sun.

The earliest kings of which we know were deified kings: god-kings. They were identified with both fire and water, the sun and the sea. They had solar titles, and lunar titles. If Dagon and Oannes were once historical figures, they were probably among the descendants of such a line of god-kings. And if such a thesis were true, they undoubtedly had possessed a greater than usual association with the water element, with the sea. In fact, certain of these kings were so thoroughly identified with the sea that they are actually remembered as sea-kings. They were the rulers of an ancient empire known as Sumeria.

Sumeria is the oldest civilization known to man. Long before Greece and Rome had attained their golden age, Sumeria was already ancient. Those in search of the roots of early history often go back to the glory days of the pharaohs of Egypt, yet Egypt too was in its infancy at a time when Sumeria had long been the center of the world. For all intents and purposes, Sumeria seems to have entered the world stage as a high civilization. It wasn't there, and then suddenly it was—complete with arts, sciences, astronomy, navigation, agriculture, and all the complexities of a highly-evolved culture. All of which leaves the modern observer to ponder exactly how such a society could appear out of nowhere and nothing into such a fully-realized entity, seemingly instantaneously. The elements that define a high culture evolve slowly and incrementally over a vast expanse of time. One can't learn to run without first knowing how to walk, and walking begins with baby steps. Yet ancient Sumeria seems to have leap-frogged over and beyond the baby steps of civilization; a feat never since repeated in the annals of mankind. How did they do it? Their explanation is quite simple and straightforward: they were taught everything they knew by a *race of gods*.

The first king of Sumeria was also the first god of Sumeria. He was a deified king named IA, and he was known as the Lord of the Flood, or Lord of the Deep Waters. The name IA served as the basis of god-names from many other cultures, including (but not limited to) Jah, Ihah, Yahweh, Jove, Jehovah, Allah, Janus, Ianus, Uranus, Ouranos, and ...Oannes. An illustration of IA from a Sumerian seal, circa 2730 BC depicts him as a bearded figure, sitting on a throne, holding vases from which water is flowing. At his feet are more vases overflowing with streams of water, and indeed the very throne on which he is seated seems to be held aloft by water. This is interesting, because a number of passages from the Christian Bible, in describing God (and his throne) would appear to be straightforward references to this very picture of IA, the first Sumerian god-king. In *Revelation 22* it says: "And then the angel showed me the river of the waters of life, as clear as crystal, *flowing from the throne of God.*" Psalms tells us that God "gathers the waters of the sea *unto jars,*" and further that, "The Lord sits *enthroned over the Flood. The Lord is King* forever." IA was a king. He was also the Lord of the Flood. And these enigmatic passages from the Bible seem to bear testimony to the fact that the Judeo-Christian Jehovah was indeed originally patterned on the far more ancient Sumerian figure of IA. In fact, many of the major figures from the Bible can be traced back to the deified kings of Sumeria. There are figures equivalent to Adam, Cain, Enoch, and even Moses; their stories are, at times, nearly identical, and the names of the figures involved bear a striking similarity to their biblical counterparts. There is the first man Adamu, a locale called Eden, the story of the Flood, and the tale of the child placed into a boat of reeds and set adrift on a river. The correspondences are so self-evident as to speak for themselves. But we are less interested in the myriad correspondences between the Sumerians and biblical history than we are in the possible clues ancient Sumeria might yield in regard to some of the

IA on his watery throne

Many of the major figures from the Bible can be traced back to the deified kings of Sumeria. There are figures equivalent to Adam, Cain, Enoch, and even Moses; their stories are, at times, nearly identical, and the names of the figures involved bear a striking similarity to their biblical counterparts.

more enigmatic aspects of the Merovingian saga vis-à-vis the Grail family. And the first clue is to be found in the depiction of the god-king IA described previously.

IA, dressed in flowing robe and crown, is seated on his throne before an audience of several people bedecked in ceremonial garb. The audience members could represent royal personages of different nations in their native dress, or they could merely be his priests or functionaries. In his right hand, IA holds aloft a vase from which water gushes forth. Emerging from the vase, and from the springs of water flowing out, we see what can clearly only be described as a fleur-de-lys. During the Middle Ages, the *fleur-de-lys* was the primary emblem of French royalty. It is to be seen in abundance on the heraldry of French and latter British royalty. It was a symbol essentially synonymous with France. And it is a symbol that pervades the church at Rennes-le-Chateau, more perhaps than the Christian cross. Most people would probably assume that an emblem so closely linked to the French identity probably arose at a time when the old French territories were coalescing into a cohesive national entity. And yet this depiction of a fleur-de-lys arising from water can be dated to 2,730 years before the birth of Christ!

Some scholars tell us that the fleur-de-lys is the stylized representation of a lily, a symbol associated with King David. Thus, the fleur-de-lys was employed as an emblem of Davidic descent. But the depiction of King IA predates King David by close to two millennia, and the rendering itself is from a period far later than IA's actual kingship. All we can reasonably surmise is that the fleur-de-lys, or lily, seems to have been an emblem of kingship dating back to the earliest period of recorded history of which we know. The clear implication would seem to be that if, as some scholars maintain, the fleur-de-lys is symbolic of a specific royal bloodline, then the Merovingians (and indeed, much of European royalty) can trace their descent back to a figure who was both the first known king, and the first known god.

IA was known as the Lord of the Flood or the Lord of the Deep Waters because he was the first post-diluvian king, and because his arrival in Sumeria coincided with the cessation of the Flood. He was said to have come from "beyond the sea" or even "out of the sea." In some versions of his myth, he descended from the heavens, and had

been appointed, as God's earthly counterpart, to be the "shepherd of mankind." In the Babylonian/Akkadian tradition he was called Ea, and was depicted as a god who was part-man, part-fish. Instead of the title Lord of the Flood, he was known to the Babylonians/Akkadians as "God of the Abyss." The Chaldeans knew him as Ea, and they too depicted him on their monuments as half-man, half-fish.

These varying traditions, so very similar and so fundamentally different, seem almost emblematic of the sort of paradox so central to the entire Merovingian mythos. While they all relate what is clearly a story pertaining to a single figure, and while the stories all obviously originated from a single source, each nonetheless possesses key elements which are *not* in agreement with one another. And yet, even the most seemingly contradictory elements of each version aren't necessarily inconsistent with any aspect of the Merovingian saga. We have a king descended from a god. That fits perfectly. We have a God associated with the sea, who is part-man, part-fish. That fits perfectly. We have stories of this god or king alternately coming from the heavens, out of the ocean, or from "the Abyss." Any of the foregoing scenarios would find numerous points of convergence with some key aspects of the Merovingian mythology.

Nineteenth century author Ignatius Donnelly has offered what might be a very straightforward explanation for the heaven/sea/abyss conundrum. According to him, the ancients perceived the lands beyond where the sun set in the west to be the underworld. Beyond the horizon existed a land of the dead, where the sun sank each day to die. Thus people could very well have been seen to be coming from the underworld, or the abyss. Conversely, people coming from beyond the horizon where the sun was reborn each dawn may have been perceived as coming forth from the heavens. And either group, coming from a land which was unseen or *unknown* to the indigenous population could very possibly have been viewed as coming out of the ocean itself. This makes sense. The ancient Sumerian kings are known as *sea kings* because they were legendary navigators. Millennia before Columbus, these sea kings had already mapped most of the world's continents.

In more recent history, white men appearing in South America were perceived as gods. Could not a people existing in the far more distant past have reached a similar conclusion about a strange race coming from beyond the distant horizon? We know from Sumerian records that this race of gods taught them about astronomy, which is fundamental to navigating the sea. And if this race first appeared following a great deluge, would it not make sense that they would appear on ships—ships in which they themselves escaped the very same massive flood? IA is, after all, the Lord of the Flood, synonymous in the minds of the Sumerians with the cataclysm which preceded his arrival. This brings us back to the drawing of IA in which he holds aloft a vase with a fleur-de-lys rising from the flowing water. If the fleur-de-lys is indeed emblematic of a royal bloodline, could not this depiction be a symbolic representation of the survival of that bloodline, rising from out of the floodwaters? If so, it would explain much of the water-based imagery pertinent to the Merovingians. One of the central images on the altar of the church at Rennes-le-Chateau is a very idiosyncratic depiction of the Grail cup. At first glance it appears straightforward enough, and yet it is highly unorthodox, because it shows the Grail chalice being born aloft on what appear to be *the waters of the Flood*. That the Grail cup is shown floating on water would be unusual in itself. But it is not merely floating calmly on still waters; the waters depicted are decidedly turbulent. This, taken in conjunction with the other ocean-based imagery to be found at Rennes-le-Chateau, convinced us that the sea played some important role in regards to this mystery. Perhaps, in the Lord of the Flood, we have found an important link in the chain; a clue that will place the whole mystery in a far broader context than the mere story of Jesus Christ and Mary Magdalen. Christ and the Magdalen are, after all, only bit players in what is plainly a far greater drama. And although they may be the best-remembered players, those who came before them and after them may have far greater things to tell us.

Writers examining the lives of Christ and Mary Magdalen in search of clues to the Grail mystery have been left with more questions than answers. And those going over the Bible with a fine-toothed comb have come up equally empty-handed. Undoubtedly the reason for this is due to the fact that the Holy Grail has virtually nothing to do with Christianity per se. Christ may have been a key figure in a long line of servants of the Grail, but its legacy is not to be found within the context of the religion founded in his name. Not a single one of the crucial clues relating to the Grail mystery can be satisfactorily explained in terms of orthodox Christianity. Indeed, it would appear that the Grail story was Christianized precisely to conceal a legacy that was wholly unchristian. It is a legacy that goes back to IA, and the mysterious race of which he was a descendant.

If the traditional Grail story a la Eschenbach, *et al* has little to do with the Christian tradition, that chapter of the mystery relating to the Priory of Sion, Berenger Sauniere and so on would seem to be even more distant still from it. The clues left behind seem to be far more specific in their meanings, while also appearing to be far less comprehensible in their possible relation to the story of the Grail family. What are we to make of Poussin's mysterious painting, *The Shepherds of Arcadia*? And why would such a seemingly simple little oil painting figure as such a pivotal clue? What of the bizarre secret society, the Priory of Sion? Though many dismiss it as a hoax, is it not perhaps too elaborate to be a mere hoax? Any hoax perpetrated to serve some functional end would hardly encompass such a vast variety of incomprehensible information and symbols. If, as some suggest, Pierre Plantard created the Priory out of whole cloth as an enticing little puzzle to serve his own political aspirations, he certainly failed miserably. Because if the Priory was nothing more than a clever cryptogram of his own devising, we can only say that he seems to have been far too clever for his own good. Mr. Plantard has now been dead for some time, and the puzzle that is the Priory of Sion persists in perplexing virtually all those who have attempted to unlock its mysteries. Academics, historians and occultists alike have all run into a brick wall in their efforts to unravel the enigma of the Priory of Sion. Having done so, they were unanimous in their appraisal that the Priory was undoubtedly a hoax. Consequently, that avenue of inquiry was dispensed with before even the most basic questions about it were answered satisfactorily. Questions such as: why are the Grand Masters called Navigators, or why do they adopt the name John as their title?

Although looking for answers to such questions within the Judeo-Christian tradition is fruitless, the tradition from which Judaism, Christianity, and so many other creeds prior to them emerged seems to contain quite a number of intriguing correspondences. The navigator title held by Priory of Sion's Grand Masters is an allusion to Sumeria's sea kings, who were legendary as navigators. Of these, the most known were the Akkadians. And Akkadians were obviously being referred to in Poussin's *The Shepherds of Arcadia*. Sumeria's sea kings were known as shepherds, a term that meant both "protector" and "shining one." Remember, their first king was said to have come from "the heavens" to serve as "*shepherd* of mankind." And the Sumerian god-king identified with Dagon was, in some records, referred to simply as the Shepherd. *The Shepherds of Arcadia*, then, can be seen as the god-kings of Akkadia; a royal dynasty of ancient Sumeria. But this is just one level of meaning, and as with so many things central to this mystery, Poussin's painting contains multiple layers of meaning.

It is well documented that *The Shepherds of Arcadia* contains a hidden pentagram, the center point of which falls exactly on the forehead of the shepherdess. The pentagram has a dual meaning, representing simultaneously both the forgotten race from which the Grail bloodline descended and that race's secret doctrine. One meaning is to be found in the Akkadia of ancient Sumeria, another in the Arcadia of ancient Greece. In Sumeria, where the pentagram originated, its pictographic image symbolized the "shining ones" or "lofty ones," terms used in reference to the deified kings. In Arcadia, the pentagram was synonymous with the secret gnosis that Hermes was said to have preserved from a race of antediluvian gods. Hermes was said to have been born in the mountains of Arcadia. Poussin's painting purports to depict Arcadia. Hermes was the patron deity of graves *and* of shepherds. So we have a painting depicting *Arcadia*, a *tomb*, and a group of *shepherds*. The clear implication is that the secret doctrine being alluded to is the royal art known as Hermeticism. And in fact, the connection between Hermeticism and the fallen angels seems to constitute a long-standing tradition. Julius Evola tells us: "Tertullian says that the ... works of nature, the secrets of metals, the virtues of plants, the forces of magical conjurations, and 'all those alien teachings that make up the science of the stars'—that is to say, the whole corpus of the ancient magico-hermetic sciences was revealed to men by the fallen angels." Tertullian's assertion is confirmed elsewhere in a statement attributed to Hermes himself: "The ancient and sacred books teach that certain angels burned with desire for women. They descended to earth and taught all the works of nature. They were the ones who created the Hermetic works, and from them proceeds the primordial tradition of this art."

Hermetic imagery recurs constantly in relation to the Grail mystery: the Cross of Lorraine, the rose-cross, the black Madonnas, the Temple of Solomon, and so on. Hermeticism seems to suffuse virtually every secret society linked to Christ and the Grail. And at Rennes-le-Chateau it is inescapable.

A third level of meaning inherent in *The Shepherds of Arcadia* is the tomb itself, located not terribly far from Rennes-le-Chateau. Poussin has given us ample clues as to who these "shepherds" were and what they believed, and he has also documented a very real location—a place where the proof which substantiates these clues can be found. Whatever constitutes the real treasure of Rennes-le-Chateau was undoubtedly buried for quite some time at the so-called "Poussin tomb." At some point, the treasure was uncovered and removed to Rennes-le-Chateau. Sauniere rediscovered it, reburied it,

Et in Arcadia Ego (*Shepherds of Arcadia*) by Nicholas Pousssin, circa 1655.

and devoted his life to leaving a tantalizing trail of clues; clues that might be decoded at some future time in which the populace in general might be far more well-disposed toward accepting a secret tradition that exists well beyond the confines of orthodoxy.

Though some disagree, Akkadia seems to be synonymous with Agade, the Sumerian capital associated with the empire's most well known leader, Sargon the Great. Sargon was so powerful a ruler that he was known as "the King of the World." One indication that Agade and Akkadia may be one and the same is that the sea-faring men of ancient Phoenicia were referred to alternately as "Gads," or "Kads." The Sumerians and Phoenicians of old never referred to themselves as Sumerians or Phoenicians, but took their names from the city-states in which they lived. According to the Sumeriologist L. A. Waddell, the term "Gad" mutated and was preserved in the name of the Goths. The term "Kad" mutated to "Catti," which was the title given to royalty in ancient Britain. Also, the word "Catti" was the source for many place names in Europe that date back to the time at which the Phoenicians had extensive trade routes, and contain the word "cat" or "cad." There are literally so many such names that to list them all would require half a page. They are to be found from the mid-east to Spain, and from North Africa to Scotland. Of interest in regard to this word "cat" or "catti" is that we had heard of it before, from a very strange figure who was staying at the same hotel as us in Rennes-le-Chateau.

The man was in the process of translating what he claimed was the oldest book in the world, a history of Atlantis. He was a linguist who had discovered the primordial language of mankind, and told us that by learning a series of fundamental linguistic principles, anyone could be taught to read and understand 40 different languages instantly (and with no memorization.) We quizzed him at length about the roots of words central to our research. When we asked him where the word Cathar came from, he explained that it referred to a people descended from the Cats and the Ari, or Aryans. He was vague as to who exactly the Cats were, but said that their name figured in the place-names of countless cities and regions, such as Catalonia, Cadiz, Caithness, and so on. They were seagoing people who had settlements throughout the known world. In light of our subsequent research, it seems likely that these "Cats" were Kads, or ancient Akkadians. The word Kad in fact shows up repeatedly in ancient placenames. Along the Phoenician coast at the time of the kingdoms of David and Solomon, there were no less than *three cities* all named Kadesh. The term Gad shows up repeatedly as well. On either side of the Straights of Gibraltar, there were once two cities both named Agadir, the most famous of which is sometimes referred to as "Gades." At the time, remember, those Straights were known as the "Firth of the Gads." So our research would seem to confirm what we were told by the mysterious stranger at Rennes-le-Chateau. We wished we could have learned more from him about this people he called the "Cats," but unfortunately our mutual language barrier prevented it. For a man who can read and understand some 40 languages, his grasp of English was spotty at best (albeit far more expert than *our* limited grasp of French.)

Conflicting chronicles list both Agade and Akkad as being the capitol of Sargon the Great's empire. Further evidence that the two were probably one and the same is that the ancient maps place both in essentially the same geographic location, not far from Babylon. Also, the maps that depict Agade don't show Akkad, and vice versa. Given the importance of Agade in the ancient world, we hypothesized that it could well have given rise to the notion of the mythical kingdoms of Asgarde and Agartha. Our guesswork has since seemingly been borne out, as we have found additional texts relating Arcadia, Akkadia, and Agartha. If Agartha is synonymous with Arcadia (and both are related to Akkadia), this could bring a whole new meaning to *The Shepherds of Arcadia*, by Nicolas Poussin. The Agarthan underworld connotation could explain why the Sumerian deified kings were also known as "Lords of the Abyss." And too, if the classical Grecian Arcadia had been named in honor of a more ancient capital of Akkadia or Agade, could not that same ancient capital have been so named in honor of a place far more ancient? The Agade/Akkad debate seems to be rooted in the fact that scholars are divided over whether this culture was essentially Semitic or Indo-European. Both camps are equally fierce in defending their agendas, and it appears that a slight difference in the spelling one way or another would tend to give credence to one side's arguments over the other's. We feel that there is substantial evidence that Agade and Akkad were synonymous. That there was probably confusion over the name at the time is evidenced in the fact that the same sea people were described as both Gads and Kads. We also feel that the controversy over who they were needn't be limited to any Semitic/Indo-European dichotomy. Perhaps this people came from someplace else entirely: a place that some ancient chronicles have called *Merou*.

The name Merou is certainly suggestive of the Merovingians, but it also ties in with another key element of this saga. The historical personage upon whom the mythic Dagon was patterned was also known as Muru, after whom numerous Sumerian cities were named. His people were known as the Muru, or the Amuru. Amuru is generally translated as meaning "people from the west," but could undoubtedly be seen to mean "people from (or descendants of) Muru/Merou" (which, from all historical accounts, lay to the west of the ancient world.) But Muru has other significant correspondences. In the Tibetan tradition, a figure equating to Muru/Dagon was said to have descended to Earth on a golden rope, to teach man his secrets. His name: Mura. And in the Koran, the fallen angels were led by two figures: Hurat and *Murat*. Again we see in widely divergent cultures the same story being retold, with the protagonist's name nearly identical— Muru, Mura, Murat. If the tale of the fallen angel (or angels) appeared in but a single major world religion, it would be all too easy to dismiss it out of hand as mere folklore. But the fact that it appears in virtually every major religion, both in the West *and* the East (Judaism, Christianity, Islam, Hinduism and Buddhism) seems indicative of the fact that we're looking at something of elemental importance. If this recurring story refers to an actual historical event, from whence came Muru, Mura and Murat? Would it not seem logical that all three could trace their genesis to a single place, the aforementioned Merou? Over the centuries, the mythic empire of Merou has been known by many names, including Mu and Lemuria. But its most well known designation is that assigned to it by Plato: Atlantis. ▢

P.R. KOENIG

HALO OF FLIES

"A story has been thought to its conclusion when it has taken its worst possible turn."
–Friedrich Duerrenmatt

Organized occultists want their "religion" to be a frozen part of society. This article intends to show how one such organization imposes intellectual conformity on sincere "seekers." As the matter is very complex, I hope that reading it is not like having a cup of tea without water... and just eating the tealeaves.

ORDO TEMPLI ORIENTIS AND GNOSTIC CATHOLIC CHURCH

The Ordo Templi Orientis (O.T.O.) is a German pseudo-masonic organization that was taken over by Aleister Crowley in the mid-1920s. While the O.T.O.'s initiatory system is a sort of Kafkaesque bureaucratic club game, it has a religiously associated section under its obedience, the so-called Gnostic Catholic Church, or "Ecclesia Gnostica Catholica" (E.G.C.). This was originally established by Crowley as the body entitled to perform the "Gnostic Mass," a theatrical ritual that he devised as a more public version of the O.T.O.'s private rites. The Gnostic Mass is Crowley's own interpretation of the Christian Eucharist. It is, needless to say, thoroughly pagan in tone, and includes symbolism from Wagner's *Parsifal*.

The American or "Caliphate" Ordo Templi Orientis founded in 1977 (I exclude here other O.T.O. groups, such as the "Typhonian" O.T.O. founded more than 10 years earlier in London or the Swiss O.T.O. from the 1950s) has continued to adapt this strand of Crowleyan doctrine within the contemporary E.G.C. In doing so it imitates Roman Catholic traditions by introducing offices like "Patriarch," "Archbishop," "Bishop," (Novitiate) "Priest" and "Priestess," and "Deacon." Nowadays, apart from the Mass itself, they have added services such as a "Baptism Ceremony for a Child," a "Baptism Ceremony for an Adult," a "Confirmation Ceremony," a "Ceremony for Ordination of a Deacon," a "Wedding Ceremony," a "Ceremony for a Greater Feast for Death," a "Basic Exorcism Rite," and a "Ceremony for Visitation and Administration of the Virtues to the Sick"; they even have a "Saintship" (though it is of note that no women appear in their litany), and "Animal Benedictions." Christian prayers are also found in association with "Caliphate" rituals: "The Litany of the Holy Name of Jesus," "The Litany of St. Joseph" and "The Litany of the Blessed Virgin Mary," for instance. While it is highly unlikely that Crowley or any of the other founders of the O.T.O. would have countenanced such flirtation with Christian orthodoxy, the "Caliphate" intends it to be taken as reference to the "*Aeonic Magus of the last Aeon, as a reminder that these Great Cycles build each upon the others*" also that the True Master Jesus was not at all deserving of the political hatchet job done on Him

Thelemites consider 'The Holy Books of Thelema' (especially the central "channeled" text of *Liber AL vel Legis* AKA *The Book of the Law*) to be their Bible and its exegesis a scholarly task.

by St. Paul. These prayers and initiation rituals are accompanied by the music of Mozart, Holst, Strauss, Mahler and the like. Obviously blissfully unaware of the traditional meaning of the expression "Wandering

Because Crowley's visionary blueprint is overshadowed by his deficient biography, a trend has started among Crowleyites of differentiating between the "man Crowley" and Crowley the "Thelemic prophet."

Bishops" (that is, bishops outside the realm of Christian orthodoxy), some of these Ecclesiatics have chosen to call themselves "Landed Bishops."

THELEMA AND LOSS OF IDENTITY

Most Crowleyan O.T.O. groups are much preoccupied, even obsessed, with his concept of *Thelema*: a new religious revelation whose key phrases are "Do what thou wilt shall be the whole of the Law," and "Love is the Law, Love under Will." This was Crowley's missionary enterprise that was supposed to sort out History, Religion, Philosophy, Magick and everyday life. That it is largely a straightforward plagiarism and distortion of Augustinus, Rabelais and Nietzsche does not appear to worry them; nor that Thelema is based on faith and individual conviction, rather than knowledge and psychology—and is therefore not truly Gnostic in nature. As a doctrine, Thelema (be it called "the new Aeon," "the new religion," the "new magick" or whatever) will generally "pretend" and "claim," but rarely try to prove a thing objectively on the basis of evidence. Therefore it could validly be claimed that Thelema is as much a prejudice as it is a belief-system.

This revisionism calls for Thelemic research so that the elements of all myths may be reduced to a table of qabalistic correspondences. The step from "finding" to "inventing" becomes methodical and mathematical, by application of the strict rules of the qabala cloaked in obscurantist terminology that has bored and puzzled many more potential followers than it has attracted. The language of Thelema is an attempt to render rational thought superfluous, and for this purpose it uses craftily manipulative phrases to camouflage it: "*The method of Science, the aim of Religion,*" and so on. Thelemites consider "The Holy Books of Thelema" (especially the central "channeled" text of *Liber AL vel Legis* AKA *The Book of the Law*) to be their Bible and its exegesis a scholarly task.

They use euphemism, irrelevance, and perversion of meaning to achieve this end: if they speak about "family," "duties," "privileges," or a desire to "make the world a nobler place," why then is Thelema so very preoccupied with things like evoking demons to destroy enemies? Thelema has to disguise itself to hide its true nature, which is "Spermo-Gnosticism" (i.e. achieving Godhead through the consumption of sperm).

As the inventor of the doctrine, Crowley is seen as infallible, and the only standard. Discussion of *The Book of the Law*, is forbidden, maybe because in his diaries Crowley identified its source of inspiration with "*Thee Satan my savior*"? Adherence to the Crowleyverse (a strict following of his "teachings," "orders," "ideas," etc.) produces, step-by-step, a state of divorce from reality. Because Crowley's visionary blueprint is overshadowed by his deficient biography, a trend has started among Crowleyites of differentiating between the "man Crowley" and Crowley the "Thelemic prophet." This limits the ability to think objectively or critically, and substitutes activism, beliefs, cultishness, ritualism and myth.

OUT OF THE CLOSETS

The occultist views himself as a rebel and a narcissist, who posits him or herself inside, as well as outside, the predominant culture. He understands himself as part of an elite, and endeavors to create himself anew. Lurking on the threshold of History, Thelema wants to communicate its ideas to the world. It evangelizes with the ulti-

If they speak about "family," "duties," "privileges," or a desire to "make the world a nobler place," why then is Thelema so very preoccupied with things like evoking demons to destroy enemies?

mate aim of destroying society's standards. It strives for world dominion and compares itself to the young Christianity that had been hunted by Rome. They say that "*If one were to substitute O.T.O. for Army, this would work very well for the Order.*"

The "Caliphate" O.T.O. has extended its sphere of activity far beyond that of the suburb of a secret Order. It may be found not just in cities, but also in geographical suburbs and villages, and has blossomed into a considerable

Internet presence in recent years. It consists of various branches, with names such as the "Mysteria Mystica Maxima," "The Esoteric Rosicrucians," "The Home of the Order of the Oriental Templars," and the "Hermetic Science College." Sometimes the ruling body of the "Caliphate" tries to borrow high-sounding names from other organizations, like that of the "Fraternitas Rosicruciana Antiqua," the "Illuminaten Orden," the "Hermetic Brotherhood of Light," "Memphis Misraim," or "Academia Masonica." They have an "Exo-Psychology Guild," "Drama and Thaumaturgy Guild," "Alcoholics Guild of O.T.O.," "Translator's Guild," "Thelemic Writer's

The occult supermarket is universally plundered and leaves only a completely devalued treasury of total subjectivity.

Guild," "Psychology Guild of O.T.O.," an "Order of the Lion" giving out "Orders of the Golden Watch" and "Orders of the Eagle." The leaders nevertheless are, of course, aware that such sub-groups make for a rather pathetic organization and who wants to be part of that? Moving Order activity away from homes and bedrooms is the most important challenge facing the current generation today. They encourage everyone to lend an air of seriousness to the Order.

Thelema as preserved and sheltered within the "Caliphate" O.T.O. claims that it is performing an educational task, with its "Colleges" of Thelema, its "Schools of Hermetic Science," its "Seminars on Gnosticism," and through the O.T.O. order structure as well. That's where their reactionary revisionism emerges like the Creature from the Black Lagoon. They want to adapt to Society at large and tame illuminating revolution with a safe mainstream tie-in. Their report on the "First National Conference" in the ballroom of the Hilton in Akron, Ohio boasts: "*How many of us, when we joined the O.T.O., imagined over a hundred Initiates dancing and drinking in formal evening-wear beneath two-ton chandeliers to big-band, disco and rock? The O.T.O. had come of age that evening.*"

There are fundamental elements in every form of human interaction. One might substitute words referring to Christianity, Christian references or derivatives for words referring to the O.T.O. in this article and still maintain the argument.

HARE RAMA HARE SUPERMARKET

Today, in the worldwide circus of the images, occultism is the continuation of fashions, of habits or mannerisms of how to display oneself: *pseudo-originality*. The occult supermarket is universally plundered and leaves only a completely devalued treasury of total subjectivity. By picking out the pieces that appeal most to him or her out of the debris left after the breakdown of the symbolic order, the occultist's cultural reality ends up consisting of slightly differing arrangements of said pieces into signs of strict hierarchies. Normal activities one might expect in joining such a group, such as experiencing, recording and processing are curbed and one is reduced to subsistence on a diet of already fixed images that work in a consciousness *dissolving* way. Common occult knowledge is repackaged and sold as a new product; Crowley's Thelema is transformed according to "Caliphate" methods into a juicy hamburger in a shiny new wrapping that you can buy at the mall. Defanged, neutered and essentially without much nutritional value.

To appeal to consumers, the "Caliphate" has produced a range of products that resemble a McDonaldized "illumination through sex-magic," a McGnosis transported through the iconic figure of Crowley as Ronald McDonald. It is hidden behind a confusing veil of euphemisms, and is preferably practiced on Sundays by means of consuming a "host" made of sexual secretions and/or blood obtained from the butcher shop (i.e. animal blood) for the public masses and those looking for titillation and codified rebellion.

The "Caliphate" O.T.O. shows itself to be a post-modern esoteric supermarket with the equivalent and equal importance it vests in a whole range of different things: qabala, T-shirts, yoga, invocations of demons and angels, sex-magic, calendars, exorcism, drugs, religion, Gnosis, videos, scandal, gossip, postcards, philosophy and pseudo-science. Egyptian mythology is revised to suit Thelemic tastes and all is reduced to the level of a soap-opera. To the uninformed observer the O.T.O. looks rather like a tiny group of people, similar to a Harry Potter reading circle, rejects from a renaissance fair or heavy metal fans in search of a naked high priestess.

MANUFACTURED GNOSIS

The development of (oc)culture is hindered by occult organizations such as the O.T.O. with their modus operandi often consisting solely of "repetitions" of rituals, signs, etc., with little original thought or practice. The individual is expected to "find themselves" in this cultural repetition, which hinders, rather than encourages, creativity.

The supreme visionary, founder of meaning, maker of images, and source of actual occult streams is Crowley. He showed his followers how the needs of lust and the wishes of the body are to be controlled. Particularly strongly, their mastering of body and consciousness is shown in their control of the euphoria of imaging through dogmatically fixed tables of values (e.g. the Qabala), and through bringing sexuality as sex magick in a form of ecstatic limitation ("fuck and make a wish").

This hierarchy allows precise control over members, and means they are under constant observation so that standardized results are produced. No experimentation is encouraged. The best way to progress has already been discovered and must therefore be followed. These restrictions have turned the "Caliphate" into an institutionalized group whose ordinary members must follow strict criteria, and pass set examinations. Huge piles of forms have to be filled out; there are tests about occult knowledge,

To appeal to consumers, the "Caliphate" has produced a range of products that resemble a McDonaldized "illumination through sex-magic"; a McGnosis transported through the iconic figure of Crowley as Ronald McDonald.

The "Caliphate" professes to provide a user-friendly method of handling occult material, abilities, knowledge, rules, and procedures. This O.T.O. has become a sort of perpetuum mobile which never permits its members a true apotheosis; they have to patiently endure a long series of initiations, which are claimed to produce illumination bit by bit. This costs long years of paying membership dues and long delays waiting for the next initiation (although most members never get further than the Third Degree). By only gradually revealing its promised secrets and adventures, this Order (firm) plays with its members' (clients) spiritual yearnings. The organization works as a dealer of the yearning itself and it is careful to rule by decree which occult methods are allowed and which are forbidden. With its efficiently organized supply of formulæ (yoga, sex-magick, "no drugs," etc.) the "Caliphate" appears to offer a permanent flow of instant mini-illuminations which run to an exactly-prescribed timetable—in other words, its hierarchical system of degrees or grades. Each initiatory degree comprises a predictable speciality within the limits of specific symbolisms and techniques. Each stage means conforming to new rules and regulations to enable or "execute" illumination. Events are interpreted according to the degree of initiation, that is: higher degrees dominate lower degrees. All Thelemites are equal, but some are more equal than others, to paraphrase Orwell.

To the uninformed observer the O.T.O. looks rather like a tiny group of people, similar to a Harry Potter reading circle, rejects from a renaissance fair or heavy metal fans in search of a naked high priestess.

passwords, grips and signs. Individual Illumination happens in a schoolroom.

Of course, it is out of the question for the rank and file to discuss the fees for membership and initiations, the group's interpretation of doctrine, or how the organization is run; the "Caliphate" is not a democratic body, and its leaders (the "Caliph" and his inner circle of friends) are not elected democratically.

WE ARE BORG ...

The greater the membership the more likely members will "behave" (as opposed to "act" or "think") and the less likely the group mind will tolerate "bad" behavior—behavior meaning adjustment to the Order's rules. Integration itself proves to be an ideology *for disintegration* into power groups which exterminate each other. He who integrates is lost. In the equating of quality with quantity, only those who introduce the most new members will rise higher in the Order. A person ceases to be *with* other people and is completely oriented towards *satisfying* the higher institutional level. By doing so, this person experiences him/herself as a part of this higher level (management), at the same time, however, relinquishing his or her own individuality.

The striking frequency of the "we"-form ("we think, we want") levels different points of view and perspectives, mixing them together into an indifferent *groupthink*. The people in the Order must be of one mind (e.g. that of the management) in their attitude to external "claimants" and critics, and must accept their position and/or grade in the

Order. Dynamic group processes create pressures to conform in uniform reactions, verbal stereotypes in passwords and stock phrases ("Love is the Law," "the fundamentalists hate us"), and standardized symbolism.

Everything has to be consistent—all members of the "Caliphate's" Fifth Degree are supposed to have a rose tattooed on their upper chest and numerologically 729 always signifies the Crowleyan version of Baphomet—a McBaphomet, in other words. Creativity and original thought are eliminated, because they are "inefficient"—and not controllable.

Flame wars and name calling abound, but even this sort of juvenile activity serves to reinforce the "Caliphate" dominance.

Making any change to their strictly limited repertoire of clichés is not a favored activity among many O.T.O. groups. For them, the status quo must be preserved at all costs: unquestioning acceptance of Crowley's omniscience as a prophet, the value of their rituals (such as the daily "Adoration of the Sun"), the routine of initiation-ceremonies and performing the Gnostic Mass every Sunday, keeping to their codes of behavior, and submitting to the restrictions concerning what is forbidden and permitted. And, of course, the near-mantric repetition of the Thelemic greeting "Do what thou wilt shall be the whole of the Law." (Their version of "Hey, how's it going?") They retreat to the old values of power and consummation in a universe that has been delivered to cults of objects, religious artifacts and meaningless jargon.

All these serve as substitute for rational analysis and experience, encouraging the prejudging of issues and intolerance of external criticism.

... AND DAMAGED

The pseudo-masonic nature of the Ordo Templi Orientis has engendered a complex grade structure, which usually takes many years to complete and pay for. It blends simple methods of "technical psychology" with religious practices, often together with an excessive emphasis on the life and character of its charismatic leader.

Unfraternal behavior between members, inflated egos, lying, game-playing, subterfuge and hysteria; all these have happened and continue to happen—causing endless in-fighting, divisions and secessions, and even court proceedings. This merely serves to reinforce the dominance

of the organizational framework. Belonging to other groups is not permitted—so membership of the "Caliphate" O.T.O. is not considered compatible with membership of, say, the "Typhonian O.T.O." or "Temple of Set." This monopolizes the marketplace in a manner very similar to the dominance of Microsoft's operating system in computers. This tendency often results in the expulsion of members who try to abandon (even slightly) Crowleyan dogmas, or legal threats to other groups which dare to use the O.T.O. name.

Unfaithful members not only face censorship but also a kangaroo court that shows plain similarity to the Spanish Inquisition: Anonymous informers, no witnesses, and no counsel for the defense. The Inquisitor is investigator, prosecutor and judge in one person. The defendants publicly have to apologize or risk expulsion.

FRANZ KAFKA'S PROCESS

"Caliphate" members live in a deliberate vagueness about the organization's labyrinthine hierarchy; just who is responsible for what—and does the left hand even know what the right one's doing? In this hierarchy's pyramid structure, it is obvious (or should be) that all members can never reach the highest degree. The highest degree exercises omni-potency and omni-competency over the group.

While officials, dignitaries and the famous enjoy only limited rights to privacy and anonymity in a democracy, it is the exact opposite in organized occult niches like the O.T.O.; the higher the O.T.O. official, the less his real name will be known, and the more pseudonymously and ritually will he exercise his power in the group. The "mundane" names of the leader or his representatives are often kept secret. They cease to be persons to meet in the real world for they lack all the many superfluous detailed characteristics, which make up a real individual. They seem to become "jobholders" in a bureaucratic club, acting on an assumption of omni-competence.

This facelessness and shapelessness has the effect that people also become faceless and shapeless. They live in a Kafkaesque world where the human being only is identified according to his or her function in the Order. As they never know all the rules of their order, they are trapped in an inner world of moods, feelings, and imaginations. This private world gets overemphasized and results in a lack of identity. Nothing remains but a dwindling whimper for attention. Certain conditions of being are defined as biased analysis, moods as programs, self-perception as cultural attainment, and pure imagination as relevation. These are the new determinations. Dogmatization infantilizes and diminishes the contents, those seeking for directness become enmeshed in a sacredized repertoire of rituals of self-dissolution, without ever effectively overcoming the ego. Coupled with sexuality and aggressivity, this repetitive theme of destructiveness is displayed on the Internet in egroups, newsgroups and chatrooms. Flame wars and name calling abound, but even this sort of juvenile activity serves to reinforce the "Caliphate" dominance.

THE ODOR OF THE O.T.O.

Fixation on Crowley, necessarily, equals stagnation. The O.T.O. functions like a piece of demo shareware with all the interesting key features disabled. It runs on a 14 day trial period which just repeats over and over again, even if you pay for the full version. "Do what thou wilt" in Crowley's O.T.O. mirrors this in anti-creativity and in the dogma of mystification; nobody must know of the central Spermo-Gnostic secret—and explicit censorship is enshrined in the statutes. There is an oligarchy (the chief and his inner circle of friends) who "owns" this knowledge, and seeks to monopolize its interpretation and transmission. Of course, anyone wishing to manipulate the market in this way must be selling the best secrets money can buy. Hence the bizarre spin-doctoring attempts to treat the "secret" of Spermo-Gnosis in the same way that Coca-Cola jealously guards its "secret recipe" It is a "trade secret" to which any reference must be denied (even when such denials look absurd) because "commercial confidentiality" must be preserved at all costs.

After all, the "central secret" was *never really a secret anyway*; everyone with an interest in the O.T.O. *already knows* it means Spermo-Gnosis. So why should anyone want to join the O.T.O., if the only ambition of those already in the Order is to reach the next degree, and what would happen if there were no more steps to achieve, if the Order was no longer a dealer of the sacred? What would be the point??

They behave as if their ancestors hadn't so much crawled out of the primordial swamp, as taken a cab.

AURA OF THE O.T.O. PHENOMENON

Occulture has become a half-baked reflection of the sort that confines itself to monstrous platitudes which multiply in a void of speculation and vagueness. Silly rumors and snobbery also serve to ornament the gossip and corruption of people who would cloak themselves as arbiters of religious wisdom. Thelemic occulture itself is now bred "in vitro" as product for the publisher's supermarket, or disembowelled at so-called "International congresses," where it's given a first-class burial. The cadaver shivers until people are sure that it'll dance again.

When Thelema faces criticism it uses a tactic of "restricted rationality" where its representatives (the "Caliph" and his friends) utilize set arguments that have the twin advantages of supporting their doctrines and excluding criticism. This tactic, augmented by the dissemination of disinformation and suppression of facts, only serves to reinforce false self-images and manufacture imaginary bogeymen.

Critics have proved dangerous to these occultists by destroying their aura: the very thing that makes them untouchable in their own eyes. Eventually, the factoids sent into orbit by occultists create a maelstrom of censorship on the Internet where spin doctors turn into pilots who surf their passengers. While they behave as if their ancestors hadn't so much crawled out of the primordial swamp, as taken a cab—they face facts that threaten their regimented happiness and carefully fenced-off security. And so they *consciously* choose ignorance as their weapon of survival. They promote benightedness, prejudice, superstition and censorship to protect their "clan" from "the world," and get stuck in the if-loop of their own labyrinth of "reality."

CYBERCATACOMBS

Thanks to the Internet, factual concerns shrink to the level of e-mail missives and second-hand opinions; knowledge becomes data hoarding, the linear becomes interactive, and proper friendship disappears in interchangeable cyber-interaction. Occulture turns into a passive audience riven by factions, which fish their pre-digested half-truths out of the limitless digital pool. This kind of McDonaldized occulture is an arena where anything goes, a breeding-ground for conspiracy theories now classified as scholarly work. Selective attention decides whether information is worthwhile or not; it doesn't matter if that information is right or wrong, or even true or false—only whether it attracts attention and as much as possible.

Never mind that when you bought the book, the "Caliphate" was not in existence: this Corporation now retroactively controls your Crowleyana.

The O.T.O.'s feuilleton mainly consists of hymnic reviews of their ideologically kindred press, of the endless celebration of Crowley and his disciples and, of course, character assasinations of Thelema's critics. Pseudo-discourse happens in complete sterility on the Internet in its vicious circle of censorship, spin-doctoring, propaganda and blatant lies. They produce an imitation of real thought-processes and new arrangements of old fantasies. Veteran spin doctors lean out of their virtual cave windows, rotating in the ruins of lust and driven by particles of supposed enlightenment in the terrain of petty bourgeoise in-fighting. It's all revealed to be so pointless!

The reduction of facts to hallucinatory speculations leaves no room for the influence of truth (whatever that may be), and results in an endless fragmented labyrinth of unlimited choices where "truth" becomes a matter of prejudice and moods. Any "true" information faces a continuing elasticity in a process of transformation and interactive reconfiguration. In the vast catacombs of hypertext it is all too easy to lose a feeling for the whole; in the nebulous atmosphere left by an absence of such an overview, connections and continuity can disappear. Where there is hypertext, there is no context.

FAHRENHEIT 418

All the concepts mentioned in the foregoing paragraphs are merely instruments serving to distract from and suppress but *one* vital fact: that the American version of the O.T.O., called the "Caliphate," exists for the purpose of providing one man's entire income by allowing him to live off the royalties from Aleister Crowley's works. This man is the leader of the "Caliphate" and is called "His Holy Majesty" "Lord Knight Caliph," etc. His strategy is to keep the O.T.O. alive as a money-milking cow—the members follow as sheep, blinded to this most salient fact.

In 1985, a rather uninformed American judge ruled in the favour of the "Caliphate," thus making way for thousands of dollars from the Crowley copyrights rolling into the bank account of this new O.T.O. group founded in 1977. The "Caliphate" not only declared itself to be "the real O.T.O." from 1985 on, but also openly implemented a scheme of three categories of so-called "historical truths" into which facts have to fit. This scheme has nothing to do with historical, academic and methodic research but nourishes the bureaucratic levels of this legally introduced hierarchy of "truths."

(1) Legally protected historical truths. "The Truth"—the "Caliphate" is the real O.T.O.—was defined by a Court. Anyone openly querying or denying this "truth" finds himself in Court—be it a mundane Court when it touches the holy copyrights, or the Inquisition room of the "Caliphate."

(2) Officially privileged historical truths. As only a handful of selected and chosen faithful and "trustworthy" people adhering to "Caliphate" "truths" have access to the primary sources in their archives, the public has to rely on their findings.

(3) Ordinary historical truths that are treated as *quantité négligeable*. "Other" historical facts without any reference to legally protected or officially privileged historical truths, e.g. what they call *distorted facts* by enemies or critics.

Threats to the income from royalties on the Crowley copyrights—which is the sole basis for the "Caliphate's" existence—have resulted in some pretty extreme and bizarre antics, as shown above. The "Caliph's" supposed omnipotence reveals his impotence at the same time. He drifts into being perceived as a parody of a ruler by the rest of society, with his titles like "Supreme King." In the end he acts like a tyrant whose slightest whim must be obeyed, and for whom everything must be sacrificed—including your freedom.

Have you heard of the Thelemic book patrol equipped with flame-throwers (i.e. lawyers)? Members who sell "secret" although published documents are brought before a Kafkaesque inquisition and eventually expelled. The open market (new and secondhand) of published books available through public libraries, manuscripts in research libraries, manuscripts held by private individuals who are not members of the O.T.O. etc., are also controlled by the Chief of the group. Never mind that when you bought the book, the "Caliphate" was not in existence: this Corporation now retroactively controls your Crowleyana.

Should you try to sell this material [even on Ebay—editor], you will receive a cease and desist order as soon as they become aware of your attempts. In this respect the "Caliphate" resembles the Church of Scientology's pursuit of any and all persons who spill their "high level" documents on the Internet and elsewhere, even as these secrets pop up like mushrooms after a morning rain.

In the context of Society, of course, the "Caliphate" is completely irrelevant. If members disobey their Order's laws, what have they to lose but the membership of the club? Gnosis? Hardly. Fact remains: Members up in arms, fighting the rules have nothing to fear in Society's context (except they have to pay for copyright infringement, but you don't have to be a club member for *that*), but the "Caliph" stands to lose everything: *his cash-cow.*

I AM THE BRAND NAME

The "Caliphate" O.T.O. is little more than a commercial concern that allows its managing director to live off the royalties generated by Aleister Crowley's writings. It isn't really the membership fees that are carved up as a rich income for the organization's chiefs, but almost entirely these royalties. Thus the "Caliphate" must continue as a withered legal appendix living parasitically on the body of

In this respect the "Caliphate" resembles the Church of Scientology's pursuit of any and all persons who spill their "high level" documents on the Internet and elsewhere, even as these secrets pop up like mushrooms after a morning rain.

the publishing. Membership is needed only in order that the chief can say, "I have a legal body that owns copyrights." This fact is whitewashed on dozens of "consciousness-expanding" Internet homepages, which show the over-egged love-and-peace pudding of the "Caliphate" up for what it is—a McO.T.O. ⌗

TAU ALLEN GREENFIELD

THE SECRET HISTORY OF MODERN WITCHCRAFT

THE LEGEND OF WITCHCRAFT AND THE ORIGIN OF WICCA

"The fact is that the instincts of ignorant people invariably find expression in some form of witch craft. It matters little what the metaphysician or the moralist may inculcate; the animal sticks to his subconscious ideas..."

–Aleister Crowley, *The Confessions of Aleister Crowley*.

"Gather together in the covens as of old, whose number is eleven, that is also my number. Gather together in public, in song and dance and festival. Gather together in secret, be naked and shameless and rejoice in my name."

–Jack Parsons, *Liber 49, The Book of Babalon*, 1946

"If you are on the Path, and see the Buddha walking towards you, kill him."

–Zen saying, paraphrased slightly

"Previously I never thought of doubting that there were many witches in the world; now, however, when I examine the public record, I find myself believing that there are hardly any..."

–Father Friedrich von Spee, S.J., *Cautio Criminalis*, 1631

"...Yet as far as Merovingian Gaul is concerned, there is no evidence to suggest that any of the pagan religions persisted beyond the 5th century, and there is no pagan religion with a 'complex set of beliefs and practices reflecting man's attitude to the supernatural' which can be identified or reconstructed from the information provided by the sources."

–Yitzhak Hen, doctoral thesis, 1995

ORIGINS IN DREAMLAND

Having spent the day musing over the origins of the modern witchcraft, I had a vivid dream. It seemed to be a cold January afternoon, and Aleister Crowley was having Gerald Gardner over to tea. It was 1945, and talk of an early end to the war was in the air. An atmosphere of optimism prevailed in the free world, but the wheezing old Magus was having none of it.

"Nobody is interested in magick any more!" Crowley ejaculated. "My friends on the Continent are dead or in exile, or grown old; the movement in America is in shambles. I've seen my best candidates turn against me....Achad, Regardie—even that gentleman out in California, what's-his-name, AMORC, the one that made all the money."

"O, bosh, Crowley," Gardner waved his hand impatiently, "all things considered, you've done pretty well for your-

"If I had it all to do over again, I would've built a religion for the unwashed masses instead of just a secret society."

self. Why, you've been called the 'wickedest man in the world' and by more than a few. And you've not, if you'll pardon the impertinence, done too badly with the ladies."

Crowley coughed, tugged on his pipe reflectively. "You know" he finally ventured, "it's like I've been trying to tell this boy Grant. A restrictive Order is not enough. If I had it all to do over again, I would've built a religion for the unwashed masses instead of just a secret society. Why, the opportunities! The women! Poor dimwit kid; he just doesn't get the point. I believe he reads Lovecraft or Poe or one of those other unsavory American fantasists too much. But you, Brother Gardner, you get what is needed."

Gardner smiled. "Precisely. And that is what I have come to propose to you. Take your *Book of the Law*, your Gnostic Mass. Add a little razzle-dazzle for the country folk. Why I know these occultists who call themselves "witches." They dance around fires naked, get drunk, have a good time. Rosicrucians, I think. Proper English country squires and dames, mostly. If I could persuade you to draw on your long experience and talents, in no time at all we could invent a popular cult that would have beautiful ladies clamoring to let us strip them naked, tie them up and spank their behinds! If, Mr. Crowley, you'll excuse my explicitness."

For all his infirmity, Aleister Crowley almost sprang to his feet, a little of the old energy flashing through his loins. "By George, Gardner, you've got something there, I should think! I could license you to initiate people into the O.T.O. today, and you could form the nucleus of such a group!"

The first time I met someone who thought she was a witch, she started going on about being a "blue of the cloak." I should've been warned right then and there.

He paced in agitation. "Yes, yes," he mused, half to Gardner, half to himself. "The Book. The Mass. I could write some rituals. An "ancient book" of magick. A "book of shadows." Priestesses, naked girls. Yes. By Jove, yes!"

Great story, but merely a dream, created out of bits and pieces of rumor, history and imagination. Don't be surprised, though, if a year or five years from now you read it

as "gospel" (which is an ironic synonym for "truth") in some new learned text on the fabled history of Wicca. Such is the way all mythologies come into being.

Please don't misunderstand me here; I use the word "mythology" in this context in its aboriginal meaning, and with considerable respect. History is more metaphor than factual accounting at best, and there are myths by which we live and others by which we die. Myths are the dreams and visions which parallel objective history.

To arrive at some perspective on what the modern mythos called, variously, "Wicca," the "Old Religion," "Witchcraft"

"Take your *Book of The Law*, your Gnostic Mass. Add a little razzle-dazzle for the country folk. Why I know these occultists who call themselves 'witches.' They dance around fires naked, get drunk, have a good time."

and "Neopaganism" is, we must firstly make a firm distinction; "witchcraft" in the popular informally defined sense may have little to do with the modern religion that goes by the same name. It has been argued by defenders of and formal apologists for modern Wicca that it is a direct lineal descendent of an ancient, indeed, prehistoric worldwide folk religion.

Some proponents hedge their claims, calling Wicca a "revival" rather than a continuation of an ancient cult. Oddly enough, there may never have been any such cult! The first time I met someone who thought she was a witch, she started going on about being a "blue of the cloak." I should've been warned right then and there.

In fact, as time has passed and the religion has spread, the claims of lineal continuity have tended to be hedged more and more. Thus, we find Dr. Gardner himself, in 1954, stating unambiguously that some witches are descendants "... of a line of priests and priestesses of an old and probably Stone Age religion, who have been initiated in a certain way (received into the circle) and become the recipients of certain ancient learning."[1]

Stated in its most extreme form, Wicca may be defined as an ancient pagan religious system of beliefs and practices, with a form of "apostolic" succession (that is, with knowledge and ordination handed on linearly from generation to generation), a more or less consistent set of rites and myths, and even a secret holy book of considerable antiquity (The Book of Shadows).

More recent writers, as we have noted, have hedged a good deal on these claims, particularly the latter. Thus we find Stewart Farrar in 1971 musing on the purported ancient text thusly: "Whether, therefore, the whole of the Book of Shadows is post-1897 is anyone's guess. Mine is that, like the Bible, it is a patchwork of periods and sources, and that since it is copied and re-copied by hand, it includes amendments, additions, and stylistic alterations according to the taste of a succession of copiers... Parts of it I sense to be genuinely old; other parts suggest modern interpolation..."[2]

As we shall discover presently, there appear to be no genuinely old copies of the Book of Shadows.

Still, as to the mythos, Farrar informs us that the "two personifications of witchcraft are the Horned God and the Mother Goddess..."[3] and that the "Horned God is not the Devil, and never has been. If today 'Satanist' covens do exist, they are not witches but a sick fringe, delayed-reaction victims of a centuries-old Church propaganda in which even intelligent Christians no longer believe...."[3]

If one is then to protest, very well, some case might be made for the Horned God being mistaken for the Christian Devil (or should that be the other way around?), but what record, prior to the advent 50 years ago of modern Wicca via Gerald Gardner, do we have of the survival of a mother goddess image from ancient times?

Wiccan apologists frequently refer to the (apparently isolated) 10th century Church document which states that "some wicked women, perverted by the Devil, seduced by the illusions and phantasms of demons, believe and profess themselves in the hours of the night to ride upon certain beasts with Diana, the goddess of pagans, or with Herodias, and an innumerable multitude of women, and in the silence of the dead of night to traverse great spaces of earth, and to obey her commands as of their mistress, and to be summoned to her service on certain nights." (Quoted in Valiente, Witchcraft For Tomorrow, Hale, 1978, p 32. and by Kramer and Sprenger in the Montague

What record, prior to the advent 50 years ago of modern Wicca via Gerald Gardner, do we have of the survival of a mother goddess image from ancient times?

Summers translation of The Hammer Of Witches). This document dates from early post-Roman Europe. Some form of intact quasi-pagan folk beliefs did survive through this period; even as late as the High Middle Ages it survived among the Vikings of Northern Europe. Human Sacrifice was practiced at Old Upsala well into the High Middle Ages. However, the historical record in Europe and later in the Americas generally suggests that, once Christian missionaries began to proselytize in a given area, conversion was astonishingly rapid and pagan beliefs and even most customs rapidly faded. In more recent times, the total conversion in a single generation documented in Mexico and Peru following the Spanish conquest provides substantial proof of the thoroughness of this process. In earlier times, such works as Yitzhak Hen's Culture And Religion In Merovingian Gaul AD 481–751 show the same pattern of rapid conversion, not just in name but in substance, both in the cities and the countryside. Of course some customs from paleopagan times exist worldwide, but there has never been any evidence of a link to modern Wicca, other than a literary one. In the mystical sense, a Piscean religion best suited a Piscean Aeon, and Christianity offered answers to the questions of death and morality in a spiritual context poorly dealt with in both the State Pagan Religion of Rome and the Celtic, Germanic and other folk beliefs of Europe.

Farrar, for his part, explains the lack of references to a goddess in the testimony at the infamous witch trials by asserting that "the judges ignored the Goddess, being preoccupied with the Satan-image of the God...."[4] But it is the evidence of that reign of terror which lasted from roughly 1484 to 1692 which brings the whole idea of a surviving religious cult into question. Authorities such as Dr. Margaret Murray to the contrary, the conventional wisdom on the witch burning mania which swept like a plague over much of Europe during the transition from medieval world to modern is that it was just that; a mania, a delusion in the minds of Christian clergymen and state authorities; that is, there were no witches, only the innocent victims of the witch hunt. Further, this humanist argument goes, the "witchcraft" of Satanic worship, broomstick riding, of Sabats and Devil-marks, was a rather late invention, borrowing but little from remaining memories of actual pre-Christian paganism. We have seen that the infamous inquisitors Kramer and Springer knew full well the early account mentioned above, and classical paganism as a literary knowledge has never been forgotten. We have seen a resurrection of this mania in the 1980s flurry over "Satanic"' cults, with as little evidence. The story still gets retold on occasion, in fresh form.

"The concept of the heresy of witchcraft was frankly regarded as a new invention, both by the theologians and by the public," writes Dr. Rossell Hope Robbins in *The Encyclopedia Of Witchcraft & Demonology,* (Crown, 1959, p 9) "Having to hurdle an early church law, the *Canon Episcopi,* which said in effect that belief in witchcraft was superstitious and heretical, the inquisitors caviled by arguing that the witchcraft of the *Canon Episcopi* and the witchcraft of the Inquisition were different...."

The evidence extracted under the most gruesome and repeated tortures resemble the Wiccan religion of today in only the most cursory fashion. Though Wicca may have been framed with the "confessions" extracted by victims of the inquisitors in mind, those "confessions"—which are more than suspect to begin with, bespeak a cult of devil worshipers dedicated to evil.

One need only read a few of the accounts of the time to realize that, had there been at the time a religion of the Goddess and God, of seasonal circles and The Book of Shadows, such would likely have been blurted out by the victims, and more than once. The agonies of the accused were, almost literally, beyond the imagination of those of us who have been fortunate enough to escape them.

The witch mania went perhaps unequaled in the annals of crimes against humanity en masse until the Hitlerian brutality of our own century. But, no such confessions were forthcoming, though the wretches accused, before the torture was done, would also be compelled to condemn their own parents, spouses, loved ones, even children. They confessed, and to anything the inquisitors wished, anything to stop or reduce the pain.

A priest, probably at risk to his own life, recorded testimony in the 1600s that reflected the reality underlying the forced "confessions" of "witches." Rev. Michael Stapirius records, for example, this comment from one "confessed witch": "I never dreamed that by means of the torture a person could be brought to the point of telling such lies as I have told. I am not a witch, and I have never seen the devil, and still I had to plead guilty myself and denounce others...." All but one copy of Father Stapirius' book were destroyed, and little wonder.

A letter smuggled from a German burgomaster, Johannes Junius, to his daughter in 1628, is as telling as it is painful even to read. His hands had been virtually destroyed in the torture, and he wrote only with great agony and no hope. "When at last the executioner led me back to the cell, he said to me, 'Sir, I beg you, for God's sake, confess something, whether it be true or not. Invent something, for you cannot endure the torture which you will be put to; and, even if you bear it all, yet you will not escape, not even if you were an earl, but one torture will follow another until you say you are a witch. Not before that,' he said, 'will they let you go, as you may see by all their trials, for one is just like another....'"[5]

For the graspers at straws, we may find an occasional line in a "confession" which is intriguing, as in the notations on the "confession" of one woman from Germany dated in late 1637. After days of unspeakable torment, wherein the woman confesses under pain, recants when the pain is removed, only to be moved by more pain to confess again, she is asked: "How did she influence the weather? She does not know what to say and can only whisper, Oh, Heavenly Queen, protect me!"

Was the victim calling upon "the Goddess"? Or, as seems more likely, upon that aforementioned transfiguration of all ancient goddesses in Christian mythology, the Virgin Mary? One more quote from Dr. Robbins, and I will cease to parade late medieval history before you.

The brutality is not that of "witches" or even of "Satanists" but rather that of the Christian Church, and the government.

It comes from yet another priest, Father Cornelius Loos, who observed, in 1592, that "Wretched creatures are compelled by the severity of the torture to confess things they have never done, and so by cruel butchery innocent lives are taken....."[6] The "evidence" of the witch trials indicates, on the whole, neither the Satanism the church and state would have us believe, nor the pagan survivals now claimed by modern Wicca; rather, they suggest only fear, greed, human brutality carried out to bizarre extremes that have few parallels in all of history. But, the brutality is not that of "witches" or even of "Satanists" but rather that of the Christian Church, and the government.

What, then, are we to make of modern Wicca? It must, of course, be observed as an aside that in a sense witchcraft or "wisecraft" has, indeed, been with us from the dawn of time, not as a coherent religion or set of practices and beliefs, but as the folk magic and medicine that stretches back to early, possibly Paleolithic, tribal shamans on to modern China's so-called "barefoot doctors."

In another sense, we can also say that ceremonial magick, as I have previously noted, has had a place in history for a very long time, and both these ancient systems of belief and practice have intermingled in the lore of modern Wicca, as apologists are quick to claim.

But, to an extent, this misses the point and skirts an essential question anyone has the right to ask about modern Wicca—namely, did Wicca exist as a coherent

Crowley, had some involvement with groups stemming from Pickingill's earlier activities, but it is only after Crowley and Gardner meet that we begin to see anything resembling the modern spiritual communion that has become known as Wicca.

"Witches," wrote Gardner in 1954, "are consummate leg-pullers; they are taught it as part of their stock-in-trade."[8] Modern apologists both of Aleister Crowley and Gerald Gardner have taken on such serious tones as well as pretensions that they may be missing places where tongues are firmly jutting against cheeks.

Both men were believers in fleshly fulfillment, not only as an end in itself but, as in the Tantric Yoga of the East, as a means of spiritual attainment. A certain prudishness has crept into the practices of post-Gardnerian Wiccans,

"Witches are consummate leg-pullers; they are taught it as part of their stock-in-trade."

creed, a distinct form of spiritual expression, prior to the 1940s; that is, prior to the meeting of minds between the old magus and venerable prophet of the occult world Aleister Crowley, and the first popularizer, if not outright inventor of modern Wicca, Gerald Brosseau Gardner?

There is certainly no doubt that bits and pieces of ancient paganism survived into modern times in folklore and, for that matter, in the very practices and beliefs of Christianity.

Further, there appears to be some evidence that "Old George" Pickingill and others were practicing some form of Satanic folk magick as early as the latter part of the last century, though even this has recently been brought into question. Wiccan writers have made much of this in the past, but just what "Old George" was into is subject to much debate.

Doreen Valiente, an astute Wiccan writer and one-time intimate of the late Dr. Gardner (and, in fact, the author of some rituals now thought by others to be of "ancient origin"), says of Pickingill that so "fierce was Old George's dislike of Christianity that he would even collaborate with avowed Satanists..."[7] What George Pickingill was doing is simply not clear.

He is said to have had some interaction with a host of figures in the occult revival of the late 19th century, including perhaps even Crowley and his teacher Bennett. It seems possible that Gardner, about the time of meeting

especially in America since the 1960s, along with a certain feminist revisionism. This has succeeded to a considerable extent in converting a libertine sex cult into a rather staid Neopuritanism.

The original Gardnerian current is still well enough known and widely enough in vogue (in Britain and Ireland especially) that one can venture to assert that what Gardnerian Wicca is all about is the same thing Crowley was attempting with a more narrow, more intellectual constituency with the magical orders under his direct influence.

These Orders had flourished for some time, but by the time Crowley "officially" met Gardner in the 1940s, much of the former's lifelong efforts had, if not totally disintegrated, at least were then operating at a diminished and diminishing level.

Through his long and fascinating career as Magus and organizer, there is some reason to believe that Crowley periodically may have wished for, or even attempted to create a more populist expression of magical religion. The Gnostic Mass, which Crowley wrote fairly early-on, had come since his death to somewhat fill this function through the O.T.O.-connected but (for a time) semi-autonomous Gnostic Catholic Church (E.G.C.).

As we shall see momentarily, one of Crowley's key followers was publishing manifestos forecasting the revival of witchcraft at the same time Gardner was being chartered by Crowley to organize an O.T.O. encampment. The O.T.O. itself, since Crowley's time, has taken on a more popular image, and is somewhat less elitist and more oriented towards international organizational efforts, thanks largely to the work under the Caliphate of the late Grady McMurtry. This contrasts sharply with the very internalized O.T.O. that barely survived during the McCarthy Era, when the late Karl Germer was in charge, and turned inward for two decades. (On the other hand, Germer when seen less as an active Grand Master and more as a Conservator of ideas and rites in a "dark age" comes off a good deal better.)

The famous Ancient and Mystic Order of the Rose Cross (AMORC), the highly successful mail-order spiritual fellowship, was an O.T.O. offspring in Crowley's time. It has been claimed that Kenneth Grant and Aleister Crowley were discussing relatively radical changes in the Ordo Templi Orientis at approximately the same time that Gardner and Crowley were interactive. Indeed, Crowley's correspondence and conversations with his eventual successor Grady McMurtry suggest that in his last years the old Magus envisioned the need for a new generation of leaders with new ideas.

Though Wiccan writers give some lip service (and, no doubt, some sincere credence) to the notion that the validity of Wiccan ideas doesn't depend upon its lineage, the suggestion that Wicca is—or, at least, started out to be, essentially a late attempt at popularizing the secrets of ritual and sexual magick Crowley promulgated through the O.T.O. and his writings, seems to evoke nervousness, if not hostility.

One notes gross animosity or a certain culpable nervousness. We hear from Wiccan writer and leader Raymond Buckland that one "of the suggestions made is that Aleister Crowley wrote the rituals ... but no convincing evidence has been presented to back this assertion and, to my mind, it seems extremely unlikely...."[9] The Wiccan rituals I have seen DO have much of Crowley in them. Yet, as we shall see presently, the explanation that "Crowley wrote the rituals for Gardner" turns out to be somewhat in error. But it is on the right track.

Doreen Valiente attempts to invoke Crowley's alleged infirmity at the time of his acquaintance with Gardner:

"It has been stated by Francis King in his *Ritual Magic In England* that Aleister Crowley was paid by Gerald Gardner to write the rituals of Gardner's new witch cult... Now, Gerald Gardner never met Aleister Crowley until the very last years of the latter's life, when he was a feeble old man living at a private hotel in Hastings, being kept alive

In his last years the old Magus envisioned the need for a new generation of leaders with new ideas.

by injections of drugs... If, therefore, Crowley really invented these rituals in their entirety, they must be about the last thing he ever wrote. Was this enfeebled and practically dying man really capable of such a tour de force?"

The obvious answer, as the late Dr. Israel Regardie's introduction to the posthumous collection of Crowley's letters, *Magick Without Tears*, implies, would seem to be yes. Crowley continued to produce extraordinary material almost to the end of his life, and much of what I have seen of the "Wiccan Crowley" is, in any case, of earlier origin.

Gerald Gardner is himself not altogether silent on the subject. In *Witchcraft Today* (p 47), Gardner asks himself, with what degree of irony one can only guess at, who, in modern times, could have invented the Wiccan rituals. "The only man I can think of who could have invented the rites," he offers, "was the late Aleister Crowley... possibly he borrowed things from the cult writings, or more likely someone may have borrowed expressions from him...." A few legs may be being pulled here, and perhaps more than a few.

As a prophet ahead of his time, as a poet and dreamer, Crowley is one of the outstanding figures of the 20th (or any) century. As an organizer, he was almost as much of a calamity as he was at managing his own finances... and personal life. As I understand the liberatory nature of the magical path, one would do well to see the difference between Crowley the prophet of Thelema and Crowley the insolvent and awkward administrator.

"The only man I can think of who could have invented the rites," he offers, "was the late Aleister Crowley... possibly he borrowed things from the cult writings, or more likely someone may have borrowed expressions from him...."

THE SECRET HISTORY OF MODERN WITCHCRAFT

Crowley very much lacked the common touch; Gardner was above all things a popularizer. Both men have been reviled as lecherous "dirty old men"—Crowley, as a seducer of women and a homosexual, a drug addict and "Satanist" rolled together.

Practices that work are of value, whether they are two years old or two thousand. Practices, myths, institutions and obligations which, on the other hand, may be infinitely ancient are of no value at all unless they work.

Gardner was, they would have it, a voyeur, exhibitionist and bondage freak with a "penchant for ritual" to borrow a line from *The Story Of O*. Both were, in reality, spiritual libertines, ceremonial magicians who did not shy away from the awesome force of human sexuality and its potential for spiritual transformation as well as physical gratification.

I will not say with finality at this point whether Wicca is an outright invention of these two divine mountebanks. If so, more power to them, and to those who truly follow in their path. I do know that, around 1945, Crowley met with Gardner, and gave him license to organize an O.T.O. encampment. This was, as it turns out, a serious effort by Crowley to establish a new O.T.O. presence in Britain. As late as May of 1947 we have seen letters from Crowley to one of his key associates urging the latter to send his followers in London to Dr. Gardner so that they might receive proper initiation in O.T.O. through Gardner's O.T.O. Camp, which Crowley anticipated being in operation in a matter of weeks. After Crowley's death his close collaborator, Lady Harris, thought Gardner to be Crowley's successor as head of the O.T.O. in Europe. Gardner claimed as much himself.

Shortly thereafter, the public face of Wicca came into view, and that is what I know of the matter: I presently have in my possession Gardner's certificate of license to organize said O.T.O. camp, signed and sealed by Aleister Crowley. The certificate and its import are examined in connection with my personal search for the original Book of Shadows in the next section of this narrative.

For now, though, let us note in the years since Crowley chartered Gardner to organize a magical encampment, Wicca has both grown in popularity and become, to my mind, something far less real than either Gardner or Crowley could have wanted or foreseen. Wherever they came from, the rites and practices which came from or through Gerald Gardner were strong, and tapped into that archetypal reality, that level of consciousness beneath the mask of polite society and conventional wisdom which is the function of True Magick.

At a popular level, this was the Tantric Sex Magick of the West. Whether this primordial access has been lost to us will depend on the awareness, the awakening or lack thereof among practitioners of the near to middle-near future. Carried to its end Gardnerian practices, like Crowley's magick, are not merely exotic; they are, in the truest sense, subversive.

Practices that *work* are of value, whether they are two years old or two thousand. Practices, myths, institutions and obligations which, on the other hand, may be infinitely ancient are of no value at all *unless* they work.

THE DEVIL, YOU SAY

Before we move on, though, in light of the furor over real and imagined "Satanism" that has overtaken parts of the popular press in recent years, I would feel a bit remiss in this account if I did not take momentary note of that other strain of left-handed occult mythology, Satanism. Wiccans are correct when they say that modern Wicca is not Satanic, that Satanism is "reverse Christianity" whereas Wicca is a separate, non-Christian religion.

Still, it should be noted, so much of our society has been grounded in the repressiveness and authoritarian moralism of what passes for Christianity that a liberal dose of "counter-Christianity" is to be expected. The Pat Robertsons of the world make possible the Anton LaVeys. In the long history of repressive religion, a certain fable of Satanism has arisen. It constitutes a mythos of its own. No doubt, misguided copycat fanatics have sometimes misused this mythos, in much the same way that Charles Manson misused the music and culture of the 1960s.

True occult initiates have always regarded the Ultimate Reality as beyond all names and description. Named "deities" are, therefore, largely symbols. "Isis" is a symbol of the long-denied female component of deity to some occultists. "Pan" or "The Horned God" or "Set" or even "Satan" are symbols of unconscious, repressed sexuality. To the occultist, there is no Devil, no "god of evil." There is, ultimately, only the Ain Sof Aur of the Qabala; the limitless light of which we are but a frozen spark. Evil, in this system, is the mere absence of light. All else is illusion.

The goal of the occult path of initiation is *balance*. In Freemasonry and High Magick, the symbols of the White Pillar and Black Pillar represent this balance between conscious and unconscious forces.

In Gardnerian Wicca, the Goddess and Horned God—and the Priestess and Priest, represent that balance. There is nothing, nothing whatever of pacts with the "Devil" or the worship of evil in any of this; that belongs to misguided ex-Christians who have been given the absurd fundamentalist Sunday school notion that one must choose the exoteric Christian version of God, or choose the Devil. Islam, Judaism and even Catholicism have at one time or another been thought "Satanic," and occultists have merely played on this bigoted symbolism, not subscribed to it.

As we have seen, Wicca since Gardner's time has been watered down in many of its expressions into a kind of mushy white-light "New Age" religion, with far less of the strong sexuality characteristic of Gardnerianism, though, also, sometimes with less pretense as well.

In any event, Satanism has popped up now and again through much of the history of the Christian Church. The medieval witches were not likely to have been Satanists, as the Church would have it, but, as we have seen, neither were they likely to have been "witches" in the Wiccan sense, either.

The Hellfire Clubs of the 18th century were mockingly Satanic, and groups like the Process Church of the Final Judgment do, indeed, have Satanic elements in their (one should remember) essentially Christian theology.

Aleister Crowley, ever theatrical, was prone to use Satanic symbolism in much the same way, tongue jutting in cheek, as he was given to saying that he "sacrificed hundreds of children each year," that is, that he was sexually active. Crowley once called a press conference at the foot of the Statue of Liberty, where he announced that he was burning his British Passport to protest Britain's involvement in World War One. He tossed an empty envelope into the water.

The most popular form of "counter-Christianity" to emerge in modern times, though, was Anton Szandor LaVey's San Francisco-based Church of Satan, founded April 30, 1966. LaVey's Church enjoyed an initial burst of press interest, grew to a substantial size, and appeared to maintain itself during the cultural drought of the 1970s. LaVey's books, *The Satanic Bible* and *The Satanic Rituals*, have remained in print for many years, and his ideas seem to be enjoying a renewal of interest, especially among younger people, punks and heavy metal fans with a death-wish mostly. By the 1980s, the Church of Satan had been largely succeeded by the Temple of Set. This is pure theater or psychodrama; more in the nature of psychotherapy than religion.

It is interesting to note Francis King's observation that before the Church of Satan began LaVey was involved in an occult group which included, among others, underground film maker Kenneth Anger, a person well known in Crowleyan circles. Of the rites of the Church of Satan, King states that "...most of its teachings and magical techniques were somewhat vulgarized versions of those of Aleister Crowley's Ordo Templi Orientis."[10] To which we might add that, as with the O.T.O., the rites of the Church of Satan and Temple of Set are manifestly potent, but hardly criminal or murderous.

LaVey, like Gardner and unlike Crowley, appears to have had "the common touch"—perhaps rather more so than Gardner. This attraction was, however, caught up in the hedonism of the 1970s, and had little to say by the end of the 20th century.

I determined to trace the Wiccan rumor to its source. As we shall see, in the very year I "fell" into being a Gnostic Bishop, I also fell into the original charters, rituals and paraphernalia of Wicca.

THE CHARTER AND THE BOOK (BEING A RADICAL REVISIONIST HISTORY OF THE ORIGINS OF THE MODERN WITCH CULT AND *THE BOOK OF SHADOWS*)

> "G. B. Gardner ... is head of the O.T.O. in Europe."
>
> –Lady Frieda Harris, letter to Karl Germer, January 2, 1948

> **By the 1980s, the Church of Satan had been largely succeeded by the Temple of Set. This is pure theater or psychodrama; more in the nature of psychotherapy than religion.**

"It was one of the secret doctrines of paganism that the Sun was the source, not only of light, but of life. The invasion of classical beliefs by the religions of Syria and Egypt which were principally solar, gradually affected the conception of Apollo, and there is a certain later identification of him with the suffering God of Christianity, Freemasonry and similar cults."

–Aleister Crowley in *Astrology*, 1974

"If GBG and Crowley only knew each other for a short year or two, do you think that would be long enough for them to become such good friends that gifts of personal value would be exchanged several times, and that GBG would have been able to acquire the vast majority of Crowley's effects after his death?"

–Merlin the Enchanter, personal letter, 1986

"...On the floor before the altar, he remembers a sword with a flat cruciform brass hilt, and a well-worn manuscript book of rituals—the hereditary Book of Shadows, which he will have to copy out for himself in the days to come..."

–Stewart Farrar in *What Witches Do*, 1971

"...the Gardnerian Book of Shadows is one of the key factors in what has become a far bigger and more significant movement than Gardner can have envisaged; so historical interest alone would be enough reason for defining it while first-hand evidence is still available..."

–Janet and Stewart Farrar in *The Witches' Way*, 1984

"It has been alleged that a Book of Shadows in Crowley's hand-writing was formerly exhibited in Gerald's Museum of Witchcraft on the Isle of Man. I can only say I never saw this on either of the two occasions when I stayed with Gerald and Donna Gardner on the island. The large, hand-written book depicted in *Witchcraft Today* is not in Crowley's handwriting, but Gerald's..."

–Doreen Valiente in *Witchcraft for Tomorrow*, 1978

"Aidan Kelly... labels the entire Wiccan revival 'Gardnerian Witchcraft'... The reasoning and speculation in Aidan's book are intricate. Briefly,

his main argument depends on his discovery of one of Gardner's working notebooks, Ye Book of Ye Art Magical, which is in possession of Ripley International, Ltd...."

–Margot Adler in *Drawing Down the Moon*, 1979

WAITING FOR THE MAN FROM CANADA

I was, for the third time in four years, waiting a bit nervously for the Canadian executive with the original Book of Shadows in the ramshackle office of Ripley's Believe It or Not Museum.

"They're at the jail," a smiling secretary-type explained, "but we've called them and they should be back over here to see you in just a few minutes."

The jail? Ah, St. Augustine, Florida. "The Old Jail," was the "nation's oldest city's" second most tasteless tourist trap, complete with cage-type cells and a mock gallows. For a moment I allowed myself to play in my head with the vision of Norm Deska, Ripley Operations Vice President and John Turner, the General Manager of Ripley's local operation and the guy who'd bought the Gerald Gardner collection from Gardner's niece, Monique Wilson, sitting in the slammer. But no, Turner apparently had just been showing Deska the town. I straightened my ice cream suit for the fiftieth time, and suppressed the comment. We were talking big history here, and big bucks, too. I gulped. The original Book of Shadows. Maybe.

It had started years before. One of the last people in America to be a fan of carnival sideshows, I was anxious to take another opportunity to go through the almost archetypally seedy old home that housed the original Ripley's Museum.

I had known that Ripley had, in the 1970s acquired the Gardner stuff, but as far as I knew it was all located at their Tennessee resort museum. I think I'd heard they'd closed it down. By then, the social liberalism of the early '70s was over, and witchcraft and sorcery were no longer in keeping with a "family style" museum. It featured a man with a candle in his head, a Tantric skull drinking cup and freak show stuff like that, but, that, apparently, was deemed suitable family fun.

I was a bit surprised, then, when I discovered some of the Gardner stuff—including an important historical document, for sale in the gift shop, in a case just opposite the little alli-

> **"You know," I suggested, "if you ever, in all this stuff, happen across a copy of The Book of Shadows in the handwriting of Aleister Crowley, it would be of considerable historical value."**

gators that have "St. Augustine, Florida—America's Oldest City" stickered on their plastic bellies for the folks back home to use as a paper-weight. The price tags on the occult stuff, however, were way out of my range.

Back again, three years later, and I decided, what the hell, so I asked the cashier about the stuff still gathering dust in the glass case, and it was like I'd pushed some kind of button.

Out comes Mr. Turner, the manager, who whisks us off to a store room which is filled, FILLED, I tell you, with parts of the Gardner collection, much of it, if not "for sale" as such, at least available for negotiation. Mr. Turner told us about acquiring the collection when he was manager of Ripley's Blackpool operation, how it had gone over well in the US at first, but had lost popularity and was now relegated for the most part to storage status.

Visions of sugarplums danced in my head. There were many treasures here, but the biggest plum of all, I thought, was not surprisingly, not to be seen.

I'd heard all kinds of rumors about the Book of Shadows over the years, many of them conflicting, all of them intriguing. Rumor #1, of course, is that which accompanied the birth (or, depending on how one looked at it, the revival) of modern Wicca, the contemporary successor of ancient fertility cults.

It revolved around elemental rituals, secret rites of passage and a mythos of goddess and god that seemed attractive to me as a psychologically valid alternative to the austere, antisexual moralism of Christianity. The Book of Shadows, in this context, was the "holy book" of Wicca, copied out by hand by new initiates of the cult with a history stretching back at least to the era of witch burnings. Rumor #2, which I had tended to credit, had it that Gerald Gardner, the "father of modern Wicca" had paid Aleister Crowley in his final years to write the Book of Shadows, perhaps whole cloth. The rumor's chief exponent was the respected historian of the occult, Francis King.

Rumor #3 had it that Gardner had written the Book himself, which others had since copied and/or stolen.

To the contrary, said rumor #4, Gardner's Museum had contained an old, even ancient copy of the Book of Shadows, proving its antiquity.

In more recent years modern Wiccans have tended to put some distance between themselves and Gardner, just as Gardner, for complex reasons, tended to distance himself in the early years of Wicca (circa 1944–1954) from the blatant sexual magick of Aleister Crowley, "the wickedest man in the world" by some accounts, and from Crowley's organization, the Ordo Templi Orientis. Why Gardner chose to do this is speculative, but I've got some idea. But, I'm getting ahead of myself.

While Turner showed me a blasphemous cross shaped from the body of two nude women (created for the 18th century infamous "Hellfire Club" in England and depicted in the *Man, Myth And Magic* encyclopedia; I bought it, of course) and a statue of Beelzebub from the dusty Garderian archives, a thought occurred to me. "You know," I suggested, "if you ever, in all this stuff, happen across a

> **It would be like finding The Book of Mormon in Joseph Smith's hand, or finding the original Ten Commandments written not by God Himself, but by Moses, pure and simple.**

copy of The Book of Shadows in the handwriting of Aleister Crowley, it would be of considerable historical value."

I understated the case. It would be like finding The Book of Mormon in Joseph Smith's hand, or finding the original Ten Commandments written not by God Himself, but by Moses, pure and simple. (Better still, eleven commandments, with a margin note, "first draft.") I didn't really expect anything to come of it, and in the months ahead, it didn't.

In the meantime, I had managed to acquire the interesting document I first mistook for Gerald Gardner's (long acknowledged) initiation certificate into Crowley's Thelemic magical Ordo Templi Orientis. To my eventual surprise, I discovered that, not only was this not a simple initiation certificate for the Minerval (probationary-lowest) degree, but, to the contrary, was a Charter for Gardner to begin his own encampment of the O.T.O., and to initiate members into the O.T.O.

In the document, furthermore, Gardner is referred to as "Prince of Jerusalem"—that is, he is acknowledged to be a Fourth Degree Perfect Initiate in the Order. This, needless to say, would usually imply years of dedicated training. Though Gardner had claimed Fourth Degree O.T.O. status as early as publication of *High Magic's Aid*, (and claimed even higher status in one edition) this runs somewhat contrary to both generally held Wiccan and contemporary O.T.O. orthodox understandings that the O.T.O. was then fallow in England.

At the time the document was written, most maintained, Gardner could have known Crowley for only a brief period, and was not himself deeply involved in the O.T.O. The document is undated but probably was drawn up around 1945.

As I said, it was once understood that no viable chapter of the O.T.O. was supposed to exist in England at that time; the only active chapter was in California, and is the direct antecedent of the contemporary authentic Ordo Templi Orientis. Karl Germer, Crowley's immediate successor, had barely escaped death in a Concentration Camp during the War, his mere association with Crowley being tantamount to a death sentence. But Crowley himself clearly expected Gardner to establish an O.T.O. Camp, and was referring followers to Gardner for initiation as late as 1947.

The German O.T.O. had been largely destroyed by the Nazis, along with other Freemasonic organizations, and Crowley himself was in declining health and power, the English O.T.O. virtually dead. A provincial Swiss branch existed, but was highly insular and tending towards schism. The Charter also displayed other irregularities of a revealing nature. Though the signature and seals are certainly those of Crowley, the text is in the decorative hand of Gerald Gardner! The complete text reads as follows:

> "Do what thou wilt shall be the law. We Baphomet X Degree Ordo Templi Orientis Sovereign Grand Master General of All English speaking countries of the Earth do hereby authorise our Beloved Son Scire (Dr.G,B,Gardner,) Prince of Jerusalem to constitute a camp of the Ordo Templi Orientis, in the degree Minerval. Love is the Law, Love under will. Witness my hand and seal Baphomet Xo"

Leaving aside the misquotation from *The Book of the Law* ("Do what thou wilt shall be the Law" instead of "Do what thou wilt shall be the whole of the Law"), which got by me for some months and probably got by Crowley when it was presented to him for signature, the document is definitely authentic. It hung for some time in Gardner's museum, possibly giving rise, as we shall see, to the rumor that Crowley wrote the Book of Shadows for Gardner. According to Doreen Valiente, and to Col. Lawrence as well, the museum's descriptive pamphlet says of this document:

"The collection includes a Charter granted by Aleister Crowley to G. B. Gardner (the Director of this Museum) to operate a Lodge of Crowley's fraternity, the Ordo Templi Orientis. (The Director would like to point out, however, that he has never used this Charter and has no intention of doing so, although to the best of his belief he is the only person in Britain possessing such a Charter from Crowley himself; Crowley was a personal friend of his, and gave him the Charter because he liked him)." This was probably written well after Wicca was developed in the form it is today identified with, at least in Britain. As I point out elsewhere, Crowley clearly took the Charter seriously, even openly envisioning it extending to a Lodge to do the entire "Man of Earth Series" of O.T.O. initiations eventually. Gardner, for his part, places a different connotation on the Charter at an earlier time, giving out the impression that it makes him the Grand Master of the O.T.O. in Europe.

Col. Lawrence ("Merlin the Enchanter"), in a letter to me dated 6 December, 1986, adds that this appeared in Gardner's booklet, *The Museum of Magic and Witchcraft*. The explanation for the curious wording of the text, taking, as Dr. Gardner does, great pains to distance himself from Crowley and the O.T.O., may be hinted at in that the booklet suggests that this display in the "new upper gallery" (page 24) was put out at a relatively late date when, as we shall discover, Gardner was making himself answerable to the demands of the new witch cult and not the long-dead Crowley and (then) relatively moribund O.T.O.

Now, the "my friend Aleister" ploy might explain the whole thing. Perhaps, as some including Ms. Valiente believe, Aleister Crowley was desperate in his last years to hand on what he saw as his legacy to someone. He recklessly handed out his literary estate, perhaps gave contradictory instruction to various of his remaining few devotees (e.g. Kenneth Grant, Grady McMurtry, Karl Germer), and may have given Gardner an "accelerated advancement" in his order.

There is, however, certainly reason to dispute this. I have read Crowley's letters to Jack Parsons and to Karl Germer, and others, including the more famous letters published as *Magick Without Tears*, and his now celebrated authorizations to Grady McMurtry—all very late writings indeed, as well as his Last Will and Testament dated June 19, 1947, only six months prior to his death, and Crowley seems intent upon an orderly process of transition of his minor financial estate and, more importantly, his substantial literary estate, to the O.T.O. leadership which, he leaves no doubt in his Will, falls to Germer, then Grand Treasurer General of the O.T.O. To the end he continues to critique what he sees as unsound thinking (letters to Parsons and Germer in 1946), and to speak of moving to California to be with Agape Lodge, by then the remaining centerpiece of the O.T.O., but also referring to Gardner's Camp in London as a virtual accomplished fact.

Ms. Valiente, a devoted Wiccan who is also a dedicated seeker after the historical truth, mentions also the claim made by the late Gerald Yorke to her that Gardner had paid Crowley a substantial sum for the document. In a letter to me dated 28th August, 1986, Ms. Valiente tells of a meeting with Yorke "...in London many years ago and mentioned Gerald's O.T.O. Charter to him, whereon he told me, 'Well, you know, Gerald Gardner paid old Crowley about [$1,500] or so for that...' This may or may not be correct..." Money or friendship do not explain the Charter.

Gardner was in the habit, after the public career of Wicca emerged in the 1950s, of downgrading any Crowleyite associations out of his past, and, as Janet and Stewart Farrar reveal in *The Witches' Way* (1984, p3) there are three distinct versions of the Book of Shadows in Gerald Gardner's handwriting which incorporate successively less material from Crowley's writings, though the last (termed "Text C" and co-written with Doreen Valiente after 1953) is still heavily influenced by Crowley and the O.T.O.

Ms. Valiente has recently uncovered a copy of an old occult magazine contemporary with *High Magic's Aid* and from the same publisher, which discusses an ancient Indian document called "The Book of Shadows" but apparently totally unrelated to the Wiccan book of the same name. Valiente acknowledges that the earliest text by Gardner known to her was untitled, though she refers to it as a "Book of Shadows."

It seems suspicious timing; did Gardner take over the title from his publisher's magazine? Ms. Valiente observed to me that the "...eastern Book of Shadows does not seem to have anything to do with witchcraft at all ... is this where old Gerald first found the expression "The Book of Shadows" and adopted it as a more poetical name for a magical manuscript than, say 'The Grimoire' or 'The Black Book'.... I don't profess to know the answer; but I doubt if this is mere coincidence...."

The claim is frequently made by those who wish to "salvage" a pre-Gardnerian source of Wiccan materials that there is a "core" of "authentic" materials. But, as the Farrars' recently asserted, the portions of the Book of Shadows "...which changed least between Texts A, B and C were naturally the three initiation rituals; because these, above all, would be the traditional elements which would have been carefully preserved, probably for centuries...."

But what does one mean by "traditional materials"? The three initiation rites, now much-described in print, all smack heavily of the crypto-Freemasonic ritual of the Hermetic Order of the Golden Dawn, the O.T.O., and the various esoteric NeoRosicrucian groups that abounded in Britain from about 1885 on, and which were, it is widely known, the fountainhead of much that is associated with Gardner's friend Crowley.

The Third Degree ritual, perhaps Wicca's ultimate rite, is, essentially, a nonsymbolic Gnostic Mass, that beautiful, evocative, erotic and esoteric ritual written and published by Crowley in the Equinox, after attending a Russian Orthodox Mass in the early part of the 20th century. The Gnostic Mass has had far-reaching influence, and it would appear that the Wiccan Third Degree is one of the most blatant examples of that influence.

Take, for example, this excerpt from what is perhaps the most intimate, most secret and most sublime moment in the entire repertoire of Wicca rituals, the nonsymbolic (that is, overtly sexual) Great Rite of the Third Degree initiation, as related by Janet and Stewart Farrar in *The Witches' Way* (p.34):

> The Priest continues: 'O Secret of Secrets, That art hidden in the being of all lives, Not thee do we adore, For that which adoreth is also thou. Thou art That, and That am I. Kiss I am the flame

The original was some mundane volume, on Asian knives or something but the inside pages had been removed, and a kind of notebook—almost a journal—had been substituted.

that burns in the heart of every man, And in the core of every star. I am life, and the giver of life. Yet therefore is the knowledge of me the knowledge of death. I am alone, the Lord within ourselves, Whose name is Mystery of Mysteries.'

Let us be unambiguous as to the importance in Wicca of this ritual; as the Farrars put it (p.31) "Third degree initiation elevates a witch to the highest of the three grades of the Craft. In a sense, a third-degree witch is fully independent, answerable only to the Gods and his or her own conscience…" In short, in a manner of speaking this is all that Wicca can offer a devotee.

With this in mind, observe the following, from Aleister Crowley's Gnostic Mass, first published in The Equinox over 80 years ago and routinely performed (albeit in the symbolic form) by me and by many other Bishops, Priests, Priestesses and Deacons in the O.T.O. and Ecclesia Gnostica (E.G.C.) today. The following is excerpted from *Gems From the Equinox*, p. 372, but is widely available in published form:

> *The Priest: O secret of secrets that art hidden in the being of all that lives, not Thee do we adore, for that which adoreth is also Thou. Thou art That, and That am I. I am the flame that burns in every heart of man, and in the core of every star. I am Life, and the giver of Life; yet therefore is the knowledge of me the knowledge of death. I am alone; there is no God where I am.*

So, then, where, apart from Freemasonry and the Thelemic tradition of Crowley and the O.T.O., is the "traditional material" some Wiccan writers seem to seek with near desperation? I am not trying to be sarcastic in the least, but even commonplace self-references used among Wiccans today, such as "the Craft" or the refrain "so mote it be" are lifted straight out of Freemasonry (see, for example, *Duncan's Ritual of Freemasonry*). And, as Doreen Valiente notes in her letter to me mentioned before, "…of course old Gerald was also a member of the Co-Masons, and an ordinary Freemason…" as well as an O.T.O. member.

THE REAL ORIGIN OF WICCA

We must dismiss with some respect the assertion, put forth by Margot Adler and others, that "Wicca no longer adheres to the orthodox mythos of the Book of Shadows."

Many, if not most of those who have been drawn to Wicca in the last three decades came to it under the spell (if I may so term it) of the legend of ancient Wicca. If that legend is false, then while reformists and revisionist apologists (particularly the peculiar hybrid spawned in the late '60s (under the name "feminist Wicca") may seek other valid grounds for their practices, we at least owe it to those who have operated under a misapprehension to explain the truth, and let the chips fall where they may.

I believe there is a core of valid experience falling under the Wiccan-Neopagan heading, but that that core is the same essential core that lies at the truths exposed by the dreaded bogey-man Aleister Crowley and the "wicked" pansexualism of Crowley's Law of Thelema. That such roots would be not just uncomfortable, but intolerable to the orthodox traditionalists among the Wiccans, but even more so among the hybrid feminist "Wiccans" may indeed be an understatement.

Neopaganism, in a now archaic "hippie" misreading of ecology, mistakes responsible stewardship of nature for nature worship. Ancient pagans did not "worship" nature; to a large extent they were afraid of it, as has been pointed out to me by folk practitioners. Their "nature rites" were to propitiate the caprice of the gods, not necessarily to honor them. The first Neopagan revivalists, Gardner, Crowley and Dr. Murray, well understood this. Neopagan Wiccans usually do not.

In introducing a "goddess element" into their theology, Crowley and Gardner both understood the yin/yang, male/female fundamental polarity of the universe. Radical feminist Neopagans have taken this balance and altered it, however unintentionally, into a political feminist agenda, centered around a near-monotheistic worship of the female principle, in a bizarre caricature of patriarchal Christianity.

I do not say these things lightly; I have seen it happen in my own time. If this be truth, let truth name its own price. I was not sure, until Norm and John got back from the Old Jail.

A couple of months earlier, scant days after hearing that I was to become a Gnostic Bishop and thus an heir to a corner of Crowley's legacy, I had punched on my answering machine, and there was the unexpected voice of John Turner saying that he had located what seemed to be the original Book of Shadows in an inventory list, locating it at Ripley's office in Toronto.

He said he didn't think they would sell it as an individual item, but he gave me the name of a top official in the Ripley organization, who I promptly contacted. I eventually made a substantial offer for the book, sight unseen, figuring there was (at the least) a likelihood I'd be able to turn the story into a book and get my money back out of it, to say nothing of the historical import.

But, as I researched the matter, I became more wary, and confused; Gardner's texts "A" "B" and "C" all seemed to be accounted for. Possibly, I began to suspect, this was either a duplicate of the "deThelemicised" post-1954 version with segments written by Gardner and Valiente and copied and recopied (as well as distorted) from hand to hand since by Wiccans the world over.

Maybe, I mused, Valiente had one copy and Gardner another, the latter sold to Ripley with the Collection. Or, perhaps it was the curious notebook discovered by Aidan Kelly in the Ripley files called *Ye Book of Ye Art Magical*, the meaning of which was unclear.

While chatting with Ms. Deska, Norm returned from his mission, we introduced in businesslike fashion, and he told me he'd get the book, whatever it might be, from the vault.

The vault?! I sat there thinking God knows what. Recently, I'd gotten a call from Toronto, and it seems the Ripley folks wanted me to take a look at what they had. I had made a considerable offer, and at that point I figured I'd had at least a nibble. As it so happened Norm would be visiting on a routine inspection visit, so it was arranged he would bring the manuscript with him.

Almost from the minute he placed it in front of me, things began to make some kind of sense. Clearly, this was *Ye Book of Ye Art Magical*. Just as clearly, it was an unusual piece, written largely in the same hand as the Charter I had obtained earlier—that is, in the hand of Gerald Gardner. Of this I became certain, because I had handwriting samples of Gardner, Valiente and Crowley in my possession. Ms. Valiente had been mindful of this when she wrote me, on August 8, 1986:

"I have deliberately chosen to write you in longhand, rather than send a typewritten reply, so that you will have something by which to judge the validity of the claim you

tell me is being made by the Ripley organization to have a copy of a "Book of Shadows" in Gerald Gardner's handwriting and mine. If this is... "Ye Book of Ye Art Magical," ... this is definitely in Gerald Gardner's handwriting. Old Gerald, however, had several styles of handwriting... I think it is probable that the whole MS. was in fact written by Gerald, and no other person was involved; but of course I may be wrong...."

At first glance it appeared to be a very old book, and it suggested to me where the rumors that a very old, possibly medieval Book of Shadows had once been on display in Gardner's Museum had emerged from.

Any casual onlooker might see *Ye Book* in this light, for the cover was indeed that of an old volume, with the original title scratched out crudely on the side and a new title tooled into the leather cover. The original was some mundane volume, on Asian knives or something (an interest of Gardner's), but the inside pages had been removed, and a kind of notebook—almost a journal—had been substituted.

As far as I could see, no dates appear anywhere in the book. It is written in several different handwriting styles, although, as noted above, Doreen Valiente assured me that Gardner was apt to use several styles. I had the distinct impression this "notebook" had been written over a considerable period of time, perhaps years, perhaps even decades. It may, indeed, date from his days in the 1930s when he linked up with a NeoRosicrucian performance theatrical troupe, that could have included among its members the legendary Dorothy Clutterbuck, who set Gardner on the path which led to Wicca.

Thinking on it, what emerges from *Ye Book of Ye Art Magical* is a developmental set of ideas. Much of it is straight out of Crowley, but it is clearly the published Crowley, the old Magus of the O.T.O. and A∴ A∴

Somewhere along the line it hit me that I was not exactly looking at the "original Book of Shadows" but, perhaps, the outline Gardner prepared over a long period of time, apparently in secret (since Valiente, a relatively early initiate of Gardner's, never heard of it nor saw it, according to her own account, until recent years, about the time Aidan Kelly unearthed it in the Ripley collection long after Gardner's death).

Turner showed me a Gardner scrapbook in Ripley's store room which was mostly cheesecake magazine photographs and articles about actresses.

Dr. Gardner kept many odd notebooks and scrapbooks that perhaps would reveal much about his character and motivations. Turner showed me a Gardner scrapbook in Ripley's store room which was mostly cheesecake magazine photographs and articles about actresses. Probably none are so evocative as *Ye Book of Ye Art Magical*, discovered hidden away in the back of an old sofa.

This is not the "ancient religion of the Wise" but the modern sayings of "the Beast 666" as Crowley was wont to style himself.

I have the impression it was essentially unknown in and after Gardner's lifetime, and that by the Summer of 1986 few had seen inside it; I knew of only Kelly and my own party. Perhaps the cover had been seen by some along the line, accounting for the rumor of a "very old Book of Shadows" in Gardner's Museum.

If someone had seen the charter unquestionably signed by Crowley ("Baphomet") but written by Gerald Gardner, and had gotten a look, as well, at *Ye Book*, they might well have concluded that Crowley had written *both*, an honest error, but maybe the source of that long-standing accusation. There is even a notation in the Ripley catalog attributing the manuscript to Crowley on someone's say-so, but I have no indication Ripley has any other such book. Finally, if the notebook is a source book of any religious system, it is not that of medieval witchcraft, but the 20th century shining sanity of the famous Magus Aleister Crowley and the Thelemic/Gnostic creed of *The Book of the Law*.

As I sat there I read aloud familiar quotations or paraphrases from published material in the Crowley-Thelemic canon. This is not the "ancient religion of the Wise" but the modern sayings of "the Beast 666" as Crowley was wont to style himself.

But, does any of this invalidate Wicca as an expression of human spirituality? It depends on where one is coming from. Certainly, the foundations of Feminist Wicca and the modern cult of the goddess are challenged with the fact that the goddess in question is Nuit, her manifestation the sworn whore, Our Lady Babalon, the Scarlet Woman. Transform what you will shall be the whole of history, but THIS makes what Marx did to Hegel look like slavish devotion.

What Crowley himself said of this kind of witchcraft is not merely instructive, but an affront to the conceits of an era.

"The belief in witchcraft," he observed, " was not all superstition; its psychological roots were sound. Women who are thwarted in their natural instincts turn inevitably to all kinds of malignant mischief, from slander to domestic destruction..."

For those who neither worship nor are disdainful of the man who "made sexuality a god" or, at least, acknowledged it as such, experience must be its own teacher. If Wicca is a sort of errant Minerval encampment of the O.T.O., gone far astray and far afield since the days Crowley gave Gardner a charter he "didn't use" but seemed to value, and a whole range of rituals and imagery that assault the senses at their most literally fundamental level; if this is true or sort of true Mythos has its place and role, but so, too, does reality.

WICCA AS AN O.T.O. ENCAMPMENT

It is of more than passing interest that the late Jack Parsons, one time (Acting) Master of Agape Lodge O.T.O. in California, began writing extensively of a revival of witchcraft from 1946 on; that is, at about the time of Crowley and Gardner's acknowledged association. Crowley referred to Dr. Gardner and his O.T.O. encampment in private correspondence almost to the time of his death, and spoke of it with optimism and enthusiasm.

When Lady Harris wrote Karl Germer that she believed Gardner was the head of the O.T.O. in Europe after Crowley's death, Germer didn't refute her; he simply indicated he hoped to see Gardner during his US visit, which he did. Furthermore, as alluded to in the previous section, Gardner himself claimed in a letter written shortly after Crowley's death that he *was*, in fact, the head of the O.T.O. in Europe.

The letter to Vernon Symonds, sent from Memphis, Tennessee where Gardner was then resident, and dated December 24, 1947, asserts that "... Aleister gave me a charter making me head of the O.T.O. in Europe. Now I want to get any papers about this that Aleister had; he had some typescript Rituals, I know. I have them, too, but I don't want his to fall into other people's hands..." I am editing Gardner's spelling with great kindness. This claim should

But, does any of this invalidate Wicca as an expression of human spirituality? It depends on where one is coming from.

be viewed with a grain of salt, but Lady Harris and Gardner were both intimate Crowley associates, and this should be kept in mind. The Charter in question referred to by Gardner is probably the one now in my possession. He almost certainly had no other. It is also noteworthy that Gardner, a ranking O.T.O. member, was resident in the US at the same time that both he and Parsons began to discuss "modern witchcraft." Both had extensive correspondence with Crowley and contact with Germer during this period.

The question of intent looms large in the background of this inquiry. If I had to guess, I would venture that Gerald Gardner did, in fact, invent Wicca more or less whole cloth, to be a popularized version of the O.T.O. Crowley, and his immediate successor Karl Germer, who also knew Dr. Gardner, likely set "old Gerald" on what they intended to be a Thelemic path, aimed at reestablishing at least a basic O.T.O. encampment in England.

It is also possible, but yet unproved, that, upon expelling Kenneth Grant from the O.T.O. in England, Germer, in the early 1950s, summoned Gardner back to America to interview him as a candidate for leading the British O.T.O. Gardner, it is confirmed, came to America, but by then Wicca, and Dr. Gardner had begun to take their own, watered-down course.

Let me close this section by quoting two interesting tidbits for your consideration.

First consider Doreen Valiente's observation to me concerning "the Parsons connection." I quote from her letter above mentioned, one of several she was kind enough to send me in 1986 in connection with my research into this matter.

We must remember that Ms. Valiente was a close associate of Gardner and is a dedicated and active Wiccan. She, of course, has her own interpretation of these matters.

The other matter of note is the question of the length of Gardner's association with the O.T.O. and with Crowley personally. My informant Col. Lawrence, tells me that he has in his possession a cigarette case which once belonged to Aleister Crowley. Inside "is a note in Crowley's hand that says simply: 'gift of GBG, 1936, A. Crowley'." (Personal letter, 6 December, 1986.)

The inscription could be a mistake, it could mean 1946, the period of the Charter. It could be a gift to Crowley from the Order GBG ("Great Brotherhood of God") of Crowley's

alienated student C. F. Russell, but the GBG closed its doors in 1938, and well before this Crowley and Russell had gone their separate ways. But, as Ms. Valiente put it in a letter to me of December 8, 1986:

> ...I did know about the existence of the O.T.O. Chapter in California at the time of Crowley's death, because I believe his ashes were sent over to them. He was cremated here in Brighton, you know, much to the scandal of the local authorities, who objected to the 'pagan funeral service.' If you are referring to the group of which Jack Parsons was a member (along with the egregious Mr. L. Ron Hubbard), then there is another curious little point to which I must draw your attention. I have a remarkable little book by Jack Parsons called Magick, Gnosticism And The Witchcraft. It is unfortunately undated, but Parsons died in 1952. The section on witchcraft is particularly interesting because it looks forward to a revival of witchcraft as the Old Religion.... I find this very thought provoking. Did Parsons write this around the time that Crowley was getting together with Gardner and perhaps communicated with the California group to tell them about it? Parsons began forecasting the "revival of Witchcraft" in the notorious "Liber 49— The Book of Babalon" written in 1946. The timing of the genesis of "The Book of Babalon"—which forecast a 'revival' of witchcraft in covens based on the number eleven (the Thelemic number of magick) rather than the traditional thirteen, seems to coincide with Crowley's O.T.O. Charter to Gardner, Gardner's U.S. visit, and also coincides rather closely with the writing of High Magic's Aid by Gardner.
>
> If your friend is right, then it would mean that old Gerald actually went through a charade of pretending to Arnold Crowther that Arnold was introducing him to Crowley for the first time—a charade which Crowley for some reason was willing to go along with. Why? I can't see the point of such a pretense; but then occultists sometimes do devious things...

Gnosticism and Wicca, the subjects of Jack Parsons' essays, republished by the O.T.O. and New Falcon Press in 1990, are the two most successful expressions to date of Crowley's dream of a popular solar-phallic religion. Maybe I'm wrong, but I think Aleister and Gerald may have cooked Wicca up. The issues for Thelemites and Wiccans here are, as I see it, two-fold:

If Wicca is the O.T.O.'s prodigal daughter, in fact, authorized directly by Crowley, how should they now relate to this?

Then too, what are we to make of and infer about all this business of a popular Thelemic-Gnostic religion? Were Crowley, Parsons, Gardner and others trying to do something of note with regard to actualizing a New Aeon here which bears scrutiny? Or is this mere speculation, and of

"The belief in witchcraft was not all superstition; its psychological roots were sound. Women who are thwarted in their natural instincts turn inevitably to all kinds of malignant mischief, from slander to domestic destruction..."

little significance for the Great Work today? If the Charter Crowley issued Gardner is, indeed, the authority upon which Wicca has been built for half a century, sometimes, I muse, the Inner Order revoked Wicca's charter in 1986, placing it, so to speak, in my hands. Since I hold it in Trust for the O.T.O., perhaps Wicca has, in symbolic form, returned home at last. It remains for the Wiccans, literally (since the charter hangs in my temple space), to read the handwriting on the wall. ⌺

Personal letters referenced in this essay:

Aleister Crowley to W.B.C., May 30, 1947
Frieda Harris to Frederic Mellinger, December 7, 1947
Gerald Gardner to Vernon Symonds, December 24, 1947
Frieda Harris to Karl Germer, January 2, 1948
Karl Germer to Frieda Harris, January 19, 1948
Doreen Valiente to Allen Greenfield, August 8, 1986
Doreen Valiente to Allen Greenfield, August 28, 1986
Doreen Valiente to Allen Greenfield, December 8, 1986

Endnotes

1. Gardner, *Witchcraft Today*, pp. 33–34.
2. Farrar, *What Witches Do*, pp. 34–35.
3. *Ibid.*, p 29.
4. *What Witches Do*, p 33.
5. *Ibid.*, pp. 12–13.
6. *Ibid.*, p 16.
7. *Tomorrow*, p 20.
8. *Witchcraft Today*, p 27.
9. Gardner, *ibid.*, introduction.
10. *Man, Myth And Magic*, p 3204.

SYMPATHY FOR THE DEVIL

MICHAEL MOYNIHAN

ANTON LAVEY
A Fireside Chat With the Black Pope

It's 1966 and drug-numbed hippies are running wild. The glare of psychedelia has begun to daze and confuse the masses, while the youth scene degenerates into one big, narcotized Love-In. What's a Luciferian outsider to do, as the rest of humanity takes a downward plunge into mobocratic misery?

If you are Anton Szandor LaVey, you come up with a sensible solution, proclaim the Year One and inaugurate history's first Church of Satan, fully aware of what kind of flak you're going to catch for it. A circle of alienated illuminati had already gathered around the charismatic LaVey, thus forming the fertile nucleus for "the ultimate conscious alternative to herd mentality and institutionalized thought," as he often described it. In LaVeyan philosophy, Satan is not a phantasm out of a Catholic exorcism, but rather a perfect symbol for the forces of Nature. It boils down more to operating within *lex talionis*, the law of retribution, than chanting mumbo-jumbo out of dusty spellbooks. But knowing wisely that every movement needs its *Mein Kampf* or *Das Kapital*, LaVey penned *The Satanic Bible*, outlining his strategies for the strong: those who would be gods among men. It's a razor-sharp, no-bullshit primer in natural and supernatural law, a tome of true heresy in the grand tradition. *The Satanic Rituals* followed hot on its heels, and by this time the Church was soaking up the international media spotlight and attracting notorious members like sexpot Jayne Mansfield, whose affair with LaVey proved legendary and, unfortunately, deadly. I'll leave it to his biographers to reveal the many facets of LaVey's vital interaction with the world of mortals—his associates, comrades, and romantic conquests were a veritable who's who of the underworld of 20th century America and beyond.

During his years in the public eye, the "Black Pope" was cheered and castigated, called everything from the world's most dangerous devil-worshipper to a mere sideshow charlatan. He's been accused of harboring fascist agendas and libertarian leanings. Initially considered to be a renegade humanist, in his later years LaVey advocated the personal use of stimulating and aesthetic artificial companions rather than suffer pointless interactions with everyday humans. Although many assume that the Church of Satan may be little more than a money-making gimmick, LaVey has

> In LaVeyan philosophy, Satan is not a phantasm out of a Catholic exorcism, but rather a perfect symbol for the forces of Nature.

always campaigned for the strict taxation of all churches, and claims that most of them could never subsist without their financial exemptions.

In the mid-1970s, tired of the media and the masses, LaVey became a deliberately elusive entity. He was the shadow looming over an already shadowy faith, who slyly handled the reigns of the beast he brought to life more than a quarter of a century ago. Giving audiences to only his closest co-conspirators, when he granted an interview it was no longer with corporate magazines or television talk shows, both of which he considered enemy missiles in the "Invisible War" for your mind and soul.

Rather than pandering for publicity, in his latter days he was happier to spend his precious time at the helm of a bank of synthesizers, conjuring deep emotions with the long-forgotten music he believed embodies the Satanic spirit. Amidst the menagerie of his feral cats Zambeezee and Cromwell, and Boaz the serpent, he and his biographer/confidant Blanche Barton lived a private, secretive life away from the madding crowd—and they smiled knowingly as LaVey's prophecies materialized one by one.

An additional by-product of this self-engineered seclusion was the multitude of unfounded rumors which swirled around his legacy, the two most common being that the Church no longer existed and that its founder passed away back in the '70s, shortly after making his initial splash. These stories couldn't have been farther from the truth, despite the wishful thinking of fearful Christians or save-the-world social activists. In 1993, at the ripe old age of 63, LaVey displayed his virility by siring a robust son, Xerxes—a magical child if ever there was one. Visiting his infamous Black House in the hills of San Francisco was an experience never forgotten, a reminder that there were still a few uniquely sentient and admirable humans left on the planet. It was during such a visit in 1994 that the following conversation took place. The version presented here is extracted from a more extensive 1994 article that ran in the (now sadly defunct) music and culture magazine *Seconds*, edited by Steven Blush and George Petros.

Anton LaVey, 1968. (Courtesy the Church of Satan)

Anton Szandor LaVey passed away on October 29, 1997. His 67 years on earth were abundantly filled with excitement, study, travel, mystery, adventure, artistry, and above all an exalted awareness of the limits of mankind's powers, both celestial and bestial. His achievements continue to inspire the next generation of modern Satanists. Since LaVey's departure, the Church of Satan has been under the guidance of High Priestess Blanche Barton. With the onset of the new millennium the active leadership was passed to the newly appointed High Priest, Peter H. Gilmore. Alongside his unflagging loyalty to LaVey's vision, Gilmore has distinguished himself as a writer and musical composer in his right, and he serves as the longstanding editor of *The Black Flame*, the church's "Official Forum."

I can understand well why some dynamic, independent, and perfectly sensible people might scoff at the idea of Satanism; I used to do so myself. Having never acknowledged Christianity in the first place, it is no wonder they feel little need for Satanism, especially as its most visible adherents seem predictably comprised of alienated teens or brash Rock and Rollers. But if the scoffers had ever happened to sit down next to LaVey in a tavern—not recognizing him, and thinking him no different from any other stranger—and strike up a conversation, the subject of Satanism probably wouldn't have even reared its head.

Talk might have ranged from that of cars, food, curious customs and human behavior, to love of animals, music, or forgotten lore of yesteryear; the conversation could have even broached upon the supernatural. Chances are they would remember it as a meeting with a charming and unpretentious fellow, possessed of a noir gleam in his eye and a penchant for off-color humor. They would

When you open your mouth, what do you have to say?
Are you going to write something interesting to read or is it just trivial?

recall him as one of the few people they'd met who seemed to truly know the score: aware of and even awed by the highest and most god-like aspirations demonstrated by exceptional personalities, but equally cognizant of the vast, turgid, and miasmal pits that most of mankind will forever wallow in, be it mentally or physically. He would have revealed himself as no starry-eyed dreamer, but rather one who knows that it has always been only a select few throughout history who are truly endowed with the ability of reaching the stars. Such scoffers would have deeply enjoyed conversing with this old curmudgeon who called himself "the Doc," and would hope that they might cross paths with this astute stranger once more, for genuinely wise men are few and far between on this earth. When reflecting on their meeting, the word "Satanic" might never even occur to them. And that, in fact, is the most sinister thing of all.

Just as Nietzsche cast a cold light on the abyss between *Übermensch* and "human, all too human" in the 19th century, LaVey was one of the most unforgiving and shining realists of the 20th. Reality is a bitter pill, and both pie-in-the-sky Christians and nose-in-the-dusty-grimoire occultniks can expect similar gastrointestinal trouble as it makes its way through their system. Those who refuse to face reality, oblivious to their own interminable foibles and mishaps, were once summed up aptly by LaVey as akin to the man who's jumped off the roof of a 20-storey building, and can be heard exclaiming as he flies past the third floor windows, "So far, so good!"

Accused of spreading the most dire diabolism to the masses, in truth LaVey was simply handing out high-voltage bullshit detectors. For those who misunderstood him and what he offered, sooner or later they'll embarrassingly find themselves sitting on a 99-cent whoopee cushion.

MM: Has the agenda of the Church of Satan altered over its history?

ASLV: No, but the tactics have changed according to the times and with respect to the needs and logistics required. What would be a form of advancement in a Satanic sense 25 years ago wouldn't be such an accomplishment now. Like recognition was important at the beginning, but that was before the era of "fifteen minutes of fame" and everyone thinking they're a big shot. When the Church of Satan started, it was the mid-60s; you had the situation of everyone thinking they're a god because they could take a drug to feel that. Now we see the results of that line of thought. But the Church of Satan said "Everyone is a god" as well. So between the psychedelic era and the Satanic counter-culture there weren't many opportunities for the average guy to be a nothing, a nobody.

MM: So "reaching God" on an LSD trip is a whole different ballgame from what you're talking about in Satanism.

ASLV: There's a very fundamental difference. For example, if someone picked up *The Satanic Bible* and found they were indeed potentially a god or goddess, they could make fools of themselves much easier than someone on drugs, since those people didn't care if anyone else even recognized it. But if someone who's a Satanist heard criticism, they might take it to heart and see they weren't quite a god yet. And at least they'd hopefully realize they weren't a zombie either.

MM: What is the next step for a Satanist after that?

ASLV: The Church of Satan claims we're already supermen, but we withhold judgment until we see what these supermen can do. When you open your mouth, what do you have to say? Are you going to write something interesting to read or is it just trivial? There are supermen and supermen—some are more superior than others. That's why there's no way Satanism can be egalitarian. That's what bothers people who come into it. If I make someone a priest it's because of them; they impress me as being qualified. It's not what they've studied; it's what they've accomplished in the real world. So the lodge head types are very frustrated when they can't come around here and be big shots. These people who join the Church of Satan and then say, "Is that all I get, a lousy red card?"—if they had a chestful of medals they'd still be a nobody. These endless occult degrees are just a substitute for achievement in the real world. It's the same thing when you get one performer who can't perform and is stupid, and they'll praise another who also can't perform. That's the conspiracy of ineptitude.

Barton: We're essentially living on a dust ball and the Satanic ethic is almost like fiddling while Rome burns. The

> **These endless occult degrees are just a substitute for achievement in the real world. It's the same thing when you get one performer who can't perform and is stupid, and they'll praise another who also can't perform. That's the conspiracy of ineptitude.**

nobility is in the fight—that's all we have. Create your world as best you can. One person can justify and fulfill their existence by being the best they can be, like a spider does. We are extremely idealistic—you'd have to be to be a Satanist—but you're insulted by Christianity. Insulted, dismayed, and the way you fight back is to be Satanist. I feel an intensity and a passion for life. The best humans are fabulous, wonderful people capable of the most incredible works of art, music, and creation. I do feel a passion of the human spirit.

It's not that I have so much against Christianity or Judaism or Buddhism, but they had better keep encouraging TV and the whole "global village" thought if they expect a changeover to total complacency. They tried to use Satanism as the last ditch to make an enemy for society but even that's falling flat.

MM: The Church of Satan emerged in the '60s, simultaneously with the "Love Generation" crowd. Compared to the Hippies, you must have looked like a pretty tough and sinister lot.

ASLV: We were the only real, disciplined counter-culture in the '60s, unless you want to include the Klan or James Madole's National Renaissance Party. The Left was established, and if it wasn't for Charles Manson's people going up to the Tate house, it might have just continued along at the same speed. Those murders didn't kill it entirely but they did put some fear into these people who were so full of acid that they felt superior to everyone.

MM: It's unfortunate, though, that Manson had to take the fall for his associates' actions.

ASLV: What can I say about Charles Manson that hasn't been said? I do feel they've made him out to be something he's not—he's not the little guy with scissors who cuts little kids' fingers off. The media keeps trotting Manson out to say things, but it's so safe. He's behind bars. Unless of course maybe he's sowing invisible seeds of rebellion in a few people's minds. But he's just been used and used as a convenient scapegoat for so long. It's redundant. There are a lot of other people who did commit murders and who may have a lot to say—like James Huberty and John Luigi Ferry—but they'll never be heard from.

MM: Getting back to Satanism, how do you respond to the hearsay and accusations that are leveled at your activities? A lot of Christians will be really disappointed to hear you haven't offered me a cup of infant's blood or a desecrated communion cracker.

ASLV: The information has been there for a quarter of a century and if they want to continue to think that way maybe it's all for the best. The material's been there and

> **"A lot of Christians will be really disappointed to hear you haven't offered me a cup of infant's blood or a desecrated communion cracker."**

so they must not really want to find out the truth. In the future the same herd behavior will be present and they'll follow Satanism. I wouldn't even now attempt to enlighten them. We still get people writing saying they can't find *The Satanic Bible* and can we please tell them about it. What rock have they been under? That's like asking about the Easter Bunny! Often these people are just psychic vampires who want to get it straight from you, knowing it'll be a drain and a redundant waste of your time. If I ever respond to these types it's only to have fun with them and tell them lies—like the chapter in *The Devil's Notebook*, "Let Me Entertain You."

MM: One of the first substantial profiles of the Church appeared in Burton Wolfe's 1974 biography of you, *The Devil's Avenger.* How did he really feel about what he witnessed?

ASLV: He was sort of a '60s well-meaning, old style liberal writer—narrow in some ways, but he was enthused about what he wrote. Some of it was a way of projecting his own views on me to get himself off the hook. That was

If they want to achieve a desired result it would behoove people to practice sex magic. There are certain rules and procedures that you apply but you have to break established rules and be blasphemous, not be afraid of boundaries that may be stifling.

his cop-out to get a disclaimer with his publisher. The truth of it was that after *The Devil's Avenger*, he became closer than ever. Later he got very bitter and misanthropic. He was a good fellow, a comrade in arms, with a good sense of humor. He did a book on the Hippies that was really blasted by them—how many books were written like that then? And he did a book on Hitler and the Nazis for young people that was really informative. He was never, at any time, antagonistic, despite what it says at the end of *The Devil's Avenger*.

MM: Early on your philosophy was described by some observers as "Humanism writ large," but you're really a rather misanthropic and illiberal fellow—which to my mind doesn't smack of Humanism at all.

ASLV: I'm a bitter man, as well I should be. I'm essentially a very happy man in an unhappy world, and that makes me dismayed. I see many areas where there doesn't have to be a problem but shit-disturbers make a point of creating one. They're my archenemy. They're pretty stupid people usually and they're people who can't enjoy life unless there's discord and disharmony. They've even tried to say that's what Satanism is based on! I rather prefer to think it's founded on innovation, a Promethean spirit, not disharmony. People complain that I'm a misanthrope but they should be glad I don't join their activities. They should be glad I'm listening to old music and watching old movies. What would they rather have me doing? Joining in on their games? They presume because I'm polite, chivalrous, and a gentleman, that's the way I'll be everywhere. What they see is what they figure they'll get—that's not necessarily the case. When we're in another's lair we treat them with respect. But we don't invite them into our lair, or if they do have to come in then we don't knuckle under. The best thing to do is stay away. I know things will piss me off in the marketplace too much, so I stay out. In the past I used to welcome these lukewarm quasi-Satanists, and make

apologies for them and take up the slack and be a gentleman, and now I don't see them mentioning Satanism in their books and literature. They've got a long way to go to even being de facto Satanists. I've talked about Humanism and said some nice things about it when I was younger. But let's turn the tables—can these humanists and their egos stand to say anything nice about me? Russia, as an atheist country, thought me aligned enough to put me in their museum. I had the Soviet Union considering me alike back then, so why should I be doing cartwheels now, just because someone 25 years later starts to act like we're not so bad. Why isn't *The Satanic Bible* in lists of influential books? That's what irks me. So why should I give these people the time of day, especially in these academic circles?

MM: Another accusation about the Church of Satan is that what you're advocating is really just a brand of Machiavellian materialism.

ASLV: I do believe in magic. I don't want to sound like Crowley or Blavatsky, and go off the deep end with the occultnik stuff. Balancing everything out is even more crafty—to know which side one's bread is buttered on, but at the same time to acknowledge the dark forces. Keep 'em guessing. Keep 'em confused and confounded 'til the stars be numbered!

MM: Your detractors often seem to be uncertain which way to go—they'll first dismiss you as little more than a sideshow carny, and then try to say you weren't even that!

ASLV: When I was first getting publicity I was stigmatized for being a roustabout, and then a couple of years later I see people coming out of the woodwork bragging about their carnival backgrounds! And then later they come around and try to say that actually I *wasn't* doing it. Don't let them see anything as an advantage because they'll try to take it away from you! The bastards! They're so devoid of anything scintillating so they want to pin that devoidness on you. As if I've been licking stamps or delivering newspapers my whole life! I worked in the carnival for a year. I helped with the lions for a season. I met people who later became famous. I just happened to be in the right place at the right time.

MM: How has the sexual climate changed a lot from the period in which you wrote *The Satanic Bible* and *The Compleat Witch*?

ASLV: I'm amazed at what I read about sex these days, that's openly and frankly discussed. Subjects like fetishism, and certain styles of clothing, that weren't discussed in the '60s, are being talked about now.

MM: How important is sex to the Satanist?

ASLV: Sex is a motivating force—it's the dance of life. But there's certainly more to life than sex. A Satanic attitude starts with the sexual. Once that is spent, the true sensualist moves to the next thing—that's where a Satanic ideology comes in. There are more productive things to do than just fucking or seeking perpetual sexual release, having this obsession with sex. I like sex and I've had my share of exploits but I can look at someone without thinking about whether or not they'd be a good lay. I can get my mind off it. Sex is the great motivator and that's why it can be sublimated into religiosity or patriotism, like in "I Love a Parade" where the guy sounds like he's having an orgasm. And these ministers rolling in the aisles—I've played for them and they're having multiple orgasms in the aisles, soiling themselves! You can't tell me they just have the Holy Spirit—it's sexual. It's been going on a long time, for centuries.

MM: What's a Satanic view on sex magic?

ASLV: If they want to achieve a desired result it would behoove people to practice sex magic. There are certain rules and procedures that you apply but you have to break established rules and be blasphemous, not be afraid of boundaries that may be stifling. You have to reach down into the secret vices of people and through imagery invoke them. If it's powerful and the shock value is there you'll reach them. Like Pygmalion when he carved the woman and she came to life because he'd invested so much energy into her. Like with my artificial people, I

down the line it will come to be. Hugh Hefner may be a great sex magician because he took a type—the Playboy bunny—and made it the standard. One man with drive and will made it that way. What's good for General Motors is good for the rest of the country! Other people who may not even know why will fall into line. You just sit back and relax and don't tug on the rope and it'll come 'round.

MM: Your dedication to the concept of artificial human companions hasn't abated, then?

ASLV: We're getting back to slavery too. You can't wipe out slavery. Everyone wants to be above someone—now they can buy a slave on the installment plan. These people can get excited about the TV characters in their living room, but they say an artificial companion won't be "real" enough—bullshit!

MM: Can someone develop a fetish for anything?

ASLV: I've known people who can spread out pictures of trains and streetcars and get sexually excited! And abandoned buildings—I can actually feel sex charges in certain locations. There's something for everyone. People are getting off right now, sitting at computers with erections.

MM: An inverted situation is when things that are touted as being the most sexual are often totally unexciting, as is the case with much of the so-called "pornography."

ASLV: The people who run these skin mags give the people what they want, but I can't find a single girl in one of them who'd even give me a tingle down there. They're like life-size Barbie dolls, so goddamn squeaky clean and sterile, sanitized and uniform. It's like they're made of injection-molded plastic. And so skinny—they look like residents of Dachau! It's just obstetrics and gynecology, really.

Hugh Hefner may be a great sex magician because he took a type–the Playboy bunny–and made it the standard. One man with drive and will made it that way.

worked and worked, inhaled the dust and fumes and invested sexual energy—they don't come to life literally but others will say they saw them move out of the corner of their eye, and later someone will show up on the doorstep who looks just like them. Explain that! If you put enough energy into your fetish you'll see others changing. People will no longer be into whips and leather corsets. I've seen it happen with my own fetishes. If you have the strength, the magical energy, and the focus, somewhere

MM: What is it that they're missing?

ASLV: *Pulchritude*—not a one of 'em has that. It's a lost word in the language. The Women's Movement caused a lot of this, not to mention creating such a boring, somber atmosphere everywhere. Try to tell a joke and they'll attempt to dig their heels in further—so humorless, these feminists!

MM: What are your views on raising children?

ASLV: I'm interested in eugenics and genetics. How people are conceived and comparing notes on conditions of birth, like how much attention is paid to a child and what kind of music they were exposed to. It's funny how so many people who share our views are not at odds with their parents, and so many liberals who should love their parents yet are at total odds with them. My parents never pushed me in any religious direction. When I wrote *The Satanic Bible* it didn't phase them—not because they were liberal, but they just didn't have an opinion. My father wasn't a musician, he couldn't tell one tune from another. But I'd hear these classical pieces and they just moved me, and I started reading because I had a thirst for knowledge. It's chromosomal. Parents can foster it or set the stage, but you can't just produce a predisposition artificially. You can have completely normal parents with a child who's exceptional. I've seen it happen so much. Even with alcoholic parents, sometimes the kids are brilliant.

TV is the single most numbing influence in a child's development and the most stultifying ingredient in their lives. It's been said so many times—that's the worst culprit. Still you have people who will say, "But there are different *kinds* of TV." What you see is just adjusted for different levels and different demographics, but the propaganda is the same. The media is always the message.

I've known people who can spread out pictures of trains and streetcars and get sexually excited!

TV is the means it gets into every home like some kind of Orwellian eye. It keeps them in line—that's good. For people of limited imagination, TV is their savior, their life. Mini-series = miseries.

MM: You must have always felt apart, ever since childhood.

ASLV: I had a torture chamber in my basement as a kid! In the crawlspace I built all these elaborate torture instruments, including a rack, straight from the middle ages. We'd find suitable victims, but then we got into some trouble, word got around, and we had to shut it down. This was just before the war and I must have been around eleven.

MM: Eugenically speaking, there has to be some good material to start with, in order for an advanced personality to develop. Most people seem pretty hopeless to improve into anything superior, especially when they've become adults.

ASLV: I'm not naive enough to believe that everyone's going to suddenly find culture, or become instantly intelligent, like these people may imagine they've accomplished who go back to school when they're 40 years old. These CEO hopefuls—I've spoken to so many of them, Lord Satan give me a break! They're no smarter and no more motivated than they were before someone gave them the ludicrous idea they could improve their minds. And they feel they're being liberated, shaking off the chains that bind them! The stupes'll always be stupes.

At this period, physical fitness is taking a back seat to mental prowess; computer technology has provided a vehicle that leads people to think they can think. All manner of "smart drugs," books on cassettes, online information, speed learning methods, give the stupes who pounded their joints jogging a chance to purchase instant IQs.

MM: And don't the exceptional people sometimes emerge from the most unlikely places?

ASLV: How can you explain the ones that do strive to be productive? What separates them from the rest? Did they have a unique chromosome of some sort? How did someone like Nat King Cole come out the way he did? What the hell has he got in his brain that makes him do that? Certain people rise above. Leni Riefenstahl dallied with Hitler and Paul Robeson with Moscow. Robeson was an accomplished Shakespearean actor and in college at Rutgers he made fullback. He excelled in everything—singer, sports figure, superman. They even named a mountain after him! But why doesn't anyone want to talk about the man? It's just like the case with Riefenstahl. There's a whole secret history of these people who just don't fit in, but are undeniably exceptional.

MM: You've mentioned the possibility of a "Satanic ethnic" which is actually genetic.

ASLV: Like Dostoyevsky's Underground Man you can sit alone for years and learn about all these experiences, but sooner or later you're going to start talking and you'll have a whole different audience and a whole new reaction. It's not going to fall on deaf ears. There are very few true underground people anymore, but it's a whole new breed, the ones who are out there. A new lost tribe. A chromosomal ethnic developing out of all these unpopular, shunned belief systems of the past. Like that hunter of

Anton LaVey and friend. 1996. (Courtesy the Church of Satan)

hunters, the guy in the Midwest who was stalking and killing hunters because he loved animals. The liberals couldn't support him, and the anti-gun people couldn't because he was obviously an expert marksman. The ecology people would shun him. This is someone in that special class. What's sort of frightening is that we get application after application from these kinds of people! So many of them are gun owners and enthusiasts, they love animals and they all talk the same way. Man is the most dangerous game. I'm not a vegetarian either. If I had to kill I suppose I would. It boils down to necessity being the supreme law.

I'll save a spider from going down a drain; I'll work overtime to save a bug. If I see a snail trying to cross a parking lot I'll help it along. What kind of a nut am I? How come humans get special dispensation?

MM: Is Satanism a revolutionary or extremist creed?

ASLV: Revolutionary, yes. "Extremist" would imply it's taking something already codified and established, and amplifying it. It's a totally different ethic—and ethnic. It's not adopting the tenets of something existing. There's a revisionist element in Satanism, but saying it's just that, or just Humanism, is too conservative.

MM: Would you consider allying the Church of Satan with any existing radical or extremist groups?

ASLV: It depends on how all-encompassing they are. In certain areas, I would answer yes. But a lot of parts of Satanism would be of no interest to them, i.e., the music, art, and aesthetics that we want to see. If that's the case then I'd say we have a common denominator only on one

level. You might have a common ground on one thing, but they couldn't find much to talk to you about. That's why I find some of them limiting. If by nature they were interested in most of the same things as we are, they would be Satanists. They'd be Satanic.

Barton: They would be eclectic, pragmatic, iconoclastic, anachronistic—that's what Satanism is. A lot of people don't ally themselves with these extremist groups because there'll be one element they can't endorse. That's not the case in Satanism, however, where there's no limited platform.

MM: Ever since the '60s, many people seem to have been imbued with an instant fear of anything that smacks of order, and this is especially true of the occultniks.

ASLV: People confuse anarchy and chaos. They think the world began in chaos—I agree. But in chaos and confusion it's an accident when something worthwhile occurs. What happens after that? The cells divide and start going off in different directions—and order forms.

Chaos here and now, is not chaos like these Chaos Magicians would like to believe. It's not the Timothy Leary "Come one, come all, it's a magical blend." It sounds utopian but it ain't the way it really is. Maybe something *developed* out of chaos, but there has to be order. There has got to be a direction there—it's not going to happen out of chaos, out of nothing, not from these disparate things that will be reconcilable in a new and terrifying way. Those with direction, plan, purpose, self-discipline—that's what leads to a conclusion. A mind held by no head is only as effective as the destination of the mind. That's why millions in the Sportpalast or the Coliseum can affect something. But people going somewhere and handfasting—they don't have the *passion*. I see no claps of thunder or lightning bolts in the sunshine in the park. These mealworms getting all together in the blinding glare just produce more glare. Wilhelm Reich was right—they just suck the energy out of the atmosphere.

People are so demoralized, desensitized, and catatonic that there can be no triumph of the will because there's no will. How can they have a will when they're sucking their life out of a cathode tube? Ten of these people out ritualizing in the woods maybe add up to one owl sitting on a branch. It's not feasible to have ten to twenty people, there are too many different agendas. But a rally with a will, a single idea—then you can manage something. ▱

SEASON OF THE WITCH

This article was originally published in MOJO magazine in "The Dark Side Issue" (Number 70, September 1999). It formed the basis of Gary Lachman's definitive book *Turn Off Your Mind: The Mystic Sixties and the Dark Side of the Age of Aquarius* (The Disinformation Company, New York, 2003)

Only a few days after the Manson murders, on the other side of America something happened that the proponents of the '60s "counterculture" had been expecting for a long time. On the weekend of August 15–17, 1969, some half-a-million people gathered at Max Yasgur's farm in upstate New York for the mother of all rock festivals, Woodstock. I was 13, stranded in New Jersey, my only link the news coming over FM radio stations. Reports of traffic jams, hordes of people, groovy vibes and scheduled performers helped create the impression—the myth—

The Tate-LaBianca killings had yet to be traced to an ex-Scientologist, maniacal hippy guru with a grudge against blacks, women and several LA pop entrepreneurs.

that something historic, even cosmic was happening. Earlier that year the mellow pop sound of The Fifth Dimension—whose name suggested the mystical tweak everything took on then—announced that, "This is the dawning of the Age of Aquarius," an anthem lifted from the tribal rock musical, *Hair*. Not long after, Donovan,

whose trippy, almost mantric *Hurdy Gurdy Man* created a sonic approximation to eternity, scored a massive hit with *Atlantis*, about "the continent that lay before the great flood in the area we now call the Atlantic Ocean."

Things cosmic, spacey and mystical were in. The UFOs were on their way, and the hippies who endured the mud and brown acid at Woodstock were the flesh and blood proof. The Tate-LaBianca killings had yet to be traced to an ex-Scientologist, maniacal hippy guru with a grudge against blacks, women and several LA pop entrepreneurs.

But if Woodstock—following 1967's San Francisco Human Be-In, the Summer of Love and the 14-Hour Technicolor Dream held at Alexandra Palace in London—was the sign that the Age of Aquarius was on its way, it was a short-lived morn. By the end of 1969, the flower generation's faith in the power of love had shrunk to a collective "What happened?" The vibes had gone nasty. The Haight soured, and so did other countercultural enclaves like New York's East Village. But the clincher came from the West Coast, where most weirdness originates in the States.

The location was American, but the main players were Brits—the event had international significance. The Rolling Stones would cap off their tour of North America with a free concert in the San Francisco Bay Area, having done one in Hyde Park that July. Peace and love were the order of the day, and the Stones uncharacteristically wanted to be part of it.

The free concert, eventually held at the disused Altamont speedway track, was a scene of intimidation, violence and murder. Hundreds of love children come to "set their soul free" were terrorized by a band of Hells Angels; at least one person was killed, and several were beaten, including Marty Balin from Jefferson Airplane. The barbarians even seemed poised to turn on the Stones themselves, the royalty who had invited them to the feast. When an annoyed Keith Richards asked the Angels to "cool it," one grabbed the mike and answered, "Fuck you!" Suddenly, it was not looking good for the Age of Aquarius.

But what's the Age of Aquarius anyway? Astronomically, an effect of a wobble in the earth's rotation; mystically, the "new age" on its way for the last century or so. The idea goes back to Plato, but it got its current meaning in the occult craze of the late 19th century, and gained pop dissemination through Haight-Ashbury astrologer Gavin Arthur in the pages of the *San Francisco Oracle*. Musically, it means those few years in the mid- to late 1960s (and into the early '70s) when "all things occultly marvelous" (as Theodore Roszak, historian of the counterculture, called it) descended on popular culture—especially music.

The 1960s witnessed an "occult revival", the likes of which hadn't been seen in the west since the fin-de-siecle days of Madame Blavatsky's Theosophical Society, and Aleister Crowley's Golden Dawn. In fact Crowley's face appears among the heroes The Beatles included on the cover of *Sgt. Pepper's Lonely Hearts Club Band* along with C. G. Jung, Edgar Allan Poe and Aldous Huxley, veteran explorers of "other worlds," and Eastern gurus like Sri Mahavatara Babaji and Paramhansa Yogananda. Three years earlier, talk of astral travel, past lives and third eyes would have met with Mod, amphetamine scorn. By 1967, they were the height of fashion.

Lysergic acid diethylamide-25 had something to do with it, likewise the shadow of the Vietnam War. But one factor has to be the publication in Paris in 1960 (published in English in 1963) of one of the decade's most influential books, *Le Matin Des Magiciens* by Louis Pauwels and Jacques Bergier. A bestseller, *The Morning of the Magicians* sparked the mass interest in "all things occultly marvellous" that characterized the time and influenced some of the leading figures in pop music. It was an influence both for the light, and for the dark.

If you go back to its roots in blues, then Robert Johnson's mythic meeting with the Devil at the crossroads is the archetype of the rock's pact with "dark forces." But some time in the mid-60s the influence of the supernatural on pop music grew beyond the occasional nod to its patron saint. Old Nick was still around—Mick Jagger would make him more fashionable than ever—but he was only part of the general fascination with the otherworldly that had taken command of the collective consciousness. UFOs, Tibet, ESP and a hundred other "occult" items were shaken together with a modish dose of hallucinogens and served up as an esoteric cocktail.

Marianne Faithfull, commenting on fellow traveler Brian Jones, recalled, "Like a lot of people at the time, myself included, he was convinced there was a mystic link between druidic monuments and flying saucers. Extra-ter-

When an annoyed Keith Richards asked the Angels to "cool it," one grabbed the mike and answered, "Fuck you!" Suddenly, it was not looking good for the Age of Aquarius.

restrials were going to read these signs from their space-ships and get the message. It was the local credo: Glastonbury, ley lines and intelligent life in outer space. I've forgotten exactly what it was we believed, but we believed it fiercely."

Weird ideas and exotic practices were the norm, and the most conspicuous form of this was the craze for all things from the mystic East.

In August 1967, The Beatles left Paddington Station for Bangor, Wales, and their short-lived romance with Maharishi Mahesh Yogi and Transcendental Meditation (leaving a huffing Cynthia Lennon behind on the platform). To their fans, the press and themselves, the giggling little man with the long beard and flowers was the newest show in town. When the Moptops memorized their mantras, and later camped out in Rishikesh, "eastern wisdom" got a huge publicity boost. The presence of other notables like Mick Jagger, Marianne Faithfull, Mia Farrow (made famous by Polanski's 1968 satanic masterpiece, *Rosemary's Baby*) and Donovan clinched it. Western mystic forms like Tarot and Qabala were on the scene. But that year India was in.

A Western convert leading the charge was ex-Harvard Doctor of Psychology, Timothy Leary. Armed with a winning smile, some Hermann Hesse novels, *The Tibetan Book Of The Dead* and a lot of LSD—as well as the cachet of a major drug bust—Leary proselytized with a wearying monotony the virtues of turning on, tuning in and dropping out. This boiled down to taking lots of acid and letting the straight world fade away in the clear light of the void, a highly attractive plan to quite a few folk—like John Lennon.

Lennon first came across Leary's LSD mysticism in March 1966 at London's legendary Indica Bookshop and Gallery, founded by Barry Miles, John Dunbar (then husband of pop chanteuse Marianne Faithfull) and Peter Asher (of Peter & Gordon). The Indica provided the avant-garde literature and esoterica that filled the bookshelves of pop cognoscenti. According to Barry Miles, Lennon turned up with McCartney, in search of a book by an unknown author, "Nitz Ga." It took Miles and Paul a few minutes to realize Lennon was interested in Nietzsche. But what really caught Lennon's eye was a copy of *The Psychedelic Experience*, Leary's tripped-out version of *The Tibetan Book of the Dead*. Lennon sank into the sofa and read "Whenever in doubt, turn off your mind, relax and float downstream." Lennon would spend the next three years attempting to do just that, mostly by taking lots of LSD and repeating the message in *Tomorrow Never Knows*, The Beatles' first psychedelic song. The ego was bad, Doctor Leary had declared, and his prescription for recovery was to blast it out of existence through repeated confrontations with the Clear Light or Void of Tibetan mysticism.

Yet by the end of the decade, Lennon had tired of Leary's rap, as he had of the Maharishi, although he agreed to pen a tune for Leary's ludicrous California gubernatorial campaign: *Come Together's* goo-goo lyrics are a late entry in Lennon's war against sense, rooted in Lewis Carroll and fuelled by Doctor Leary's medicine. "Nonsense" is a potent tool for stimulating altered states of consciousness—just ask Andre Breton and the surrealists. "Toe jam football," "spinal cracker" and other jabberwockery create a weird sense of unspecific menace, the shadows closing around the Aquarian Age. By the time of his first solo album in 1970, Lennon was finished with magic altogether. In "God," his consciousness flushed out to a bare minimum by his latest obsession, Arthur Janov's Primal Scream Therapy, Lennon renounced the entire pantheon of '60s ideology. "I don't believe in magic," he sang. I Ching, Tarot, Buddha, Jesus—even The Beatles didn't survive his austere renunciation. The dream and the decade were over.

By the autumn of '69, the Beatle myth had descended into the ghoul-ish hysteria surrounding the "Paul is dead"

hoax, and not too long after The Beatles themselves were a thing of the past. Their old rivals, meanwhile, were only just getting into their devilish stride.

Paul Devereux, author of *The Long Trip: A Prehistory Of Psychedelia*, recalls a "white-suited Mick Jagger" breezing into Watkins Bookshop off London's Charing Cross Road and carrying out "a stack of occult books." The prime literary influence on the Stones' seminal 1968 song *Sympathy For The Devil* was, in fact, a novel, a copy of which was a gift to Mick from girlfriend Marianne Faithfull: *The Master And Margarita* by Mikhail Bulgakov, in which the devil causes havoc in Stalinist Moscow. Jagger takes Bulgakov's smarmy prince of darkness and gives him a mic stand, linking a smoking-jacketed Satan to such archetypal bloodlettings as the Crucifixion and the Kennedy assassination. Whether Jagger and Richards were artists tapping into the Zeitgeist or merely pandering to the love generation's latent violence is debatable. Legend has it that a year later at Altamont the Stones were just kicking into *Sympathy* as Meredith Hunter was knifed, while the Midnight Rambler is chums with the Boston Strangler and *Gimme Shelter* reeks of impending apocalypse. It all started three years earlier at a chic, bohemian address in Kensington, West London.

Home to Rolling Stone Brian Jones and his actress-model-girlfriend Anita Pallenberg, 1 Courtfield Road was, according to regular visitor and Mick Jagger's then girlfriend Marianne Faithfull:

"A veritable witches' coven of decadent illuminati, rock princelings and hip aristos," including art dealer Robert Fraser; designer Michael Rainey; and Stash Klossowski, son of the painter Balthus and author of works on alchemy and hermeticism. "In my mind's eye I open the door," she recalls. "Peeling paint, clothes, newspapers, and magazines strewn everywhere. A grotesque little stuffed goat standing on an amp, a Moroccan tambourine, lamps draped with scarves, a pictograph painting of demons. There's Brian in his finest Plantagenet satins. On the battered couch, an artfully reclining Keith is perfecting his gorgeous slouch. At the center, like a phoenix on her nest of flames, the wicked Anita. Desultory intellectual chitchat, drugs, hip aristocrats, languid dilettantes and high naughtiness. I knew I was on my path."

Faithfull's self-titled autobiography, a saga of sexual and pharmaceutical excess, is littered with mystical rhetoric—and a few close encounters. Like her prophecy of Brian Jones' death through a toss of the I Ching ("Death by Water," she called it, although the I Ching has no such hexagram) and her own visitation by a deceased Brian as she lay unconscious in Sydney, her stomach full of Tuinals. Jones himself was a devotee of the Master Musicians of Joujouka of Morocco, whose hypnotic drone is dedicated to the Great God Pan; on a visit to Tangiers to record them, the decaying pop star had a vision of himself as a sacrificial goat. During a kif binge, while watching a goat being prepared for its dispatch, Jones whispered continually to an amused Brion Gysin, "That's me, that's me." Out in LA in 1968 to mix *Beggars Banquet*, Keith Richards and Anita Pallenberg (who was reputed to own a collection of human relics, including a voodoo doll of Brian Jones, for use against those who incurred her displeasure) would head out to the weird landscape of Joshua Tree in the Southern California desert with LA country-rocker Gram Parsons and various supplies, looking for UFOs. "It was a great spot," Richards recalled of their night at Cap Rock. "There was a kind of barber's chair right on top, where Leary used to sit. We rustled up some mescaline and peyote and tried to talk with the local Indians." Anita Pallenberg remembers "binoculars, loads of blankets, and a big stash of coke." But did they really believe in UFOs? "Well, it was all part of that period. We were just looking for something."

One of the Stones' occult-dabbling playmates was the avant-garde filmmaker, Kenneth Anger, a self-styled warlock and devotee of Aleister Crowley (Of the "magicians" fashionable in the mystic '60s, Crowley had the most appeal; his appetite for weird sex and heavy drugs made him the perfect prophet of the "repressionless" decade.) Kenneth Anger was one of the "crazy West Coast Magus types" who popped up in Swinging London (he claimed to have seen Brian Jones's "supernumary witch's tit"—Keith and Mick were supposed to have them too).

In 1967 Anger lived in San Francisco with actor-cum-singer Bobby Beausoleil in an old house called the Russian Embassy. There they devoted themselves to some hands-on experience of Crowley's so-called "magick"—a practice Beausoleil may have put to unsavory use as a henchman for Charles Manson, when he murdered Gary Hinman at the start of the Family's spree. Beausoleil played the lead in an ongoing film project of Anger's, *Lucifer Rising*, telling

him he believed he was the Devil. At the time, 1967, Beausoleil, like Charlie later, was getting into rock music, playing lead guitar and sitar for The Magick Powerhouse Of Oz, an 11-piece rock ensemble formed by Beausoleil to create the soundtrack to Anger's occult film. (In Crowley's

One of the Stones' occult-dabbling playmates was the avant-garde filmmaker, Kenneth Anger, a self-styled warlock and devotee of Aleister Crowley.

qabalistic system, 11 is a powerful number, symbolizing the double phallus of homoerotic sex magic.) He would also have a brief stint as guitarist with Arthur Lee's Love. During one performance Anger flipped and smashed a caduceus-headed cane that supposedly had belonged to The Great Beast, Crowley himself. Beausoleil and Anger fell out, and Bobby split with Anger's car, camera equipment and some footage of *Lucifer Rising*. He rode into the future and a murder rap.

Anger thought the Stones' concerts were demonic invocations, calling on powers that Crowley and other magi had tapped. Their music, he said, was the perfect accompaniment for sex magic—"music to fuck to." Besotted with the androgynous Mick, Anger saw him as Lucifer, and Keith as his familiar, Beelzebub. He wanted them for his still unfinished epic, with Jagger now in the lead (apparently Beausoleil had skipped with his own scenes).

John Michel, author of *The View Over Atlantis* (1969), the book that put Glastonbury and ley lines on the countercultural map, dallied with the Courtfield Road set (they all loved his 1967 tome *The Flying Saucer Vision*). Michel remembers a trip in Keith's Bentley to a church in Hereford where Anger did something "unmentionable." There was other weirdness too: late night acid runs to Stonehenge, or to Primrose Hill, to join up the ley lines. "Keith and Anita decided to have a pagan marriage ceremony at dawn on Hampstead Heath. Kenneth Anger would be the priest," Keith's biographer Victor Bockris alleges. "They planned all this out, then one day Keith came downstairs and found that the front doors at Redlands (his Sussex house) had been taken off their hinges overnight and been painted gold, a symbolic color to do with invasion by black magic, then replaced on their hinges. He had the most sophisticated lock system possible and there was no way to explain how this had been done without anyone hearing it. So he flipped out completely. He said to Anita, 'I don't care what Kenneth says, I don't want any more to do with this.'"

Eventually, according to Faithfull, both Keith and Mick tired of Anger's eccentricities. When Anger, peeved at Jagger's lack of response, took to tossing copies of William Blake through Mick's window at his home in Chelsea's Cheyne Walk, the spell was broken. Jagger threw his stack of occult books from Watkins on the fire,

In the film, dosed with mushrooms, Chas undergoes a personality change, metamorphosing into Turner. In reality, the stoned Chas on the screen is Fox, unknowingly spiked with acid by Cammell, Pallenberg and Jagger—or so the story goes.

but not before Anger squeezed the soundtrack for his film *Invocation Of My Demon Brother* out of Jagger and his new Moog synthesizer. (In a 1976 interview in *Crawdaddy* magazine, Anger remarked of Jagger: "At the time I asked him he could still have just been able to play the part (of Lucifer), but not now; he's into too much of a performance now in every sense of the word. After Altamont he got scared of becoming too closely identified with that whole Satanic Majesties thing. I noticed that when he married Bianca, he was wearing a prominent cross...")

Another familiar face at Courtfield Road (and fellow player in Kenneth Anger's ongoing magnum opus *Lucifer Rising*, playing the Egyptian god Osiris opposite Marianne Faithfull's Lilith) was Donald Cammell. His father, Charles Richard Cammell, had befriended Aleister Crowley and written a book about him (in later life Donald would talk of being bounced on the ageing mage's knee). With script unseen and with no film experience, in 1968 Warner Brothers bought Cammell's idea of a film starring Mick Jagger, thinking they'd be getting a pop-rock romp, along the lines of The Beatles' "mystic" comedy, *Help!* (Ringo, remember, is on the run from the murderous devotees of the Hindu goddess Kali.) But what Cammell and co-director Nicholas Roeg delivered was something else again. Shelved and then shamefacedly drip-fed by Warners into the arthouse circuit, *Performance* today is acclaimed as a classic. It is also an exercise in calculated darkness.

This is the plot: In the London of Reggie and Ronnie Kray, Chas (played by James Fox) is a professional sadist on the run from his gangland boss. Looking for a hideout, he finds the dilapidated Notting Hill mansion of fading rock star Turner (played by Jagger). There he's caught in a drugged-out web of personality crises and sexual ambiguity, featuring Jagger, Anita Pallenberg and the 16 year-old Michele Breton. When *Performance* finally premiered in

1971, John Simon, critic for *New York* magazine, called it "the most loathsome film of all," while Cammell remarked: "This movie was finished before Altamont and Altamont actualized it." Warners objected to the cold violence and hot sex; both came across as too real. Both were. Outtakes of some of the sex scenes between Pallenberg and Jagger won first prize at an Amsterdam pornography festival. And some of the cast and crew were "real" gangland characters, like David Litvinoff, an East End chancer. Friend of the Krays as well as of artists Francis Bacon and Lucian Freud, Litvinoff was hired as "Director of Authenticity," and helped the fastidious Fox get into his role.

For Marianne Faithfull, the film was a "psycho-sexual lab run by Cammell, with James Fox the prime experimental animal." Jagger once told Faithfull that he was "into disturbed states of mind," with *Performance* his big opportunity. Allegedly, Mick wanted to "do Fox in," and throughout shooting would play mind games with the insecure actor. In the film, dosed with mushrooms, Chas undergoes a personality change, metamorphosing into Turner. In reality, the stoned Chas on the screen is Fox, unknowingly spiked with acid by Cammell, Pallenberg and Jagger—or so the story goes. Just as creepily, Cammell was recreating on film a ménage a trois between himself, his wife and Michele Breton. He was also recreating a ménage a quatre between Jagger and Marianne Faithfull, and Fox and his girlfriend, Andee Cohen. Finally, Jagger's character, Turner, is based on a composite Brian Jones and Keith Richards. Like the man said, "I am he as you are he and we are all together."

Along with Crowley, Cammell's other major influence was the Argentine writer Jorge Luis Borges, who specialized in blurring the boundary between reality and fantasy. Cammell wanted to create a Borgesian world on the set of *Performance*, and for Fox the experience was traumatic. At the end of filming, a shattered Fox abandoned his career and took to distributing fundamentalist Christian pamphlets door to door. Nor was he the only one to suffer. While Jagger and Anita performed, her boyfriend Keith Richards fumed outside in his car; after the affair, he became a heavy heroin user. Michele Breton, Turner's androgynous waif, became a heroin addict too, eventually ending up in a psychiatric clinic in Germany. Pallenberg also became a heroin addict, lost

Keith, and entered a downward spiral. As for Cammell, he saw *Performance* as an albatross. He only made two more films before shooting himself in the head in 1996, eerily reprising *Performance's* closing shot of the bullet boring through Turner's brain, arriving at a picture of Borges. Litvinoff likewise later committed suicide. Jagger walked away in one piece, but there was hell to pay later at Altamont.

■　■　■　■

1963: The world was about to be conquered by those symbols of youth, innocence and optimism, The Beatles. Meanwhile, a darker British invasion was getting underway. From a Church of Scientology premises in the West End, an occult group would emerge that would have links with the pop aristocracy from London to LA: The Process Church of the Final Judgment, commonly known merely as the Process.

Strange reactions follow the mention of their name. Pete Brown, poet, musician and friend of Graham Bond, the legendary '60s bandleader who became obsessed with Holy Magick and died under a train at Finsbury Park station, remembers them as "the nutters in the black capes." Novelist Robert Irwin, whose *Satan Wants Me* takes place against the occult drugscape of Swinging London, recalled the occasional deflowered virgin at Process gatherings, but expresses doubts that there were any virgins in London then. Ed Sanders, of the legendary Fugs and author of *The Family*, in which he speculates on a connection between the Process and Manson, commented, "The traces of evil are faint after 30 years. Why revive them?" Advice perhaps taken by Marianne Faithfull who, despite a cheerful lack of reticence about much else in her autobiography, doesn't even mention her appearance in the infamous "Fear" issue of *The Process* magazine in 1967, in which she was photographed holding a flower and looking quite dead.

What was it about these guys?

In 1963, Robert Moore and Mary Ann MacLean met at the Hubbard Institute of Scientology, on Fitzroy Street, London. Both were training to be "auditors." They married soon after, and in 1964 left Scientology to set up their own system, Compulsions Analysis. They also adopted

the name DeGrimston. Robert had been trained as an architect, while Mary Anne had been married to the American boxing champion, Sugar Ray Robinson, before moving to London and running a prostitution ring. Red-haired, with long, silver fingernails, she had connections to the Profumo scandal, and entertained influential men; one of her clients became a lawyer for the Process.

In March 1966, the DeGrimstons were successful enough at siphoning off the excess cash of neurotic English youth to lease a mansion on Balfour Place in Mayfair. Members felt compelled to donate their worldly possessions to the couple, who lived on the top floor. In August that year, the cult decamped to Xtul, Mexico, on the north coast of Yucatan. There they apparently discovered Satan. Returning to London in 1967 and funded by a member's inheritance, they turned their Mayfair mansion into a Satanic palace, complete with all-night coffee bar, movie house and book store, where they sold issues of their magazine, *The Process* (editorial policy: Hitler, Satan and gore). Processeans went around in black capes, turtlenecks, and silver crosses. They held telepathy classes, talked about the coming world conflagration and got on

> **From a Church of Scientology premises in the West End, an occult group would emerge that would have links with the pop aristocracy from London to LA: The Process Church of the Final Judgment, commonly known merely as the Process.**

their soap box in Hyde Park, preaching apocalypse. They attracted enough attention for the *Sunday Telegraph* to run an article about them.

They began to target pop-aristos as possible converts. Paul McCartney, actor Richard Harris, then owner of Crowley's old London address, Tower House (for which Great Beast devotee Jimmy Page later outbid David Bowie) were approached. But their big catch was Marianne Faithful. "Because of my father, I was quite open to ideas of group mind and power," she admits today. "I grew up on a commune, so had already been exposed to ideas of this sort. All I did was an interview for their magazine. I was attracted to them at first, mostly because they took me seriously, when nobody else did. The Process people were very admiring of me. They must have recognized that I have got magic powers. All through my life people like this have been trying to get their hands

"John Michel, the Holy Grail and flying saucers were OK, but there was something almost like fascism about the Process."

The Beach Boys' *Friends*, and as a B-side of *Bluebirds Over The Mountain*.

on me. I thought I was being quite sophisticated, but the boys—Mick, Christopher (Gibbs) and the others—told me I had made a mistake. On one level it was a bit like *The Prisoner*—all these handsome young men in black turtle-necks—but before I went any further a warning bell went off and I backed away. I had a strong feeling that it wasn't OK, and that it seemed to have something to do with brainwashing. John Michel, the Holy Grail and flying saucers were OK, but there was something almost like fascism about the Process."

Late '67 the Process hit the States; in LA they sidled up to members of the West Coast rock establishment—just as Charlie Manson would soon do. John Phillips and Mama Cass of Mamas And The Papas were approached. So was Warren Beatty. It's just possible they had a relationship with Sirhan Sirhan, later convicted of Bobby Kennedy's assassination (Sirhan spoke of "an occult group from London" that he "really wanted to go to London to see"). Another Hollywood figure the Process approached was Terry Melcher. Too late: he had his hands full with Charlie Manson's gonorrhea-laden hippy chicks at Dennis Wilson's Brentwood mansion.

Among other LA rockers Melcher might have seen there was Neil Young, who recalled sharing a couch with Linda Kasabian and Patricia Krenwinkle, "singing a song. A lot of pretty well known musicians around LA knew him (Charlie), though they'd probably deny it now. He was great. He was unreal. He was really, really good. Scary. Put him with a band that was as free as he was. No one was ever going to catch up with Charlie Manson 'cos he'd make up the songs as he went along." And yet... "there was just something about him that stopped anybody from being around him for too long—he was too intense. He was one of those guys that wouldn't let you off the hook." Young was impressed enough with Manson's music to suggest to Mo Ostin, head of Warner Brothers, that he sign him. It never happened, though Manson did manage to land a tune with The Beach Boys. His *Cease To Exist*, with its echoes of "turn off your mind" (Charlie, too, thought the ego was bad) appeared as *Never Learn Not To Love* on

By the by, Manson's jail pal at Ohio State Penitentiary in the early '60s, Phil Kaufmann, later turns up as Gram Parsons' roadie (picking up Marianne Faithfull at LAX in summer '69). This same Kaufmann once put the hex on Charlie, after the Family "creepy-crawled" The Flying Burrito Brothers' house in Beverly Glen—the band returned to their house once and found the furniture had been moved around. Phil recognized Charlie's tricks, and put a tombstone with Manson's name and date of birth on it on the lawn; the date of death he left open. They didn't return. A few years later Kaufmann would take Gram Parsons' body from LAX out to the desert in Joshua Tree National Monument and burn it in a pagan ceremony.

Nor were the Process and Manson's Family alone in the California occult underworld. In 1966, Anton LaVey inaugurated the Church of Satan in San Francisco; members would include Sammy Davis Jr. and Jayne Mansfield, later decapitated in a freak car accident. LaVey's brand of the satanic combined '50s film noir atmospherics with a carnival huckster pitch. Even here there's a Manson connection. Susan Atkins, who killed the pregnant Sharon Tate, worked for a while as a dancer in LaVey's Topless Witches Review, a vampire girlie show in LA. Weirder still, LaVey was hired as "consultant" for Roman Polanski's 1968 film *Rosemary's Baby* and played the Devil.

■ ■ ■ ■

In 1969 Jim Morrison said, "expose yourself to your deepest fear. After that fear has no power, and the fear of freedom shrinks and vanishes. You are free." By that summer of '69, fear sent the affluent and decadent denizens of LA's Sunset Strip scurrying out of clubs like the Whisky A Go Go and into heavily secured safe houses. Eyes peered through bamboo-shaded windows for any

A few years later Kaufmann would take Gram Parsons' body from LAX out to the desert in Joshua Tree National Monument and burn it in a pagan ceremony.

sign of the maniac who had it in for the rich and privileged. Heavy drugs like cocaine and heroin, and now Manson, had turned the Good Vibrations of surfin' '66 into a fringe-jacketed Apocalypse Now. No-one picked up on this aura of imminent collapse like The Doors.

From the beginning The Doors were about altered states of consciousness. The name comes from William Blake, by way of Aldous Huxley. Blake unlocked the doors of perception with poetry. Huxley used psychedelics. Morrison brought the two together, creating a kind of rock theatre-of-cruelty-cum-mystery ritual, with the singer as sacrificial god.

If John Lennon was the tripped-out mystic and Jagger suave Jack Scratch, Morrison was the prehistoric shaman, letting rip the ancient gods within. "I obey the impulses everyone else has but won't admit to," he said, intoning the ethos of total liberation that was blowing itself out in those final days of '69, echoing Robert DeGrimston: "Release the fiend that lies dormant within you, for he is strong and ruthless and his power is far beyond the bounds of human frailty," as he wrote in one of his epistles to the Process. In the spring of '68, an issue of The Process magazine hit the Strip. The cover showed a satanic ceremony, a naked girl surrounded by hooded cultists. With his taste for topless bars and things demonic, it's reasonable to guess that Jim would have seen it being sold on his journeys to and from the Alta Cienega Hotel in West Hollywood, a short roll down the hill from the Strip. Black capes in the warm California sun would be hard to miss.

Did Morrison step into the Galaxy Club, Omnibus or The Melody Room? If so, he may have come across Chuck Summers, alias Charlie Manson. Chuck hung at the Galaxy Club, just up the street from Jim's regular haunt, the Whisky; the area was claimed by the biker gangs that Charlie and the Process wanted to recruit to the cause.

Morrison had been into magic and ritual for years, first passing through the doors of perception via film. In his collection of jottings made during his UCLA film school days, later published as The Lords, Morrison wrote of "Yoga powers": "To make oneself invisible and small. To become gigantic and reach to the farthest things... To summon the dead. To exalt senses and perceive inaccessible images." This last hits the Rimbaud-esque note that Morrison brought to rock'n'roll, a coupling of the rock star and the poet that later shamans like Patti Smith would emulate. "There are no longer dancers," Jim complained. "We have been metamorphosized from a mad body dancing on the hillside to a pair of eyes staring in the dark..."

The Lords is full of references to the occult roots of cinema. "Cinema derives not from painting ... but from ancient wiz-

ardry." It is the "heir of alchemy, last of an erotic science..." The Lords themselves are a kind of secret society, a hidden hand arranging events behind the scenes. "Fear the Lords who are secret among us." A later collection of poetry, The New Creatures, is dominated by images of sacrifice and mutilation, evoking "the wet dreams of an Aztec king."

Nor was Jim the only mystic Door. Robby Krieger and John Densmore were into transcendental meditation. Ray Manzarek's account of his time with band, Light My

> ## "I am interested in anything about revolt, disorder, chaos, especially activity that seems to have no meaning."
> ### –Jim Morrison

Fire, drips with esoterica (Tibetan bardos, the Qabala, you name it): he and Jim exemplified the aesthetic dialectic of Nietzsche—Morrison the wild, mad ecstatic (Dionysus) to Manzarek's translucent dreamer (Apollo). Ray doesn't stop there. He was the true psychedelic savant, on 150 mics of LSD invoking the Russian philosopher P. D. Ouspensky and the Fourth Dimension to describe the experience.

And then Jim quit acid and hit the bottle. Morrison saw himself in that unhappy company of the drunk poet—Poe, Fitzgerald, Malcolm Lowry. The bottle opened doors within him that led down to the archetypes—the sun, sea, moon, stars, the long snake, the ancient lake. It brought him down to the dark, watery roots, the swampy, earthy realm of the shadow. "I am interested in anything about revolt, disorder, chaos, especially activity that seems to have no meaning," he wrote for an Elektra publicity release in 1967. He saw himself as the shaman, who would "intoxicate himself ... put himself into a trance by dancing, drinking, taking drugs...." The shaman would go on a "mental travel and describe his journeys to the rest of the tribe."

The shaman is also a healer, who takes on himself the sickness of the tribe, and through sacrifice, cures it. There's an atmosphere of finality around The Doors' music, some of which can be chalked up to generic adolescent morbidity, but not all. The End. Break On Through. Funeral pyres. Killers on the roam. When The Music's Over. Blood in the streets. We must, he tells us, "think of The Doors as a séance in an environment which has become hostile to life."

In 1968, the film *The Unknown Soldier* premiered at the old Fillmore East in New York's East Village. It depicts the sacrificial death of Morrison, tied to a stake and shot. Blood pours from his mouth, drenching flowers at his feet. 1968 was that kind of year: Bobby Kennedy, Martin Luther King, race riots, the Chicago Democratic

For his marriage to Patricia Kennely on Midsummer Night, 1970, the couple had a Wicca ceremony. Led by a high priestess of a coven, Jim and Patricia prayed and invoked the Moon goddess, then cut their arms, mixed their blood with wine and drank it, before stepping over a broomstick.

Convention, the student revolts in Paris and Cornell, Street Fighting Man. Another celluloid effort, *HWY,* is a dark version of Jack Kerouac's *On The Road*, with Morrison as a maniac hitchhiker on a killing spree in the desert, a theme later reprised in *Riders On The Storm*. (During the filming in LA, Jim called his poet friend Michael McClure in San Francisco. When McClure answered, Morrison said, "I wasted him," then hung up.) Afterwards he was filmed urinating from a ledge on the top of the 17-storey 9000 Building on Sunset Boulevard. As Nitz Ga said, "Live dangerously."

There's an eerie photo of Morrison from the infamous Miami performance. Black-shirted, with long dark hair, thick beard and shades, Morrison holds a white lamb; the image evokes suggestions of some weird ritual slaughter, Jim's get-up not that far removed from Process haute couture. He did dabble in a few standard occult exercises. For his marriage to Patricia Kennely on Midsummer Night, 1970, the couple had a Wicca ceremony. Led by a high priestess of a coven, Jim and Patricia prayed and invoked the Moon goddess, then cut their arms, mixed their blood with wine and drank it, before stepping over a broomstick. Later, during rehearsals for *LA Woman*, Morrison got into an affair with Ingrid Thompson, a Valkyrie-like beauty from Scandinavia. Both were heavily into coke at the time, and one night, after going through nearly a film can's worth, Ingrid remarked to Jim that she sometimes drank blood. Jim insisted they have some immediately. Ingrid managed to slice her palm. Jim caught it in a champagne glass. They made love, smearing themselves, then danced.

Oh, and during the night of the Tate killings the previous year, the caretaker of 10050 Cielo Drive, William Garretson, said he didn't hear any screams because he was listening to music: The Doors.

By the end of the decade, the occult explosion had turned into a mystical Big Bang. Jimi Hendrix was into flying saucers, and wanted to create a music that could "open people's eyes to cosmic forces." Speculating on the occult properties of music, he studied theories of sound-color resonance that harkened back to Theosophical composers like Alexandre Scriabin. At his famous Rainbow Bridge concert on Maui, the audience was seated according to their astrological sign, and chanted "Om" before Hendrix began to wail. The Grateful Dead, pioneers of acid spirituality, went on an "occult world tour" in the early '70s, taking them to the Pyramids.

Thirty years on, the occult still attracts attention. Marilyn Manson has relations with The Church Of Satan; Boyd Rice and Marc Almond too, so I'm told. And Trent Reznor of Nine Inch Nails moved into 10050 Cielo Drive, pulled in his equipment and recorded his most recent album there. It's called *Downward Spiral*... ⟁

Thanks for their help: Marianne Faithfull, Ian Macdonald, David Dalton, David Sinclair, Pete Brown, Harry Shapiro, Ed Sanders, John Michel, Neil Spencer, Robert Irwin, Barry Miles, Victor Bockris, Sid Griffin and Jenny Fabian.

OCCULT WAR

THE ADVENT OF AHRIMAN
An Essay on the Deep Forces Behind the World-Crisis

ABSTRACT: A powerful spiritual being, called "Ahriman" (or "Satan"), will incarnate in a human body. The terms "soul" and "spirit" have clear meanings. Earthly/cosmic evolution is an outcome of the deeds of the Gods. The central event of earth-evolution was the Incarnation of Christ. Spiritual powers of opposition are active: Lucifer, Ahriman, Sorat. Ahriman is the inspirer of materialistic science and commercialism, and permeates modern culture with deadening forces. Ordinary scientific thinking is only semiconscious; we can, however, make thinking conscious. The spirits of opposition are necessary in the Gods' evolutionary design. Ahriman manifests especially at 666-year intervals; the contemporary is 1998 AD = 3x666. Goethean science is a life-positive alternative to Ahrimanic science. Ahriman-in-the-flesh will likely present himself as the Christ. The Christ does not reappear in a physical body, but in a super-physical, ethereal form. Ahriman may incarnate "macrocosmically" in our computers. Mankind will acquire new faculties of thinking-consciousness and clairvoyance. Ahriman seeks to pervert these faculties, and to divert mankind and the earth from their destined paths in the Gods' evolutionary plan. Ahrimanic secret societies influence politics, finance, and culture.

AUTHOR'S PREFACE

I wish to bring before the public some information about tremendous events approaching. I am aware that much talk in this vein is already on the Internet, and that there is generally a sense "in the air" that something big is happening, with the new Millennium, the end of the Mayan calendar, etc. I believe that this sense of "something in the air" is a correct perception, albeit sometimes highly distorted. Most of the information in this essay is not new; it has been open to the public at least since the aftermath of the First World War. Yet it has not reached the wide public that needs to hear it. I hope to make this important information available to many around the world who have not yet encountered it and who might put it to good use. I claim no special knowledge concerning these matters; I have merely drawn on published sources. I expect no one to take my word for anything. I do ask the readers to read and think through this information, to follow the leads that I give, and do their own investigations. Conscientious investigations might well cause some intellectual upheavals, and change the course of some lives; and this is exactly what is needed, many times over, around the world.

This essay is based, directly or indirectly, on the "spiritual science" or "Anthroposophy" promulgated by Rudolf Steiner (1861–1925) in the first quarter of the 20th century. I say "based on" because this exposition can only be grossly oversimplified, and must contain whatever misunderstandings that derive from my own grasp of the subject matter. The reader must assume that this essay is almost wholly derivative; it contains scarcely any original ideas of my own. In the interest of readability, I do not provide full citations in

19th century devil

I realize that many are not inclined to take seriously the possibility of such an event, or to believe that such matters are known, or can be known. Nevertheless, again I ask the reader to read this essay with an open mind, at least open enough to take in the thoughts and concepts. I will give a few epistemological considerations which support the notion that such matters can be known. And I will give some references which will help the readers to conduct their own epistemological researches, and thus to be able to make an informed estimation of this report. This is a matter of some importance; it is essential for the future of mankind and the earth that as many people as possible become wakeful and not be caught sleeping by the impending events.

SPIRIT AND SOUL

Since this essay speaks of "spiritual" matters, I would like to bring into focus the concept of "spirit," along with the concepts of "soul" and "body." (I follow Steiner's exposition in his *Theosophy*.) The "body," of course, is the physical form, perceptible by the outer senses, in the world that is usually perceived in common by people's outer senses. By "soul" I mean the inner world of subjective feelings and sensations of a Man (or animal). The sensation of an outer sense-perception (such as the green of grass), as well as feelings (such as pleasure or pain), are in the soul. Also, the inner being acts through the soul by the will, though the will is not usually conscious. We might say that the physical world acts on the soul through sensation; the soul lives in its own feelings, and acts upon the world through the will. We (generally) experience sensations in wakefulness, feelings as if in a dream, and will as if in deep, unconscious sleep.

the text. If I did, almost every sentence would be footnoted. It is probable that hundreds, or thousands, of people in this world are better qualified than I to write this notice. I wrote it because I was not aware that anyone else was writing it, and it needed to be written, and published.

The events of which I speak are the approaching incarnation of a powerful, super-human spiritual being, following the concomitant political, social, economic, and cultural events. Preparations for this incarnation have been building to a climax over the past four centuries or more, and the climax is approaching soon. This being is called "Ahriman" (from the ancient Persian name *Angra Mainyu*, given by the prehistoric Zarathustra). We might consider Ahriman to be the same being usually called "Satan" except that the concept of "Satan" is much confused and misunderstood. Therefore, in this essay I will use the name "Ahriman" and will attempt to give a clearer understanding of his nature and aims than one generally obtains.

Ahriman is the inspirer of materialistic science and commercialism, and permeates modern culture with deadening forces.

In addition to living in the inner world of the soul, the Man can live in the world of thought. Through thinking, we make contact with the being of the things of the world. By "spirit" I mean the essence of thought. Contrary to common misconception, thought is not subjective, but objective, in that it belongs to the whole world, accessible to all. Many people can grasp the same thought and through that thought contact the same objective reality, though they do not (usually) experience each other's sensations and feelings. As the physical world interacts with the soul, so also does the spirit; we can call forth thoughts by our acts of will, and the thoughts give us feelings. Much of the confusion about the supposed subjectivity of thinking arises from the subjectivity of feelings and sensations connected with thinking, as well as from the fact that much of what usually passes for thinking is hardly thinking at all, but a kind of semi-conscious, automatic pseudo-thinking. (In modern times, people experience thinking as if it comes, usually automatically, out of themselves, yet, paradoxically, thinking in essence is objective and universal [as we can best see in mathematics]. I will say more about this below.) Thus, through our experience of thinking, we can attach an experiential, "empirical" meaning to the concept of "spirit." (All this should, of course, be taken as only a bare introduction to a vast, deep subject. For now, I am trying only to counter the widespread opinion that "soul" and "spirit" are nebulous, meaningless terms.) And while it is usually true that we hardly experience our thinking, thinking may be intensified so that it becomes conscious, and this development of consciousness may lead to the perception of the world and beings of soul and spirit—and thus become the basis of "spiritual science."

SPIRITUAL BEINGS AND EARTHLY EVOLUTION

Following the communications of this spiritual science, I will posit that spiritual beings, known as "angels," live invisibly (to us, usually) and involve themselves in earthly affairs. (This idea has been gaining acceptance in the general culture in recent years, with a surge of interest in angels.) I will also posit the existence of other spiritual beings, higher and more advanced than the angels, called the "archangels" in theology or angelology. Modern spiritual research (by Steiner), as well as ancient tradition (from Dionysius the Areopagate, pupil of St. Paul) speaks of at least nine orders of angels and supra-angelic beings—which, taken together, are called the "hierarchies," sometimes the "choirs of angels," or sometimes the "Gods" (other, still higher Beings are not discussed here). Some of the names given to the nine hierarchies, in ascending order, are:

- Angels (Angeloi, Sons of Twilight, Sons of Life; all Men have individual angels as guardians and carriers of their eternal Selves)

- Archangels (Archangeloi, Spirits of Fire; the "folk-spirits" are of this rank)

- Archai (singular "Arche"; Spirits of Personality, Primal Beginnings, Principalities; the "Time Spirit" or "Zeitgeist" is of this rank)

- Exusiai (Spirits of Form, Powers, Authorities; the "Elohim" and "Jehovah" are of this rank)

- Dynamis (Spirits of Motion, Mights, Virtues)

- Kyriotetes (Spirits of Wisdom, Dominions)

- Thrones (Spirits of Will)

- Cherubim (Spirits of Harmony)

- Seraphim (Spirits of Love)

Although the doctrines of Dionysius were long considered to be heretical, the existence of these Hierarchical beings is mentioned in the Bible. Angels, of course, are mentioned in many places. Some other examples:

- *Archangels - Jude v.9; I Thes. 4: 16*

- *Thrones, Dominions, Principalities, Powers - Rom. 8: 38; Col. 1: 16, 2: 15; Eph. 1: 21, 3: 10*

- *Cherubim - Gen. 3: 24; Ex. 25: 18–20,22; Num. 7: 89; Ezk. 9: 3, ch. 10; Ps. 18: 10*

- *Seraphim - Isa. 6: 21*

These spirits are not all "angelic," in the sense of "good and holy." Some, sometimes, oppose the regular, good world-order. Ahriman ("the Unjust Prince of this World") is a "retarded" Spirit of Form, working as an Arche, opposing (in a sense) the good world order. (Yet, this opposition is not purely "evil," as I will discuss below.) Since Ahriman is a spirit of opposition, we might begin to understand his nature by understanding what he opposes: the Gods' plan of earthly and human development. But the situation is not as simple as a two-sided contest; basic to competent understanding of the world-process is the recognition of at least three kinds of spiritual influence upon the evolution of mankind and the cosmos. (We must be clear that this "evolution" is something very different from the random, meaningless, material process conceived by the Darwinists and suchlike theorists. I mean by "evolution" a thoroughly purposeful, thought-filled process of development initiated and guided by spiritual beings.)

The normal Gods (the regular hierarchies) create and nurture the evolvement of the world and mankind, so as to bring about the possibility of Men attaining the status of divinity as "Spirits of Freedom and Love"—the tenth hierarchy. (At the present stage of evolution, the Man progresses through alternating periods of earth-lives and purely spiritual lives: birth, death, and reincarnation.) As the name implies, essential to the fulfillment of mankind's task is the realization of "freedom," meaning not so much political freedom as spiritual freedom—that Men should become independent, unique individuals acting consciously as the originators of their own deeds. Occult wisdom, independently rediscovered and made public by Steiner explains this evolution as being created and guided through seven great cosmic ages. We are now in the fourth great age, called the "Earth" Age (All ages' names here are given in order of succession). The previous three ages are called "Saturn," "Sun," and "Moon." Again, these are past ages of cosmic development, not to be confused with the present-day heavenly bodies of the same names. The same holds for the three future ages: "Jupiter," "Venus," and "Vulcan." The great Earth Age comprises seven lesser ages, of which we are in the fifth. These five are called "Polarian," "Hyperborean," "Lemurian," "Atlantean," and "Post-Atlantean." And the Post-Atlantean Age comprises seven cultural epochs, of which, again, we are in the fifth. The previous four are called "Indian," "Persian," "Egypto-Chaldean," and "Greco-Roman." Recorded history begins only with the Egypto-Chaldean Epoch; what is generally known of ancient Indian and Persian culture derives from records made in the third epoch. These names of epochs do not imply that nothing important was happening in other regions of the earth, but that the archetypal evolutionary impulses of the times were centered in the regions designated. The epochs last approximately 2160 years; and the present, fifth post-Atlantean epoch began about 1413 AD. Neither are these epochs considered to be sharply differentiated; transitions happen gradually, future developments being prepared in advance, and past influences lingering after.

The central event of the Earth Age occurred during the Greco-Roman Epoch, in Palestine. It was the incarnation of a very high spiritual Being, a God of the normal current, called the "Christ"—culminating in the events surrounding the Crucifixion: the "Mystery of Golgatha." This Event was the turning point of Earth-evolution from descent from spirit into matter, toward ascent back to the spirit, with the fruits gained from the sojourn into matter (Steiner himself did not begin with a Christian world-view. He independently, and unexpectedly, rediscovered the "mystical fact" of Christianity during the course of his consciously clairvoyant experiences).

Besides the normal Gods, a host of abnormal spiritual beings, called "Luciferic," also influences earthly evolution. In a sense, these oppose the normal Gods' plans for evolution. The Luciferic beings try to draw mankind away from the normal earth-evolution to their own abnormal psychic-spiritual cosmos of light. In the human soul they inspire pride, egotism, disinterest in one's fellow Men, fiery emotionalism, subjectivity, fantasy, and hallucination. In the human intellect they inspire generalization, unification, hypothesizing, and the building of imaginative pictures beyond reality. Human speech and thought are Luciferic in origin; so are human self-consciousness and the capacity for independence and rebellion against the normal Gods' world-order. Also, the susceptibility to disease originated from Luciferic influence. A high spiritual being, in a sense the leader of the Luciferic host, "Lucifer" himself, incarnated in a human body, in the region of China, in the Third Millennium BC. This event brought about a revolution in human consciousness.

Human speech and thought are Luciferic in origin; so are human self-consciousness and the capacity for independence and rebellion against the normal Gods' world-order.

Before then, Men could not use the organs of intellect and lived by a kind of instinct. Lucifer was the first to grasp by the intellect the wisdom of the Mysteries theretofore revealed by the Gods to mankind in other forms of consciousness. The effects of this incarnation inspired the wisdom of Pagan culture, up through the Gnosis of the early centuries AD, and lingered even into the early 19th century. This wisdom should not be considered to be false in itself; it is good or evil depending on who holds it, and for what purposes it is used. The great Pagan initiates took it upon themselves to enter into the Luciferic influence and turn it to the good of mankind. Only through the Luciferic influence has mankind risen above the status of childishness. (Apart from the Pagan culture of Nature-wisdom was the Hebraic culture, which [in a sense] separated the Man from Nature, and which prepared an hereditary current to provide a body for the incarnation of Christ. In Pagan culture the Man felt membered into the starry cosmos, without what we now know as moral impulses. Moral impulses in the human soul were prepared by Hebrewism and furthered by Christianity. Christianity is also a culmination and fulfillment of Pagan wisdom. Here "Christianity" means not so much "organized religion" as the deeds and continuing influence of the Christ-Being and His hosts, not necessarily confined to formal-religious organizations.)

Ahriman lives upon lies; he is a spirit of untruth, the "Father of Lies."

A third spiritual influence working into human and earthly evolution is the Ahrimanic. The intention of Ahriman, and his hosts, is to freeze the earth into complete rigidity, so that it will not pass over to the Jupiter, Venus, and Vulcan ages, and to make the Man into an entirely earthly being—unindividualized, unfree, and divorced from the normal Gods' cosmos. The essential Ahrimanic tendency is to materialize; to crystallize; to darken; to silence; to bring living, mobile forces into fixed form—in other words, to kill that which is living. This tendency in itself, within proper bounds, is not evil; the dead, material world is necessary for the regular Gods' plan of human and cosmic development. The Ahrimanic tendency is evil only when it exceeds proper bounds, when it reaches into what should be alive—and Ahriman does try to exceed proper bounds. Again, the basic reality of the world is spiritual beings together with their deeds, but Ahriman promotes the illusion, the lie, that matter is the basic reality, or the only reality. In fact, Ahrimanic spirits, not "atoms" or "ultimate particles," are the reality behind the apparently material world. Ahriman lives upon lies; he is a spirit of untruth, the "Father of Lies."

AHRIMAN IN MODERN TIMES

In the present, fifth cultural epoch the Ahrimanic influence in human culture is reaching a climax. The modern scientific revolution, since the 15th century, has been inspired largely by Ahriman. He is the inspirer of amoral, atheistic, mechanistic materialism, and the kind of cleverness that goes with it. The regular Gods' intent for the present epoch (also called the "Consciousness Soul Epoch") is that mankind should develop increased consciousness, together with the individuality and spiritual freedom that go with that consciousness. Ahriman opposes this; he wants the Man to live from unconscious instincts as an unindividualized, impulsive animal—clever, but an animal nonetheless. (Ahriman is the teacher of the lie that the Man is an animal: Darwinism and similar theories.)

To the modern mind it might seem a contradiction to say Ahriman opposes increased consciousness but promotes intelligence and science. This is because the modern mind is so immured in what is generally considered to be "scientific thinking" that it has almost no conception of the true nature of conscious thinking. The fact is that the "scientific" thinking normal in this epoch, no matter how clever, is hardly conscious at all (possibly with some relatively rare exceptions at moments of "insight" or mathematical discovery).

In the kind of consciousness usual in our "scientific" culture, we become conscious only of the fixed results of the thinking, after it has been accomplished; we are not (usually) conscious of the thinking-process itself. And since it is unconscious, it is not our free action; it is automatic. When we think in the manner usual in our epoch, we are sentient automata, acting from instinct. And this is what Ahriman wants: he wants to stamp out all traces and all possibility of free, individualized human consciousness; he wants the Man not to be an individual, but only a member of a general species of pseudo-mankind—to be a clever, earth-bound animal, an "homunculus."

As indicated, Ahriman is the inspirer of the most extreme kind of "scientific" materialism: the doctrine that there is no spirit or soul in the world; that life itself is not in fact alive, but is only a complex of mechanical processes; that reality is at base only quantitative, that there is no reality in the qualitative—color, sound, etc.; even that the human's inner being is a confluence of material forces. On the emotional level, he works in the human subconscious instincts, inspiring fear, hatred, lust for power, and destructive sex impulses. On the mental level, he inspires rigid, automatic thinking: thinking almost entirely without thoughts, but thinking tremendously strongly in the language, in the literal words, which easily become empty words, which in turn easily become lies. This "abstract" thinking is devoid of any conscious, inner activity and devoid of any real connection to living experience, and creates a darkened consciousness without light, color, or images.

THE DEGRADATION OF LANGUAGE

According to Steiner, it is characteristic of the present culture of Ahrimanic scientism and Anglo-American economic imperialism that language has lost its instinctive spiritual meaning; that is, the connection is lost between the literal word and the spiritual impulse that constitutes meaning.

Without real, spiritual content, language consists only of "empty phrases," such as *rule by the will of the people, the free world, individual freedom*, and so on. These phrases are largely devoid of reality in our socio-political structure; here the pervasive actuality is the power of money over Men and over life. And where the empty phrase rules in language, mere conventions—rather than living human contact—rule in social life, and mere routine—rather than lively human interest—rules in economic life. And: "It is only a short step from the empty phrase to the lie." Again, this is especially true in politics and economics, for the prevalence of empty words makes possible the falsification of realities—a potent weapon in the hands of those with occult, conscious intentions to manipulate people for devious ends. In our time, people en masse act as if they are possessed by evil forces, because, in a way, they are. The demons of materialism

The prevalence of empty words makes possible the falsification of realities—a potent weapon in the hands of those with occult, conscious intentions to manipulate people for devious ends.

speak through empty words. A language in which the demons of materialism have taken the place of human spiritual impulses can lead only to destruction.

Certainly Steiner was not the only one to notice this aspect of modern language. George Orwell was perhaps the most prominent writer to decry this trend. See, for instance, his classic essay "Politics and the English Language." He envisioned the dehumanization of language becoming deliberately intensified in the "newspeak" of the Ahrimanic nightmare 1984. Having no apparent knowledge of spiritual science, and working with only keen observation and a love of truth, he saw what was happening in the political discourse of Western Europe and carried to extremes in the totalitarian regimes.

On the socio-political level, the antidote for this poison of empty words is the liberation of cultural life, especially education, from political and financial power. (As outlined in Steiner's concept of the "threefold commonwealth": the separation of the political-rights state, the spiritual-cultural sphere, and the economic sector—along with the elimination of egotism and coercion from the economy.) On the individual-personal level, the antidote is the infusion of active, creative thought into language, thus creating a language in which the words point to the thoughts, evoking living thinking in the listeners. If we do not put effort into creating our original thoughts, then ready-made pseudo-thoughts, trite words and phrases, come automatically to mind and carry us along with them, resulting in "thinking almost entirely without thoughts." (Steiner). We can at least make the effort to resist these ready-made phrases and generalizations that effortlessly come to mind, and to form mental pictures of particular people, things, and events—and further, to make original word-formations describing these things and pictures from varying

points of view. The essential point is that we not let our speaking and writing be determined by unconscious influences, but that we call forth *through our own efforts* new, original thought-creations and convey them with original, fluid, artistic word-formations. We will not always fully succeed; we are not all poets all the time; but if we consciously make this effort, then we will go far toward recovering the lost human-spirituality of language, and consequently, toward the humanization of culture. And, not incidentally, we will thus progress toward living consciously in the thinking-free-of-literal-words that is the "language" of the spirit-soul world in which we will live after death—"Men must learn to see through words; they will have to acquire the capacity to grasp the gesture in language." [From *Symptom to Reality in Modern History*, p. 124]

THE AHRIMANIZATION OF CULTURE

In the social-cultural sphere, Ahriman's influence is apparent everywhere, especially strong and growing stronger throughout the later part of the 20th century and continuing at an accelerated pace still to this day. Chief among the Ahrimanic trends are:

- Antagonistic nationalism based on ethnicity. (Moderate folk-nationalism was a progressive principle in the past, but ethnic nationalism is retrogressive and destructive today.)

- Dogmatic party politics, engendering hatred and bitterness arising from the refusal to see other, equally valid (or invalid) points of view.

- The subjugation of cultural life (e.g. medicine, education, research, criminal jurisprudence) to political and economic power.

- The mechanization of the political state, bound by rigid laws everywhere, with little place for free human initiative.

- In everyday life: Philistinism, tedium, and alienation, lack of interest in one's work, even in intellectual work. (Ahriman wants knowledge to be devoid of warm human interest and connection, to be stored in libraries and not to live in human souls.)

- In medicine: materialistic, mechanistic (and atrocious) experimentalism and treatment, without understanding of the living human individual. (The related practice of embalming corpses tends to bind the human entity to earth; this is an Ahrimanic reflection of ancient Egyptian mummification.)

- In social science: blind acceptance of statistics, and the belief that the satisfaction of economic needs by itself will secure human welfare.

- In economics: the subjugation of all living and human interests to the inhuman, impersonal mechanism of profit-seeking, to the "artificial person" of the corporation (In the USA this has reached such a state that the humanizing influence of the labor movement is being obliterated, and the exigencies of "making a living," along with other destructive Ahrimanic trends, are destroying the human family—this in the so-called "richest country in the world." (A perspicacious American folk-wisdom has coined the phrase "*the Almighty Dollar.*") The Ahrimanic "Mammon" is archetypally the god of "filthy lucre" and of the power of money over life, as well as of all low and dark forces; his hosts also attack the human body and soul to corrupt and destroy them.)

- In the Christian religion: narrow, simplistic interpretation of the Gospels, without appreciation for the occult wisdom needed for an approach to the deep mysteries of the Christ Being.

- In literature: books inspired directly by Ahriman, works of great intelligence that further Ahriman's goals (e.g. some parts of Nietzsche's *Antichrist* and *Ecce Homo*).

- In techniques: very refined developments, but directed only at satisfying animal needs, promoting human immersion in the sense-world to the exclusion of the supersensible.

- In world-view: humans as animals, animals (and all living things) as mechanisms, the non-existence of soul and spirit, and the non-existence of moral reality: amoralism.

Obviously, these impulses are running amok in this world, more so all the time. They are, in fact, approaching a climax; they are preparations for the incarnation of Ahriman himself in a human body.

GOOD AND EVIL

To sum up this description of the triad of spiritual streams: The conflicts of human and spiritual life do not derive from a simple, two-sided war between good and evil. It was one of the great insights of Steiner to renew the ancient teaching of the "Golden Mean," of good as the middle way between opposing extremes. Lucifer is too warm, too flighty, too unstable; he inspires human fanaticism, false mysticism, hot-bloodedness, and the tendency to flee earthly reality for hallucinatory pleasures. Ahriman is too cold, too hard, too rigid; he tries to make people dry, prosaic, philistine, materialistic in thought and in deed—and hardens what would be healthily mobile, supple thoughts, feelings, and even bodies. Christ, as the Exemplar of the regular Gods, represents the middle way between the too-much and the too-little, holding the opposites in balance—and leading mankind to find the healthy middle way. Seen this way, Lucifer and Ahriman are not purely evil; they both bring to human and earthly evolution forces that are needed for good, healthy development and the fulfillment of the Gods' plans. Evil results only when events get out of balance and run to extremes. However, neither do Lucifer and Ahriman simply oppose each other; in a sense, they work together in opposition to the Gods' intent for evolution; they both work to prevent mankind and the earth from pro-

In the USA this has reached such a state that the humanizing influence of the labor movement is being obliterated, and the exigencies of "making a living," along with other destructive Ahrimanic trends, are destroying the human family.

gressing together to the New Jupiter. Lucifer draws human spirits away from earthly embodiment toward his own psychic-spiritual "planet" of light; Ahriman pushes the individual human spirit out of the human organism and away from the earth, so that only a hardened, mechanized, ghostly human organism, devoid of free individuality and living an instinctive-but-clever animalistic species-life remains on the hardened "cosmic slag" of the earth (surrounded with Old Moon forces). Mankind's rightful task for the present is to lead lives of healthy, progressive alternation between the earthly and the cosmic (life, death, and rebirth), so as to lead the earth over to New Jupiter—the profound mystery of evil is that in a higher sense, in the long run, it serves the good. Not to imply that we would be justified in doing evil with the rationalization that good would result: "...it must needs be that offences come; but woe to that man by whom the offence cometh!" [Matthew 18: vii]

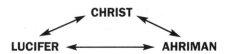

The true picture of the workings of evil might be even more complex than outlined above. Steiner did make some statements which might be interpreted as indicating a third stream of spirits of opposition: the "Asuras" (a borrowed Eastern term), which are retarded Archai who work to destroy the human "I" or the Ego itself. The Asuras might be agents of the actual Antichrist, the Sun-Demon, known to occultism as "Sorat" (or "Sorath"). In some passages Steiner does identify the Apocalyptic Beast 666 as Sorat, not clearly differentiating the Ahrimanic and Soratic principals. While it seems true that the numerological interpretation of the Hebrew spelling of "Sorat" gives the number 666, still the position of Sorat in relation to Lucifer and Ahriman is not altogether clear (to this writer). A possible solution to this question might follow from the imagery of the Apocalypse: Michael casts the Dragon out of heaven; immediately afterwards arise the two "beasts"—the first from the sea (Lucifer) and the second from the land (Ahriman). Thus Lucifer and Ahriman appear on earth as two beings or principles, but they are the progeny of the one spirit of opposition—the Dragon—in Heaven. If we identify the Dragon, the Antichrist, as Sorat, we can picture Lucifer and Ahriman as the left and right hands of Sorat. Christ strives to hold Lucifer and Ahriman in balance so that they serve the good, while Sorat strives to keep them out of balance, so that they work for destruction. While Lucifer seeks to draw the human "I"—the Ego to his own planet, and Ahriman seeks to harden the earth and the human organism so that no Ego can live in a human on earth, Sorat—through the Asuras—seeks to destroy the Ego itself, along with the earth. Sorat uses Lucifer and Ahriman as spirits of seduction to mask his own true intention of pure destruction. And Sorat manifests in social evolution as pure destruction, especially in the wars and mass murders of our time. Thus, the true picture might look something like this:

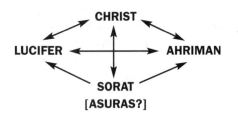

> These impulses are running amok in this world, more so all the time. They are, in fact, approaching a climax; they are preparations for the incarnation of Ahriman himself in a human body.

WHERE AND WHEN?

Steiner says that the Ahrimanic incarnation will happen in the West in the Third Millennium. In his nomenclature "West" means primarily Britain and English-speaking America. There is ample reason to suspect that the destined place for this event is (North) America, for the effect of the American natural environment on the human body and soul especially favors Ahrimanic tendencies. According to Steiner's insights, each of the various regions of the earth has its unique effect upon the human organism. In America, the Ahrimanic influence is strong, rising from the center of the earth, carried by electromagnetism. This strengthens the entity known to occultism as the human "double" or "Doppelgänger." This Doppelgänger is an Ahrimanic soul-being with intelligence and will, but with no individual, spiritual ego, and tending to bind the human soul to the body, hardening human thinking, feeling, and willing. All Men have a Doppelgänger living in their nerve-electricity, infusing into their souls all sorts of degrading, depressing impulses, as well as instigating internal illnesses. (Electricity is the "sub-natural," rigidifying shadow of soul forces.) The Ahrimanic tendencies in America are well known even to those whose perception is unenlivened by occult knowledge; American culture has long been famous for its violence and "hard-boiled" materialism, and its degeneracy and decadence.

As to exactly when Ahriman's incarnation will happen, Steiner (as far as I am aware) does not give a precise time. In at least one passage he seems to indicate the end of the Third Millennium; in other places he indicates the early part of that millennium. In many places he points to a great crisis at the end of the 20th century, even a "War of All against All," when mankind might well "stand at the grave of civilization." In any case, it seems highly likely that a major Ahrimanic onslaught—either the incarnation or birth of Ahriman himself, or the advent of the "false prophet" of the Apocalypse, or some other attack—occurs around 1998 AD (approximately). To see why this is so, we need to do a few simple calculations, based on the occult principle of meaningful rhythms in history. (Let the skeptical reader be a true skeptic and suspend judgment, and take in the following discussion with a mind open to possibilities unsuspected by the materialistic mind.)

SOME OCCULT HISTORY

Unknown to history, but revealed by Steiner's spiritual research, while the Incarnation of Christ was happening in Palestine another stupendous drama played out in Mexico. A high initiate of the negative Mysteries, the most advanced "black magician" in the world, had reached, by repeated ritual murders of an especially horrible kind, the threshold of knowledge of certain deep, cosmic secrets. This knowledge would have given him the ability, as was his intention, of achieving the Ahrimanic goals of completely rigidifying the earth, so as to draw it out of the progressive development toward the New Jupiter, and of binding human organisms as automata in that "slag" of the earth. He was thwarted in this intention by the incarnate high Sun-being "Vitzliputzli," who caused the black magician to be crucified at the same time as the Crucifixion of Jesus Christ—a shattering reflection in the American continent of the Events in Palestine. (Since then the soul of this black magician has been held in a kind of "prison.")

Recall that the Greco-Roman Epoch ran approximately 2160 years, from 747 BC to 1413 AD. The midpoint of this epoch was 1413 AD minus 2160/2 = 333 AD. Consider (as an hypothesis) the occult teaching that events in history occur at times that, as it were, reflect and balance the events equidistant in time from a midpoint. Taking 333 AD as the midpoint, the fulcrum of the balance, and on one side the Birth in Palestine, on the other side of the scales would be 333 AD + 333 = 666 AD. The big event, known to history, of the 7th century was the rise of Islam. Another event, not so famous but still known to history, was the transfer of ancient Greek philosophy (especially Aristotle's works, probably including the lost work on alchemy) to the Academy of Jundi Sabur (near present-day Baghdad). Following the expulsion of the philosophers from Syrian Edessa in 489 AD and from Athens in 529 AD, the philosophers had found refuge in what was then the Persian Empire, and at that Academy they pursued their calling. Then this knowledge passed to the Islamic Arabs, and science of a particular bent reached a high development under them, while Europe was in the "Dark Ages." Only gradually, over many centuries, did this science pass over to Europe, where it developed into the modern scientific revolution. Again, the trend of modern science, as it has in fact developed, is Ahrimanic. The direct ancestor of scientific materialism was this Arabian science, which was itself derived from the Academy of Jundi Sabur. Thus, on the other side of the 333 AD midpoint from the Birth in Palestine was the rise of an active materialistic, anti-Christian worldview in Jundi Sabur.

Occult history (as given by Steiner) reveals how this came about: Sorat intended to approach physical manifestation in 666 AD at Jundi Sabur, and to bestow upon the philosophers there a super-human knowledge. This knowledge was to consist of everything that mankind, under the plan of the regular Gods, was to learn through its own efforts by the height of the present, Consciousness Soul Epoch. This epoch began in 1413 AD, so its midpoint will be 2493 AD. In other words, Sorat wanted to give to mankind, prematurely and without the requisite human effort and experience, the knowledge that would be right and healthy for mankind to achieve through work and evolution by the middle of the Third Millennium. The regular Gods' plan for the Consciousness Soul Epoch is for mankind to acquire, through self-education and self-discipline, the free, conscious, individualized human personality. If the mankind of the 7th century had been given this advanced knowledge at that immature stage of development, when people could not think in full consciousness, the result would have been disastrous. Just consider how much evil mankind has done with the science we have acquired up to now, at our present stage of maturity (or

> **A high initiate of the negative Mysteries, the most advanced "black magician" in the world, had reached, by repeated ritual murders of an especially horrible kind, the threshold of knowledge of certain deep, cosmic secrets.**

immaturity), and then try to imagine what the relatively primitive people of the 7th century would have done with the science of 2493 AD. This picture is bad enough, but we need to recall Steiner's occult insights to begin to get the whole picture. If Sorat had succeeded, we humans would have lost the possibility of developing our true nature, and would have become egotistic, animalistic automata, with no possibility of further development. We would have become earth-bound, and the Earth could never then pass over to the Jupiter, Venus, and Vulcan stages. The normal Gods' plan would have been thwarted and Men could not become the Spirits of Freedom and Love. However, the rise of Islam thwarted this plan of Sorat. It is a deep, mysterious paradox that Islam, which was, and is, opposed to Christianity in many ways, also in effect worked jointly with the Christ-impulse in history, by blanketing, by "skimming the cream off," this Sorat-science, and by watering it down. Still, this science survived, and has worked on into the present day, but the worst was averted, for those times. The weakened Jundi Sabur impulse, as a distorted quasi-Aristotelianism, passed to the Arabs, over Africa and Spain, to France, England, and through the monasteries (e.g. Roger Bacon) back over to the Continent. The "Realism" of the Medieval scholastics (especially the revived Aristotelianism of Thomas Aquinas) opposed this Arabian influence, somewhat correctly seeing it as inimical to Christianity; but with the decline and decadence of Medieval Aristotelianism, and with the dawn of modern, anti-Aristotelian "empiricism" (e.g. Francis Bacon), the diluted, but still powerful, Sorat-science came to dominate world-culture.

BACONIAN AND GOETHEAN SCIENCE

The true spirit of this kind of scientism can be illustrated by a telling metaphor coined early in this epoch by scientism's seminal spokesman, Francis Bacon. He said, propounding scientific experimentalism, that we must put Nature on the rack and force Her to answer the questions we put to Her. This figure will speak volumes to those who meditate upon it: We, seeking information for whatever motives, are to torture the Goddess who gave us birth and nurture, so as to cause Her, through unbearable pain and injury, to blurt out secrets which She, in her wisdom, conceals from the impure and self-seeking. In much of so-called "physiological research" and "medical training" this is hardly even a metaphor; the torture unto death is quite literal. The usual victims are animals, but all too many "researchers" are not above using human "subjects" when they can get enough power over them. And even a slight whiff of occult knowledge shows us a deeper meaning: The central rite of "Satanism" or "black magic"—sometimes crude, sometimes sophisticated—is the deliberate, ritual torture and killing of animals and, at a more advanced level, of humans. When done in a precise way, this practice confers knowledge and power upon the practitioner; also, it affects the whole earth, hardening and rigidifying it, to the characteristic Ahrimanic purpose. Thus we can see the hordes of "researchers" and medical students—who hurt, injure, and "sacrifice" animals—as undergoing an unconscious, Ahrimanic black magic initiation, which hardens, brutalizes, and Ahrimanizes their souls, and

through them also the culture, and even the earth itself. (*Sacrifice* is the actual word they commonly use, not thinking which "god" they sacrifice unto.) Vivisection is truly the archetypal act of modern science as it is generally understood and practiced.

In contrast to our Baconian science, there does exist a little-known scientific trend, inaugurated by the German poet Johann Wolfgang von Goethe. In the general culture he is known primarily as the author of *Faust;* but he was also a scientist, known for (if known at all) the prediction of the discovery of the intermaxillary bone in humans, or, less often, for his anti-Newtonian theory of color. His mode of scientific thinking was quite different from the Baconian-Ahrimanic mode, and likewise he illustrated it with a telling metaphor. He said (in paraphrase) that we must approach Nature as a reverent lover, and, perhaps, She will whisper to us Her intimate secrets. The contrast to Bacon's metaphor could hardly be more stark. Also, the Goethean method of scientific investigation, in contrast to amoral experimentalism, is a method of self-improvement and self-development—a reverent meditating upon the facts of experience, in the hope that they will speak. This scientific method has, of course, been all but buried under the Baconian-Ahrimanic avalanche, even in Goethe's own country. And it was no mere accident that Steiner's first professional appointment was to edit Goethe's scientific writings, in the Goethe-Schiller Archive in Weimar. Steiner and his successors have developed and expanded the Goethean method to an amazing extent, giving us a reasonable hope for renewed life in our deadened, death-dealing scientific culture. Steiner too has been almost totally ignored by scientists in the West, slightly less so in Central Europe. Also, the practice of Goethean-Steinerean science has vast implications for the soul of the practitioner, as well as for the whole earth. Spiritual science sees soul and spirit in Nature, in a real, practical way, completely consistent with the "empirical" facts. It reverently approaches the scientific laboratory as

The 666-year rhythm continued further; another period ended in 1332 AD. Around this time (circa 1312) the cruel suppression of the Knights Templar began.

a holy place, and the experiment as a sacrament, as a revelation of the Creator-Spirits through the sacred symbols of Nature. This is consistent only with the moral development of the scientist, and with the furtherance of the Gods' plan of human and cosmic evolution.

666 AGAIN

The 666-year rhythm continued further; another period ended in 1332 AD. Around this time (circa 1312) the cruel suppression of the Knights Templar began. Little is known to history of the true nature of the Templars, because of their secretive nature and the distortions passed to history by their triumphant enemies. But these Knights did cultivate an esoteric Christianity that, although somewhat flawed, had the potential of bringing about a more humane civilization in Europe. This possibility was thwarted by the power of the French King, Philip the Fair, and his allies in the Church. Philip, through the torture and killing of the Templars, and through the material inspiration from their looted gold, attained a kind of Ahrimanic initiation-knowledge, but he died soon thereafter. The Templars were either killed or driven underground, and Medieval culture declined until the Renaissance and Reformation. The Templar-impulse did continue underground, to pass over to the "Lodges," especially York and Scottish Rite Freemasonry. These Lodges worked in opposition to Roman Catholicism (at least until the end of the 18th century, when Freemasonry and esoteric-political Catholicism united in opposition to Napoleon), but the esoteric content of Freemasonry became decadent and Ahrimanized. Nevertheless, many of the modern institutions of "liberal republican democracy" (such as freedom of speech, religion, and the press) are very largely due to the influence of Freemasonry, especially in the USA.

And, of course, another 666-year cycle ended around 1998 AD. As stated already, it is apparent that the Ahrimanic influence in culture is building to some kind of climax. Indeed, as is obvious to all with eyes to see, that civilization in the USA, despite (or because of) the triumphant march of technology, human culture and civilization are decaying (regardless of erstwhile "rising economic indicators"). It is an easy guess that the decades after 1998 AD are a propitious period for a major Ahrimanic manifestation: perhaps the appearance of Ahriman himself; or since 1998 = 3x666 years since the Birth of the body for the incarnation of Christ, perhaps the body was born which is to be the vehicle for Ahriman, possibly 30 years later; or perhaps some other major event, such as the advent of the "false prophet" of the Apocalypse.

(These are approximate times only; the outer effects of occult [="hidden"] events may manifest only gradually. In 1998 we did not see newspaper headlines announcing a spectacular, "supernatural" event. But if we had been alive in 666 AD or 1332 AD neither would we have likely been informed by the then contemporary analogues of headlines that any major, "supernatural" events had occurred. Those manifestations of evil did not fully succeed according to the "plan"; other influences intervened and moderated the outcomes. The occult machinations were hardly known to the public. Such may also be true in the present: the actual course of events depends on many contending forces, and upon the consciousness and will of Men; and the crux of the struggle will likely be hidden ["occult"] to the wide public. We will live and/or die in the outer effects of the occult causes, as uncomprehending [most of us, probably] as is usual in social cataclysms. This essay is an attempt to lessen the incomprehension, and to lighten the mental atmosphere of this planet, even a little. Surely, as "thoughts are things," even a slight change in consciousness can influence physical events in the right direction.)

Steiner repeatedly pointed to the turn of the Millennium as a time of crisis. (As is the turn of every millennium: every 1000 years Lucifer and Ahriman work together with special power.) Also, the Dutch Anthroposophist Bernard Lievegoed, in his deathbed testament, made the following remarks:

"From indications by Rudolf Steiner, we have to assume that in the year 1998 Ahriman will play an important role ... it is a part of the development of the earth and of mankind that Ahriman will at one time be on earth in a physical body. In lectures, Rudolf Steiner has mentioned a time in the third millennium: 'before even a part of the third millennium after Christ has passed'. However, he said at a meeting of young people in Breslau, that Ahriman will do everything in his power to advance this moment as much as he can. Steiner then mentions the year 1998. It will depend on all of mankind together whether Ahriman will succeed in this or not.... Whether he will succeed in this will depend on the question whether there will be enough people who see through his designs.... In 1916 Rudolf Steiner said that at the beginning of the 21st century, evil will appear in a form which at that time [1916] could not yet be described.... My estimate is that the nadir of this battle will fall around the years 2020 to 2040. Then the abyss of the demons will open. National Socialism and Bolshevism will pale in comparison with this. Millions of people will perish." [The Battle for the Soul; pp. 98–113]

A cynic might say that these predictions allow for plenty of "wiggle room" for the incarnation of Ahriman: 1998 to the first part of the new millennium, or even the end of this millennium. I will concede that the predicted time is not very precise, but I believe nevertheless that it is highly likely that this incarnation will manifest in the next few years to half-century or century. And even without occult insight, one who observes the present social/cultural decline can hardly avoid seeing some kind of wrenching changes approaching.

Again, it is not certain that Ahriman's incarnation will be immediately known to the public: Steiner warns that Ahriman wants mankind to be unconscious of his true nature and to see his advent as progressive and good

In 1916 Rudolf Steiner said that at the beginning of the 21st century, evil will appear in a form which at that time [1916] could not yet be described.

for human welfare. Says Steiner: "*If Ahriman were able to slink into a humanity unaware of his coming, that would gladden him most of all. It is for this reason that the occurrences and trends in which Ahriman is working for his future incarnation must be brought to light.*" Ahriman will establish a (possibly secret) school for powerful "magic" arts and clairvoyance. The technical applications of this highly intelligent spirit will indeed look like "magic" to us, even as advanced as we might consider our science to be—for Ahriman's understanding is not limited by the crude materialism he foists upon mankind. And the clairvoyance bestowed upon Ahriman's pupils will be effortless, not won through the long preparation of soul-purification and self-discipline of legitimate occultism. It will give spirit-vision, but the visions will be subjective and deceptive; people will see differing, conflicting visions of the soul/spirit worlds, and will fall into confusion and conflict. Ahriman-in-the-flesh will be an overwhelmingly powerful and impressive figure, when he reveals himself. And it seems probable that, as the Father of Lies, he will present himself as that which he is most certainly not: Christ, in His Second Coming. And again, it is America, where many religious people are expecting the Second Coming in a physical body, which will be especially susceptible to Ahriman's deceptions. It is entirely possible that they who cling to the Gospels with a superficially literalistic interpretation closed to occult insight will be the very people who will be the false Christ's followers.

THE TRUE SECOND COMING

Another tremendous revelation from Steiner's spiritual science concerns the true nature of the Second Coming of Christ. Steiner was adamant that the physical incarnation of Christ can happen once and only once. "Just as a pair of scales can have only one balancing-point, so in Earth evolution the event of Golgatha can take place only once." The amazing fact is that the Second Coming is happening now, but that most of mankind is unaware of it. (Actually, the term "second coming" is not in the New Testament; the Greek word is *parousia*, meaning roughly "active presence." It was this "presence" that Saul/Paul experienced on the road to Damascus; Paul being mankind's "premature birth" of the coming new experience of Christ. *Parousia* was translated into Latin as *adventus*, which means *arrival*, thus helping to give rise to the expectation of a physical arrival of Christ. The original Greek term seems in consonance with Steiner's explanation. See Emil Bock's *St. Paul*.) In fact, it is the driving force behind the "apocalyptic" convulsions and struggles of our time. For, as the picture is given in the Apocalypse of John, the bottomless pit is opened, Michael casts the dragon and his hosts onto the earth, the vials of wrath are poured out, and Babylon is overthrown—all in preparation for Christ's triumph that brings the New Heaven and New Earth. Most of us are unaware of this present Second Coming because it is not happening in the visible, material world, but in the "ethereal" region of the Earth. "Ethereal" means the system of "formative forces," bordering on the physical, that raise inert matter to the realm of the living. Plants, animals, and humans all have ethereal, formative-force "bodies," and when the ethereal body forsakes the physical body, the physical body becomes ordinary matter; in other words, it dies. The earth, being the body of a living Being, also has a formative-force body, the "ethereal earth." These ethereal forces manifest especially in weather phenomena, such as cloud formation. (It is a false, Ahrimanic science that sees cloud formation as a merely material process of evaporation and condensation of "water molecules"; this is rather a process of de-materialization and re-materialization through the workings of the ethers.)

With these concepts, we can see new meaning in the Bible verses concerning the Ascension and Return of Christ. "... [A] cloud received him out of their sight" (Acts

It is America, where many religious people are expecting the Second Coming in a physical body, which will be especially susceptible to Ahriman's deceptions.

I;9) seems to be saying that Christ ascended into the ethereal, formative-force region of the earth. And the statement that He "...so shall come in like manner as ye have seen him go into heaven" (Acts I;11) seems to say that He shall return from the ethereal regions: "Behold he cometh with clouds...." (Rev. I;7) Steiner's assertion that Christ shall not come again in the flesh seems to be in consonance with the Bible: "Then if any man shall say unto you, Lo, here is Christ, or there; believe it not.... Wherefore if they shall say unto you, Behold, he is in the desert; go not forth; behold he is in the secret chambers; believe it not." (Matt. XXIV;23,26) On the contrary, the Second Coming shall be a tremendous event, not limited to a particular location: "For as the lightning cometh out of the east, and shineth even unto the west; so also shall the coming of the Son of man be." (Matt. XXIV; 27) The ethereal is super-physical, not bound by the laws of material space; Christ's appearance in the ethereal earth is everywhere-at-once. And since the ethereal is super-physical, some degree of super-physical vision, or "clairvoyance," is needed to see into it. Few people at the present stage of evolution have that kind of clairvoyance, and some may have it only sporadically. But the Second Coming is only at its beginning; true clairvoyance (as opposed to the deceptive Ahrimanic clairvoyance) will reveal to consciousness the ethereal Christ in the centuries to come. Ahriman dreads human consciousness of the ethereal Christ, and fights against it. It is essential for us to grasp the fact that he who shall come in the flesh is not Christ, but Ahriman: "For there shall arise false Christs, and false prophets, and shall show great signs and wonders...." (Matt. XXIV; 24)

Steiner revealed the occult notion that since the beginning of the present reign of the Sun-Archangel Michael as the Time Spirit in 1879 AD, the human ethereal body is becoming less closely bound to the physical body, thus opening the possibility of new clairvoyance. 1933 AD (two 950-year cycles of the precession of the nodes of Saturn since the Crucifixion and Resurrection in 33 AD) would have been an especially propitious time for the beginning of widespread perception of the ethereal Christ. But this was hindered by the rise to power of Hitler—one expression of Sorat himself "rising from the Abyss"—and by the many convulsions and distractions around the same time in earth-life. What was hindered in 1933 might again become propitious around 2000–2100 AD (a reflection of the calling of Abraham around 2000–2100 BC). We may speculate that Ahriman and Sorat will oppose this new Christ-consciousness by even more horrendous hindrances.

THE OCCULT MEANING OF THE COMPUTER

A very interesting theory (by David B. Black) interprets the progressive mechanization of culture not only as an Ahrimanic influence, but as the actual "macrocosmic incarnation" of Ahriman: This is being brought to completion through the development of the electronic computer. Black traces the milestones in the evolution of the computer as reflections of the spiritual events in the heavens. For example, in the 1840s, around the time of Jehovah's abandonment of human blood-bound thinking to Ahriman, Boolean algebra was developed. The year 1879—the time of Michael's accession as Time Spirit and the final expulsion of the "dragon" onto earth—saw the publication of Frege's *Begriffschrift*, a great milestone in the development of "formal logic": the separation of logic from the spiritual "Word." Also in 1879: Edison invented the electric light (light is separated from the sun and plunged into the "sub-earthly": "Electricity is Ahrimanic 'light'"); Trotsky and Stalin were born; Merganthaler invented the Linotype machine; Bessemer introduced the hard-steel process; and the US Census Bureau hired Herman Hollerith, who developed the first large-scale punched-card tabulating machine. The Christ's "coming in the clouds" was reflected on earth in the early 1930s by the publication of Gödel's "incompleteness theorem," which demonstrated that a truly-thinking machine is impossible, but which also led to the development of "recursion theory," which is the essential conceptual framework for "artificial intelligence" and "artificial life." Also in 1930, by a fortuitous comedy of errors, the planet Pluto was discovered. Pluto, of course, is the god of the underworld, and the discovery of "his" planet was a synchronistic harbinger of the unleashing of the sub-material "powers of the pit" upon earth: later transits of Saturn and Uranus to Pluto's discovery position marked the bombing of Hiroshima and the explosion of the first H-bomb.

As is well known, the development of the electronic computer proceeded exponentially, from von Neumann's development of the "stored program" to the desktop and the laptop. A lesser-known development was the "Josephson effect," which allows the construction of semi-conductors from superconducting materials. Thus, electrical circuits can operate without "Luciferic" heat, and Ahriman, whose nature is "freezing cold," can completely enter into electrical devices. As superconducting computers become more common, Ahrimanic beings higher than "elementals" might actually incarnate in them, since no physical energy is consumed in a superconducting circuit. (Ahrimanic "elemental spirits" inhabit our artificial machines, just as normal "elementals" [or "nature spirits": gnomes, undines, sylphs, salamanders] work in and throughout the living processes of Nature.) Black sums up: "Sunless light and Wordless logic intertwined, and out of them came the computer." Thus, while Ahriman incarnates "microcosmically" in a human body, we might also face the "macro-cosmic" literal incar-nation of Ahriman in our machines.

glimpse into the motives of the sophisticated "Satanists" or "black magicians." Ahriman's acolytes seek a kind of "immortality" in the slag-earth-surrounded-with-Old-Moon-forces, but an immortality with egotistic, earthly con-sciousness instead of the cosmic consciousness of the individualized spiritual Ego.

Today it is essential that more of this wisdom become generally known, if human culture is not to succumb to Ahriman.

AN EVOLUTIONARY LEAP

The incarnation of high spiritual beings in human bodies has the special significance that new possibilities for human development are opened up, because, as it were, the way is cleared by these high-spiritual-beings-in-the-flesh being the first to accomplish these developments. Lucifer was the first to use the organs of intellect. Christ was the first to redeem the "fallen" death-prone human body with the Resurrection Body. Likewise, Ahriman-in-the-flesh will try to inaugurate a new human capacity, for his own ends: he wishes to bring the shadowy, brain-bound, semi-conscious, clever Ahrimanic "thinking" into the human ethereal body. This would be an especially evil development if it is carried into the average human organ-ism. It is normal and healthy, at the present stage of human evolution, for the human ethereal body to dissolve into the wide cosmos in the days immediately following death (after "one's whole life passes before one's eyes"). Afterwards the human soul-and-spirit entity rises to higher regions, where it is purified and prepared for a new earth-life. But materialism in the earth-life hardens the ethereal body so that it does not dissolve, but remains near the earth for a longer time, while the dead human entity serves Ahriman. Only slowly and in unconsciousness do such dead spirits enter the spirit-worlds to prepare for a new incarnation. Ahriman wishes to be the first to so hard-en the ethereal body so that it becomes the vehicle of automatic, intellectual thinking-devoid-of-will, and thus to make it possible to keep human ethereal bodies perma-nently in the region of the earth. Then the earth would become so hardened that it would not pass over to the Jupiter Age, and humans would become clever, animalis-tic, ghostly, earth-bound creatures. The Gods' plan for human and earthly evolution would be thwarted. Steiner put it this way: "Ahriman works against the word 'Heaven and earth shall pass away, but My words shall not pass away.' He wills that the words shall be thrown away, that heaven and earth shall continue on." Here we can get a

The regular Gods intend that in the present epoch people should indeed think free of the physical brain, but with free, conscious, self-created thinking. This development would gradually open the possibility of the reintegration of mankind into the spiritual cosmos, and further the pass-ing of the earth over to the New Jupiter. Mankind could eventually rise to the rank of Spirits of Freedom and Love, and not sink to the level of earth-bound, animalistic, clever automata. To put it mildly: a lot is at stake here.

TURNING EVIL TO GOOD

But Ahriman's incarnation need not be an evil event, as he wishes it to be. This incarnation is necessary in human and earthly evolution, and it can be turned toward the good, if mankind meets it in the right way: On the mundane level, we can remedy Ahrimanic tedium in the work-life and the intellectual life, by filling them with warm, Luciferic enthusiasm, by finding what is interesting in them, by getting ourselves interested in objective, impersonal facts and processes. On the psychological level, we can remedy Luciferic subjectivity and fiery emo-tionalism by observing ourselves coolly, as we would an external natural process.

On a higher level, we can become more aware of the meaning of our own lives, and of the world-process, by studying and filling ourselves with the modern form of cos-mic wisdom, given by spiritual science (mainly from Steiner, in my opinion, but from others also). This is a renewal of wisdom that was formerly kept hidden, or "occult," in the Mysteries. Today it is essential that more of this wisdom become generally known, if human culture is not to succumb to Ahriman. Just as the ancient Initiates entered into the Luciferic wisdom and rescued it for the good of mankind, now must mankind, with the conscious-ness gained from spiritual science and from the Ethereal Christ, enter into the coming Ahrimanic knowledge and

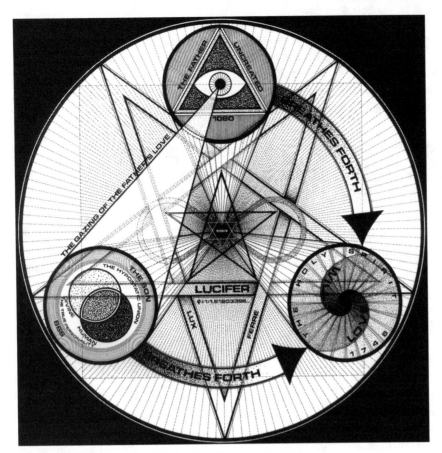

Get Thee Behind Me, Satan, Paul Laffoley, 20" x 20", India ink on paper.
From the collection of Richard Metzger

turn it to good purpose. The Ahrimanic knowledge will show what cleverness can, and cannot, produce from earthly forces. If we meet Ahriman consciously, we can acquire through him the realization that the Earth is becoming old and must decline physically, eventually to die and enter the spiritual worlds, to be reborn as the New Jupiter. And through this decline, mankind is to be lifted above the earthly, as the seed survives the dying plant in winter, to sprout and grow in the Spring.

THE EPOCH OF CONSCIOUSNESS

The fundamental principle in this, the Consciousness Soul Epoch, is the emergence in the Man of conscious, individualized, independent thinking. Concurrent with the emergence of this soul-force (as a by-product, as it were) are wider possibilities for the workings of the forces of Death and Evil. But these workings are (as is characteristic of Ahriman) so falsified that, for example, the cultural institutions that are generally regarded as most beneficial—education and medicine—are in fact among the worst carriers of evil (not to imply that these institutions

should be shunned or destroyed, but purified and renewed—in part by their liberation from money and politics). When this epoch has run its course (if it will have fulfilled its potentials), human culture will be vastly changed. For example, the distinction between "civilized" and "primitive" peoples will have been erased, and a kind of moral "socialism" will have become instinctive.

Our specific task for the Consciousness Soul Epoch is to acquire three great truths, the same truths that Sorat wished to foist upon mankind in the 7th century, with his own slant. We might presume that Ahriman-in-the-flesh will likewise try to insert them into our culture and distort them to his own ends. It is the task of an alert and conscious mankind, schooled in spiritual science and led by the Christ, to gain these three truths through our own striving and to use them for the good development of the earthly creation.

The first truth concerns the Mystery of Birth and Death: that the human soul in the physical world has but the semblance of the true soul-life that it had before conception and will have again after death. The life in the sense-world interrupts the supersensible soul-life in the world-between-death-and-rebirth, so that we can gain, for the spirit, that which can be gained only in the sense-world. To see this truth, we must "look Lucifer in the eye," and thus see through the distortions and illusions he spreads over the human soul. The destiny of the "East" (meaning the Slavic regions and eastwards) is to give rise to a "eugenic occultism": the knowledge of how, through astrological regulation of conception, to bring the right human entities to birth at the right time and place for forward evolution, or conversely, to bring in the wrong entities, for the hindrance of right evolution. Thus, this eugenic occultism can cause great good or great harm, depending on how it is used.

The second truth concerns the Mystery of the Body: that the human body is not a lump of matter, but a form, which is spiritual in origin, and through which interchanging substances are constantly in flux. This knowledge will lead to a true medical art, the essence of which is to keep intact the natural healing forces of the body. The destiny of the

"Middle" (meaning Central Europe) is to give rise to this "hygienic occultism"—which, of course, can lead to great good, but can also cause great harm if it is used without strict conscientiousness.

The third truth concerns the Mystery of Matter: that the reality behind "material substance" is not "atoms," "molecules," or "ultimate particles," but is spirit—to be exact: Ahrimanic spirits, in rhythmic inter-relations. The true picture of "solid matter" is not a machine, but a rainbow: a ghostly appearance, an outcome of spiritual processes. Modern physics, in some advanced theorizing, may have made some halting moves toward this truth, but the dead, mechanistic world-conception still holds sway over the scientism which dominates world-culture. This scientism is the Ahrimanic lie, the descendant of the Jundi Sabur influence, which, even though weakened, banished soul and spirit from the scientific world-view. To see through this lie, we must "look Ahriman in the eye"—a dangerous undertaking if we are not prepared by spiritual science. The destiny of the West (meaning primarily the English-speaking world) is to give rise to a "mechanistic occultism," which will bring about fantastic machine forces, based on rhythm and resonance (The lost, fabled "Keely motor" was a start in this direction). But the introduction of such machine forces would cause harm to society if the political, cultural, and economic spheres are not made mutually independent, and if egotism is not banished from the economy.

Ahriman seeks to divert and pervert these three destined developments of the Consciousness Soul Epoch, through the activity of angels who rejected the Christ influence during the Egypto-Chaldean Epoch. In the present times, the "Christian" angels pour pictures of spirit-realities into the deep regions of the human soul-organism. If the Man does not take up these pictures consciously, they sink down into the ethereal body and act as unconscious instincts through the influence of the Ahrimanic angels. These unconscious instincts work against the three progressive evolutionary trends in the following ways:

1. Perverting the Eugenic Occultism, destructive sex impulses affect the whole social life, working against the development of conscious human brotherhood, and making a mankind entirely egotistical and entirely controlled by instinctive urges carried in the blood.

2. Perverting the Hygienic Occultism, medicine becomes materialistic and can be used to heal or harm, according to egotistic purposes.

3. Perverting the Mechanistic Occultism, powerful, Keely-like machine forces are employed, controlled not by the "vibrations" of good people (seeking the liberation of the workers), but by egotistic people for the evil purpose of attaining power and control over the masses.

The first two perversions are readily apparent in modern society; the third has yet to emerge in public. Again, the direction that these three trends of the present epoch will take depends upon human consciousness and will.

SOME OCCULT POLITICS

Some powerful, Ahrimanic secret societies linked to the Lodges in Britain and the USA strive to keep their version of this third truth (of the spirituality of matter) as their own secret and to ensure that the wider public knows only a crude atheistic-mechanistic scientism, in which spirit and soul have no place. (In more recent times, one can notice that the "crude materialism" given to the public is beginning to be replaced by a more quasi-esoteric materialism.) These societies also strive to guide political and economic trends over the world so that the budding potentialities of the Middle and Eastern peoples come under their domination. The history of modern times has very largely been the story of the outworkings of this struggle. The crimes of the secret Anglo-American power groups include the instigation of the First World War and the consequent establishment of the Bolshevik regime in the East. These power groups believe that the English-speaking peoples are destined to justifiably dominate the East-Slavs in this, the fifth cultural epoch, for the purpose of guiding their nascent potentialities, which should blossom to lead the world-culture in the sixth epoch—just as the Romans, during the fourth epoch, dominated and educated Britain for her future leadership in the fifth epoch. Some truth does lie behind this concept: this is the epoch of the consciousness soul, and the English-speaking peoples are gifted to develop the consciousness soul in an instinctive way, and it is true that the Slavs are destined to lead world-culture in the sixth epoch. But these power groups seek, through illegitimate

But much depends on us, on mankind. We need to become conscious of these power groups, as well as their deeper aims and the aims of Ahriman himself.

means, to guide toward illegitimate, Ahrimanic ends these inherent potentialities, which are loosely "written into" destiny. Many historians and "paranoid right-wing conspiracy nuts" have, solely through common sense and open-eyed observation of external events, discerned some of the outworkings of the influence of these secret societies through their semi-secret instruments: the Council on Foreign Relations, the Order of Skull and Bones (whose members included George Bush, Averell Harriman, and an amazing number of powerful Americans), the Rhodes Scholarships, the Round Table, etc. But these observers, lacking occult knowledge, can only guess at the true aims of the secret power groups. The "Anglophile" societies may disagree among themselves about means and details, but essentially they aim to gain world-domination for themselves (though certainly not for the good of the masses of the English-speaking peoples) and to influence all cultural trends in an Ahrimanic direction.

Now, in "post-Cold War" Europe, the Anglo-Americans and the Jesuit-Catholic power groups apparently are working together to make the basic arrangements of this part of the "New World Order": Central Europe, from France to Poland, is to be dominated by the Jesuit interests, while the "East" (meaning roughly the regions historically Orthodox Christian) is to be dominated by the Anglo-American "West." This arrangement furthers the aims of the Anglo-Americans by preventing cultural collaboration between Central Europe and the Eastern Slavs, thus preventing the rise of a strong, healthy, and independent Central European culture that could mediate and balance the East and the West. Thus, the present push toward the "New World Order" in Europe is a continuation of the long-standing Anglo-American policy of obliterating Central Europe (especially Germany) as a political/cultural force and of controlling the future-seeds being prepared in East-Europe—the same policy that led to First World War and the Bolshevik Revolution.

The deeper, Ahrimanic aim of the Anglo-Americans is to defeat the Gods' plan for Earth-evolution, by turning Earth into a heap of dark, frozen, cosmic slag, haunted by an earthbound mankind of ghostly homunculi—and to secure for themselves a privileged place in this Ahrimanic world-order: an Ahrimanic immortality, with earthly consciousness and with power over the uninitiated.[1]

But much depends on us, on mankind. We need to become conscious of these power groups, as well as their deeper aims and the aims of Ahriman himself. If we do not acquire this alert consciousness, Ahriman might have his way, and the future of the earth, and of mankind, will be dark and bleak. The earth's future, as well as our own, is our responsibility. Any real progress toward a healthy social order depends on mankind's development of a new kind of thinking. The present, Ahrimanic, brain-bound pseudo-thinking is inherently anti-social; it (subconsciously) tries to dominate other people and put them to sleep. Most present anti-social aspects of society proceed from anti-social consciousness; the brain-bound pseudo-thinking is determined by subjective, unconscious instincts, not by concurrence with the objective truth, not by the meaning-process of the thinking itself. An anti-social society is a physical picture of the anti-social human consciousness. If human consciousness becomes harmonious with objective reality, then a truly social society will be possible. Again, it all depends on human consciousness—and will. ◻

Endnote

1. The late Professor Carroll Quigley, mentor of the young Wm. Jefferson Clinton, wrote the fairly well-known tome *Tragedy and Hope*, and the lesser-known work *The Anglo-American Establishment*, in which he described, from a sympathetic point of view, some of the machinations of semi-secret "Anglophile" (his word) power groups. Prominent among these "Anglophile" groups was the secret society organized by Cecil Rhodes around 1891. Its members included Wm. T. Stead (a spiritualist known to Annie Besant of the Theosophical Society), Lord Esher (an advisor to Queen Victoria), the Earl of Rosebury, Nathan Rothschild, Alfred Milner (whose posts included Colonial Secretary, and War Minister during the First World War), H. A. L. Fisher (sometime Education Minister), and A. J. Balfour. I do not imply that Quigley, or Clinton (or all those working for the goals of these power groups) were, or are, fully aware of the deeper aims *behind* the "Anglophiles," but that they are more or less knowingly, or unknowingly, under the influence of the occultists and will usually act in the way desired by these occultists. Altogether, of those who work in accordance with the aims of what may be loosely called the "Anglo-American power groups" (e.g. the Freemasons (or at least some factions of them), C.F.R., Round Table, Rhodes Scholarships, Skull and Bones, and their associated political and economic instruments)—or of the Jesuits—very few are aware of the true, occult aims. This is true even of most of the "initiated," for the ceremonial magic of the initiation-rituals works on the ethereal bodies of the acolytes so as to make those lower initiates into receptive, unsuspecting instruments for the wishes of the few who are more aware. This process might loosely be likened to a sophisticated kind of "post-hypnotic suggestion." In general, we should hold suspect any secret society that practices ceremonial magic and is administered by higher "grades." Nor do I wish to imply that one super-secret power group on earth "controls everything"; various occult power groups, arrayed in various and shifting alliances and antagonisms, vie for their various aims. The centers of the conspiracies do not lie on the physical plane, and no matter how great their power, they are not omnipotent. Again, the primal force behind present-day turmoil is the Coming of the Ethereal Christ. As an old saying goes: "Where there is bright light, there are deep shadows."

JULIUS EVOLA'S COMBAT MANUALS FOR A REVOLT AGAINST THE MODERN WORLD

Passport photo of Julius Evola, circa 1940. Collection of Gaspare Cannizzo. Published in *Julius Evola: Scritti per Vie della Tradizione 1971-1974*, Edizioni di Vie Tradizione, Palermo, Italy

Julius Evola (1898–1974) is one of the most challenging esotericists of the 20th century. His bold and disconcerting proclamations have earned him great admirers and vicious detractors, for few can remain impartial when confronted with Evola's harsh verdict on modern life. Fewer still are probably prepared to accept his counterposed ideal of a sacrally ordered society where all aspects of life reflect a parallel and transcendental "world of Tradition." Rather than fading away into obscurity, though, Evola's works continue to elicit a growing level of interest. And while he is still relatively unknown in America, European intellectuals have long been aware of his writings. Mircea Eliade, the famous scholar of religion and myth, praised Evola's "astounding knowledge," and Marguerite Yourcenar recognized the "prodigious wealth of erudite detail" that informed his elucidations. Novelist Herman Hesse read Evola in the early 1930s and called him "a dazzling and interesting, but very dangerous author." René Guénon, a fellow Traditionalist and lifelong correspondent of Evola's, curiously likened the latter's utterances to the "cry of an eagle." But this is appropriate, for Evola would recognize the keen-eyed eagle as a traditional symbol of the divine *imperium* and, in the poetic realm, as the companion of Nietzsche's lonely mountaineer, Zarathustra.

He was born Giulio Césare Andrea Evola in 1898 to an aristocratic Sicilian family, but little is known of his youth or upbringing. This is due to Evola's aversion against disclosing the circumstantial details of his life, even in autobiographical writings. As a young man Evola developed an interest in art, and in the writings of Nietzsche, Otto Weininger, and

Carlo Michelstaedter. After the outbreak of World War I he joined the Italian army, serving as an officer in a mountain artillery unit; these military and alpine experiences would leave a lasting impression and serve as a strong inspiration for some of his later spiritual writings. Following the war he came into contact with literary and artistic iconoclasts of the time such as Giovanni Papini, F. T. Marinetti, and Tristan Tzara. Through his association with Tzara, Evola became a leading Italian exponent of the Dada "anti-art" movement, producing poetry and paintings. During this artistic period he experimented with drugs and also underwent a period of severe depression; he later claimed to have just barely averted suicide by immersing himself in the early Buddhist text the *Majjhima-Nikaya*.

In Evola's subsequent philosophical period he absorbed and built upon the works of the German Idealists, along with more volatile ideas drawn from Nietzsche, Schopenhauer, and Max Stirner. These studies resulted in his detailed expositions (1925–1930) of "Magical Idealism" and a theory and phenomenology of the "Absolute Individual." In these works Evola posited the existence of an Absolute Self—a liberated higher Self which the awakened, active individual may become aware of and identify with only through disciplined ascetic practices that lead to this enlightenment.

HGA

Evola's studies of Tantra (*The Yoga of Power*, 1925) and Hermeticism (*The Hermetic Tradition*, 1931) are rooted in a similar perspective, and explore how these doctrines may be understood as symbolic and practical tools for transcendent self-realization. In the latter half of the 1920s he formed associations with figures such as the esotericist Arturo Reghini (who influenced Evola's 1928 anti-Christian polemic *Pagan Imperialism*) and the French Traditionalist René Guénon, and involved himself in the UR Group, an eclectic magical order whose membership included a host of significant Italian literary and cultural figures. The profound influence of Guénon resulted in Evola's resolute identification with the Traditionalist movement, a perspective that would remain with him for the rest of his life. In 1935 he published his own Traditionalist *magnum opus* entitled *Revolt Against the Modern World*.

Throughout the Fascist period Evola wrote profusely as a journalist, occasionally coming under fire from various sides for his criticisms of the regime's shortcomings, which he saw evidenced in its plebian sloganeering and tendency toward compromise, especially with the Catholic Church.

Consequently he began to look abroad for ideological allies, lecturing in Germany and engaging in fruitful exchanges with the loosely knit circles of the Conservative Revolution movement.

During World War II Evola published his important study of early Buddhist texts, *The Doctrine of Awakening* (1943). When the Allies invaded Rome in 1944, he escaped to Vienna where he may have worked briefly doing research on secret societies for a department of the S.S. Amid the storm of a Russian bombardment in 1945 he walked alone through the streets of the city in order to silently "question his fate" and was injured by shrapnel, which damaged his spinal cord and left him permanently crippled.

From 1948 on, his physical condition confined him to an apartment in Rome where he received visitors, some of them young neo-fascists in search of an ideological guru. They called him *il magico barone*, the "magical baron," in reference to his aristocratic title and esoteric pursuits. In these postwar years Evola continued to write, penning critical commentaries on the Fascist and National Socialist era as well as a book entitled *Men Among the Ruins* (1953) detailing his idealized socio-political visions from a Traditionalist perspective. In 1951 he was arrested for allegedly "glorifying Fascism" and inspiring young extremist groups through his writings; in the ensuing trial he was acquitted of all charges. In *Ride the Tiger* (1961) he advanced the concept of apoliteia, advocating a detached spiritual bearing that rose above temporal political entanglements. This was one further step in Evola's revolt against what he considered to be an utterly degenerate and unsalvageable modern world. He also authored an important study of transcendent sexual dynamics entitled *The Metaphysics of Sex* (1958; the English translation has recently been reissued as *Eros and the Mysteries of Love*), and completed his spiritual autobiography, *The Cinnabar Path* (1963). After stoically enduring an extended period of physical pain in his final years, he died in June of 1974. His final request was to be brought to a window overlooking the Janiculum, the hill where a temple to Janus had stood in pagan Rome, in order that he might die upright. For Evola this was emblematic of the heroic manner in which a man should confront his mortal end. In accordance with his wishes he was given no Christian funeral and his cremated ashes were later deposited in an icy crevasse on Monte Rosa.

Evola worked adeptly with occult ideas and Hermetic doctrines throughout his life. It was during his years with the UR Group that such ideas were applied practically in the context of an organized magical order. Much of this work was documented and elaborated upon in the UR Group's journals, which were subsequently collected into three volumes under Evola's editorial guidance. These texts reveal the workings and ideas of a European tradition that certainly rivals the better-known doctrines of Aleister Crowley or the Golden Dawn, not just in complexity, but also in its goals and imaginal intensity. In terms of attitude and eclectic approach, it foreshadows contemporary Chaos Magic in many respects. Joscelyn Godwin, a highly regarded scholar of the history of esotericism, has even gone so far as to call the UR Group's writings "the highest magical teaching ever set before the public."

The following two essays are slightly revised translations drawn from *Introduction to Magic: Rituals and Practical Techniques for the Magus* (trans. Guido Stucco, Inner Traditions, 2001), which is the first volume of the UR Group's material to appear in English. In the original publications, all of the UR Group members assumed magical pseudonyms. Both of the following pieces (credited to "Ea" and "Iagla," respectively) were almost certainly written by Evola himself.

In order to begin to understand Evola's perspective, one must step outside of the modernist mindset entirely. This is no easy task. It requires a Nietzschean "re-evaluation of all values" and an heretical break from the humanistic worldview that informs all aspects of the present popular discourse. To a Traditionalist, notions such as "evolution" and "progress" are simply pernicious modern delusions. In contrast, Evola adhered to the traditional doctrine of cyclical ages and was convinced that humanity is now enduring the dark age of the Kali Yuga, as it is called in Hindu terminology. This is equivalent to the ancient Greek "Age of Iron" or the Germanic Ragnarok, in which all social bonds are severed and even siblings turn against one another. It is an epoch of confusion and unchecked egoism, with materialism and scientism in full ascendancy as culture degenerates to little more than crass commercialism and superficiality. For the awakened individual who recognizes that all external institutions are bankrupt and disintegrating, the best option for survival amid the prevailing conditions is the active and disciplined development of one's own spiritual armor. Evola's words are directed toward those few he hopes capable of forming a latter-day *kshatriya*, or sacral warrior caste, while the present cycle of destruction inevitably plays itself out.

ON THE MAGICAL VIEW OF LIFE - "EA"

Self-overcoming, aside from being the objective of rituals, is connected to a renewed, heroicized perception of the world and of life, not as an abstract concept of the mind, but as something that pulsates in the rhythm of one's own blood. It is the sensation of the world as power, or the sensation of the world as a sacrificial act. A great freedom, with action as the sole law. Entities everywhere composed of strength, and, at the same time, a cosmic breathing, a sense of height, of *airiness*.

Action needs to be liberated. It must be realized in and of itself, disinfected from mental fever, cleansed of hatred and craving. These truths must penetrate the soul: *there is no place to go to, nothing to ask for, nothing to hope for, nothing to fear*. The world is *free*: goals and reasons, "evolution," fate or providence—all that is fog, an invention by beings who did not yet know how to walk on their own and needed crutches and supports.

These truths must penetrate the soul: *there is no place to go to, nothing to ask for, nothing to hope for, nothing to fear.*

Now you will be left to yourself. You must perceive yourself as a *center of strength* and know the action that is no longer dictated by this or that object, but for the sake of itself. You will no longer be moved: detached, you will move. The objects around you will cease to be objects of desire for you—they will become objects of action. Gravitating around things that no longer exist, the impulses of an irrational life will finally become extinguished: what will fall away too is the sense of effort, the habit of running around, of doing, the painful seriousness and need, the tragic sentiment and the Titanic bond—in other words, the great disease itself, namely the *human* sense of life. A superior calm will ensue. From this will come action, pure and purifying action: it is an action ready, at any time and in any place, to assume any direction. It is a flexible action, free toward itself, superior to winning and losing, success and failure, selfishness and altruism, happiness and misery; action released from bonds, from identification, from attachment.

In such an action you will be able to find *purification*, since according to it the "individual" no longer counts and because it takes you beyond both abstract knowledge and the irrational impetus of inferior forces. Not

Hatred tranforms and prevents you from controlling the influence of your opponent; worse yet it opens you to his own influence, which you can instead know and paralyze, if you remain calm, without reacting.

ghosts of concepts and ideas and "values"—but rather a *vision without reference points*, with *reality itself* as its sole direct object. Action awakened as an *elementary* thing, simple, unrestrained. The power to command and the power to obey: both absolute, to be quintessentialized in the requisite manner for evocations and identifications, as for those immediate, immaterial encounters with "presences," in which some may ascend and disappear, powerful and invisible, while others precipitate into bodily forms.

In ordinary life it is necessary to follow a discipline capable of realizing the uselessness of all sentimentalism and all emotional complications. In their place, a clear gaze and an appropriate action. As with a surgeon, instead of compassion and mercy, an operation that solves the problem. As with a warrior or athlete, instead of fear and irrational agitation in the face of danger, the instant resolve to do what lies within one's power. Mercy, fear, hope, impatience, anxiety—these are all spiritual *cave-ins* that nourish occult and vampiric powers of negation.

Take compassion for instance: it eliminates none of the other person's misfortune, but allows it to perturb your spirit. If you are able to do so, then act: assume the person of the other and give him your strength. Otherwise, detach yourself. It is the same with hatred: when you hate, you degrade yourself. If you desire, if your sense of justice demands it, tear down and cut away, without your spirit becoming perturbed. Moreover, remember that by hating, you decline. Hatred tranforms and prevents you from controlling the influence of your opponent; worse yet it opens you to his own influence, which you can instead know and paralyze, if you remain calm, without reacting. Those who want the *knowledge* and the *power* of good

and evil must slay their "passion" for "good" or for "evil." They need to be able to give as a pure act, as an absolute gift, not for the enjoyable feeling of sympathy or mercy; they need to be able to strike down without hatred. "In the strong ones I am the strength that is free from desire and passion"—*balam balvatâm asmi kâmarâgavivarjitam*—this is what Krishna says about himself as that *force* and *purity* over which nothing has power, before which even the law of action and reaction can no longer take hold.[1] As soon as that fever, the dark force of instinct, of craving or aversion, removes one from this central inner disposition, even the greatest of gods meets their ruin.

Detachment, silence, solitude—this is what prepares the liberation of this view of life and of the world.

Distance between human beings. Not to recognize oneself in others: never feeling superior, equal, or inferior to them. In this world, beings are alone, without law, with no escape, without excuse, clothed only in their strength or weakness: peaks, stones, sand. This is the first liberation of one's view of life. To overcome the brotherly contamination, the need to love and to feel loved, to feel together, to feel equal and connected with others. Purge yourself of this. At a certain point you will no longer feel united with somebody because of blood, affections, country, or human destiny. You will feel united only with those who

At a certain point you will no longer feel united with somebody because of blood, affections, country, or human destiny. You will feel united only with those who are on your same path, which is not the human path, for it has no regard for human ways.

are on your same path, which is not the human path, for it has no regard for human ways.

When you look around, try to perceive the *voice of what is inanimate*. "How beautiful they are, these free forces that have not yet been stained by the spirit!" (Nietzsche)

Do not say these forces are "not yet," but rather "*no longer*" stained with "spirit," and understand that by "spirit" is meant what is "unreal"—in other words, everything that man with his sentiments, thoughts, fears, and hopes has projected onto nature in order to render it more intimate, or in order to make it speak the same language.

Abandon all this and try to understand the message of things, especially where they appear foreign, naked, mute—where they have no soul because they are something greater than "soul." This is the first step toward the liberation of one's view of the world. On the plane of *magic* you will know a world that has returned to its free, intensive, and essential state, a state in which nature is not nature, nor is the spirit "spirit"; in which there are no things, men, speculations about "gods"—but rather *powers*—and life is an heroic affair at every moment, composed of symbols, illuminations, commands, ritual and sacrificial actions.

In this world there is no longer a "here" or a "there," or attachment; everything is infinitely equal and infinitely diverse, and action originates from itself, pure and hidden. The "Wind," the "Breath" (the Breath of the Hermetic "Great Green") carries upon it everything in the sense of a sacrifice, an offering, a luminous and marvelous ritual, among zones of an activity as calm as the deepest sleep, and immobility as intense as the most vehement tornado.

Here that which is "human" melts away as a dark memory of misery and as the specter of a long nightmare. The Angel awakens, the Ancient Ice:[2] immobility and a vertiginously slow pace resolve every tension. This is the threshold and the transfiguration. Beyond it lies—the world of the eternal.

■ ■ ■ ■

SERPENTINE WISDOM "IAGLA"

They burn with fire—we burn with water;
they wash with water—we wash with fire.
—Van Helmont

Occultism has an extremely subtle "virtue." It is "serpentine." And it is also essential.

In general, people have their clichés, their ethical, religious, or social ideals, their opinions about Strength, Wisdom, and Greatness. But occultism is altogether a very different thing. It is elusive and cannot be measured. It comes from the opposite direction to the one that everyone is looking toward. Thus it goes unnoticed; or if it is noticed, it disconcerts. It robs those who believed they were secure, who thought they had their feet on the ground, of their certainties.

The occultist is an entity that cannot be measured by ordinary standards. Nobody knows what he is really capable of, nor what his action consists of. His path is impenetrable. You may be his best friend, his companion, and even his lover; you may think you own his heart, his affection, or his devotion. And yet, he will be an *other*, besides the one you already know. You will become aware of this "other" one only when you enter his domain. Then you will feel as if you had been walking along the edge of an abyss.

Never mind the fact that today in the West there are countless people who declare themselves to be occultists, Masters, Initiates, etc., and who would be very unhappy if one were not aware of their presumed quality. Let me repeat that, with some remarkable exceptions, it is rare for a true initiate to come forward and to reveal himself outside his own circle. The real initiate lives in a

Occultism is altogether a very different thing. It is elusive and cannot be measured.

state that categorically *destroys* any dependency on people. What the latter say or think about him, and whether the opinion they form of him is accurate or not—these things no longer concern him. Due to an "irresistible" inclination, people want others to "know" who they are (or worse yet, what they *think* they are). When they act, they want everyone else to know about it too; the absence of reactions and a natural impassibility in the face of an unjust comment or action are not typical of them. An

Do they wish to strike him on the cheek? Let them. He will even turn the other cheek: he only plays those games in which he is the one dictating all the rules.

occultist finds all this to be puerile. He *does not exist*. Let others try to grasp at air, if that is what they enjoy. He can pull the rug from under their feet, and he will do it when the occasion arises, without them even realizing where the action came from, or if there even *was* an action at all. Do they wish to strike him on the cheek? Let them. He will even turn the other cheek: he only plays those games in which he is the one dictating *all* the rules. He is at the mercy of no one. He alone decides what reactions must arise in himself due to other people's words, actions, or qualities. Call him a hero, call him a coward: he does not care either way. He is only concerned with what effects follow from these thoughts of others, what their consequences are for his game. He cares only for making some things *occur*: he calmly and coolly establishes the means and the conditions, he acts, and that is all. He does not adhere to his action as if it were his *own*. Above all he does not talk about it, nor does he care about the outcome. The action is a mere instrument. He is immune from the mania of "self-affirmation."

The more an occultist progresses, the more deeply his center recedes, and the more that those whom he acts upon will have the perfect illusion of being free. How well known this characteristic of occultism is these days, I do not know. It does not help for it to be known; it is preferable if it escapes notice. However, I know that too often in the West occultism is distorted by alien viewpoints and by profane prejudices. People *know* little and talk much. Thus the risk for mistakes and misunderstandings is great. Yet we should not give any support to those who do not even know where the true principles lie, and for whom occultism is just another excuse for games and manias with which they divert the public. In our writings we have often referred to the "will," "action," and the "Self"... But I am not sure if our readers understand that here, will is not will, action is not action, and the Self is not the Self.

About 2,500 years ago, a little book was written in China. In this book, the principles of a *subtle* and *Hermetic* wis-

dom are set forth in a clear, cool, and lucid form: I am talking, of course, about Lao-tzu's *Tao-te Ching*. It may be helpful here to recall the main themes of this practical wisdom, which is timeless and boundless. It is an unequivocal reference point. It is very dangerous, yet absolute. I know of nothing more absolute. It has a sense of *surgery*. An essential clearsightedness. No echo of human limitations and manias. Here, one can breathe and fully be.

Although it may be based in legend, Confucius's encounter with Lao-tzu, narrated by Cho-Hong in the *Si Sien Chuen*, is very meaningful. According to Cho Hong, Confucius, who tried to involve Lao-tzu in his preoccupation with customs, morality, and tradition, received such answers from him that, when reflecting several years later on this encounter, he wrote: "It is possible to set a trap in order to catch animals; it is possible to catch fish with nets and to shoot birds with arrows. But how will one capture the dragon that flies in the air above the clouds?"

This is how the maxims of the *Tao-te Ching* gradually define the nature of the Fulfilled One, the Ambiguous, the Subtle, the Elusive. The text begins in this manner:[3] "The Way that is the Way is not the ordinary way. The Name that is the Name is not the ordinary name." Men *steal* life; they are outside the center and draw outside of it the virtues that should remain deep and invisible. They construct the puppet of "personality," instead of *being*; then they grasp it, clinging tenaciously to it like beasts. Eternally they accumulate, absorb, hold onto, and "affirm": Me! Me! Me! The mask, the grimace, become everything. They do not realize that this is fever, error, mania. *Death* lies in wait within the shell they erected. And death cuts them down. They are larvae ejected from the Great Game.

This is what the Fulfilled One says: true affirmation, absolute individuality, are not the affirmation or the individuality known to men; rather, the latter are a way of illusion and corruption. People talk of possessing, and know not what possession is. They talk of "strength," but what they refer to is a mere fairy tale. The Fulfilled One says: only by losing itself can the Self *become individualized*, ceasing to "affirm" in order to really be *individuals and Lords of the Self*. One cannot have while hanging on; one cannot become sharper by grasping. The Fulfilled One disappears—in this way he reveals. He empties himself—in this way he achieves absolute being. In order to reach the peak, he conceals his Self. By giving away, he earns; by giving away, he is wealthy. He lets go, dissolves, and ascends. He lets go of the ray of success, abolishes splendor, and *fixes* himself in the invisible origin. Concentrated, he achieves—scattered, he fails. From fullness he shifts to "emptiness." There lies the essence of fullness, just as in the center lies the essence of the wheel. From movement he proceeds to what, as the real cause of motion, is itself motionless. From being to that which, in its incorporeity, is nonbeing. "Self," "non-Self," "will"—all manias! Earnings become a loss. He who stands on his toes does not grow taller, nor does a random jerking of the legs make one go anywhere.

Those who expose themselves, create a chance to be stricken down.

He who places himself in the spotlight remains in the dark; he who thinks he has arrived finds himself pushed back: to exhibit oneself is to be dependent; to take care of oneself is to decay; to exert oneself is useless, insane, and takes one even further from the path. The more he "affirms" and the more he goes outside, the more he affirms nothingness.

Unless you quit the game of resistance, of ownership, of *your* will, you will not cease to be fooled: the Path is something else. To will without willing to will; to act without willing to act; to achieve without doing; to do without being the doer; to elevate oneself without dominating. Straight, but flexible, clear though not shining—this is what Lao-tzu says. To truly be consists in not *wishing* to be. Lao-tzu turns all human "values" upside down. He smiles at you as if you were a little child when you wear the mask of "conqueror," "Übermensch," or of him who "breaks but does not bend." How naive! Concerning water, he says: there is nothing in the world like water, ready to assume any form—and yet nothing is more capable of defeating what is strong and rigid. Water cannot be tamed because it adapts itself to all things; because it offers no resistance, it cannot be captured. The "virtue" of Heaven imitates it. What is flexible triumphs over what is rigid, and what is weak triumphs over what is strong. The tools of death are strong and hard; the tools of life are subtle and flexible. The former are below, the latter are above. The latter direct the former; the incorporeal penetrates matter's impenetrability.

Those who expose themselves, create a chance to be stricken down. The strong tree is the one that is felled … Failing is occasioned by "willing," loss is made possible by attachment; there is no action that does not provoke a reaction. Thus, a good wrestler does not use violence; a good winner does not struggle; a good walker leaves no traces; a good director does not direct; a good guard does not need locks, a good capturer does not use ropes. A truly winning army does not need to "fight"—it has never even considered the struggle or the possibility of having to struggle. See how bewildering all this is? Against this you cannot find a hold, you find no resistance although you feel a force against which you can do nothing, a force that first of all takes away the possibility of a struggle, because a sword cannot strike air, and a net cannot catch water. Those who have been "bitten by the Dragon" possess this strength: they direct worldly affairs through this strength, operating with it, remaining invisible and silent behind the scenes. To them, people are nothing (just as people are nothing to the impersonal powers of nature): they utilize them like instruments—says Lao-tzu—without experiencing love or hatred, good or ill. Does a builder behave any differently toward the stones he uses? The infinitely wide square no longer has corners; the infinitely wide container is bottomless; the infinitely acute sound is no longer audible; the infinitely wide image no longer has a form. This is the teaching of Lao-tzu. The lack of traces is the trace of his Perfect One. In the immensity of the strength of his spirit, compared to the limited consciousness of human beings, he appears to hardly know he exists. In the guise of weakness, he has true strength; he knows he is powerful, yet appears as weak. He knows he is enlightened, yet appears as small and mediocre. He dulls what is sharp, clarifies what is confused, tones down his shining nature, and is outwardly identical with what is ordinary. He progresses without advancing; he absorbs without conquering; he possesses without owning. Becoming like everybody else, he becomes different from everybody. As he goes on, he is as prudent as one who crosses a winter stream, vigilant as one who knows he is surrounded by enemies; cold as a stranger; ephemeral as a melting snowflake; rough as a tree trunk; wide as the great valleys; impenetrable as deep water; inaccessible as solitary peaks. He arrives at his destination without walking; he penetrates without looking; achieves without willing; acts without doing; he simply vanishes. He is

Do you know what your "heroes," your "martyrs," and your "men of character" are? Creatures of vanity, nothing more.

obeyed without making commands; he wins without struggle; he draws people to himself without calling for them. How disheartening to those who uphold the myth of manhood based on muscles and iron strength: for this alone is the *true* man, the *absolute* man! Within himself he absorbs the ambiguous virtue of the female. Lao-tzu talks about the invisible magic of the feminine, which in a feline fashion attracts and absorbs man's action into itself; and he compares it to the image of dark, hidden valleys, drawing the water of the alpine peaks to themselves in an irresistible way.

"The Way that is the Way is not the ordinary way," indeed. Do you know what your "heroes," your "martyrs," and your "men of character" are? Creatures of vanity, nothing more. "I break but do not bend": what you mean is that for the sake of the "beautiful gesture" and for the proud satisfaction I feed my ego, I sacrifice *reality*. What a child! Lao-tzu does not hide behind the smoke screen of the "heroic" and the "tragic." Cool and lucid, he only cares to *fulfill*. You advance? He pulls back and then returns like the wave: "It is better to step back a foot than to gain an inch: among two combatants, the one who wins is the one who does not fight." Do you put forth an obstacle, or an "affirmation?" He lets you go ahead, goes underground and cuts you down at the root. He anticipates that which is not yet manifest; acts upon that which is still weak; resolves a crisis before it erupts. He withdraws; he aims at acting where there are no conditions or defenses, where there is no "cause," in other words, where there is nothing against which an effect may react.

"Just as the fish could not live if it left the dark abysses, likewise the ordinary person cannot know the weapon of this lordly wisdom." –Lao-tzu

Lao-tzu says: people do not know what *action* is. Today we have the religion of "effort," "becoming," "action." What matters is not to arrive, but to "aim at the infinite," the "struggle," the "eternal aspiration." Men need action in order to be *aware* of themselves, rather than to *attain*. The more they are caught, excited, and carried away, the happier they are. Thus they *feel* more, because naturally they *need* to "feel themselves" … What a disaster, the day they no longer encounter *resistance*! They would burst like the soap bubbles they are. *And this is exactly what happens at death*, when the solid shell that helped them to "reflect" their consciousness is broken; then the knot is untied and dissolved into the infinite ether, in which there is no support or direction, namely into the dragon's domain.

To level out, be silent, to disappear; the voice without words; sight without objects; possession without touch; action without movement. This the way of the Tao. Is it a paradox? Is it nonsense? These are mere words, which swarm around the royal elephant like so many tiny flies. But pay attention to what Lao-tzu says, you who wishes to reach the other bank of the river: "Just as the fish could not live if it left the dark abysses, likewise the ordinary person cannot know the weapon of this lordly wisdom." ⛎

Endnotes

1. *Bhagavad Gita*, 2:38, 47–8; 3:30; 7:11.
2. Evola is making an untranslatable word-play here in the Italian, using the words *angelo* (angel) and *antico gelo* (ancient ice).
3. The English version here closely follows the translation of Lao-tzu edited by Evola, *Il libro della Via e della Vita di Laotze*, Carabba, Lanciano, 1921.

JULIUS EVOLA

THE OCCULT WAR
Excerpt From
Men Among the Ruins

Various causes have been adduced to explain the crisis that has affected and still affects the life of modern peoples: historical, social, socioeconomic, political, moral, and cultural causes, according to different perspectives. The part played by each of these causes should not be disputed. However, we need to ask a higher and essential question: are these *always* the first causes and do they

The occult war is a battle that is waged imperceptibly by the forces of global subversion, with means and in circumstances ignored by current historiography.

have an inevitable character like those causes found in the material world? Do they supply an ultimate explanation or, in some cases, is it necessary to identify influences of a higher order, which may cause what has occurred in the West to appear very suspicious, and which, beyond the multiplicity of individual aspects, suggest that there is the same logic at work?

The concept of *occult war* must be defined within the context of the dilemma. The occult war is a battle that is waged imperceptibly by the forces of global subversion, with means and in circumstances ignored by current historiography. The notion of occult war belongs to a three-dimensional view of history: this view does not regard as essential the two superficial dimensions of time and space (which include causes, facts, and visible leaders) but rather emphasizes the dimension of *depth*, or the "subterranean" dimension in which forces and influences often act in a decisive manner, and which, more often not

than not, cannot be reduced to what is merely human, whether at an individual or a collective level.

Having said that, it is necessary to specify the meaning of the term *subterranean*. We should not think, in this regard, of a dark and irrational background that stands in relation to the known forces of history as the unconscious stands to consciousness, in the way the latter relationship is discussed in the recently developed "Depth Psychology." If anything, we can talk about the unconscious only in regard to those who, according to the three-dimensional view, appear to be history's *objects* rather than its *subjects*, since in their thoughts and conduct they are scarcely aware of the influences that they obey and the goals they contribute toward achieving. In these people, the center falls more in the unconscious and the preconscious than in the clear reflected consciousness, no matter what they—who are often men of action and ideologues— believe. Considering this relation, we can say that the most decisive actions of the occult war take place in the human unconscious. However, if we consider the true

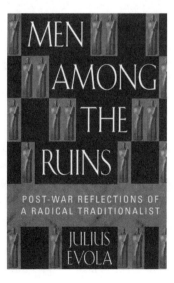

MEN AMONG THE RUINS

POST-WAR REFLECTIONS OF A RADICAL TRADITIONALIST

JULIUS EVOLA

These forces are sometimes referred to in a moralistic fashion as "forces of evil," or in a theological fashion as the "forces of the Antichrist."

agents of history in the special aspects we are now discussing, things are otherwise: here we cannot talk of the subconscious or the unconscious, for we are dealing with intelligent forces that know very well what they want and the means most suited to achieve their objectives.

The third dimension of history should not be diluted in the fog of abstract philosophical or sociological concepts, but rather should be thought of as a "backstage" dimension where specific "intelligences" are at work.

An investigation of the secret history that aspires to be positivist and scientific should not be too lofty or removed from reality. However, it is necessary to assume as the ultimate reference point a dualistic scheme not dissimilar from the one found in an older tradition. Catholic historiography used to regard history not only as a mechanism of natural, political, economic, and social causes, but rather as the unfolding of divine Providence, to which hostile forces are opposed. These forces are sometimes referred to in a moralistic fashion as "forces of evil," or in a theological fashion as the "forces of the Antichrist." Such a view has a positive content, provided it is purified and emphasized by bringing it to a less religious and more metaphysical plane, as was done in Classical and Indo-European antiquity: forces of the *cosmos* against forces of *chaos*. To the former corresponds every-

thing that is form, order, law, spiritual hierarchy, and tradition in the higher sense of the word; to the latter correspond every influence that disintegrates, subverts, degrades, and promotes the predominance of the inferior over the superior, matter over spirit, quantity over quality. This is what can be said in regard to the ultimate reference points of the various influences that act upon the realm of tangible causes behind known history. These must be kept into account, though with some prudence. Let me repeat: aside from this necessary metaphysical background, let us never lose sight of concrete history.

Methodologically speaking, we need to be careful to prevent valid insights from degenerating into fantasies and superstition, and not develop the tendency to see an

occult background everywhere and at all costs. In this regard, every assumption we make must have the character of what are called "working hypotheses" in scientific research—as when something is admitted provisionally, thus allowing the gathering and arranging of a group of apparently isolated facts, only to confer on them a character not of hypothesis but of truth when, at the end of a serious inductive effort, the data converge in validating the original assumption. Every time an effect outlasts and transcends its tangible causes, a suspicion should arise, and a positive or negative influence behind the stages should be perceived. A problem is posited, but in analyzing it and seeking its solution, prudence must be exercised. The fact that those who have ventured in this direction have not restrained their wild imaginations has discredited what could have been a science, the results of which could hardly be overestimated. This too meets the expectations of the hidden enemy.

This is all I have to say concerning the general premises proper to a new three-dimensional study of history. Now let us return to what I said earlier on. After considering the state of society and modern civilization, one should ask if this is not a specific case that requires the application of this method; in other words, one should ask whether some situations of real crisis and radical subversion in the modern world can be satisfactorily explained through "natural" and spontaneous processes, or whether we need to refer to something that has been concerted, a still unfolding plan devised by forces hiding in the shadows.

"The world is governed by people entirely different from the ones imagined by those who are unable to see behind the scenes." –Disraeli

In this particular domain, many red flags have gone up: too many elements have concurred to alarm the less superficial observers. In the middle of the past century, Disraeli wrote these significant and often quoted words: "The world is governed by people entirely different from the ones imagined by those who are unable to see behind the scenes." Malinsky and De Poncins, when considering the phenomenon of revolution, have remarked that in our age, where it is commonly acknowledged that every disease of the individual organism is caused by bacteria, people pretended that the diseases of the social body, namely revolutions and disorder, are spontaneous, self-generated phenomena, rather than the effect of invisible agents, acting in society the way bacteria and pathogenic germs act in the organism of the individual.

WEAPONS IN THE OCCULT WAR

For practical purposes, too, it is very important to recognize the instruments of the occult war, namely the means employed by the secret forces of global subversion to conceal their action, prevent their opponents' action, and continue to exercise their influence. I will now say something in this regard, drawing inspiration from some of the points developed by René Guénon, who was one of the most perceptive people in reference to the secret backgrounds of many upheavals of modern times.

Let us begin with the tool of *scientific suggestion*. I believe that the so-called "scientific" method of considering events and history is more the consequence of a suggestion spread in modern culture by antitraditional forces in order to conceal their action than the natural orientation of a short-sighted mentality. Those who believe that history is only made by the men on the stage and determined by the most evident economic, social, political, and cultural factors, do not see and do not seek any other explanation; and yet this is exactly what every force operating in secret desires. A civilization dominated by the positivist prejudice offers the most fertile ground to an action arising from what I have called the "third dimension." In great part this is the case of modern civilization. It is a civilization rendered myopic and defenseless by the positivist, rationalist, and scientist prejudice. We have scarcely begun to expose all the ideas that remain at the basis of the modern mentality and education; these ideas are not so much errors and limitations as they are suggestions spread and promoted for precise reasons by antitraditional forces.

I have already mentioned some non-positivist views of the course of events that introduce various entities, such as the "absolute Spirit," or the *élan vital*, or "History." In this we can see an example of the possible application of a second instrument of the occult war, namely the *tactic of replacement*. This tactic is employed every time there is the danger of an awakening on the part of "history's objects," or when some ideas that facilitate the occult game of the forces of global subversion have lost their power of suggestion. In the above-mentioned case, such confused philosophical views act as a sort of bait for

Often the tactic of replacement develops efficaciously in the form of a *tactic of counterfeits*.

those who are unsatisfied with positivist views, so that their eyes may not look in the direction where they should. Due to the vagueness of these notions, the field is not any less concealed than by positivist blindness. People will play around with "philosophical ideas" while the plan continues to unfold.

Often the tactic of replacement develops efficaciously in the form of a *tactic of counterfeits*. It may happen that after the effects of the destructive work reach the material plane, they become so visible as to provoke a reac-

Those who believe that history is only made by the men on the stage and determined by the most evident economic, social, political, and cultural factors, do not see and do not seek any other explanation; and yet this is exactly what every force operating in secret desires.

tion, and thus ideas and symbols are employed for a defense and a reconstruction. In the best case they are values of the traditional past, which come back to life thanks to this existential reaction of a society or civilization threatened by dissolution. Then the occult war is not waged in a direct manner; often attention is paid to promoting only distortions and counterfeits of these ideas. In this way, the reaction is contained, deviated, or even led in the opposite direction.

Such a tactic may be employed in various domains, from the spiritual and cultural to the political. An example is given by "traditionalism." I have already discussed what the term *tradition* signifies in the higher sense of the word: it is the form bestowed by forces from above upon the overall possibilities of a given cultural area and specific period, through super-individual and even antihistorical values and through elites that know how to derive an authority and natural prestige from such values. In our days it often happens that a confused desire to return to "tradition" is purposely channeled to the form of "traditionalism." The content of this "traditionalism" consists of habits, routines, surviving residues and vestiges of what once was, without a real understanding of the spiritual world and of what in them is not merely factual but has a character of perennial value. Thus, such non-traditional, or should we say, "traditionalist" attitudes offer an easy target to the enemy, whose attack mounted against traditionalism is only the opening barrage preceding an attack against Tradition itself: to this purpose the slogans of "anachronism," "anti-history," "immobilism" and "regression" are employed. Thus, reaction is paralyzed as the maneuver leads successfully to the preestablished goal.

From the general plane it is easy to shift to particular cases, since recent history is full of them. Thus, in the political context, the Roman idea with its symbols, the

demic specialization, is often affected by this maneuver. The results seem to be for the most part something distorted; this severely limits the positive influence that various aspects of the legacy of ancient Eastern spirituality are liable to exercise, provoking the reaction of the most obtuse and inappropriate "defenses of the West." Another example consists in the milieus that, when it comes to

Another method is the tactic of ricochet. This tactic is employed in cases where the traditional forces being targeted take the initiative through an action against other traditional forces, an action that eventually ricochets back at its promoters.

"Aryan" idea, and the idea of the Empire or Reich—to all this, the tactic of misleading substitutions and counterfeits has been applied with deprecative effects that cannot elude an attentive observer. Therefore, it is possible to understand the validity of the points I made in the first chapter.

Fourth, we must point out the *tactic of inversion*. Let us take a typical example. The secret forces of global subversion knew exactly that the basis of the order to be destroyed consisted in the supernatural element—that is, in the spirit—conceived not as a philosophical abstraction or as an element of faith, but as a superior reality, as a reference-point for the integration of everything that is human. After limiting the influence that could be exercised in this regard by Christianity, through the spread of materialism and scientism, the forces of global subversion have endeavored to conveniently divert any tendency toward the supernatural arising outside the dominant religion and the limitation of its dogmas. So-called "neo-spiritualism,"[1] not only in its more deleterious spiritualist forms, but also in its pseudo-Eastern and occultist forms (not to mention the theories concerning the unconscious, the irrational, and so on), is greatly influenced by the tactic of inversion. Instead of rising toward what is beyond the person as a really supernatural element, here we remain in the subpersonal and in the infrarational, according to an inversion that quite often has sinister characteristics.

The results achieved in this way are twofold. First, it was easy to extend the discredit that in numerous cases rightly affected these ideas to different ideas which might appear related, even though in their innermost essence they have nothing in common; thus, the latter genuine ideas are put in a condition to no longer pose a threat. A good part of what the West has learned about the East, outside the dry and sterile domain of philology and aca-

symbols and esotericism, can think only of Masonry or Theosophy, even when the reference goes back to ancient and noble traditions that have nothing to do with the latter; the positivist and rationalist prejudice of a certain critical "culture" identifies all this as superstition and fantasy, thus completing the smear campaign. This is the case with some militant Catholic apologetics that see only naturalism and pantheism in everything outside their perspective; these are misunderstandings and effects of an interplay of concordant actions and reactions, to which several representatives of Catholicism are liable.

The second result does not concern the domain of ideas but rather the practical and concrete domain. The inverted tendencies toward the spiritual and the supernatural can favor the emergence of dark forces, and be resolved in a deceitful action against the human personality. Many reactions against rationalism and intellectualism lead exactly to this, especially the theories of the unconscious, which through psychoanalysis have either generated a well-established practice or encouraged various forms of morbid fascination.

Another method is the *tactic of ricochet*. This tactic is employed in cases where the traditional forces being targeted take the initiative through an action against other traditional forces, an action that eventually ricochets back at its promoters. For instance, the secret forces of global subversion, through opportune infiltrations or suggestions, may induce the representatives of a certain tradition to believe that the best way to strengthen it consists in either undermining or discrediting other traditions. Those who do not realize what is going on and who, because of material interests, attack Tradition in likeminded people, sooner or later must expect to see Tradition attacked in themselves, by ricochet. The forces of global subversion rely very much on this tactic; thus, they attempt in every possible way to cause any higher idea to give in to the tyranny of individual interests or proselytizing, prideful, and power-hungry tendencies. They know perfectly well that this is the best way to destroy every unity and solidarity and to favor a state of affairs in which their overall scheme will be implemented. They know well that there is an objective law of immanent justice and that "the mills of God grind slowly, but they grind exceeding fine," and thus they act accordingly; they wait for the fruits of these inconsiderate initiatives to mature, and then they intervene.

In the political domain, the case of every Machiavellian employment of revolutionary forces falls within this category. Shortsighted political leaders have often believed that to arouse or to support revolution in hostile nations is, in certain circumstances, an excellent means to benefit their own people. Without realizing it, or becoming aware of it too late, they have obtained the opposite result. While they thought that they were using the revolution as a means, it was the revolution that used them as tools; eventually, the revolution spread to other countries, catching up with the politicians who unleashed it and wiping them out. Modern history has been in part the theater of a subversion that has tragically spread in this way.[2]

Thus, we can never emphasize too much that unconditioned loyalty to an idea is the only possible protection from occult war; where such loyalty falls short and where the contingent goals of "real politics" are obeyed, the front of resistance is already undermined. The ricochet should be seen in an analogous context, in the case of "peoples' right to self-determination." This principle, after having been employed by modern democracies as an ideological instrument during World War II, eventually affected white peoples, thus putting an end to Europe's prestige and preeminence.

When the secret forces of world subversion are fearful of exposure or realize that, due to special circumstances, the direction imparted from backstage has become obvious, at least in its major effects, they employ the *scapegoat tactic*. They try to shift the enemy's attention onto elements that are responsible only partially, or in a subordinated fashion, for their own wrongful deeds. A reaction is then unleashed against those elements, which then become the scapegoats. Thus, after a pause, the secret front may resume its work, because its opponents

believe that they have identified the enemy and dealt with it. [Regarding the] *Protocols of the Elders of Zion*, I have mentioned a possible case of such tactics in reference to the part attributed to Jews and Masons. Thus, we must beware of any unilaterality and never lose sight of the overall picture of the secret front.

Let us now discuss the *tactic of dilution*, which constitutes a particular aspect of the "tactic of surrogates." The main example that I will now introduce must be prefaced with the following: the process that has led to the current crises has remote origins and has developed in several phases.[3] In each of these phases the crisis was already present, though in a latent or potential form. The theory of "progress" may be regarded as one of the suggestions spread by the secret forces of world subversion so that attention would be diverted from the origins, and the process of dissolution could proceed, carried forth by the illusion of the triumphs of technological-industrial civilization. The tragic events of recent times have provoked a partial awakening from this hypnosis. Many people have begun to realize that the march of so-called progress paralleled a race toward the abyss. Thus, to stop and return to the origins as the only way to restore a normal civiliza-

Shortsighted political leaders have often believed that to arouse or to support revolution in hostile nations is, in certain circumstances, an excellent means to benefit their own people. Without realizing it, or becoming aware of it too late, they have obtained the opposite result.

tion, has been the inspiring vision for many. Next, the occult front employed new means to prevent any radical reaction. Here too it employed the slogans of "anachronism" and "reactionary and retrograde forces"; then it caused the forces that aimed at a return to the origins to be led toward stages in which the crisis and the disease were present in less extreme forms, though still clearly visible. This trap worked as well. The leaders of world subversion naturally know that, once this is done, there is no longer a real danger: it is enough to wait and soon we will be back at the starting point, by following processes analogous to the ones that have already occurred, but now without the possibility of any resistance to the dissolution.

There are many historical examples of this tactic, which should be rather instructive for those who hope to assume the initiative of a reconstructive action. As a first example, we should examine closely some traits of modern nationalism. We know about the revolutionary, subversive, and anti-hierarchical function that the collectivist-demagogic concept of "nation" has played against the previous forms of European civilization and political organization. The reference point of many people who have fought against the various Internationals (especially against the communist International) has been the concept of the nation; care was rarely taken to define such a concept in a way that would no longer represent what needed to be opposed.

In this regard, it will suffice to recall what I have said elsewhere[4] about the opposition existing between popular nationalism and the spiritual nation, between national State and traditional State. In the first case, nationalism has a leveling and antiaristocratic function; it is like the prelude to a wider leveling, the common denominator of which is no longer the nation, but rather the International. In the second case, the idea of the nation may serve as the foundation for a new recovery and an important first reaction against the internationalist dissolution; it upholds a principle of differentiation that still needs to be further carried through toward an articulation and hierarchy within every single people. But where the awareness of this opposition is lacking, in the case of indiscriminate nationalism, there is a danger of being subjected to the tactic of dilution: this danger, incidentally, has already occurred. It is in view of this—that is, in view of such a possible meaning of nationalistic orientation—that Soviet communism, while opposing nationalism as a counterrevolutionary phenomenon, favors and supports it in the non-

ural and inevitable inner development. The second example concerns the cultural domain. I have already discussed the meaning of psychoanalytical theories in the context of the modern subversion. Among those who are capable of a healthy discernment there has been a reaction against the coarsest forms of this pseudo-science, which correspond to pure or "orthodox" Freudianism. The tactic of dilution was employed again; the formulation and spread of a spiritualized psychoanalysis for more refined tastes was furthered. The result was that those who react against Freud and his disciples no longer do so against Jung, without realizing that what is at work here is the same inversion, though in a more dangerous form because it is subtler, and a contaminating exegesis ventures more decidedly into the domain of spirituality than in the case of Freud.

Another tactic consists in the *deliberate misidentification of a principle with its representatives*. In many regards the decay of traditional institutions began with the corruption of their worldly representatives. The effective dissolution and destruction has been made possible by the confusion between principles and people; this is another weapon of the occult war. When the representatives of a given principle prove to be unworthy of it, the criticism of them extends immediately to the principle itself and is especially directed against it. Instead of acknowledging that some individuals are not at the level of the principle, and instead of requiring that they be replaced by qualified individuals, in order to restore a situation of normalcy, it is claimed that the principle itself is false, corrupt, or passé, and that it should be replaced with a different principle. In almost every revolution this tactic has played a major role. It may also be characterized as that of portraying a crisis *in* the system as a crisis *of* the system. Examples of this kind are so prevalent that I hardly need mention them. The attack against monarchies and aristocracies has

Another tactic consists in the deliberate misidentification of a principle with its representatives. In many regards the decay of traditional institutions began with the corruption of their worldly representatives.

followed this path. Marxism has applied the same device, using the injustices of capitalism as a pretext in order to attack free-market economy and to proclaim a collectivist economy. In the spiritual domain the examples are numerous. The Lutheran Reformation used the corruption of the representatives of the Roman Church in order to question the principle of authority and many fundamental beliefs of the Catholic tradition, thus shifting over from people to principles.

Marxist areas inhabited by the so-called "underdeveloped" peoples, who are the alleged victims of colonialism, waiting for further developments to lead to the stage in which it will be able to reap its fruits.

I will mention here two more examples of the tactic of dilution. The first concerns the socioeconomic domain and is connected to all the "national" and social-conformist versions of Marxism; it is the same disease in diluted form. This is also the case of "socializing" theories, which are Trojan horses to be introduced into the citadel, not in order to conquer it with a direct attack, but rather through a nat-

Finally, I wish to mention one more instrument of the secret war, though it refers to a very particular domain:

the tactic of the *replacing infiltrations*. It is used in cases where a certain spiritual or traditional organization falls into such a state of degeneration that its representatives know very little of its true, inner foundation, or the basis of its authority and prestige. The life of such an organization may then be compared to the automatic state of a sleepwalker, or living body deprived of its soul. In a sense a spiritual "void" has been created which can be filled, through infiltrations, by other subversive forces. These forces, while leaving the appearances unchanged, use the organization for totally different purposes, which at times may even be the opposite of those which were originally its own. We should also not rule out the case where such infiltrated elements work for the destruction of the organ-

Endnotes

1. More commonly referred to now as the "New Age" movement. [Editor's note]
2. Recent decades of overt and covert US foreign policy ploys are disturbingly illustrative in this regard. [Editor's note]
3. See *Revolt Against the Modern World*, trans. Guido Stucco, Inner Traditions, 1995, part II ("Genesis and Face of the Modern World").
4. See chapter three of *Men Among the Ruins*. [Editor's note]

These forces, while leaving the appearances unchanged, use the organization for totally different purposes, which at times may even be the opposite of those which were originally its own.

ization which they now control—for example by creating new scandals, liable to give rise to serious repercussions. In this particular case what is employed on the outside is the previously mentioned tactic of mistaking the representatives for the principle. Even the knowledge of this can cast light on many phenomena of the past and present.

I hope that having limited myself to only a few examples and having primarily discussed principles will not prevent the reader from recognizing the multiple possibilities of application of those same principles in various spheres, for there is no sphere in which the occult war has not in some manner been undertaken and is not still being waged today. The most important sphere for the application of the knowledge of the weapons of the occult war, is the inner one: the world of one's own thoughts. It is here that one needs to be on guard; it is here that one should be able to recognize the subtle influences that try to suggest ideas and reactions to us in certain situations. If this can be accomplished, even if it is still not possible to identify the enemy in our midst, it would at least bar to him the main paths of his secret action. ⛢

[Sections excerpted from *Men Among the Ruins: Postwar Reflections of a Radical Traditionalist* by Julius Evola, trans. Guido Stucco, Inner Traditions, 2001, pp. 235–51. The same chapter also contains Evola's interesting commentaries on the infamous conspiratorial tract *The Protocols of the Elders of Zion*.]

SECRET OF THE ASSASSINS

After the death of the Prophet Mohammad, the new Islamic community was ruled in succession by four of his close Companions, chosen by the people and called the Rightfully-guided Caliphs. The last of these was Ali ibn Abu Talib; the Prophet's son-in-law.

Ali had his own ardent followers among the faithful, who came to be called Shi'a or "adherents." They believed that Ali should have succeeded Mohammad by right, and that after him his sons (the Prophet's grandsons) Hasan

The highly evolved mysticism of the sect was at once its special attraction and its major limitation.

and Husayn should have ruled; and after them, their sons, and so on in quasi-monarchial succession.

In fact except for Ali none of them ever ruled all Islamdom. Instead they became a line of pretenders, and in effect heads of a branch of Islam called Shiism. In opposition to the orthodox (Sunni) Caliphs in Baghdad these descendants of the Prophet came to be known as the Imams.

To the Shiites an Imam is far more, far higher in rank than a Caliph. Ali ruled by right because of his spiritual greatness, which the Prophet recognized by appointing him his successor (in fact Ali is also revered by the sufis as "founder" and prototype of the Moslem saint). Shiites differ from orthodox or Sunni Moslems in believing that this spiritual pre-eminence was transferred to Ali's descendants through Fatima, the Prophet's daughter.

The sixth Shiite Imam, Jafar al-Sadiq, had two sons. The elder, Ismail, was chosen as successor. But he died before his father. Jafar then declared his own younger son Musa the new successor instead.

But Ismail had already given birth to a son—Mohammad ibn Ismail—and proclaimed him the next Imam. Ismail's followers split with Jafar over this question and followed Ismail's son instead of Musa. Thus they came to be known as Ismailis.

Musa's descendants ruled "orthodox" Shiism. A few generations later, the Twelfth Imam of this line vanished without trace from the material world. He still lives on the spiritual plane, whence he will return at the end of this cycle of time. He is the "Hidden Imam," the Mahdi foretold by the Prophet. "Twelver" Shiism is the religion of Iran today.

The Ismaili Imams languished in concealment, heads of an underground movement which attracted the extreme mystics and revolutionaries of Shiism. Eventually they emerged as a powerful force at the head of an army, conquered Egypt and established the Fatimid dynasty, the so-called anti-Caliphate of Cairo.

The early Fatimids ruled in an enlightened manner, and Cairo became the most cultured and open city of Islam. They never succeeded in converting the rest of the Islamic world however; in fact, even most Egyptians failed to embrace Ismailism. The highly evolved mysticism of the sect was at once its special attraction and its major limitation.

Hassan Sabbah's lair. Picture taken in Alamut 1986. Part of a PHAUSS project with CM von Hausswolff. Photo Erik Pauser

In 1074 a brilliant young Persian convert arrived in Cairo to be inducted into the higher initiatic (and political) ranks of Ismailism. But Hasan-i Sabbah soon found himself embroiled in a struggle for power. The Caliph Mustansir had appointed his eldest son Nizar as successor. But a younger son, al-Mustali, was intriguing to supplant him. When Mustansir died, Nizar—the rightful heir—was imprisoned and murdered.

Hasan-i Sabbah had intrigued for Nizar, and now was forced to flee Egypt. He eventually turned up in Persia again, head of a revolutionary Nizari movement. By some clever ruse he acquired command of the impregnable mountain fortress of Alamut ("Eagle's Nest") near Qazvin in Northwest Iran.

Hasan-i Sabbah's daring vision, ruthless and romantic, has become a legend in the Islamic world. With his followers he set out to recreate in miniature the glories of Cairo in this barren multichrome forsaken rock landscape.

In order to protect Alamut and its tiny but intense civilization Hasan-i Sabbah relied on assassination. Any ruler or politician or religious leader who threatened the Nizaris went in danger of a fanatic's dagger. In fact Hasan's first major publicity coup was the murder of the Prime Minister of Persia, perhaps the most powerful man of the era (and according to legend, a childhood friend of Sabbah's).

Once their fearful reputation was secure, the mere threat of being on the eso-terrorist hit list was enough to deter most people from acting against the hated heretics. One theologian was first threatened with a knife (left by his pillow as he slept), then bribed with gold. When his disciples asked him why he had ceased to fulminate against Alamut from his pulpit he answered that Ismaili arguments were "both pointed and weighty."

Since the great library of Alamut was eventually burned, little is known of Hasan-i Sabbah's actual teachings. Apparently he formed an initiatic hierarchy of seven circles based on that in Cairo, with assassins at the bottom and learned mystics at the top.

Ismaili mysticism is based on the concept of ta'wil, or "spiritual hermeneutics." Ta'wil actually means "to take something back to its source or deepest significance." The Shiites had always practiced this exegesis on the Koran itself, reading certain verses as veiled or symbolic allusions to Ali and the Imams. The Ismailis extended ta'wil much more radically. The whole structure of Islam appeared to them as a shell; to get at its kernel of meaning the shell must be penetrated by ta'wil, and in fact broken open completely.

The structure of Islam, even more than most religions, is based on a dichotomy between exoteric and esoteric. On the one hand there is Divine Law (shariah), on the other hand the Spiritual Path (tariqah). Usually the Path is seen as the esoteric kernel and the Law as the exoteric shell. But to Ismailism the two together present a totality which

In order to protect Alamut and its tiny but intense civilization Hasan-i Sabbah relied on assassination.

in its turn becomes a symbol to be penetrated by ta'wil. Behind Law and Path is ultimate Reality (haqiqah), God Himself in theological terms—Absolute Being in metaphysical terms.

This Reality is not something outside human scope; in fact if it exists at all then it must manifest itself completely on the level of consciousness. Thus it must appear as a man, the Perfect Man—the Imam. Knowledge of the Imam is direct perception of Reality itself. For Shiites the Family of Ali is the same as perfected consciousness.

Once the Imam is realized, the levels of Law and Path fall away naturally like split husks. Knowledge of inner meaning frees one from adherence to outer form: the ultimate victory of the esoteric over the exoteric.

Knowledge of inner meaning frees one from adherence to outer form: the ultimate victory of the esoteric over the exoteric.

The "abrogation of the Law" however was considered open heresy in Islam. For their own protection Shiites had always been allowed to practice taqqiya, "permissible dissimulation" or Concealment, and pretend to be orthodox to escape death or punishment. Ismailis could pretend to be Shiite or Sunni, whichever was most advantageous.

For the Nizaris, to practice Concealment was to practice the Law; in other words, pretending to be orthodox meant obeying the Islamic Law. Hasan-i Sabbah imposed Concealment on all but the highest ranks at Alamut, because in the absence of the Imam the veil of illusion must naturally conceal the esoteric truth of perfect freedom.

In fact, who was the Imam? As far as history was concerned, Nizar and his son died imprisoned and intestate. Hasan-i Sabbah was therefore a legitimist supporting a non-existent pretender! He never claimed to be the Imam himself, nor did his successor as "old Man of the Mountain," nor did his successor. And yet they all preached "in the name of Nizar." Presumably the answer to this mystery was revealed in the seventh circle of initiation.

Now the third Old Man of the Mountain had a son named Hasan, a youth who was learned, generous, eloquent and loveable. Moreover he was a mystic, an enthusiast for the deepest teachings of Ismailism and Sufism. Even during his father's lifetime some Alamutis began to whisper that young Hasan was the true Imam; the father heard of these rumors and denied them. I am not the Imam, he said, so how could my son be the Imam?

In 1162 the father died and Hasan (call him Hasan II to distinguish him from Hasan-i Sabbah) became ruler of Alamut. Two years later, on the seventeenth of Ramazan (August 8) in 1164, he proclaimed the Qiyamat, or Great Resurrection. In the middle of the month of Fasting, Alamut broke its fast forever and proclaimed perpetual holiday.

The resurrection of the dead in their bodies at the "end of time" is one of the most difficult doctrines of Islam (and Christianity as well). Taken literally it is absurd. Taken symbolically however it encapsulates the experience of the mystic. He "dies before death" when he comes to realize the separative and alienated aspects of the self, the ego-as-programmed-illusion. He is "reborn" in consciousness but he is reborn in the body, as an individual, the "soul-at-peace."

When Hasan II proclaimed the Great Resurrection which marks the end of Time, he lifted the veil of concealment and abrogated the religious Law. He offered communal as well as individual participation in the mystic's great adventure, perfect freedom.

He acted on behalf of the Imam, and did not claim to be the Imam himself. (In fact he took the title of Caliph or "representative.") But if the family of Ali is the same as perfect consciousness, then perfect consciousness is the same as the family of Ali. The realized mystic "becomes" a descendant of Ali (like the Persian Salman whom Ali adopted by covering him with his cloak, and who is much revered by sufis, Shiites and Ismailis alike).

In Reality, in haqiqah, Hasan II was the Imam because in the Ismaili phrase, he had realized the "Imam-of-his-own-being." The Qiyamat was thus an invitation to each of his followers to do the same, or at least to participate in the pleasures of paradise on earth.

The legend of the paradisal garden at Alamut where the houris, cupbearers, wine and hashish of paradise were enjoyed by the Assassins in the flesh, may stem from a folk memory of the Qiyamat. Or it may even be literally true. For the realized consciousness this world is no other than paradise, and its bliss and pleasures are all permitted. The Koran describes paradise as a garden. How logical then for wealthy Alamut to become outwardly the reflection of the spiritual state of the Qiyamat.

In 1166 Hasan II was murdered after only four years of rule. His enemies were perhaps in league with conservative elements at Alamut who resented the Qiyamat, the dissolving of the old secret hierarchy (and thus their own power as hierarchs) and who feared to live thus openly as heretics. Hasan II's son however succeeded him and established the Qiyamat firmly as Nizari doctrine.

If the Qiyamat were accepted in its full implications however it would probably have brought about the dissolution and end of Nizari Ismailism as a separate sect.

Hasan II as Qa'im or "Lord of the Resurrection" had released the Alamutis from all struggle and all sense of legitimist urgency. Pure esotericism, after all, cannot be bound by any form.

Hasan II's son, therefore, compromised. Apparently he decided to "reveal" that his father was in fact and in blood a direct descendant of Nizar. The story runs that after Hasan-i Sabbah had established Alamut, a mysterious emissary delivered to him the infant grandson of Imam Nizar. The child was raised secretly at Alamut. He grew up, had a son, died. The son had a son. This baby was born on the same day as the son of the Old Man of the Mountain, the outward ruler. The infants were surreptitiously exchanged in their cradles. Not even the Old Man knew of the ruse. Another version has the hidden Imam committing adultery with the Old Man's wife, and producing as love-child the infant Hasan II.

The Ismailis accepted these claims. Even after the fall of Alamut to the Mongol hordes the line survived and the present leader of the sect, the Aga Khan, is known as the 49th in descent from Ali (and pretender to the throne of

The legend of the paradisal garden at Alamut where the houris, cupbearers, wine and hashish of paradise were enjoyed by the Assassins in the flesh, may stem from a folk memory of the Qiyamat.

Egypt!). The emphasis on Alid legitimacy has preserved the sect as a sect. Whether it is literally true or not, however, matters little to an understanding of the Qiyamat.

With the proclamation of the Resurrection, the teachings of Ismailism were forever expanded beyond the borders imposed on them by any historical event. The Qiyamat remains as a state of consciousness which anyone can adhere to or enter, a garden without walls, a sect without a church, a lost moment of Islamic history that refuses to be forgotten, standing outside time, a reproach or challenge to all legalism and moralism, to all the cruelty of the exoteric. An invitation to paradise. ◘

SORCERY

"Chaos never died. No listen, what happened was this: they lied to you, sold you ideas of good and evil, gave you distrust of your body and shame for your prophethood of Chaos, invented words of disgust for your molecular love, mesmerized you with inattention, bored you with civilization and all its usurious emotions." So speaketh Hakim Bey, philosopher of the Temporary Autonomous Zone (T.A.Z.), Ontological Anarchism and Immediatism (meaning both "without mediation" and *now*). Bey's "Radio Sermonettes" on WBAI (New York) called for "Poetic Terrorism," "A Congress of Weird Religions" and "Black Magic as Revolutionary Action." Little is known about Bey and few have seen him. He is rumored to live in a squalid opium den in New York's Chinatown or else in a silver Gulfstream trailer somewhere in the New Jersey Pine Barrens. But this is just speculation –*RM*

The universe wants to play. Those who refuse out of dry spiritual greed and choose pure contemplation forfeit their humanity—those who refuse out of dull anguish, those who hesitate, lose their chance at divinity—those who mold themselves blind masks of Ideas and thrash around seeking some proof of their own solidity end by seeing out of dead men's eyes.

Sorcery: the systematic cultivation of enhanced consciousness or non-ordinary awareness and its deployment in the world of deeds and objects to bring about desired results.

The universe wants to play.

The incremental openings of perception gradually banish the false selves, our cacophonous ghosts—the "black magic" of envy and vendetta backfires because Desire cannot be forced. Where our knowledge of beauty harmonizes with the *ludus naturae*, sorcery begins.

No, not spoon-bending or horoscopy, not the Golden Dawn or make-believe shamanism, astral projection or the Satanic Mass—if it's mumbo jumbo you want go for the real stuff, banking, politics, social science—not that weak Blavatskian crap.

Sorcery works at creating around itself a psychic/physical space or openings into a space of untrammeled expression—the metamorphosis of quotidian place into angelic sphere. This involves the manipulation of symbols (which are also things) and of people (who are also symbolic)—the archetypes supply a vocabulary for this process and therefore are treated as if they were both real and unreal, like words. Imaginal Yoga.

If it's mumbo jumbo you want go for the real stuff, banking, politics, social science —not that weak Blavatskian crap.

The sorcerer is a Simple Realist: the world is real—but then so must consciousness be real since its effects are so tangible. The dullard finds even wine tasteless but the sorcerer can be intoxicated by the mere sight of water. Quality of perception defines the world of intoxication— but to sustain it and expand it to include *others* demands activity of a certain kind—sorcery. Sorcery breaks no law of nature because there is no Natural Law, only the spontaneity of *natura naturans*, the Tao. Sorcery violates laws which seek to chain this flow—priests, kings, hierophants, mystics, scientists and shopkeepers all brand the sorcerer *enemy* for threatening the power of their charade, the tensile strength of their illusory web.

A poem can act as a spell and vice versa—but sorcery refuses to be a metaphor for mere literature—it insists that symbols must cause events as well as private epiphanies. It is not a critique but a re-making. It rejects all eschatology and metaphysics of removal, all bleary nostalgia and strident futurismo, in favor of a paroxysm or seizure of *presence*.

Sorcery violates laws which seek to chain this flow—priests, kings, hierophants, mystics, scientists and shopkeepers all brand the sorcerer enemy for threatening the power of their charade.

Incense and crystal, dagger and sword, wand, robes, rum, cigars, candles, herbs like dried dreams—the virgin boy staring into a bowl of ink—wine and ganja, meat, yantras and gestures—rituals of pleasure, the garden of houris and sakis—the sorcerer climbs these snakes and ladders to a moment which is fully saturated with its own color, where mountains are mountains and trees are trees, where the body becomes all time, the beloved all space.

The tactics of ontological anarchism are rooted in this secret Art—the goals of ontological anarchism appear in its flowering. Chaos hexes its enemies and rewards its devotees ... this strange yellowing pamphlet, pseudonymous and dust-stained, reveals all ... send away for one split second of eternity. ☐

HAKIM BEY

MEDIA HEX
The Occult Assault on Institutions

The levels of Immediatist organization:

1) The gathering. Could be anything from a party to a riot. Can be planned or unplanned but depends on spontaneity to "really happen." Examples: anarchist gathering, neo-pagan celebration, Rave, brief urban riot or spontaneous demo. Of course the best gatherings become TAZ's such as some of the Be-Ins of the '60s, the early Rainbow Tribe gatherings, or the Stonewall Riot.

2) The horizontal potlach. A one-time meeting of a group of friends to exchange gifts. A planned orgy might fall into this category, the gift being sexual pleasure—or a banquet, the gift being food.

3) The Bee. Like a quilting bee, the Immediatist Bee consists of a group of friends meeting regularly to collaborate on a specific project. The Bee might serve as an organizing committee for a gathering or potlach, or as a creative collaborative, an affinity group for direct action, etc. The Bee is like a Passional Series in Fourier's system, a group united by a shared passion which can only be realized by a group.

4) When the Bee acquires a more-or-less permanent membership and a purpose larger than just a single project—an on-going project, let's say—it can either become a "club" or Gesellschaft organized non-hierarchically for open activity, or else a "Tong" organized non-hierarchically but clandestinely for secret activity. The Tong is of more immediate interest to us now for tactical reasons, and also because the club operates in danger of "institutionalization" and hence (in Ivan Illich's phrase), "paradoxical counter-productivity." (That is, as the institution approaches rigidity and monopoly it begins to have the opposite effect from its original purpose. Societies founded for "freedom" become authoritarian, etc.) The traditional Tong is also subject to this trajectory, but the Immediatist Tong is built, so to speak, to auto-destruct when no longer capable of serving its purpose.

5) The TAZ can arise out of any or all of the above forms singly, in sequence, or in complex patterning. Although I've said the TAZ can last as briefly as one night or as long as a couple of years, this is only a rough rule, and probably most examples fall in between. A TAZ is more than any of the first four forms, however, in that while it lasts it fills the horizon of attention of all its participants, it becomes (however briefly) a whole society.

6) Finally, in the uprising, the TAZ breaks its own borders and flows (or wants to flow) out into the "whole world," the entire immediate time/space available. While the uprising lasts, and has not been terminated by defeat or by changing into "Revolution" (which aspires to permanence), the Insurrection keeps the consciousness of most of its adherents spontaneously tuned in to that elusive other mode of intensity, clarity, attention, individual and group realization, and (to be blunt) that happiness so characteristic of great social upheavals such as the Commune, or 1968. From the existential point of view (and here we invoke Stirner, Nietzsche, and Camus), this happiness is actually the purpose of the uprising.

We've long since grown weary of quibbling over terms, and if you don't know what we mean by "necessary beauty" you may as well stop reading here.

The goals of the Immediatist organization are:

1) Conviviality: the coming together in physical closeness of the group for the synergistic enhancement of its membership's pleasures.

2) Creation: the collaborative production, direct and unmediated, of necessary beauty, outside all structures of hypermediation, alienation, commodification.[1] We've long since grown weary of quibbling over terms, and if you don't know what we mean by "necessary beauty" you may as well stop reading here. "Art" is only a possible sub-category of this mystery and not necessarily the most vital.

3) Destruction: We'd go farther than Bakunin, and say that there is no creation without destruction. The very notion of bringing some new beauty into being implies that an old ugliness has been swept away or blown up. Beauty defines itself in part (but precisely) by destroying the ugliness which is not itself. In our version of the Sorelian myth of social violence, we suggest that no Immediatist act is

The very notion of bringing some new beauty into being implies that an old ugliness has been swept away or blown up.

completely authentic and effective without both creation and destruction: the whole Immediatist dialectic is implied in any Immediatist "direct action," both the creation-in-destruction and the destruction-in-creation. Hence "poetic terrorism," for example; and hence the real goal or telos of all our organizational forms is:

4) The construction of values. The Maslovian "peak experience" is value-formative on the individual level; the existential factuality of the Bee, Tong, TAZ or uprising permits a "revaluation of values" to flow from its collective intensity. Another way of putting it: the transformation of everyday life.

The link between the organization and the goal is the tactic. In simple terms, what does the Immediatist organization do? Our "strategy" is to optimize conditions for the emergence of the TAZ (or even the Insurrection)—but what specific actions might be carried out to construct this strategy? Without tactics, the Immediatist organization might as well disperse at once. "Direct action" should further the "cause" but also must itself hold all the potential for the flowering of the cause within itself. In fact, each act must be in potentia both aimed at the goal and identical with the goal. We cannot use tactics which are limited to mediation; each action must immediately realize the goal, at least in some respect, lest we find ourselves working for abstractions and even simulations of our purpose. And yet the many different tactics and actions should also add up to more than the sum of their parts, and should give birth to the TAZ or the Uprising. Just as ordinary organizations cannot provide the structures we need, so ordinary tactics cannot satisfy our demand for both immediate and insurrectionary "situations."

Conviviality is both a tactic and a goal. Noble in itself, it may serve as both form and content for such organizational modes as the gathering, the potlach, the banquet. But conviviality by itself lacks the transformative energy that generally arises only out of a complex of actions which includes what we've called "destruction" as well as "creation." The ideal Immediatist organization aims at this more complex goal, and gains conviviality as a necessary structure along with it. In other words, gathering together in a group to plan a potential TAZ for an even larger group is already an Immediatist act involving conviviality—like the kingdom of heaven, is "added unto" all sincere striving for more exalted break-throughs. It would seem that the quintessential Immediatist act or tactic however will involve simultaneous creation and destruction rather than just conviviality—hence the Bee and Tong are "higher" organizational forms than the gathering and potlach.

In the Bee the emphasis is on creation—the quilt, so to speak—the collaborative art project, the group's act of generosity toward itself and toward reality rather than toward an "audience" of mediated consumers. Of course the Bee can also consider and undertake destructive or "criminal" actions. But when it does so it has perhaps already taken the first step toward becoming a secret society or Immediatist Tong. Hence I think that the Tong is the most complex (or "highest") form of Immediatist organization which can be pre-determined to a significant degree. The TAZ and the uprising depend finally on many factors for the "organization" process to achieve without "luck." As

I've said, we can maximize possibilities for the TAZ or the insurrection but we cannot really "organize" them or make them happen. The Tong however can be clearly defined and organized and can carry out complex actions, both material and symbolic, both creative and destructive. The Tong cannot guarantee the TAZ, much less the insurrection, but it can surely gratify many or most immediate desires of lesser complexity—and after all it might succeed in precipitating the great event of the TAZ, the Commune, the "restoration of the Ming" as Great Festival of Consciousness, the objective correlative of all desire.

Keeping all this in mind let us try to imagine—and then criticize—possible tactics for the Immediatist group, and ideally for the well-organized semi-permanent Tong or virtually clandestine action group or affinity web, capable of attempting fully-evolved complex direct actions in an articulated strategy. Each such action must simultaneously damage or destroy some real and or imaginal time/space of "the enemy," even as it simultaneously creates for its perpetrators the strong chance of peak expe-

We're talking about real-time direct actions which must be carried out "against" identifiable nodes of real-time power. Discussion of abstract enemies such as "the state" will get us nowhere.

rience or "adventure": each tactic thus in a sense moves to appropriate and detourne the enemy's space, and eventually to occupy and transform it. Each tactic or action is already potentially the whole "Path" of autonomy in itself, just as each invocation of the Real already contains the entirety of the spiritual path (according to the "gnosis" of Ismailism and heterodox Sufism).

But wait! First: who is "The Enemy"? It's all very well to mutter about conspiracies of the Establishment or the networks of psychic control. We're talking about real-time direct actions which must be carried out "against" identifiable nodes of real-time power. Discussion of abstract enemies such as "the state" will get us nowhere. I am not oppressed (or alienated) directly by any concrete entity called the state, but by specific groups such as teachers, police, bosses, etc. A "Revolution" may aim at overthrowing a "state." But the Insurrection and all its Immediatist action-groups will have to discover some target which is not an idea, a piece of paper, a "spook" that enchains us with our own bad dreams about power and impotence. We'll play at the war of images, yes. But images arise

from or flow through specific nexuses. The spectacle has a structure, and the structure has joints, crossings, patterns, levels. The Spectacle even has an address—sometimes—maybe. It's not real in the same way the TAZ is real. But it's real enough for an assault.

Because the Immediatist texts have largely been addressed to "artists" as well as "non-authoritarians" and because Immediatism is not a political movement but a game, even an aesthetic game, it would seem inescapably obvious that we should look for the enemy in the media, especially in those media we find to be directly oppressive. For example for the student the oppressive and alienating medium is "education," and the nexus (the pressure point) must therefore be the school. For the artist the direct source of alienation would seem to be the complex we usually call the Media, which has usurped the time and the space of art as we wish to practice it—which has redefined all creative communicativeness as an exchange of commodities or of alienating images—which has poisoned "discourse." In the past the alienating medium was the church and the insurrection was expressed in the language of heretical spirituality vs. organized religion. Now the Media plays the role of the Church in the circulation of images. As the Church once concocted a false scarcity of sanctity or salvation, so the Media constructs a false scarcity of values, or "meaning." As the Church once tried to impose its monopoly on the spirit, the Media wants to re-make language itself as pure mind, divorced from the body. The media denies meaning to corporeality, to everyday life, just as the Church once defined the body as evil and everyday life as sin. The Media defines itself, or its discourse, as the real universe. We mere consumers live in a skull-world of illusion, with TVs as eye-sockets through which we peer at the world of the living, the "rich and famous," the real. Just so did religion define the world as illusion and heaven only as real—real, but so far away. If insurrection once spoke to the Church as heresy, so it must speak now to the Media. Once, the revolting peasants burned churches. But what exactly are the churches of the Media?

It's easy to feel nostalgia for such a once-magnificent enemy as the Roman Catholic Church. I've even tried to convince myself that today's washed-out sex-hating charade is still worth conspiring against. Infiltrate the church; fill up the tractate shelf with beautiful porno flyers labeled "This is the Face of God"; hide dada/voodoo objects under the pews and behind the altar; send occult manifestos to the Bishop and clergy; leak satanic scares to the idiot press; leave evidence incriminating the Illuminati. An even more satisfying target might be the Mormons, who are completely enthralled by hypermediated CommTech and yet intensely sensitive to "black magic."[2] Televangelism offers an especially tempting mix of media

itself, but even so it could never erase the experience of the liberated neighborhood and its people—and chances are the Media would after all remain silent, since the whole event would seem too complex for it to digest and shit out as "news."

As the Church once concocted a false scarcity of sanctity or salvation, so the Media constructs a false scarcity of values, or "meaning."

and bad religion. But when it comes to real power, the churches feel quite empty. The god has abandoned them. The god has his own talk-show now, his own corporate sponsors, his own network. The real target is the Media.

The "magical assault" however still holds promise as a tactic against this new church and "new inquisition"—precisely because the Media, like the church, does its work through "magic," the manipulation of images. In fact our biggest problem in assaulting the Media will be to invent a tactic which cannot be recuperated by Babylon and turned to its own power-advantage. A breathless "live-news" report that CBS had been attacked by radical sorcerers would simply become part of the "spectacle of dissidence," the sub-Manichean drama of the discourse of simulation. The best tactical defense against this co-optation will be the subtle complexity and aesthetic depth of our symbolism, which must contain fractal dimensions untranslatable into the flat image-language of the tube. Even if "they" try to appropriate our imagery, in other words, it will carry an unexpected "viral" subtext which will infect all attempts at recuperation with a nauseating malaise of uncertainty—a "poetic terror."

One simple idea would be to blow up a TV transmission tower and then take credit for the action in the name of the American Poetry Society (who ought to be blowing up TV towers); but such a purely destructive act lacks the creative aspect of the truly Immediatist tactic. Each act of destruction should ideally also be an act of creation.[3] Suppose we could blank TV transmission in one neighborhood and at the same time sage a miraculous festival, liberating and transforming the local mall into a one-night TAZ—then our action would combine destruction and creation in a truly Immediatist "direct action" of beauty and terror—Bakuninesque, Situationistic, real Dada at last. The media might try to distort it and appropriate its power for

Such an immensely complicated action would lie beyond the capabilities of all but the richest and most fully-developed Immediatist Tong. But the principle can be applied at lower levels of complexity. For example, imagine that a group of students wish to protest the stupefying effect of the education-medium by disrupting or shutting down school for some time. Easily done, as many bold high school saboteurs have discovered. Carried out as a purely negative action, however, the gesture can be interpreted by authority as "delinquency" and thus its energy can be recuperated to the benefit of Control. The saboteurs should make a point of simultaneously providing valuable information, beauty, a sense of adventure. At the very least anonymous leaflets about anarchism, home schooling, media critique or something of the sort can be "left at the scene" or distributed to other students, faculty, even press. At best, an alternative to school itself should be suggested, through conviviality, festival, liberated learning, shared creativity.[4]

Getting back to the project of a "magical assault" on the Media, or media-hex: it too should combine in one gesture (more or less) both the creative and destructive elements of the effective Immediatist artwork or work of poetic terrorism. In this way it will (we hope) prove too complex for the usual recuperation-process. For example, it would be futile to bombard the Media-target with images of horror, bloodshed, serial murder, alien sex abuse, S&M splatter and the like, since the Media itself is the chief purveyor of all such imagery. Guignol demi-satanism fits right into the spectrum of horror-as-control where most broadcasting occurs. You can't compete with the "News" for images of disgust, repulsion, atavistic panic, or gore. The Media (if we can personify it for a moment) might at first be surprised that anyone would bother to mirror this crap back at the Media—but it would have no occult effect.[5]

Let us imagine (another "thought-experiment!") that an Immediatist cabal of some size and seriousness has

We mere consumers live in a skull-world of illusion, with TVs as eye-sockets through which we peer at the world of the living, the "rich and famous," the real.

somehow gotten hold of the addresses (including fax, phone, email, or whatever) of the executive and creative staff of a TV show we might feel represented a nadir of alienation and psychic poison (say "NYPD Blue"). In "The Malay Black Djinn Curse" I suggested sending packages of dada/voodoo objects to such people, along with warnings that their place of work had been cursed. At that time

I was reluctant to recommend curses against individuals. I would now however recommend even worse.

I was reluctant to recommend curses against individuals. I would now however recommend even worse. Moreover, for these media moghouls I might well favor the kind of creepy Moslem/heretic jungle reptile imagery I outlined in the "Black Djinn" operation—since the Media show such fear of "Moslem" terror and such bigotry against Moslems—but I would now make the whole scenario and imagery far more complex. The TV execs and writers should be sent objects as exquisite and disturbing as surrealist "boxes," containing beautiful but "illegal" images of sexual pleasure,[6] and intricate spiritual symbolism, evocative images of autonomy and pleasure in self-realization, all very subtle, convoluted, mysterious; these objects must be made with real artistic fervor and the highest inspiration, but each one meant only for one person—the victim of the hex.

The recipients may well be disturbed by these anonymous "gifts" but will probably neither destroy them nor even discuss them at once. No harm to our scheme if they do. But these objects may well look too fine, too "expensive" to destroy—and too "dirty" to show to anyone else. Next day, the victims each receive a letter explaining that their receipt of the objects effected the delivery of a curse. The hex will cause them to come to know their true desires, symbolized by the magical objects. They will also now begin to realize they are acting as enemies of the human race by commodifying desire and working as the agents of soul-Control. The magic art-objects will weave into their dreams and desires, making their jobs now seem not only poisonously boring but also morally destructive. Their desires so magically awakened will ruin them for work in the Media—unless they turn to subversion and sabotage. At best they can quit. This might save their sanity at the expense of their meaningless "careers." If

they remain in Media they will waste away with unsatisfied desire, shame, and guilt. Or else become rebels, and learn to fight against the Eye of Babylon from within the idol's belly. Meanwhile their "show" has been picked for total black magic assault by a group of Shiite terrorist sorcerers, or the Libyan Voodoo Hit squad, or something of the sort. Of course it would be nice to have an inside agent to plant "clues" and to spy out information, but some variation on this scheme can be carried out without active infiltration of the institution. The initial assault might perhaps be followed up with mailings of anti-Media propaganda, and even Immediatist tracts. If possible, of course, some bad luck could be produced for the victims or for their institution. Pranks, you know. But again, this is not necessary, and may even get in the way of our pure experiment in mind-fuck and image-manipulation. Let the bastards produce their own bad luck out of their inner sadness at being such evil assholes, out of their atavistic superstition (without which they wouldn't be such media-wizards), out of their fear of otherness, out of their repressed sexuality. You can be sure they will—or at least, that they'll remember the "curse" every time something bad happens to them.

The general principle can be applied to media other than television. A computer company for example might be cursed through its computers by a talented hacker, although one would have to avoid Sci-Fi scenarios such as William Gibson's haunted cyberspace—too baroque. Advertising companies run on pure magic, film-makers, PR firms, art galleries, lawyers, even politicians.[7] Any oppressor who works through the image is susceptible to the power of the image.

It should be stressed that we are not describing the Revolution here, or revolutionary political action, or even the Uprising. This is merely a new kind of neo-hermetic agit-prop, a proposal for a new kind of "political art," a project for a Tong of rebel artists, an experiment in the game of Immediatism. Others will struggle against oppression in their own fields of expertise, work, discourse, life. As artists we choose to struggle within "art," within the world of the Media, against the alienation which oppress-

Their desires so magically awakened will ruin them for work in the Media—unless they turn to subversion and sabotage. At best they can quit. This might save their sanity at the expense of their meaningless "careers."

es us most directly. We choose to battle where we live, rather than theorize about oppression elsewhere. I've tried to suggest a strategy and imagine certain tactics which would further it. No other claims are made and no further details should be divulged. The rest is for the Tong.

I'll admit that my own taste might run toward an even more violent approach to Media than proposed here in this text. People talk about "taking over" TV stations, but not one of them has succeeded. It might make more sense to shoot TV sets in electronic shop windows, ludicrous as it seems, than to dream of taking over the studios. But I draw the line at suggesting attentats against News fascists, or even killing Geraldo's dog, for several reasons which still seem sufficient to me. For one, I have taken to heart Nietzsche's remarks on the inferiority and futility of revengism as a political doctrine. Mere reaction is never a sufficient response—much less a noble path. Moreover, it wouldn't work. It would be seen as an "attack on free speech." The project proposed here includes within its structure the possibility of actually changing something—even if it's only a few "minds." In other words it has a constructive aspect integrally bound up with a destructive aspect, so that the two cannot be separated. Our dada/voodoo object is both an attack and a seduction in one, and both motives will be thoroughly explained in the accompanying flyers or letters. After all, there's the chance we might convert someone. Of course, we may easily fail here too. All our efforts could end up in the trash, forgotten by minds too well armored even to feel a moment's unease. This is, after all, merely a thought experiment, or an experiment in thought. If you like you could even call it merely a form of aesthetic criticism directed at the perpetrators rather than the consumers of bad art. The time for real violence is not yet, if only because the production of violence remains the monopoly of the Institutions. There's no point in sticking one's head up and waving a gun if one is facing a star wars death beam satellite.[8] Our task is to enlarge the cracks in the pseudo monolith of social discourse, gradually uncovering bits of empty spectacle, labeling subtle forms of mind-control, charting escape routes, chipping away at crystallizations of image suffocation, banging on pots and pans to wake a few citizens from media trance, using the intimate media[9] to orchestrate our assaults on Big Media and its Big Lies, learning again how to breathe together, how to live in our bodies, how to resist the image-heroin of "information." Actually what I've called "direct action" here

might better be known as indirect action, symbolic, viral, occult and subtle rather than actual, wounding, militant, and open. If we and our natural allies enjoy even a little success, however, the superstructure may eventually lose so much coherence and assurance that its power will start to slip as well. The day may come (who would've thought that one morning in 1989 Communism would evaporate?), the day may come when even too-late Capitalism begins to melt down—after all it's only outlasted Marxism and fascism because it's even more stupid—one day the very fabric of the consensus may start to unravel, along with the economy and the environment. One day the colossus may tremble and teeter, like an old statue of Stalin in some provincial town square. And on that day perhaps a TV station will be blown up and will stay blown up. Until then:—one, ten, a thousand occult assaults on the institutions. ⚲

Let the bastards produce their own bad luck out of their inner sadness at being such evil assholes.

Endnotes

1. I'm not using the term hypermedia here in the sense assigned to it by our comrades at Xexoxial Endarchy, who call hypermedia simply the appropriation of all creative media to single effect (i.e., the next stage beyond "mixed media") ... I'm using "hyper-mediation" to mean representation exacerbated to the point of an immiserating alienation, as in the image of the commodity.
2. Mormonism was founded by rogue Freemason occultists, and Mormon leaders remain extremely susceptible to hints of a buried past coming back to haunt them. The Roman Catholic Church might treat a "magical assault" with a millenial shrug of Italianate sophistication—but Mormons would go for their guns.
3. It's important not to get caught, as this neutralizes any power we might have gained or sought to express, and even turns our own power against us. A good Immediatist action should be relatively impeccable, to coin an oxymoron. Getting expelled from High-school might spoil the effect. Immediatism wants to be a martial art, not a road to martyrdom.
4. A Note on the Architecture of the TAZ. Obviously the TAZ usually leaves not a wrack behind. Building isn't its top priority. And yet all lived space is architecture—built space, made space—and the TAZ by definition has presence in real time and space. The nomad encampment should perhaps serve as the primordial prototype. Tents, trailers, RV's, houseboats. The old traveling tent circus or carnival might offer a model for TAZ architecture. In an urban setting the squat becomes the commonest possible space for our purposes, but in America at any rate the law of property makes the squat almost by definition a poor space. The TAZ wants rich space, not so much rich in articulation (as in the space of control, the official building of capital, religion, state) but rich in expression. The temporary playful spaces proposed by Situationist and urbanist radicals in the '60s had some potential but finally proved too expensive and too planned. The ur-TAZ architecture is that of the Paris Commune. The microneighborhood is closed off by barricades. The identical houses of the poor are then connected by driving passageways through all connecting walls on the ground floor. These passageways remind us of Fourier's arcades, by which the Planasterians would circulate

through their communal palace, from private to public space and back again. The Commune city-block became a fortified TAZ with public military space on ground level (and roofs) and private space on upper stories, with the enclosed streets as festival-space. This plan influences the architecture of P.M.'s bolo'bolo where the commune-block becomes a more permanent urban utopian commune. As for the TAZ, it is effected by a kind of closure, but one paradoxically shot through with openings. It escapes the asphyxiating enclosure of Capital, and the tragic ugliness of industrial space. Its architecture is smooth, not striated—hence the tent not the prison, the passageway not the portal, the barricade, not Haussman's boulevards.

5. The trouble with most "transgressive" art is that it transgresses none of the Consensus values—it merely exaggerates them, or at best exacerbates them. Aesthetic obsession with "Death" makes a perfect commodity (image-without-substance), since the delivery of the meaning of the image would actually put an end to the consumer. To buy death is to buy either failure or fascism—a brink upon which Bataille himself teetered with sickening lack of balance. I say this despite admiration for Bataille.

6. This will prevent the images from ever appearing on TV or in news photos. It will also, coincidentally, make a statement about the relation between "beauty" and "obscenity," and between "art" and "censorship," etc., etc.

7. Generally not worth attacking as "politicians," since they are after all mere "paper tigers"—but perhaps worth attacking as paper tigers.

8. All praise to the activists who destroyed such a satellite in California with axes. Unfortunately they were caught, and punished by having their salaries seized to pay off the cost of destruction. Not good.

9. The intimate media by definition don't reach the mass unconscious like TV, movies, newspapers. They can still "speak" to the individual. FM radio, cable public access video, small press, CDs and cassette tapes, software and other CommTech can be used as intimate media. Here the Xexoxial Endarchy's idea of "hypermedia" as a tool for insurrection finds its true role. There exist two contending factions within non-authoritarian theory at present: the anti-tech primitivists (Fifth Estate, Anarchy: A Journal of Desire Armed, John Zerzan) and the pro-Tech futurologists (including both left-wing anarcho-syndicalists and right-wing anarcho-libertarians). I find all the arguments vastly informative and inspiring. In TAZ and elsewhere I've attempted to reconcile both positions in my own thinking. I would now suggest that the question proposed by these arguments cannot be answered except in the process-of-becoming of an active praxis (or politique) of desire. Let us imagine that "the Revolution" has taken place. We're free to decide our level of technology, in a spectrum ranging from pre-Ice-Age primitive to post-industrial Sci Fi. Will the neo-paleolithics force the futurists to give up their tech? Will the space cadets force the Zerzanites to buy VR rigs? Piously, one hopes not. The question will rather be: how much do we desire the hunting/gathering life? Or the CyberEvolutionary life? Do we desire computers enough to forge the silicon chips ourselves? Because after the Revolution no one will accept alienated work. On this, all non-authoritarian tendencies agree. You want a forest full of game? You are responsible for its fecundity and wildness. You want a spaceship? You are responsible for its manufacture, from mining the ore to black smithing the nose cone. By all means form a commune or network. By all means demand that my level of tech doesn't interfere with yours. Other than these few ground-rules for avoiding civil war, non-authoritarian society can depend on nothing but desire to shape its techne'. As Fourier would put it, the level of economic complexity of utopian society will be in harmony with the totality of all Passions. I can't predict what exactly might emerge. All I can imagine is what I'm capable of desiring to the point of willing its realization.

Personally (as a matter of taste) I envision something very like bolo'bolo: infinite variety within the basic revolutionary context of positive freedom. By definition there could be no such thing as a NASA-bolo or a Wall Street-bolo, because NASA and Wall Street depend on alienation to exist. I would expect something like low-tech or "appropriate" tech (envisioned by '60s theorists such as Illich) to become the Utopian average, with extreme wings occupying a restored Wild(er)ness on the one hand, and the Moon on the other … In any case, it's all science fiction. In my writing I try to envision tactics which can be used now by any non-authoritarian tendency. Both the "Tong" and the assault on Media should appeal to both the primitivists and the techies. And I discuss the use of both magic and computers because both exist in the world I inhabit, and both will be used in the liberating struggle. Not only the future but even the present holds too much possibility, too many resources, a superabundant-redundant excess of potentials, to be limited by ideology. A theory of technology is too constraining. Immediatism offers instead an aesthetics of technology, and prefers praxis to theory.

DR. STEPHEN EDRED FLOWERS

THE SECRET OF THE GOTHICK GOD OF DARKNESS

There is a Secret God, a Hidden God, who dwells in a spiraling tower fortress and who has guided and overseen our development from time immemorial—and who has remained concealed but very close to us awaiting the "future" time of reawakening. The time of the reawakening is near. Already we have heard the distant claps of thunder which signal the coming storm.

The legacy of the Dark Gothick God is one which can guide those chosen by him to a state of development wherein they have attained a permanent (immortal) consciousness which is free to act or not act in the material universe as it desires. This consciousness becomes privy to all manner of secrets of life *and* death and life in death. The price for this attainment is contained in the cost of attaining it—for one who has been so chosen there can be no rest, no respite from the Quest which is, and remains, the Eternal Work.

Because the *way* in which knowledge of this Dark Gothick God is passed from generation to generation contradicts the favored methods of the so-called "major religions" of the world—the religions of the "book," i.e. Judaism, Christianity and Islam—this knowledge and its methods have been forbidden and made increasingly taboo for all of the centuries since the cunning ideological conversion of Europe by Christianity.

Books can be burned, religious leaders can be killed—but the blood endures.

The time of the reawakening is near.

THE GOTHICK GOD

In the past ten or fifteen years our European culture (including the "colonies" of western European cultures such as those in North America and Australia) have witnessed a revival of an æsthetic "Gothick Kulture." This revival, or reawakening, of the Gothick spirit in many respects follows the characteristics of all the previous revivals.

The word "Gothick" is the key to understanding the nature and character of the spirit behind the æsthetic. (Here I use the "-k" spelling for æsthetic reasons as well as to differentiate the cultural movement from designations of

Books can be burned, religious leaders can be killed— but the blood endures.

architecture or literary history—more commonly spelled in the standard way.) "Gothick" is ultimately derived from the name of an ancient Germanic nation—the Goths.

These Goths came out of the far North (from present-day Götland in Sweden) and swept down into southern Europe beginning about 150 CE. They split into two major groups along the way: the Visigoths and the Ostrogoths. In the south they established kingdoms in present-day Spanish Italy (with its capital in Ravenna) and southern France (with its capital in present-day Toulouse). This latter kingdom, under pressure from the Franks, moved its capital to the present-day Spanish city of Toledo. In all of these regions the Goths established many secret traditions at the highest levels of society. The tip of this secret iceberg is revealed when you see how many names of nobility are derived from Gothic forms. Some of the more familiar examples of these would be Frederico, Adolfo, Carlo, Ricardo....

The mystery of what happened to the lost treasure of Rome (including the "Lost Ark") can be solved through knowledge of Visigothic secret history. But that is a story for another time. Eventually the Goths were militarily defeated by a coalition of the Roman Catholic Church and the king of the Franks, who was the first Germanic king to convert to Roman Catholicism. All others before him, including many Goths, had "converted" to their own brand of esoteric "Gothic Christianity." The final end to overt Gothic rule in Spain came with the Muslim invasion in 711 CE. But their secret traditions lived on.

He dwells in deep darkness and travels to the most forbidden zones of the multiverse in his eternal search for increasing knowledge.

The Goths gained a reputation in their own time, and through subsequent ages, as a sort of "master-race." In ancient Scandinavia the word *gotar* was used as an honorific title for heroes, as even today members of the noble class in modern Spain are referred to as *godos* ("Goths"). As time went on, some of the secret Gothic tradition merged with some of the established traditions of the peoples among whom they disappeared, while other parts of it were submerged in the cultural "underclass" of peasants, vagabonds and heretics.

Four to five centuries after their official "demise" an æsthetic in memorial to the spirit of the Goths was created in northern Europe—later art historians even named the style "Gothic." But nowhere the Goths had been remained unmarked by their prestige and secret tradition. This dark and mysterious Gothick past of superhuman qualities loomed as a secret alternative to the bright and rational Classical past which was used as a model for both Christian theologians of the Middle Ages and rational humanists of the Renaissance.

It is in this cultural framework that the Romantic movement began to grow in the 1700s. The Classical models had failed the avant-garde of the day. They looked to a more distant past, as a way of looking into a deeper, more mysterious, and at the same time more *real*, level of themselves. When the French looked beyond their Medieval Christian roots they found the Romans, and

hence the word "Roman-tic" aptly described what it was they were looking for. In northern Europe, however, the term "Romantic" was generally found wanting by the adventurous souls who saw nothing of the *deep-past = deep-self* formula in the word. It was still remembered that our noble past was not Roman, but *Gothick* (by now the word "Gothick" was also a synonym for "Germanic" or "Teutonic").

The Gothick world was a world of the distant and powerful past, shrouded in mist and swathed in darkness—a nightside world of dream and nightmare. The Gothick images conjured by the artists of the day—poets such as Burger, Novalis, Byron and Hugo, or painters such as Fuseli, Arbo and Doré—acted as doorways for opening the world to the Gothick steam. The dead came alive once more and walked among the living—and upon the living begat the children of darkness.

This process has continued from those nights to these, branching out in ever wider circles to encompass more aspects of life. But at the level of what might be called "popular culture" traces can be seen that connect Ann Radcliffe's *The Mysteries of Udulpho* to M. G. Lewis' *The Monk* to C. R. Maturin's *Melmoth* to E. A. Poe's tales and poetry to R. W. Chambers' *The King in Yellow* to Bram Stoker's *Dracula* and on to Hanns Heinz Ewers, H. P. Lovecraft and Anne Rice. All in their own ways, wittingly or unwittingly, have contributed to the descent of the Gothick God of Darkness in popular culture.

In many respects Stoker's famous novel, *Dracula*, was a "warning" of an "evil influence" from the Gothick past—*Die Toten reiten schnell!* Stoker has his evil nobleman declare his kinship with the northern Berserkers who fought with the "spirit which Thor and Wodin [*sic*] gave them," and even obliquely refers to the Gothic tradition reported by Jordanes in his *Getica* that the Huns were the offspring of Gothic sorceresses, known as *Haljurûnas* (Hel-Runes) and devils that roamed the steppes.

Neither was this influence lost on the American writer H. P. Lovecraft, who, when he was feeling more "heroic" in his younger days, strongly identified with the Gothick heritage. In a letter from October of 1921 he wrote: "I am essentially a Teuton and barbarian; a Xanthochroic Nordic from the forests of Germany or Scandinavia ... I am a son of Odin and brother to Hengist and Horsa ..."

The most important god of the ancient Goths was their most distant ancestor, which the Gothic histories record as one named *Gauts*. Old Norse literature provides the key to discovering a more familiar identity of this God. There we find this name among the many given to the God Óðhinn or Woden (as he was known among the Anglo-Saxons). Óðhinn is called the All-Father, and Gautr is at the head of the genealogy of the Gothic kings just as Woden is at the head of the genealogies of all the pre-Norman English kings.

This God—or ultimate præterhuman ancestor—is a wise and dark communicator. He is the master of all forms of mysterious communication by means of signs and symbols. In ancient times a system of such symbols for communication was discovered and called "Runes." In order to learn these the God hung himself for nine nights on a tree and thereby encountered the realm of Death—and from that spear-tip point which is the interface between Life and Death he at once comprehended the Runes—the Mysteries of the World.

These Runes form a system of semiotic elements which are not only potent in a purely abstract or theoretical way, but which are, by their very nature, connected to the physical universe and the realm of generation and regeneration.

Even in ancient times, when Woden was acknowledged as the High-God of the Germanic peoples, he was not a very *popular* God. He hid himself from most, and many were glad of it. Then and even now he dwells in deep darkness and travels to the most forbidden zones of the multiverse in his eternal search for increasing knowledge.

As with the ancient Goths, Woden's most essential role is as the All-Father, as the progenitor of a continuous bloodline—and through that bloodline the forger of a permanent link with humanity. The importance of *blood* as a symbol of what is at the heart of what is going on in a more mysterious way is essential. The mystery and the secret of Woden is not that "knowledge" of him is passed along through clandestine cults (though this too occurs), or even through the rediscovery of old books and texts (though this happens)—but rather that such knowledge is actually *encoded* in a mysterious way in the DNA, in the very genetic material, of those who are descended from him. This, in and of itself, is an awful secret to bear—and once grasped it is a secret that has driven more than one man mad.

Runic (Mysterious) information is stored "in the blood" where it lies concealed and dormant until the right stimulus is applied from the outside which signals its activation. In this way, knowledge can seem to have been eradicated, but yet resurface again with no apparent, or apparently natural, connection between one manifestation and other subsequent remanifestations.

Scientists have more recently discovered the phenomenal platform for this noumenal process in the form of the double helix of the DNA molecule.

THE SECRET

The Gothick obsession is an obsession with the Mystery of Darkness. It is no accident, or if it is an "accident" it is a meaningful synchronicity, that the name of the mythic sorceresses of Gothic history that gave birth to the Huns was *Haljurûnas*, which literally translated from the Gothic would be: "The Mysteries of Death." The Gothick offspring have always sought to pry into the Mysteries of Life and Death, to penetrate to the depth of the Self and to the outermost reaches of the darkened and chaotic world. Boldly forging into the Darkness to seek the Grail of Undefiled Wisdom, to *Seek the Mysteries*, is the highest Quest of the Gothick Children of the Night. There is great power in the Quest, and in the Quest alone.

The Gothic word for "mystery" is *rûna*. When the Gothic bishop Ulfilas translated the Christian Bible into Gothic for use in the Gothic cult, he translated the Greek word *mystêrion* (μυστηριον) with the Gothic *rûna*.

The practical power of this at once simple and obscure idea of mystery was once well illustrated in an episode of the once popular American television series, *Unsolved Mysteries*. One day an out-of-work father took his sons fishing in a remote forest area where they discovered some stones in the river carved with a variety of arcane symbols. The father and his sons were deeply struck by the signs—What could they mean? Who could have carved them? They went home filled with a sense of mystery and awe. Within a short time business opportunities poured the father's way and the family was soon prosperous. They attributed their good fortune to the power of the

In the coming years the value and power of the concept of pure Mystery, or the Hidden, will become more apparent as the ways of the Gothick God of Darkness begin to unfold.

stones. (Experts from a nearby university determined that the signs were carved recently and were not Amerindian pictographs, though they appeared to be imitations of similar designs.) Indeed, the family had come by their turn of good fortune from the stones—but not because of the particular shapes or qualities of the signs themselves but rather because of the *sense of mysterious power* which had struck the father and sons upon seeing the stones in the first place.

In the coming years the value and power of the concept of pure Mystery, or the Hidden, will become more apparent as the ways of the Gothick God of Darkness begin to unfold.

That which links this world with that of the Mysterious Gothick realm is clearly symbolized by the blood. But do not mistake the *symbol* for the entirety of the thing itself—although it, as a true symbol, is a *fractum* of the thing itself. The Gothick heritage, the heritage of power and knowledge, is encoded information which is by some as yet unknown paraphysical process passed from generation to generation. Knowledge of this mode of transmitting information is among the greatest taboos in our contemporary society. The reason for this is that it represents the single greatest challenge to the Christian *and* Modern establishments with their dependence on conventional modes for transmitting information (especially the written

In his landmark work *The Postmodern Condition*, the French critic Jean-François Lyotard has some interesting things to say about the character of knowledge and the unknown in the coming years:

> Postmodern science—by concerning itself with such things as undecidables, the limits of precise control, conflicts characterized by incomplete information, 'fracta,' catastrophes and pragmatic paradoxes—is theorizing its own evolution as discontinuous, catastrophic, non rectifiable, and paradoxical. It is changing the meaning of the word knowledge, while expressing how such change can take place. It is producing not the known, but the unknown. (p. 60)

Among the unknown things which will be produced in the Unmanifest zone, which the profane call the "future," will be the engendering of a new Gothick realm which will be none other than the remanifestation of the elder realm. As yet it lives in crimson darkness, but in the spiraling tower the Gothick God waits and watches as those who will call his realm forth work their wills upon the world.

Reyn til Rûna! ⚲

When the right constellation of individuals with this knowledge are present the Age of Dependence—on Medieval Churches or Modern Governments—will begin to come to an end.

word). The forbidden secret of the Gothick God is that you can be informed from within, by means of innate structures, which are stimulated by actual experience in the framework of objective intellectual knowledge (undefiled wisdom). When the right constellation of individuals with this knowledge are present the Age of Dependence—on Medieval Churches or Modern Governments—will begin to come to an end.

The Gothick God of Darkness is the Unknown God, the Hidden God—and hence the God of unknown and hidden things. His actions are hidden because he is hidden. Mere words cannot reveal this information, only Words (the hidden forms behind certain key concepts) can do this. It is these which hold the secrets of eternal consciousness and power beyond death. Look, you see it before you now! If you see it, you must work to realize it within—and having mastered it there, to realize it without.

CONTRIBUTORS

Brian Barritt, to the best of his recollection, has been called a genius by at least three different people, but then he has been called many other things as well. Over the years he has been an author, painter, prisoner, dope fiend, comedian, Krautrocker, occultist, raving maniac and Beatnik, and has known many notable figures including William Burroughs, Alexander Trochi, Ash Ra Tempel, H.R. Giger, Sergius Golowin and Timothy Leary. Amazingly, and this defies all logic and reason, he is about the only notable figure from this Beatnik era to survive into the 21st century. Needless to say, he is still up to no good. His website is www.brianbarritt.com.

Hakim Bey (No information available)

Brian Butler is a writer, producer, and musician living in Los Angeles. He has extensively researched and practiced western magic for 20 years and is considered an expert in occultism. A former member of the Golden Dawn, he now heads his own Magical Order with newly revised rituals based on the teachings of Cameron, C. F. Russell and Charles Stansfeld Jones. Interested aspirants may contact him directly by email: znees@yahoo.com.

Vere Chappell began his study and practice of the occult arts in 1985. In 1989 he joined the Ordo Templi Orientis, and led one of its local bodies in Los Angeles for eight years. In 1997 he was appointed to the post of Grand Treasurer General for the O.T.O. within the United States, in which capacity he continues to serve today. He is also a Bishop of the Gnostic Catholic Church and performs the Gnostic Mass monthly. Mr. Chappell has a Bachelor's Degree in Cognitive Science from UCLA and an MBA from Pepperdine University. He is a senior partner in a technology consulting firm and also owns an Internet production company. His interests include cognitive psychology, photography, occult history and esoteric sexuality. He has travelled extensively throughout Europe and the United States, including recent research trips to Great Britain, France, and Italy. Mr. Chappell lives in Southern California with his lovely wife and priestess, Lita-Luise, and their two feline familiars.

Joe Coleman's paintings are unflinching autopsies of the human condition. Wielding his single-hair brush like a scalpel, Coleman forces us to join him in a brutal project to document the frailties and cruelties of the flesh and the bizarre junctions between saint and sinner, sacred and profane, holy and horrifying. In tortured self-portraits, apocalyptic "humanscapes" and portraits of historical figures from outlaw hero John Dillinger to *Gangs of New York*-era mercenary Albert Hicks to outsider artist Henry Darger, Joe Coleman packs his images with fascinating information and excruciating, hallucinatory detail. Joe Coleman's paintings have been exhibited at the American Visionary Art Museum, the Hieronymus Bosch Museum, and the Wadsworth Athenaeum.

Erik Davis is a San Franciso-based writer currently working on a cultural history of California spirituality. His book *TechGnosis: Myth, Magic, and Mysticism in the Age of Information* became a cult hit after being released in the fall of 1998, and has been translated into numerous languages. Davis is a contributing editor for *Wired* and *Trip* magazines and has contributed essays to a number of recent collections, including *Zig Zag Zen: Buddhism and Psychedelics*, *Sound Unbound*, *Prefiguring Cyberculture*, and *Radical Spirit*. Davis appeared in Craig Baldwin's underground film, *Specters of the Spectrum*, and has lectured internationally on technoloculture, electronic music, and spiritual weirdness. Some of his work can be accessed at www.techgnosis.com, and he can be reached at erik@techgnosis.com.

Nevill Drury was born in Hastings, England, in 1947 but has lived most of his life in Australia. He has been interested in western magic and consciousness research for over 30 years and has written widely on shamanism and the western esoteric tradition, as well as on contemporary art. He holds a Masters degree in anthropology from Macquarie University in Sydney and is the author of over 40 books, including *Exploring the Labyrinth*, *Sacred Encounters*, *The Elements of Shamanism*, *Pan's Daughter* and *The Dictionary of the Esoteric*. His work has been published in fifteen languages.

Stephen Edred Flowers is the world's leading expert on esoteric, or "radical" Runology. He has written or translated nearly 40 books on this and related subjects. In 1980 he founded the Rune-Gild, the world's most influential initiatory organization dedicated to Rune-Work on the Odian path. His work in Runology extends into academic pursuits and in 1984 he received a Ph.D. from the University of Texas at Austin with a dissertation entitled Runes and Magic. He has recently founded the Woodharrow Institute for Germanic and Runic Studies. Edred is also the owner of Runa-Raven Press and lives with his wife, Crystal, at Woodharrow near Austin, Texas. His work is devoted to seeking the principle of RUNA—the Mystery—as understood in the mythic idiom of the Germanic peoples.

Michael Goss, of Irish-Dutch parentage, spent his formative years in the Navy town of Portsmouth in the South of England. He started out as a photographer and occasional journalist before founding Delectus Books, in 1988; a publishing house and bookseller, which he still runs while occasionally editing books for other publishers (www.delectus-books.co.uk). Michael has one of the finest archives of erotica in private hands and is always looking to add new material on his travels. He currently spends his time between his London base and frequent trips to the Amazon in Colombia.

John Grigsby Geiger was born in Ithaca, New York, and graduated in history from the University of Alberta. He is the author of *Chapel of Extreme Experience*, the true story of how the discovery of flicker potentials, and scientific observations about strange patterns, organized hallucinations, and even the displacement of time derived from stroboscopic light, very nearly resulted in a Dream Machine in every suburban living room. It is published in the US by Soft Skull. His other books include the international bestseller *Frozen In Time*, about the role lead poisoning played in the destruction of the 1845 Franklin Expedition. His work has been translated into seven languages.

T Allen Greenfield is 56, married, father of three, native of Augusta, Georgia. A world traveler and writer since his middle teen years, he has taken a decidedly unconventional approach to already highly unconventional subjects. The author of half a dozen books on offbeat, controversial and esoteric topics, Greenfield has been a UFO field investigator, radical political activist, professional psychic, science fiction buff, occultist and theologian. He professes only two fundamentals: Scientific Illuminism, or the method of science employed in pursuit of the aims of religion, and that the world as-it-is is sufficiently unsatisfactory that exploration of almost any ethical out-of-the-box alternative, however outré, is worth the effort. He would like it known that he had no influence, or say, on the title of this anthology and his opinions are his own and do not reflect or represent the opinions of any organization.

Phil Hine became widely-known as a proponent of Chaos Magic, a (post)modern magical current based on the idea that beliefs are tools, not ends in themselves. In keeping with this spirit, Phil no longer has much to do with Chaos Magic. Gravitating to Chaos groups in Yorkshire in the '80s, Phil published a series of booklets on "Urban Shamanism," and a magic primer that recently became *Condensed Chaos* (New Falcon, 1995)—described by William Burroughs as "the most concise statement of the logic of modern magic." He has also written *Prime Chaos* (New Falcon, 1999) and *The Pseudonomicon* (Chaos International, 1998). He spent some time editing the now defunct *Chaos International* magazine, as well as *Pagan News*, which he edited intermittently between 1988 and 1992. He has contributed to numerous other publications.

Peter-R. Koenig, a victim of two petit-bourgeois sins, gluttony and anger, is Swiss-born but lives exclusively on http://www.cyberlink.ch/~koenig where his occult histories are located for your reading pleasure.

Gary Lachman is the author of *Turn Off Your Mind: The Mystic Sixties and the Dark Side of the Age of Aquarius* (The Disinformation Company, 2003). A founding member of Blondie, as Gary Valentine he was responsible for some of the group's early hits and is the author of *New York Rocker: My Life in The Blank Generation With Blondie, Iggy Pop and Others 1974–1981* (Sidgwick & Jackson). His most recent book is *A Secret History of Consciousness* (Anthroposophic Press). A frequent contributor to *Fortean Times*, *MOJO*, *The Guardian* and *Times Literary Supplement*, his new CD, *Tomorrow Belongs to You*, is available from Overground Records (www.overground.co.uk) and his forthcoming books include *A Dark Muse: The Dedalus Book of the Occult* (Dedalus) and *The Sly Man: The Story of Gurdjieff and Ouspensky* (Quest Books). Born in New Jersey, after lengthy sojourns in New York and Los Angeles, he moved to London in 1996.

Paul Laffoley was born in Cambridge, Massachusetts, in 1940. He spoke his first word, "Constantinople," at six months, then remained silent until the age of four (having been diagnosed as slightly autistic), when he began to draw and paint. He has continued as a self-taught artist to the present. He was dismissed from the Harvard Graduate School of Design, but managed to apprentice with the sculptor Mirko Baseldella, before going to New York to apprentice with the visionary architect Frederick Kiesler. He formed the Boston Visionary Cell, Inc. in 1971. He has participated in over two hundred exhibits, nationally and internationally. In 1990, he became a registered architect.

BOOK OF LIES

348

Tim Maroney is a software architect, occult scholar, spiritual practitioner, and bon vivant living in Berkeley, California. His studies in the sciences bring a unique perspective to his intimate treatment of mysticism and the occult. Tim has been a professional writer for over 20 years, appearing in *Gnosis*, *d e v e l o p* and other magazines and newspapers. He pioneered creative writing on computer networks; some of his published and network essays are collected at www.maroney.org. Tim has studied Western occultism and Eastern religion since childhood, and began yoga, meditation and ritual in 1978. He is an ordained Gnostic Priest and a confirmed skeptic. He practices ritual in the Ordo Templi Orientis, Neo-Pagan Witchcraft, and the Golden Dawn tradition. His biographical introduction to *The Book of Dzyan* was called "the most insightful and balanced discussion of Blavatsky's writings to date" by leading Theosophical historian K. Paul Johnson. Tim is working on his second book, *Scientific Meditations*.

Robert S. Mason was born 1948 and resides in Virginia. He has studied Anthroposophy since 1982 with no formal training. Opinions expressed are his own and he represents no organization, Anthroposophical or otherwise.

Born in 1946, author and explorer **Terence McKenna** spent over 25 years in the study of the ontological foundations of shamanism and the ethno-pharmacology of spiritual transformation. McKenna graduated from the University of California at Berkeley with a distributed major in Ecology, Resource Conservation and Shamanism. After graduation he traveled extensively in the Asian and New World Tropics, becoming specialized in the shamanism and ethno-medicine of the Amazon Basin. With his brother Dennis, he is the author of *The Invisible Landscape* and *Psilocybin: The Magic Mushroom Growers' Guide*. Other books include a study of the impact of psychotropic plants on human culture and evolution, *Food of the Gods*, and a book of essays and conversations, *The Archaic Revival*. His *True Hallucinations* is a narrative of spiritual adventure set in the jungles of the Colombian Amazon. Terence McKenna died on April 3, 2000.

Richard Metzger is the co-founder of The Disinformation Company and for two seasons hosted and directed the Disinformation TV series that ran on Britain's Channel 4 network. A 2-DVD set and a companion book of the series, *Disinformation: The Interviews*, are published by The Disinformation Company.

John S. Moore, born 1948, is a freelance scholar and maverick philosopher now living in Islington North London. He studied philosophy at King's College, University of London 1966–69. He has published several papers on Nietzsche, as well as on other figures like Crowley, Bulwer-Lytton, Schopenhauer, and Wittgenstein. He has also published three volumes of poetry.

Grant Morrison is highly regarded as one of the most original and inventive writers in the comics medium. His revisionist Batman book *Arkham Asylum* (with artist Dave McKean) has sold over 500,000 copies worldwide and won numerous awards, making it the most successful original graphic novel to be published in America. He has written comics for 25 years and has contributed groundbreaking and best-selling runs of popular stories for the major companies including DC Comics characters *JLA*, *Doom Patrol*, *Animal Man* and Marvel Comics' *X-Men* and *Fantastic Four*. In addition he has created a number of revolutionary new series including *Zenith*, *Sebastian O*, *The Invisibles*, *Marvel Boy* and the cult classics *Kill Your Boyfriend* and *The Mystery Play*. In July 1997, he was the first comic book writer to be included as one of Entertainment Weekly's top 100 creative people in America. Current projects include "Sleepless Knights," an original screenplay for Steven Spielberg's DreamWorks SKG and his first novel, *The IF*. He has recently finished working with Universal on a "Battlestar Galactica" computer game and others, including original concepts, are in discussion with various developers. He is currently writing the critically acclaimed, best-selling monthly, *New X-Men* for Marvel Comics and an original 13-part social-surrealist series *The Filth* for DC/Vertigo. He lives and works in Glasgow, Scotland.

Michael Moynihan was born in 1969 in New England. He is an artist, musician, author, and editor. He has traveled and performed music throughout Western Europe, as well as in Japan. The latest release of his and Annabel Lee's music project Blood Axis is *Absinthe: La Folie Verte*, a collaboration with the French group Les Joyaux de la Princesse. His record label Storm has recently issued a 2-CD retrospective of the seminal psychedelic Industrial band Factrix, as well as a debut album from Sangre Cavallum, a Northern Portuguese/Galician traditional ensemble. His book *Lords of Chaos* (Feral House), co-written with Didrik Søderlind, has been an independent best-seller and was recently translated into German. In addition to authoring essays for *Apocalypse Culture II* (Feral

House), and contributing entries to the reference work *The Encyclopedia of Religion and Nature* (Continuum), he recently edited two books by the Italian traditionalist Julius Evola, *Introduction to Magic* and *Men among the Ruins* (both published by Inner Traditions), as well as a volume of K. M. Wiligut's occult writings entitled *The Secret King* (translated by Stephen E. Flowers and published by Dominion/Rûna-Raven). He is also a co-editor of *Rûna*, an esoteric British periodical which focusses on the ancient culture of Northern Europe, and *TYR*, an annual book-format journal of "Myth, Culture, and Tradition" published in Atlanta. Email: dominion@pshift.com

Mark Pesce is widely known as the co-inventor of VRML, which brought virtual reality to the World Wide Web nearly a decade ago. The author of five books, he's most proud of *The Playful World* (www.playfulworld.com), an exploration of the relationship between technology, language, and childhood. Pesce has taken initiation in several magical orders, and can proudly say that he's been thrown out of every one of them.

Daniel Pinchbeck is the author of *Breaking Open the Head: A Psychedelic Journey into the Heart of Contemporary Shamanism* (Broadway Books). A founder of Open City Magazine, he has written for the *New York Times Magazine, Rolling Stone, Esquire, Wired,* and many other publications. He can be contacted through his website, www.breakingopenthehead.com.

Genesis Breyer P-Orridge, born in Manchester, England, 1950. Member of Kinetic action group Exploding Galaxy/Transmedia Exploration, 1969–70. Conceived and founded seminal British "performance art" group COUM TRANSMISSIONS, 1969; pioneer co-founder (with Cosey Fanni Tutti, Peter Christopherson, Chris Carter) of Throbbing Gristle, 1975; co-founder (with Alex Fergusson) of hyperdelic acid house innovators Psychic TV, 1981; founded spoken word/ambient music performance group Thee Majesty 1999. Invented the term/genre Industrial Music (with Monte Cazazza) September 3rd, 1975, releasing more than 200 CDs of experiments in music to date. Has worked and collaborated with Beatnik writers William S. Burroughs and Brion Gysin; radical queer filmmaker Derek Jarman; psychedelic guru Dr. Timothy Leary and many other luminaries. Early pioneer/innovator of Acid House/Rave Movement in UK and USA from early 80s–mid-90s. Early champion of Internet and commentator on its media virus cultural implications, often collaborating with Douglas Rushkoff, Richard Metzger and other leading figures in Cyberia. He has published thousands of articles, texts, interviews covering the functional and metaphysical implications and strategies of popular culture. Also explored human behavior, ritual, and personality modification through splintering of expectation in private magical situations to create neo-shamanic collaged paintings called "Sigils." Currently resides in the New York area as an author, cultural engineer/commentator and fine artist. Has performed his improvised "Expanded Poetry" as THEE MAJESTY (with guitarist Bryin Dall, guitarist Lady J. and tabla player Larry Thrasher) at arts festivals and music venues all over the USA and Europe since 1998. A monograph on his fine art *Painful But Fabulous* (Soft Skull Press, NYC) has been published and exhibitions, installations and lectures are held across Europe and the USA. Website at: www.genesisp-orridge.com.

Boyd Rice is a writer, musician and lecturer whose lifelong interest in the occult began at an early age. Since the 1980s, his reputation as an esotericist has earned him frequent guest spots on television and talk radio, both in the United States and throughout Europe. His career as an avant-garde musician and recording artist has spanned more than a quarter of a century, and his pioneering work in the field of industrial music has established him as one of the founding fathers of the genre. For the last six years he has devoted his time almost exclusively to researching the bloodline of the Holy Grail, and the attendant myths and folklore associated with it. His frequent travels to Europe have allowed him to investigate personally many sites and monuments connected to the Grail mythos.

Tracy Twyman, the editor and creator of *Dagobert's Revenge*, is a prolific writer, publisher, and film producer, as well as a recognized expert on ancient and medieval history, secret societies and the occult. Since 1996, she has been the publisher of *Dagobert's Revenge* magazine, and has written extensively on the subjects of Freemasonry, the Knights Templar, the Priory of Sion, Rosicrucianism, Hermeticism, conspiracies, and esoterica. In addition, she has written for a number of other publications, including *Hustler, Seconds, Propaganda,* and *Paranoia*, and has appeared on a number of television and radio programs. She has a Bachelor of Arts in Film and Video, and has produced several short films and videos.

Donald Tyson is a Canadian from Halifax, Nova Scotia. Early in life he was drawn to science by an intense fascination with astronomy, building a telescope by hand when he was eight. He began university seeking a science degree, but became disillusioned with the aridity and futility of a mechanistic view of the universe and shifted his major to English. After graduating with honors he has pursued a writing career. Now he devotes his life to the attainment of a complete gnosis of the art of magic in theory and practice. His purpose is to formulate an accessible system of personal training composed of East and West, past and present, that will help the individual discover the reason for one's existence and a way to fulfill it.

Peter Lamborn Wilson's reputation goes back to as early as the late '60s when he wandered North Africa, India and Asia, spending a long time in Iran for his voluminous reading of Islamic heretical texts and studying the historical and mystical dimensions of Sufism. Wilson has writen on early American spiritual anarchism and published some pseudonymous manifestos and books (*Temporary Autonomous Zone*). As an underground intellectual he is involved in a range of initiatives, including bi-weekly broadcasting his "Moorish Orthodox Radio Crusade" on WBAI, regular lectures at the New York Open Center, being a member of the Autonomedia collective, and author of "high and low" publications from science fiction zines to "Studies in Mystical Literature" and his collection of essays "Sacred Drift."

Robert Anton Wilson is the co-author, with Robert Shea, of the underground classic *The Illuminatus! Trilogy*, which won the 1986 Prometheus Hall of Fame Award. His other writings include *Schrodinger's Cat Trilogy*, called "the most scientific of all science fiction novels," by New Scientist, and several nonfiction works of Futurist psychology and guerilla ontology, such as *Prometheus Rising* and *The New Inquisition*. Wilson, who sees himself as a Futurist, author, and stand-up comic, regularly gives seminars at Esalen and other New Age centers. Wilson has made both a comedy record (*Secrets of Power*) and a punk rock record (*The Chocolate Biscuit Conspiracy*), and his play *Wilhelm Reich in Hell* was performed at the Edmund Burke Theatre in Dublin, Ireland. His novel *Illuminatus!* was adapted as a 10-hour science fiction rock epic and performed under the patronage of Her Majesty Queen Elizabeth II at Great Britain's National Theatre, where Wilson appeared briefly on stage in a special cameo role. Robert Anton Wilson is also a former editor at *Playboy* magazine. ⌁

ARTICLE HISTORIES

"Pop Magic!" by Grant Morrison originally appeared at www.grant-morrison.com. Used by permission of the author.

"The Executable Dreamtime" by Mark Pesce was written especially for this volume.

"Thee Splinter Test" by Genesis P-Orridge originally appeared in *Rebels and Devils*, edited by Dr. Christopher Hyatt, New Falcon Publications, Tempe, Arizona. Used by permission of the author.

"Memento Mori: (Remember You Must Die)" by Paul Laffoley was written especially for this volume.

"Joe is in the Details" by Joe Coleman was written especially for this volume.

"Are You Illuminated?" by Phil Hine is taken from *Condensed Chaos*, New Falcon Publications, Tempe, Arizona, and used by their kind permission.

"Tryptamine Hallucinogens and Consciousness" by Terence McKenna is taken from *The Archaic Revival* (pp 34–47), HarperSanFrancisco, 1992. Copyright 1991 Terence McKenna. Reprinted by permission of HarperCollins Publishers Inc.

The extended excerpt from *Breaking Open The Head* by Daniel Pinchbeck is used by kind permission of Broadway Books, a division of Random House, Inc., New York, 2002. Published in the British Commonwealth by Flamingo, 2003, and again used with their kind permission.

"Kick That Habit: Brion Gysin, His Life & Magick" by Michael R. Goss originally appeared in *Isis Nuit*, Mandrake of Oxford (www.mandrake.uk.net), 1993.

"Who is There William Burroughs" by John Geiger was written especially for this volume.

"Magick Squares and Future Beats" by Genesis P-Orridge was written especially for this volume.

"Austin Osman Spare: Divine Draughtsman" by Nevill Drury is from *The History of Magic in the Modern Age*, Constable, 2000. Used by permission of the author.

"Virtual Mirrors in Solid Time" by Genesis P-Orridge originally appeared in *Rapid Eye*, Rapid Eye Publishing, Brighton, 1989. Used by permission of the author.

"Calling Cthulu: H. P. Lovecraft's Magick Realism" by Erik Davis originally appeared in a shorter form in *Gnosis* magazine, Fall, 1995. Used by permission of the author.

"Full Moon at Bou Saada" and "Bou Saada Decoded" by Brian Barritt are from *The Road of Excess*, PSI Publishing, London 1998. Used by permission of the author.

"Robert Anton Wilson on Leary and Crowley," an excerpt from *Cosmic Trigger* was originally published in 1977 by And/Or Press; Falcon Press, 1986; New Falcon 2002. Used by permission of the author.

"Six Voices on Crowley" by Tim Maroney originally appeared on www.maroney.org and this expanded version was prepared especially for this volume.

"Aleister Crowley as Guru" by John S. Moore originally appeared in *Chaos International* magazine #17, 1994. Used by permission of the author.

"The Enochian Apocalypse" by Donald Tyson originally appeared in *Gnosis* magazine, Summer 1996. Used by permission of the author.

"The Crying of Liber 49: Jack Parsons, Antichrist Superstar" by Richard Metzger originally appeared in *21.C* magazine.

"Cameron: The Wormwood Star" by Brian Butler was written especially for this volume.

"Ida Craddock: Sexual Mystic and Martyr for Freedom" by Vere Chappell was originally presented at the Second National O.T.O. Conference, August 7, 1999 and also appears online at www.idacraddock.org along with other materials relating to Ida Craddock.

"Rosaleen Norton: Pan's Daughter" by Nevill Drury from *The History of Magic in the Modern Age*, Constable, 2000. Used by permission of the author.

"Magical Blitzkrieg: Hitler and the Occult" by Tracy Twyman originally appeared in her *Dagobert's Revenge* magazine, volume 2, #2.

"That Which Has Fallen" by Boyd Rice originally appeared in *Dagobert's Revenge* magazine, volume 4, #1.

"Halo of Flies" by Peter-R. Koenig was written especially for this volume.

"The Secret History of Modern Witchcraft" by Tau Allen Greenfield has appeared in several different places and in several forms.

"Anton LaVey: A Fireside Chat with the Black Pope" by Michael Moynihan originally appeared in *Seconds* magazine, 1994. Used by permission of the author.

"Season of the Witch" by Gary Lachman originally appeared in *MOJO*, September 1999. Used by permission of the author.

"The Advent of Ahriman" by Robert Mason originally appeared in a longer version on various Internet websites.

"Julius Evola's Combat Manuals for a Revolt Against the Modern World" by Michael Moynihan was written especially for this volume.

"On the Magical View of Life" by "Ea" (Julius Evola) is taken from *Introduction to Magic*, Julius Evola and the UR Group; Guido Stucco, translator; Michael Moynihan, editor. Inner Traditions, Rochester, Vermont, 2001. English translation copyright 2001 by Inner Traditions International, 1-(800) 246-8648.

"Serpentine Wisdom" by "Iagla" (Julius Evola) is taken from *Introduction to Magic*, Julius Evola and the UR Group; Guido Stucco, translator; Michael Moynihan, editor. Inner Traditions, Rochester, Vermont, 2001. English translation copyright 2001 by Inner Traditions International, 1-(800) 246-8648.

"Occult War" by Julius Evola from *Men Among the Ruins*, Guido Stucco, translator; Michael Moynihan, editor. Inner Traditions, Rochester, Vermont, 2002. English translation copyright 2002 by Inner Traditions International, 1-(800) 246-8648.

"Secret of the Assassins" by Peter Lamborn Wilson from *Scandal: Essays in Islamic Heresy*, Autonomedia, NY, 1988. Used by permission of the author.

"Sorcery" by Hakim Bey from *T.A.Z. The Temporary Autonomous Zone*, Autonomedia, NY, Anti-copyright 1985, 1991. Used by permission of the author.

"Media Hex: The Occult Attack on Institutions" by Hakim Bey from *T.A.Z. The Temporary Autonomous Zone*, Autonomedia, NY, Anti-copyright 1985,1991. Used by permission of the author.

"The Secret of the Gothick God of Darkness" by Dr. Stephen Edred Flowers originally appeared on October 31, 1994 in *Fringeware Review* #6(66). Used by permission of the author.

HOW DID A DECADE OF LOVE AND PEACE END IN ALTAMONT AND THE MANSON FAMILY?

TURN
OFF
YOUR MIND
The Mystic Sixties and the Dark Side of the Age of Aquarius
By Gary Lachman

GARY LACHMAN EXPLORES THE SINISTER DALLIANCE OF ROCK'S HIGH ROLLERS AND A NEW WAVE OF OCCULTISTS, TYING TOGETHER JOHN LENNON, TIMOTHY LEARY, MICK JAGGER, BRIAN WILSON, CHARLES MANSON, ANTON LAVEY, JIM MORRISON, L. RON HUBBARD AND MANY MORE CULTURAL ICONS.

THE 1960S WERE A TIME OF REVOLUTION—POLITICAL, SOCIAL, PSYCHEDELIC, SEXUAL. BUT THERE WAS ANOTHER REVOLUTION THAT MANY HISTORIANS FORGET: THE RISE OF A POWERFUL CURRENT THAT PERMEATED POP CULTURE AND HAS BEEN A CENTRAL INFLUENCE ON IT EVER SINCE. IT WAS A MAGICAL REVOLUTION—A REVIVAL OF THE OCCULT. GARY LACHMAN HERE CHARTS THIS EXPLOSION, ITS RISE AND FALL, AND ITS ENDURING LEGACY.

"A REALLY WELL-RESEARCHED, WELL-WRITTEN BOOK ABOUT THE MOMENT OF DESTINY FROM WHICH I FOR ONE WAS GLAD TO ESCAPE ALIVE."
—MARIANNE FAITHFUL

TURN OFF YOUR MIND:
THE MYSTIC SIXTIES AND THE DARK SIDE OF THE AGE OF AQUARIUS

By Gary Lachman • Published by The Disinformation Company
Trade paperback • 430 pp • $19.95 • ISBN 0-9713942-3-7

WHAT DO CNN, YOUR HISTORY TEACHER, AND THE WHITE HOUSE HAVE IN COMMON?

Daniel Ellsberg • Howard Zinn • Greg Palast • Gary Webb • Jim Hougan • Paul Krassner • Thomas Szasz • Howard Bloom • William Blum • And More Than 35 Others! Edited by Russ Kick

ABUSE YOUR ILLUSIONS

THE DISINFORMATION GUIDE TO MEDIA MIRAGES AND ESTABLISHMENT LIES

ALL OF THEM HAVE KEPT SHOCKINGLY IMPORTANT FACTS FROM YOU:

- THE US MILITARY FACES A HUGE RAPE CRISIS.

- THE MOST POPULAR KIND OF ANTIDEPRESSANTS CAN CAUSE SUICIDE.

- THE NATION OF PANAMA WAS CREATED AS A GET-RICH SCHEME BY WALL STREET.

- THE ATLANTA CHILD-KILLER WAS CONVICTED OF ONLY TWO MURDERS—OF ADULTS.

- ISLAMIC GROUPS ARE CENSORING CRITICAL MATERIAL IN AMERICA.

- CORPORATIONS HAVE CLAIMED THE "RIGHT" TO LIE.

- THE US AND OTHER ALLIES MASSACRED GERMAN POWS AND CIVILIANS DURING AND AFTER WWII.

- THE FOOD DROPS IN AFGHANISTAN WERE A COMPLETE FIASCO.

...AND THAT'S NOT ALL!

ABUSE YOUR ILLUSIONS:
THE DISINFORMATION GUIDE TO MEDIA MIRAGES AND ESTABLISHMENT LIES

Edited by Russ Kick • Published by The Disinformation Company
Oversize paperback • 350 pp • $24.95 • ISBN 0-9713942-4-5

STILL
ESSENTIAL

YOU ARE BEING LIED TO THE DISINFORMATION GUIDE TO MEDIA
DISTORTION, HISTORICAL WHITEWASHES AND CULTURAL MYTHS

Edited by Russ Kick • Published by The Disinformation Company
Oversized softcover • 400 pp • $24.95 • ISBN 0-9664100-7-6

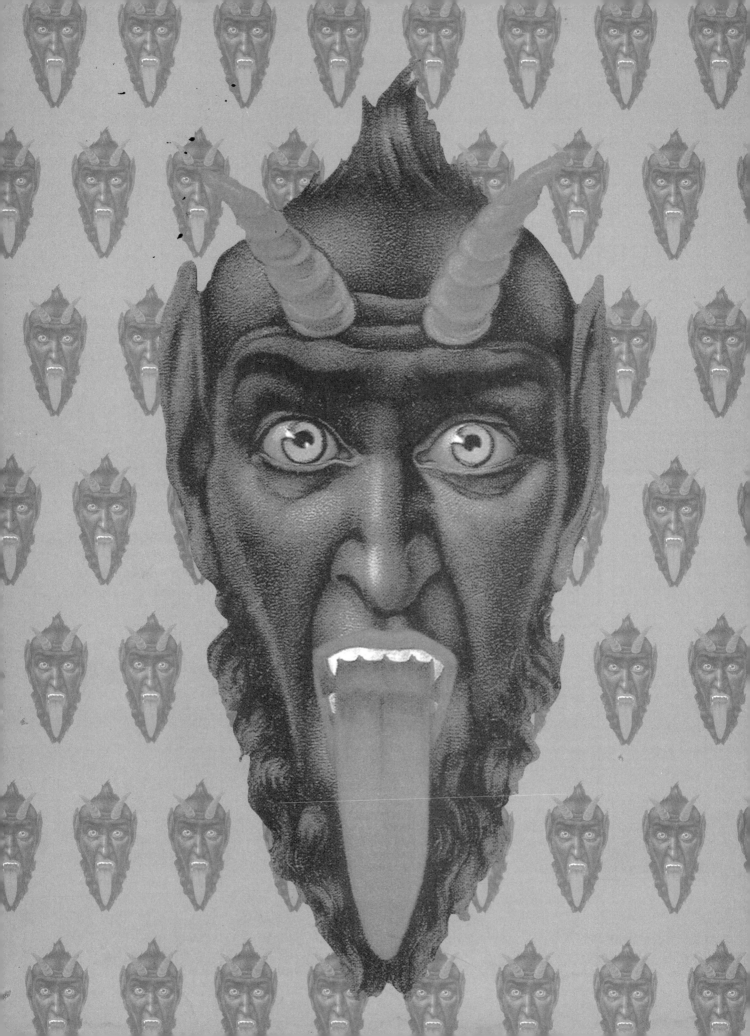